U0881824

湖北统计年鉴

HUBEI STATISTICAL YEARBOOK

2020

（总第36期）

湖 北 省 统 计 局
国家统计局湖北调查总队 编

中国统计出版社
China Statistics Press

©中国统计出版社有限公司 2020
版权所有。未经许可，本书的任何部分不得以任何方式在世界任何地区以任何文字翻印、拷贝、仿制或转载。

©2020 China Statistics Press Co.,Ltd.
All rights reserved. No part of the publication may be reproduced or transmitted in any form or by any means, electronic or mechanical, including photocopying, recording, or any information storage and retrieval system, without written permission from the publisher.

图书在版编目（CIP）数据

湖北统计年鉴. 2020 = Hubei Statistical Yearbook 2020 : 汉英对照 / 湖北省统计局，国家统计局湖北调查总队编. -- 北京 : 中国统计出版社，2020.9
ISBN 978-7-5037-9250-2

Ⅰ. ①湖… Ⅱ. ①湖… ②国… Ⅲ. ①统计资料—湖北—2020—年鉴—汉、英 Ⅳ. ①C832.63-54

中国版本图书馆 CIP 数据核字(2020)第 162390 号

湖北统计年鉴-2020

作　　者/ 湖北省统计局　国家统计局湖北调查总队
责任编辑/ 钟钰
责任校对/ 程文懿　张文怡
装帧设计/ 刘亚非
出版发行/ 中国统计出版社有限公司
地　　址/ 北京市丰台区西三环南路甲 6 号
邮政编码/ 100073
电　　话/ 邮购（010）63376909　书店（010）68783171
网　　址/ http://www.zgtjcbs.com
印　　刷/ 武汉市盛宏源印务有限公司
经　　销/ 新华书店
开　　本/ 890mm×1240mm　1/16
字　　数/ 1100 千字
印　　张/ 35.5
版　　别/ 2020 年 9 月第 1 版
版　　次/ 2020 年 9 月第 1 次印刷
定　　价/ 380.00 元　Price:380.00yuan(RMB)

本书附同版本 CD-ROM 一张，光盘内容以书面文字为准。
如有印装差错，由本社发行部调换。

《湖北统计年鉴-2020》

编委会和编辑工作人员

编委会

主　　任： 朱　慧　刘顺国

副 主 任： 叶　青　吴中志　张　静　蔡受清　崔永红　叶福生　陈小清　刘　凡　阳俊雄　时明国　张小青　程良世

编　　委： 李团中　王　博　刘　洪　马泽明　刘水国　舒振斌　龚其民

（以下以姓氏笔划为序）

王行刚　王兴华　王光纯　王　楠　尹汉华
邓智红　乐友来　龙江舫　卢　薇　叶祯祥
付春晖　付晓芳　刘传勇　李良华　朱利明
刘　荣　许晓红　杜云波　汪　军　陈志明
吴晓秦　宋　雪　张永云　张在金　张利阳
肖　强　明　峰　金　锐　周家庆　周银华
周雁峰　贺　宾　胡先红　唐军华　倪群峰
盛少华　舒　猛　谢名义　谢余强　蒋宇飞
雷炳建　魏尚平

编辑工作人　　员

总 编 辑： 张利阳　周家庆

副总编辑： 邓有成　胡树泉

执行编辑： 刘　颖　程文懿　张文怡

英文翻译： 刘　颖

封面设计： 刘亚非

光盘设计： 熊　威

Hubei Statistical Yearbook -2020

EDITORIAL BOARD AND STAFF

I. Editorial Board

Chairman: Zhu Hui   Liu Shunguo

Vice - chairman: Ye Qing   Wu Zhongzhi   Zhang Jing   Cai Shouqing
Cui Yonghong   Ye Fusheng   Chen Xiaoqing   Liu Fan
Yang Junxiong   Shi Mingguo   Zhang Xiaoqing   Cheng Liangshi

Editorial Board: Li Tuanzhong   Wang Bo   Liu Hong   Ma Zeming
Liu Shuiguo   Shu Zhenbin   Gong Qimin

(in order of the number of strokes of the Chinese character of the surname)

Wang Xinggang   Wang Xinghua   Wang Guangchun   Wang Nan
Yin Hanhua   Deng Zhihong   Le Youlai   Long Jiangfang
Lu Wei   Ye Zhenxiang   Fu Chunhui   Fu Xiaofang
Liu Chuanyong   Li Lianghua   Zhu Liming   Liu Rong
Xu Xiaohong   Du Yunbo   Wang Jun   Chen Zhiming
Wu Xiaoqin   Song Xue   Zhang Yongyun   Zhang Zaijing
Zhang Liyang   Xiao Qiang   Ming Feng   Jin Rui
Zhou Jiaqing   Zhou Yinhua   Zhou Yanfeng   He Bin
Hu Xianhong   Tang Junhua   Ni Qunfeng   Sheng Shaohua
Shu Meng   Xie Mingyi   Xie Yuqiang   Jiang Yufei
Lei Bingjian   Wei Shangping

II. Editorial Staff

Editor-in-chief: Zhang Liyang   Zhou Jiaqing

AssociateEditors-in-chief: Deng Youcheng   Hu Shuquan

Executive Copy-Editor: Liu ying   Cheng Wenyi   Zhang Wenyi

EnglishTranslators: Liu ying

CoverDesigner: Liu Yafei

CD-ROMDesigner: Xiong Wei

编 者 说 明

一、《湖北统计年鉴—2020》是一本信息密集的资料工具书。通过大量数据，全面地记载和反映了湖北省2019年经济、社会、科技、文化等方面的发展情况。具有信息量大、权威性强、适用性广等特点。

二、本年鉴包括综合、人口、从业人员和职工工资、固定资产投资、能源生产和消费、物价指数、人民生活、资源和环境、城市概况、农业、工业、建筑业、运输和邮电、国内贸易、对外经济贸易和旅游、财政和金融、科技和教育、文化和体育、卫生和社会服务、公共管理、长江经济带、县市概况、附录等23个部分。

三、2020年的湖北统计年鉴，篇章结构与《中国统计年鉴》保持一致，参照执行了国家统计局《省级统计年鉴指标体系目录》，采用了最新的国民经济行业分类标准和指标口径，并对英文注释和指标解释进行了全面修订。2020年湖北统计年鉴大量选用第四次全国经济普查数据。

四、本年鉴对过去发表的统计资料重新予以审核，凡与本年鉴资料有出入的，均以本年鉴为准。本年鉴中统计公报的数据为初步数，若与年鉴数据不一致，请以年鉴数据为准。

五、年鉴中指标的使用要结合文中的指标解释，以及注解合理使用，以免发生错误。

六、《湖北统计年鉴》公开出版以来，受到国内外读者的爱护与支持，对本年鉴的内容和编辑工作提出了许多宝贵意见，为此，我们特表谢意。由于水平有限，编辑工作中难免有疏误之处，竭诚欢迎读者批评指正。

COMPLIERS NOTES

I. *Statistical Yearbook of Hubei 2020* is an information–intensive data reference book. In a comprehensive manner, it records and reflects the economic, social, technological and cultural developments among other aspects in Hubei province in 2019, featuring a large amount of information, authority, wide applicability and so on.

II. The yearbook contains twenty–three chapters: general survey, population, employment and wages, fixed–assets investment, energy production and consumption, price index, the lifehood of people and natural resources and the environment, city overview, agriculture, industry, construction, transportation, post and telecommunication services, domestic trade, foreign economy and tourism, government finance and banking education, science and culture, sports, health and social services, public management, Yangtze River Economic Zone, overviews of counties and cities as well as the appendix.

III. Hubei statistical yearbook 2020 features a structure in line with *China Statistical Yearbook,* with reference to the implementation of the Provincial Statistics Index System Directory. The yearbook adopts the latest industrial categorization standards and indicator range, while the English notes and the interpretation of indicators have been revised thoroughly. In 2020, the yearbook adopts a large number of data of the Fourth National Economic Census.

IV. The yearbook adopts the updated statistical data based on the review of the past publications. Should any discrepancy arise, the yearbook shall prevail. Data of the statistical communique in the yearbook are the initial count. If that is not consistent with data of the yearbook, the latter shall prevail.

V. For any use of the indicators in the yearbook, please refer to the explanatory notes and annotations, so as to avoid mistakes.

VI. Since publication, *Statistical Yearbook of Hubei* has received concern and support from domestic and foreign readers, who also offer a number of valuable suggestions concerning the content and editorial work, for which we hereby express our gratitude. It is undeniable that editing work is subject to human erros and we thereby sincerely welcome criticisms and corrections from readers.

目 录
CONTENTS

特 载

Specifically Stated

1 综 合

General Survey

2 人 口

Population

3 就业人员和职工工资

Employment and Wages

4 固定资产投资

Investment in Fixed Assets

5 对外经济贸易和旅游

International Trade and Economic Cooperation & Tourism

6 能 源

Energy

7 财政和金融

Government Finance and Banking

8 价 格

Price

9 居民生活

People's Livelihoods

10 城市概况

City Overview

11 资源和环境

Resources and Environment

12 农 业

Agriculture

13 工 业

Industry

14 建筑业

Construction

15 交通运输、邮电

Transport, Postal and Telecommunication Services

16 国内贸易

Domestic Trade

17 科技和教育

Science, Technology and Education

18 卫生和社会服务

Public Health and Social Services

19 文化和体育

Culture and Sports

20 公共管理及其他

Public Managementand Other

21 "长江经济带"国民经济和社会发展主要指标

Main Indicators of National Economic and Social Development by Yangtze River Economic Zone

22 县域经济主要指标

Main Economic Indicators of Counties

附录 全国分省主要指标

Major Indicators by Region

特　　载

Specifically stated

2019年湖北省国民经济和社会发展统计公报

湖 北 省 统 计 局
国家统计局湖北调查总队

2019年,在省委省政府坚强领导下,全省上下以习近平新时代中国特色社会主义思想为指导,全面贯彻党的十九大和十九届二中、三中、四中全会精神,牢记"四个着力""四个切实"重要嘱托,统筹推进"五位一体"总体布局,协调推进"四个全面"战略布局,坚持稳中求进工作总基调,坚持新发展理念,始终把打好三大攻坚战作为高质量发展的重中之重,把全面深化改革开放作为关键一招,把保障和改善民生作为第一目标,克难攻坚、勇毅笃行,推动全省经济在高质量发展的道路上行稳致远。

一、综合

2019年,全省完成生产总值45828.31亿元,增长7.5%。其中,第一产业完成增加值3809.09亿元,增长3.2%;第二产业完成增加值19098.62亿元,增长8.0%;第三产业完成增加值22920.60亿元,增长7.8%。三次产业结构由2018年的8.5∶41.8∶49.7调整为8.3:41.7:50.0。在第三产业中,交通运输仓储和邮政业、批发和零售业、住宿和餐饮业、金融业、房地产业、其他服务业增加值分别增长9.4%、5.3%、8.5%、7.1%、5.6%、9.2%。

价格运行保持平稳。湖北居民消费价格上涨3.1%,涨幅比上年提高1.2个百分点。其中,城市上涨3.0%,农村上涨3.2%。分类别看,八大类商品价格七涨一降。其中,食品烟酒价格上涨7.0%,衣着价格上涨1.6%,居住价格上涨1.9%,生活用品及服务价格上涨0.4%,交通和通信价格下降0.7%,教育文化和娱乐价格上涨2.5%,医疗保健价格上涨1.8%,其他用品和服务价格上涨2.6%。湖北工业生产者出厂价格上涨0.2%,工业生产者购进价格下降0.7%。

市场主体发展加快。全省新登记市场主体90.03万户,其中,新登记私营企业25.13万户,新登记个体工商户62.73万户。

就业保持稳定。年末全省就业人员3548万人,其中城镇就业人员2090万人。全年全省城镇新增就业92.15万人,比上年多增0.19万人。年末全省城镇登记失业率为2.44%,比上年末下降0.11个百分点。

图1 2015-2019年湖北城镇新增就业人数

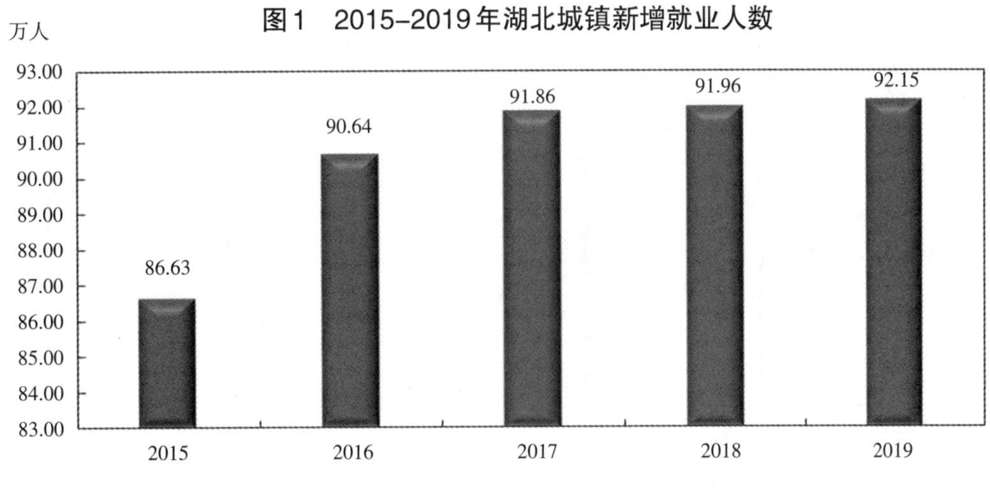

劳动生产率稳步提高。全省全员劳动生产率为12.86万元/人,比上年提高8.5%。

脱贫攻坚成效明显。按照每人每年2300元(2010年不变价)的农村贫困标准计算,年末农村贫困人口5.8万人,比上年末减少92.5万人;贫困发生率0.14%,比上年下降2.26个百分点。

图2 2015-2019年末湖北减贫人口和贫困发生率

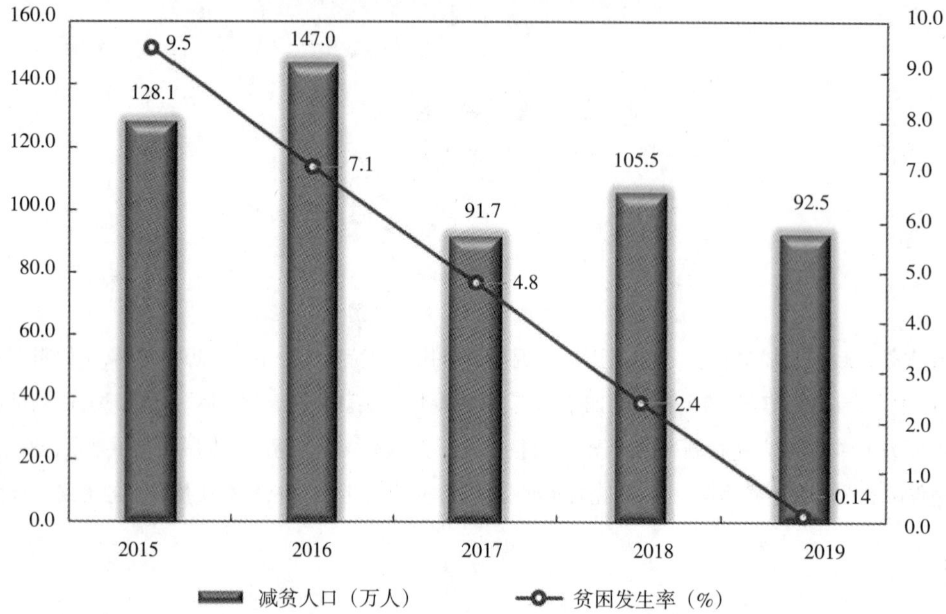

二、农业

全年全省农林牧渔业增加值4014.00亿元,按可比价格计算,比上年增长3.5%。

粮食产能保持稳定。全省粮食总产量2724.98万吨,下降4.0%,连续7年稳定在500亿斤以上;种植面积4608.60千公顷,下降4.9%。

图3 2015-2019年湖北粮食产量

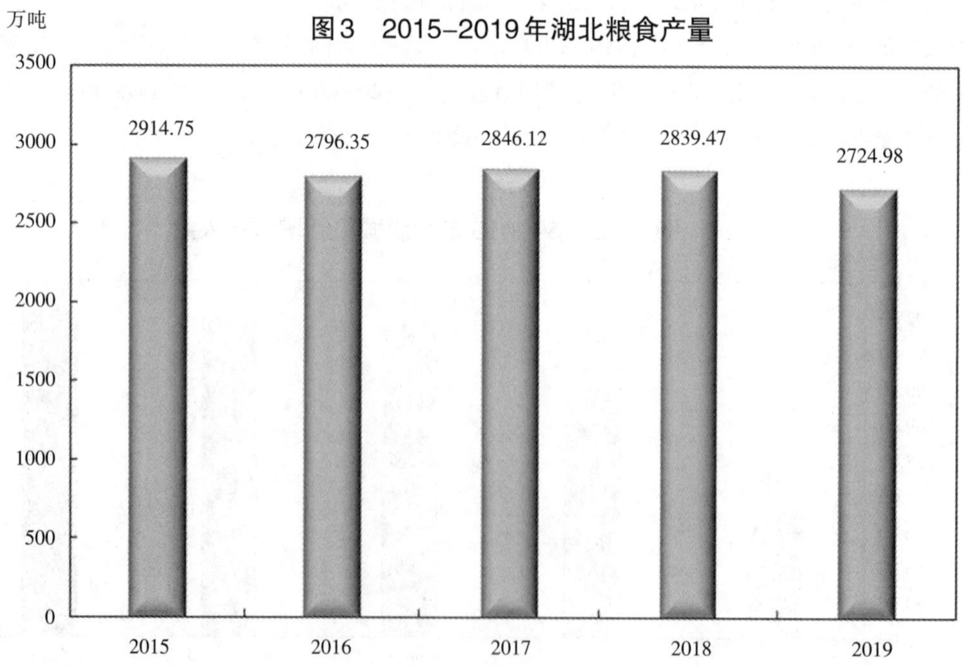

特色优势经济作物增长较快。蔬菜及食用菌产量4086.71万吨,增长3.1%;茶叶产量35.25万吨,增长6.9%;园林水果(不含

果用瓜)产量661.04万吨,增长0.9%。

畜禽养殖深度调整。受非洲猪瘟疫情影响,生猪出栏3189.24万头,下降26.9%;牛出栏109.52万头,增长1.1%;羊出栏615.93万只,增长1.1%;家禽出笼59394.01万只,增长11.5%;禽蛋产量178.75万吨,增长4.2%。

水产品生产形势趋稳,全年渔业恢复性增长,水产品总产量469.08万吨,增长2.4%。

表1　　2019年全省主要农产品产量

单位:万吨

产品名称	产量	比上年增长(%)
粮食	2724.98	-4.0
棉花	14.36	-3.8
油料	313.95	3.8
# 油菜籽	211.35	2.9
茶叶	35.25	6.9
园林水果(不含果用瓜)	661.04	0.9
蔬菜及食用菌	4086.71	3.1

三、工业和建筑业

工业生产保持稳定增长。年末全省规模以上工业企业达到15589家。规模以上工业增加值增长7.8%。其中,国有及国有控股企业增长4.4%;集体企业下降6.7%;股份制企业增长8.5%;外商及港澳台投资企业增长3.4%;其他经济类型企业增长4.3%。轻工业增长6.8%;重工业增长8.2%。

制造业增长7.9%,高于规模以上工业0.1个百分点。高技术制造业增长14.4%,快于规模以上工业6.6个百分点,占规模以上工业增加值的比重达9.5%,对规模以上工业增长的贡献率达17.0%。其中,计算机、通信和其他电子设备制造业增长19.0%,电气机械和器材制造业增长11.0%。

全年规模以上工业销售产值增长7.8%,产品销售率为97.2%,出口交货值下降0.4%。全年规模以上工业企业实现利润2867.8亿元,增长4.0%。

表2　　2019年全省规上工业主要产品产量及其增速

产品名称	单位	产量	比上年增长(%)
白酒	万千升	63.0	4.7
啤酒	万千升	128.2	-5.4
卷烟	亿支	1273.8	-0.2
布	亿米	57.2	-0.8
硫酸(折100%)	万吨	848.9	-1.4
农用氮、磷、钾化学肥料(折纯)	万吨	558.3	14.6
化学药品原药	万吨	19.8	0.6
中成药	万吨	32.1	-22.9
发电量	亿千瓦小时	2896.40	4.4
#水电	亿千瓦小时	1330.27	-8.0
水泥	万吨	11622.8	6.0
平板玻璃	万重量箱	10299.4	9.9
生铁	万吨	2765.2	-1.3

产品名称	单位	产量	比上年增长（%）
粗钢	万吨	3611.5	1.0
钢材	万吨	3771.6	2.3
十种有色金属	万吨	85.8	11.0
#精炼铜	万吨	53.6	5.3
工业机器人	套	10440.0	7.1
汽车	万辆	224.0	-7.4
#新能源汽车	辆	60554.0	-8.9
发电机组	万千瓦	120.3	-22.1
锂离子电池	万只(自然只)	108588.0	28.2
房间空气调节器	万台	2110.9	14.1
微型计算机设备	万台	1270.2	14.3
显示器	万台	1519.4	29.7
移动通信手持机	万台	3920.0	-10.2

建筑业稳步发展。全年全省具有总承包和专业承包资质建筑企业完成总产值16979.59亿元，增长12.2%；实现利润723.24亿元，增长15.2%。新开工房屋建筑施工面积38058.62万平方米，下降4.3%。

四、固定资产投资

全省完成固定资产投资(不含农户)增长10.6%，其中房地产开发投资增长8.9%。商品房销售面积8602.04万平方米，下降3.0%；实现商品房销售额7751.79亿元，增长2.9%。按产业划分，全省一、二、三次产业投资分别增长18.6%、6.2%、13.2%。全省316个省级在建重点建设项目全年完成投资2924.45亿元。

图4　2019年湖北三次产业投资占固定资产投资(不含农户)比重

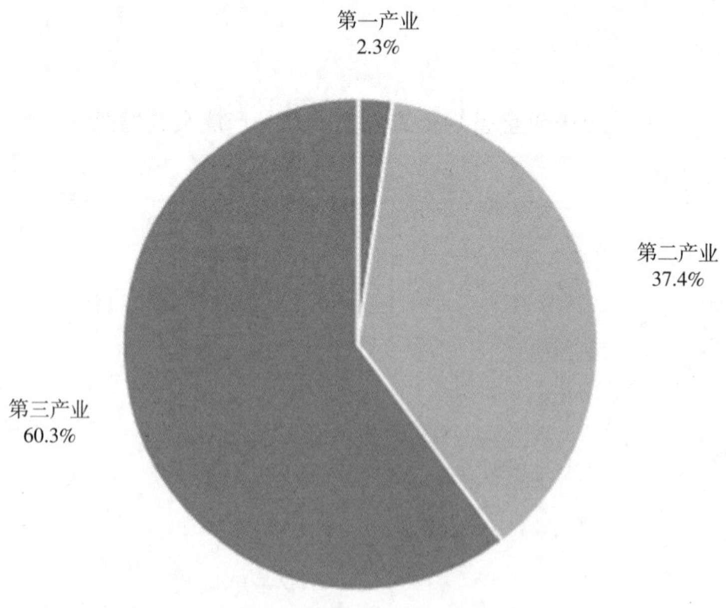

全省亿元以上新开工项目3952个，亿元以上项目完成投资增长10.6%。

五、国内贸易

全年全省实现社会消费品零售总额20224.23亿元，增长10.3%。分城乡看，城镇实现零售额16933.99亿元，增长10.2%；乡村实现零售额3290.24亿元，增长11.2%。其中，限额以上企业（单位）实现消费品零售额8633.84亿元，增长9.0%。

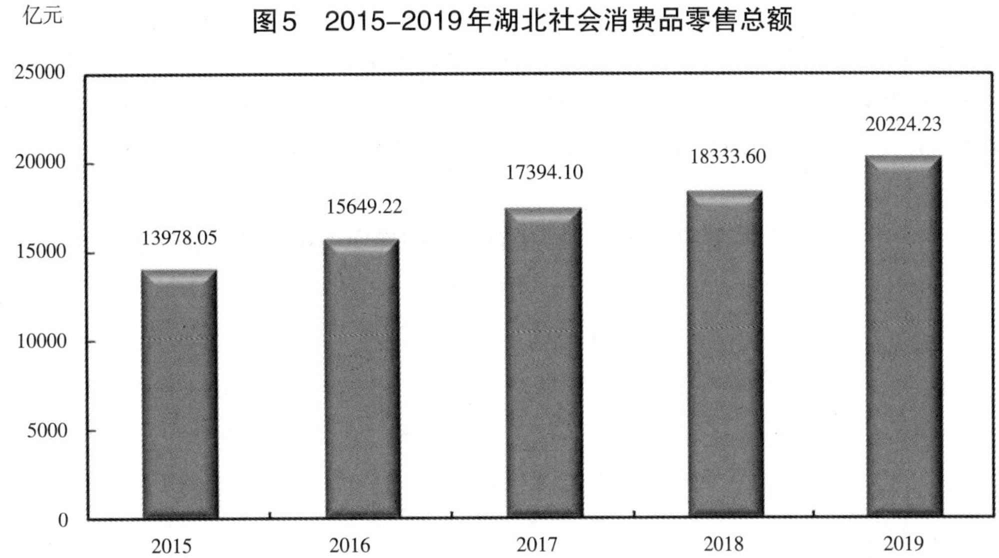

图5 2015-2019年湖北社会消费品零售总额

2019年，全省网上零售额达到2860.0亿元，比上年增长10.1%，其中实物商品网上零售额2384.4亿元，增长17.7%，占社会消费品零售总额的比重为11.8%。

六、对外经济

全年全省实现货物进出口总额3943.6亿元，增长13.1%，其中，进口1458.7亿元，增长18.2%；出口2484.9亿元，增长10.3%。对"一带一路"沿线国家进出口总额1183.3亿元，比上年增长22.4%。

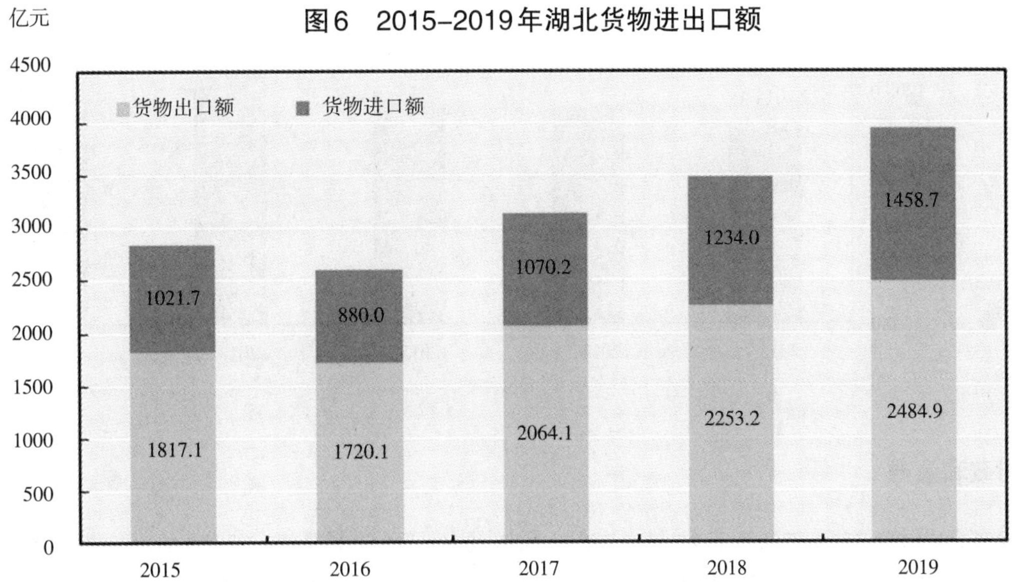

图6 2015-2019年湖北货物进出口额

新批外商直接投资项目446个。全年实际使用外资129.07亿美元，增长8.1%。其中，"一带一路"沿线国家对湖北直接投资新设立企业60家，增长9.1%。

七、交通运输和邮电通信

全年全省完成货物周转量7237.85亿吨公里，比上年增长8.4%；旅客周转量1386.79亿人公里，下降2.2%；公路总里程达289029.20公里，增长5.1%；高速公路里程达6860.32公里，增长7.8%；港口完成货物吞吐量3.07亿吨，增长26.7%。

全省邮政业务总量458.51亿元，增长32.8%。其中，快递业务量16.85亿件，快递业务收入173.89亿元。全省电信业务总量3365.93亿元，增长65.4%。长途光缆线路总长度达到3.08万公里；移动电话交换机容量达9043.50万户；固定电话用户518.93万户；移动电话用户达到5688.02万户；全省电话普及率为104.9部／百人，移动电话普及率为96.1部/百人；固定互联网宽带接入用户1708.32万户，比上年增加227.59万户；移动互联网用户接入流量38.27亿GB，比上年增长75.3%。

图7　2015-2019年湖北快递业务量及其增长速度

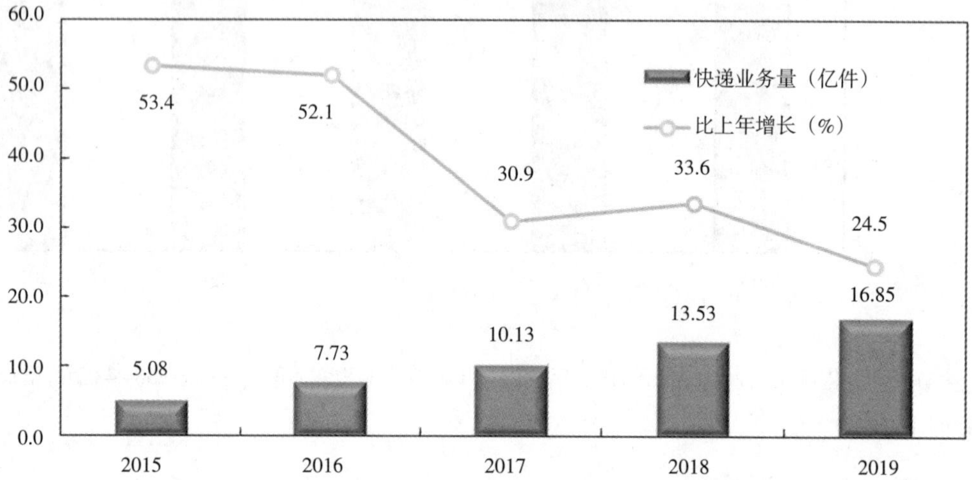

图8　2015-2019年湖北年末固定互联网宽带接入用户数

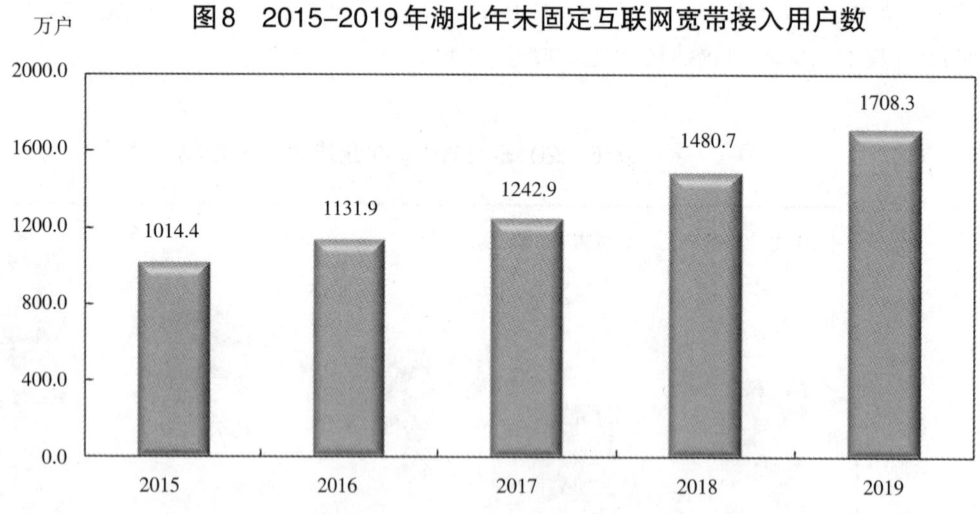

八、财政和金融

全年全省完成财政总收入5786.86亿元，增长1.8%。其中，地方一般公共预算收入3388.39亿元，增长2.5%。在地方一般公共预算收入中，税收收入2530.64亿元，增长2.7%。地方一般公共预算支出7967.73亿元，增长9.8%。

图9 2015-2019年湖北一般公共预算收入

注：图中2015年至2018年数据为湖北一般公共预算收入决算数，2019年为进度数据。

年末全省金融机构人民币各项存款余额59747.70亿元，比年初增加4362.04亿元。其中，住户存款29804.55亿元，增加3475.43亿元。金融机构人民币各项贷款余额50663.96亿元，比年初增加6094.07亿元。其中，住户贷款16584.11亿元，增加2472.19亿元；非金融企业及机关团体贷款34075.24亿元，增加3623.68亿元。

全年实现保费收入1728.57亿元，增长17.5%。其中，财产险保费收入397.85亿元，增长13%；人身险保费收入1330.72亿元，增长18.9%。支付各类赔款及给付512.26亿元，增长9.8%，其中，财产险赔付支出210.43亿元，增长15.4%；人身险赔付支出301.82亿元，增长6.2%。

九、教育和科学技术

2019年，全省普通高等教育本专科招生46.0万人，在校生150.1万人，毕业生38.4万人；研究生招生5.5万人，在校研究生16.0万人，毕业生3.9万人；各类中等职业教育招生17.9万人，在校生47.5万人，毕业生14.0万人；普通高中招生30.1万人，在校生85.2万人，毕业生27.4万人；普通初中在校生165.4万人，小学在校生376.5万人，幼儿园在园幼儿177.8万人。

科学研究和技术开发取得新的成果。全年共登记重大科技成果1597项。其中，基础理论成果136项，应用技术成果1401项，软科学成果60项。全年共签订技术合同39511项，技术合同成交金额1449.6亿元，合同金额比上年增长17.2%。

2019年末，全省共建有225家省级工程研究中心（工程实验室）、528家省级企业技术中心。

全省共有国家级检验检测中心35个；累计有14101家企业通过ISO9000体系认证；企业获得强制性认证证书14873张。法定计量技术机构有91个，强制检定计量器具234万台件。

全省天气雷达观测站点有14个，卫星云图接受站点17个。地震遥测台网3个，地震台站47个。

十、文化、卫生和体育

2019年末，全省共有国有艺术表演团体87个，群艺馆、文化馆125个，公共图书馆115个，博物馆200个。电影放映管理机构103个，放映单位1837个。广播电台5座，电视台5座，广播电视台79座，有线电视用户1073.3万户。全年出版全国性和省级报纸7.4亿份，各类期刊1.1亿册，图书2.8亿册。

全省共有医疗卫生机构35432家，其中医院1028家，基层医疗卫生机构33856家，专业公共卫生机构484家；全省共有卫生计生人员总数52.6万人，其中执业（助理）医师15.4万人，注册护士19.4万人；全省共有医疗卫生机构床位40.4万张，其中医院床位28.9万张，社区卫生服务机构床位1.6万张，卫生院床位8.2万张。

全年全省运动健儿在国际比赛中共获得冠军103项次、亚军66项次、季军62项次，其中奥运会项目最高水平比赛冠军14项次、亚军5项次、季军8项次；在各类全国比赛中，获冠军230项次、亚军218项次、第三名275项次，其中，全运会项目全国最高水平比赛中冠军46项次、亚军40项次、第三名47项次。全年销售体育彩票106.0亿元。

十一、人口、居民生活和社会保障

年末全省常住人口5927万人，其中，城镇3615.47万人，乡村2311.53万人。城镇化率达到61%。全年出生人口67.21万人，出生率为11.35‰；死亡人口41.93万人，死亡率为7.08‰，人口自然增长率为4.27‰。

图10 2015–2019年湖北常住人口城镇化率

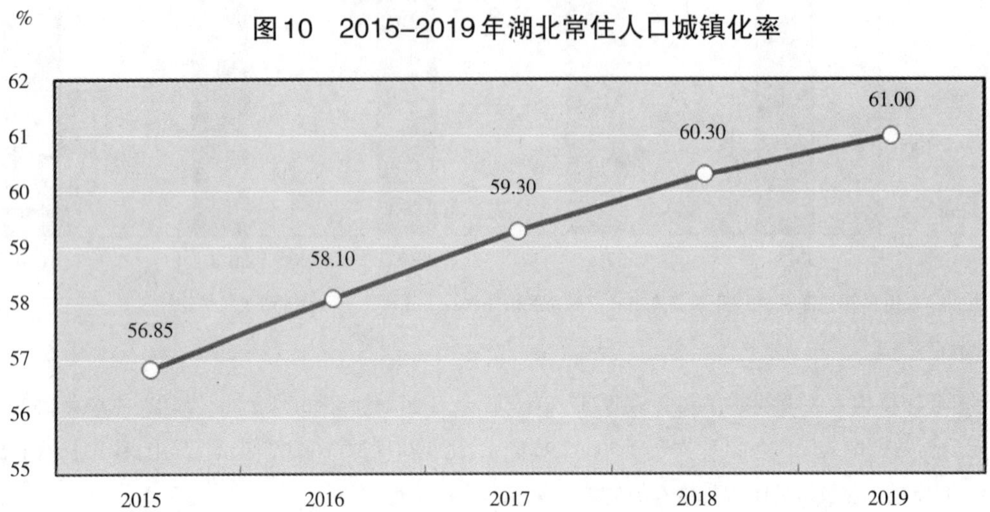

居民收入稳定增长。湖北城镇常住居民人均可支配收入37601元，增长9.1%；湖北农村常住居民人均可支配收入16391元，增长9.4%。

社会保障进一步加强。年末全省参加城镇职工基本养老保险1690.8万人，其中，在职职工1110.7万人，离退休人员580.1万人；参加城乡居民基本养老保险2345.4万人；参加城镇职工基本医疗保险1093.2万人；参加城乡居民基本医疗保险4469.4万人；参加工伤保险717.3万人；参加生育保险577.7万人；参加失业保险人数619.5万人，年末领取失业保险金人数6.2万人。

全年全省城镇居民最低生活保障对象31.8万人，农村居民最低生活保障人数139.3万人，国家抚恤、补助各类优抚对象40.3万人。社会福利事业不断发展。年末全省养老（含社区）床位数41.4万张，社区服务中心、站共计11575个。全年销售社会福利彩票81.2亿元。

十二、节能降耗、资源环境

全省继续大力推进节能降耗工作，单位GDP能耗继续保持下降态势，年初确定的2%的下降目标顺利完成。

全省主要河流的179个地表水水质监测断面中，水质优良为Ⅰ～Ⅲ类的占89.4%，水质较差为Ⅳ类、Ⅴ类的占9.5%，水质污染严重为劣Ⅴ类的占1.1%。全省主要湖泊、水库的32个水域中，水质优良为Ⅰ～Ⅲ类水域占50.0%，水质较差为Ⅳ类、Ⅴ类的占50.0%，无劣Ⅴ类水域。

全省完成造林面积29.92万公顷，其中人工造林面积9万公顷，占全部造林面积的30%。森林抚育面积26.7万公顷。截至2019年底，全省国家级自然保护区22个。

注：本公报所列数据为统计快报数。

2019 Statistics Bulletin of the National Economic and Social Development of Hubei Province

Hubei Provincial Bureau of Statistics
Survey Office of the National Bureau of Statistics in Hubei

In 2019, under the strong leadership of the provincial party committee and government, the whole province follows the guidance of Xi Jinping Thought on Socialism with Chinese Characteristics for a New Era, fully implements the guiding principles of the Party's 19th National Congress and the second, third, and fourth plenary sessions of its 19th Central Committee. Bearing in mind important entrustment of the "Four Efforts" and the "Four Practical", we implement the five-sphere integrated plan and the four-pronged comprehensive strategy, continue to follow the general principle of pursuing progress while ensuring stability, and applied the new development philosophy. We always take the three critical battles as the top priority of high-quality development, comprehensively deepen reform and opening up as key measures, ensure and improve people's livelihood as the first goal. We've overcome difficulties, bravely and resolutely, and promoted the province's economy to go up the road of high-quality development stability.

I General

In 2019, the whole province registered a GDP of 4.582831trillion yuan, representing an increase of 7.5% over the previous year. The primary industry saw the value-added stand at 380.909 billion yuan, rising by 3.2%; the secondary industry saw the value-added stand at 1.909862 trillion yuan, rising by 8.0%; the tertiary industry saw the value-added stand at 2.29206 trillion yuan, rising by 7.8%. The composition of the three industries has been transformed into 8.3:41.7:50.0 from 8.5：41.8：49.7 in 2018. Among the tertiary industry, transport, warehousing and postal services, wholesale and retail, hotels and catering services, finance, real estate and other services have witnessed the value-added grow by 9.4%, 5.3%, 8.5%,7.1%, 5.6%, and 9.2% respectively.

The price level remained basically stable. Consumer prices in Hubei rose by 3.1%, 1.2 percentage points higher than the previous year. Within this category, urban consumer price increased by 3.0%, and rural 3.2%. For the price of the main eight kinds of commodities, the price of seven commodities have risen to varying degrees, except for the prices of traffic and communication, which fell by 0.7% from the previous year. In details, the prices of food, tobacco and wine rose by 7.0%, clothing 1.6%, residence1.9%, articles of daily use and services 0.4%, education, culture and entertainment 2.5%, medical care 1.8%, and other articles for use and services 2.6%. In Hubei, the industrial producer factory prices rose by 0.2% while the industrial producer purchase prices fell by 0.7%.

Market entities speeded up development. The whole province now has a total of 900.3 thousand newly-registered market entities, specifically 251.3 thousandnewly-registered private enterprises and 627.3 thousand newly-registered privately or individually-owned businesses.

Employment remained stable. At the end of the year, the province employed 35.48 million people, including 20.9 million urban employment. Throughout the year, there was 921.5 thousand new employment in cities and towns in the province, which included an increase of 1.9 thousand over the previous year.The registered urban unemployment rate was 2.44% at the end of the year, 0.11 percentage points lower than at the end of the previous year.

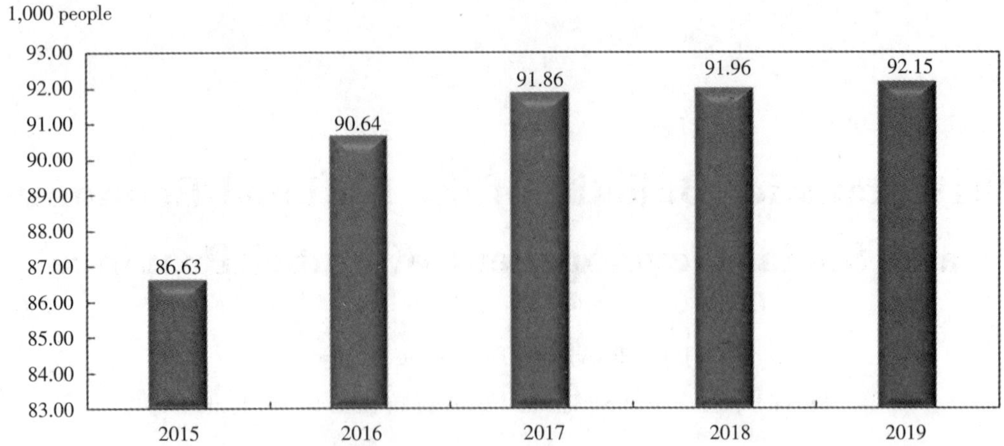

Figure 1 Number of New Urban Employment in Hubei Province from 2015 to 2019

Labor productivity has risen steadily. The overall labor productivity of the whole province was 128.6 thousand yuan per person, an increase of 8.5% over the previous year.

The effect of poverty reduction is obvious.According to the rural poverty standard of 2.3 thousand yuan per person per year (2010 constant price), there were 58.0 thousand rural poverty–stricken people at the end of the year, 925.0 thousand less than the end of the previous year, and the incidence of poverty was 0.14%, 2.26 percentage points lower than that of the previous year.

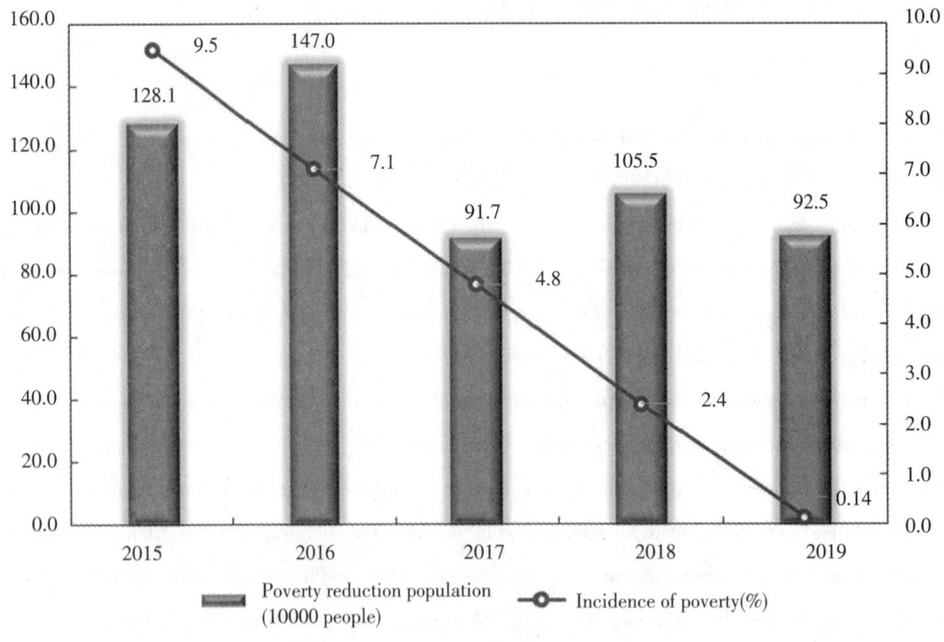

Figure 2 Poverty Reduction Population and Poverty Incidence Rate in Hubei Province at the end of the year from 2015 to 2019

II Agriculture

The value added of agriculture, forestry, animal husbandry and fishery in the whole province reached 401.4 billion yuan, up by 3.5% over the previous year at comparable prices.

Grain production remained stable. The whole province' s grain output was 27.2498 million tons, down by 4.0%, yet maintaining an output of over 50 billion jin for the seventh consecutive years. The planted area was 4.6086 million hectares, down by 4.9 %.

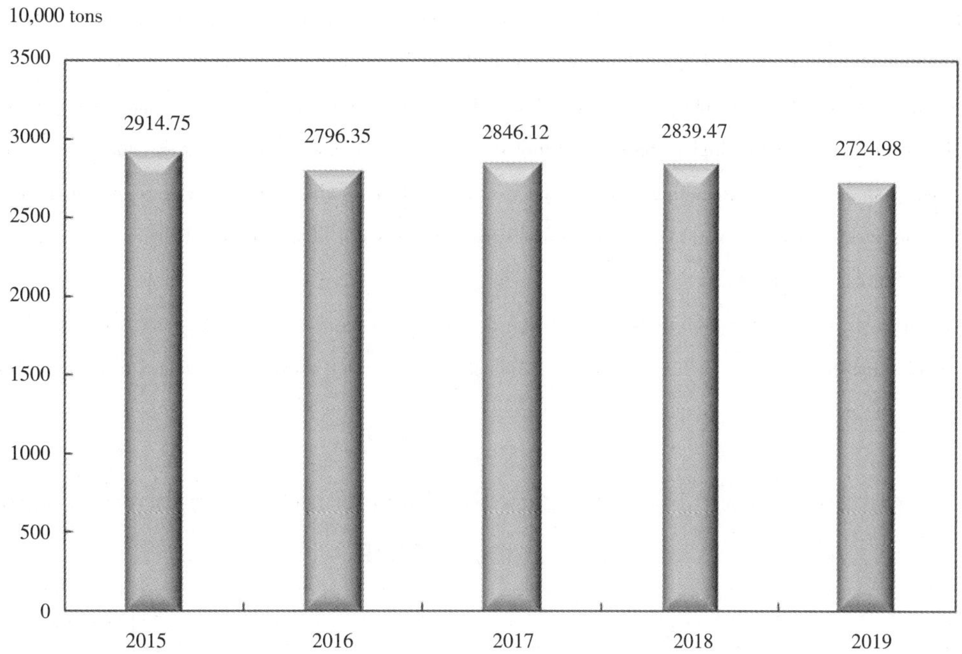

Figure 3 Grain Output of Hubei Province from 2015 to 2019

Cash crops with distinctive advantages grew rapidly. The output of vegetables and edible fungi was 40.8671million tons, up by 3.1%; the output of tea was 352.5 thousand tons, up by 6.9%; the output of garden fruits (excluding melons) was 6.6104million tons, up by 0.9%.

Livestock and poultry breeding adjusted deeply. Due to the African swine fever, the number of live pigs for sales was 31.8924 million, down by 26.9%. A total of 1.0952 million heads of cattle and 6.1593 million heads of sheep were full-grown and ready for slaughter, up by 1.1% and 1.1%, respectively. 593.9401 million fowls were delivered to the slaughterhouse, up by 11.5%; The output of poultry eggs was 1.7875 million tons, up by 4.2%.

The situation of aquatic products production has stabilized, and the fishery industry has been growing in a restorative way throughout the year. The total output of aquatic products was 4.6908 million tons, up by2.4%.

Table 1 Output of Main Agricultural Productions in 2019

Unit: 10,000 ton

Item	Output	YoY Growth Rate (%)
Grain	2724.98	-4.0
Cotton	14.36	-3.8
Oil	313.95	3.8
#Rapeseed	211.35	2.9
Tea	35.25	6.9
Garden fruits (excluding melons)	661.04	0.9
vegetables and edible fungi	4086.71	3.1

III Industry and Construction

Industrial production increased steadily. By the end of the year, there were 15.589 thousand industrial enterprises above designated size across the province. The value added of industries above designated size rose by 7.8%. In terms of different types of organizations, the value added of–state–owned and state–holding enterprises increased by 4.4%, that of collective enterprises down by 6.7%, that of–joint–stock enterprises grew by 8.5%, that of enterprises with foreign, Hong Kong, Macao and Taiwan investors increased by 3.4%; Other types of businesses grew by 4.3%. Light industry grew by 6.8% and heavy industry 8.2%.

Manufacturing grew by 7.9%, 0.1 percentage points lower than that of industries above designated size. High–tech manufacturing grew by 14.4%, 6.6 percentage points higher than that of industries above designated size, accounting for 9.5% of the value added of industries above designated size and contributing 17.0% to the growth of industries above designated size. Among them, the computer, communication and other electronic equipment manufacturing industry increased by 19.0%, and the electrical machinery and equipment manufacturing industry increased by 11.0%.

Throughout the year, the output value of industries above designated size increased by 7.8%, the product sales rate was 97.2% and the export delivery value decreased by 0.4%. The profits of industrial enterprises above designated size reached 286.78 billion yuan, up by 4.0 %.

Table 2 Output and Growth Rate of Major Products of Industriesabove Designated Size in Hubei in 2019

Item	Unit	Output	YoY Growth Rate (%)
quor	10,000 kiloliters	63.0	4.7
Beer	10,000 kiloliters	128.2	-5.4
Cigarette	100 million	1273.8	-0.2
Cloth	100 million meters	57.2	-0.8
Sulfuric acid (100%)	10,000 tons	848.9	-1.4
Agricultural nitrogen, phosphorus and potassium chemical fertilizer (pure)	10,000 tons	558.3	14.6
Chemical ingredients	10,000 tons	19.8	0.6
Chinese patent medicine	10,000 tons	32.1	-22.9
Power generation	100 million kw/h	2896.40	4.4
# Water and electricity	100 million kw/h	1330.27	-8.0
Cement	10,000 tons	11622.8	6.0
Plate glass	10,000 weight cases	10299.4	9.9
Pig iron	10,000 tons	2765.2	-1.3
Crude steel	10,000 tons	3611.5	1.0
Steel products	10,000 tons	3771.6	2.3
Ten kinds of non–ferrous metals	10,000 tons	85.8	11.0
# Refined copper	10,000 tons	53.6	5.3
Industrial robot	set	10440.0	7.1
Automobile	10,000 vehicles	224.0	-7.4
# New Energy Vehicle	vehicle	60554.0	-8.9
Generator set	10,000 kilowatts	120.3	-22.1
Lithium ion battery	10,000tons(Nature only)	108588.0	28.2
Room air conditioner	10,000sets	2110.9	14.1
Microcomputer equipment	10,000 sets	1270.2	14.3
Monitor	10,000 sets	1519.4	29.7
Mobile communication device	10,000 sets	3920.0	-10.2

The construction industry has developed steadily. In the whole year, the total output value of construction enterprises with general contracting and professional contracting qualifications reached 1.697959 trillion yuan, up by 12.2%; registering a profit of 72.324 billion yuan, up by 15.2%. We have begun work on new housing construction covering 380.5862 million square meters, down by 4.3%.

IV Fixed Assets Investment

The fixed-assets investment (excluding rural households) in the province increased by 10.6%. Investment in real estate development increased by 8.9%. The floor space of commercial buildings sold was 86.0204 million square meters, down by 3.0%.The sales of commercial buildings reached 775.179 billion yuan, up by 2.9%. In regard to specific industries, the primary, secondary and tertiary industrial investment in the province increased by 18.6%, 6.2% and 13.2%, respectively. A total of 316 key construction projects under construction in the province registered an investment of 292.445 billion yuan.

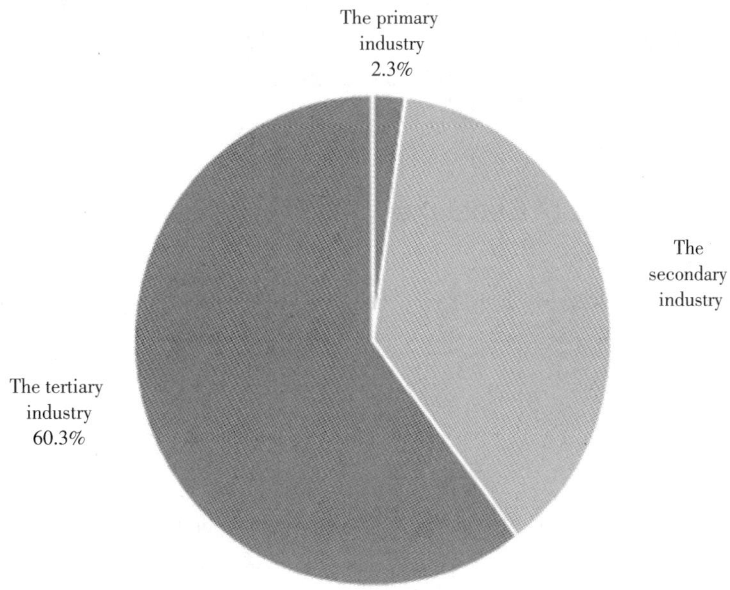

Figure 4 Proportion of Investment in Three Industries in Fixed Assets Investment (excluding Farmers) in 2019

The number of newly launched projects of over 100 million yuan stood at 3,952, with a 10.6% increase of investment into projects of over 100 million yuan.

V Domestic Trade

The total annual retail sales of consumer goods in the province reached 2.022423 trillion yuan, up by 10.3%. If we categorize them according to the business location, the retail sales in urban areas reached 1.693399 trillion yuan, up by 10.2%, while that in rural area reached 329.024 billion yuan, up by 11.2%. Among them, retail sales of consumer goods by enterprises (units) above the quota reached 863.384 billion yuan, up by 9.0%.

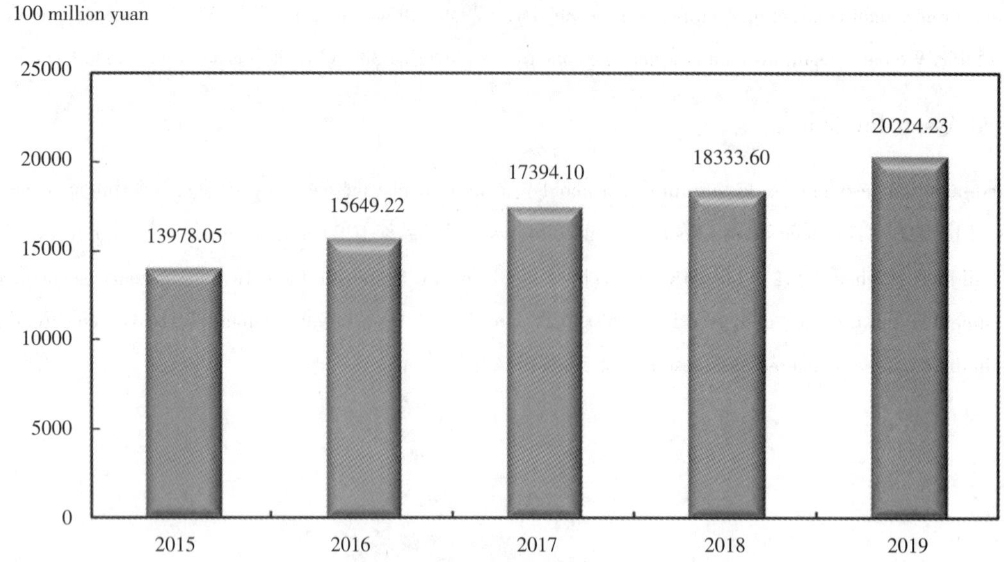

Figure 5 Total Retail Sales of Consumer Goods in Hubei Province from 2015 to 2019

In 2019, the provincial online retail sales reached 286.0 billion yuan, an increase of 10.1% over the previous year. Specifically, the online retail sales of physical goods reached 238.44 billion yuan, an increase of 17.7%, accounting for 11.8% of the total retail sales of consumer goods.

VI Foreign Trade

The annual imports and exports in the province reached 394.36 billion yuan, up by 13.1%. Specifically, imports rose by 18.2% to 145.87 billion yuan, while exports grew by 10.3% to 248.49 billion yuan. For the countries along the line of "one belt, one road", the total volume of imports and exports is 118.33 billion yuan, an increase of 22.4% over the previous year.

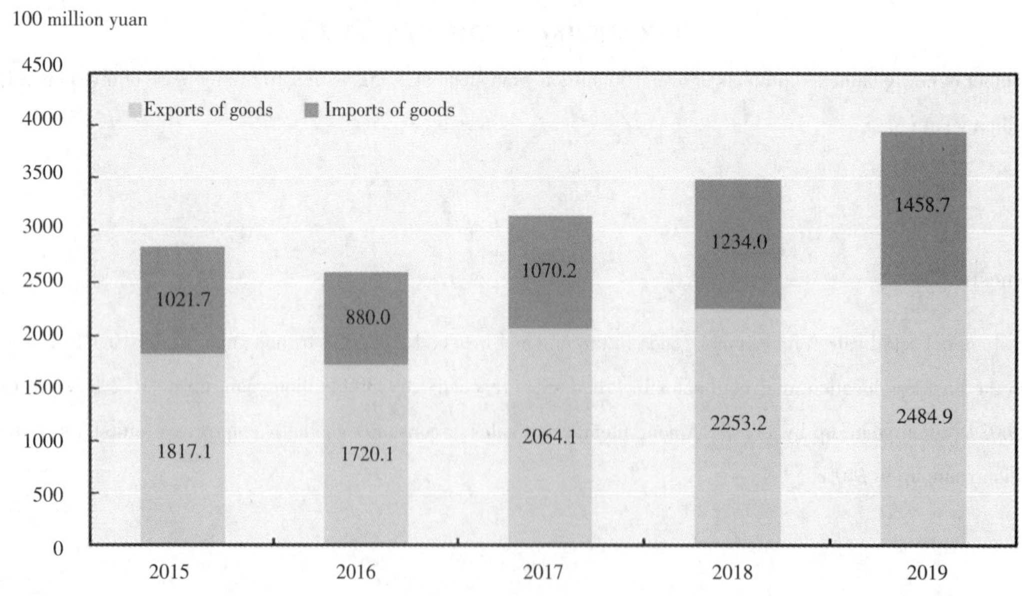

Figure 6 Total Import and Export Volume of Goods in Hubei Province from 2015 to 2019

There were 446 newly approved FDI projects. The value of foreign investment in actual use in the whole year stood at12.907 billion dollars, up by 8.1%. Among them, there were 60 newly established enterprises, which the countries along the line of "one belt, one road" have direct investment in Hubei, up by 9.1%.

VII Transport & Postal and Telecommunications Services

The turnover of freight traffic in the whole province was 723.785 billion ton-kilometers, up by 8.4% over the previous year. Passenger turnover was 138.679 billion person-kilometers, down by 2.2%; the total length of roads reached 289.0292 thousand kilometers, up by 5.1%, while expressways measured 6.86032 thousand kilometers, up by7.8%. The port completed 307 million tons of cargo throughput, up by 26.7%.

The province's postal service delivered a total revenue of 45.851 billion yuan, up by 32.8%. Among them, the express business volume was 1.685 billion pieces, and the express business income was 17.389 billion yuan. The telecommunications business generated 336.593 billion yuan, up by 65.4%. The total length of long-distance fiber-optical cable reached 30.8 thousand kilometers. The capacity of mobile telephone exchange reached 90.435 million; 5.1893 million households use landline phones, while mobile phone reached 56.8802 million people. The telephone penetration rate of the whole province was 104.9 units per 100 people, and the mobile phone penetration rate was 96.1 per 100 people. There were 17.0832 million fixed Internet broadband users, an increase of 2.2759 million over the previous year, and mobile Internet users' access flow was 3.827 billion GB, an increase of 75.3% over the previous year.

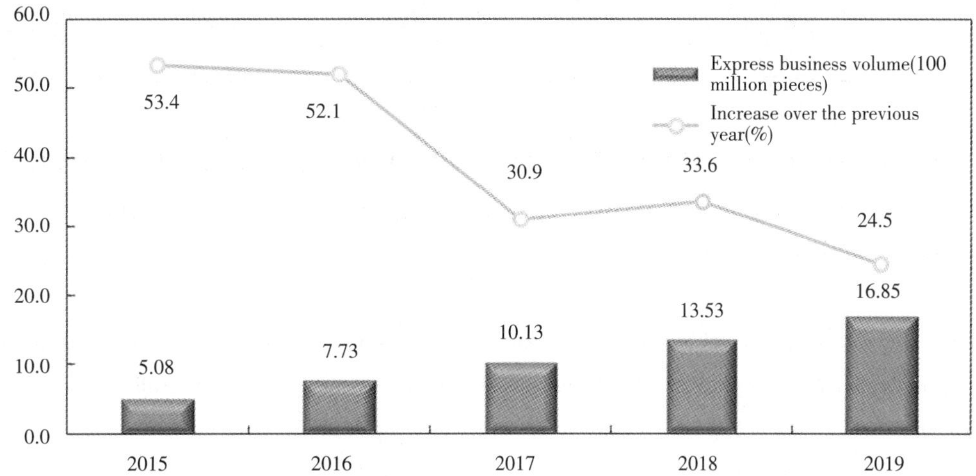

Figure 7 Express Business Volume and Growth Rate in Hubei from 2015 to 2019

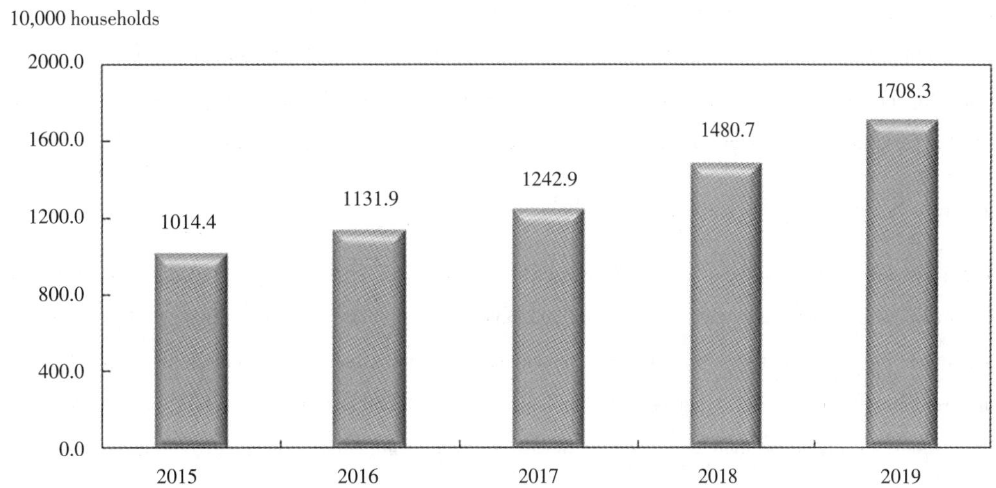

Figure 8 Fixed Internet Broadband Access Users in Hubei Province at the end of the year from 2015 to 2019

VIII Government Revenue & Finance

The annual revenue of the whole province stood at 578.686 billion yuan, up by 1.8%, including 338.839-billion-yuan revenue in the local general public budget, up by 2.5%. Concerning the revenue in the local general public budget, tax revenue totaled 253.064 billion yuan, up by 2.7%. Government expenditures for the year totaled 796.773 billion yuan, up by 9.8%.

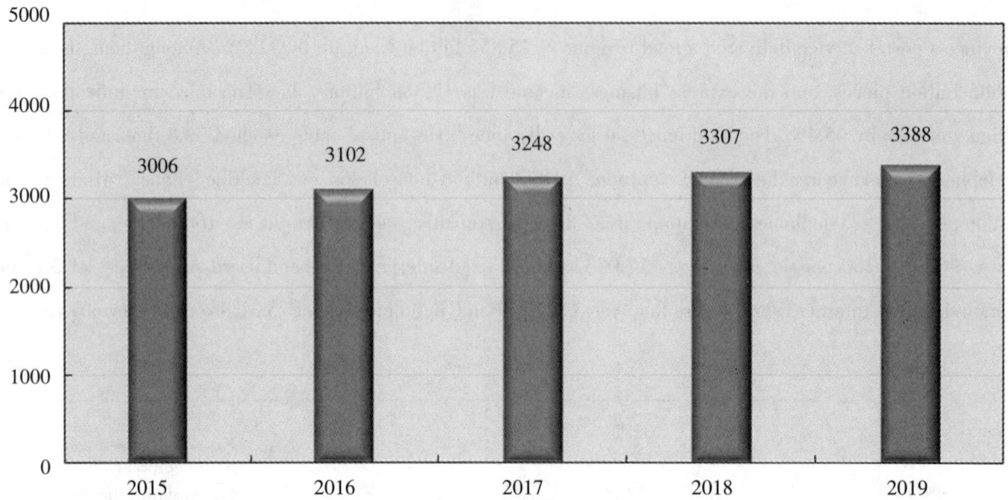

Figure 9 General Public Budget Revenue in Hubei from 2015 to 2019

Note: The data in the figure from 2015 to 2018 are the final accounts of Hubei's general public budget revenue, and the figure in 2019 is the progress data.

At the end of the year, RMB deposits balance in provincial financial institutions was5.97477 trillion yuan, an increase of 436.204 billion yuan over the beginning of the year. Specifically, household deposits amounted to 2.980455 trillion yuan, an increase of 347.543 billion yuan. The outstanding loans of financial institutions amounted to 5.06639 trillion yuan, an increase of 609.407 billion yuan over the beginning of the year. Of this amount, household loans amounted to 1.658411 trillion yuan, an increase of 247.219 billion yuan, while loans to non-financial enterprises and government organs and organizations totaled 3.407524 trillion yuan, an increase of 362.368 billion yuan.

The annual insurance premiums totaled 172.857 billion yuan, up by 17.5%. Specifically, property insurance companies reaped 39.785 billion yuan in premiums, up by 13%, while life insurance companies earned 133.072 billion yuan, up by 18.9%. Indemnities and various types of payments amounted to 51.226 billion yuan, up by 9.8%. Property insurance companies paid 21.043 billion yuan for indemnity, up by 15.4%, while life insurance companies spent 30.182 billion yuan on the said category, up by 6.2%.

IX Education, Science and Technology

In 2019, the province's general higher education enrolls 460.0 thousand students, 1501.0 thousand students and 384.0 thousand graduates; the province saw the enrollment of 55.0 thousand graduate students, totaling 160.0 graduate students and 39.0 thousand graduates; the province saw the enrollment of 179.0 thousand secondary vocational education students, totaling 475.0 thousand students and 140.0 thousand graduates; There are 301.0 thousand students enrolled in ordinary senior high schools, totaling 852.0 thousand students in school and 274.0 thousand graduates; there are 1.654 million students in junior high schools, 3.765 million students in primary schools and 1.778 million children in kindergartens.

New achievements were made in scientific research and technological development. A total of 1.597 thousand major scientific and technological achievements were registered, including 136 basic theories, 1.401 thousand applied technologies and 60 results in soft science. A total of 39.511thousand technology contracts were signed, involving 144.96 billion yuan, an increase of 17.2% over the previous year.

By the year-end of 2019, the province has established 225 provincial-level engineering research centers (engineering laboratories) and 528 provincial-level enterprise technology centers.

There are 35 national inspection and testing centers in the province. A total of 14.101thousand enterprises have obtained the ISO9000 system certification. Corporations have obtained 14.873 thousand compulsory certificates. The number of legal metrological technical institutions is 91, with 2.34 million units of measuring instruments subject to compulsory verification.

There are 14 weather radar observation stations and 17 satellite image receiving stations, as well as 3 seismic telemetry networks and 47 seismic stations.

X Culture, Public Health and Sports

By the end of 2019, the province has 87 state-owned art troupes, 125 art and cultural centers, 115 public libraries and 200 museums. There are 103 film projection management organizations and 1.837 thousand projection units. There are 5 radio stations, 5 television stations and 79 radio and television stations. 10.733 million households have subscribed cable TV. It published 740 million copies of national and provincial newspapers, 110 million copies of periodicals and 280 million copies of books.

There are 35.432 thousand medical and health institutions in the province, including 1028 hospitals, 33.856 thousand grassroots medical and health institutions, and 484 professional public health institutions. There are 526.0 thousand health and family planning personnel in the province, including 154.0 thousand practicing (assistant) physicians and 194.0 thousand registered nurses. The province has 404.0 thousand beds in medical and health institutions, including 289.0 thousand beds in hospitals, 16.0 thousand beds in community health service institutions and 82.0 thousand beds in health centers.

In the whole year, athletes in the province ended up winning 103 champion titles, runner-up 66 times and third place 62 times in the international competitions, including 14 gold medals, 5 silver medals and 8 bronze medals in the Olympic Games. In all kinds of national competitions, they garnered 230 championships, 218 runner-upsand 275 third places, including 46 gold medals, 40 silver medals and 47 bronze medals in the National Games. The annual sports lottery sales totaled 10.6 billion yuan.

XI Population, Life and Social Security

By the end of the year, there were 59.27 million permanent residents in the province, with 36.1547 million in urban areas and 23.1153 million in rural areas. The urbanization rate reached 61 percent. There were 672.1 thousand births and 419.3 thousand deaths, with birth and death rates of 11.35 and 7.08 per 1000, respectively, and thus a natural population growth rate of 4.27 per thousand.

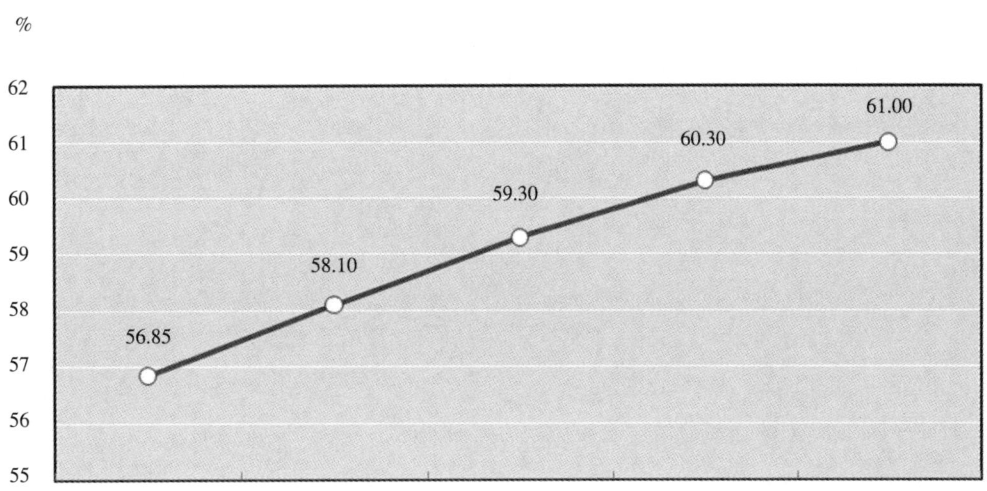

Figure 10 The Urbanization Rate of Hubei Permanent Population from 2015 to 2019

Personal income grew steadily. The per capita disposable income of permanent urban residents in Hubei was 37.601 thousand yuan, up by 9.1%; that of permanent rural residents in Hubei was 16.391 thousand yuan, up by 9.4%.

Social security was further strengthened. By the end of the year, 16.908 million people have participated in the basic endowment insurance for urban workers, including 11.107 million employees and 5.801 million retirees. 23.454 million people have participated in the basic endowment insurance for urban and rural residents; 10.932 million people have participated in the basic medical insurance for urban workers; 44.694 million people have participated in the basic medical insurance for urban and rural residents; 7.173 million people are covered by work-related injury insurance,and 5.777 million people by maternity insurance; 6.195 million people have participated in unemployment insurance and 62.0 thousand received unemployment insurance compensation at the end of the year.

Throughout the year, 318.0 thousand urban residents and 1.393 million rural residents received the minimum living allowances, and the entitled group of 403.0 thousand people has received special pensions and subsidies by the state. Social welfare programs have continued developing. At the end of the year, there were 414.0 thousand beds for all kinds of social welfare in the province, and 11.575 thousand community service centers and stations in cities and towns. The annual social welfare lottery sales totaled 8.12 billion yuan.

XII Energy Saving and Consumption Reduction, Resources and Environment

The province continued rolling out efforts to conserve energy and cut consumption. As a result, energy consumption per unit of GDP continued declining, and the 2% target set at the beginning of the year was successfully met.

Among the 179 surface water quality monitoring sections of the main rivers in the province, 89.4% of the surface water quality monitoring sections are of good quality, 9.5% are of class IV and V with poor water quality, and 1.1% are of serious water pollution. Among the 32 main lakes and reservoirs in the province, 50.0% of the 32 waters are of good water quality, 50.0% are of class IV and V with poor water quality, and there is no inferior class V water area.

The afforestation area of the whole province is 299.2 thousand hectares, including 90.0 thousand hectares of artificial afforestation area, accounting for 30% of the total afforestation area. The forest tending area is 267.0 thousand hectares. By the end of 2019, there are 22 national nature reserves in the province.

Notes: Data in this Bulletin are express data.

1 综合

General Survey

资料整理人员：程文懿　周　真　王喜锋
闵胜男　金　花

综 合
General Survey

从数字看2019年的湖北
Statistic about Hubei in 2019

湖 北 的 地 位
Position of Hubei in the Country

地区生产总值45828.31亿元	Gross Domestic Production: 4582.831billion yuan	占全国的4.63%
#第三产业22920.60亿元	Tertiary Industry: 2292.060 billion yuan	占全国的4.29%
人均地区生产总值77387元	Per Capita Regional GDP:77387 yuan	相当于全国的109.16%
社会消费品零售总额22722.31亿元	Total Retail Sales of Social Consumption: 2272.231 billion yuan	占全国的5.52%
进出口总额571.28亿美元	Total Imports and Exports: 57.128 billion US dollars	占全国的1.25%
#出口总额359.80亿美元	Total Exports: 35.980 billion US dollars	占全国的1.44%
实际外商直接投资129.07亿美元	Actual Foreign Direct Investment: 12.907 billion US dollars	占全国的9.34%
粮食产量2724.98万吨	Grain: 27.2498 million tons	占全国的4.10%
钢产量3771.58万吨	Rolled Steel: 37.7158 milliom tons	占全国的3.13%
发电量2896.40亿千瓦小时	Electricity: 289.640 billion kwh	占全国的3.86%
城镇居民人均可支配收入37601元	Per Capita Disposable Income of Urban Residents: 37601 yuan	相当于全国的88.77%
农村居民人均可支配收入16391元	Per Capita Net Incomes of Rural Residents:16391 yuan	相当于全国的102.31%

湖 北 的 人 口
Population of Hubei

常住人口	Population of Permanent Residents	5927.00万人
从业人员	Employment	3548.00万人
#在岗职工人数	Staff and Workers	1089.16万人
出生人口	Birth Population	67.21万人
死亡人口	Death Population	41.93万人
城镇人口	Urban Population	3615.47万人
乡村人口	Rural Population	2311.53万人
人口密度	Density of Population	319人/平方公里

湖 北 的 经 济 发 展
Economic Development of Hubei

		1979-2019年平均增长(%)
地区生产总值	Regional Gross Production	10.4
第一产业	Primary Industry	4.6
第二产业	Second Industry	12.2
第三产业	Tertiary Industry	12.2
财政收入	Government Revenue	12.1
货物运输量	Cargo Transport Volume	7.4
社会消费品零售总额	Total Retail Sales of Social Consumption	15.3
出口总额	Total Exports	14.1

湖 北 的 一 天
One Day in Hubei

地区生产总值	Gross Domestic Product	125.56亿元
第一产业	First Industry	10.44亿元
第二产业	Second Industry	52.32亿元
第三产业	Tertiary Industry	62.80亿元
地方公共财政收入	Local Government Public Finance Income	9.28亿元
货物运输量	Freight Traffic	515.46万吨
竣工房屋面积	Floor Space of Building Completed	92.90万平方米
社会消费品零售总额	Total Retail Sales of Social Consumption	62.25亿元
出口总额	Total Exports	9875.53万美元
出版报纸	Newspapers Published	201.89万份
邮寄函件	Letters and Correspondents Delivered	17.89万件

1-1 土地面积与行政区划
Land Area and Administrative Division

项目	单位	Item	unit	2000	2005	2010	2015	2017	2018	2019
常住人口	(万人)	Population of the Whole Province	(10 000 persons)	5646	5710	5724	5852	5902	5917	5927
土地面积	(万平方公里)	Land Area	(10 000 sq.km)			18.59	18.59	18.59	18.59	18.59
耕地面积	(千公顷)	Cultivated Area	(1000 hectares)			5312.3	5255	5235.91	5235.4	
行政区划		Adinimisrtative Division								
省辖市	(个)	Municipality	(unit)	12	12	12	12	12	12	12
自治州	(个)	Autonomous	(unit)	1	1	1	1	1	1	1
林区	(个)	Forest Zone	(unit)	1	1	1	1	1	1	1
县级市	(个)	City	(unit)	24	24	24	24	24	25	25
省辖行政单位	(个)	Adinimistrative Units under the Jurisdiction of Province	(unit)	3	3	3	3	3	3	3
县	(个)	County	(unit)	41	39	40	39	39	38	38
乡政府	(个)	Local Government	(unit)	476	217	201	168	165	163	162
镇政府	(个)	Township Government	(unit)	853	737	742	761	761	762	760
办事处	(个)	Office	(unit)	145	163	211	304	308	310	327
村民委员会	(个)	Village Community	(unit)	32400	26678	26018	25343	24312	23571	23202
村民小组	(个)	Village Groups	(unit)	259250	212587	209598	208546	206786	205059	203005

注：耕地面积数据来源于自然资源部门。
Note: Statistics of cultivated area sources from the Department of Natural Resources of Hubei Province.

1-2 市、州行政区划
Administrative Division of Cities and Prefectures

单位:个　　(2019年底)(by the End of 2019)　　(unit)

地区	Region	县级市 Cities	县 Counties	区 Districts	乡政府 Village Government	镇政府 Township Government	村民委员会 Village Community	村民小组 Village Groups
全 省	Total	25	38	39	162	760	23202	203005
武汉市	Wuhan			13	3	1	1889	16574
黄石市	Huangshi	1	1	4	1	27	787	7867
十堰市	Shiyan	1	4	3	34	72	1807	10013
荆州市	Jingzhou	3	3	2	12	88	1499	17839
宜昌市	Yichang	3	5	5	19	67	1348	8100
襄阳市	Xiangyang	3	3	3	4	74	2286	14457
鄂州市	Ezhou			3	3	18	324	4023
荆门市	Jingmen	2	1	2	2	48	1320	9963
孝感市	Xiaogan	3	3	1	23	72	2271	22440
黄冈市	Huanggang	2	7	1	16	99	4026	37457
咸宁市	Xianning	1	4	1	12	52	903	9636
恩施自治州	Enshi	2	6		30	53	2312	22255
随州市	Suizhou	1	1	1		37	848	8481
仙桃市	Xiantao	1				15	633	4502
天门市	Tianmen	1			1	21	528	6336
潜江市	Qianjiang	1				10	354	2736
神农架林区	Shennongjia				2	6	67	326

注:乡政府、镇政府、村民委员会、村民小组数只涉及农村生产经营单位数。
Note:The number of village government, township government, village community and village groups only refers to the number of units run by village production peration.

1-3 全省法人和产业活动单位数(2019年)
Number of Legal Entities and Industrial Activity Units of Hubei(2019)

指 标 名 称	Item	法人单位数(个) Corporation Units	规模、资质或限额以上单位 Unit of Scale, Qualification or Above	产业活动单位数(个) Number of Economic Activities Units
总计	**Total**	**1006949**	**41822**	**1123200**
一、按地区分组	**Grouped by Region**	**1006949**	**41822**	**1123200**
武汉市	Wuhan	313160	11784	341581
黄石市	Huangshi	42467	1884	47171
十堰市	Shiyan	51881	2312	59965
宜昌市	Yichang	83482	3951	92855
襄阳市	Xiangyang	100529	4045	108532
鄂州市	Ezhou	19601	882	21720
荆门市	Jingmen	42438	2259	48089
孝感市	Xiaogan	49987	2257	59105
荆州市	Jingzhou	63217	2980	70540
黄冈市	Huanggang	67006	2932	78405
咸宁市	Xianning	44783	1993	49235
随州市	Suizhou	24929	1448	28611
恩施州	Enshi	58084	1084	66969
仙桃市	Xiantao	16644	838	18169
潜江市	Qianjiang	11164	506	12876
天门市	Tianmen	15153	603	16470
神农架	Shennongjia	2424	64	2907
二、按国民经济行业门类分组	**Grouped by Sector**	**1006949**	**41822**	**1123200**
农、林、牧、渔业	Farming, Forestry, Animal husbandary and Fishery	72337		73160
采矿业	Mining	2711	400	2885
制造业	Manufacturing	100949	14656	102968
电力、热力、燃气及水生产和供应业	Power, Gas and Water Production and Supply	5593	425	8177
建筑业	Construction	74766	4974	80531
批发和零售业	Transportaation, Storage and Post	276178	8456	309877
交通运输、仓储和邮政业	Information Transmission, Computer Service and software	25438	1365	33100
住宿和餐饮业	Wholesale and Retail Sale	18322	2413	22544
信息传输、软件和信息技术服务业	Hotel and Catering	50017	664	55029
金融业	Banking	2804		13036
房地产业	Real Estate	34986	4862	40125
租赁和商务服务业	Leasing and Commerical Service	113373	1212	122317
科学研究和技术服务业	Scietific Research, Polytechnical Service and Geological Prospecting	62116	848	67200
水利、环境和公共设施管理业	Water Conservancy, Environment and Public Facility Management	9742	233	10969
居民服务、修理和其他服务业	Resident Service and Others	20763	254	22248
教育	Education	27838	245	30791
卫生和社会工作	Health Care, Social Security and Social Welfare	12768	278	19766
文化、体育和娱乐业	Culture, Sports and Recreation	24354	537	25696
公共管理、社会保障和社会组织	Public Management and Social Organization	71894		82781

1-3 续表1 continued

指标名称	Item	法人单位数（个）Corporation Units	规模、资质或限额以上单位 Unit of Scale, Qualification or Above	产业活动单位数（个）Number of Economic Activities Units
总计	**Total**	**1006949**	**41822**	**1123200**
三、按登记注册类型分组	**Grouped by Type of Registration**	**1006949**	**41822**	**1123200**
内资	Inner Funded	1003187	40664	1113074
国有	State-owned	55323	631	77455
集体	Collective-owned	8763	232	13140
股份合作	Share Holding Cooperative	481	18	717
联营	Joint Funded	737	15	956
国有联营	State Joint owned	86	1	127
集体联营	Collective Joint-owned	267	6	374
国有与集体联营	State - owned and Collective Joint-owned	71	5	86
其他联营	Other Joint-owned	313	3	369
有限责任公司	Co. Ltd	56764	13510	73561
国有独资公司	State-owned Solely Funded Co.	1731	642	4087
其他有限责任公司	Other Co. Ltd	55033	12868	69474
股份有限公司	Share Holding Co.Ltd.	4478	1542	15053
私营	Private - owned Enterprises	735852	24400	784531
私营独资	Private Solely Funded Enterprises	81839	865	83631
私营合伙	Private Partnership Enterprises	9552	140	9862
私营有限责任公司	Private Co. Ltd	640039	22277	684591
私营股份有限公司	Private Share Holding Co.Ltd.	4422	1118	6447
其他内资	Others	140789	316	147661
港澳台商投资	Hongkong, Macao and Taiwan Funded Enterprises	1661	515	4034
与港澳台商合资经营	Joint Venture with Hongkong, Macao and Taiwan	617	179	656
与港澳台商合作经营	Cooperate with Hongkong, Macao and Taiwan Funded	22	6	29
港澳台商独资	Enterprises Solely Funded by Hongkong, Macao and Taiwan	974	292	3223
港澳台商投资股份有限公司	Share Holding Co.Ltd. with Hongkong, Macao and Taiwan Investment	28	22	70
其他港、澳、台商投资	Other Hongkong, Macao and Taiwan Investment	20	16	56
外商投资	Foreign Funded Enterprises	2101	643	6092
中外合资经营	Sino - Foreign Joint Funded Enterprises	759	293	909
中外合作经营	Sino - Foreign Cooperative Funded Enterprises	20	6	25
外资企业	Foreign Solely Funded Enterprises	1120	297	4107
外商投资股份有限公司	Foreign Funded Share Holding Co.Ltd.	135	15	933
其他外商投资	Other Foreign Investment	67	32	118
四、按机构类型分组	Grouped by Type	1006949	41822	1123200
企业	Enterprise	804822	41429	896145
事业单位	Public Institution	39815	35	53304
机关	Government Agency	9879		14861
社会团体	Mass Organization	13291		13321
民办非企业单位	Private Non Enterprise Unit	19589	201	19428
基金会	Foundation	142		142
居委会	Neighborhood Committee	4981		5138
村委会	Village Committee	24989		25143
农民专业合作社	Farmer Specialized Cooperative	81117	136	81470
其他组织机构	Others	8324	21	14248

注：规模、资质或限额以上单位不包括省属重点服务业和投资专业法人单位。

Note: The units above the scale, qualification or above do not include the key service industries and the specialized legal person units of investment under the province.

1–4 国民经济和社会发展总量与速度指标

指标	Item	总量指标		
		1978	1990	2000
人口与就业	**Population and Employment**			
人口 (万人)	**Population** (10 000 persons)			
年末人口	Population at Year-end	4574.91	5439.29	5646.00
城镇人口	Urban	690.23	1551.51	2285.11
乡村人口	Rural	3884.68	3887.78	3360.89
就业 (万人)	**Employment (10 000 persons)**			
就业人数	Employment	1910.40	3040.40	3384.90
职工人数	Staff and Workers	457.34	698.55	677.96
#国有单位	State-owned Units	371.56	524.12	506.11
宏观经济	Marcoeconomy			
国民核算 (亿元)	**National Accounting** (100 million yuan)			
地区生产总值	Gross Domestic Products	151.00	824.38	3545.39
第一产业	First Industry	61.11	289.45	662.30
第二产业	Second Industry	63.71	313.39	1437.38
第三产业	Tertiary Industry	26.18	221.54	1445.71
支出法地区生产总值	Gross Domestic Expenditures			
#最终消费	Final Consumption Expenditures	81.70	535.49	2030.07
居民消费	Resident Consumption	74.70	434.62	1594.08
政府消费	Government Consumption Expenditures	7.00	100.87	436.00
资本形成总额	Gross Capital Formation	43.13	261.95	1882.47
固定资本形成	Fixed Capital Formation	31.40	147.13	1451.85
存货增加	Changes in Stock	11.72	114.82	430.62
固定资产投资 (亿元)	**Investment in Fixed Assets** (100 million yuan)			
固定资产投资总额	Total Investment in Fixed Assets	33.58	144.44	1421.55
#国有单位	State-Owned Units	33.19	100.35	857.01
集体单位	Collective-owned Units	0.39	15.59	128.32
财政 (亿元)	**Public Finance** (100 million yuan)			
地方一般公共预算收入	Local Public Financial Revenue	31.38	77.85	214.35
地方一般公共预算支出	Local Public Financial Expenditures	29.98	84.82	368.77
物价(上年=100)	Price (preceding year = 100)			
商品零售价格总指数	General Retail Price Index	100.5	102.9	97.8
居民消费价格指数	General Consumer Price Index	100.3	104.2	99.0
利用外资 (亿美元)	**Utilization of Foreign Capital** (100 million dollars)			
实际外商直接投资	Actual Foreign Direct Investment		0.29	9.44
产 业	**Industry**			
农业	**Agriculture**			
农林牧渔业总产值 (亿元)	Gross Output Value of Farming, Forestry, Animal Husbandry and Fishery (100 million yuan)	84.46	402.23	1125.64
主要农产品产量 (万吨)	Output of Major Farm Products (10 000 tons)			
粮食	Grain	1725.60	2475.03	2218.49
棉花	Cotton	36.67	51.73	30.43
油料	Oil-Bearing Crops	23.71	95.75	269.98
糖料	Sugar Crops	8.73	34.66	101.66
蚕茧	Silkworm Cocoons	0.47	0.79	1.22
肉类产量	Output of Meat	64.00	146.85	271.19
水产品	Aquatic Products	11.00	70.98	234.34

注：1.人口数除1982年、1990年、2000年、2010年是以人口普查为基数推算外，1982年及以后为人口抽样调查推算数。

2.2000年以前数据是总人口数，2001年以后数据为常住人口数。

3.2017年地区生产总值数据根据第三次农业普查数据进行调整，历史数据未调整。

4.从2016年，固定资产投资总额对2015年基数进行调整，且不再包含农户投资。

5.根据第三次全国农业普查结果对农业相关数据进行了修订，其中水产数据修订到2012年，产值、增加值、粮食、畜牧、经济作物数据修订到2007年。

Aggregate Indicators on National Economic and Social Development and Growth Rates

Aggregate Data			速度指标 Indices and Growth Rates								
			2019年比下列各年增长(%) Increases					年平均增长(%) Average Annual Growth Rate			
2010	2018	2019	1978	1990	2000	2010	2018	1979~2019	1991~2019	2001~2019	2011~2019
5723.77	5917.00	5927.00	29.6	9.0	5.0	3.6	0.2	0.6	0.3	0.3	0.4
2844.95	3567.95	3615.47	423.8	133.0	58.2	27.1	1.3	4.1	3.0	2.4	2.7
2878.82	2349.05	2311.53	-40.5	-40.5	-31.2	-19.7	-1.6	-1.3	-1.8	-2.0	-2.4
3645.00	3580.00	3548.00	85.7	16.7	4.8	-2.7	-0.9	1.5	0.5	0.2	-0.3
685.21	1060.63	1089.16	138.2	55.9	60.7	59.0	2.7	2.1	1.5	2.5	5.3
277.60	228.75	221.51	-40.4	-57.7	-56.2	-20.2	-3.2	-1.3	-2.9	-4.3	-2.5
16114.59	42021.95	45828.31	5698.4	1865.8	599.9	124.9	7.5	10.4	10.8	10.8	9.4
2147.00	3548.17	3809.09	544.5	237.4	129.1	44.1	3.2	4.6	4.3	4.5	4.1
7869.02	17573.87	19098.62	11029.2	3152.5	801.8	135.0	8.7	12.2	12.8	12.3	10.0
6098.57	20899.91	22920.60	11337.6	2472.7	651.0	138.2	9.7	12.3	11.8	11.2	10.1
7363.80											
5136.78											
2227.02											
8684.17											
8373.40											
310.77											
10802.69											
3768.95											
602.80											
1011.23	3307.08	3388.57	10698.5	4252.7	1480.9	235.1	2.5	12.1	13.9	15.6	14.4
2501.40	7258.27	7970.21	26485.1	9296.6	2061.3	218.6	9.8	14.6	17.0	17.6	13.7
103.1	101.2	102.6	2.1	-0.3	4.9	-0.5	1.3	0.1	0.0	0.3	-0.1
102.9	101.9	103.1	2.8	-1.1	4.1	0.2	1.1	0.1	0.0	0.2	0.0
40.50	119.41	129.07		44406.9	1267.3	218.7	8.1		23.4	14.8	13.7
3407.64	6207.83	6681.85	218.9	74.2	0.3	52.7	3.5	2.9	1.9	0.0	4.8
2304.26	2839.47	2724.98	57.9	10.1	22.8	18.3	-4.0	1.1	0.3	1.1	1.9
47.41	14.93	14.36	-60.8	-72.2	-52.8	-69.7	-3.8	-2.3	-4.3	-3.9	-12.4
302.28	302.48	313.95	1224.1	227.9	16.3	3.9	3.8	6.5	4.2	0.8	0.4
28.37	27.77	27.90	219.6	-19.5	-72.6	-1.7	0.5	2.9	-0.7	-6.6	-0.2
0.68	0.40	0.38	-19.1	-51.9	-68.9	-44.1	-5.0	-0.5	-2.5	-6.0	-6.3
383.48	430.95	349.20	445.6	137.8	28.8	-8.9	-19.0	4.2	3.0	1.3	-1.0
353.00	458.40	469.54	4168.5	561.5	100.4	33.0	2.4	9.6	6.7	3.7	3.2

Note: a)Data of 1982,1990,2000.and 2010 are based on population census, and data of other years are based on sampling survey.
b)Data before 2000 refer to total population. Data after 2001 refer to permanent residents.
c)The GDP data for 2017 were adjusted according to the data of the third agricultural census, and historical data were not adjusted.
d)Since 2016,the basic number of 2015 is adjusted and famer investment is no longer included in the social fixed assets investment.
e)According to the results of the third national agricultural census, the relevant agricultural data were revised, including aquatic product data to 2012, output value,added value, grain, animal husbandry, cash crop data to 2007.

1-4 续表1 continued

指 标		Item		总量指标		
				1978	1990	2000
工业		**Industry**				
主要工业产品产量	(万吨)	Output of Major Industrial Products	(10000 tons)			
粗 钢		Steel		307.97	629.25	895.92
成品钢材		Rolled-Steel		184.63	533.07	811.10
发电量	(亿千瓦小时)	Electricity	(100 million kWh)	91.64	340.39	538.11
原煤		Coal		644.01	924.26	389.34
农用氮、磷、钾化学肥料(折纯)		Chemical Furtilizers		27.62	132.07	221.11
化学农药原药(折有效成分100%)		Chemical Pesicide		2.97	1.07	5.18
水泥		Cement		328.65	987.00	2460.92
化学纤维		Chemical Fiber		0.48	2.48	9.82
布	(亿米)	Cloth	(100 million meter)	6.70	14.09	17.15
汽车	(万辆)	Automobile	(10000 Units)	0.80	11.38	19.57
建筑业		**Construction**				
建筑业企业职工平均人数	(万人)	Average Number of Employed Persons	(10000 persons)	25.94	41.88	82.76
建筑业总产值	(亿元)	Gross Output Value	(100 million yuan)	11.11	49.30	454.35
施工房屋面积	(万平方米)	Floor Space of Building Under Construction	(10 000 sq.m)	596.00	1684.90	6256.50
竣工房屋面积	(万平方米)	Floor Space of Building Completed	(10 000 sq.m)	297.40	785.90	3150.10
交通运输		**Transportation**				
货运量	(万吨)	Freight Traffic	(10 000 tons)	10199.08	10916.10	40949.00
#铁路		Railway		3513.00	3901.00	6558.00
公路		Highway		3556.00	2941.00	27863.00
水运		Waterway		3130.00	3784.00	6270.00
客运量	(万人)	Passenger Capacity	(10000 persons)	12009.20	32145.93	31593.00
#铁路		Railway		2854.00	2107.00	3469.00
公路		Highway		7429.00	27333.00	27184.00
水运		Waterway		1722.00	2693.00	679.00
港口货物吞吐量	(万吨)	Volume of Freight Handled at Seaports	(10 000 tons)			4113.46
邮电通信业		**Postal Telecommunication Services**				
邮电业务总量	(亿元)	Total Business Revenue	(100 million yuan)	0.56	4.80	116.60
函件	(亿件)	Number of Letters Delivered	(100 million pieces)	1.18	2.39	3.62
年末移动电话用户	(万户)	Number of Local Telephone Users	(10 000 units)			
国际互联网用户	(万户)	Internet Users	(10 000 units)			
国内商业		**Domestic Commerce**				
社会消费品零售总额	(亿元)	Total Retail Sales of Consumer Goods	(100 million yuan)	59.84	326.36	1789.35
对外经济贸易和旅游		**Foreign Trade and Tourism**				
进出口总额	(亿美元)	Total Imports and Exports	(100 million ollars)	1.73	11.90	32.10
进口		Imports		0.14	1.18	12.79
出口		Exports		1.59	10.72	19.31
入境旅游人数	(万人次)	Number of Tourists Received	(10 000 persons)	1.01	15.57	45.08
金融保险		**Banking and Insurance**				
金融机构存款	(亿元)	Deposits of Banking System	(100 million yuan)	42.16	406.56	3037.22
金融机构贷款	(亿元)	Loans of Banking System	(100 million yuan)	96.78	732.77	3147.77
国内保险保费收入	(亿元)	Domestic Premium	(100 million yuan)		6.19	60.53

注:2017年因铁路运输调整统计方法,货运量和客运量相关数据与前期不可比。

Aggregate Data			速度指标 Indices and Growth Rates								
			2019年比下列各年增长(%) Increases					年平均增长(%) Average Annual Growth Rate			
2010	2018	2019	1978	1990	2000	2010	2018	1979~2019	1991~2019	2001~2019	2011~2019
2498.67	3469.20	3594.73	1067.2	471.3	301.2	43.9	3.6	6.2	6.2	7.6	4.1
2894.72	3681.92	3769.26	1941.5	607.1	364.7	30.2	2.4	7.6	7.0	8.4	3.0
2028.67	2754.03	2896.40	3060.6	750.9	438.3	42.8	5.2	8.8	7.7	9.3	4.0
1291.71	58.46	38.53	-94.0	-95.8	-90.1	-97.0	-34.1	-6.6	-10.4	-11.5	-32.3
899.08	484.14	558.32	1921.4	322.7	152.5	-37.9	15.3	7.6	5.1	5.0	-5.2
19.71	19.97	18.48	522.2	1627.1	256.8	-6.2	-7.5	4.6	10.3	6.9	-0.7
8982.87	10901.08	11622.84	3436.5	1077.6	372.3	29.4	6.6	9.1	8.9	8.5	2.9
11.66	25.90	26.52	5425.0	969.4	170.1	127.4	2.4	10.3	8.5	5.4	9.6
46.38	56.09	57.15	753.0	305.6	233.2	23.2	1.9	5.4	4.9	6.5	2.3
172.29	241.90	223.97	27896.3	1868.1	1044.5	30.0	-7.4	14.7	10.8	13.7	3.0
170.71	254.34	251.25	868.6	499.9	203.6	47.2	-1.2	5.7	6.4	6.0	4.4
4344.39	15133.87	16979.59	152731.6	34341.4	3637.1	290.8	12.2	19.6	22.3	21.0	16.4
25046.72	88238.10	92042.23	15343.3	5362.8	1371.1	267.5	4.3	13.1	14.8	15.2	15.6
12813.44	32691.00	33907.92	11301.5	4214.5	976.4	164.6	3.7	12.2	13.9	13.3	11.4
97006.94	203704.00	188143.00	1744.7	1623.5	359.5	93.9	-7.6	7.4	10.3	8.4	7.6
10145.00	4116.00	5480.00	56.0	40.5	-16.4	-46.0	33.1	1.1	1.2	-0.9	-6.6
71020.00	163145.00	143549.00	3936.8	4781.0	415.2	102.1	-12.0	9.4	14.3	9.0	8.1
15832.00	36432.00	39105.00	1149.4	933.4	523.7	147.0	7.3	6.4	8.4	10.1	10.6
105415.50	98719.70	88926.43	640.5	176.6	181.5	-15.6	-9.9	5.0	3.6	5.6	-1.9
7281.30	15700.40	17216.06	503.2	717.1	396.3	136.4	9.7	4.5	7.5	8.8	10.0
96873.00	80989.51	69584.36	836.7	154.6	156.0	-28.2	-14.1	5.6	3.3	5.1	-3.6
375.80	647.79	631.63	-63.3	-76.5	-7.0	68.1	-2.5	-2.4	-4.9	-0.4	5.9
18782.67	34620.55	30660.74			645.4	63.2	-11.4			11.2	5.6
1028.09	2380.51	3824.44	682835.7	79575.8	3180.0	272.0	60.7	24.0	25.9	20.2	15.7
1.00	0.74	0.65	-44.9	-72.8	-82.0	-35.0	-12.6	-1.4	-4.4	-8.6	-4.7
3454.70	5569.79	5688.02				64.6	2.1				5.7
459.40	1480.73	1708.32				271.9	15.4				15.7
7013.90	18333.60	22722.31	37871.8	6862.3	1169.9	224.0	23.9	15.6	15.8	14.3	14.0
259.07	528.02	571.28	32922.0	4700.7	1679.7	120.5	8.2	15.2	14.3	16.4	9.2
114.65	187.14	211.49	150964.3	17822.9	1553.6	84.5	13.0	19.5	19.6	15.9	7.0
144.42	340.89	359.80	22528.9	3256.3	1763.3	149.1	5.5	14.1	12.9	16.6	10.7
181.74	405.11	450.02	44456.4	2790.3	898.3	147.6	11.1	16.0	12.3	12.9	10.6
21568.31	55371.19	59747.70	141616.6	14595.9	1867.2	177.0	7.9	19.4	18.8	17.0	12.0
14136.58	44340.54	50663.96	52249.6	6814.0	1509.5	258.4	14.3	16.5	15.7	15.7	15.2
500.33	1470.92	1728.57		27825.2	2755.7	245.5	17.5		21.4	19.3	14.8

Note: Due to the statistics method of railway transportation has been adjusted, the data related to freight traffic and passenger traffic in 2017 can not be compared with the previous

1-4 续表 2 continued

指标	Item	总量指标 Aggregate Data 1978	1990	2000	2010	2018
教育、科技、文化	**Education, Science and Technology,Culture and**					
教育	**Education**					
高等学校本专科在校学生 (万人)	Students Enrollment in Institutions of Higher Eduction (10 000persons)	4.94	13.04	34.66	129.69	143.59
中等职业学校在校学生 (万人)	Students Enrollment in Specialized Secondary Schools (10 000persons)	5.36	1458.00	27.86	90.38	36.94
普通中学在校学生 (万人)	Students Enrollment in Regular Secondary Schools (10 000persons)	372.38	211.56	350.93	341.83	241.13
小学在校学生 (万人)	Students Enrollment in Primary Schools (10 000persons)	765.73	623.06	667.74	365.55	366.58
文化	**Culture**					
图书出版量 (亿册)	Books Published (100 million copies)	1.62	4.02	2.88	2.75	2.68
杂志出版量 (亿册)	Magazines Issued (100 million copies)	0.09	0.73	2.20	3.01	1.19
报纸出版量 (亿份)	Newspaper Issued (100 million copies)	1.97	6.24	13.42	18.17	8.99
家庭、生活、环境	**Family, People's Livelihood and Environment**					
家庭	**Family**					
城镇居民平均每户家庭人口 (人)	Average Household size in Urban Areas (person)	4.32	3.47	3.14	2.93	3.00
农村居民平均每户常住人口 (人)	Average Household size in Rural Areas (person)	6.02	4.67	4.11	3.98	3.08
居住	**Housing**					
城镇居民人均住房建筑面积(平方米)	Per Capita Net Floor Space of Urban Residents (sq.m)		9.80	13.90	33.20	45.00
农村居民人均住房面积 (平方米)	Per Capita Net Floor Space of Rural Residents (sq.m)		25.73	30.11	40.99	57.76
生活	**People's Livelihood**					
城镇居民人均可支配收入 (元)	Per Capita Annual Disposbale Income of Urban Residents (yuan)	325.00	1427.20	5524.50	16058.00	34454.63
农村居民人均可支配收入 (元)	Per Capita Annual Disposbale Income of Rural Residents (yuan)	110.52	670.80	2268.50	5832.00	14977.82
居民储蓄存款余额 (亿元)	Saving Deposit (100 million yuan)	6.96	244.38	1908.80	9851.00	26315.35
工资	**Wages**					
工资总额 (亿元)	Total Wages of Staff and Workers (100 million yuan)	25.89	131.24	405.34	1870.51	6330.24
职工平均工资 (元)	Average Wages of Staff and Workers (yuan)	581	1903	7565	28092	60561
卫生	**Health Care**					
卫生机构数 (个)	Number of Health Care Organizations (unit)	5940	10472	11065	34269	36397
#医院	Hospitals	1817	2024	2041	602	996
床位数 (万张)	Number of Hospital Beds (10 000 units)	11.52	16.34	14.96	20.04	39.35
#医院	Hospitals	10.34	13.16	12.99	13.50	28.15
卫生技术人员数 (万人)	Number of Medical Technical Personels (10 000 persons)	14.06	20.92	23.88	25.58	41.08
#执业(助理)医师	Licensed(assitant) Doctors	5.82	8.68	10.30	9.95	15.19
环境	**Environment**					
污染治理项目本年完成投资(亿元)	Investment for the Pollution Treatment projects Completed (100 million yuan)		1.81	8.52	27.74	13.74
本年施工污染治理项目数 (个)	Number of Pullution Treatment Project Under Construction (unit)		1545	851	226	187
工业废水排放量 (亿吨)	Volume of Industrial Waste Water Discharged (100 million tons)		16.23	10.67	9.46	4.58

注：卫生机构数从2009年起包含村卫生室数量。

	速 度 指 标 Indices and Growth Rates								
	2019年比下列各年增长(%) increases					年平均增长(%) Average Annual Growth Rate			
2019	1978	1990	2000	2010	2018	1979~2019	1991~2019	2001~2019	2011~2019
149.81	2932.6	1048.8	332.2	15.5	4.3	8.7	8.8	8.0	1.6
39.19	631.2	-97.3	40.7	-56.6	6.1	5.0	-11.7	1.8	-8.9
250.59	-32.7	18.4	-28.6	-26.7	3.9	-1.0	0.6	-1.8	-3.4
376.48	-50.8	-39.6	-43.6	3.0	2.7	-1.7	-1.7	-3.0	0.3
3.17	95.7	-21.1	10.1	15.3	18.3	1.7	-0.8	0.5	1.6
1.05	1066.7	43.8	-52.3	-65.1	-11.8	6.2	1.3	-3.8	-11.0
7.37	274.1	18.1	-45.1	-59.4	-18.0	3.3	0.6	-3.1	-9.5
3.01	-30.3	-13.3	-4.1	2.7	0.3	-0.9	-0.5	-0.2	0.3
3.08	-48.8	-34.0	-25.1	-22.6		-1.6	-1.4	-1.5	-2.8
46.3		372.4	233.1	39.5	2.9		5.5	6.5	3.8
58.68		128.1	94.9	43.2	1.6		2.9	3.6	4.1
37601.36	11469.6	2534.6	580.6	134.2	9.1	12.3	11.9	10.6	9.9
16390.86	14730.7	2343.5	622.5	181.1	9.4	13.0	11.7	11.0	12.2
29804.55	428126.3	12096.0	1461.4	202.6	13.3	22.6	18.0	15.6	13.1
6944.45	26722.9	5191.4	1613.2	271.3	9.7	14.6	14.7	16.1	15.7
64661	11029.3	3297.8	754.7	130.2	6.8	12.2	12.9	12.0	9.7
35479	497.3	238.8	220.6	3.5	-2.5	4.5	4.3	6.3	0.4
1034	-43.1	-48.9	-49.3	71.8	3.8	-1.4	-2.3	-3.5	6.2
40.65	252.9	148.8	171.7	102.8	3.3	3.1	3.2	5.4	8.2
29.12	181.6	121.3	124.2	115.7	3.5	2.6	2.8	4.3	8.9
41.95	198.4	100.5	75.7	64.0	2.1	2.7	2.4	3.0	5.7
15.50	166.3	78.6	50.5	55.8	2.0	2.4	2.0	2.2	5.0

Note: The number of health institutions has included the number of village clinics since 2009.

1-5 国民经济和社会发展结构指标
Composition Indicators on National Economic and Social Development

单位:% (%)

指 标	Item	1978	2000	2005	2010	2017	2018	2019
人口与就业	**Population and Employment**							
人 口	**Population**							
城乡结构	Urban and Rural Structure							
城镇	Urban	14.6	40.5	43.2	49.7	59.3	60.3	61.0
乡村	Rural	85.4	59.5	56.8	50.3	40.7	39.7	39.0
性别结构	Sexual Structure							
男	Male	51.3	52.1	51.8	51.4	50.8	50.8	50.8
女	Female	48.7	47.9	48.2	48.6	49.2	49.2	49.2
就 业	**Employment**							
产业结构	Industrial Structure							
第一产业	First Industry	77.0	48.0	47.7	46.4	35.4	34.0	32.8
第二产业	Second Industry	14.1	20.8	20.5	20.7	23.2	23.4	23.7
第三产业	Tertiary Industry	8.9	31.2	31.8	32.9	41.4	42.6	43.5
经济类型结构	Structrues by Ownership							
城镇单位从业人员	Staff and Workers Employed in Urban Units							
国有单位	State-Owned	81.2	74.7	62.1	40.4	38.5	37.8	36.3
城镇集体单位	Collective-Owned	18.8	14.3	8.0	3.1	1.8	1.7	1.7
其他单位	Others		11.0	29.9	56.5	59.7	60.5	62.0
宏观经济	**Macroeconomy**							
国民核算	**National Accounting**							
地区生产总值产业结构	Industrial Structure							
第一产业	First Industry	40.5	18.7	16.3	13.3	10.0	9.0	8.3
第二产业	Second Industry	42.2	40.5	43.4	48.8	43.5	43.4	41.7
第三产业	Tertiary Industry	17.3	40.8	40.3	37.9	46.5	47.6	50.0
地区生产总值支出结构	Domestic Expenditures							
最终消费	Total Consumption	54.0	54.0	54.6	45.7	48.4		
居民消费	Residents Consumption	49.4	42.4	42.0	31.9	36.0		
政府消费	Government Consumption Expenditures	4.6	11.6	12.6	13.8	12.5		
资本形成总额	Gross Capital Formation	28.5	50.1	45.3	53.9	58.8		
固定资本	Fixed Capital Formation	20.8	38.6	43.2	52.0	58.0		
存货增加	Changes in Stock	7.7	11.5	2.1	1.9	0.8		
净出口	Net Exports	17.4	-4.0	0	0.4	-7.2		
投 资	**Investment**							
经济类型结构	Structrues by Ownership							
国有经济	State-Owned	98.8	60.3	38.7	34.9	28.9	20.6	19.5
集体经济	Collective-Owned	1.2	9.0	2.8	5.6	1.6	0.4	0.4
其他	Others		30.7	58.5	59.5	69.5	79.0	80.1
资金来源结构	Structure of Funded Sources							
国家预算资金	State Budget	77.2	10.0	9.0	8.0	7.3	6.1	5.4
国内贷款	Domestic Loans	0.4	17.2	16.7	16.4	9.7	11.3	10.5
利用外资	Foreign Investment		2.0	2.5	1.4	0.2	0.2	0.4
自筹资金	Fundraising	18.0	54.9	52.7	62.1	67.2	61.2	62.4
其他投资	Others	4.3	15.9	19.1	12.2	15.7	21.2	21.3

1-5 续表 1 continued

指 标	Item	1978	2000	2005	2010	2017	2018	2019
财 政	**Finance**							
地方公共支出结构	Local Public Financial Expenditure Structure							
#一般公共服务	#General Public Service				12.6	10.6	10.2	10.0
教育	Education				14.7	16.3	14.7	14.4
社会保障和就业	Social Security and Employment				14.7	16.2	16.1	15.9
利用外资	**Foreign Investment**							
实际外商直接投资结构	Actual Foreign Direct Investment							
合资经营企业	Joint Venture		63.4	40.8	35.3	37.3	33.7	38.7
合作经营企业	Cooperation		3.0	4.8	1.6	1.4	0.5	1.1
独资经营企业	Sole Proprietorship Business		33.6	34.5	63.1	56.5	60.6	55.1
外商投资股份制企业	Joint-stock Enterprises with Foreign Investment			0.9		2.6	3.8	2.6
产业经济	**Industrial Economy**							
农 业	**Agriculture**							
农林牧渔业产值结构	Agricultural Output Value Structure							
农业	Agriculture	77.3	54.7	52.5	55.3	48.3	48.9	48.7
林业	Forestry	4.9	3.6	2.1	1.9	3.5	3.8	3.9
牧业	Animal Husbandry	12.8	30.1	30.7	25.9	24.1	22.3	22.8
渔业	Fishery	0.8	11.6	13.3	13.5	17.8	17.8	17.2
农林牧渔服务业	Agriculture,Animal Husbandry and Fishery service			1.4	3.4	6.3	7.2	7.4
工 业	**Industry**							
工业产值按经济类型分	Industrial Output by Type							
#国有企业	#State-owned Enterprises	77.3	35.3	25.3	21.0	3.1	3.0	3.4
集体企业	Collective Enterprises	22.7	18.4	1.8	0.9	0.2	0.2	0.2
港澳台商投资企业	Hong Kong, Macao And Taiwan Invested Enterprises		4.2	4.3	5.1	4.3	4.2	4.4
外商投资企业	Foreign-invested Enterprises		6.8	18.3	15.0	12.8	11.6	11.4
工业产值按轻重分	Industrial Output Divided by Weight							
轻工业	Light Industry	47.1	38.4	24.8	27.5	34.2	34.6	34.4
重工业	Heavy Industry	52.9	61.6	75.2	72.5	65.8	65.4	65.6
建筑业	**Building Industry**							
建筑业总产值结构	Gross Output Value Structure							
国有经济	State-owned Economy	88.6	58.6	57.6	52.6	47.4	44.5	47.5
地方	Local	42.8	23.5	19.9	9.5	9.9	8.0	10.1
中央	Central	45.6	35.1	37.7	43.1	37.5	36.6	37.4
其它经济	Other Economic		14.3	37.3	45.9	52.6	55.5	52.5
运输业	**Transport**							
货运量结构	Cargo Structures							
铁路	Railway	34.4	16.0	16.9	10.5	3.7	2.0	2.9
公路	Highway	34.9	68.0	66.5	73.2	77.4	80.1	76.3
水运	Water Transport	30.7	15.3	15.8	16.3	18.9	17.9	20.8

1-5 续表 2 continued

指 标	Item	1978	2000	2005	2017	2018	2019
国内商业	**Domestic Trade**						
社会消费品零售总额结构	Total Retail Sales of Consumer Goods						
#批发零售贸易业	Wholesale and Retail Sale	85.1	61.9	81.5	89.0	89.0	89.1
住宿及餐饮业	Hotel and Catering	2.8	10.8	13.1	10.1	10.3	10.5
其他	Others	12.1	27.3	5.4	0.9	0.7	0.4
对外经济贸易和国际旅游	**Foreign Trade and Tourism**						
进出口总额	Total Imports and Exports						
#出口	Exports	8.1	39.8	51.1	65.9	64.6	63.0
进口	Imports	91.9	60.2	48.9	34.1	35.4	37.0
海外旅游人数结构	Structure of Tourists						
外国人	Foreigners	47.3	79.3	75.9	75.5	75.8	77.8
港澳台同胞	Compatriots from Hongkong, Macao and Taiwan	52.7	20.7	24.1	24.5	24.2	22.2
教育、科技、文化	**Education,Science and Culture**						
教 育	**Education**						
在校学生结构	Structure of Students Enrollment						
大学生	College and University Students	0.4	3.3	10.4	19.3	19.1	19.2
中学生	Secondary School Students	32.6	33.3	45.7	31.8	32.1	32.3
小学生	Primary School Students	67.0	63.4	43.9	48.9	48.8	48.5
专任教师结构	Full-Time Teacher by Type						
大学	College and Universities	2.9	11.9	17.5	17.3	17.3	17.3
中学	Secondary Schools	39.6	38.9	44.5	40.5	40.5	40.5
小学	Primary Schools	57.5	49.2	38.0	42.2	42.2	42.2
科 技	**Science and Technology**						
R&D经费支出结构	Expenditure On R&D						
基础研究	Basic Research			4.6	4.0	3.7	4.5
应用研究	Applied Research			20.0	12.8	13.2	12.5
实验发展	Expenditure Development			71.3	83.2	83.1	83.0
生活、环境	People´s Livelihood and Environment						
生 活	People´s Livelihood						
城镇居民消费结构	Consumption Structutre of Urban Residents						
食品	Food		38.3	39.0	30.8	28.1	27.8
衣着	Clothing		11.4	12.0	7.3	7.3	7.1
居住	Residence		14.1	10.2	21.9	22.5	22.4
其他	Others		36.2	38.8	40.0	42.2	42.7
农村居民消费结构	Consumption Structutre of Rural Residents						
食品	Food	70.8	53.2	49.1	28.6	28.2	27.2
衣着	Clothing	12.0	4.8	5.1	5.4	5.6	5.4
居住	Residence	8.9	11.5	12.8	21.6	21.2	21.3
其他	Others	8.3	30.5	33.0	44.4	45.0	46.1

1-6 湖北国民经济占全国的比重(2019)
Proportion of Hubei´s National Economy in China (2019)

指　　标		Item		全 国 Country	湖北 Hubei	湖北占全国的比重(%) Percentage to the Country
土地面积	(万平方公里)	Ground space	(10 000 sq.km.)	960.00	18.59	1.94
年末常住人口	(万人)	Population	(Year-end)	140005	5927	4.23
地区生产总值	(亿元)	Local Gross Production	(100 million yuan)	990865.1	45828.31	4.63
第一产业		First Industry		70466.7	3809.09	5.41
第二产业		Second Industry		386165.3	19098.62	4.95
第三产业		Tertiary Industry		534233.1	22920.60	4.29
人均地区生产总值	(元)	Local Gross Production Per Capita	(yuan)	70892	77387	相当于全国109.16 %
投资	(亿元)	Investment	(100 million yuan)			
#房地产开发		Development of Real Estate		132194.26	5111.73	3.87
地方公共财政收入	(亿元)	Local Public Financial Revenue		101076.82	3388.57	3.35
社会消费品零售总额	(亿元)	Total Retail Sales of Social Consumption	(100 million yuan)	411649.02	22722.31	5.52
进出口总额	(亿美元)	Total Imports and Exports	(100 million dollars)	45761.26	571.28	1.25
#出口		Exports		24990.29	359.80	1.44
实际外商直接投资	(亿美元)	Actual Foreign Direct Investment	(100 million dollars)	1381.35	129.07	9.34
普通高等学校本专科在校生	(万人)	Students Enrollment in Institutions of Higher Eductioan	(10 000 persons)	3031.53	149.81	4.94
医院卫生机构床位数	(万张)	Number of Hospital Beds	(10 000 units)	880.70	40.65	4.62
卫生技术人员	(万人)	Number of Medical Technical Personnels	(10 000 persons)	1015.40	41.95	4.13
#执业(助理)医师		Professional (assistant) Doctors		386.70	15.50	4.01
在岗职工平均工资	(元)	Average Wages of Employee		90501	64661	相当于全国71.45 %
城镇居民人均可支配收入	(元)	Per Capita Disposable Income of Urban Residents	(yuan)	42359	37601	相当于全国88.77%
农村居民人均可支配收入	(元)	Per Capita Net Incomes of Rural Residents	(yuan)	16021	16391	相当于全国102.31 %
工农业主要产品产量	(万吨)	Output of Major Products in Argriculture and Industry				
粮食		Grain		66384.3	2725.0	4.10
棉花		Cotton		588.9	14.4	2.44
油料		Oil-Bearing Crops		3493.0	314.0	8.99
粗钢		Crude steel		99634.2	3594.7	3.61
钢材		Steel		120477.4	3769.3	3.13
发电量	(亿千瓦小时)	Electricity	(100 million kWh)	75034.3	2896.4	3.86
原煤		Coal		384633.2	38.5	0.01
农用氮、磷、钾化学肥料(折纯)		Agricultural Nitrogen, Phosphorus and Potassium Fertilizer		5731.2	558.3	9.74
水泥		Cement		235012.1	11622.8	4.95
生铁		Pig Iron		80936.5	2765.2	3.42
布	(亿米)	Cloth	(100 million meter)	575.6	57.2	9.94
汽车	(万辆)	Moter Vehicles	(10 000 units)	2552.8	224.0	8.77

注:全国数据使用国家统计年鉴数据,湖北数据使用第四次经济普查后的数据。

Note:National data use national statistical yearbook data, and data of Hubei use the data after the fourth economic census.

1-7 全省人均国民经济主要指标

指 标	Item	1990
地区生产总值 (元)	Gross Domestic Product (yuan)	1541.17
第一产业	First Industry	541.12
第二产业	Second Industry	583.90
第三产业	Tertiary Industry	416.15
地方公共财政预算收入 (元)	Government Revenue (yuan)	145.54
地方财政支出 (元)	Government Expenditure (yuan)	158.57
社会消费品零售额 (元)	Total Retail Sales of Consumer Goods (yuan)	610.00
进出口总额 (美元)	Total Imports and Exports (US.dollars)	22.24
#出口	Exports (US.dollars)	20.04
农村居民可支配收入 (元)	Net Income of Rural Residents (yuan)	671.00
城镇居民可支配收入 (元)	Disposable Income of Urban Residents (yuan)	1427.00
居民储蓄存款 (元)	Outstanding Amount of Saving Deposits of Urabn And Rural Residents (yuan)	455.00
在校大学生数 (人/万人)	Number of Students Enrollment in Institutions of Higher Education (person/10 000 persons)	24.38
医院病床数 (张/万人)	Hospital Beds (bed/10000 persons)	24.60
卫生技术人员数 (人/万人)	Number of Medical Technical Personnels (person/10000 persons)	39.11
#执业(助理)医师	Professional (assitant) Doctors	16.22
主要工农业产品产量 (千克)	Output of Major Industrial and Agricultural Products (kg)	
粮 食	Grain	467.10
棉 花	Cotton	9.76
油 料	Oil-Bearing Crops	18.07
钢 材	Steel	100.60
原 煤	Coal	174.43
发电量 (千瓦小时)	Electricity (kWh)	639.62

注：2010年之后农产品产量根据第三次农业普查数据进行调整。

Major Per Capita Indicators of Hubei´s

2000	2005	2010	2015	2017	2018	2019
6121.17	11342.32	28359.43	52014.57	63179.77	71109.15	77386.54
1143.47	1875.54	3570.85	5330.93	5987.88	6004.18	6432.10
2473.66	4836.66	13541.45	23260.32	26663.03	29738.34	32250.28
2504.03	4630.12	11247.13	23423.32	30528.85	35366.63	38704.15
376.61	658.36	1767.30	5151.97	5511.90	5596.21	5722.00
1647.93	1368.21	4371.64	10446.47	11591.99	12282.38	13458.64
3144.00	5197.00	11743.40	24003.84	29514.04	31023.94	38369.32
56.40	159.40	452.77	781.42	785.76	893.52	964.68
33.93	78.02	252.40	500.78	517.51	576.85	607.56
2268.00	3099.00	5832.27	11843.89	13812.09	14977.82	16390.86
5524.00	8786.00	16058.37	27051.47	31889.42	34454.63	37601.36
3209.00	7929.00	17211.00	33539.49	40744.06	44531.00	50329.00
60.89	177.54	226.66	241.48	237.35	242.99	252.97
22.42	17.00	23.59	42.27	45.73	47.63	49.17
41.96	37.69	44.71	63.01	67.82	69.51	70.84
17.40	14.90	17.39	23.20	25.04	25.71	26.17
372.92	382.00	402.71	499.64	482.93	480.49	460.15
5.12	6.26	8.25	5.16	3.12	2.53	2.42
45.38	51.50	52.83	54.29	52.21	51.19	53.01
136.34	278.04	505.90	586.45	52.87	623.05	635.95
64.45	83.80	225.75	130.00	52.87	9.89	6.51
904.54	2204.00	3545.46	3944.98	4325.14	4660.34	4890.92

Note:Production of agricultural products after 2010 is adjusted according to the data of the third agricultural census.

1-8 湖北的一天
One Day in Hubei

指　标		Item		2000	2005	2010	2015	2018	2019
每天创造的财富		**Daily Production**							
地区生产总值	(亿元)	Gross Domestic Products		9.71	17.86	44.15	81.87	107.85	125.56
			(100 million yuan)						
第一产业		First Industry		1.81	2.96	5.88	9.07	9.72	10.44
第二产业		Second Industry		3.94	7.70	21.56	37.68	46.82	52.32
第三产业		Tertiary Industry		3.96	7.20	16.71	35.12	51.32	62.8
地方公共财政预算收入	(亿元)	Government Revenue	(100 million yuan)	0.59	1.03	2.77	8.23	9.06	9.28
粮食	(万吨)	Grain	(10 000 tons)	6.08	5.97	6.31	7.99	7.78	7.47
肉类产量	(吨)	Meat	(tons)	7429.86	9387.12	10506.30	12155.07	11806.85	9567.12
水产品	(吨)	Aquatic Products	(tons)	6420.27	8713.15	9671.23	12487.67	12558.90	12864.11
粗 钢	(万吨)	Steel	(10 000 tons)	2.45	4.31	6.85	8.00	9.50	9.85
成品钢材	(万吨)	Rolled-Steel	(10 000 tons)	2.22	4.34	7.93	9.37	10.09	10.33
发电量	(亿千瓦小时)	Electricity	(100 million kWh)	1.47	3.44	5.56	6.31	7.55	7.94
水泥	(万吨)	Cement	(10 000 tons)	6.74	12.36	24.61	30.93	29.87	31.84
布	(万米)	Cloth	(10 000 meters)	470.00	573.00	1270.69	2187.67	1536.74	1565.78
每天消费量		**Daily Consumption**							
最终消费	(亿元)	Final Consumption	(100 million yuan)	5.56	9.99	20.25	37.81		
居民消费	(亿元)	Resident Consumption	(100 million yuan)	4.37	7.63	14.07	27.86		
城镇居民每人		Per Capita Living Expenditure of Urban		1.19	2.36	6.17	9.95		
消费性支出	(元)	Residents	(yuan)	12.72	18.46	31.37	49.84		
#食品消费		Food Consumption							
农村居民每人		Per Capita Living Expenditure of Rural		4.88	7.19	12.14	15.97		
生活消费支出	(元)	Residents	(yuan)	4.26	6.66	11.21	26.86		
#食品消费		Food Consumption							
政府消费	(亿元)	Government Consumption Expenditure		2.27	3.27	4.83	8.09		
			(100 million yuan)						
社会消费品零售总额	(亿元)	Total Retail Sales of Consumer Goods		4.90	8.12	18.41	38.37	50.23	62.25
			(100 million yuan)						
每天其他经济活动		**Other Daily Economic Acitivities**							
货物运输量	(万吨)	Freight Traffic	(10 000 tons)	112.19	136.78	265.77	439.43	558.09	515.46
旅客运输量	(万人)	Passenger Traffic	(10 000 persons)	86.56	195.61	288.81	286.83	270.46	243.63
竣工房屋面积	(万平方米)	Floor Space of Housing Completed		8.63	18.90	35.11	73.49	89.56	92.90
			(10 000 sq.m)						
出版报纸	(万份)	Newspapers Published	(10 000 pieces)	367.67	536.16	497.80	423.39	246.33	201.89
函件	(万件)	Letters Delivered	(10 000 pieces)	99.00	41.64	27.40	18.63	20.38	17.89
进出口总额	(万美元)	Total Imports and Exports	(10 000 USD)	879.45	2490.96	7097.81	12489.32	14466.42	15651.64
#出口		Exports		529.04	1219.18	3956.71	8003.84	9339.38	9875.53
实际外商直接投资	(万美元)	Actual Foreign Direct Investment		258.63	598.63	1109.59	2451.51	3271.51	3536.29
			(10 000 USD)						
每天人口变动和婚姻		**Daily Population Changes and Marriages**							
出生人数	(人)	Birth	(persons)	1582	1441	1625	1716	1871	1841
死亡人数	(人)	Death	(persons)	979	940	944	932	1135	1149
结婚对数	(对)	Marriage	(couple)	969	1080	1564	1570	1199	1067
离婚对数	(对)	Divorce	(couple)	58	146	244	396	485	516

1-9 地区生产总值
Gross Domestic Product

本表按当年价格计算 (At current price)

年 份 Year	地区生产总值(亿元) Total Output (100 million yuan)	第一产业 Primary Industry	第二产业 Secondary Industry		第三产业 Tertiary Industry			人均地区生产总值(元) Per Capita GDP (yuan)	人均地区生产总值(美元) Per Capita GDP (USD)
				工业 Industry	建筑业 Contruction		#金融业 Banking	#房地产业 Real Estate		
1952	24.51	13.90	3.82	3.17	0.66	6.79			90.13	34.44
1955	34.05	18.14	7.43	6.25	1.20	8.48			117.88	47.88
1957	48.86	24.33	11.56	9.03	2.56	12.97			162.17	65.87
1962	52.13	29.30	10.60	9.10	1.53	12.23			161.47	65.59
1965	72.43	37.74	21.10	17.36	3.80	13.59			209.26	85.00
1970	88.15	44.41	26.82	21.79	5.11	16.92			221.78	90.09
1975	120.10	53.71	45.36	32.68	12.80	21.03			274.30	139.50
1978	151.00	61.11	63.52	52.17	11.54	26.37	4.54	1.42	332.03	210.53
1980	199.38	71.22	91.39	75.63	16.04	36.77	5.51	2.83	427.98	279.67
1985	396.26	144.44	173.78	152.88	21.47	78.04	10.71	4.61	808.11	275.19
1986	442.04	163.61	187.35	164.93	23.03	91.08	13.68	5.97	885.96	256.59
1987	517.77	183.99	223.79	197.66	26.87	109.99	17.09	7.39	1018.42	273.61
1988	626.52	214.66	270.34	244.17	27.08	141.52	20.82	8.88	1215.93	326.68
1989	717.08	239.07	299.43	276.47	23.99	178.58	28.14	9.18	1373.22	364.72
1990	824.38	289.45	312.33	284.15	29.24	222.60	33.77	11.36	1541.17	322.20
1991	913.38	279.30	358.64	327.50	32.36	275.44	40.30	13.61	1668.03	313.34
1992	1088.39	303.00	443.11	402.59	42.02	342.28	48.07	17.22	1962.45	355.86
1993	1325.83	346.39	535.83	475.44	62.16	443.61	52.22	25.63	2360.53	409.67
1994	1700.92	501.44	655.47	580.80	76.83	544.01	56.83	37.85	2991.34	347.07
1995	2109.38	619.77	777.64	680.92	99.26	711.97	60.86	42.07	3671.40	439.64
1996	2499.77	716.34	920.68	805.53	118.15	862.75	65.37	62.23	4310.99	811.22
1997	2856.47	767.92	1068.40	929.91	141.95	1020.15	69.68	69.65	4883.80	589.13
1998	3114.02	778.22	1195.20	1041.20	157.88	1140.60	74.14	81.78	5287.04	638.60
1999	3229.29	653.99	1310.20	1139.52	174.92	1265.10	78.81	85.01	5452.46	658.65
2000	3545.39	662.30	1432.75	1243.24	194.14	1450.34	81.49	99.40	6121.17	739.41
2001	3880.53	692.17	1569.33	1360.10	214.29	1619.03	88.48	122.49	6865.76	829.50
2002	4212.82	707.00	1704.41	1473.00	236.89	1801.41	96.95	145.17	7436.58	898.46
2003	4757.45	798.35	1949.76	1682.16	273.86	2009.34	107.31	176.80	8378.00	1012.20
2004	5546.78	1008.87	2273.53	1955.61	325.21	2264.38	115.85	199.62	9745.73	1177.48
2005	6469.66	1069.81	2758.83	2410.42	357.39	2641.02	118.52	235.26	11342.32	1384.61
2006	7531.80	1125.52	3270.80	2863.47	418.00	3135.48	161.79	333.55	13210.21	1691.73
2007	9451.39	1331.44	4128.89	3597.37	544.92	3991.06	316.57	495.05	16593.03	2206.08
2008	11497.46	1716.03	5066.19	4406.90	675.70	4715.24	364.38	661.46	20153.30	2902.09
2009	13192.14	1717.32	6035.52	5212.66	842.27	5439.30	439.41	713.42	23081.34	3376.39
2010	16226.94	2043.20	7748.26	6750.66	1022.73	6435.48	508.50	766.12	28359.43	4189.30
2011	19942.45	2469.20	9766.13	8551.19	1246.78	7707.12	602.70	893.63	34737.59	5378.33
2012	22590.89	2674.82	11152.55	9771.03	1417.91	8763.52	769.06	1014.77	39162.50	6203.96
2013	25378.01	2883.73	11846.30	10227.36	1657.03	10647.98	1033.11	1484.94	43838.33	7078.92
2014	28242.13	3001.59	13007.91	11174.22	1875.40	12232.63	1196.39	1698.70	48630.44	7916.66
2015	30344.00	3109.93	13569.49	11677.26	1957.78	13664.58	1588.78	1879.93	52014.57	8351.19
2016	33353.00	3406.46	14527.01	12480.47	2109.18	15419.53	1975.11	2231.70	56836.37	8556.73
2017	37235.00	3528.96	15713.86	13431.59	2342.51	17992.18	2255.19	2794.30	63179.77	9357.47
2018	42021.95	3548.17	17573.87	14849.55	2781.41	20899.91	2554.00	3320.08	71109.15	10745.78
2019	45828.31	3809.09	19098.62	16087.33	3073.13	22920.60	2783.57	3680.34	77386.54	11217.88

注:2018年四经普后,所有历史数据按最新产业、行业分类进行了修订。

Note:After the fourth national economic census in 2018, all historical data were revised according to the latest industry and trade classification.

1-10 地区生产总值指数(1952年=100)

Indices of Gross Domestic Product(preceding year=100)

按可比价计算，上年=100 (In comparable price, preceding year=100)

年 份	地区生产总值(%)	第一产业	第二产业			第三产业			人均地区生产总值(%)
				工业	建筑业		*金融业	*房地产业	
Year	Total Output (%)	Primary Industry	Secondary Industry	Industry	Contruction	Tertiary Industry	Banking	Real Estate	Per Capita GDP (%)
1953	114.0	107.4	129.4	141.0	93.3	122.7			111.6
1955	127.1	135.5	104.9	100.2	139.2	127.1			124.8
1957	107.4	106.4	115.3	109.5	146.0	102.6			104.7
1962	100.9	112.3	84.0	92.7	50.5	94.0			99.0
1965	118.1	111.5	132.5	124.5	196.4	114.9			115.5
1970	126.9	112.2	161.2	151.2	222.0	111.3			123.4
1975	111.4	94.5	139.0	135.2	152.5	116.0			110.0
1978	113.5	103.4	128.4	131.9	112.2	107.4			112.1
1980	106.4	86.9	123.5	126.7	107.0	111.0	97.4	160.6	105.1
1985	116.2	108.3	124.7	124.7	124.3	79.8	112.4	112.3	115.1
1986	105.5	103.3	105.2	103.9	116.8	155.2	120.5	122.2	103.7
1987	108.4	103.1	111.3	112.9	99.0	110.7	114.5	113.4	106.4
1988	107.8	94.9	113.7	115.1	101.5	114.3	107.0	105.6	106.4
1989	104.5	105.2	102.1	104.2	81.3	109.3	121.8	93.2	103.1
1990	105.0	107.5	99.0	99.5	92.8	114.8	108.9	109.7	102.5
1991	106.6	95.1	111.1	111.6	106.1	115.4	114.4	114.7	104.1
1992	114.1	108.2	116.6	117.5	107.5	116.9	111.5	117.8	112.7
1993	113.0	105.8	116.7	116.1	123.3	115.2	112.0	119.4	111.6
1994	113.7	107.1	119.0	119.2	117.6	112.4	107.7	127.3	112.3
1995	113.2	108.9	116.3	116.0	118.5	112.5	107.3	121.0	112.0
1996	111.6	104.5	115.8	115.7	116.6	111.3	107.3	116.5	110.6
1997	111.9	106.9	113.4	113.5	112.3	113.5	103.4	110.3	110.9
1998	108.6	99.4	111.1	110.9	113.9	111.5	107.0	117.9	107.8
1999	107.8	101.9	108.3	108.3	107.5	111.0	103.7	106.1	107.2
2000	108.6	102.5	109.1	109.0	110.7	111.5	105.6	116.8	111.0
2001	108.9	102.5	109.9	110.2	108.5	110.8	107.4	122.1	111.6
2002	109.2	102.0	110.1	110.0	110.5	111.4	108.4	114.5	108.9
2003	109.7	105.8	110.1	110.1	110.6	110.8	110.1	119.0	109.4
2004	110.8	107.6	113.5	113.5	113.4	109.4	105.2	113.2	110.5
2005	112.1	104.1	115.0	115.9	109.6	112.2	104.1	108.5	111.9
2006	113.3	105.1	116.1	116.5	113.7	113.6	135.1	129.4	113.3
2007	114.6	104.7	116.3	115.4	122.9	116.4	166.8	131.6	114.7
2008	113.4	106.0	116.7	117.0	114.8	112.5	110.8	117.4	113.3
2009	113.7	105.2	116.9	115.7	124.6	112.9	122.5	114.6	113.5
2010	114.7	104.6	119.8	121.0	112.6	111.8	110.0	109.7	114.6
2011	114.1	104.4	117.9	119.1	109.9	112.6	112.8	104.4	113.7
2012	111.2	104.7	113.4	113.6	111.4	110.4	126.1	105.0	110.7
2013	110.2	105.3	110.6	110.9	111.6	111.1	115.3	109.9	109.8
2014	109.7	104.8	110.2	110.2	110.9	110.3	114.7	106.6	109.4
2015	108.6	104.5	108.3	108.6	106.1	110.1	130.7	106.5	108.1
2016	108.1	103.9	107.8	107.7	107.8	109.5	123.6	108.1	107.5
2017	107.8	103.6	107.1	107.2	106.2	109.5	109.0	113.3	107.4
2018	107.8	102.9	106.8	107.1	104.2	109.9	105.0	106.3	107.6
2019	107.5	103.2	108.0	108.3	105.8	107.8	107.1	105.6	107.2

注:2018年四经普后,所有历史数据按最新产业、行业分类进行了修订。

Note:After the fourth national economic census in 2018, all historical data were revised according to the latest industry and trade classification.

1-11 地区生产总值指数(1952年=100)

Indices of Gross Domestic Product(year of 1952=100)

按可比价计算,1952=100 (In comparable price, 1952 = 100)

年 份 Year	地区生产总值(%) Total Output (%)	第一产业 Primary Industry	第二产业 Secondary Industry	工业 Industry	建筑业 Contruction	第三产业 Tertiary Industry	#金融业 Banking	#房地产业 Real Estate	人均地区生产总值(%) Per Capita GDP (%)
1953	114.0	107.4	129.4	141.0	93.3	122.7			111.6
1955	121.6	115.7	152.3	168.4	102.2	118.2			114.4
1957	169.5	143.7	280.1	295.2	233.2	172.0			153.0
1962	141.6	129.9	223.7	257.9	116.2	124.2			119.2
1965	205.6	161.3	490.0	538.8	339.3	161.1			161.5
1970	242.8	158.4	705.8	745.7	581.7	202.1			166.1
1975	320.1	185.0	1126.0	1165.0	998.6	258.7			198.8
1978	398.9	204.4	1615.6	1857.3	928.0	313.6			238.5
1980	490.6	211.1	2256.6	2637.9	1175.6	398.2	110.8	179.8	286.4
1985	869.8	341.6	4108.2	5129.6	1386.7	565.8	186.6	253.4	482.4
1986	917.7	352.8	4321.8	5329.7	1619.7	878.2	224.8	309.7	500.2
1987	994.7	363.8	4810.2	6017.2	1603.5	972.1	257.4	351.2	532.1
1988	1072.3	345.2	5469.2	6925.8	1627.6	1111.1	275.4	370.8	565.9
1989	1120.6	363.2	5584.0	7216.7	1323.2	1214.5	335.4	345.6	583.6
1990	1176.6	390.4	5528.2	7180.6	1227.9	1394.2	365.3	379.2	598.2
1991	1254.3	371.3	6141.8	8013.5	1302.9	1608.9	417.9	434.9	622.9
1992	1431.1	401.7	7161.3	9415.9	1400.6	1880.8	466.0	512.3	701.7
1993	1617.2	425.0	8357.3	10931.8	1726.9	2166.7	521.9	611.7	783.1
1994	1838.7	455.2	9945.2	13030.7	2030.8	2435.4	562.1	778.7	879.4
1995	2081.5	495.7	11566.2	15115.7	2406.5	2739.8	603.1	942.2	985.0
1996	2322.9	518.0	13393.7	17488.8	2806.0	3049.4	647.1	1097.7	1089.4
1997	2599.3	553.7	15188.5	19849.8	3151.2	3461.1	669.1	1210.7	1208.1
1998	2822.9	550.4	16874.4	22013.4	3589.2	3859.1	716.0	1427.4	1302.4
1999	3043.1	560.9	18274.9	23840.6	3858.4	4283.6	742.5	1514.5	1396.1
2000	3304.8	574.9	19938.0	25986.2	4271.2	4776.2	784.0	1769.0	1549.7
2001	3598.9	589.3	21911.8	28636.8	4634.3	5292.1	842.1	2159.9	1729.5
2002	3930.0	601.1	24124.9	31500.5	5120.9	5895.4	912.8	2473.1	1883.4
2003	4311.2	635.9	26561.5	34682.0	5663.7	6532.1	1005.0	2943.0	2060.4
2004	4776.8	684.3	30147.3	39364.1	6422.6	7146.1	1057.2	3331.4	2276.8
2005	5354.8	712.3	34669.4	45623.0	7039.2	8017.9	1100.6	3614.6	2547.7
2006	6067.0	748.6	40251.2	53150.8	8003.5	9108.3	1486.9	4677.3	2886.6
2007	6952.7	783.8	46812.2	61336.0	9836.3	10602.1	2480.1	6155.3	3310.9
2008	7884.4	830.8	54629.8	71763.2	11292.1	11927.4	2748.0	7226.4	3751.2
2009	8964.6	874.1	63862.3	83030.0	14070.0	13466.0	3366.3	8281.4	4257.7
2010	10282.4	914.3	76507.0	100466.3	15842.8	15055.0	3702.9	9084.7	4879.3
2011	11732.2	954.5	90201.7	119655.3	17411.2	16951.9	4176.9	9484.4	5547.7
2012	13046.2	999.3	102288.8	135928.5	19396.1	18714.9	5267.0	9958.7	6141.4
2013	14376.9	1052.3	113131.4	150744.7	21646.1	20792.3	6072.9	10944.6	6743.2
2014	15771.4	1102.8	124670.8	166120.6	24005.5	22933.9	6965.6	11666.9	7377.1
2015	17127.8	1152.5	135018.4	180407.0	25469.8	25250.2	9104.0	12425.3	7974.6
2016	18515.1	1197.4	145549.9	194298.3	27456.5	27649.0	11252.6	13431.7	8572.7
2017	19959.3	1240.5	155883.9	208287.8	29158.8	30275.7	12265.3	15218.1	9207.1
2018	21516.2	1276.5	166484.0	223076.2	30383.4	33272.9	12878.6	16176.9	9906.8
2019	23129.9	1317.3	179802.8	241591.6	32145.7	35868.2	13793.0	17082.8	10620.1

注:1.2018年四经普后,所有历史数据按最新产业、行业分类进行了修订。

2.金融业、房地产业指数以1978年为100。

Note:a)After the fourth national economic census in 2018, all historical data were revised according to the latest industry and trade classification.

b)The index of financial industry and real estate industry was 100 in 1978.

1-12 地区生产总值构成
Composition of Gross Domestic Product

本表按当年价格计算 (At current prices)

年 份 Year	地区生产总值(%) Total Output (%)	第一产业 Primary Industry	第二产业 Secondary Industry	工业 Industry	建筑业 Contruction	第三产业 Tertiary Industry	#金融业 Banking	#房地产业 Real Estate
1952	100	56.7	15.6	12.9	2.7	27.7		
1955	100	53.3	21.8	18.4	3.5	24.9		
1957	100	49.8	23.7	18.5	5.2	26.5		
1962	100	56.2	20.3	17.5	2.9	23.5		
1965	100	52.1	29.1	24.0	5.2	18.8		
1970	100	50.4	30.4	24.7	5.8	19.2		
1975	100	44.7	37.8	27.2	10.7	17.5		
1978	100	40.5	42.1	34.5	7.6	17.4	3.0	0.9
1980	100	35.7	45.8	37.9	8.0	18.5	2.8	1.4
1985	100	36.4	43.9	38.6	5.4	19.7	2.7	1.2
1986	100	37.0	42.4	37.3	5.2	20.6	3.1	1.4
1987	100	35.5	43.2	38.2	5.2	21.3	3.3	1.4
1988	100	34.3	43.1	39.0	4.3	22.6	3.3	1.4
1989	100	33.3	41.8	38.6	3.3	24.9	3.9	1.3
1990	100	35.1	37.9	34.5	3.5	27.0	4.1	1.4
1991	100	30.6	39.3	35.9	3.5	30.1	4.4	1.5
1992	100	27.8	40.7	37.0	3.9	31.5	4.4	1.6
1993	100	26.1	40.4	35.9	4.7	33.5	3.9	1.9
1994	100	29.5	38.5	34.1	4.5	32.0	3.3	2.2
1995	100	29.4	36.9	32.3	4.7	33.7	2.9	2.0
1996	100	28.7	36.8	32.2	4.7	34.5	2.6	2.5
1997	100	26.9	37.4	32.6	5.0	35.7	2.4	2.4
1998	100	25.0	38.4	33.4	5.1	36.6	2.4	2.6
1999	100	20.2	40.6	35.3	5.4	39.2	2.4	2.6
2000	100	18.7	40.4	35.1	5.5	40.9	2.3	2.8
2001	100	17.8	40.5	35.0	5.5	41.7	2.3	3.2
2002	100	16.8	40.4	35.0	5.6	42.8	2.3	3.4
2003	100	16.8	41.0	35.4	5.8	42.2	2.3	3.7
2004	100	18.2	41.0	35.3	5.9	40.8	2.1	3.6
2005	100	16.5	42.7	37.3	5.5	40.8	1.8	3.6
2006	100	15.0	43.4	38.0	5.5	41.6	2.1	4.4
2007	100	14.1	43.7	38.1	5.8	42.2	3.3	5.2
2008	100	14.9	44.1	38.3	5.9	41.0	3.2	5.8
2009	100	13.0	45.8	39.5	6.4	41.2	3.3	5.4
2010	100	12.6	47.7	41.6	6.3	39.7	3.1	4.7
2011	100	12.4	49.0	42.9	6.3	38.6	3.0	4.5
2012	100	11.8	49.4	43.3	6.3	38.8	3.4	4.5
2013	100	11.4	46.7	40.3	6.5	41.9	4.1	5.9
2014	100	10.6	46.1	39.6	6.6	43.3	4.2	6.0
2015	100	10.3	44.7	38.5	6.5	45.0	5.2	6.2
2016	100	10.2	43.6	37.4	6.3	46.2	5.9	6.7
2017	100	9.5	42.2	36.1	6.3	48.3	6.1	7.5
2018	100	8.5	41.8	35.3	6.6	49.7	6.1	7.9
2019	100	8.3	41.7	35.1	6.7	50.0	6.1	8.0

注:2018年四经普后,所有历史数据按最新产业、行业分类进行了修订。

Note:After the fourth national economic census in 2018, all historical data were revised according to the latest industry and trade classification.

1-13 三次产业贡献率

Share of the Contributions of the Three Strata of Industry to the Increase of the GDP

单位：% 本表按可比价格计算 (In comparable price) (%)

年 份 Year	地区生产总值 Gross Domestic Product	第一产业 Primary Industry	第二产业 Second Industry	#工 业 Industry	第三产业 Tertiary Industry
1992	100	18.0	48.2	46.4	33.8
1993	100	13.3	51.7	45.9	35.0
1994	100	14.4	57.9	53.4	27.7
1995	100	17.7	53.7	48.6	28.6
1996	100	9.8	60.9	55.5	29.3
1997	100	13.7	52.3	48.3	34.0
1998	100	-1.6	61.0	54.5	40.6
1999	100	5.0	51.1	47.1	43.9
2000	100	5.7	51.4	46.3	42.9
2001	100	5.3	45.1	40.0	49.6
2002	100	3.8	44.6	38.5	51.6
2003	100	9.8	42.9	37.0	47.3
2004	100	11.2	51.4	44.7	37.4
2005	100	5.2	52.4	48.0	42.4
2006	100	6.4	51.8	46.3	41.8
2007	100	5.0	49.0	40.4	46.0
2008	100	6.3	55.0	48.7	38.7
2009	100	5.0	56.2	45.6	38.8
2010	100	3.8	63.3	57.8	32.9
2011	100	3.9	60.6	56.4	35.5
2012	100	4.8	59.0	52.9	36.2
2013	100	5.6	52.3	47.5	42.1
2014	100	5.1	53.2	46.8	41.7
2015	100	5.2	48.8	44.8	46.0
2016	100	4.9	42.8	36.5	52.3
2017	100	4.6	40.5	35.4	54.9
2018	100	3.6	38.3	34.7	58.1
2019	100	3.9	46.8	42.2	49.3

注:2018年四经普后,所有历史数据按最新产业、行业分类进行了修订。
Note:After the fourth national economic census in 2018, all historical data were revised according to the latest industry and trade classification.

1-14 三次产业拉动率
Contribution of the Three Strata of Industry to GDP Growth

单位:百分点　　本表按可比价格计算(In comparable price)　　(percentage point)

年 份 Year	地区生产总值 Gross Domestic Product	第一产业 Primary Industry	第二产业 Second Industry	#工 业 Industry	第三产业 Tertiary Industry
1992	14.1	2.5	6.8	6.5	4.8
1993	13.0	1.7	6.7	6.0	4.6
1994	13.7	2.0	7.9	7.3	3.8
1995	13.2	2.3	7.1	6.4	3.8
1996	11.6	1.1	7.1	6.4	3.4
1997	11.9	1.6	6.2	5.7	4.1
1998	8.6	-0.1	5.2	4.7	3.5
1999	7.8	0.4	4.0	3.7	3.4
2000	8.6	0.5	4.4	4.0	3.7
2001	8.9	0.5	4.0	3.6	4.4
2002	9.2	0.4	4.1	3.5	4.7
2003	9.7	0.9	4.2	3.6	4.6
2004	10.8	1.2	5.6	4.8	4.0
2005	12.1	0.6	6.4	5.8	5.1
2006	13.3	0.8	6.9	6.2	5.6
2007	14.6	0.7	7.2	5.9	6.7
2008	13.4	0.8	7.4	6.5	5.2
2009	13.7	0.7	7.7	6.2	5.3
2010	14.7	0.6	9.3	8.5	4.8
2011	14.1	0.6	8.5	8.0	5.0
2012	11.2	0.5	6.6	5.9	4.1
2013	10.2	0.6	5.3	4.8	4.3
2014	9.7	0.5	5.2	4.5	4.0
2015	8.6	0.4	4.2	3.8	4.0
2016	8.1	0.4	3.5	3.0	4.2
2017	7.8	0.3	3.2	2.8	4.3
2018	7.8	0.3	3.0	2.7	4.5
2019	7.5	0.3	3.5	3.2	3.7

注:2018年四经普后,所有历史数据按最新产业、行业分类进行了修订。
Note:After the fourth national economic census in 2018, all historical data were revised according to the latest industry and trade classification.

1-15 市、州生产总值(2019)
Gross Domestic Product of Cities and Prefectures (2019)

单位:亿元 (100 million yuan)

地 区	Regions	地区生产总值 Gross Domestic Product	第一产业 Primary Industry	第二产业 Secondary Industry	第三产业 Tertiary Industry
武 汉	Wuhan	16223.21	378.99	5988.88	9855.34
黄 石	Huangshi	1767.19	103.82	900.38	762.99
十 堰	Shiyan	2012.72	171.46	884.18	957.08
宜 昌	Yichang	4460.82	416.05	2054.15	1990.62
襄 阳	Xiangyang	4812.84	449.25	2329.24	2034.35
鄂 州	Ezhou	1140.07	100.49	550.30	489.28
荆 门	Jingmen	2033.77	242.89	961.50	829.38
孝 感	Xiaogan	2301.40	310.37	983.30	1007.73
荆 州	Jingzhou	2516.48	434.58	933.77	1148.13
黄 冈	Huanggang	2322.73	403.01	876.56	1043.16
咸 宁	Xianning	1594.98	200.00	704.90	690.08
随 州	Suizhou	1162.23	156.22	544.08	461.93
恩施州	Enshi	1159.37	180.94	299.43	679.00
仙 桃	Xiantao	868.47	92.51	400.72	375.24
潜 江	Qianjiang	812.63	80.82	407.94	323.87
天 门	Tianmen	650.82	85.32	306.93	258.57
神农架	Shennongjia	32.86	2.37	10.16	20.33

1-16 市、州生产总值指数(2019)
Indices of Gross Domestic Product of Cities and Prefectures (2019)

(上年=100,单位:%) (preceding year = 100,%)

地 区	Regions	地区生产总值 Gross Domestic Product	第一产业 Primary Industry	第二产业 Secondary Industry	第三产业 Tertiary Industry
武 汉	Wuhan	107.4	103.0	106.5	108.2
黄 石	Huangshi	108.2	103.4	108.9	108.1
十 堰	Shiyan	107.0	103.5	106.3	108.5
宜 昌	Yichang	108.1	103.3	109.6	107.5
襄 阳	Xiangyang	107.9	103.3	109.1	107.6
鄂 州	Ezhou	107.8	103.4	107.9	108.8
荆 门	Jingmen	107.5	103.2	107.9	108.4
孝 感	Xiaogan	108.0	103.3	109.1	108.5
荆 州	Jingzhou	107.5	103.3	108.1	108.8
黄 冈	Huanggang	106.8	103.2	107.6	107.6
咸 宁	Xianning	108.1	103.3	108.9	108.8
随 州	Suizhou	107.8	103.3	109.0	107.9
恩施州	Enshi	106.6	103.5	105.5	108.1
仙 桃	Xiantao	107.7	103.3	108.6	107.9
潜 江	Qianjiang	107.9	103.3	108.5	108.3
天 门	Tianmen	107.7	103.2	108.8	107.9
神农架	Shennongjia	107.3	103.8	107.5	107.7

1-17 市、州民营经济增加值(2019)
Value Added of Private Economy (2019)

地 区	Regions	增加值(亿元) Value-Added (100 million yuan)		占GDP比重(%) Percentage(%)	
		2018	2019	2018	2019
全 省	Total	22770.22	25038.73	54.2	54.6
武 汉	Wuhan	6370.17	6963.61	42.7	42.9
黄 石	Huangshi	925.80	1017.36	57.5	57.6
十 堰	Shiyan	906.92	1048.81	48.7	52.1
宜 昌	Yichang	2539.62	2825.89	62.9	63.3
襄 阳	Xiangyang	2324.84	2544.85	52.8	52.9
鄂 州	Ezhou	709.36	799.21	67.9	70.1
荆 门	Jingmen	1166.28	1276.77	62.1	62.8
孝 感	Xiaogan	1359.99	1500.84	64.6	65.2
荆 州	Jingzhou	1155.33	1289.23	50.0	51.2
黄 冈	Huanggang	1578.71	1693.97	72.8	72.9
咸 宁	Xianning	960.45	1058.84	66.0	66.4
随 州	Suizhou	717.20	786.58	67.5	67.7
恩施州	Enshi	479.01	510.35	44.3	44.0
仙 桃	Xiantao	582.83	632.16	72.8	72.8
潜 江	Qianjiang	551.77	601.75	73.9	74.0
天 门	Tianmen	428.67	472.86	71.7	72.7
神农架	Shennongjia	13.26	15.65	43.8	47.6

注:2018年数据根据四经普结果进行修订。
Note:The data in 2018 are revised according to the results of the fourth national economic census.

主要统计指标解释

平均增长速度 计算平均增长速度有两种方法：一种是习惯上经常使用的“水平法”，又称几何平均法，是以间隔期最后一年的水平同基期水平对比来计算平均每年增长(或下降)速度；另一种是“累计法”，又称代数平均法或方程法，是以间隔期内各年水平的总和同基期水平对比来计算平均每年增长(或下降)速度。在一般正常情况下，两种方法计算的平均每年增长速度比较接近；但在经济发展不平衡、出现大起大落时，两种方法计算的结果差别较大。

国民经济行业分类自 2012年定期报表开始使用新的《国民经济行业分类》(GB/T4754-2011)。该分类是由国家统计局组织修订，国家质量监督检验检疫总局和中国国家标准化管理委员会于2011年4月29日发布。这次修订是在2002年分类标准的基础上，参照联合国《全部经济活动的国际标准产业分类》(ISIC/Rev.4)进行的。修订后的《国民经济行业分类》(GB/T4754-2012)共有门类20个，大类96个，中类432个，小类1094个

企业(单位)登记注册类型 是以在工商行政管理机关登记注册的各类企业为划分对象，以工商行政管理部门对企业登记注册的类型为依据，将企业登记注册类型分为内资企业、港澳台商投资企业和外商投资企业三大类。内资企业包括国有企业、集体企业、股份合作企业、联营企业、有限责任公司、股份有限公司、私营公司和其他企业；港澳台商投资企业和外商投资企业分别包括合资经营企业、合作经营企业、独资经营企业和股份有限公司。对不在工商行政管理部门进行登记注册的行政机关、事业单位和社会团体，主要按其经费来源和管理方式进行划分。

国有企业 指企业全部资产归国家所有，并按《中华人民共和国企业法人登记管理条例》规定登记注册的非公司制的经济组织。不包括有限责任公司中的国有独资公司。

集体企业 指企业资产归集体所有，并按《中华人民共和国企业法人登记管理条例》规定登记注册的经济组织。

股份合作企业 指以合作制为基础，由企业职工共同出资入股，吸收一定比例的社会资产投资组建，实行自主经营，自负盈亏，共同劳动，民主管理，按劳分配与按股分红相结合的一种集体经济组织。

联营企业 指两个及两个以上相同或不同所有制性质的企业法人或事业单位法人，按自愿、平等、互利的原则，共同投资组成的经济组织。联营企业包括国有联营企业、集体联营企业、国有与集体联营企业和其他联营企业。

有限责任公司 指根据《中华人民共和国公司登记管理条例》规定登记注册，由两个以上、五十个以下的股东共同出资，每个股东以其所认缴的出资额对公司承担有限责任，公司以其全部资产对其债务承担责任的经济组织。有限责任公司包括国有独资公司以及其他有限责任公司。

股份有限公司 指根据《中华人民共和国公司登记管理条例》规定登记注册，其全部注册资本由等额股份构成并通过发行股票筹集资本，股东以其认购的股份对公司承担有限责任，公司以其全部资产对其债务承担责任的经济组织。

私营企业 指由自然人投资设立或由自然人控股，以雇佣劳动为基础的营利性经济组织。包括按照《公司法》、《合伙企业法》、《私营企业暂行条例》规定登记注册的私营有限责任公司、私营股份有限公司、私营合伙企业和私营独资企业。

其他企业 指上述企业之外的其他内资经济组织。

与港澳台商合资经营企业 指港澳台地区投资者与内地企业依照《中华人民共和国中外合资经营企业法》及有关法律的规定，按合同规定的比例投资设立、分享利润和分担风险的企业。

与港澳台商合作经营企业 指港澳台地区投资者与内地企业依照《中华人民共和国中外合作经营企业法》及有关法律的规定，依照合作合同的约定进行投资或提供条件设立、分配利润和分担风险的企业。

港澳台商独资经营企业 指依照《中华人民共和国外资企业法》及有关法律的规定，在内地由港澳台地区投资者全额投资设立的企业。

港澳台商投资股份有限公司 指根据国家有关规定，经原外经贸部依法批准设立，其中港、澳、台商的股本占公司注册资本

的比例达25% 以上的股份有限公司。凡其中港、澳、台商的股本占公司注册资本的比例小于25%的，属于内资企业中的股份有限公司。

中外合资经营企业 指外国企业或外国人与中国内地企业依照《中华人民共和国中外合资经营企业法》及有关法律的规定，按合同规定的比例投资设立、分享利润和分担风险的企业。

中外合作经营企业 指外国企业或外国人与中国内地企业依照《中华人民共和国中外合作经营企业法》及有关法律的规定，依照合作合同的约定进行投资或提供条件设立、分配利润和分担风险的企业。

外资企业 指依照《中华人民共和国外资企业法》及有关法律的规定，在中国内地由外国投资者全额投资设立的企业。

外商投资股份有限公司 指根据国家有关规定，经原外经贸部依法批准设立，其中外资的股本占公司注册资本的比例达25% 以上的股份有限公司。凡其中外资股本占公司注册资本的比例小于25%的，属于内资企业中的股份有限公司。

行政机关、事业单位和社会团体 参照企业登记注册类型，主要按其经费来源和管理方式划分。具体规定如下：

(1)行政机关：包括国家机关和政党机关，原则上均列为“国有”。但有特殊规定的，如供销社等，则列为“集体”。

(2)事业单位：包括经国家机构编制部门和有关业务主管部门批准成立的各类事业单位，不包括实行企业化管理的事业单位。事业单位的划分办法如下：

①由国家财政预算拨款或列入财政预算外资金管理以及经费主要来源于国有主管部门或国有上级单位的事业单位，列为“国有”。

②经费主要来源于集体单位的事业单位，列为“集体”。

③公民个人(或个人合伙)开办的事业单位，列为“私营”。

④上述以外的其他事业单位，如果其经费来源不明确，按管理方式进行归类。

(3)社会团体：包括经民政部门批准成立以及未纳入社会团体管理条例范围的工会、妇联等各类社会团体。社会团体的划分办法如下：

①未纳入民政部社会团体管理条例范围的工会、妇联、共青团、青联、工商联、科协、侨联等社会团体，国家拨款设立的基金会或基金管理组织以及经费主要来源于国有业务主管部门或国有上级单位的社会团体，列为“国有”。

②经费主要来源于集体单位的社会团体，列为“集体”。

③公民个人(或个人合伙)开办的社会团体，划为“私营”。

④上述以外的其他社会团体，如果其经费来源不明确，改按管理方式进行归类。

地区生产总值(GDP) 指按市场价格计算的一个地区所有常住单位在一定时期内生产活动的最终成果。地区生产总值有三种表现形态，即价值形态、收入形态和产品形态。从价值形态看，它是所有常住单位在一定时期内生产的全部货物和服务价值超过同期投入的全部非固定资产货物和服务价值的差额，即所有常住单位的增加值之和；从收入形态看，它是所有常住单位在一定时期内创造并分配给常住单位和非常住单位的初次收入之和；从产品形态看，它是所有常住单位在一定时期内最终使用的货物和服务价值减去货物和服务流进价值。在实际核算中，地区生产总值有三种计算方法，即生产法、收入法和支出法。三种方法分别从不同的方面反映地区生产总值及其构成。

国民总收入(GNI) 即国民生产总值，指一个国家(或地区)所有常住单位在一定时期内收入初次分配的最终结果。一国常住单位从事生产活动所创造的增加值在初次分配中主要分配给该国的常住单位，但也有一部分以生产税及进口税(扣除生产和进口补贴)、劳动者报酬和财产收入等形式分配给非常住单位；同时，国外生产所创造的增加值也有一部分以生产税及进口税(扣除生产和进口补贴)、劳动者报酬和财产收入等形式分配给该国的常住单位，从而产生了国民总收入的概念。它等于国内生产总值加上来自国外的净要素收入。与国内生产总值不同，国民总收入是个收入概念，而国内生产总值是个生产概念。

三次产业 三产业的划分是世界上较为常用的产业结构分类，但各国的划分不尽一致。我国的三次产业划分是：

第一产业是指农、林、牧、渔业。

第二产业是指采矿业，制造业，电力、煤气及水的生产和供应业，建筑业。

第三产业是指除第一、二产业以外的其他行业。

劳动者报酬 指劳动者因从事生产活动所获得的全部报酬。包括劳动者获得的各种形式的工资、奖金和津贴,既包括货币形式的,也包括实物形式的,还包括劳动者所享受的公费医疗和医药卫生费、上下班交通补贴、单位支付的社会保险费、住房公积金等。对于个体经济来说,其所有者所获得的劳动报酬和经营利润不易区分,这两部分统一作为劳动者报酬处理。

生产税净额 指生产税减生产补贴后的余额。生产税指政府对生产单位从事生产、销售和经营活动以及因从事生产活动使用某些生产要素(如固定资产、土地、劳动力)所征收的各种税、附加费和规费。生产补贴与生产税相反,指政府对生产单位的单方面转移支出,因此视为负生产税,包括政策亏损补贴、价格补贴等。

固定资产折旧 指一定时期内为弥补固定资产损耗按照规定的固定资产折旧率提取的固定资产折旧,或按国民经济核算统一规定的折旧率虚拟计算的固定资产折旧。它反映了固定资产在当期生产中的转移价值。各类企业和企业化管理的事业单位的固定资产折旧是指实际计提的折旧费;不计提折旧的政府机关、非企业化管理的事业单位和居民住房的固定资产折旧是按照统一规定的折旧率和固定资产原值计算的虚拟折旧。原则上,固定资产折旧应按固定资产当期的重置价值计算,但是目前我国尚不具备对全社会固定资产进行重估价的基础,所以暂时只能采用上述办法。

营业盈余 指常住单位创造的增加值扣除劳动者报酬、生产税净额和固定资产折旧后的余额。它相当于企业的营业利润加上生产补贴,但要扣除从利润中开支的工资和福利等。

支出法地区生产总值 是从最终使用的角度反映一个地区一定时期内生产活动最终成果的一种方法,包括最终消费支出、资本形成总额及货物和服务净流出三部分。计算公式为:

支出法国内生产总值=最终消费支出+资本形成总额+货物和服务净流出

最终消费支出 指常住单位为满足物质、文化和精神生活的需要,从本国经济领土和国外购买的货物和服务的支出。它不包括非常住单位在本国经济领土内的消费支出。最终消费支出分为居民消费支出和政府消费支出。

居民消费支出 指常住住户在一定时期内对于货物和服务的全部最终消费支出。居民消费支出除了直接以货币形式购买的货物和服务的消费支出外,还包括以其他方式获得的货物和服务的消费支出,即所谓的虚拟消费支出。居民虚拟消费支出包括如下几种类型:单位以实物报酬及实物转移的形式提供给劳动者的货物和服务;住户生产并由本住户消费了的货物和服务,其中的服务仅指住户的自有住房服务和付酬的家庭雇员提供的家庭和个人服务;金融机构提供的金融媒介服务;保险公司提供的保险服务。

政府消费支出 指政府部门为全社会提供的公共服务的消费支出和免费或以较低的价格向居民住户提供的货物和服务的净支出,前者等于政府服务的产出价值减去政府单位所获得的经营收入的价值,后者等于政府部门免费或以较低价格向居民住户提供的货物和服务的市场价值减去向住户收取的价值。

资本形成总额 指常住单位在一定时期内获得减去处置的固定资产和存货的净额,包括固定资本形成总额和存货增加两部分。

固定资本形成总额 指生产者在一定时期内获得的固定资产减处置的固定资产的价值总额。固定资产是通过生产活动生产出来的,且其使用年限在一年以上、单位价值在规定标准以上的资产,不包括自然资产。可分为有形固定资本形成总额和无形固定资本形成总额。有形固定资本形成总额包括一定时期内完成的建筑工程、安装工程和设备工器具购置(减处置)价值,以及土地改良、新增役、种、奶、毛、娱乐用牲畜和新增经济林木价值。无形固定资本形成总额包括矿藏的勘探、计算机软件等获得减处置。

存货增加 指常住单位在一定时期内存货实物量变动的市场价值,即期末价值减期初价值的差额,再扣除当期由于价格变动而产生的持有收益。存货增加可以是正值,也可以是负值,正值表示存货上升,负值表示存货下降。存货包括生产单位购进的原材料、燃料和储备物资等存货,以及生产单位生产的产成品、在制品和半成品等存货。

货物和服务净流出 指货物和服务流出减货物和服务流进的差额。流出包括常住单位向非常住单位出售或无偿转让的各种货物和服务的价值;流进包括常住单位从非常住单位购买或无偿得到的各种货物和服务的价值。由于服务活动的提供与使用同时发生,一般把常住单位从非常住单位得到的服务作为流进,非常住单位从常住单位得到的服务作为流出。

Explanatory Notes on Main Statistical Indicators

Average Annual Growth Rate Two methods for calculating average annual growth rate are applied, one is often called level approach, or the method of calculating geometric average, which is derived by comparing the level of the last year of the interval with that of the beginning year; the other is called accumulative approach or algebraic average or equation method, which is derived by the summation of the actual figure of each year in the interval divided by the figure in the base year. Usually the results calculated by the two methods are fairly close, but they differed sharply when uneven economic development occurred with striking fluctuations in growth.

Industrial Classification of the National Economy The new Industrial Classification of the National Economy (GB/T 4754–2011) is introduced starting from the compilation of 2012 annual statistics. The revision, based on the 2002 classification, was organized by the National Bureau of Statistics taking into consideration of the International Standards of the Industrial Classification of All Economic Activities (ISIC/Rev.4) of the United Nations. The new Classification was promulgated by the National Administration of Quality Supervision, Inspection and Quarantine and the Standardization Administration of the People's Republic of China on April 29, 2011. The revised version of the Industrial Classification of the National Economy (GB/T 4754–2012) is composed of 20 sections, 96 divisions, 432 groups and 1094 classes.

Registration Status of EnterprisesEnterprises are classified into 3 categories, namely domestic–funded enterprises, enterprises with investment from Hong Kong, Macau and Taiwan, and enterprises with foreign investment, in the light of the registration status of an enterprise in industrial and commercial administration agencies. Domestic–funded enterprises include state–owned enterprises, collective–owned enterprises, cooperative enterprises, joint ownership enterprises, limited liability corporations, share–holding corporations Ltd., private enterprises and other enterprises. Included in the enterprises with investment from Hong Kong, Macau and Taiwan and enterprises with foreign investment are joint–venture enterprises, cooperative enterprises, sole investment enterprises and share–holding corporations Ltd. For government agencies, institutions and social organizations which are not requested to be registered in industrial and commercial administration agencies, they are classified mainly by their sources of funds and way of management.

State–owned Enterprises refer to non–corporation economic units where the entire assets are owned by the state and which have registered in accordance with the Regulation of the People's Republic of China on the Management of Registration of Corporate Enterprises. Excluded from this category are sole state–funded corporations in the limited liability corporations.

Collective–owned Enterprises refer to economic units where the assets are owned collectively and which have registered in accordance with the Regulation of the People's Republic of China on the Management of Registration of Corporate Enterprises.

Cooperative Enterprises refer to a form of collective economic units (enterprises) where capitals come mainly from employees as their shares, with certain proportion of capital from the outside, where production is organized on the basis of independent operation, independent accounting for profits and losses, joint work, democratic management, and a distribution system that integrates remuneration according to work with dividend according to capital share.

Joint Ownership Enterprises refer to economic units established by two or more corporate enterprises or corporate institutions of the same or different ownership, through joint investment on the basis of equality, voluntary participation and mutual benefits. They include state joint ownership enterprises, collective joint ownership enterprises, joint state–collective enterprises, other joint ownership enterprises.

Limited Liability Corporations refer to economic units established with investment from 2–50 investors and registered in accor–

dance with the Regulation of the People's Republic of China on the Management of Registration of Corporations, each investor bearing limited liability to the corporation depending on its share of investment, and the corporation bearing liability to its debt to the maximum of its total assets. Limited liability corporations include exclusive state–funded limited liability corporations and other limited liability corporations.

Share–holding Corporations Ltd. refer to economic units registered in accordance with the Regulation of the People's Republic of China on the Management of Registration of Corporations, with total registered capitals divided into equal shares and raised through issuing stocks. Each investor bears limited liability to the corporation depending on the holding of shares, and the corporation bears liability to its debt to the maximum of its total assets.

Private Enterprises refer to profit–making economic units invested and established by natural persons, or controlled by natural persons using employed labour. Included in this category are private limited liability corporations, private share–holding corporations Ltd., private partnership enterprises and private–funded enterprises registered in accordance with the Corporation Law, Partnership Enterprises Law and Interim Regulations on Private Enterprises .

Other Domestic–funded Enterprises refer to domestic–funded economic units other than those mentioned above.

Cooperative Enterprises with Funds from Hong Kong Macau and Taiwan established by investors from Hong Kong, Macau and Taiwan with enterprises in the mainland of China in accordance with the Law of the People's Republic of China on Sino–foreign Cooperative Enterprises and other relevant laws, where the investment or provision of facilities, and the share of profits and risks is stipulated in the cooperative contract.

Enterprises with Sole (exclusive) Investment from Hong Kong, Macau and Taiwan refer to enterprises established in the mainland of China with exclusive investment from investors from Hong Kong, Macau and Taiwan in accordance with the Law of the People's Republic of China on Foreign–Funded Enterprises and other relevant laws.

Share–holding Corporations Ltd. with Investment from Hong Kong, Macau and Taiwan refer to share–holding corporations Ltd. established with the approval from the former Ministry of Foreign Trade and Economic Relations in line with relevant state regulations, where the share of investment from Hong Kong, Macau or Taiwan businessmen exceeds 25% of the total registered capital of the corporation. In case the share of investment from Hong Kong, Macau or Taiwan is less than 25% of the total registered capital, the enterprise is to be classified as domestic–funded share–holding corporation Ltd.

Joint–venture Enterprises with Foreign Investment refer to enterprises jointly established by foreign enterprises or foreigners with enterprises in the mainland of China in accordance with the Law of the People's Republic of China on Sino–foreign Joint Venture Enterprises and other relevant laws, where the share of investment, profits and risks is stipulated in the contract.

Cooperation Enterprises with Foreign Investment refer to enterprises jointly established by foreign enterprises or foreigners with enterprises in the mainland of China in accordance with the Law of the People's Republic of China on Sino–foreign Cooperative Enterprises and other relevant laws, where the investment or provision of facilities, and the share of profits and risks is stipulated in the cooperative contract.

Enterprises with Sole (exclusive) Foreign Investment refer to enterprises established in the mainland of China with exclusive investment from foreign investors in accordance with the Law of the People's Republic of China on Foreign–Funded Enterprises and other relevant laws.

Share–holding Corporations Ltd. with Foreign Investment refer to share–holding corporations Ltd. established with the approval from the Ministry of Foreign Trade and Economic Relations in line with relevant state regulations, where the share of investment from foreign investors exceeds 25% of the total registered capital of the corporation. In case the share of foreign investment is less than 25% of the total registered capital, the enterprise is to be classified as domestic–funded share–holding corporation Ltd.

Government Agencies, Institutions and Social Organizations are classified into following categories by source of funds and way of management taking reference of the registration status of enterprises:

(1) Government agencies: include state and party agencies, classified in principle as state–owned. There are exceptions, such as supply and marketing cooperatives which are classified as collective–owned.

(2) Institutions: include institutions of various types established with the approval by organization and staffing departments of the government, but exclude institutions where enterprise management system is introduced. Institutions are further classified as follows:

(a) Institutions whose main budget is listed in the government budget appropriations or extra–budget funds, or allocated from the budget of their competent government agencies. Such institutions are classified as state–owned.

(b) Institutions whose budget mainly comes from collective units. Such institutions are classified as collective–owned.

(c) Institutions other than those mentioned above whose source of budget is not clear. Such institutions are classified by way of management.

(3) Social organizations: include social organizations established with the approval from the Ministry of Civil Affairs, and organizations that are not covered by social organization management regulations such as trade unions, womens federations etc.. Social organizations are further classified as follows:

(a) Social organizations that are not covered by social organization management regulations of the Ministry of Civil Affairs such as trade unions, womens federations, communist youth leagues, youth associations, industrial and commerce associations, scientists associations, overseas Chinese associations, etc., foundations and fund management organizations established with funds from the state, and social organizations whose funds mainly come from the budget of their competent government agencies. Such institutions are classified as state–owned.

(b) Social organizations whose budget mainly comes from collective units. Such institutions are classified as collective–owned.

(c) Social organizations established by individual or a group of citizens, which are classified as private.

(d) Social organizations other than those mentioned above whose source of budget is not clear. Such organizations are classified by way of management.

Gross Domestic Product (GDP) refers to the final products at market prices produced by all resident units in a country (or a region) during a certain period of time. Gross domestic product is expressed in three different forms, i.e. value, income, and products respectively. GDP in its value form refers to the total value of all goods and services produced by all resident units during a certain period of time, minus the total value of input of goods and services of the nature of non–fixed assets; in other term, it is the sum of the value–added of all resident units. GDP in the form of income includes the income created by all resident units and distributed to resident and non–resident units. GDP in the form of products refers to the value of all goods and services for final consumption by all resident units minus the net exports of goods and services during a given period of time. In the practice of national accounting, gross domestic product is calculated with three approaches, i.e. production approach, income approach and expenditure approach, which reflect gross domestic product and its composition from different aspects.

Gross National Income (GNI) also known as gross national product, refers to the final result of the primary distribution of the income created by all the resident units of a country (or a region) during a certain period of time. The value–added created by the resident units of a country engaged in production activities is distributed, during the primary distribution, mainly to the resident units of that country, while part of it is distributed to the non–resident units in the form of production tax and import duties (minus subsidies to production and import), remuneration for the labourers and property income. At the meantime, a part of the value–added created abroad is distributed to the resident units of the country in the form of production tax and import duties (minus subsidies to production and import), remuneration for the labourers and property income. The concept of gross national income is thus developed, which equals to the gross domestic product plus the net factor income from abroad. Unlike the gross domestic product which is a concept of production, the gross national income is a concept of income.

Three Industries Classification of economic activities into three branches of industries is a common practice in the world, although the grouping varies to some extent form country to country. In China economic activities are categorized into following industries:

Primary industry: refers to agriculture, forestry, animal husbandry and fishery.

Secondary industry: refers to mining and quarrying, manufacturing, production and supply of electricity, water and gas, and construction.

Tertiary industry: refers to all other economic activities not included in primary or secondary industry.

Labourers Remuneration refers to the whole payment of various forms earned by the labourers from the productive activities they are engaged in. It includes wages, bonuses and allowances the labourers earned in monetary form and in kind. It also includes the free medical services provided to the labourers and the medicine expenses, traffic subsidies and social insurance, housing fund paid by the employers. As the individual economy is concerned, since the labourers remuneration is not easily distinguished from the operating profit, both are treated as labourers remuneration.

Net Taxes on Production refers to the difference of the taxes on production minus the subsidies on production. The taxes on production refers to the various taxes, extra charges and fees levied on the production units on their production, sale and business activities as well as on the use of some factors of production, such as fixed assets, land and labour force in the production activities they are engaged in. In contrast to the taxes on production, the subsidies on production refer to the unilateral government transfer to the production units and are therefore regarded as negative taxes on production. They include subsidies on the loss due to implementation of government policies, price subsidies, etc.

Depreciation of Fixed Assets refers to the depreciation of fixed assets of a given period, drawn in accordance with the stipulated depreciation rate for the purpose of compensating the wear loss of the fixed assets or the depreciation of fixed assets calculated in a fictitious way in accordance with the stipulated unified depreciation rate in the national economic accounting system. It reflects the value of transfer of the fixed assets in the production of the current period. The depreciation of fixed assets in various enterprises and institutions managed as enterprises refers to the depreciation expenses actually drawn. In government agencies and institutions not managed as enterprises which do not draw the depreciation expenses, as well as for the houses of residents, the depreciation of fixed assets is the imputed depreciation, which is calculated in accordance with the stipulated unified depreciation rate. In principle, the depreciation of fixed assets should be calculated on the basis of the re-purchased value of the fixed assets. However, there is no actual condition to re-evaluate all the fixed assets in China. Therefore, the above-mentioned methods are temporarily adopted at present.

Operating Surplus refers to the balance of the value added created by the resident units deducting the labourers remuneration, net taxes on production and the depreciation of fixed assets. It is equivalent to the business profit of the enterprises plus subsidies on production, but the wages and welfare expenses paid from the profits should be deducted.

GDP by Expenditure Approach refers to the method of measuring the final results of production activities of a country (region) during a given period from the perspective of final use. It includes final consumption expenditure, total capital formation and net export of goods and services, i.e.:

GDP by expenditure approach = final consumption expenditure + total capital formation + net export of goods and services

Final ConsumptionExpenditure refers to the total expenditure of resident units for purchases of goods and services from domestic economic territory and abroad to meet the requirements of material, cultural and spiritual life. It excludes the expenditure of non-resident units on consumption in the economic territory of the country. The final consumption expenditure is broken down into household consumption expenditure and government consumption expenditure.

Households ConsumptionExpenditure refers to the total expenditure of resident households on the final consumption of goods and services. In addition to the consumption of goods and services bought by the households directly with money, the households consumption expenditure also includes expenditure on goods and services obtained by the households in other ways, i.e. the so-called imputed consumption expenditure, which includes the following: (a) the goods and services provided to the households by the employer in the form of payment in kind and transfer in kind; (b) goods and services produced and consumed by the households themselves, in which the services refer only to the owner-occupied housing and domestic and individual services provided by the paid household workers; (c) financial intermediate services provided by financial institutions; (d) insurance services provided by insurance companies.

Government ConsumptionExpenditure refers to the expenditure on the consumption of the public services provided by the government to the whole society and the net expenditure on the goods and services provided by the government to the households free of charge or at low prices. The former equals to the output value of the government services minus the value of operating income obtained by the government departments. The latter equals to the market value of the goods and services provided by the government free of charge or at low prices to the households minus the value received by the government from the households.

Total Capital Formation refers to the fixed assets acquired minus those disposed of and the net value of inventory, including the total fixed capital formation and the increase in inventory.

Total Fixed Capital Formation refers to the value of fixed assets acquired minus those disposed of during a given period. Fixed assets are the assets produced through production activities with specified unit value which could be used for over one year, excluding natural assets. Total fixed capital formation can be categorized into total tangible capital formation and total intangible capital formation. The total tangible capital formation include the value of the construction projects, installation projects completed and the equipment, apparatus and instruments purchased as well as the value of land improved, the value of draught animals, breeding stock, animals for milk, wool and for recreational purpose, and the newly increased forest with economic value during a given period. The total intangible capital formation includes the prospecting of minerals, the acquisition of computer software minus the disposal of them.

Increase in Inventory refers to the market value of the change in inventory of resident units during a given period, i.e. the difference of value between the beginning and the end of the period minus the current gains due to the change in prices. The increase in inventory can be positive or negative. A positive value indicates the increase in inventory while a negative value indicates the decrease in stock. The inventory includes the raw materials, fuels and reserve materials purchased by the production units as well as the inventory of finished products, semi-finished products, work-in-progress, etc.

Outflow of Goods and Services refers to the difference of the exports of goods and services minus the imports of goods and services. The imports include the value of various goods and services sold or gratuitously transferred by the resident units to the non-resident units. The imports include the value of various goods and services purchased or gratuitously acquired by the resident units from the non-resident units. Because the provision of services and the use of them happen simultaneously, the acquisition of services by the resident units from abroad is usually treated as import while the acquisition of services by non-resident units in this country is usually treated as export. The export and import of goods are calculated at FOB.

2 人口

Population

资料整理人员：刘　通

2-1 人 口 数
Population

单位:万人 (年底数)(number at year-end) (10 000 persons)

年份 Year	户籍人口 Total Population	男 Male	女 Female	常住人口 Total Population	男 Male	女 Female
1952	2745.0	1414.6	1330.4			
1957	3062.4	1579.7	1482.7			
1965	3504.5	1793.3	1711.2			
1975	4408.2	2261.7	2146.5			
1980	4684.5	2401.8	2282.7			
1985	4931.0	2540.0	2391.0	4980.8	2566.3	2414.5
1986	4989.0	2573.4	2415.6	5047.8	2603.3	2444.5
1987	5058.1	2608.7	2449.4	5120.3	2640.3	2480.0
1988	5144.2	2652.1	2492.1	5184.9	2673.1	2511.8
1989	5223.9	2694.6	2529.3	5258.8	2712.5	2546.3
1990	5373.5	2771.5	2602.0	5439.3	2805.5	2633.8
1991	5446.8	2805.4	2641.4	5512.3	2839.1	2673.2
1992	5513.6	2841.2	2672.4	5579.9	2862.3	2717.6
1993	5590.5	2880.9	2709.6	5653.5	2913.3	2740.2
1994	5656.8	2915.6	2741.2	5718.8	2947.5	2771.3
1995	5727.1	2952.1	2775.0	5772.1	2959.6	2812.5
1996	5776.3	2979.5	2796.8	5825.1	3004.8	2820.3
1997	5838.8	3014.0	2824.8	5872.6	3016.6	2856.0
1998	5890.6	3039.9	2850.7	5907.2	3032.6	2874.6
1999	5942.5	3061.8	2880.7	5938.0	3031.9	2906.1
2000	5936.0	3066.1	2869.9	5646.0	2939.3	2706.7
2001	5956.6	3073.2	2883.4	5658.0	2919.1	2738.9
2002	5978.2	3086.2	2892.0	5672.0	2928.1	2743.9
2003	6000.5	3109.9	2890.6	5685.0	2946.3	2738.7
2004	6001.3	3107.8	2893.5	5698.0	2950.7	2747.3
2005	5984.1	3102.4	2881.7	5710.0	2960.2	2749.8
2006	6038.3	3129.6	2908.7	5693.0	2950.6	2742.4
2007	6084.9	3154.0	2930.9	5699.0	2953.9	2745.1
2008	6110.8	3167.5	2943.3	5711.0	2960.2	2750.8
2009	6141.9	3185.5	2956.4	5720.0	2966.6	2753.4
2010	6176.0	3202.0	2974.0	5723.8	2939.3	2784.5
2011	6164.1	3194.0	2970.1	5758.0	2956.0	2802.0
2012	6165.4	3194.0	2971.4	5779.0	2963.9	2815.1
2013	6170.6	3199.5	2971.1	5799.0	2972.0	2827.0
2014	6162.3	3198.1	2964.2	5816.0	2980.3	2835.7
2015	6138.9	3190.1	2948.8	5851.5	2984.5	2867.0
2016	6156.8	3200.4	2956.3	5885.0	2997.2	2887.8
2017	6141.8	3191.1	2950.7	5902.0	2996.8	2905.2
2018	6172.9	3206.5	2966.4	5917.0	3004.4	2912.6
2019	6177.8	3208.7	2969.1	5927.0	3009.5	2917.5

2-2 人口城乡构成
Composition of Urban and Rural Population

单位:万人 (年底数)(number at year-end) (10 000 persons)

年份 Year	总人口 Total Population	城镇人口 Urban Population	乡村人口 Rural Population
1952	2745.00	271.41	2416.17
1957	3062.41	411.69	2650.72
1965	3504.54	485.06	3019.48
1975	4408.15	626.22	3781.93
1980	4684.45	786.49	3897.96
1985	4980.81	1464.65	3516.16
1986	5047.83	1187.23	3860.60
1987	5120.27	1288.61	3831.66
1988	5184.94	1389.99	3794.95
1989	5258.83	1491.37	3767.46
1990	5439.29	1551.51	3887.78
1991	5512.33	1433.06	4079.27
1992	5579.85	1637.68	3942.17
1993	5653.48	1731.66	3921.82
1994	5718.81	1604.13	4114.68
1995	5772.07	1800.89	3971.18
1996	5825.13	1965.40	3859.73
1997	5872.60	1834.60	4038.00
1998	5907.23	1884.41	4022.82
1999	5938.03	1990.17	3947.86
2000	5646.00	2285.11	3360.89
2001	5658.00	2308.50	3349.50
2002	5672.00	2348.20	3323.80
2003	5685.00	2387.70	3297.30
2004	5698.00	2427.30	3270.70
2005	5710.00	2466.70	3243.30
2006	5693.00	2493.50	3199.50
2007	5699.00	2524.70	3174.30
2008	5711.00	2581.40	3129.60
2009	5720.00	2631.20	3088.80
2010	5723.77	2844.51	2879.26
2011	5758.00	2984.32	2773.68
2012	5779.00	3091.77	2687.23
2013	5799.00	3161.03	2637.97
2014	5816.00	3237.80	2578.20
2015	5851.50	3326.58	2524.92
2016	5885.00	3419.19	2465.81
2017	5902.00	3499.89	2402.11
2018	5917.00	3567.95	2349.05
2019	5927.00	3615.47	2311.53

注:1981年及以前数据为户籍统计数;1982、1990、2000、2010年数据为当年人口普查时点数据;其余年份数据为年度人口抽样调查推算数据(下相关表同)。

Note:The data of 1981 and before are the household registration statistics; the data of 1982, 1990, 2000 and 2010 are the census time point data of that year; the data of other years are the estimated data of annual population sampling survey (the same as the relevant table below).

2-3 全省人口自然变动
Natural Change of Population

年 份 Year	人口变动数(万人) Number of Population Changed (10 000 persons)			变动系数(‰) Growth Rates		
	出生数 Number of Birth	死亡数 Number of Death	自然增长数 Number of Nature Growth	出生率 Birth Rate	死亡率 Death Rate	自然增长率 Natural Growth Rate
1965	121.48	34.75	86.73	35.10	10.04	25.06
1975	90.80	34.52	56.28	20.74	7.88	12.86
1980	94.84	32.59	62.25	20.36	7.00	13.36
1985	97.83	37.37	60.46	19.95	7.62	12.33
1986	107.09	39.45	67.64	21.01	7.74	13.27
1987	108.56	36.12	72.44	21.43	7.13	14.30
1988	97.62	32.95	64.67	19.08	6.44	12.64
1989	110.13	36.24	73.89	21.09	6.94	14.15
1990	114.40	38.66	75.74	21.60	7.30	14.30
1991	113.34	40.30	73.04	20.70	7.36	13.34
1992	105.60	38.08	67.52	19.05	6.87	12.18
1993	112.55	38.92	73.63	20.04	6.93	13.11
1994	103.31	37.98	65.33	18.17	6.68	11.49
1995	92.96	39.70	53.26	16.18	6.91	9.27
1996	93.24	40.18	53.06	16.08	6.93	9.15
1997	86.62	39.13	47.49	14.81	6.69	8.12
1998	74.09	39.46	34.63	12.58	6.70	5.88
1999	68.52	37.73	30.79	11.57	6.37	5.20
2000	57.76	35.75	22.01	9.71	6.01	3.70
2001	50.84	36.27	14.57	8.51	6.07	2.44
2002	50.10	36.90	13.20	8.38	6.17	2.21
2003	49.50	35.60	13.90	8.26	5.94	2.32
2004	50.66	36.23	14.43	8.43	6.03	2.40
2005	52.60	34.30	18.30	8.74	5.69	3.05
2006	54.80	35.90	18.90	9.08	5.95	3.13
2007	55.69	36.12	19.57	9.19	5.96	3.23
2008	55.98	39.51	16.47	9.21	6.50	2.71
2009	57.80	36.58	21.22	9.48	6.00	3.48
2010	59.30	34.46	24.84	10.36	6.02	4.34
2011	59.67	34.52	25.15	10.39	6.01	4.38
2012	63.45	35.30	28.15	11.00	6.12	4.88
2013	64.14	35.60	28.54	11.08	6.15	4.93
2014	68.88	40.42	28.46	11.86	6.96	4.90
2015	62.65	34.01	28.64	10.74	5.83	4.91
2016	70.65	40.90	29.75	12.04	6.97	5.07
2017	74.26	41.31	32.95	12.60	7.01	5.59
2018	68.28	41.42	26.86	11.54	7.00	4.54
2019	67.21	41.93	25.29	11.35	7.08	4.27

2-4 分市、州、县年底人口数(2019)
Population of Cities, Prefectures and Counties of Hubei at Year-end(2019)

单位: 万人 (10 000 persons)

地 区	Region	户籍人口(万人) Total Population	常住人口(万人) Population of Permnant Residents	地 区	Region	户籍人口(万人) Total Population	常住人口(万人) Population of Permnant Residents
全 省	**Province**	**6177.84**	**5927.00**	丹江口市	Danjiangkou	46.25	44.54
武汉市	**Wuhan**	**906.40**	**1121.20**	**宜昌市**	**Yichang**	**390.94**	**413.79**
江岸区	Jiang'an	78.59	96.28	西陵区	Xiling	39.94	55.06
江汉区	Jianghan	51.36	72.98	伍家岗区	Wujiagang	19.70	25.18
硚口区	Qiaokou	53.99	86.89	点军区	Dianjun	10.40	11.25
汉阳区	Hanyang	71.79	67.00	猇亭区	Xiaoting	5.04	6.78
武昌区	Wuchang	110.34	128.54	夷陵区	Yiling	52.64	54.11
青山区	Qingshan	45.96	52.90	远安县	Yuan'an	18.99	18.39
洪山区	Hongshan	121.96	171.29	兴山县	Xingshan	16.38	16.60
东西湖区	Dongxihu	35.50	60.13	秭归县	Zigui	36.86	35.40
汉南区	Hannan	11.67	13.60	长阳县	Changyang	38.59	38.20
蔡甸区	Caidian	46.95	78.49	五峰县	Wufeng	19.60	19.00
江夏区	Jiangxia	64.69	98.70	宜都市	Yidu	38.64	38.41
黄陂区	Huangpi	116.33	102.80	当阳市	Dangyang	46.46	46.40
新洲区	Xinzhou	97.29	91.60	枝江市	Zhijiang	47.70	49.01
黄石市	**Huangshi**	**273.34**	**247.17**	**襄阳市**	**Xiangyang**	**589.78**	**568.00**
黄石港区	Huangshigang	20.86	22.84	襄城区	Xiangcheng	46.55	51.44
西塞山区	Xisai mountainous	20.33	23.82	樊城区	Fancheng	81.02	91.22
下陆区	Xialu	16.03	18.60	襄州区	Xiangzhou	100.10	92.15
铁山区	Tieshan	4.76	5.60	南漳县	Nanzhang	57.03	54.64
大冶市	Daye	99.68	91.28	谷城县	Gucheng	59.58	51.12
阳新县	Yangxin	111.69	85.03	保康县	Baokang	26.62	25.86
十堰市		**346.07**	**339.80**	老河口市	Laohekou	51.09	48.27
茅箭区	Maojian	30.10	42.56	枣阳市	Zaoyang	111.95	100.52
张湾区	Zhangwan	25.85	39.32	宜城市	Yicheng	55.84	52.78
郧阳区	Yunyang	63.18	57.17	**鄂州市**	**Ezhou**	**111.56**	**105.97**
郧西县	Yunxi	51.61	43.10	梁子湖区	Liangzihu	19.20	14.57
竹山县	Zhushan	45.96	41.68	华容区	Huarong	26.85	25.13
竹溪县	Zhuxi	35.72	31.40	鄂城区	Echeng	65.51	66.27
房 县	Fang	47.41	40.03				

2-4 续表 Continued

单位: 万人 (10 000 persons)

地 区	Regions	户籍人口 Total Population	常住人口 Permnant Population	地 区	Regions	户籍人口 Total Population	常住人口 Permnant Population
荆门市	**Jingmen**	**290.95**	**289.75**	蕲春县	Hanchun	100.75	78.22
东宝区	Dongbao	35.46	37.91	黄梅县	Huangmei	103.17	86.94
掇刀区	Zhuodao	29.63	33.59	麻城市	Macheng	115.39	88.04
京山市	Jingshan	62.63	62.17	武穴市	Wuxue	82.32	65.40
沙洋县	Shayang	59.29	55.98	**咸宁市**	**Xianning**	**305.28**	**254.84**
钟祥市	Zhongxiang	103.94	100.10	咸安区	Xian'an	63.04	53.15
孝感市	**Xiaogan**	**515.15**	**492.10**	嘉鱼县	Jiayu	36.54	31.98
孝南区	Xiaonan	95.74	93.03	通城县	Tongcheng	52.69	41.73
孝昌县	Xiaochang	66.97	59.96	崇阳县	Congyang	51.09	40.85
大悟县	Dawu	62.47	62.48	通山县	Tongshan	48.78	37.77
云梦县	Yunmeng	57.11	53.74	赤壁市	Chibi	53.15	49.36
应城市	Yingcheng	64.65	60.66	**随州市**	**Suizhou**	**249.48**	**222.10**
安陆市	Anlu	61.23	58.40	曾都区	Zengdu	66.20	63.92
汉川市	Hanchuan	106.98	103.83	随县	Sui	92.07	80.66
荆州市	**Jingzhou**	**637.16**	**557.01**	广水市	Guangshui	91.21	77.52
沙市区	Shashi	52.66	66.64	**恩施州**	**Enshi Prefecture**	**402.10**	**339.00**
荆州区	Jingzhou	54.88	58.54	恩施市	Enshi	81.30	78.36
公安县	Gong'an	98.91	83.78	利川市	Jianli	91.88	67.45
监利县	Jianli	156.55	100.72	建始县	Jianshi	50.96	42.40
江陵县	Jianglin	39.05	33.88	巴东县	Badong	48.60	43.19
石首市	Shishou	61.50	56.01	宣恩县	Xuan'en	35.76	30.92
洪湖市	Honghu	91.32	80.68	咸丰县	Xianfeng	38.54	31.14
松滋市	Songzi	82.29	76.76	来凤县	Laifeng	33.44	25.02
黄冈市	**Huanggang**	**737.81**	**633.30**	鹤峰县	Hefeng	21.62	20.55
黄州区	Huangzhou	35.41	39.78	**省直管单位**	**Jurisdictional**		
团风县	Tuanfeng	36.71	34.61	仙桃市	Xiantao	152.92	114.01
红安县	Hong'an	64.80	60.92	潜江市	Qianjiang	100.50	96.61
罗田县	Luotian	59.25	55.27	天门市	Tianmen	160.51	124.74
英山县	Yingshan	39.76	36.39	**神农架林区**	**Shennongjian**	**7.87**	**7.61**
浠水县	Xishui	100.25	87.73				

主要统计指标解释

人口数 指一定时点、一定地区范围内有生命的个人总和。

年度统计的年末人口数指每年12月31日24时的人口数。

城镇人口和乡村人口 城镇人口是指居住在城镇范围内的全部常住人口；乡村人口是除上述人口以外的全部人口。

出生率(又称粗出生率) 指在一定时期内(通常为一年)一定地区的出生人数与同期内平均人数(或期中人数)之比，用千分率表示。本资料中的出生率指年出生率，其计算公式为：

$$出生率=\frac{年出生人数}{年平均人数}\times 1000‰$$

式中：出生人数指活产婴儿，即胎儿脱离母体时(不管怀孕月数)，有过呼吸或其他生命现象。年平均人数指年初、年底人口数的平均数，也可用年中人口数代替。

死亡率(又称粗死亡率) 指在一定时期内(通常为一年)一定地区的死亡人数与同期内平均人数(或期中人数)之比，用千分率表示。本资料中的死亡率指年死亡率，其计算公式为：

$$死亡率=\frac{年死亡人数}{年平均人数}\times 1000‰$$

人口自然增长率 指在一定时期内(通常为一年)人口自然增加数(出生人数减死亡人数)与该时期内平均人数(或期中人数)之比，用千分率表示。计算公式为：

$$人口自然增长率=\frac{本年出生人数-本年死亡人数}{年平均人数}\times 1000‰$$

$$=人口出生率-人口死亡率$$

Explanatory Notes on Main Statistical Indicators

Total Population refers to the total number of people alive at a certain point of time within a given area.

The annual statistics on total population is taken at midnight, the 31st of December.

Urban Population and Rural Population Urban population refer to all people residing in cities and towns, while rural population refer to population other than urban population.

Birth Rate (or Crude Birth Rate) refers to the ratio of the number of births to the average population (or mid-period population) during a certain period of time (usually a year), expressed in ‰. Birth rate in the chapter refers to annual birth rate. The following formula is used:

Birth Rate = (Number of Births/Average Number of Population) × 1000‰

Number of births in the formula refers to live births, i.e. when a baby has breathed or showed any vital phenomena regardless of the length of pregnancy.

Annual average number of population is the average of the number of population at the beginning of the year and that at the end of the year. Sometimes it is substituted by the mid-year population.

Death Rate (or Crude Death Rate) refers to the ratio of the number of deaths to the average population (or mid-period population) during a certain period of time (usually a year), expressed in ‰. Death rate in the chapter refers to annual death rate. The following formula is used:

Death Rate= (Number of Deaths/Annual Average Number of Population) × 1000‰

Natural Growth Rate of Population refers to the ratio of natural increase in population (number of births minus number of deaths) in a certain period of time (usually a year) to the average population (or mid-period population) of the same period, expressed in ‰. The following formula is applied:

Natural Growth Rate of Population = [(Number of Births–Number of Deaths)/Average Number of Population] × 1000‰

Natural Growth Rate of Population = Birth Rate–Death Rate

3 就业人员和职工工资

Employment and Wages

资料整理人员：刘　通

3-1 全社会从业人员
Total Employed Persons for the Whole Society

单位：万人 (10 000 person)

年份 Year	合计 Total	按城乡分 Grouped by Areas		按产业分 Grouped by Industries		
		城镇 Urban	乡村 Rural	第一产业 Primary Industry	第二产业 Secondary Industry	第三产业 Tertiary Industry
1952	1020.30	141.60	878.70			
1965	1404.20	222.70	1181.60			
1970	1618.50	278.00	1340.80			
1975	1802.50	381.70	1420.80			
1978	1910.40	458.00	1452.30	1470.60	269.00	170.80
1980	1986.90	507.20	1479.70	1453.70	286.30	247.00
1985	2238.10	637.60	1600.50	1383.30	485.40	369.50
1990	3040.40	890.80	2149.60	1859.80	628.50	552.10
1991	3082.70	909.40	2173.30	1897.40	623.00	562.30
1992	3118.60	923.10	2195.50	1869.00	650.90	598.70
1993	3157.60	940.90	2216.70	1818.80	684.60	654.20
1994	3196.90	980.10	2216.80	1760.50	717.10	719.30
1995	3232.50	1015.00	2217.50	1697.00	743.50	792.00
1996	3275.50	1050.80	2224.70	1677.10	746.80	851.60
1997	3311.20	1070.50	2240.70	1663.20	752.00	896.00
1998	3328.20	1093.60	2234.60	1612.50	705.60	1010.10
1999	3358.10	1110.50	2247.60	1612.60	697.80	1047.70
2000	3384.90	1123.80	2261.10	1625.10	702.40	1057.40
2001	3414.50	1148.70	2265.80	1639.00	706.80	1068.70
2002	3443.00	1177.00	2266.00	1652.60	704.10	1086.30
2003	3476.00	1211.00	2265.00	1661.50	712.60	1101.90
2004	3507.00	1245.00	2262.00	1672.90	720.30	1113.80
2005	3537.00	1271.00	2266.00	1687.30	725.00	1124.70
2006	3564.00	1297.00	2267.00	1694.70	732.40	1136.90
2007	3584.00	1322.00	2262.00	1697.00	740.10	1146.90
2008	3607.00	1337.00	2270.00	1707.91	730.42	1168.67
2009	3622.00	1357.00	2265.00	1702.30	736.60	1183.10
2010	3645.00	1382.60	2262.40	1691.10	754.70	1199.20
2011	3672.00	1413.00	2259.00	1678.10	771.12	1222.78
2012	3687.00	1430.60	2256.40	1638.90	781.60	1266.50
2013	3692.00	1438.00	2254.00	1582.00	793.80	1316.20
2014	3687.50	1437.60	2249.90	1487.00	834.30	1366.20
2015	3658.00	1935.00	1723.00	1404.00	834.00	1420.00
2016	3633.00	2074.00	1559.00	1338.00	837.00	1458.00
2017	3610.00	2086.00	1524.00	1278.00	839.00	1493.00
2018	3580.00	2088.00	1492.00	1216.00	840.00	1524.00
2019	3548.00	2090.00	1458.00	1164.00	841.00	1543.00

注：因2015年开展全国1%人口抽样调查，根据调查结果对部分数据进行修正，使2015年全省全社会从业人员数据产生较大波动。

3-2 分行业城镇单位从业人员数(2019)
Number of Employed Persons in Urban Units by Sector(2019)

单位：人 (person)

行业	Sector	城镇全部单位 All the Units In Urban Area	国有经济单位 State Owned Units	城镇集体单位 Urban Collective Owned Units	其他经济单位 Other Units	城镇私营单位 Urban Private Units
总计	**Total**	**11402632**	**2372609**	**112494**	**4052462**	**4865067**
农、林、牧、渔业	Farming,Forest,Herd, ishery	167323	87670	301	2019	77333
采矿业	Mining and Quarrying	132395	291	753	39164	92187
制造业	Manufacturing	3406955	34615	25689	1282579	2064072
电力、燃气及水的生产和供应业	Power, Gas and water production and supply	186804	90935	2382	52711	40776
建筑业	Construction	2209055	47581	27319	1121965	1012190
批发和零售业	Wholesale and Retail sale	1036258	31719	12175	325433	666931
交通运输、仓储和邮政业	Transportation, storage and post	414548	79358	2341	228170	104679
住宿和餐饮业	Hotel and Catering	328101	8739	990	78641	239731
信息传输、软件和信息技术服务业	Information Transmission, Software and Computer Services	228080	12108	42	168683	47247
金融业	Banking	210428	33574	3428	165043	8383
房地产业	Real Estate	313903	8881	1920	166225	136877
租赁和商务服务业	Leasing and Commerical Services	297491	32121	5041	140165	120164
科学研究、技术服务业	Scietific Research, polytechnical	208196	67965	1795	99932	38504
水利、环境和公共设施管理业	Water Conservance, Environment and Public Facilities Management	138341	80815	9643	27063	20820
居民服务、修理和其他服务业	Resident Service and Others	97336	9925	259	15085	72067
教育	Education	760998	623544	7600	74604	55250
卫生和社会工作	Health, Social Security and	439763	366158	10057	40497	23051
文化、体育和娱乐业	Culture, Sports and Entertainment	103772	34025	750	24192	44805
公共管理、社会保障和社会组织	Public management, social security and social organization	722885	722585	9	291	

注:城镇全部单位统计范围含城镇私营单位(后表未经特别注明均同此口径)。

Note: All Statistics of Units in Urban Areas of 2010 including all the private run unit. (The following tables if without specific notes are considered the same standard with this one.)

3-3 分行业在岗职工人数(2019)
Number of Staff and Workers by Sector(2019)

单位：人 (person)

行业	Sector	城镇全部单位 All the Units In Urban Area	国有经济单位 State Owned Units	城镇集体单位 Urban Collective Owned Units	其他经济单位 Other Units	城镇私营单位 Urban Private Units
总计	**Total**	**10891623**	**2215089**	**106034**	**3705433**	**4865067**
农、林、牧、渔业	Farming, Forest, Herd, Fishery	152928	73516	291	1788	77333
采矿业	Mining and Quarrying	127559	265	750	34357	92187
制造业	Manufacturing	3374241	29868	25479	1254822	2064072
电力、燃气及水的生产和供应业	Power, Gas and water production and supply	184147	89218	2374	51779	40776
建筑业	Construction	2025984	34924	25837	953033	1012190
批发和零售业	Wholesale and Retail sale	1019100	29841	11750	310578	666931
交通运输、仓储和邮政业	Transportation, storage and post	401474	76988	2315	217492	104679
住宿和餐饮业	Hotel and Catering	319601	8569	978	70323	239731
信息传输、软件和信息技术服务业	Information Transmission, Software and Computer Services	188772	11626	42	129857	47247
金融业	Banking	168888	29383	3380	127742	8383
房地产业	Real Estate	306474	8190	1840	159567	136877
租赁和商务服务业	Leasing and Commerical Services	283583	31516	4411	127492	120164
科学研究、技术服务业	Scietific Research, polytechnical	198929	65290	1671	93464	38504
水利、环境和公共设施 管理业	Water Conservance, Environment and Public Facilities Management	124326	71177	7002	25327	20820
居民服务、修理和其他服务业	Resident Service and Others	95451	9216	257	13911	72067
教育	Education	724295	590340	7348	71357	55250
卫生和社会工作	Health, Social Security and	417557	345881	9568	39057	23051
文化、体育和娱乐业	Culture, Sports and Entertainment	100554	31788	734	23227	44805
公共管理、社会保障和社会组织	Public management, social security and social organization	677760	677493	7	260	

3-4 分行业在岗女职工人数(2019)
Number of Female Staff and Workers by Sector(2019)

单位：人 (person)

行业	Sector	城镇全部单位(不含私营单位) All the Units In Urban Area	国有经济单位 State Owned Units	城镇集体单位 Urban Collective Owned Units	其他经济单位 Urban Private Units
总计	**Total**	**2327722**	**977833**	**36077**	**1313812**
农、林、牧、渔业	Farming, Forest, Herd, Fishery	30029	29456	83	490
采矿业	Mining and Quarrying	10599	85	139	10375
制造业	Manufacturing	483256	9398	5146	468712
电力、燃气及水的生产和供应业	Power, Gas and water production and supply	42283	24810	604	16869
建筑业	Construction	149070	6717	3774	138579
批发和零售业	Wholesale and Retail sale	193503	8848	7025	177630
交通运输、仓储和邮政业	Transportation, storage and post	81412	27764	757	52891
住宿和餐饮业	Hotel and Catering	54299	3770	671	49858
信息传输、软件和信息技术服务业	Information Transmission, Software and Computer Services	71799	4328	17	67454
金融业	Banking	95938	12537	1510	81891
房地产业	Real Estate	72834	2953	721	69160
租赁和商务服务业	Leasing and Commerical Services	55125	10623	2037	42465
科学研究、技术服务业	Scietific Research, polytechnical	49034	21236	415	27383
水利、环境和公共设施管理业	Water Conservance, Environment and Public Facilities Management	45608	29882	4092	11634
居民服务、修理和其他服务业	Resident Service and Others	13145	4034	162	8949
教育	Education	368868	315366	4475	49027
卫生和社会工作	Health, Social Security and	256230	224161	4231	27838
文化、体育和娱乐业	Culture, Sports and Entertainment	26435	13774	211	12450
公共管理、社会保障和社会组织	Public Management、social security and Social Organization	228255	228091	7	157

3-5 城镇登记失业人数及失业率
Number of Registered Unemployed Persons and Unemployment Rate in Urban Area

单位：万人 (10 000 person)

年份 Year	年末城镇登记失业人数 The Number of Unemployeed in Urban Areas by the End of Year	年末城镇登记失业率(%) Year End Unemployment registered Rate %
1978	20.03	4.19
1980	15.54	2.97
1990	12.66	1.72
1991	14.20	1.88
1992	16.89	2.17
1993	17.96	2.20
1994	21.06	2.90
1995	24.45	3.10
1996	28.25	3.50
1997	29.83	3.50
1998	31.33	3.30
1999	33.10	3.30
2000	36.64	3.50
2001	42.15	4.00
2002	44.66	4.30
2003	49.34	4.30
2004	49.37	4.20
2005	52.60	4.33
2006	52.56	4.22
2007	46.72	4.21
2008	55.07	4.20
2009	55.25	4.21
2010	55.65	4.18
2011	55.11	4.10
2012	42.26	3.83
2013	40.26	3.49
2014	37.88	3.10
2015	33.43	2.64
2016	32.91	2.41
2017	37.07	2.59
2018	36.14	2.55
2019	37.63	2.44

3-6 职工平均工资及指数

年份 Year	平均货币工资(元) Average Money Wages (yuan)					指数(上年=100) Indices(preceding year=100)	
	合计 Total	国有经济单位 State Owned Units	城镇集体经济单位 Urban Collective Owned	其他经济单位 Other Units	城镇私营单位 Urban private units	货币工资 Money Wages	国有经济单位 State Owned Units
1978	581	592	532			104.5	104.5
1980	719	744	619			116.0	115.9
1990	1903	2045	1467	2259		111.7	107.6
1992	2370	2532	1837	2575		113.9	114.4
1993	2933	3141	2183	3248		123.8	124.1
1994	4050	4348	2845	4352		138.1	138.4
1995	4685	4991	3308	5093		115.7	114.8
1996	5099	5411	3590	5754		108.8	108.4
1997	5401	5741	3731	5740		105.9	106.1
1998	6436	6783	4748	6166		108.7	109.1
1999	6991	7381	5001	6681		108.6	108.8
2000	7565	7989	5090	7327		108.2	108.2
2001	8619	9133	5677	8035		113.9	114.3
2002	9611	10403	6534	8180		111.5	113.9
2003	10692	11806	7137	8698		111.2	113.5
2004	11855	13096	7608	10270		110.9	110.9
2005	13330	14774	8663	11572		112.4	112.8
2006	15172	17078	9848	13098		113.8	115.6
2007	17397	21971	12921	16829		114.7	128.7
2008	19597	24756	14840	20293		112.6	112.7
2009	23709	30032	19181	23528	15615	121.0	121.3
2010	28092	35981	24429	28799	18626	118.5	119.8
2011	32050	40345	26988	34354	20788	114.1	112.1
2012	35179	43438	33551	38675	23037	109.8	107.7
2013	38720	46126	34181	43975	25898	110.1	106.2
2014	43217	55071	37599	48163	28534	111.6	119.4
2015	47320	60615	41152	52060	31051	109.5	110.1
2016	51415	68983	44154	56461	34167	108.7	113.8
2017	55903	78423	49064	61286	37142	108.7	113.7
2018	60561	85712	52514	70512	40126	108.3	109.3
2019	64661	91665	55560	76157	43536	106.8	106.9

注:1998年以后为在岗职工平均工资。2007年以后统计范围含城镇全部私营单位。

Average Wages and Indices of Staff and Workers

指数(上年=100) Indices(preceding year=100)							
			实际工资 Real Wages				
城镇集体经济单位 Urban Collective Owned	其他经济单位 OtherUnits	城镇私营单位 Urban private units		国有经济单位 State Owned Units	城镇集体经济单位 Urban Collective Owned	其他经济单位 OtherUnits	城镇私营单位 Urban private units
106.4			104.2	103.9	106.1		
116.4			108.6	108.5	109.0		
107.1	107.1		107.8	108.3	104.4	103.9	
110.5	109.0		103.1	103.5	100.0	98.7	
118.8	126.1		106.6	106.8	102.3	108.6	
130.3	134.0		108.7	109.0	102.6	105.5	
116.3	117.0		96.3	95.6	96.8	97.4	
108.5	113.0		95.1	94.0	95.3	99.9	
103.9	99.8		97.6	96.6	95.9	96.6	
109.2	99.1		110.2	110.2	110.8	100.5	
105.3	108.4		110.0	111.0	107.4	110.6	
101.8	109.7		109.3	109.3	102.7	110.8	
111.5	109.7		113.6	114.0	111.2	109.3	
115.1	101.8		112.0	114.4	115.6	102.2	
109.2	106.3		108.8	111.1	106.8	104.0	
106.6	118.1		105.7	105.7	101.6	112.6	
113.9	112.7		109.2	109.6	110.7	109.5	
113.7	113.2		112.0	113.8	111.9	111.4	
131.2	128.5		109.4	122.8	125.2	122.6	
114.9	120.6		106.0	106.0	108.0	113.4	
129.3	115.9		121.8	122.2	130.2	116.8	
127.4	122.4	119.3	115.1	116.4	123.8	119.0	115.9
110.5	119.3	111.6	107.8	106.0	104.4	112.8	105.5
124.3	112.6	110.8	106.7	104.6	120.8	109.4	107.7
101.9	113.7	112.4	107.1	103.3	99.1	110.6	109.4
110.0	109.5	110.2	109.4	117.1	107.8	107.4	108.0
109.4	108.1	108.8	107.9	108.4	107.8	106.5	107.2
107.3	108.5	110.0	106.3	111.4	105.0	106.1	107.7
111.1	108.5	108.7	107.1	112.0	109.5	106.9	107.1
107.0	115.1	108.0	106.4	107.4	105.1	113.2	106.1
105.8	108.0	108.5	103.7	103.8	102.7	104.9	105.4

Notes:Data after 1998 refers to average wages and indices of employed staff and workers.Statistics of 2007 involves all the private run units in urban areas.

3-7 分行业在岗职工平均工资(2019)
Average Wages of Staff and Worker on the Job by Sector(2019)

单位：元 (yuan)

行业	Sector	城镇全部单位 All the Units In Urban Area	国有经济单位 State Owned Units	城镇集体单位 Urban Collective Owned Units	其他经济单位 Other Units	城镇私营单位 Urban Private Units
总计	**Total**	**64661**	**91665**	**55560**	**76157**	**43536**
农、林、牧、渔业	Farming, Forest, Herd, Fishery	35859	36770	41538	41656	34844
采矿业	Mining and Quarrying	56938	45100	39565	91211	43497
制造业	Manufacturing	54338	69406	57996	71819	43386
电力、燃气及水的生产和供应业	Power, Gas and water production and supply	91077	105226	51233	105037	39653
建筑业	Construction	57477	53669	45133	68496	47636
批发和零售业	Wholesale and Retail sale	49656	89545	41271	64590	40850
交通运输、仓储和邮政业	Transportation, storage and post	76200	77535	42581	91947	42168
住宿和餐饮业	Hotel and Catering	42416	56435	43098	51755	39140
信息传输、软件和信息技术服务业	Information Transmission, Software and Computer Services	96628	71363	43286	114854	51050
金融业	Banking	113495	106796	84656	119800	52651
房地产业	Real Estate	60848	69730	52370	70173	49364
租赁和商务服务业	Leasing and Commerical Services	51379	50595	64271	61937	39740
科学研究、技术服务业	Scietific Research, polytechnical	103610	90795	56202	136453	48791
水利、环境和公共设施管理业	Water Conservance, Environment and Public Facilities Management	61839	67832	56327	68654	34034
居民服务、修理和其他服务业	Resident Service and Others	42677	68382	60700	52570	37422
教育	Education	90733	97797	73254	70433	42172
卫生和社会工作	Health, Social Security and	92050	97491	73950	79186	41741
文化、体育和娱乐业	Culture, Sports and Entertainment	64181	90185	59175	75880	38545
公共管理、社会保障和社会组织	Public Management, social security and Social Organization	97166	97171	67833	84731	

主要统计指标解释

经济活动人口 指在16周岁及以上，有劳动能力，参加或要求参加社会经济活动的人口。包括就业人员和失业人员。

就业人员 指在16周岁及以上，从事一定社会劳动并取得劳动报酬或经营收入的人员。这一指标反映了一定时期内全部劳动力资源的实际利用情况，是研究我国基本国情国力的重要指标。

单位就业人员 指报告期末最后一日24时在各类单位工作，并取得工资或其他形式劳动报酬的人员数。该指标为时点指标，不包括最后一日当天及以前已经与单位解除劳动合同关系的人员，是在岗职工、劳务派遣人员及其他从业人员之和。从业人员不包括：

1.离开本单位仍保留劳动关系，并定期领取生活费的人员；

2.在本单位实习的各类在校学生；

3.本单位因劳务外包而使用的人员。

在岗职工 指在本单位工作且与本单位签订劳动合同，并由单位支付各项工资和社会保险、住房公积金的人员，以及上述人员中由于学习、病伤、产假等原因暂未工作仍由单位支付工资的人员。在岗职工还包括：

1.应订立劳动合同而未订立劳动合同人员（如使用的农村户籍人员）；

2.处于试用期人员；

3.编制外招用的人员，如临时人员；

4.派往外单位工作，但工资仍由本单位发放的人员（如挂职锻炼、外派工作等情况）。

在岗职工平均工资 指单位在岗职工在一定时期内平均每人所得的货币工资。它表明一定时期在岗职工工资收入的高低程度，是反映在岗职工工资水平的主要指标。计算公式为：

$$\text{平均工资}=\frac{\text{报告期实际支付的全部在岗职工工资总额}}{\text{报告期全部在岗职工平均人数}}$$

平均工资指数 指报告期在岗职工平均工资与基期平均工资的比率，是反映不同时期在岗职工货币工资水平变动情况的相对数。计算公式为：

$$\text{平均工资指数}=\frac{\text{报告期在岗职工平均工资}}{\text{基期在岗职工平均工资}}\times 100\%$$

平均实际工资指数 在岗职工平均实际工资指扣除物价变动因素后的在岗职工平均工资。在岗职工平均实际工资指数是反映实际工资变动情况的相对数，表明职工实际工资水平提高或降低的程度。计算公式为：

$$\text{平均实际工资指数}=\frac{\text{报告期职工平均工资指数}}{\text{报告期城镇居民消费价格指数}}\times 100\%$$

城镇登记失业人员 指有非农业户口，在一定的劳动年龄内(16周岁至退休年龄)，有劳动能力，无业而要求就业，并在当地就业服务机构进行求职登记的人员。

城镇登记失业率 城镇登记失业人员与城镇单位就业人员(扣除使用的农村劳动力、聘用的离退休人员、港澳台及外方人员)、城镇单位中的不在岗职工、城镇私营业主、个体户主、城镇私营企业和个体就业人员、城镇登记失业人员之和的比。

$$\text{城镇登记失业率}=\frac{\text{城镇登记失业人数}}{（\text{城镇单位就业人员}-\text{使用的农村劳动力}-\text{聘用的离退休人员}-\text{聘用的港澳台及外方人员}）}\times 100\%$$

Explanatory Notes on Main Statistical Indicators

Economically Active Population refers to the population aged 16 and over who are capable to work, are participating in or willing to participate in economic activities, including employed persons and unemployed persons.

Employed Persons refer to the persons aged 16 and over who are engaged in social working and receive remuneration payment or earn business income. This indicator reflects the actual utilization of total labour force during a certain period of time and is often used for the research on China's economic situation and national power.

Persons Employed in Various Units refer to all the persons working in government agencies of various levels, political and party organizations, social organizations, enterprises and institutions, and receiving wages or other forms of payment. They include fully-employed staff and workers, re-employed retirees, teachers in schools run by the local people, foreigners and Chinese compatriots from Hong Kong, Macao, and Taiwan working in various units, part-time employees, employees of other units working temporarily at current posts, and employees holding the second job, but exclude staff and workers who have left their working units while keeping their labour contract (employment relation) unchanged. This indicator reflects the total number of laborers actually engaged in production or other operations in various units.

Staff and Workers refer to persons working in, and receive payment from units of state ownership, collective ownership, joint ownership, share holding ownership, foreign ownership, and ownership by entrepreneurs from Hong Kong, Macao, and Taiwan, and other types of ownership and their affiliated units. They do not include 1) persons employed in township enterprises, 2) persons employed in private enterprises, 3) urban self-employed persons, 4) retirees, 5) re-employed retirees, 6) teachers in the schools run by the local people, 7) foreigners and persons from Hong Kong, Macao and Taiwan who work in urban units, and 8) other persons not to be included by relevant regulations. (Data of 1998 and afterward refer to fully employed staff and workers. Other related statistics such as total wage bill and average wage are adjusted since 1998 accordingly).

Average Wage refers to the average wage in money terms per person during a certain period of time for staff and workers in enterprises, institutions, and government agencies, which reflects the general level of wage income during a certain period of time and is calculated as follows:

Average Wage = Total Wages of Staff and Workers at Reference Time /Average Number of Staff and Workers at Reference Time.

Average Wage Indices refers to the ratio of average wage of staff and workers in the report period to that in the base period, which reflects the change of wage of staff and workers at the different period. It is calculated as follows:

Average Wage Indices = Average Wage of Staff and Workers at Reference Time / Average Wage of Staff and Workers at Base Period x 100%

Average Real Wage Indices average real wage of staff and workers refers to the average wage of staff and workers after removing the effects of the price changes and average real wage indices of staff and workers refers to the change of real wage, which reflects the relative increasing or decreasing level of real wage of staff and workers, which is calculated as follows:

Average Real Wage Indices = Average Wage Indices of Staff and Workers at the Reference Time / Urban Consumer Price Indices at Reference Time × 100%

Registered Urban Unemployed Persons refer to the persons with non-agricultural household registration at certain working ages (16-50 years for male and 16-45 years for females), who are capable of work, unemployed and willing to work, and have been registered at the local employment service agencies to apply for a job.

Registered Urban Unemployment Rate refers to the ratio of the number of the registered unemployed persons to the sum of the number of persons employed in various units (minus the rural labour force, retirees, and Hong Kong, Macao, Taiwan or foreign employ–ees they employ) laid–off workers in urban units, owners and employees in urban private enterprises, urban self–employed individuals and the registered urban unemployed persons. The formula is as follows:

Registered urban unemployment rate = number of registered urban unemployed persons ÷ (number of persons employed in urban units – rural labour force employed retirees employed – Hong Kong, Macao, Taiwan or foreign employees employ + laid–off workers + owners and employees in urban private enterprises + self–employed individuals in urban areas + registered urban unemployed persons) × 100%.

4 固定资产投资

Investment in Fixed Assets

资料整理人员：肖 悦 张 萍

固定资产投资

Investment in Fixed Assets

2019

固定资产投资	Urban Investment	10.6 %
#房地产开发	Real Estate Development	8.9 %

2009-2019年固定资产投资增速(%)

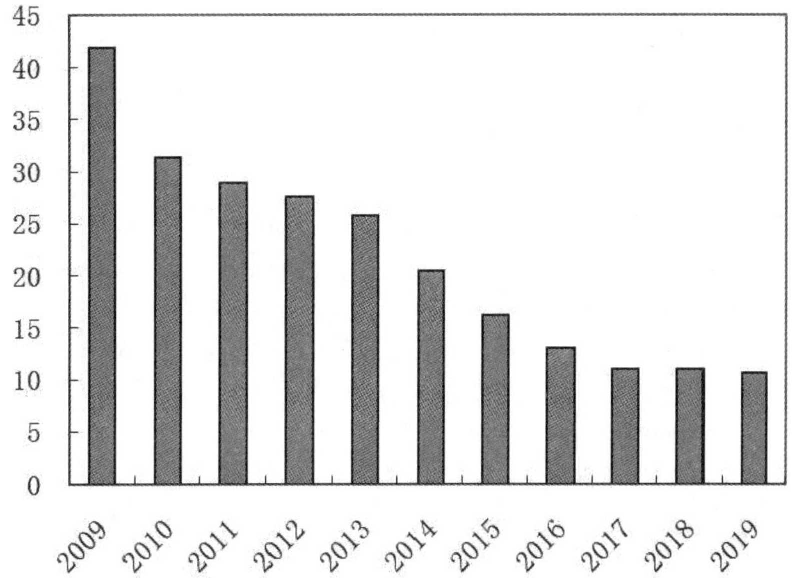

附:固定资产投资完成额构成(%)

		2007	2009	2010	2011	2012	2013	2014	2015	2016	2017	2018	2019
国有投资	State-Owned	39.9	38.1	34.9	29.1	25.8	24.4	23.3	23.9	27.2	28.9	20.6	19.5
集体投资	Collective-Owned	3.4	5.0	5.6	5.1	4.4	4.0	3.3	2.6	2.3	1.6	0.4	0.4
私营个体投资	Individuals	19.9	21.6	23.2	25.6	28.6	32.6	34.8	35.6	31.8	31.9	33.7	31.9
外商港澳台商投资	Foreign, HK, Macao and Taiwan	6.8	4.9	4.2	4.5	4.1	3.1	2.7	2.9	2.7	3.0	3.2	3.9
其他	Others	30.0	30.4	32.1	35.7	37.1	35.9	35.9	35.0	36.0	34.6	42.1	44.3

注:从2011年起固定资产投资统计口径调整为计划总投资500万元及以上项目,取消城镇农村公布口径,其他年份未做相应调整。2016年对2015年基数进行了调整。从2016年起,固定资产投资不包含农户投资。

Note:Since 2011, the fixed assets investment accounts for investment over 5 million yuan, canceling town and countryside. Other years' statistics do not correspond to this adjustment.The basic number of 2015 is adjusted in 2016. Since 2016,farmer investment isn't induded in the fixed assets investment.

4-1 固定资产投资主要指标

指 标	Item	1990	2000	2005	2008
投资总额(亿元)	**Total Investment (100 million yuan)**	**144.44**	**1421.55**	**2834.75**	**5798.56**
按经济类型分	**Grouped by Ownership**				
国有经济	State-owned Units	100.35	857.01	1095.71	2273.83
集体经济	Collective-owned Units	15.59	128.32	79.47	253.32
#农村	Rural Area	9.59	98.95	26.55	65.02
私营个体经济	Individuals	28.50	221.43	554.27	1201.53
#农村	Rural Area	23.62	106.65	135.95	190.19
联营经济	Joint-ownership Economic Units		3.94	19.56	15.05
股份制经济	Share Holding Co.Ltd.		86.29	232.34	462.81
有限责任公司	Limited Liability Corporations		53.33	557.21	1109.43
港澳台投资经济	Economic Units Funded by Hongkong, Macao and Taiwan		36.57	92.68	160.62
外商投资经济	Foreign Funded Enterprise Units		23.90	116.23	178.60
其他经济	Others		10.76	87.28	143.37
按资金来源分	**Grouped by Source of Finance**				
国家预算内资金	State Budgetary Apporpriations	11.38	141.48	255.76	570.17
国内贷款	Domestic Loans	22.22	243.90	474.21	894.57
利用外资	Foreign Investment	4.79	28.28	71.34	57.02
自筹资金	Fund Raising	92.96	781.50	1492.66	3677.00
其他资金来源	Others	13.09	226.39	540.78	599.80
按构成分	**Grouped by Usage of Funds**				
建筑安装工程	Construction Installation	92.64	814.66	1696.80	3568.96
设备工器具购置	Purchase of Equipments and Instruments	41.02	371.56	642.86	1245.73
其他费用	Others	10.78	235.33	495.09	983.87
按产业分	**Grouped by Industry**				
#住宅	Residential Housing	39.61	290.24	510.04	901.26
第一产业	Primary Industry	12.16	103.05	92.88	231.25
第二产业	Second Industry	67.41	521.58	1086.34	2344.36
第三产业	Tertiary Industry	64.87	796.92	1655.53	3222.95
房屋建筑面积(万平方米)	**Floor Space of Building** (10000 sq.m)				
施工面积	Floor Space under Construction	5103.48	9920.42	12572.00	16417.07
#住宅	Residential Housing	3507.53	6831.02	8401.20	9896.66
竣工面积	Floor Space Completed	4169.12	7508.96	7863.85	7551.82
#住宅	Residential Housing	3058.40	5417.38	5627.67	4679.96
商品房销售面积(万平方米)	**Floor Space of Commercial House (sq.m)**	**130.53**	**612.05**	**1708.02**	**1941.62**

注:2006年投资总额(城镇投资)不含城镇工矿区私人建房投资(下同)。由于方法制度调整,按可比口径计算,2005年扣除城镇工矿区私人建房投资基数应为2788.92亿元;从2011年起固定资产投资统计口径调整为计划总投资500万元及以上项目,取消城镇农村公布口径,其他年份未做相应调整。从2017年起,三次产业采用新的划分标准。

Major Indicators of Investment in Fixed Assets

2009	2010	2011	2014	2015	2016	2017
8211.85	**10802.69**	**12935.02**	**25001.77**	**29191.06**	**29503.88**	**31872.57**
3124.90	3768.95	3764.22	5829.79	6983.99	8021.33	9199.68
411.18	602.80	660.59	820.75	754.53	677.42	524.02
77.50	99.23	137.69	117.04	143.42	—	—
1771.61	2510.61	3307.47	8708.83	10386.49	9386.11	10168.42
240.48	301.05	365.51	698.73	940.57	—	—
11.32	19.89	22.49	11.84	13.38	64.03	36.84
659.79	896.87	987.66	1238.81	1125.37	983.55	986.38
1648.26	2221.99	3056.98	6026.42	6634.45	8614.44	8621.09
202.38	207.81	253.89	343.93	393.90	443.65	484.72
200.79	245.92	328.55	333.45	459.38	344.86	479.99
181.62	327.85	553.17	1687.95	2439.57	968.49	1371.45
711.98	868.46	663.18	1107.45	1339.03	1829.24	2326.38
1432.98	1768.79	1707.46	2874.92	2907.66	3068.40	3078.89
68.33	147.03	189.26	78.99	46.86	59.01	65.59
4956.65	6703.61	8800.61	18732.35	22470.65	20623.21	21408.69
1041.91	1314.80	1574.51	2208.06	2426.86	3924.02	4993.03
5025.62	6701.91	8056.53	18185.42	21826.03	22876.58	23772.98
1753.28	2308.73	2812.91	4292.85	4845.70	4124.21	4891.02
1432.95	1792.05	2065.58	2523.50	2519.33	2503.08	3208.57
1127.28	1417.95	1750.16	3461.65	3853.52	3434.85	3555.18
321.59	393.00	440.91	799.35	997.94	889.94	912.24
3097.68	4169.92	5526.40	10733.09	12146.51	12224.54	13236.47
4792.58	6239.77	6967.71	13469.32	16046.61	16389.40	17723.86
20142.81	25284.83	31388.88	58064.39	58095.72	44198.73	42087.64
11762.06	14486.90	16337.96	27199.41	29006.34	24286.60	23849.67
9772.28	11802.18	14585.68	21175.37	22992.18	8878.64	7172.55
5556.71	6785.61	7375.38	8702.01	9381.09	3582.22	3094.58
2718.30	**3508.61**	**4187.62**	**5601.98**	**6244.55**	**7427.16**	**8155.21**

Note: In 2006 the investment (town investment) does not contain town private house industrial investment.(same below) Because of method adjustment, according to comparable caliber, 2005's investment base should be 278.892 billion yuan deducting industrial town private house. Since 2011, the fixed assets investment accounts for investment over 5 million yuan, canceling town and countryside. Other years' statistics do not correspond to this adjustment. Since 2017, the division of three industries emploies a new standard.

4-2 固定资产投资额
Investment in Fixed Assets

单位:亿元 (100 million yuan)

年 份 Year	投资额 Investment	#房地产开发 Real Estate Development	#国有经济 State Owned Units	#集体经济 Collective Owned Units	#私营个体 Individuals
"六五"时期 Period of the Six-Year Plan	**315.82**		**207.57**	**49.41**	**58.84**
1985	102.91		61.66	17.44	23.81
"七五"时期 Peroid of the Seven-Year Plan	**680.12**	**5.94**	**435.32**	**94.17**	**150.64**
1986	111.44		66.42	15.89	29.13
1987	140.08		85.32	22.31	32.46
1988	160.46		102.21	24.60	33.64
1989	123.70		81.02	15.78	26.91
1990	144.44	5.94	100.35	15.59	28.50
"八五"时期 Peroid of the Eight-Year Plan	**2211.67**	**254.77**	**1497.69**	**190.04**	**261.87**
1991	168.19	7.88	119.07	19.49	29.63
1992	240.73	12.55	182.86	22.52	35.35
1993	383.18	37.01	275.84	30.62	40.37
1994	593.07	76.20	401.16	44.83	56.62
1995	826.50	121.13	518.76	72.58	99.90
"九五"时期 Peroid of the Nine-Year Plan	**6022.80**	**634.60**	**3425.23**	**573.74**	**943.77**
1996	984.38	118.40	593.32	96.50	124.78
1997	1083.60	126.47	567.60	107.12	160.56
1998	1231.10	131.23	661.94	116.92	194.52
1999	1302.17	123.87	745.36	124.88	242.48
2000	1421.55	134.63	857.01	128.32	221.43
"十五"时期 Peroid of the Ten-Year Plan	**10321.69**	**1354.15**	**4817.55**	**541.41**	**1806.78**
2001	1551.75	151.24	918.21	126.41	249.59
2002	1695.22	178.64	963.18	121.42	263.00
2003	1883.59	239.04	888.72	109.05	303.90
2004	2356.38	337.28	951.73	105.06	436.02
2005	2834.75	447.95	1095.71	79.47	554.27
"十一五"时期 Peroid of the Eleven-Year Plan	**32919.93**	**4999.84**	**12449.99**	**1533.63**	**7020.48**
2006	3572.69	564.76	1473.70	110.67	636.25
2007	4534.14	723.73	1808.61	155.66	900.48
2008	5798.56	892.67	2273.83	253.32	1201.53
2009	8211.85	1200.44	3124.90	411.18	1771.61
2010	10802.69	1618.24	3768.95	602.80	2510.61
"十二五"时期 Peroid of the Twelve-Year Plan	**104385.93**	**16124.98**	**25912.37**	**3796.30**	**33879.07**
2011	12935.02	2066.48	3764.22	660.59	3307.47
2012	16504.17	2539.46	4265.95	733.92	4712.60
2013	20753.91	3286.02	5068.42	826.51	6763.68
2014	25001.77	3983.79	5829.79	820.75	8708.83
2015	29191.06	4249.23	6983.99	754.53	10386.49
"十三五"时期 Peroid of the Thirteen-Year Plan					
2016	29503.88	4296.38	8021.33	677.42	9386.11
2017	31872.57	4574.89	9199.68	524.02	10168.42

注:房地产开发投资统计制度从1990年开始建立。从2011年起固定资产投资统计口径调整为计划总投资500万元及以上项目,取消城镇农村公布口径,其他年份未做相应调整。

Note: The statistical system of real estate development investment is established in 1990. Since 2011, the fixed assets investment accounts for investment over 5 million yuan, canceling town and countryside. Other years' statistics do not correspond to this adjustment.

4-3 按登记注册类型分固定资产投资增幅

Growth Rate of Investment in Fixed Assets by Registration Status

单位:%

指 标	Item	2016	2017	2018	2019
总 计	**Total**	**13.1**	**11.0**	**11.0**	**10.6**
内资企业	Domestic Funded Enterprises	13.9	10.6	11.5	9.8
国有企业	State-owned Enterprises	7.6	10.3	12.9	4.4
集体企业	Collective-owned Enterprises	-41.1	-5.5	-30.9	-3.5
股份合作企业	Share Holding Cooperative Enterprises	251.8	-39.9	-63.0	-34.2
联营企业	Joint Owned Enterprise	45.6	-41.5	-21.6	-6.3
国有联营	State Joint ownership	-93.0	127.0	54.0	15.4
集体联营	Collective Joint Ownership	16.2	-61.7	-25.5	22.9
国有与集体联营	Joint State-Collective	90.4	33.8	21.6	-97.1
其他联营企业	Other Joint Owned Enterprise	770.5	-63.5	-48.3	29.0
有限责任公司	Co. Ltd	56.5	10.5	6.4	18.9
国有独资公司	Solely State Funded Co.	348.0	50.3	-2.4	16.8
其他有限责任公司	Other Co. Ltd	40.1	3.6	8.9	19.5
股份有限公司	Share Holding Co.Ltd.	-4.3	3.7	11.5	-0.2
私营企业	Private - owned enterprises	9.5	11.0	22.8	4.8
其他企业	Others	-59.0	42.6	-20.1	10.1
港、澳、台商投资企业	Hongkong, Macao and Taiwan Funded	18.0	10.1	-1.4	43.4
合资经营企业	Joint Funded Enterprises	37.2	31.8	-18.5	58.6
合作经营企业	Cooperative Operation Enterprises	334.7	-74.1	0.3	-33.5
独资经营企业	Solely Funded Enterprises	5.9	1.3	3.3	48.6
股份有限公司	Share Holding Co.Ltd.	-56.6	344.7	84.0	-48.6
外商投资企业	Foreign Invested Enterprises	-8.2	40.3	-0.6	24.2
合资经营企业	Joint Funded Enterprises	38.8	25.1	-29.8	39.4
合作经营企业	Cooperative Operation Enterprises	-100.0			
独资企业	Solely Funded Enterprises	-48.2	122.8	58.3	2.9
股份有限公司	Share Holding Co.Ltd.	-52.2	35.9	21.7	2.4
个体经营	Individual Investment	-0.6	50.8	27.2	2.0
个体户	Individual Self-Employed	60.6	55.1	19.1	18.8
个人合伙	Individual Pattenership	-59.9	34.0	79.2	-70.1

注:从2011年起固定资产投资统计口径调整为计划总投资500万元及以上项目,取消城镇农村公布口径,其他年份未做相应调整。

Note: Since 2011, the fixed assets investment accounts for investment over 5 million yuan, canceling town and countryside. Other years' statistics do not correspond to this adjustment.

4-4 按构成分固定资产投资增幅(2019)
Growth Rate of Investment in Fixed Assets by Composition of Investment(2019)

单位:%

行 业	Sector	全部投资 Investment	建筑安装工程 Construction and Installation	设备工器具购置 Purchases of Equipments and Instruments	其他 Others
总 计	**Total**	**10.6**	**10.8**	**12.4**	**7.1**
农、林、牧、渔业	Farming, Forestry, Animal Husbandry and Fishery	17.0	13.4	38.3	21.5
农业	Farming	23.2	18.7	56.4	21.8
林业	Forestry	6.6	-3.5	-19.5	62.5
畜牧业	Animal Husbandry	8.1	4.2	5.4	57.8
渔业	Fishery	23.2	18.7	83.5	-17.3
农、林、牧、渔专业及辅助性活动	Professional and Support for Agriculture, Forestry, Animal Husbandry and Fishery	7.3	10.2	20.5	-48.8
采矿业	Mining	0.3	3.5	-8.1	-4.7
制造业	Manufacturing	10.0	7.8	13.0	20.8
农副食品加工业	Processing of Food from Agriculture Products	-0.5	-2.8	2.3	19.8
食品制造业	Manufacture of Foods	-16.9	-13.6	-23.4	-30.7
酒、饮料和精制茶制造业	Manufacture of Liquor,Beverages and Refined Tea	-0.2	-8.0	17.3	22.5
烟草制品业	Manufacture of Tobacco	-18.2	-21.7		-74.2
纺织业	Manufacture of Textile	16.9	19.8	10.6	25.2
纺织服装、服饰业	Manufacture of Textile, Wearing Apparel and Accessaries	38.8	45.5	22.4	25.0
皮革、毛皮、羽毛及其制品和制鞋业	Manufacture of Leather, Fur, Feather and Related Products and Footwear	-13.9	-15.9	-17.8	41.2
木材加工和木、竹、藤、棕、草制品业	Processing of Timber, Manufacture of Wood, Bamboo, Rattan, Palm and Straw Products	26.8	40.5	9.2	-5.1
家具制造业	Manufacture of Furniture	34.3	39.1	21.1	25.4
造纸和纸制品业	Manufacture of Paper and Paper Products	0.6	-2.4	22.0	-41.4
印刷和记录媒介复制业	Printing and Reproduction of Recording Media	-8.4	-20.0	43.8	16.5
文教、工美、体育和娱乐用品制造业	Manufacture of Articles for Culture, Education, Arts and Crafts Sport and Entertainment Activities	-15.9	-11.9	-24.8	-34.3
石油、煤炭及其他燃料加工业	Processing of Petroleum, Coal and Other Fuels	-17.2	-7.2	-36.0	14.9
化学原料和化学制品制造业	Manufacture of Raw Chemical Materials and Chemical Products	18.1	13.3	24.4	34.0
医药制造业	Manufacture of Medicines	-10.3	-7.6	-11.9	-34.3
化学纤维制造业	Manufacture of Chemical Fibres	40.4	59.9	36.7	-47.3
橡胶和塑料制品业	Manufacture of Rubber and Plastic Products	10.7	26.7	-5.5	-26.1
非金属矿物制品业	Manufacture of Non-metallic Mineral Products	11.8	10.3	18.7	-5.3
黑色金属冶炼和压延加工业	Smelting and Pressing of Ferrous Metals	18.6	2.5	52.7	20.8
有色金属冶炼和压延加工业	Smelting and Pressing of Non-ferrous Metals	10.0	12.2	-4.8	159.5
金属制品业	Manufacture of Metal Products	29.4	27.7	27.3	69.9
通用设备制造业	Manufacture of General Purpose Machinery	14.9	15.2	9.7	43.0
专用设备制造业	Manufacture of Special Purpose Machinery	0.2	6.4	-12.0	-28.4
汽车制造业	Manufacture of Automobiles	3.4	4.8	-5.2	49.2
铁路、船舶、航空航天和其他运输设备制造业	Manufacture of Railway, Ship, Aerospace and Other Transport Equipment	9.8	-3.6	7.6	113.2
电气机械和器材制造业	Manufacture of Electrical Machinery and Apparatus	-18.6	-14.5	-29.4	-0.8
计算机、通信和其他电子设备制造业	Manufacture of Computers, Communication and Other Electronic Equipment	38.6	8.2	77.6	90.0
仪器仪表制造业	Manufacture of Measuring Instruments and Machinery	40.1	45.9	6.7	112.0
其他制造业	Other Manufacture	66.2	54.6	373.3	-62.4
废弃资源综合利用业	Utilization of Waste Resources	55.5	53.9	46.2	137.1
金属制品、机械和设备修理业	Repairing Service of Metal Products, Mechanical Equipment	106.2	98.7	132.0	122.7
电力、热力、燃气及水生产和供应业	Production and Supply of Electricity, Heat, Gas and Water	-7.2	-4.3	-10.5	-28.2
电力、热力生产和供应业	Production and Supply of Electric Power and and Heat Power	0.3	6.2	-9.7	-11.2
燃气生产和供应业	Production and Supply of Gas	-7.0	2.2	-9.7	-71.3
水的生产和供应业	Production and Supply of Water	-16.5	-14.8	-13.9	-48.6

注:从2011年起固定资产投资统计口径调整为计划总投资500万元及以上项目,取消城镇农村公布口径,其他年份未做相应调整。从2018年起执行新的国民经济行业代码(GB/T4754-2017)。

Note: Since 2011, the fixed assets investment accounts for investment over 5 million yuan, canceling town and countryside. Other years' statistics do not correspond to this adjustment.Since 2018,a new national economy industry code(GB/T4754-2017)is implemented.

4-4 续表 continued

单位:%

行 业	Sector	全部投资 Investment	建筑安装工程 Construction and Installation	设备工器具购置 Purchases of Equipments and Instruments	其他 Others
建筑业	Construction	-97.5	-99.2	-88.9	-100.0
交通运输、仓储和邮政业	Transport, Storage and Post	5.4	4.1	22.6	9.1
铁路运输业	Railway Transport	-29.4	-44.3	349.4	16.2
道路运输业	Road Transport	12.6	12.2	18.3	14.3
水上运输业	Water Transport	-19.1	-8.3	-43.8	-60.7
航空运输业	Air Transport	158.6	171.0	143.3	99.0
管道运输业	Transport via Pipelines	-26.5	-22.6	-100.0	-100.0
多式联运和运输代理业	Intermodality and Forwarding Agency	-19.8	-18.8	-49.1	202.5
装卸搬运和仓储业	Loading, Unloading and Storage	-11.4	-7.4	-5.4	-53.0
邮政业	Post	5168.3	4800.1	376.4	23769.2
信息传输、软件和信息技术服务业	Information Transmission, Software and Information Technology Service	58.6	88.9	28.0	-49.3
电信、广播电视和卫星传输服务	Telecom, Radio and Tv and Satellite Transmission Service	24.6	54.2	-4.4	15.0
互联网和相关服务	Internet and Related Service	126.2	191.0	94.7	-85.4
软件和信息技术服务业	Software and Information Technology	12.4	11.9	8.2	33.3
批发和零售业	Wholesale and Retail Trades	-6.5	-7.3	-20.9	27.3
住宿和餐饮业	Hotels and Catering Services	15.2	11.4	6.7	91.4
金融业	Financial Intermediation	-16.1	35.8	-52.3	1977.0
房地产业	Real Estate	8.1	7.7	31.8	7.5
租赁和商务服务业	Leasing and Commercial Services	14.2	11.6	-7.6	72.7
租赁业	Leasing	-21.8	18.0	-62.7	-96.3
商务服务业	Business Services	15.0	11.5	-2.7	81.5
科学研究和技术服务业	Scientific Research and Technical Services	27.5	34.8	22.8	-38.3
水利、环境和公共设施管理业	Management of Water Conservancy, Environment and Public Facilities	18.0	23.2	14.5	-23.5
水利管理业	Management of Water Conservancy	13.6	15.0	1.6	-2.3
生态保护和环境治理业	Ecological Protection and Environment Treatment	44.4	49.8	38.1	13.6
公共设施管理业	Management of Public Facilities	16.4	22.4	13.0	-29.5
土地管理业	Management of Land	-15.8	-15.3	-48.5	57.3
居民服务、修理和其他服务业	Service to Households, Repair and Others Services	-12.1	-14.7	-15.0	16.7
教育	Education	61.4	62.0	57.1	59.6
卫生和社会工作	Health Care and Social Service	-2.1	-5.9	6.0	63.9
卫生	Health	-7.4	-11.1	0.6	72.2
社会工作	Social Service	15.6	10.4	56.2	53.4
文化、体育和娱乐业	Culture, Sports and Entertainment	69.6	68.8	81.0	67.0
广播、电视、电影和影视录音制作业	Radio, Television, Motion Picture and Videotape Programme	24.8	33.2	-36.6	2.4
文化艺术业	Culture and Art Activities	7.3	3.7	64.2	50.4
体育	Sports Activities	-13.4	-2.9	-42.6	-59.4
娱乐业	Entertainment	109.5	107.7	106.6	128.5
公共管理、社会保障和社会组织	Public Management, Social Security and Social Organization	-27.4	-34.9	19.9	-45.9

4-5 按建设性质分固定资产投资增幅(2019)

Growth Rate of Investment in Fixed Assets by Type of Construction(2019)

单位:%

行 业	Sector	全部投资 Investment	新建 New Construction	扩建 Expension	改建和技术改造 Reconstruction and Technical Transformation
总 计	**Total**	**10.6**	**11.8**	**3.8**	**12.4**
农、林、牧、渔业	Farming, Forestry, Animal Husbandry and Fishery	17.0	21.0	5.7	-35.3
农业	Farming	23.2	25.3	10.4	-16.5
林业	Forestry	6.6	17.6	-45.0	-29.0
畜牧业	Animal Husbandry	8.1	13.8	-15.2	-18.6
渔业	Fishery	23.2	24.2	279.5	-73.9
农、林、牧、渔专业及辅助性活动	Professional and Support for Agriculture, Forestry, Animal Husbandry and Fishery	7.3	13.4	2.5	-35.8
采矿业	Mining	0.3	-20.7	-39.2	32.3
制造业	Manufacturing	10	10.2	-2.0	14.9
农副食品加工业	Processing of Food from Agriculture Products	-0.5	5.9	-19.7	6.8
食品制造业	Manufacture of Foods	-16.9	-24.4	-54.4	11.4
酒、饮料和精制茶制造业	Manufacture of Liquor,Beverages and Refined Tea	-0.2	-9.8	8.3	3.4
烟草制品业	Manufacture of Tobacco	-18.2	-1.6		-47.1
纺织业	Manufacture of Textile	16.9	29.4	10.6	5.7
纺织服装、服饰业	Manufacture of Textile, Wearing Apparel and Accessaries	38.8	66.3	26.6	9.1
皮革、毛皮、羽毛及其制品和制鞋业	Manufacture of Leather, Fur, Feather and Related Products and Footwear	-13.9	8.5	-73.1	-25.8
木材加工和木、竹、藤、棕、草制品业	Processing of Timber, Manufacture of Wood, Bamboo, Rattan, Palm and Straw Products	26.8	26.0	-22.3	89.6
家具制造业	Manufacture of Furniture	34.3	27.8	41.2	49.6
造纸和纸制品业	Manufacture of Paper and Paper Products	0.6	-15.3	77.9	-0.9
印刷和记录媒介复制业	Printing and Reproduction of Recording Media	-8.4	10.5	-6.0	-21.9
文教、工美、体育和娱乐用品制造业	Manufacture of Articles for Culture, Education, Arts and Crafts Sport and Entertainment Activities	-15.9	-12.3	39.2	-57.3
石油、煤炭及其他燃料加工业	Processing of Petroleum, Coal and Other Fuels	-17.2	-35.0	-18.7	8.5
化学原料和化学制品制造业	Manufacture of Raw Chemical Materials and Chemical Products	18.1	24.2	19.6	10.2
医药制造业	Manufacture of Medicines	-10.3	-3.7	-26.8	-16.2
化学纤维制造业	Manufacture of Chemical Fibres	40.4	94.5	41.7	-35.1
橡胶和塑料制品业	Manufacture of Rubber and Plastic Products	10.7	-11.0	34.3	28.8
非金属矿物制品业	Manufacture of Non-metallic Mineral Products	11.8	12.2	-2.8	21.5
黑色金属冶炼和压延加工业	Smelting and Pressing of Ferrous Metals	18.6	-72.1	-50.1	159.0
有色金属冶炼和压延加工业	Smelting and Pressing of Non-ferrous Metals	10.0	47.0	-16.6	-11.3
金属制品业	Manufacture of Metal Products	29.4	44.1	7.1	25.6
通用设备制造业	Manufacture of General Purpose Machinery	14.9	34.6	-15.2	5.7
专用设备制造业	Manufacture of Special Purpose Machinery	0.2	-26.1	-27.4	61.7
汽车制造业	Manufacture of Automobiles	3.4	6.6	-23.3	14.4
铁路、船舶、航空航天和其他运输设备制造业	Manufacture of Railway, Ship, Aerospace and Other Transport Equipment	9.8	-18.3	31.2	77.9
电气机械和器材制造业	Manufacture of Electrical Machinery and Apparatus	-18.6	-24.2	-15.2	-12.4
计算机、通信和其他电子设备制造业	Manufacture of Computers, Communication and Other Electronic Equipment	38.6	39.1	42.4	11.3
仪器仪表制造业	Manufacture of Measuring Instruments and Machinery	40.1	78.7	-16.5	28.4
其他制造业	Other Manufacture	66.2	-15.0	539.6	15.6
废弃资源综合利用业	Utilization of Waste Resources	55.5	52.8	153.1	47.4
金属制品、机械和设备修理业	Repairing Service of Metal Products, Mechanical Equipment	106.2	60.6		-14.3
电力、热力、燃气及水生产和供应业	Production and Supply of Electricity, Heat, Gas and Water	-7.2	-8.0	8.8	-28.5
电力、热力生产和供应业	Production and Supply of Electric Power and and Heat Power	0.3	2.7	-16.2	-8.9
燃气生产和供应业	Production and Supply of Gas	-7	-30.8	66.1	40.5
水的生产和供应业	Production and Supply of Water	-16.5	-17.3	63.8	-54.2

4-5 续表 continued

单位:%

行 业	Sector	全部投资 Investment	新建 New Construction	扩建 Expension	改建和技术改造 Reconstruction and Technical Transformation
建筑业	Construction	-97.5	-99.1	-100.0	-100.0
交通运输、仓储和邮政业	Transport, Storage and Post	5.4	5.3	27.8	-14.3
铁路运输业	Railway Transport	-29.4	-25.1	-100.0	-95.0
道路运输业	Road Transport	12.6	11.7	39.0	-5.2
水上运输业	Water Transport	-19.1	-7.1	-32.2	-86.8
航空运输业	Air Transport	158.6	72.4	566.0	338.0
管道运输业	Transport via Pipelines	-26.5	-26.5		
多式联运和运输代理业	Intermodality and Forwarding Agency	-19.8	-17.6	-4.8	-100.0
装卸搬运和仓储业	Loading, Unloading and Storage	-11.4	-6.0	-8.2	-51.4
邮政业	Post	5168.3	4408.2		
信息传输、软件和信息技术服务业	Information Transmission, Software and Information Technology Service	28.6	62.6	15.5	-7.2
电信、广播电视和卫星传输服务	Telecom, Radio and Tv and Satellite Transmission Service	24.6	34.7	39.3	-98.9
互联网和相关服务	Internet and Related Service	126.2	129.2		10.1
软件和信息技术服务业	Software and Information Technology	12.4	17.3	-81.6	-25.7
批发和零售业	Wholesale and Retail Trades	-6.5	1.5	-37.2	-53.1
住宿和餐饮业	Hotels and Catering Services	15.2	19.5	-37.2	32.9
金融业	Financial Intermediation	-16.1	44.8		14.1
房地产业	Real Estate	8.1	9.2	21.0	-29.6
租赁和商务服务业	Leasing and Commercial Services	14.2	18.3	-39.5	0.6
租赁业	Leasing	-21.8	-15.2	-71.3	
商务服务业	Business Services	15.0	19.1	-36.9	0.6
科学研究和技术服务业	Scientific Research and Technical Services	27.5	19.0	-41.1	615.8
水利、环境和公共设施管理业	Management of Water Conservancy, Environment and Public Facilities	18.0	15.6	15.7	51.0
水利管理业	Management of Water Conservancy	13.6	18.6	-14.5	-6.5
生态保护和环境治理业	Ecological Protection and Environment Treatment	44.4	25.6	41.2	24736
公共设施管理业	Management of Public Facilities	16.4	14.4	18.4	43.8
土地管理业	Management of Land	-15.8	-23.9	201.2	10.7
居民服务、修理和其他服务业	Service to Households, Repair and Others Services	-12.1	-16.6	24.8	26.4
教育	Education	61.4	61.3	113.9	-37.4
卫生和社会工作	Health Care and Social Service	-2.1	-7.7	28.4	-19.0
卫生	Health	-7.4	-17.0	48.2	-17.5
社会工作	Social Service	15.6	21.2	-23.4	-25.7
文化、体育和娱乐业	Culture, Sports and Entertainment	69.6	73.4	67.4	23.8
广播、电视、电影和影视录音制作业	Radio, Television, Motion Picture and Videotape Programme	24.8	33.4	93.3	-36.2
文化艺术业	Culture and Art Activities	7.3	20.2	20.3	-77.1
体育	Sports Activities	-13.4	-13.2	32.1	-27.0
娱乐业	Entertainment	109.5	113.9	73.5	135.8
公共管理、社会保障和社会组织	Public Management, Social Security and Social Organization	-27.4	-34.1	-71.4	35.9

4-6 按行业分施工投产项目个数(2019)
Number of Projects under Construction and Put into Production by Sector (2019)

行业	Sector	施工项目(个) Number of Projects under Construction (unit)	#新开工 Newly Started	全部建成投产项目(个) Completion and Put into Production of All Projects (unit)	项目建成投产率(%) Rate of Completion and Put into Production (%)
总计	**Total**	**23852**	**11416**	**12473**	**52.3**
农、林、牧、渔业	Farming, Forestry, Animal Husbandry and Fishery	1475	716	865	58.6
农业	Farming	747	341	445	59.6
林业	Forestry	95	42	44	46.3
畜牧业	Animal Husbandry	244	118	156	63.9
渔业	Fishery	171	85	108	63.2
农、林、牧、渔专业及辅助性活动	Professional and Support for Agriculture, Forestry, Animal Husbandry and Fishery	218	1130	112	51.4
采矿业	Mining	246	139	147	59.8
制造业	Manufacturing	9519	5011	5148	54.1
农副食品加工业	Processing of Food from Agriculture Products	847	486	489	57.7
食品制造业	Manufacture of Foods	247	131	130	52.6
酒、饮料和精制茶制造业	Manufacture of Liquor,Beverages and Refined Tea	337	176	186	55.2
烟草制品业	Manufacture of Tobacco	7	1	4	57.1
纺织业	Manufacture of Textile	408	228	227	55.6
纺织服装、服饰业	Manufacture of Textile, Wearing Apparel and Accessaries	299	181	178	59.5
皮革、毛皮、羽毛及其制品和制鞋业	Manufacture of Leather, Fur, Feather and Related Products and Footwear	71	37	45	63.4
木材加工和木、竹、藤、棕、草制品业	Processing of Timber, Manufacture of Wood, Bamboo, Rattan, Palm and Straw Products	205	112	121	59.0
家具制造业	Manufacture of Furniture	209	105	94	45.0
造纸和纸制品业	Manufacture of Paper and Paper Products	132	58	91	68.9
印刷和记录媒介复制业	Printing and Reproduction of Recording Media	94	62	58	61.7
文教、工美、体育和娱乐用品制造业	Manufacture of Articles for Culture, Education, Arts and Crafts Sport and Entertainment Activities	78	41	43	55.1
石油、煤炭及其他燃料加工业	Processing of Petroleum, Coal and Other Fuels	64	33	29	45.3
化学原料和化学制品制造业	Manufacture of Raw Chemical Materials and Chemical Products	675	370	336	49.8
医药制造业	Manufacture of Medicines	370	158	147	39.7
化学纤维制造业	Manufacture of Chemical Fibres	24	7	15	62.5
橡胶和塑料制品业	Manufacture of Rubber and Plastic Products	364	213	190	52.2
非金属矿物制品业	Manufacture of Non-metallic Mineral Products	1225	678	720	58.8
黑色金属冶炼和压延加工业	Smelting and Pressing of Ferrous Metals	127	74	72	56.7
有色金属冶炼和压延加工业	Smelting and Pressing of Non-ferrous Metals	127	64	61	48.0
金属制品业	Manufacture of Metal Products	515	283	292	56.7
通用设备制造业	Manufacture of General Purpose Machinery	453	244	245	54.1
专用设备制造业	Manufacture of Special Purpose Machinery	465	209	266	57.2
汽车制造业	Manufacture of Automobiles	943	458	556	59.0
铁路、船舶、航空航天和其他运输设备制造业	Manufacture of Railway, Ship, Aerospace and Other Transport Equipment	83	41	46	55.4
电气机械和器材制造业	Manufacture of Electrical Machinery and Apparatus	463	215	207	44.7
计算机、通信和其他电子设备制造业	Manufacture of Computers, Communication and Other Electronic Equipment	431	210	168	39.0
仪器仪表制造业	Manufacture of Measuring Instruments and Machinery	64	29	34	53.1
其他制造业	Other Manufacture	31	15	19	61.3
废弃资源综合利用业	Utilization of Waste Resources	150	87	75	50.0
金属制品、机械和设备修理业	Repairing Service of Metal Products, Mechanical Equipment	11	5	4	36.4
电力、热力、燃气及水生产和供应业	Production and Supply of Electricity, Heat, Gas and Water	925	367	484	52.3
电力、热力生产和供应业	Production and Supply of Electric Power and and Heat Power	357	143	172	48.2
燃气生产和供应业	Production and Supply of Gas	92	40	53	57.6
水的生产和供应业	Production and Supply of Water	476	184	259	54.4

4-6 续表 continued

行　业	Sector	施工项目(个) Number of Projects under Construction (unit)	新开工 Newly Started	全部建成投产项目(个) Completion and Put into Production of All Projects (unit)	项目建成投产率(%) Rate of Completion and Put into Production (%)
建筑业	Construction	2	2	2	100.0
交通运输、仓储和邮政业	Transport, Storage and Post	2184	1022	949	43.5
铁路运输业	Railway Transport	32	8	8	25.0
道路运输业	Road Transport	1817	872	792	43.6
水上运输业	Water Transport	54	15	20	37.0
航空运输业	Air Transport	21	8	5	23.8
管道运输业	Transport via Pipelines	3	1	1	33.3
多式联运和运输代理业	Intermodality and Forwarding Agency	18		8	44.4
装卸搬运和仓储业	Loading, Unloading and Storage	228	107	111	48.7
邮政业	Post	11	8	4	36.4
信息传输、软件和信息技术服务业	Information Transmission, Software and Information Technology Service	99	37	51	51.5
电信、广播电视和卫星传输服务	Telecom, Radio and Tv and Satellite Transmission Service	42	18	20	47.6
互联网和相关服务	Internet and Related Service	32	11	17	53.1
软件和信息技术服务业	Software and Information Technology	25	8	14	56.0
批发和零售业	Wholesale and Retail Trades	476	252	300	63.0
住宿和餐饮业	Hotels and Catering Services	360	186	202	56.1
金融业	Financial Intermediation	23	13	18	78.3
房地产业	Real Estate	976	269	430	44.1
租赁和商务服务业	Leasing and Commercial Services	284	139	135	47.5
租赁业	Leasing	11	6	7	63.6
商务服务业	Business Services	273	133	128	46.9
科学研究和技术服务业	Scientific Research and Technical Services	217	89	118	54.4
水利、环境和公共设施管理业	Management of Water Conservancy, Environment and Public Facilities	4475	1981	2264	50.6
水利管理业	Management of Water Conservancy	612	255	312	51.0
生态保护和环境治理业	Ecological Protection and Environment Treatment	389	165	202	51.9
公共设施管理业	Management of Public Facilities	3415	1533	1705	49.9
土地管理业	Management of Land	59	28	45	76.3
居民服务、修理和其他服务业	Service to Households, Repair and Others Services	169	81	113	66.9
教育	Education	689	312	397	57.6
卫生和社会工作	Health Care and Social Service	415	168	236	56.9
卫生	Health	296	108	181	61.1
社会工作	Social Service	119	60	55	46.2
文化、体育和娱乐业	Culture, Sports and Entertainment	1042	516	476	45.7
广播、电视、电影和影视录音制作业	Radio, Television, Motion Picture and Videotape Programme	33	12	21	63.6
文化艺术业	Culture and Art Activities	143	62	69	48.3
体育	Sports Activities	102	43	49	48.0
娱乐业	Entertainment	762	399	336	44.1
公共管理、社会保障和社会组织	Public Management, Social Security and Social Organization	273	113	137	50.2

4-7 按国民经济行业分的固定资产投资增幅
Growth Rate of Investment in Fixed Assets by National Economic Sector

单位:%

行业	Sector	2018	2019
总 计	**Total**	**11.0**	**10.6**
农、林、牧、渔业	Farming, Forestry, Animal Husbandry and Fishery	-1.4	17.0
农业	Farming	6.2	23.2
林业	Forestry	-51.9	6.6
畜牧业	Animal Husbandry	5.3	8.1
渔业	Fishery	11.9	23.2
农、林、牧、渔专业及辅助性活动	Professional and Support for Agriculture, Forestry, Animal Husbandry and Fishery	4.6	7.3
采矿业	Mining	68.0	0.3
制造业	Manufacturing	15.6	10.0
农副食品加工业	Processing of Food from Agriculture Products	6.5	-0.5
食品制造业	Manufacture of Foods	9.3	-16.9
酒、饮料和精制茶制造业	Manufacture of Liquor,Beverages and Refined Tea	-11.2	-0.2
烟草制品业	Manufacture of Tobacco	-79.6	-18.2
纺织业	Manufacture of Textile	10.2	16.9
纺织服装、服饰业	Manufacture of Textile, Wearing Apparel and Accessaries	22.6	38.8
皮革、毛皮、羽毛及其制品和制鞋业	Manufacture of Leather, Fur, Feather and Related Products and Footwear	27.0	-13.9
木材加工和木、竹、藤、棕、草制品业	Processing of Timber, Manufacture of Wood, Bamboo, Rattan, Palm and Straw Products	22.7	26.8
家具制造业	Manufacture of Furniture	6.4	34.3
造纸和纸制品业	Manufacture of Paper and Paper Products	49.6	0.6
印刷和记录媒介复制业	Printing and Reproduction of Recording Media	46.9	-8.4
文教、工美、体育和娱乐用品制造业	Manufacture of Articles for Culture, Education, Arts and Crafts Sport and Entertainment Activities	-15.7	-15.9
石油、煤炭及其他燃料加工业	Processing of Petroleum, Coal and Other Fuels	56.3	-17.2
化学原料和化学制品制造业	Manufacture of Raw Chemical Materials and Chemical Products	12.4	18.1
医药制造业	Manufacture of Medicines	7.7	-10.3
化学纤维制造业	Manufacture of Chemical Fibres	29.5	40.4
橡胶和塑料制品业	Manufacture of Rubber and Plastic Products	15.0	10.7
非金属矿物制品业	Manufacture of Non-metallic Mineral Products	32.6	11.8
黑色金属冶炼和压延加工业	Smelting and Pressing of Ferrous Metals	0.7	18.6
有色金属冶炼和压延加工业	Smelting and Pressing of Non-ferrous Metals	10.9	10.0
金属制品业	Manufacture of Metal Products	0.5	29.4
通用设备制造业	Manufacture of General Purpose Machinery	2.7	14.9
专用设备制造业	Manufacture of Special Purpose Machinery	34.2	0.2
汽车制造业	Manufacture of Automobiles	12.4	3.4
铁路、船舶、航空航天和其他运输设备制造业	Manufacture of Railway, Ship, Aerospace and Other Transport Equipment	44.5	9.8
电气机械和器材制造业	Manufacture of Electrical Machinery and Apparatus	25.9	-18.6
计算机、通信和其他电子设备制造业	Manufacture of Computers, Communication and Other Electronic Equipment	31.7	38.6
仪器仪表制造业	Manufacture of Measuring Instruments and Machinery	-16.4	40.1
其他制造业	Other Manufacture	-68.1	66.2
废弃资源综合利用业	Utilization of Waste Resources	65.4	55.5
金属制品、机械和设备修理业	Repairing Service of Metal Products, Mechanical Equipment	-63.4	106.2
电力、热力、燃气及水生产和供应业	Production and Supply of Electricity, Heat, Gas and Water	9.5	-7.2
电力、热力生产和供应业	Production and Supply of Electric Power and and Heat Power	-11.7	0.3
燃气生产和供应业	Production and Supply of Gas	17.7	-7.0
水的生产和供应业	Production and Supply of Water	53.4	-16.5

4-7 续表 continued

单位:%

行业	Sector	2018	2019
建筑业	Construction	-32.7	-97.5
交通运输、仓储和邮政业	Transport, Storage and Post	11.2	5.4
铁路运输业	Railway Transport	10.9	-29.4
道路运输业	Road Transport	12.4	12.6
水上运输业	Water Transport	17.1	-19.1
航空运输业	Air Transport	-69.1	158.6
管道运输业	Transport via Pipelines	-18.3	-26.5
多式联运和运输代理业	Intermodality and Forwarding Agency	-2.6	-19.8
装卸搬运和仓储业	Loading, Unloading and Storage	21.4	-11.4
邮政业	Post	-77.6	5168.3
信息传输、软件和信息技术服务业	Information Transmission, Software and Information Technology Service	55.3	58.6
电信、广播电视和卫星传输服务	Telecom, Radio and Tv and Satellite Transmission Service	63.5	24.6
互联网和相关服务	Internet and Related Service	143.3	126.2
软件和信息技术服务业	Software and Information Technology	-5.8	12.4
批发和零售业	Wholesale and Retail Trades	16.6	-6.5
住宿和餐饮业	Hotels and Catering Services	7.7	15.2
金融业	Financial Intermediation	13.4	-16.1
房地产业	Real Estate	3.5	8.1
租赁和商务服务业	Leasing and Commercial Services	-28.1	14.2
租赁业	Leasing	21.8	-21.8
商务服务业	Business Services	-28.8	15.0
科学研究和技术服务业	Scientific Research and Technical Services	14.3	27.5
水利、环境和公共设施管理业	Management of Water Conservancy, Environment and Public Facilities	12.1	18.0
水利管理业	Management of Water Conservancy	-1.5	13.6
生态保护和环境治理业	Ecological Protection and Environment Treatment	56.5	44.4
公共设施管理业	Management of Public Facilities	12.6	16.4
土地管理业	Management of Land	-59.2	-15.8
居民服务、修理和其他服务业	Service to Households, Repair and Others Services	-18.4	-12.1
教育	Education	28.0	61.4
卫生和社会工作	Health Care and Social Service	33.7	-2.1
卫生	Health	18.0	-7.4
社会工作	Social Service	142.5	15.6
文化、体育和娱乐业	Culture, Sports and Entertainment	159.8	69.6
广播、电视、电影和影视录音制作业	Radio, Television, Motion Picture and Videotape Programme	-78.5	24.8
文化艺术业	Culture and Art Activities	1.9	7.3
体育	Sports Activities	263.5	-13.4
娱乐业	Entertainment	453.2	109.5
公共管理、社会保障和社会组织	Public Management, Social Security and Social Organization	-33.4	-27.4

4-8 按资金来源和构成分固定资产投资

Investment in Fixed Assets by Funds Source and Composition

年 份	按资金来源分 Grouped by Source of Finance					按构成分 Grouped by Use of Funds		
Year	国家预算内资金 State Budgetary Appropriations	国内贷款 Domestic Loans	利用外资 Foreign Investment	自筹资金 Fund Raising	其他资金来源 Others	建筑安装工程 Construction Installation	设备工器具购置 Purchases of Equipment and Instruments	其他费用 Others
投资额(亿元) Investment (100 million yuan)								
1990	11.38	22.22	4.79	92.96	13.09	92.64	41.02	10.78
1995	58.40	173.47	88.71	422.92	83.00	454.40	248.51	123.59
1998	85.18	225.95	33.86	703.44	182.66	695.55	323.47	212.08
1999	108.18	207.61	36.57	730.92	218.89	771.24	329.26	201.67
2000	141.48	243.90	28.28	781.50	226.39	814.66	371.56	235.33
2001	174.03	241.96	29.89	874.60	231.27	890.60	419.20	241.95
2002	200.95	280.11	63.22	717.24	433.69	974.73	418.55	301.94
2003	150.20	291.60	57.41	786.40	597.98	1059.98	463.23	360.38
2004	197.03	383.78	64.74	1182.36	528.47	1409.25	537.25	409.88
2005	255.76	474.21	71.34	1492.66	540.78	1696.80	642.86	495.09
2006	378.79	708.39	79.32	1902.71	503.48	2252.72	717.10	602.87
2007	472.98	790.84	88.37	2470.28	711.66	2857.31	896.36	780.47
2008	570.17	894.57	57.02	3677.00	599.80	3568.96	1245.73	983.87
2009	711.93	1432.89	68.32	4956.88	1041.83	5025.62	1753.28	1432.95
2010	868.46	1768.79	147.03	6703.61	1314.80	6701.91	2308.73	1792.05
2011	663.18	1707.46	189.26	8800.61	1574.51	8056.52	2812.91	2065.59
2012	784.27	1964.14	131.64	11812.15	1811.96	11054.16	3162.99	2287.02
2013	886.58	2720.19	66.82	14823.15	2257.17	14312.25	3856.68	2584.98
2014	1107.45	2874.92	78.99	18732.35	2208.06	18185.42	4292.85	2523.50
2015	1339.03	2907.66	46.86	22470.65	2426.86	21826.03	4845.70	2519.33
2016	1829.24	3068.40	59.01	20623.21	3924.02	22876.58	4124.21	2503.08
2017	2326.38	3078.89	65.59	21408.69	4993.03	23772.98	4891.02	3208.57
构成(%) Composition (%)								
1990	7.9	15.4	3.3	64.4	9.0	64.1	28.4	7.5
1995	7.1	21.0	10.7	51.2	10.0	58.6	30.3	11.1
1998	6.9	18.4	2.8	57.1	14.8	70.2	18.4	11.4
1999	8.3	15.9	2.8	56.1	16.9	63.4	26.5	10.1
2000	10.0	17.2	2.0	55.0	15.8	64.3	23.9	11.8
2001	11.2	15.6	1.9	56.4	14.9	64.8	24.3	10.9
2002	11.9	16.5	3.7	42.3	25.6	64.4	23.6	12.1
2003	8.0	15.5	3.0	41.8	31.7	60.9	23.4	15.7
2004	8.4	16.3	2.7	50.2	22.4	63.9	20.8	15.3
2005	9.0	16.7	2.5	52.7	19.1	59.9	22.7	17.4
2006	10.6	19.8	2.2	53.3	14.1	63.1	20.1	16.8
2007	12.6	19.7	1.3	81.1	13.2	78.7	27.5	21.7
2008	9.8	15.4	1.0	63.4	10.4	61.5	21.5	17.0
2009	8.7	17.4	0.8	60.4	12.7	61.2	21.4	17.4
2010	8.1	16.4	1.4	62.1	12.0	62.0	21.4	16.6
2011	5.1	13.2	1.5	68.0	12.2	62.3	21.7	16.0
2012	4.8	11.9	0.8	71.6	11.0	67.0	19.2	13.9
2013	4.3	13.1	0.3	71.4	10.9	69.0	18.6	12.4
2014	4.4	11.5	0.3	74.9	8.9	72.7	17.2	10.1
2015	4.6	10.0	0.2	77.0	8.3	74.8	16.6	8.6
2016	6.2	10.4	0.2	69.9	13.3	77.5	14.0	8.5
2017	7.3	9.7	0.2	67.2	15.7	74.6	15.3	10.1
2018	6.1	11.3	0.2	61.2	21.2	74.2	13.8	12.0
2019	5.4	10.5	0.4	62.4	21.3	74.3	14.0	11.7

注:从2011年起固定资产投资统计口径调整为计划总投资500万元及以上项目,取消城镇农村公布口径,其他年份未做相应调整。

Note: Since 2011,the fixed assets investment statistical adjustment plan for a total investment of 5 million yuan RMB and the above project, cancel the town and countryside,other years did not do corresponding adjustment.

4-9 按国民经济行业分的改建和技术改造投资增幅
Growth Rate of Investment in Reconstruction and Technological Transformation by National Economic Sector

单位：%

行业	Sector	2018	2019
总 计	**Total**	**32.6**	**12.4**
农、林、牧、渔业	Farming, Forestry, Animal Husbandry and Fishery	-43.0	-35.3
农业	Farming	-28.5	-16.5
林业	Forestry	-99.2	-29.0
畜牧业	Animal Husbandry	108.6	-18.6
渔业	Fishery	83.5	-73.9
农、林、牧、渔专业及辅助性活动	Professional and Support for Agriculture, Forestry, Animal Husbandry and Fishery	137.0	-35.8
采矿业	Mining	106.9	32.3
制造业	Manufacturing	41.9	14.9
农副食品加工业	Processing of Food from Agriculture Products	48.1	6.8
食品制造业	Manufacture of Foods	26.2	11.4
酒、饮料和精制茶制造业	Manufacture of Liquor,Beverages and Refined Tea	56.6	3.4
烟草制品业	Manufacture of Tobacco		-47.1
纺织业	Manufacture of Textile	42.5	5.7
纺织服装、服饰业	Manufacture of Textile, Wearing Apparel and Accessaries	38.0	9.1
皮革、毛皮、羽毛及其制品和制鞋业	Manufacture of Leather, Fur, Feather and Related Products and Footwear	59.4	-25.8
木材加工和木、竹、藤、棕、草制品业	Processing of Timber, Manufacture of Wood, Bamboo, Rattan, Palm and Straw Products	-0.4	89.6
家具制造业	Manufacture of Furniture	12.7	49.6
造纸和纸制品业	Manufacture of Paper and Paper Products	146.1	-0.9
印刷和记录媒介复制业	Printing and Reproduction of Recording Media	270.5	-21.9
文教、工美、体育和娱乐用品制造业	Manufacture of Articles for Culture, Education, Arts and Crafts Sport and Entertainment Activities	79.2	-57.3
石油、煤炭及其他燃料加工业	Processing of Petroleum, Coal and Other Fuels	60.7	8.5
化学原料和化学制品制造业	Manufacture of Raw Chemical Materials and Chemical Products	45.2	10.2
医药制造业	Manufacture of Medicines	10.7	-16.2
化学纤维制造业	Manufacture of Chemical Fibres	10.3	-35.1
橡胶和塑料制品业	Manufacture of Rubber and Plastic Products	34.1	28.8
非金属矿物制品业	Manufacture of Non-metallic Mineral Products	52.7	21.5
黑色金属冶炼和压延加工业	Smelting and Pressing of Ferrous Metals	10.0	159.0
有色金属冶炼和压延加工业	Smelting and Pressing of Non-ferrous Metals	11.3	-11.3
金属制品业	Manufacture of Metal Products	-12.7	25.6
通用设备制造业	Manufacture of General Purpose Machinery	42.4	5.7
专用设备制造业	Manufacture of Special Purpose Machinery	35.4	61.7
汽车制造业	Manufacture of Automobiles	24.9	14.4
铁路、船舶、航空航天和其他运输设备制造业	Manufacture of Railway, Ship, Aerospace and Other Transport Equipment	276.9	77.9
电气机械和器材制造业	Manufacture of Electrical Machinery and Apparatus	44.0	-12.4
计算机、通信和其他电子设备制造业	Manufacture of Computers, Communication and Other Electronic Equipment	249.0	11.3
仪器仪表制造业	Manufacture of Measuring Instruments and Machinery	94.3	28.4
其他制造业	Other Manufacture	-10.4	15.6
废弃资源综合利用业	Utilization of Waste Resources	60.4	47.4
金属制品、机械和设备修理业	Repairing Service of Metal Products, Mechanical Equipment	-61.6	-14.3
电力、热力、燃气及水生产和供应业	Production and Supply of Electricity, Heat, Gas and Water	27.3	-28.5
电力、热力生产和供应业	Production and Supply of Electric Power and and Heat Power	-24.6	-8.9
燃气生产和供应业	Production and Supply of Gas	21.6	40.5
水的生产和供应业	Production and Supply of Water	161.4	-54.2

4-9 续表 continued

单位:%

行业	Sector	2018	2019
建筑业	Construction	-88.2	-100.0
交通运输、仓储和邮政业	Transport, Storage and Post	4.0	-14.3
铁路运输业	Railway Transport	234.4	-95.0
道路运输业	Road Transport	-13.3	-5.2
水上运输业	Water Transport	304.6	-86.8
航空运输业	Air Transport		338.0
管道运输业	Transport via Pipelines		
多式联运和运输代理业	Intermodality and Forwarding Agency	367.3	-100.0
装卸搬运和仓储业	Loading, Unloading and Storage	428.7	-51.4
邮政业	Post	-100.0	
信息传输、软件和信息技术服务业	Information Transmission, Software and Information Technology Service	-16.8	-7.2
电信、广播电视和卫星传输服务	Telecom, Radio and Tv and Satellite Transmission Service	17.3	-98.9
互联网和相关服务	Internet and Related Service	-14.3	10.1
软件和信息技术服务业	Software and Information Technology	-68.1	-25.7
批发和零售业	Wholesale and Retail Trades	103.6	-53.1
住宿和餐饮业	Hotels and Catering Services	-27.6	32.9
金融业	Financial Intermediation	-64.1	14.1
房地产业	Real Estate	80.6	-29.6
租赁和商务服务业	Leasing and Commercial Services	-55.8	0.6
租赁业	Leasing	-100.0	
商务服务业	Business Services	-55.3	0.6
科学研究和技术服务业	Scientific Research and Technical Services	-67.5	615.8
水利、环境和公共设施管理业	Management of Water Conservancy, Environment and Public Facilities	-3.3	51.0
水利管理业	Management of Water Conservancy	4.5	-6.5
生态保护和环境治理业	Ecological Protection and Environment Treatment	157.1	247.6
公共设施管理业	Management of Public Facilities	-11.3	43.8
土地管理业	Management of Land	-92.0	10.7
居民服务、修理和其他服务业	Service to Households, Repair and Others Services	12.4	26.4
教育	Education	-34.5	-37.4
卫生和社会工作	Health Care and Social Service	174.9	-19.0
卫生	Health	122.4	-17.5
社会工作	Social Service		-25.7
文化、体育和娱乐业	Culture, Sports and Entertainment	329.8	23.8
广播、电视、电影和影视录音制作业	Radio, Television, Motion Picture and Videotape Programme	-16.6	-36.2
文化艺术业	Culture and Art Activities	192.4	-77.1
体育	Sports Activities	188.4	-27.0
娱乐业	Entertainment		135.8
公共管理、社会保障和社会组织	Public Management, Social Security and Social Organization	-45.6	35.9

4-10 房地产开发投资主要指标
Major Indicators of Investment in Real Estate Development

指　标	Item	1990	1995	2000	2005	2010
企业个数(个)	**Number of Enterprises (unit)**	**129**	**571**	**1052**	**1990**	**3556**
内资	Inner Funded	129	404	848	1782	3395
#国有	State - owned	129	292	380	228	187
集体	Collective-owned		51	105	74	66
港澳台投资	Funded by Enterprises from Hongkong, Macao and Taiwan		68	149	129	106
外商投资	Foreign Funded		99	55	79	55
投资完成额(亿元)	**Investment Completed This Year**	**5.94**	**121.13**	**134.63**	**447.95**	**1618.24**
按构成分	Grouped by Use of Funds					
#建筑安装工程	Construction Projects	5.45	89.56	99.59	315.15	1059.26
设备工器具购置	Installation Projects		4.47	2.83	4.68	29.07
按工程用途分	Grouped by Use of Projects					
#住宅	Residential Houses	4.70	61.78	93.15	317.65	1040.25
#经济适用房屋	Economical Houses		7.44	23.53	13.49	40.33
资金来源	Grouped by Source of Finance	5.94	138.88	117.88	513.44	2219.50
国内贷款	Domestic Loans	1.21	39.01	18.08	100.41	415.43
利用外资	Foreign Investments		16.35	1.15	1.82	97.29
自筹投资	Fund Raising	3.72	41.26	47.27	186.95	784.39
其他投资	Others	1.01	42.26	51.38	224.26	922.40
房屋建筑面积(万平方米)	**Floor Space of Building (10000 sq.m)**					
施工面积	Floor Space Under Construction	390.11	2049.30	2102.86	4804.35	11589.44
#住宅	Residential Buildings	325.82	1299.03	1673.84	4012.13	9172.43
竣工面积	Floor Spaace Completed	183.91	518.88	843.55	1627.03	2541.21
#住宅	Residential Buildings	156.77	427.19	733.27	1411.67	2129.33
土地开发及购置(万平方米)	**Land Development and Purchase** (10000sq.m)					
本年土地开发面积	Area of Land development This Year		903.00	469.28	941.26	
本年土地购置面积	Area of Land Purchased This Year		719.00	838.12	1530.64	1422.06
商品房销售情况	**Selling of Commercial Houses**					
房屋销售面积(万平方米)	Floor Psace of Selling Houses (10000sq.m)	130.53	240.00	612.05	1708.02	3508.61
#住宅	Residential Buildings	112.67	211.00	571.04	1549.19	3236.88
#经济适用房	Economic Houses		40.00	172.99	111.31	99.48
商品房销售额(亿元)	Sales Value of Commercial House	6.93	31.00	83.74	386.57	1313.20
#住宅					335.19	1134.94

注：本表资金来源均为资金到位数；从2010年起本年土地开发面积指标取消；从2011年起经济适用房分组指标取消。

Note: The source of capital in this table are the number of achieved funds; From 2010 the land development indicators of this year had been canceled.From 2011 the group index of affordable housing had been canceled.

4-10 续表 continued

指　标	Item	2011	2015	2016	2017	2018	2019
企业个数(个)	**Number of Enterprises (unit)**	**3648**	**4212**	**4280**	**4039**	**4300**	**4275**
内资	Inner Funded	3505	4107	4173	3936	4195	4180
#国有	State - owned	189	134	74	61	41	43
集体	Collective-owned	66	14	15	11	11	9
港澳台投资	Funded by Enterprises from Hongkong, Macao and Taiwan	96	78	83	76	72	64
外商投资	Foreign Funded	47	27	24	27	33	31
投资完成额(亿元)	**Investment Completed This Year**	**2066.48**	**4249.23**	**4296.38**	**4574.89**	**4676.12**	**5111.73**
按构成分	Grouped by Use of Funds						
#建筑安装工程	Construction Projects	1407.17	3243.50	3377.98	3232.22	3122.66	3457.70
设备工器具购置	Installation Projects	36.29	68.09	75.45	102.53	72.23	94.99
按工程用途分	Grouped by Use of Projects						
#住宅	Residential Houses	1334.42	3020.54	3012.35	3235.42	3453.66	3954.72
#经济适用房屋	Economical Houses						
资金来源	Grouped by Source of Finance	2864.05	4880.42	5696.35	6438.19	7388.38	6824.77
国内贷款	Domestic Loans	462.25	777.89	1031.66	976.97	1150.01	1065.73
利用外资	Foreign Investments	39.03	0.90	0.80	1.15	0.00	10.33
自筹投资	Fund Raising	1195.28	2357.67	2175.22	2257.39	2520.42	2094.25
其他投资	Others	1167.49	1743.96	2488.67	3202.68	276.81	212.21
房屋建筑面积(万平方米)	**Floor Space of Building (10000 sq.m)**						
施工面积	Floor Space Under Construction	13922.07	28296.28	29879.88	30510.48	31281.35	33825.07
#住宅	Residential Buildings	11013.30	20906.65	21803.01	22479.79	23362.74	25540.84
竣工面积	Floor Spaace Completed	3221.05	2785.17	3127.49	3219.72	2770.46	2558.60
#住宅	Residential Buildings	2728.39	2193.44	2348.38	2433.72	2088.15	2019.29
土地开发及购置(万平方米)	**Land Development and Purchase** (10000sq.m)						
本年土地开发面积	Area of Land development This Year						
本年土地购置面积	Area of Land Purchased This Year	1582.27	729.91	648.64	676.44	956.58	784.90
商品房销售情况	**Selling of Commercial Houses**						
房屋销售面积(万平方米)	Floor Psace of Selling Houses (10000sq.m)	4187.62	6244.55	7427.16	8155.21	8858.35	8602.04
#住宅	Residential Buildings	3788.68	5647.72	6789.21	7363.67	8094.76	7967.09
#经济适用房	Economic Houses						
商品房销售额(亿元)	Sales Value of Commercial House	1878.73	3661.37	4994.05	6258.92	7525.89	7751.79
#住宅		1569.32	3198.53	4383.81	5380.31	6585.94	6903.7

4-11 按登记注册类型分房地产开发投资(2019)
Investment in Real Estate Development by Registration Status(2019)

单位:亿元 (100 million yuan)

项 目	Item	总计 Total	内资 Inner Funded	国有 State - owned	集体 Collective -owned	港澳台商投资 Hongkong, Macao and Taiwan Funded	外商投资 Foreign nvestment
企业个数(个)	**Number of Enterprises (unit)**	**4275**	**4180**	**43**	**9**	**64**	**31**
#亏损企业个数	Loss- Making Enterprises	1772	1725	19	1	31	16
本年完成投资	**Investment Completed This Year**	**5111.73**	**4861.40**	**60.43**	**5.15**	**189.61**	**60.71**
按构成分	Grouped by Use of Funds						
建筑工程	Construction Projects	3068.78	2932.95	27.00	4.68	89.38	46.46
安装工程	Installation Projects	388.92	381.56	0.45	0.03	5.75	1.60
设备工器具购置	Purchase of Equipment, Tools and Instruments	94.99	94.16	0.42	0.03	0.81	0.02
其他费用	Other Funds	1559.04	1452.73	32.56	0.40	93.67	12.63
#土地购置费	Purchase of Land	1361.50	1263.88	30.46		87.17	10.45
按构成用途分	Grouped by Use of Projects						
住宅	Residential Buildings	3954.72	3785.64	38.65	2.40	130.27	38.81
#经济适用房	Economical Houses						
别墅、高档公寓	Villa, Top Grade Flat	82.00	78.44	0.44		3.56	
办公楼	Office Building	233.01	203.95	0.56	0.04	20.02	9.04
商业营业用房	Business Buildings	497.50	466.94	4.07	2.12	18.88	11.68
其他	Others	426.50	404.87	17.15	0.58	20.44	1.19
本年新增固定资产	**Newly Increased Fixed Assets This Year**	**1068.14**	**1059.28**	**8.43**		**8.86**	**0.01**
资金来源	**Finance Sources**	**6824.77**	**6482.88**	**73.07**	**2.51**	**237.25**	**104.64**
国内贷款	Domestic Loans	1065.73	955.67	2.51	1.51	91.50	18.56
利用外资	Foreign Investments	10.33	0.70			9.64	
自筹资金	Fund Raising	2094.25	2037.33	32.87	4.66	44.21	12.71
定金及预收款	Deposit and Pre Payment	2316.71	2188.17	16.10	2.37	68.15	60.38
个人按揭贷款	Individual Mortgage Loans	1125.54	1090.46	11.84	3.10	22.99	12.09
其他到位资金	Others	212.21	210.56	9.76	0.64	0.76	0.89
土地开发(万平方米)	**Land Development (10000 sq.m)**						
待开发土地面积	Area of Land to be Developed	2252.60	2178.90	9.55		68.83	4.87
本年购置土地面积	Area of Land Purchased This Year	784.90	768.16	6.82		13.86	2.89
本年土地成交价款	Value of Land Transaction	419.46	347.10	4.06		70.00	2.36

注:本表资金来源均为资金到位数,从2010年起土地开发投资额和本年土地开发面积指标取消。
Note: The sources of capital in this table are the number of achieved funds. From 2010, the indicators of investment and area of land development had been canceled.

4-12 市、州固定资产投资增幅
Growth Rate of Investment in Fixed Assets of Cities and Prefectures

单位:%

市、州	Cities and Prefectures	2011	2012	2013	2014	2015	2016	2017	2018	2019
全 省	**Total**	**28.9**	**27.6**	**25.8**	**20.4**	**16.2**	**13.1**	**11.0**	**11.0**	**10.6**
武汉市	Wuhan Municipality	22.5	20.1	19.1	16.5	10.3	-2.8	11.0	10.6	9.8
黄石市	Huangshi Municipality	34.1	25.2	28.7	21.3	17.6	10.2	14.0	11.1	12.6
十堰市	Shiyan Municipality	30.8	34.5	30.5	21.9	17.8	18.0	16.6	11.7	11.8
宜昌市	Yichang Municipality	33.7	34.3	29.4	22.1	18.2	18.8	-19.1	11.3	12.1
襄阳市	Xiangyang Municipality	42.5	40.1	29.9	22.5	19.3	18.7	15.3	11.5	12.1
鄂州市	Ezhou Municipality	37.9	34.6	28.1	21.1	17.3	17.0	15.3	10.8	12.2
荆门市	Jingmen Municipality	40.8	35.7	28.5	21.6	18.0	18.9	16.9	11.5	12.0
孝感市	Xiaogan Municipality	37.2	35.7	29.3	22.0	18.8	17.3	7.5	11.4	12.3
荆州市	Jingzhou Municipality	38.0	36.1	29.3	22.0	18.0	18.0	11.5	11.0	11.7
黄冈市	Huanggang Municipality	35.5	34.9	28.8	21.4	18.1	13.4	8.1	11.0	11.3
咸宁市	Xianning Municipality	41.3	34.6	28.9	20.5	17.5	17.6	16.5	11.3	11.7
随州市	Suizhou Municipality	40.8	34.9	28.4	22.3	18.1	17.7	16.3	11.2	11.3
恩施自治州	Enshi Prefecture	37.3	29.7	25.4	20.5	17.3	17.0	15.5	11.2	11.0
仙桃市	Xiantao Municipality	39.5	36.2	30.1	22.1	18.9	18.8	16.9	11.9	11.4
潜江市	Qianjiang Municipality	37.5	36.0	29.3	21.8	17.9	16.3	16.7	11.3	12.4
天门市	Tianmen Municipality	37.3	36.1	30.3	21.5	17.9	17.8	16.4	11.3	4.3
神农架林区	Shennongjia Forest Zone	36.9	27.2	28.1	20.7	16.9	15.3	9.2	10.2	10.2

注:2006年固资资产(城镇投资)不含城镇工矿区私人建房投资(下同)。由于方法制度调整,按可比口径计算,2005年扣除城镇工矿区私人建房投资基数应为2788.92亿元,各市、州固资资产未做调整。从2011年起固定资产投资统计口径调整为计划总投资500万元及以上项目,取消城镇农村公布口径,其他年份未做相应调整。

Note: In 2006 the investment (town investment) does not contain town private house industrial investment (the same below). Because method system adjustment, the comparable caliber calculation, 2005 deduct industrial town private house should be 278.892 billion yuan investment base; Since 2011,the fixed assets investment statistical adjustment plan for a total investment of 5 million yuan RMB and the above project, cancel the town and countryside,other years did not corresponding adjustment.

4-13 市、州民间固定资产投资增幅

Growth Rate of Non-governmental Investment in Fixed Assets of Cities and Prefectures

单位:%

市、州	Cities and Prefectures	2018	2019
全　省	**Total**	**11.4**	**11.6**
武汉市	Wuhan	11.8	8.0
黄石市	Huangshi	13.0	12.7
十堰市	Shiyan	20.6	17.4
宜昌市	Yichang	12.8	17.1
襄阳市	Xiangyang	8.1	10.3
鄂州市	Ezhou	12.3	6.9
荆门市	Jingmen	16.4	13.2
孝感市	Xiaogan	9.6	9.0
荆州市	Jingzhou	1.6	10.0
黄冈市	Huanggang	4.4	11.7
咸宁市	Xianning	18.8	19.6
随州市	Suizhou	16.1	10.3
恩施自治州	Enshi	14.3	23.4
仙桃市	Xiantao	21.9	7.4
潜江市	Qianjiang	3.7	15.2
天门市	Tianmen	11.1	3.8
神农架林区	Shennongjia	-23.4	0.0

4-14 市、州基础设施投资增幅

Growth Rate of Infrastructure Investment of Cities and Prefectures

单位:%

市、州	Cities and Prefectures	2019
全　省	**Total**	**14.7**
武汉市	Wuhan	12.9
黄石市	Huangshi	23.0
十堰市	Shiyan	28.1
宜昌市	Yichang	16.1
襄阳市	Xiangyang	31.1
鄂州市	Ezhou	17.4
荆门市	Jingmen	9.9
孝感市	Xiaogan	10.0
荆州市	Jingzhou	12.1
黄冈市	Huanggang	5.1
咸宁市	Xianning	21.0
随州市	Suizhou	31.4
恩施自治州	Enshi	2.2
仙桃市	Xiantao	60.4
潜江市	Qianjiang	28.2
天门市	Tianmen	50.5
神农架林区	Shennongjia	8.7

注:从2017年起技术改造投资统计口径调整为改建和技术改造投资,其他年份未做相应调整。

Note: Since 2017, the technical transformation investment statistics is adjusted to investment in alteration and technical transformation.

4-15 市、州工业投资增幅

Growth Rate of Industrial Investment in Fixed Assets of Cities and Prefectures

单位:%

市、州	Cities and Prefectures	2018	2019
全　省	**Total**	**15.8**	**8.1**
武汉市	Wuhan	12.1	16.3
黄石市	Huangshi	19.3	6.8
十堰市	Shiyan	19.0	10.3
宜昌市	Yichang	18.5	10
襄阳市	Xiangyang	17.3	4
鄂州市	Ezhou	14.5	-9.8
荆门市	Jingmen	12.2	12.2
孝感市	Xiaogan	18.6	10
荆州市	Jingzhou	16.2	-0.2
黄冈市	Huanggang	14.7	5.2
咸宁市	Xianning	20.9	10.7
随州市	Suizhou	14.9	8.6
恩施自治州	Enshi	27.0	11.4
仙桃市	Xiantao	19.9	11.1
潜江市	Qianjiang	14.6	-7.7
天门市	Tianmen	10.1	-5.5
神农架林区	Shennongjia	109.4	-34.3

注:从2017年起技术改造投资统计口径调整为改建和技术改造投资,其他年份未做相应调整。
Note: Since 2017, the technical transformation investment statistics is adjusted to investment in alteration and technical transformation.

4-16 市、州技术改造投资增幅

Growth Rate of Investment of Technical Transformation of Cities and Prefectures

单位:%

市、州	Cities and Prefectures	2018	2019
全　省	**Total**	**32.6**	**12.4**
武汉市	Wuhan	34.3	44.6
黄石市	Huangshi	41.8	21
十堰市	Shiyan	27.3	7.4
宜昌市	Yichang	83.4	26.4
襄阳市	Xiangyang	34.3	18
鄂州市	Ezhou	17.4	10.2
荆门市	Jingmen	17.6	-4
孝感市	Xiaogan	23.5	-15.7
荆州市	Jingzhou	38.6	15.9
黄冈市	Huanggang	48.8	-20.4
咸宁市	Xianning	10.2	39.8
随州市	Suizhou	1.7	-5.8
恩施自治州	Enshi	12.9	30.3
仙桃市	Xiantao	24.0	-21.4
潜江市	Qianjiang	8.9	-9.2
天门市	Tianmen	50.5	-2.7
神农架林区	Shennongjia	112.2	-1.9

注:从2017年起技术改造投资统计口径调整为改建和技术改造投资,其他年份未做相应调整。
Note: Since 2017, the technical transformation investment statistics is adjusted to investment in alteration and technical transformation.

4-17 市、州房地产开发投资
Investment in Real Estate Development of Cities and Prefectures

单位:亿元 (100 million yuan)

市、州	Cities and Prefectures	2011	2012	2013	2014	2015	2016	2017	2018	2019
全　省	**Total**	**2066.48**	**2539.46**	**3286.02**	**3983.79**	**4249.23**	**4296.38**	**4574.89**	**4676.12**	**5111.73**
武汉市	Wuhan	1282.25	1574.86	1905.60	2353.63	2581.79	2517.44	2686.34	2780.13	2966.21
黄石市	Huangshi	42.51	56.04	84.68	115.77	130.14	132.37	156.29	149.13	170.57
十堰市	Shiyan	52.00	76.64	101.11	90.80	83.01	87.28	66.50	76.95	95.34
宜昌市	Yichang	135.97	176.59	203.18	194.60	241.89	244.18	197.85	256.30	263.63
襄阳市	Xiangyang	144.97	186.19	301.94	330.94	334.58	340.76	336.49	287.36	263.53
鄂州市	Ezhou	18.82	11.65	22.78	20.39	21.09	22.88	29.23	36.71	59.41
荆门市	Jingmen	55.65	64.31	87.79	123.98	118.11	100.39	94.36	111.64	140.37
孝感市	Xiaogan	56.40	74.95	111.13	136.35	171.58	160.02	175.66	181.36	198.18
荆州市	Jingzhou	55.80	54.89	76.79	134.17	113.33	151.53	238.12	194.51	270.68
黄冈市	Huanggang	62.15	78.57	132.73	174.27	200.05	265.73	284.33	238.66	268.16
咸宁市	Xianning	65.46	84.96	112.06	109.14	59.94	56.99	62.74	65.92	54.42
随州市	Suizhou	24.68	19.79	29.23	33.98	28.77	24.05	38.04	39.95	57.67
恩施自治州	Enshi	35.47	40.28	57.06	91.54	100.99	130.75	131.50	142.70	171.94
仙桃市	Xiantao	16.34	15.66	26.62	24.80	22.66	19.23	35.87	39.72	44.15
潜江市	Qianjiang	5.75	9.15	18.11	22.58	15.60	21.06	23.25	30.61	34.00
天门市	Tianmen	12.26	14.93	15.24	26.84	25.68	21.73	18.34	43.56	52.70
神农架林区	Shennongjia								0.91	0.77

4-18 按构成分的固定资产投资

Investment in Fixed Assets by Composition of Investment

单位:亿元 (100 million yuan)

年 份 In copies	全省 建筑安装工程 Building installation	全省 设备工具器具购置 Equipment tools, equipment purchase	全省 其他费用 Other expenses	#地方 建筑安装工程 Building installation	#地方 设备工具器具购置 Equipment tools, equipment purchase	#地方 其他费用 expenses Other
1978	20.30	9.98	3.30	9.89	4.51	0.48
1980	23.85	9.76	1.89	14.01	4.55	0.97
"六五"时期	**216.19**	**83.11**	**16.52**	**155.63**	**59.71**	**7.43**
1985	67.53	28.67	6.71	54.64	23.00	3.39
"七五"时期	**434.43**	**195.59**	**50.10**	**352.24**	**152.75**	**32.96**
1990	92.64	41.02	10.78	73.58	29.31	7.11
"八五"时期	**1300.95**	**606.68**	**304.04**	**972.09**	**429.78**	**178.69**
1991	108.07	45.11	15.01	86.74	33.68	10.64
1992	149.34	68.03	23.36	119.61	51.46	15.94
1993	227.25	98.91	57.02	174.02	74.17	39.83
1994	361.89	146.12	85.06	261.27	99.72	49.60
1995	454.40	248.51	123.59	330.45	170.75	62.68
"九五"时期	**3392.01**	**1596.34**	**1034.45**	**2593.68**	**1108.81**	**598.32**
1996	510.52	307.89	165.97	392.06	218.14	82.28
1997	600.04	264.16	219.40	405.69	171.97	201.38
1998	695.55	323.47	212.08	556.36	230.59	101.48
1999	771.24	329.26	201.67	594.41	248.78	94.54
2000	814.66	371.56	235.33	645.16	239.33	118.64
"十五"时期	**6031.36**	**2481.09**	**1809.24**	**5317.08**	**1883.69**	**1216.75**
2001	890.60	419.20	241.95	739.97	276.93	124.89
2002	974.73	418.55	301.94	829.11	303.57	155.49
2003	1059.98	463.23	360.38	945.58	363.78	243.47
2004	1409.25	537.25	409.88	1282.71	416.98	307.87
2005	1696.80	642.86	495.09	1519.71	522.43	385.03
"十一五"时期	**20406.53**	**6921.20**	**5592.20**	**18649.08**	**5890.61**	**4859.93**
2006	2252.72	717.10	602.87	1918.63	601.90	477.07
2007	2857.31	896.36	780.47	2492.24	756.58	660.27
2008	3568.97	1245.73	983.86	3226.13	971.37	819.50
2009	5025.62	1753.28	1432.95	4683.30	1472.52	1243.52
2010	6701.91	2308.73	1792.05	6328.78	2088.24	1659.57
"十二五"时期	**73434.38**	**18971.13**	**11980.42**	**71272.16**	**18040.47**	**11545.96**
2011	8056.52	2812.91	2065.59	7626.28	2520.40	1950.61
2012	11054.16	3162.99	2287.02	10609.45	2942.10	2192.00
2013	14312.25	3856.68	2584.98	13934.73	3702.30	2508.97
2014	18185.42	4292.85	2523.50	17765.47	4160.35	2425.92
2015	21826.03	4845.70	2519.33	21336.23	4715.32	2468.46
"十三五"时期						
2016	22876.58	4124.21	2503.08	22349.47	3980.74	2421.55
2017	23772.98	4891.02	3208.57	23194.42	4678.76	3083.96

4-19 按三次产业划分的固定资产投资

Investment in Fixed Assets by Three Strata of Industry

单位:亿元 (100 million yuan)

年 份 In copies	全省 第一产业 The first industry	全省 第二产业 The second industry	全省 第三产业 The third industry	地方 第一产业 The first industry	地方 第二产业 The second industry	地方 第三产业 The third industry
1978	2.24	25.28	6.06	2.24	8.80	3.85
1980	2.11	22.75	10.64	2.03	9.98	7.52
六五时期	**24.77**	**155.02**	**136.03**	**24.05**	**83.83**	**114.89**
1985	8.37	47.42	47.12	8.09	31.48	41.46
七五时期	**49.76**	**335.53**	**294.83**	**47.24**	**245.00**	**245.71**
1990	12.16	67.41	64.87	11.61	46.30	52.09
八五时期	**78.98**	**1074.06**	**1058.63**	**73.97**	**674.84**	**831.75**
1991	12.48	77.95	77.76	12.12	55.25	63.69
1992	12.42	121.00	107.31	11.04	87.18	88.79
1993	11.89	170.93	200.36	10.10	114.05	163.87
1994	14.97	302.49	275.61	14.38	173.32	222.89
1995	27.22	401.69	397.59	26.11	220.95	316.82
九五时期	**272.08**	**2298.38**	**3452.34**	**271.69**	**1265.99**	**2763.13**
1996	29.76	451.28	503.34	29.73	272.79	389.96
1997	41.02	436.04	606.54	41.02	269.87	468.15
1998	59.48	450.16	721.46	59.48	234.94	594.01
1999	71.22	439.32	791.63	71.22	227.20	639.31
2000	70.60	521.58	829.37	70.24	261.19	671.70
十五时期	**416.79**	**3952.90**	**5969.82**	**414.74**	**2724.92**	**5277.86**
2001	77.48	590.01	902.08	77.33	323.55	740.91
2002	80.08	648.81	966.33	79.02	375.77	833.38
2003	88.80	714.81	1079.98	88.35	489.49	974.99
2004	77.55	912.93	1365.90	77.16	684.54	1245.86
2005	92.88	1086.34	1655.53	92.88	851.57	1482.72
十一五时期	**1202.88**	**12641.78**	**19075.27**	**1197.58**	**10748.83**	**17471.71**
2006	107.64	1317.12	2147.93	107.56	1044.17	1845.87
2007	149.40	1710.74	2674.00	148.72	1395.28	2365.09
2008	231.25	2346.32	3220.99	230.95	1859.42	2926.62
2009	321.59	3097.68	4792.58	319.58	2656.02	4442.25
2010	393.00	4169.92	6239.77	390.77	3793.94	5891.88
十二五时期	**3354.26**	**44874.29**	**56157.36**	**3351.93**	**43109.22**	**54397.45**
2011	440.91	5526.40	6967.71	440.51	5032.88	6623.90
2012	525.45	7281.04	8697.68	525.13	6891.67	8326.75
2013	590.61	9187.25	10976.04	589.28	8883.83	10672.89
2014	799.35	10733.09	13469.32	799.07	10432.00	13120.68
2015	997.94	12146.51	16046.61	997.94	11868.84	15653.23
十三五时期						
2016	889.94	12224.54	16389.40	885.93	11929.18	15936.64
2017	912.24	13236.47	17723.86	911.18	12831.31	17214.65

主要统计指标解释

全社会固定资产投资 是以货币形式表现的在一定时期内全社会建造和购置固定资产的工作量以及与此有关的费用的总称。该指标是反映固定资产投资规模、结构和发展速度的综合性指标,又是观察工程进度和考核投资效果的重要依据。全社会固定资产投资按登记注册类型可分为国有、集体、个体、联营、股份制、外商、港澳台商、其他等。

固定资产投资 指各种登记注册类型的企业、事业、行政单位及个体户进行的计划总投资500万元及500万元以上的建设项目投资、房地产开发投资、城镇和工矿区私人建房投资。

固定资产投资的资金来源 根据固定资产投资的资金来源不同,分为国家预算内资金、国内贷款、利用外资、自筹资金和其他资金。

(1)国家预算内资金:分为财政拨款和财政安排的贷款两部分。包括中央财政的基本建设基金(分经营性基金和非经营性基金两部分)、专项支出(如煤代油专项等)、收回再贷、贴息资金,财政安排的挖潜改造和新产品试制支出、城建支出、商业部门简易建筑支出、不发达地区发展基金等资金中用于固定资产投资的资金;地方财政中由国家统筹安排的资金等。

(2)国内贷款:指报告期固定资产投资单位向银行及非银行金融机构借入的用于固定资产投资的各种国内借款,包括银行利用自有资金及吸收的存款发放的贷款、上级主管部门拨入的国内贷款、国家专项贷款(包括煤代油贷款、劳改煤矿专项贷款等)、地方财政专项资金安排的贷款、国内储备贷款、周转贷款等。

(3)利用外资:指报告期收到的用于固定资产建造和购置的国外资金(包括设备、材料、技术在内)。包括对外借款(外国政府、国际金融组织贷款、出口信贷、外国银行商业贷款、对外发行债券和股票)、外商直接投资及外商其他投资。不包括我国自有外汇资金(国家外汇、地方外汇、留成外汇、调剂外汇和中国银行自有资金发行的外汇贷款等)。计算利用外资时,需要折算成人民币,折算中所使用的外汇汇率按现汇计算,即按使用外汇时的汇率计算。

(4)自筹资金:指固定资产投资单位报告期收到的,由各地区、各部门及企、事业单位筹集用于固定资产投资的预算外资金,包括中央各部门、各级地方和企、事业单位的自筹资金。

(5)其他资金:指在报告期收到的除以上各种资金之外其他用于固定资产投资的资金,包括企业或金融机构通过发行各种债券筹集到的资金、群众集资、个人资金、无偿捐赠的资金及其他单位拨入的资金等。

固定资产投资按国民经济行业分 根据建设项目建成投产后的主要产品或主要用途及社会经济活动性质来确定国民经济行业。一般情况下,一个建设项目或一个企业、事业单位只能属于一种国民经济行业。

固定资产投资按隶属关系分 是按建设单位或企业、事业、行政单位的主管上级机关确定的。

(1)中央:是指中共中央、人大常委会和国务院各部、委、局、总公司以及直属机构直接领导的建设项目和企业、事业、行政单位。这些单位的固定资产投资计划由国务院各部门直接编制和下达,建设中所需物资、主要设备以及建设中的问题都由中央有关部门安排和解决。

(2)地方:是由省(自治区、直辖市)、地区(州、盟、省辖市)、县(旗、县级市)三级政府及业务主管部门直接领导和管理的建设项目、企业、事业、行政单位。地方项目还包括不隶属以上各级政府及主管部门的建设项目和企业、事业单位,如外商投资企业和无主管部门的企业等。

固定资产投资按建设性质分 根据整个建设项目情况来确定。建设项目的性质一般分为新建、扩建、改建和技术改造、迁建、恢复。房地产开发单位、农村投资、城镇工矿区私人建房投资不划分建设性质。

(1)新建:一般指从无到有"平地起家"开始建设的企业、事业和行政单位或建设项目。现有企业、事业、行政单位一般不属于新建。但如有的单位原有基础很小,经过建设后新增的固定资产价值超过该企、事业、行政单位原有固定资产价值(原值)三倍以上的也应作为新建。

(2)扩建:指在厂内或其他地点,为扩大原有产品的生产能力(或效益)或增加新的产品生产能力,而增建主要的生产车间(或主要工程)、分厂、独立的生产线。行政、事业单位在原单位增建业务用房(如学校增建教学用房、医院增建门诊部、病房等)也作为扩建。

现有企、事业单位为扩大原有主要产品生产能力或增加新的产品生产能力,增建一个或几个主要生产车间(或主要工程)、分厂，同时进行一些更新改造工程的，也应作为扩建。

(3)改建和技术改造：指现有企业、事业单位，对原有设施进行技术改造或更新(包括相应配套的辅助性生产、生活福利设施)的建设项目。现有企业、事业单位为适应市场变化的需要，而改变企业的主要产品种类(如军工企业转产民用品等)的建设项目，应作为改建。原有产品生产作业线由于各工序(车间)之间能力不平衡，为填平补齐充分发挥原有生产能力而增建不增加本企业主要产品设计能力的车间，也应作为改建。技术改造是指企业、事业单位在现有基础上，用先进的技术代替落后的技术，用先进的工艺和装备代替落后的工艺和装备，以改变企业落后的技术经济面貌，实现以内涵为主的扩大再生产，达到提高产品质量、促进产品更新换代、节约能源、降低消耗、扩大生产规模、全面提高社会经济效益的目的。技术改造具体包括以下内容：机器设备和工具的更新改造；生产工艺改革、节约能源和原材料的改造；厂房建筑和公共设施的改造；劳动条件和生产环境的改造等。

固定资产投资按构成分 固定资产投资活动按其工作内容和实现方式分为建筑安装工程，设备、工具、器具购置，其他费用三个部分。

(1)建筑安装工程(建筑安装工作量)：指各种房屋、建筑物的建造工程和各种设备、装置的安装工程。包括各种房屋建造工程；各种用途设备基础和各种工业窑炉的砌筑工程及金属结构工程；为施工而进行的各种准备工作和临时工程以及完工后的清理工作等；铁路、道路的铺设，矿井的开凿及石油管道的架设等；水利工程；防空地下建筑等特殊工程；列入房屋工程预算内的暖气、卫生、通风、照明、煤气等设备的价值及装设油饰工程；列入建筑工程预算内的各种管道(蒸汽、压缩空气、石油、给排水等管道)、电力、电讯电缆导线等的敷设工程；以及各种机械设备的安装工程；为测定安装工程质量，对设备进行的试运工作；房地产开发单位进行的商品房屋开发建设工程、土地开发工程。

在安装工程中，不包括被安装设备本身的价值。

(2)设备、工具、器具购置：指建设单位或企、事业单位购置或自制的，达到固定资产标准的设备、工具、器具的价值。新建单位及扩建单位的新建车间，按照设计或计划要求购置或自制的全部设备、工具、器具，不论是否达到固定资产标准均计入“设备、工具、器具购置”中。

(3)其他费用：指在固定资产建造和购置过程中发生的，除上述几项内容以外的各种应分摊计入固定资产的费用。

施工项目 指报告期内进行过建筑或安装施工活动的项目。凡是报告期内施过工的建设项目，不论施工时间长短，均作为施工项目统计。施工项目个数可以反映一定时期固定资产投资的实际规模，与同期全部建成投产项目个数相比，可以从建设速度的角度反映固定资产投资的效果。根据建设项目施工活动的不同性质，施工项目又分为：本年正式施工项目、本年收尾项目和以前年度全部停缓建项目。

全部建成投产项目 工业项目指设计文件规定形成生产能力的主体工程及其相应配套的辅助设施全部建成，经负荷试运转，证明具备生产设计规定合格产品的条件，并经过验收鉴定合格或达到竣工验收标准，与生产性工程配套的生活福利设施可以满足近期正常生产的需要，正式移交生产的建设项目。非工业项目指设计文件规定的主体工程和相应的配套工程全部建成，能够发挥设计规定的全部效益，经验收鉴定合格或达到竣工验收标准，正式移交使用的建设项目。

新增生产能力(或工程效益) 指通过固定资产投资活动而增加的设计能力(或工程效益)，该指标是以实物形态表现的反映固定资产投资成果的指标，也是考核投资经济效果的重要依据之一。

房屋建筑面积 指房屋建筑物勒脚以上外墙外围的水平截面面积，包括房屋建筑物的有效面积和结构面积。该指标是从实物形态上反映建设规模和建设成果的重要指标之一，也是检查工程形象进度、计算工程造价、分析投资效果、研究施工任务和建筑材料之间平衡情况的重要依据。

住宅建筑面积 指施工和竣工房屋建筑面积中供居住用的房屋建筑面积。

施工面积 指报告期内施工的全部房屋建筑面积。包括本期新开工的面积和上期开工跨入本期继续施工的房屋面积，以及上期已停建在本期恢复施工的房屋面积。本期竣工和本期施工后又停缓建的房屋，其建筑面积仍计入本期房屋施工面积中。

竣工面积 指在报告期内房屋建筑按照设计要求已经全部完工，达到住人和使用条件，经验收鉴定合格(或达到竣工验收标准)，正式移交使用单位的各栋房屋建筑面积的总和。

房屋建筑面积竣工率 指一定时期内房屋竣工面积占同期房屋施工面积的比率。是从房屋建筑施工速度的角度反映投资效果的指标。

新增固定资产 指报告期内已经完成建造和购置过程，并已交付生产或使用单位的固定资产价值。该指标是表示固定资产投资成果的价值指标，也是反映建设进度，计算固定资产投资效果的重要指标。

项目建设投产率 指一定时期内全部建成投产项目个数与同期施工项目个数的比率。该指标是从建设单位建设速度的角度反映投资效果的指标。

固定资产交付使用率 指一定时期新增固定资产与同期完成投资额的比率。该指标是反映固定资产动用速度,衡量建设过程中宏观投资效果的综合指标。由于新增固定资产是较长时期内形成的结果,而投资额则是当年完成的,因此,该指标一般适宜于反映较长时期内固定资产的动用情况。

商品房销售面积 指报告期内出售商品房屋的合同总面积(即双方签署的正式买卖合同中所确定的建筑面积)。由现房销售建筑面积和期房销售建筑面积两部分组成。

商品房销售额 指报告期内出售商品房屋的合同总价款(即双方签署的正式买卖合同中所确定的合同总价)。该指标与商品房销售面积同口径,由现房销售额和期房销售额两部分组成。

Explanatory Notes on Main Statistical Indicators

Total Investment in Fixed Assets in the Whole Country refers to the volume of activities in construction and purchases of fixed assets and related fees, expressed in monetary terms. It is a comprehensive indicator which shows the size, structure and growth of the investment in fixed assets, providing basis for observing the progress of construction projects and evaluating results of investment. Total investment in fixed assets in the whole country includes, by type of ownership, the investment by the state-owned units, collective units, individuals, joint ownership units, share-holding units, as well as investment by businessmen from foreign countries and from Hong Kong, Macao and Taiwan, and by other units.

Investment in Fixed Assets refers to construction projects involving a total planned investment of 500,000 yuan and over by enterprises and institutions of various types of ownership, by administrative units and by individuals, investment in real estate development, and housing investment by individuals in urban areas and in industrial and mining areas.

Sources of Funds for Investment in Fixed Assets include fund from state budget, domestic loans, foreign investment, self-raised funds, and others depending on the source of investment.

(1) Fund from state budget consists of budgetary appropriation and loans from state budget. More specifically, it includes, from the budget of the central government, capital construction fund (operation fund and non-operational fund), special expenses (e.g. expenses on substituting petroleum with coal), loans from repayment, discount fund, expenses on innovation and trial production of new products, expenses on urban construction, expenses on temporary construction by trade departments, development fund for less developed areas, as well as local budgetary fund transferred from the central budget.

(2) Domestic loans refer to loans of various forms borrowed by investing units from banks and non-bank financial institutions during the reference period for the purpose of investment in fixed assets, including loans issued by banks from their self-owned funds and deposit, loans appropriated by higher responsible authorities, special loans by government (including loan for substituting petroleum with coal, special loan for reform-through-labour coal mines), loans arranged by local government from special funds, domestic reserve loan, and working loan, etc..

(3) Foreign Investment refers to foreign funds received during the reference period for the construction and purchase of investment in fixed assets (covering equipment, materials and technology), including foreign borrowings (loans from foreign governments and international financial institutions, export credit, commercial loans from foreign banks, issue of bonds and stocks overseas), foreign direct investment and other foreign investment. Excluded in this category are capitals in foreign exchanges owned by China (foreign exchanges owned by the central and local governments, foreign exchanges retained by enterprises, foreign exchanges by enterprises through regulating mechanism, loans in foreign exchanges issued by the Bank of China with its own fund, etc.). In calculating the utilization of foreign capitals, foreign currencies are converted into Chinese Renminbi applying the current exchange rate when the foreign capitals are actually used.

(4) Self-raised funds refer to extra-budgetary funds for investment in fixed assets received by investing units from central govern-

ment ministries, local governments, enterprises and institutions, including their self-raised funds.

(5) Others refer to funds for investment in fixed assets received from the sources other than those listed above, including capitals raised through issuing bonds by enterprises or financial institutions, funds raised from individuals and through donations, and funds transferred from other units.

Investment in Fixed Assets by Sector The classification of construction projects by sector is determined by the major products or the purpose of the projects when they are put into production or use, and by the nature of their social economic activities. In general, one project or one enterprise or institution can only be classified into one sector.

Investment in Fixed Assets by Jurisdiction of Management refers to the classification of investment by the competent authorities under which investment is made by construction units, enterprises, institutions or administrative units.

(1) Central investment refers to the investment in projects or by enterprises, institutions or administrative units which are under the direct leadership and management of the CPC Central Committee, the NPC Standing Committee, the State Council and of the national commissions, ministries, agencies and state-owned large corporations. Various ministries and departments of the State Council prepare and implement plans for investment in fixed assets by those departments, and arrange and ensure the supply of materials and key equipment required for the projects.

(2) Local investment refers to the investment in projects or by enterprises, institutions or administrative units which are under the direct leadership and management of departments under the provincial, prefecture and county governments. Also included are projects by foreign-invested enterprises and enterprises without competent managing authorities.

Investment in Fixed Assets by Type of Construction The construction projects in general can be classified, by the type of construction, into new construction, expansion, reconstruction and technical transformation, moving and restoration. However, investment by type of construction is not applied to investment by real-estate development units, investment in rural areas and investment in housing by urban individuals.

(1) New construction in general refers to newly constructed enterprises, institutions, administrative agencies or independent projects from scratch. Construction in the existing enterprises, institutions or agencies is not considered as new construction. In case the assets of the existing unit is quite small, and the value of newly added fixed assets exceeds the original value of assets by three times, the expansion will be considered as new construction.

(2) Expansion refers to construction of new major production workshop, branch factory or independent production line within a factory or in other locations, for the purpose of increasing the production capacity (or improving efficiency) of the original products. Newly constructed houses for the operation of institutions and administrative organizations (such as the newly constructed buildings for teaching in schools, buildings for clinics or wards in hospitals, etc.) are also classified as expansion.

Also included in the expansion are investments by existing enterprises or institutions in building major production line(s) or branch factory(ies) along with some work on innovation, for the purpose of expending the production capacity of original products or producing new products.

(3) Reconstruction refers to construction projects by existing enterprises or institutions in innovation or technical transformation of the old facilities (including auxiliary production equipment and welfare facilities). Also considered as reconstruction is the construction of new workshops by the existing enterprises or institutions to change the variety of products to meet the market demand (such as the production of civil products by defence industries), or to bring the designed production capacity into full play through a more balanced production process on production lines. Technical transformation refers to replacement of old technology or equipment by new technology or equipment, in order to expand the reproduction through improvement of technology contents in production, to improve product quality, to promote new products, to save energy and reduce consumption and to improve overall social-economic efficiency. Contents of technical transformation include: updating of machinery, equipment and tools; reforming production process by using energy or materials saving technology; construction of factory workshops and transformation of public facilities; improvement of working conditions and environment, etc.

Investment in Fixed Assets by Structure By their contents, investment activities are classified into 3 categories, i.e. construction and installation, purchase of equipment and instrument, and other expenses.

(1) Construction and installation (work volume of construction and installation) refers to the construction of various houses and buildings and installation of various kinds of equipment and instruments. They include construction of various houses; equipment foundations, industrial kilns and stoves, and metal structure work; preparation works for project construction, and clearing up works post project construction; pavement of railways and roads, drilling of mines and putting up of oil pipes; construction of projects of water conservancy; construction of underground air-raid shelters and construction of other special projects; value of equipment for heating, sanitation, ventilation, lighting, gas, painting, etc. that are covered by the budget of housing projects; laying out of various pipelines (for steam, compressed air, petroleum, tap water and sewage) and lines for electric power and for communications; installation of various machinery equipment, testing operation for pre-testing the quality of installation projects, and land and other development work conducted by real estate developers for commercial housing. The value of equipment installed is not included in the value of installation projects.

(2) Purchase of equipment and instruments refers to the total value of equipment, tools, and instruments purchased or self-produced which come up to standards for fixed assets by the construction units or investing enterprises or institutions. Equipment, tools and instruments purchased or self-produced for new workshops by newly established or expanded units are categorized as "purchase of equipment and instruments" no matter whether they come up to the standards for fixed assets.

(3) Other expenses refer to expenses occurring during the construction or purchase of fixed assets other than those mentioned above.

Projects under Construction refer to projects with construction and installation activities undertaken in the reference period. All projects that have construction activities undertaken during the reference period are reported as projects under construction irrespective of the length of construction work. The number of projects under construction can reflect the actual size of investment in fixed assets during a given period, and when compared with the number of projects completed and put into use during the same period, it demonstrates the results of investment in fixed assets. Depending on the nature of construction activities, projects under construction can also be classified into projects under construction in current year, winding-up projects in current year and stopped or suspended projects in previous years (with preservation work in current year).

Projects Completed and Put into Use Industrial projects refer to the major projects and accessory facilities completed which result in forming production capacity and have been checked and accepted while the living and welfare facilities have been completed and can ensure normal production and formally put into production. Non-industrial projects refer to the major projects and accessory facilities completed which possess the designed capacity and have been checked, accepted and formally put into production.

Newly Increased Production Capacity(or Project Efficiency) refers to the increase of designed capacity (or project efficiency) through investment in fixed assets, which reflects the accomplishment of investment in fixed assets in kind and serves as important basis for evaluating the economic efficiency of investment.

Floor Space of Buildings under Construction refers to total floor space of the horizontal section of outer walls above the plinth of the building, including the effective area and the area occupied by the structure. This indicator is one of the important indicators in physical terms to reflect the scale and accomplishment of the construction industry, and important basis for monitoring the progress, calculating the cost, analyzing the efficiency and studying the supply of building materials in relation with the construction projects.

Floor Space of Residential Buildings refers to the floor space of the residential buildings among the total space of buildings under construction or completed.

Floor Space under Construction refers to total floor space of all buildings under construction during the reference period, including floor space of newly started buildings during the reference period, floor space of construction extended from the previous period to the current period, and floor space of construction suspended during the previous period and resumed in the current period. Floor space of construction completed in the current period, and floor space of construction started and then suspended in the current period are also included in the floor space under construction of the current year.

Floor Space of Buildings Completed refers to the floor space of all buildings completed in the reference period, which have been appraised and accepted (or come up to the designed standards) and have been transferred to the owners for use.

Completion Rate of Floor Space of Buildings refers to the ratio of the floor space of buildings completed in certain period of time to the floor space of buildings under construction in the same period. This indicator reflects the investment result from the perspective of the speed of construction.

Newly Increased Fixed Assets refer to the newly increased value of fixed assets, constructed or purchased, that have been transferred to the investors. This is an indicator that demonstrates the results of investment in fixed assets in monetary terms, and an important indicator to reflect the speed of construction and to calculate the efficiency of investment.

Rate of Construction Projects Completed and Put into Use refers to the ratio of the number of construction projects completed and put into use in certain period of time to the number of projects under construction in the same period. This reflects the investment efficiency from the perspective of the speed of projects construction.

Rate of Projects of Fixed Assets Completed and Put into Operation refers to the ratio of the newly increased fixed assets to the total investment made in the same period. This is a comprehensive indicator reflecting the speed of the employment of fixed assets and the investment efficiency at the macro-level. As the newly increase fixed assets is the result of a long period while the investment is completed in the current year, this indicator is expected to be used to reflect the employment of fixed assets over a long period of time.

Area of Commercial Housing Sold refers to total contracted area of commercial housing (i.e. area of floor space as designated in the formal contracts signed by both sides) during the reference time. It constitutes floor space of completed housing and floor space of future housing.

Value of Commercial Housing Sold refer to total value of contracts (i.e. value of sales/purchase for selling/purchase of commercial housing as designated in the contracts signed by both sides) during the reference time. It has the same coverage as the area of commercial housing sold, constituting completed housing and floor space of future housing

5 对外经济贸易和旅游

International Trade and Economic Cooperation & Tourism

资料整理人员：王　芳

5-1 对外经济主要指标

Major Indicators of International Trade and Economic Cooperation

单位:万美元 (USD 10 000)

指 标	Item	1995	2000	2005	2010	2015	2017	2018	2019
进出口总额	**Total Imports and Exports**	**340920**	**320249**	**905475**	**2593211**	**4560531**	**4630863**	**5280245**	**5712847**
进口总额	Total Imports	142484	127369	462607	1149031	1638490	1580938	1871372	2114883
出口总额	Total Exports	198435	192880	442868	1444180	2922041	3049925	3408873	3597964
合同外商直接投资项目(个)	**Contracted Projets of Foreign Direct Investment (uint)**	**881**	**331**	**520**	**306**	**274**	**272**	**418**	**446**
合同外商直接投资	**Contracted Value of Foreign Direct Investment**	**108847**	**106583**	**211023**	**278627**	**416112**	**860726**	**1481727**	**1624612**
实际外商直接投资	**Actual Value of Foreign Direct Investment**	**62253**	**94368**	**218475**	**405015**	**894801**	**1099392**	**1194095**	**1290746**
对外经济合作	**Economic Cooperation with Foreign Countries &Regions**								
合同金额	Contracted Value	7300	36706	35953	776945				
#对外承包工程	#Contracted Projects			27952	765547	1145362	1486979	1488185	1663154
对外劳务合作	Labor Services			5568	11398				
完成营业额	Value of Tornover Fulfilled	4100	15815	31843	327164				
#对外承包工程	#Contracted Projects			28852	319979	523369	707516	643554	661042
对外劳务合作	Labor Services			2601	7186				

5-2 对外贸易进出口总额

Total Imports and Exports of International Trade

单位:万美元 (USD 10 000)

年 份 Year	合 计 Total	进 口 Imports	出 口 Exports
1992	174533	58696	115837
1995	340920	142484	198435
1996	286287	133684	152603
1997	320668	128583	192084
1998	283189	112478	170711
1999	268107	116729	151378
2000	320249	127369	192880
2001	357720	178041	179679
2002	395314	185488	209826
2003	510930	245393	265537
2004	676581	338361	338219
2005	905475	462607	442868
2006	1176219	550157	626063
2007	1489647	669593	820054
2008	2070567	899676	1170891
2009	1725102	727222	997880
2010	2593211	1149031	1444180
2011	3358693	1405233	1953460
2012	3196409	1256525	1939884
2013	3638928	1355160	2283768
2014	4306401	1641821	2664580
2015	4560531	1638490	2922041
2016	3939760	1332470	2607290
2017	4630863	1580938	3049925
2018	5280245	1871372	3408873
2019	5712847	2114883	3597964

注:根据海关统计有关文件规定2008年年终数据部分调整。

Note:According to the provisions of the relevant documents to customs statistics data portion of the 2008 year-end adjustments.

5-3 按贸易方式和经济类型分的进出口总额

单位:万美元

项 目	Item	2000		2005	
		进口 Imports	出口 Exports	进口 Imports	出口 Exports
总 计	**Total**	**127369**	**192880**	**462607**	**442868**
按贸易方式分	**Grouped by Type of Trade**				
一般贸易	General Trade	91576	138907	340768	350354
来料加工装配贸易	Processing and Assembling Trade	20136	13265	15428	22381
进料加工贸易	Raw Material Input Processing Trade	32803	14154	54328	71920
来料加工装配进口的设备	Processing and Assembling Import Equipment Provided With Material	6		18	
外商作为投资进口的设备	Goods as Invested for Import Equipments	8602		45087	
租赁贸易	Leasing Trade			114	
出料加工贸易	Raw Material Output Processing Trade				
易货贸易	Repalce Goods with Goods				
保税仓库进出境货物	Import and Export Goods of Protcetive Tariff Storage	105		8028	33
按经济类型分	**Grouped by Ownership**				
#国有企业	#State-Owned Enterprises	64805	140826	221963	213955
集体企业	Collective-Owned Enterprises	1255	9124	5719	20033
外商投资企业	Foreign-funded Enterprises	61691	42901	190170	130579
民营企业	Private-Owned Enterprises	111	240	45839	80397

Total Imports and Exports by Type of Trade and Ownership

(USD10000)

2010		2015		2017		2018		2019	
进口 Imports	出口 Exports	进口 Imports	出口 Exports	进口 Imports	出口 Exports	进口 Imports	出口 Exports	进口 Imports	出口 Exports
1149031	**1444180**	**1638490**	**2922041**	**1580938**	**3049925**	**1871372**	**3408873**	**2114883**	**3597964**
841306	829994	1088411	1961768	1259178	2165126	1445928	2605974	1620005	2829499
28304	32269	11584	53984	12628	62825	15420	69122	12830	62977
210483	518911	487467	744388	195337	645362	245421	543998	255398	525648
348		29		12		320		62	
43809		8312		7322		10820		5015	
5	144		10	1	6	2051	133	1986	32
320	212	913	607	455	196	1259	963	1137	773
20511	16794	16030	16982	42934	15173	73606	30460	66714	30066
513134	472230	401246	574791	519061	524856	575181	609771	791391	493809
4021	16161	1398	18099	2091	19548	2902	19531	2731	16251
534565	569501	556216	674909	560356	657865	637159	725349	610226	738358
93032	386177	679603	1653454	499430	1847656	654283	2048247	703447	2331576

5-4 进出口商品主要国别和地区
Imports and Exports Value by Countries and Regions

单位:万美元 (USD 10 000)

国家(地区)	Countries (Regions)	2018			2019		
		进出口 Imports and Exports	进口 Imports	出口 Exports	进出口 Imports and Exports	进口 Imports	出口 Exports
亚 洲	**Asia**	**2031049**	**786485**	**1244565**	**2349294**	**1033749**	**1315546**
#香港	#Hongkong	432999	1582	431417	362591	2097	360494
日本	Japan	415400	308448	106952	491288	375261	116027
韩国	Korea, Rep.	267292	153784	113508	341507	218231	123276
台湾省	Taiwan Province	214532	136351	78181	277656	189381	88275
印度	India	206728	19208	187519	202698	24095	178603
越南	Vietnam	173473	41554	131919	208442	63360	145083
泰国	Thailand	121662	47964	73698	136041	51710	84331
马来西亚	Malaysia	100355	37902	62453	164160	40638	123522
新加坡	Singapore	98609	39692	58917	164911	68976	95935
非 洲	**Africa**	**216442**	**103703**	**112739**	**273474**	**142076**	**131399**
欧 洲	**European**	**378367**	**163141**	**215227**	**397458**	**161540**	**235919**
#德国	#Germany	201061	97284	103777	192698	100946	91752
法国	France	78710	36074	42636	84964	22928	62037
荷兰	Netherland	98596	29783	68814	119796	37666	82130
南美洲	**South America**	**209776**	**69781**	**139995**	**197590**	**51247**	**146343**
#巴西	#Brazil	209776	69781	139995	197590	51247	146343
北美洲	**North America**	**794790**	**186567**	**608223**	**754509**	**182811**	**571697**
#美国	#United States of America	708586	170605	537981	674413	170831	503582
墨西哥	Mexico	86204	15962	70242	80096	11981	68115
大洋洲	**Occeania**	**167262**	**120666**	**46596**	**151664**	**101862**	**49802**
#澳大利亚	#Australia	167262	120666	46596	151664	101862	49802
附:东南亚国家联盟	**Association of Southeast-Asia Nations**	**641132**	**187729**	**453403**	**849962**	**249385**	**600577**
欧洲联盟	**European Union**	**772593**	**268015**	**504578**	**813381**	**258166**	**555215**
亚太经济合作组织	**Asia-Pacific Economic Cooperation**	**3294493**	**1356011**	**1938482**	**3630053**	**1582658**	**2047395**

5-5　合同外商直接投资项目
Number of Foreign Direct Investment's Contracted Projects

单位:个　　　　(unit)

指　标	Item	1990	1995	2000	2005	2010	2015	2016	2017	2018	2019
合　计	**Total**	**99**	**881**	**331**	**520**	**306**	**274**	**235**	**272**	**418**	**446**
合资经营企业	Equity Joint Venture	17	577	156	203	108	101	92	127	192	191
合作经营企业	Contractual Joint Venture	75	44	16	29	5	4	1	3	1	3
外资企业	Wholly Foreign-owned Enterprise	7	260	158	285	193	168	139	134	224	250
外商投资股份制企业	FDI Shareholding Inc.			1	3		1	3	3	1	2
合伙企业	Partnership								5		

5-6　合同外商直接投资金额
Value of Foreign Direct Investment's Contracted Projects

单位:万美元　　　　(USD 10 000)

指　标	Item	1990	1995	2000	2005	2010	2015	2016	2017	2018	2019
合　计	**Total**	**3947**	**108847**	**106583**	**211023**	**278627**	**416112**	**334118**	**860726**	**1481727**	**1624612**
合资经营企业	Equity Joint Venture	1364	68923	27936	51010	132679	78912	124301	235632	965332	526689
合作经营企业	Contractual Joint Venture	2464	7899	48711	24480	3319	11078	1171	144791	29597	71190
外资企业	Wholly Foreign-owned Enterprise	119	32025	29936	132897	235498	313337	195939	321903	477066	716197
外商投资股份制企业	FDI Shareholding Inc.				2636	33519	12785	12707	3528	9732	310536
合伙企业	Partnership								154872		

5-7 实际外商直接投资金额
Actual Value of Foreign Direct Investment

单位:万美元 (USD 10 000)

指 标	Item	1990	1995	2000	2004	2005	2010
合 计	**Total**	**2900**	**62253**	**94368**	**207126**	**218475**	**405015**
合资经营企业	Equity Joint Venture	2492	40259	59879	130048	65472	132679
合作经营企业	Contractual Joint Venture	85	5012	2789	11741	5089	3319
外资企业	Wholly Foreign-owned Enterprise	323	16982	31700	62155	75305	235498
外商投资股份制企业	FDI Shareholding Inc.					2739	33519
合伙企业	Partnership						

5-7 续表 continued

单位:万美元

指 标	Item	2013	2014	2015	2016	2017	2018	2019
合 计	**Total**	**688847**	**792792**	**894801**	**1012889**	**1099392**	**1194095**	**1290746**
合资经营企业	Equity Joint Venture	223950	300982	329123	359083	410416	402894	499461
合作经营企业	Contractual Joint Venture	3758	759	4261	7480	15178	5529	14738
外资企业	Wholly Foreign-owned Enterprise	442107	440949	548452	548867	621377	723081	711424
外商投资股份制企业	FDI Shareholding Inc.	19032	35969	9325	56625	28789	44838	33459
合伙企业	Partnership					243		

5-8 按行业分外商直接投资(2019)
Foreign Direct Investment Grouped by Sector(2019)

行 业	Item	项目(个) Number of Projects (unit)	合同外资(万美元) Contracted Foreign Capital (USD 10 000)	实际投资(万美元) Actual Foreign Investment (USD 10 000)
总 计	**Total**	**446**	**1624612**	**1290746**
农、林、牧、渔业	Agriculture, Forestry, Animal Husbandry and Fishery	9	241979	2866
采矿业	Mining	1	3925	
制造业	Manufactruring	118	499833	623071
电力、燃气及水的生产和供应业	Production and Supply of Electricity,Heat, Gas and Water	12	31874	58295
建筑业	Construction	6	100816	5611
交通运输、仓储和邮政业	Transport, Storage and Post	10	6714	47203
信息传输、软件和信息技术服务业	Information Transmision, Software and and Information Technology	46	68418	38673
批发和零售业	Wholesale and Retail Trades	92	72474	46224
住宿和餐饮业	Hotels and Catering Services	10	3161	9996
金融业	Financial Intermediation	32	29584	4456
房地产业	Real Estate	9	106848	251988
租赁和商务服务业	Leasing and Business Services	36	439750	161537
科学研究和技术服务业	Scientific Research and Technical Services	32	20366	15100
水利、环境和公共设施管理业	Management of Water Conservancy, Environment and Public Facilities	1	2290	15870
居民服务、修理和其他服务业	Sevice to Households,Repair and Other Services	7	-4725	3
教育	Education	4	-969	60
卫生和社会工作	Health and Social Service	6	1341	102
文化、体育和娱乐业	Culture, Sports and Entertainment	15	933	9691

5-9 年末登记外商投资企业行业分布情况(2019)
Industry Distribution of Registered Foreign-invested Enterprises at Year-end(2019)

单位:个 (unit)

行 业	Item	企业数 Number of Enterprises
总 计	**Total**	**446**
农、林、牧、渔业	Agriculture, Forestry, Animal Husbandry and Fishery	9
采矿业	Mining	1
制造业	Manufactruring	118
电力、燃气及水的生产和供应业	Production and Supply of Electricity,Heat, Gas and Water	12
建筑业	Construction	6
交通运输、仓储和邮政业	Transport, Storage and Post	10
信息传输、软件和信息技术服务业	Information Transmision, Software and and Information Technology	46
批发和零售业	Wholesale and Retail Trades	92
住宿和餐饮业	Hotels and Catering Services	10
金融业	Financial Intermediation	32
房地产业	Real Estate	9
租赁和商务服务业	Leasing and Business Services	36
科学研究和技术服务业	Scientific Research and Technical Services	32
水利、环境和公共设施管理业	Management of Water Conservancy, Environment and Public Facilities	1
居民服务、修理和其他服务业	Sevice to Households,Repair and Other Services	7
教育	Education	4
卫生和社会工作	Health and Social Service	6
文化、体育和娱乐业	Culture, Sports and Entertainment	15

5-10 对外承包工程和劳务合作

Contracted Projects and Labor Services Cooperation with Foreign Countries or Regions

年份 Year	Item	合同金额 (万美元) Contracted Value (USD 10 000)	实际完成营业额 (万美元) Value of Turnover Fulfilled (USD 10 000)	年末在外人数(人) Number of Persons Working Abroad at Year-end (person)
对外承包工程	**Contracted Projects**			
2003		17900	28552	1759
2004		28027	25334	2199
2005		27952	28852	2365
2006		56930	36266	2671
2007		183749	54416	5950
2008		318872	142456	9145
2009		526671	256368	10546
2010		765547	319978	17655
2011		631308	406741	13961
2012		726900	456194	16404
2013		1021254	520733	20801
2014		1269954	579636	31957
2015		1145362	523369	16406
2016		1263523	511109	20274
2017		1486979	707516	13830
2018		1488185	643554	10594
2019		1663154	661042	11520
对外劳务合作	**Labor Cooperation**			
2003		823	1783	3136
2004		1565	1597	3583
2005		5568	2601	5143
2006		6331	4379	7602
2007		6520	5340	8704
2008		6016	6856	6239
2009		6208	6988	4602
2010		11398	7186	4717
2011		7965	8261	3425
2012		11045	9669	8258
2013		12286	18194	8296
2014				
2015				
2016				
2017				
2018				
2019				
对外设计咨询	**Design Consulting**			
2002		541	267	42
2003		507	650	28
2004		475	1517	72
2005		390	2433	91
2006		983	452	90
2007		5423	2511	461
2008		6531	2804	22

注:2009年起"对外设计咨询"指标数并入"对外承包工程"中;"年末在外人数(人)"修订为"劳务外派人数(人)"。

Note: From 2009, "Design and Consultation" index number combined into the "International Contractors"; "outer (person) at the end of the year" to "manning (person)".

5-11 湖北旅游主要指标
Major Indicators of Hubei's Tourism

年份 Year	旅游总收入 (亿元) Total Earnings of Tourism (100 million yuan)	国内旅游收入 (亿元) Earnings from Domestic Tourism (100 million yuan)	国内游客 (万人次) Number of Domestic Tourists (10 000 persons-time)	外汇收入 (万美元) Foreign Exchange Earnings (USD 10 000)	入境游客 (万人次) Number of Overseas Vistor Arrivals (10 000 persons-time)
1982				299.60	2.00
1983				355.30	2.40
1984				731.30	5.40
1985				1008.60	8.50
1986	3.47	2.50	1262	1166.00	10.50
1987	3.67	2.40	1184	1545.00	12.20
1988	3.56	2.40	1208	1411.80	11.30
1989	3.99	3.10	1034	1085.50	8.20
1990	4.56	2.70	890	2263.20	15.60
1991	5.83	3.90	984	2350.00	17.00
1992	9.03	5.40	1071	4432.20	26.30
1993	13.26	9.50	1350	4588.90	23.10
1994	18.09	13.00	1500	6211.40	24.70
1995	24.00	18.00	1700	7316.90	27.10
1996	163.28	153.00	3152	12545.60	36.90
1997	193.92	180.00	3600	16977.50	58.00
1998	217.24	210.00	4044	8831.40	29.60
1999	247.11	238.50	4659	10498.50	30.50
2000	282.26	270.30	5478	14572.10	45.10
2001	353.66	337.20	6064	20075.20	66.80
2002	407.48	384.20	6670	28390.90	102.40
2003	342.77	331.60	5684	13626.90	40.50
2004	410.00	394.20	6849	19240.40	61.20
2005	473.15	450.80	7630	27636.30	82.60
2006	539.74	514.24	8459.78	32000.38	105.57
2007	640.87	609.40	10135.00	41264.00	131.81
2008	744.19	713.43	11678.00	44255.31	118.75
2009	1004.48	969.63	15065.18	51020.22	133.46
2010	1460.53	1409.48	20946.00	75116.49	181.74
2011	1992.89	1931.80	27154.87	94018.00	213.52
2012	2629.54	2553.55	34230.00	120296.72	264.72
2013	3205.61	3130.13	40621.04	121892.18	267.96
2014	3752.11	3675.98	46900.00	123851.30	277.07
2015	4308.76	4206.02	50668.24	167190.01	311.76
2016	4879.24	4764.18	56930.83	187238.97	337.56
2017	5514.90	5372.79	63499.86	210473.63	368.14
2018	6178.00	6021.42	53556.28	237968.93	405.11
2019	6927.38	6743.99	60143.70	265415.75	450.02

注：按照文化和旅游部统计督查整改意见，对2018年度旅游总收入、国内旅游收入、国内旅游人数进行了调整。

Note: According to the opinions of the Ministry of Culture and Tourism, Total Earnings of Tourism ,Earnings from Domestic Tourism and Number of Domestic Tourists in 2018 were adjusted.

5-12 接待入境旅游人数
Number of Entrance Tourists

单位:人次 (person-times)

年份 Year	总计 Total	外国人 Foreigners	港澳台同胞 Compatroits from Hongkong, Maco and Taiwan	#港澳同胞 #Compatroits from Hongkong, Macao	#台湾同胞 #Compatroits from Taiwan
1982	19775	15126	4649		
1983	24200	18903	5297		
1984	53800	40496	13304		
1985	84598	68103	16495		
1986	105300	83570	21730		
1987	122390	82029	40361		
1988	113051	78206	34845	19725	15120
1989	81781	49511	32270	13908	18362
1990	155734	36374	119360	11560	107800
1991	170121	53055	117066	12645	104421
1992	263401	72691	190323	14054	176269
1993	230883	84552	146331	28460	117871
1994	247212	133343	113869	56417	57452
1995	270890	172869	98021	42785	55236
1996	368877	243595	125282	58949	66333
1997	580223	359700	220523	64466	156057
1998	295643	209402	86241	30337	55904
1999	305408	224748	80660	30935	49725
2000	450805	357352	93453	42928	53162
2001	667818	542737	125081	48417	76664
2002	1024312	755718	268594	49113	219481
2003	405214	323151	82063	40294	41769
2004	611859	501873	109986	57086	52900
2005	825700	626805	198895	107141	91754
2006	1055752	857028	198724	110246	88478
2007	1318179	1077189	240990	140384	100606
2008	1187549	926625	260924	152631	108293
2009	1334634	1017620	317014	182616	134398
2010	1817416	1385457	431959	241430	190529
2011	2135247	1601129	534118	291487	242631
2012	2647163	1929571	717592	410921	306671
2013	2679623	2047316	632307	365184	267123
2014	2770689	2132562	638127	363810	274317
2015	3117592	2397892	719700	377115	342585
2016	3375628	2546454	829174	390797	438377
2017	3681433	2779487	901946	427834	474112
2018	4051128	3070321	980807	438550	542257
2019	4500182	3499353	1000829	415709	585120

5-13 入境旅游外汇收入
Foreign Exchange Earnings from Inbound Tourism

年份 Year	外汇收入(万美元) Foreign Exchange Earnings (USD 10 000)	发展指数(1978年为100) Development Index (year1978=100)	同比 Comparision Percentage (±%)	人均天花费(美元) Expenditures Per Capita a day (USD)
1982	299.64	129.85	82.00	
1983	355.30	153.98	18.58	
1984	731.30	316.92	105.83	
1985	1008.58	327.69	37.92	
1986	1166.00	505.31	15.61	
1987	1545.00	669.56	32.50	
1988	1411.75	611.81	-8.62	
1989	1085.45	470.40	-23.11	
1990	2263.18	980.79	108.50	
1991	2350.00	1018.42	3.84	
1992	4432.16	1920.76	88.60	
1993	4588.88	1988.68	3.54	
1994	6211.42	2691.84	35.36	125.10
1995	7316.86	3170.90	17.80	155.70
1996	12545.60	5436.88	71.46	167.04
1997	16977.51	7357.53	35.33	168.52
1998	8831.43	3827.27	-47.98	162.87
1999	10498.49	4549.72	18.88	166.31
2000	14572.13	6315.12	38.80	166.58
2001	20075.16	8699.96	37.76	164.25
2002	28390.95	12303.77	41.42	160.57
2003	13626.93	5905.50	-52.00	160.57
2004	19240.41	8338.21	51.00	169.92
2005	27636.30	11976.73	43.64	170.14
2006	32000.38	13867.99	15.79	177.16
2007	41264.00	17882.56	28.95	181.68
2008	44255.31	19178.90	7.25	197.56
2009	51020.22	22110.60	15.29	193.43
2010	75116.49	32553.20	47.23	192.84
2011	94018.00	40744.53	25.16	195.36
2012	120296.72	52132.92	27.95	193.04
2013	121892.18	52824.35	1.33	194.44
2014	123851.30	53675.70	1.61	192.34
2015	167190.01	72458.19	34.99	214.30
2016	187238.97	81143.65	11.99	198.95
2017	210473.63	91212.84	12.41	209.34
2018	237968.93	103124.63	13.06	233.10
2019	265415.75	115023.07	11.50	211.63

5-14 接待入境旅游者天数

Number of Days Receiving Inbound Tourists

单位:人天 (person/day)

年 份 Year	总计 Total	外国人 Foreigners	港澳台同胞 Compatroits from Hongkong, Maco and Taiwan	#港澳同胞 #Compatroits from Hongkong, Macao	#台湾同胞 #Compatroits from Taiwan
1981	22946	15282	7664		
1982	29016	24188	4828		
1983	29830	25298	4532		
1984	107600	37806	69794		
1985	143815	115774	28041		
1986	186379	139677	46702		
1987	167035	115219	51816		
1988	190486	132301	58185	35505	22680
1989	127891	79217	48674	20862	27812
1990	178737	49487	129250	11960	117290
1991	235595	74913	160682	17450	143232
1992	351591	101878	249713	18973	230740
1993	324350	142240	182110	49959	132151
1994	472467	231716	240751	117889	122862
1995	501038	317246	183792	86910	96882
1996	729968	477152	252816	131993	120823
1997	949661	591127	358534	111291	247243
1998	513569	366348	147221	61491	85730
1999	622037	478486	143551	57765	85786
2000	852455	676130	176325	81432	94893
2001	1208938	891787	317151	93376	223775
2002	1712230	1232818	479412	86427	392985
2003	799824	603001	196823	98230	98593
2004	1069442	849071	220371	118234	102137
2005	1513678	1135995	377683	194122	183561
2006	1824387	1502277	322110	176901	145209
2007	2342786	1926484	416302	233946	182356
2008	2217172	1734211	482961	243638	239323
2009	2640362	2025972	614390	338898	275492
2010	3750746	2868024	882722	481484	401238
2011	4596252	3494098	1102154	581193	520961
2012	5934359	4424239	1510060	822210	687850
2013	6009111	4581165	1427946	802642	625304
2014	6370867	4926991	1443876	805502	638374
2015	7248536	5634388	1614448	833216	781232
2016	8026469	6119616	1901053	906834	994219
2017	9267815	7198608	2069207	985599	1083608
2018	10209040	7931912	2277128	1008464	1268664
2019	11319394	8818976	2500418	1045213	1455205

注:2000年国家不再设“华侨”指标,“华侨”人数含在“外国人”中。

Note:The item of "overseas Chinese" is cancled by state since 2000, The number of "Overseas Chinese" is included in the number of "Foreigner".

5-15 湖北国内旅游接待人数及收入
Number of Domestic Tourist Received and Earnings in Hubei

年份 Year	接待人数(万人次) Number of Tourists Received (10 000person-times)	同比(±%) Comparision Percentage (±%)	旅游收入 (亿元) Earnings (100 million yuan)	同比(±%) Comparision Percentage (±%)	人均花费(元) Expenditures Per Capita (yuan)	
					全国 The Whole Nation	湖北 Hubei
1987	1184	-6.18	2.37	-6.0		
1988	1208	2.03	2.42	2.1		
1989	1034	-14.40	3.10	28.1		
1990	890	-13.92	2.67	-13.9		
1991	984	10.56	3.93	47.2		
1992	1071	8.84	5.36	36.4		
1993	1350	26.05	9.50	77.2		
1994	1500	11.11	13.00	36.8		
1995	1700	13.33	18.00	38.5		
1996	3152	85.41	152.95		256	485
1997	3600	14.21	180.00	17.7	328	500
1998	4044	12.33	210.03	16.7	344	519
1999	4659	15.21	238.50	13.6	394	511
2000	5478	17.58	270.31	13.3	427	493
2001	6064	10.70	337.18	24.7	450	556
2002	6670	9.99	384.24	14.0	441	576
2003	5684	-14.78	331.60	-13.7	395	583
2004	6849	20.50	394.22	18.9	550	576
2005	7630	11.40	450.76	14.3	436	591
2006	8460	10.88	514.24	14.1	447	607
2007	10135	19.80	609.40	18.5	482	601
2008	11678	15.2	713.43	17.1	511	610
2009	15065	29.0	969.63	35.9	535	644
2010	20946	39.0	1409.48	45.4	598	673
2011	27155	29.6	1931.80	37.1	731	711
2012	34230	26.1	2553.55	32.2	766	746
2013	40621	18.6	3130.13	22.6	806	771
2014	46900	15.5	3752.11	17.1	839	782
2015	50668	12.7	4206.02	14.3	857	830
2016	56931	12.4	4764.18	13.3	888	837
2017	63500	11.5	5372.79	12.8		846
2018	53556	13.8	6021	15.2		1124
2019	60144	12.3	6744	12.0		1121

注:按照文化和旅游部统计督查整改意见,对2018年度接待人数、旅游收入进行了调整。
Note: According to the opinions of the Ministry of Culture and Tourism, Number of Tourists Received and Earnings in 2018 were adjusted.

5-16 湖北旅游总收入
Total Earnings of Tourism in Hubei

年份 Year	旅游总收入 Total Earnings of Tourism 绝对额(亿元) (100 million yuan)	旅游总收入 Total Earnings of Tourism 同比(±%) Comparision Percentage (±%)
1997	193.92	18.8
1998	217.27	12.0
1999	247.11	13.7
2000	282.26	14.2
2001	353.64	24.9
2002	407.52	15.2
2003	342.77	-15.9
2004	410.00	19.6
2005	473.15	15.4
2006	539.74	14.1
2007	640.87	18.7
2008	744.19	16.1
2009	1004.48	35.0
2010	1460.53	45.4
2011	1992.89	36.5
2012	2629.54	32.0
2013	3205.61	21.9
2014	3752.11	17.1
2015	4308.76	14.8
2016	4888.51	13.5
2017	5514.90	12.8
2018	6178.00	12.0
2019	6927.38	12.1

注:按照文化和旅游部统计督查整改意见,对2018年度旅游总收入进行了调整。
Note: According to the opinions of the Ministry of Culture and Tourism, Total Earnings of Tourism in 2018 was adjusted.

主要统计指标解释

货物进出口总额 指实际进出我国关境的货物总金额。包括对外贸易实际进出口货物,来料加工装配进出口货物,国家间、联合国及国际组织无偿援助物资和赠送品,华侨、港澳台同胞和外籍华人捐赠品,租赁期满归承租人所有的租赁货物,进料加工进出口货物,边境地方贸易及边境地区小额贸易进出口货物,中外合资企业、中外合作经营企业、外商独资经营企业进出口货物和公用物品,到、离岸价格在规定限额以上的进出口货样和广告品(无商业价值、无使用价值和免费提供出口的除外),从保税仓库提取在中国境内销售的进口货物,以及其他进出口货物。该指标可以观察一个国家在对外贸易方面的总规模。我国规定出口货物按离岸价格统计,进口货物按到岸价格统计。

商品收发货人所在地进、出口额 指所在地海关注册登记的有进出口经营权的企业实际进、出口额。

商品目的地进口额和商品货源地出口额 目的地进口额指进口货物的消费、使用或最终抵运地的实际进口额;货源地出口额指出口货物的产地或原始发货地的实际出口额。

外商直接投资 指外国企业和经济组织或个人(包括华侨、港澳台胞以及我国在境外注册的企业)按我国有关政策、法规,用现汇、实物、技术等在我国境内开办外商独资企业、与我国境内的企业或经济组织共同举办中外合资经营企业、合作经营企业或合作开发资源的投资(包括外商投资收益的再投资),以及经政府有关部门批准的项目投资总额内企业从境外借入的资金。

对外承包工程 根据《对外承包工程管理条例》,对外承包工程是指中国的企业或者其他单位承包境外建设工程项目的活动。

对外劳务合作 指组织劳务人员赴其他国家或地区为国外的企业或机构工作的经营性活动。

入境游客 指报告期内来中国(大陆)观光、度假、探亲访友、就医疗养、购物、参加会议或从事经济、文化、体育、宗教活动的外国人、港澳台同胞等游客(即入境旅游人数)。统计时,入境游客按每入境一次统计1人次。入境旅游人数包括入境过夜游客和入境一日游游客。

国内游客 指报告期内在中国(大陆)观光游览、度假、探亲访友、就医疗养、购物、参加会议或从事经济、文化、体育、宗教活动的中国(大陆)居民人数,其出游的目的不是通过所从事的活动谋取报酬。统计时,国内游客按每出游一次统计1人次。

国内旅游收入 指国内游客在国内旅行、游览过程中用于交通、参观游览、住宿、餐饮、购物、娱乐等全部花费。

国际旅游(外汇)收入 指入境旅游的外国人、华侨、港澳同胞和台湾同胞在中国大陆旅游过程中发生的一切旅游支出,其对于国家来说就是国际旅游(外汇)收入。

Explanatory Notes on Main Statistical Indicators

Total Imports and Exports at Customs refer to the real value of commodities imported into and exportedacross the border of China. They include the actual imports and exports through foreign trade, imported and exported goods under the processing and assembling trades and materials, supplies and gifts as aid given gratis between governments and by the United Nations and other international organizations, and contributions donated by overseas Chinese, compatriots in Hong Kong and Macao and Chinese with foreign citizenship, leasing commodities owned by tenant at the expiration of leasing period, the imported and exported commodities processed with imported materials, commodities trading in border areas, the imported and exported commodities and articles for public use of the Sino-foreign joint ventures, cooperative enterprises and ventures with sole foreign investment. Also included are import or export of samples and advertising goods for which CIF or FOB value are beyond the permitted ceiling (excluding goods of no trading or use value and free commodities for export), imported goods sold in China from bonded warehouses and other imported or exported goods. The indicator of the total imports and exports at customs can be used to observe the total size of external trade in a country. In accordance with the stipulation of the Chinese government, imports are calculated at CIF, while exports are calculated at FOB.

Import or Export Value by Location of China' s Foreign Trade Managing Units refers to actual value of imports and exports carried out by corporations which have been registered by the local Customshouse and are vested with right to run import export business.

Import Value of Commodities by the Places of their Destination and Export Value of Commodities by the Places of their Origin in China The former indicator refers to the value of import commodities of the places of their consumption, utilization or the places of their final destination. The latter indicator refers to the value of export commodities of the places of their origin or the places of the commodities dispatched.

Foreign Direct Investment refers to the investments inside China by foreign enterprises and economic organizations or individuals (including overseas Chinese, compatriots from Hong Kong, Macao and Taiwan, and Chinese enterprises registered abroad), following the relevant policies and laws of China, for the establishment of ventures exclusively with foreign own investment, Sino-foreign joint ventures and cooperative enterprises or for co-operative exploration of resources with enterprises or economic organizations in China. It includes the re investment of the foreign entrepreneurs with the profits gained from the investment and the funds that enterprises borrow from abroad in the total investment of projects which are approved by the relevant department of the government.

Overseas Contracted Projects refer to activities of contracting overseas contruction projects by Chinese enterprises or any other units,which are stipulated in the Regulations on Administration of Foreign Contracted Project.

Overseas Labour Services refer to operational activities of organizing labour force to go abroad providing services to foreign enterprises or agencies.

Overseas Vistor Arrivals refer to thenumber of tourists of foreigners,Chinese compatriots from Hong Kong,Macao and Taiwan who come to China (mainland)within the reference period for sight-seeing,vacation,visitingrelatives,medicaltreatment,shopping, attending conference, or to engage in economic, cultural, sports and religious activities(namely the number of overseas visitor arrivals).In compiling statistics, each arrival is counted as one person-time.The number of overseas visitor arrivals includes inbound overnight tourists and one-day tourists.

Number of Domestic Tourists refers to the number of Chinese (mainland) residentswho travel within China (mainland) for sight-seeing,vacation,visitingrelatives,medical treatment, shopping, attending conference,or to engage in economic,cultural,sports and religious activities.In compiling statistics,each time of travelling is counted as one person-time.

Incomefrom Domestic Tourism refer to expenditure of domestic tourists on transportation,sighting,accommodation,food,shopping and entertainment while they travel.

Foreign Exchange Earnings from International Tourism refer to the total expenditures of foreigners, overseas Chinese, Chinese compatriots from Hong Kong, Macao and Taiwan during their stay in the mainland of China, which are earnings of foreign exchange from international tourism from the point of view from China.

6 能源

Energy

资料整理人员：苏　畅　高　媛

6-1 工业能源生产量
Output of Industrial Energy Production

产品		Item		2016	2017	2018	2019
原煤	(万吨)	Coal	(10 000 ton)	547.42	311.59	58.46	38.53
原油	(万吨)	Crude Oil	(10 000 ton)	58.09	55.50	54.25	53.62
天然气	(亿立方米)	Natural Gas	(100 million cu.m)	1.31	1.27	5.09	4.89
水电	(亿千瓦时)	Water and Electricity	(100 million KW/h)	1379.30	1459.22	1430.89	1330.27

说明：原煤、原油、天然气以及水电产量为规模以上工业生产量。
Note: Raw coal, crude oil, natural gas and hydropower output are the above scale industrial production.

6-2 规模以上工业能源消费量
Energy Consumption of Industry above Designated Size

产品		Item		2016	2017	2018	2019
能源消费量合计	(万吨标煤)	Total	(10000 tons standardized coal)	13954.63	14159.66	14074.61	15019.74
原煤	(万吨)	Coal	(10000 ton)	7433.21	7116.78	7704.97	8718.65
洗精煤	(万吨)	Cleaned Coal	(10000 ton)	1253.29	1250.16	1251.52	1162.50
其他洗煤	(万吨)	Other Washed Coal	(10000 ton)	23.86	16.12	22.31	20.77
煤制品	(万吨)	Moulded Coal	(10000 ton)	10.25	11.52	8.72	12.51
焦炭	(万吨)	Coke	(10000 ton)	1095.31	1062.32	1131.70	1115.52
其他焦化产品	(万吨)	Other Coked Products	(10000 ton)	1.68	0.73	0.50	0.26
焦炉煤气	(亿立方米)	Coke-oven Gas	(100 million cu.m)	35.69	36.23	32.92	30.35
高炉煤气	(亿立方米)	Bblast Furnace Gas	(100 million cu.m)	316.25	352.79	358.70	357.85
其他煤气	(亿立方米)	Other Gases	(100 million cu.m)	22.64	24.63	23.46	25.37
天然气	(亿立方米)	Natural Gas	(100 million cu.m)	25.69	28.20	33.73	36.27
原油	(万吨)	Crude Oil	(10000 ton)	1239.61	1427.76	1419.60	1515.43
汽油	(万吨)	Gasoline	(10000 ton)	12.08	8.00	7.08	6.16
煤油	(万吨)	Kerasene	(10000 ton)	1.14	1.02	0.61	0.74
柴油	(万吨)	Diesel Oil	(10000 ton)	48.76	44.35	43.23	42.99
燃料油	(万吨)	Fuel Oil	(10000 ton)	4.22	3.29	3.08	6.43
液化石油气	(万吨)	LPG	(10000 ton)	27.33	34.37	36.59	38.12
炼厂干气	(万吨)	Dry Gas	(10000 ton)	36.44	41.84	37.99	38.54
其他石油制品	(万吨)	Other Petroleum Products	(10000 ton)	638.38	684.37	238.24	254.19
热力	(万百万千焦)	Heat	(10 billion kilo-joule)	7860.91	8875.93	9206.97	9668.64
电力	(亿千瓦时)	Electricity	(100 million kW/h)	1311.43	1290.62	1298.95	1350.86
其他燃料	(万吨标准煤)	Other Fuels	(10000 tons standardized coal)	23.21	22.00	20.93	19.65

注：能源消费量包括加工转换投入量，且为当量值。
Note: The conversion of energy consumption, including processing input, and when the money is.

6-3 规模以上工业分行业能源消费量(2019)
Energy Consumption of Industry above Designated Size by Sector(2019)

行业	Item	原煤消费量(万吨) Coal Consumption (10000 tons)	汽油消费量(万吨) Gasoline Consumption (10000tons)	柴油消费量(万吨) Diesel Consumption (10000tons)	电力消费量(亿千瓦小时) Electricity Consumption (100million kw/h)
总消费量	**Total Consumption**	**8718.65**	**6.16**	**42.99**	**1350.86**
采矿业	**Mining**	**115.55**	**0.49**	**10.33**	**29.15**
煤炭开采和洗选业	Mining and Washing of Coal	83.86	0.00	0.00	0.15
石油和天然气开采业	Extraction of Petroleum and Natural Gas	9.92	0.05	0.54	8.13
黑色金属矿采选业	Mining and Processing of Ferrous Metal Ores	3.79	0.03	0.21	6.90
有色金属矿采选业	Mining and Processing of Non-Ferrous Metal Ores	0.00	0.01	0.04	2.16
非金属矿采选业	Mining and Processing of Non-metal Ores	14.73	0.23	2.76	10.19
开采辅助活动	Mining Auxiliary	3.12	0.18	6.78	1.52
其他采矿业	Mining of Other Ores	0.12	0.00	0.00	0.10
制造业	**Manufacturing**	**3031.61**	**5.47**	**31.46**	**1084.17**
农副食品加工业	Processing of Food from Agricultural Products	19.85	0.34	2.69	36.02
食品制造业	Manufacture of Foods	37.68	0.07	0.18	14.58
酒、饮料和精制茶制造业	Manufacture of Wine, Beverages and Tea	9.98	0.13	0.23	11.08
烟草制品业	Manufacture of Tobacco	0.00	0.00	0.01	1.64
纺织业	Manufacture of Textile	4.57	0.09	0.31	62.83
纺织服装、服饰业	Manufacture of Textile Wearing Apparel	1.04	0.07	0.18	5.61
皮革、毛皮、羽毛及其制品和制鞋业	Manufacture of Leather, Fur, Feather and Related and Footware	0.05	0.02	0.00	2.49
木材加工和木、竹、藤、棕、草制品业	Processing of Timber, Manufacture of Wood, Bamboo, Rattan, Palm, and Straw Products	1.08	0.05	0.19	10.04
家具制造业	Manufacture of Furniture	0.03	0.02	0.13	1.98
造纸和纸制品业	Manufacture of Paper and Paper Products	101.38	0.06	1.81	26.96
印刷和记录媒介复制业	Printing and Reproduction of Recording Media	8.36	0.08	0.25	9.95
文教、工美、体育和娱乐用品制造业	Manufacture of Articles for Culture, Education, Art, Sport and Entertainment	4.26	0.02	0.19	10.99
石油加工、炼焦和核燃料加工业	Processing of Petroleum, Coking and Nuclear Fuel	9.16	0.01	0.02	15.41
化学原料和化学制品制造业	Manufacture of Raw Chemical Materials and Chemical Products	1071.56	0.16	2.13	217.71
医药制造业	Manufacture of Medicines	72.70	0.08	0.62	30.38
化学纤维制造业	Manufacture of Chemical Fibres	18.72	0.00	0.01	3.26
橡胶和塑料制品业	Manufacture of Rubber and Plastics	7.95	0.67	0.50	22.44
非金属矿物制品业	Manufacture of Non-metal Mineral Products	999.25	0.30	9.92	136.32
黑色金属冶炼和压延加工业	Smelting an Processing of Ferrous Metals	607.67	0.03	0.84	198.94
有色金属冶炼和压延加工业	Smelting an Processing of Non-ferrous Metals	41.09	0.04	0.48	27.30
金属制品业	Manufacture of Metal Products	8.41	0.22	2.24	29.91
通用设备制造业	Manufacture of General Purpose Machinery	0.27	0.26	2.65	17.20
专用设备制造业	Manufacture of Special Purpose Machinery	0.73	0.30	1.82	13.22
汽车制造业	Manufacture of Automobile	1.96	1.80	2.56	83.74
铁路、船舶、航空航天和其他运输设备制造业	Manufacture of Realway, Ship, Aircraft and Other Transport Equipment	0.59	0.08	0.12	3.32
电气机械和器材制造业	Manufacture of Electrical Machinery and Equipment	0.07	0.22	0.26	35.88
计算机、通信和其他电子设备制造业	Manufacture of Computers, Communication Equipment and Other Electronic Equipment	0.06	0.12	0.04	45.93
仪器仪表制造业	Manufacture of Measuring Instruments	0.00	0.18	0.01	1.62
其他制造业	Manufacture of Other Products	0.00	0.02	0.00	0.48
废弃资源综合利用业	Recycling and Disposal of Waste	3.16	0.01	0.34	6.51
金属制品、机械和设备修理业	Repairing of Metal Products and Mechanical Equipment	0.00	0.06	0.74	0.45
电力、燃气及水生产和供应业	**Electric Power, Gas and Water Production and Supply**	**5571.49**	**0.20**	**1.21**	**237.54**
电力、热力生产和供应业	Production and Supply of Electric Power and Heat Power	5571.49	0.07	1.17	219.96
燃气生产和供应业	Production and Supply of Gas	0.00	0.03	0.02	7.47
水的生产和供应业	Production and Supply of Water	0.00	0.09	0.01	10.11

6-4 全社会综合能源平衡表(等价值)
Overall Energy Balance Sheet for the Whole Society (Equivalence Value)

单位:万吨标准煤 (10000 tons standardized coal)

项 目	Item	2016	2017	2018	2019
一、可供量	**Quantity Available**	**15897**	**16180**	**16682**	**17316**
一次能源生产量	Primary Energy Production	5336	5341	5331	4892
外省(区、市)调入量	Engery moblized from other Province	13402	13571	14045	14879
进口量	Import Volume		20	114	262
本省(区、市)调出量(-)	Engery moblized to other Province	2572	2675	2665	2588
出口量(-)	Output Volume		45	67	51
年初年末库存差额	Storage Balance Difference between the Beginning and the End of the Year	-269	-31	-75	-78
年初库存量	Storage Volume at the Beginning of the Year	536	804	834	911
年末库存量(-)	Storage Volume by the End of the Year	804	835	909	989
二、消费量	**Consumption**	**15897**	**16180**	**16682**	**17316**
消费量分组一	Consumption Group 1.	**15897**	**16180**	**16682**	**17316**
1.农、林、牧、渔业	Agriculture, Forestry, Animal Husbandary, Fishing	416	415	426	452
2.工 业	Industry	9525	9533	9488	9574
3.建筑业	Construction	370	382	395	424
4.交通运输、仓储和邮政业	Transport communication, Storage, Post Service	1919	1959	2003	2220
5.批发、零售业和住宿、餐饮业	Wholesale,Retail Sale, Hotel and Catering Industry	757	805	876	909
6.其 他	Others	858	865	1015	1093
7.生活消费	Living Consumption	2052	2222	2480	2644
消费量分组二	**Consumption Group 2.**	**15897**	**16180**	**16682**	**17316**
1.终端消费	Terminal Consumption	15701	16123	16665	17321
#工业	Industry	9328	9476	9472	9580
2.加工转换损失	Loss in Processing	-137	-287	-361	-391
火力发电损失	Loss in Thermal Power Generation				
供热损失	Loss in Heating	232	166	139	123
洗选煤损失	Loss in Coal Seperation	2	1		2
炼焦损失	Loss in Coke Making	34	34	37	34
炼油及煤制油损失	Loss in Oil Refining	55	48	54	41
制气损失	Loss in Gas Drying				
天然气液化损失	Loss in Natural gas liquefaction	7	4	5	1
煤制品加工损失	Loss in Coal Products Processing				
回收能	Recuperated Energy	-468	-541	-597	-591
3.损失量	Loss in Processing	334	344	378	386
三、平衡差额	**Balance**				

注:根据第四次全国经济普查结果对2018及之前年度数据进行了修订。
Note:Based on the results of the fourth national economic census, the data of 2018 and previous years are revised.

6-5 全社会煤炭平衡表
Coal Balance Sheet for the Whole Society

单位:万吨 (10 000 tons)

项　目	Item	2016	2017	2018	2019
一、可供量	**Quantity Available**	**10740**	**10721**	**11100**	**11768**
生产量	Primary Energy Production	594	315	119	41
外省(区、市)调入量	Engery moblized from other Province	10180	10385	11007	11716
进口量	Import Volume		28	20	51
本省(区、市)调出量(－)	Engery moblized to other Province				
出口量(–)	Output Volume				
年初年末库存差额	Storage Balance Difference between the Beginning and the End of the Year	–34	–7	–47	–40
年初库存量	Storage Volume at the Beginning of the Year	576	610	617	664
年末库存量(–)	Storage Volume by the End of the Year	610	617	664	703
二、消费量	**Consumption**	**10740**	**10721**	**11100**	**11768**
消费量分组一	**Consumption Group 1.**	**10740**	**10721**	**11100**	**11768**
1.农、林、牧、渔业	Agriculture, Forestry, Animal Husbandary, Fishing	206	206	196	190
2.工　业	Industry	9352	9360	9791	10493
3.建筑业	Construction	47	46	36	35
4.交通运输、仓储和邮政业	Transport communication, Storage, Post Service	52	49	44	45
5.批发、零售业和住宿、餐饮业	Wholesale,Retail Sale, Hotel and Catering Industry	262	257	253	246
6.其　他	Others	274	270	264	258
7.生活消费	Living Consumption	546	534	516	501
消费量分组二	**Consumption Group 2.**	**10740**	**10721**	**11100**	**11768**
1.终端消费	Terminal Consumption	5403	5257	4802	4618
#工业	Industry	4016	3895	3493	3344
2.用于加工转换	Coal Used for Processing	5336	5464	6299	7150
火力发电	Thermal Power Generation	3624	3724	4510	5356
供　热	Heating	445	485	537	591
洗煤损耗	Loss in Washing Coal	15	5		41
炼　焦	Coke Making	1253	1250	1252	1163
炼油及煤制油	Oil Refining and Coal Preparation				
制　气	Air Drying				
型煤加工损耗	Loss in Standardlized Coal Processing				
3.损失量	Loss				
三、平衡差额	**Balance**				

注:根据第四次全国经济普查结果对2018及之前年度数据进行了修订。
Note:Based on the results of the fourth national economic census, the data of 2018 and previous years are revised.

6-6 全社会石油平衡表
Petroleum Balance Sheet for the Whole Society

单位:万吨 (10000 tons standardized coal)

项 目	Item	2016	2017	2018	2019
一、可供量	**Quantity Available**	**2526**	**2601**	**2707**	**2927**
生产量	Primary Energy Production	58	56	54	54
外省(区、市)调入量	Engery moblized from other Province	2645	2605	2670	2783
进口量	Import Volume			68	169
本省(区、市)调出量(-)	Engery moblized to other Province	7	16	14	31
出口量(-)	Output Volume		32	47	36
年初年末库存差额	Storage Balance Difference between the Beginning and the End of the Year	-170	-12	-26	-12
年初库存量	Storage Volume at the Beginning of the Year	41	211	223	248
年末库存量(-)	Storage Volume by the End of the Year	211	223	248	260
二、消费量	**Consumption**	**2526**	**2601**	**2707**	**2927**
消费量分组一	**Consumption Group 1.**	**2526**	**2601**	**2707**	**2927**
1.农、林、牧、渔业	Agriculture, Forestry, Animal Husbandary, Fishing	107	107	111	120
2.工 业	Industry	568	595	612	628
3.建筑业	Construction	174	177	182	195
4.交通运输、仓储和邮政业	Transport communication, Storage, Post Service	1117	1146	1159	1288
5.批发、零售业和住宿、餐饮业	Wholesale,Retail Sale, Hotel and Catering Industry	125	127	137	147
6.其 他	Others	114	106	145	159
7.生活消费	Living Consumption	322	343	360	388
消费量分组二	**Consumption Group 2.**	**2526**	**2601**	**2707**	**2927**
1.终端消费	Terminal Consumption	2477	2554	2676	2895
#工业	Industry	519	547	581	597
2.加工转换损失	Coal Used for Processing	49	47	31	31
火力发电损失	Thermal Power Generation	2	3	3	3
供热损失	Heating	3	4	4	5
炼油损耗	Loss in Oil Refining	44	40	24	24
制 气	Gas Making				
3.损失量	Loss				
三、平衡差额	**Balance**				

注:根据第四次全国经济普查结果对2018及之前年度数据进行了修订。
Note:Based on the results of the fourth national economic census, the data of 2018 and previous years are revised.

6-7 全社会电力平衡表
Electricity Balance Sheet for the Whole Society

单位:亿千瓦时 (100 million kw/h)

项 目	Item	2016	2017	2018	2019
一、可供量	**Quantity Available**	**1960**	**2021**	**2166**	**2323**
生产量	Production Capacity	2479	2606	2830	2958
火力发电	Thermal Power Generation	1017	1043	1239	1470
水力发电、核发电、其它发电	Hydroelectricity Generation, Nuclearpower Generation, and others	1463	1563	1591	1488
外省(区、市)调入量	Engery moblized from other Province	297	282	204	205
进口量	Import Volume				
本省(区、市)调出量(-)	Engery moblized to other Province	815	868	867	840
出口量(-)	Output Volume				
二、消费量	**Consumption**	**1960**	**2021**	**2166**	**2323**
消费量分组一	**Consumption Group 1.**	**1960**	**2021**	**2166**	**2323**
1.农、林、牧、渔业	Agriculture, Forestry, Animal Husbandary, Fishing	30	30	33	40
2.工 业	Industry	1312	1321	1349	1421
3.建筑业	Construction	29	32	37	40
4.交通运输、仓储和邮政业	Transport communication, Storage, Post Service	47	54	62	69
5.批发、零售业和住宿、餐饮业	Wholesale,Retail Sale, Hotel and Catering Industry	93	98	110	115
6.其 他	Others	135	149	180	202
7.生活消费	Living Consumption	315	338	395	436
消费量分组二	**Consumption Group 2.**	**1960**	**2021**	**2166**	**2323**
1.终端消费	Terminal Consumption	1851	1907	2040	2194
#工业	Industry	1203	1206	1223	1291
2.输配电损失量	Distribution Loss	109	114	126	129
三、平衡差额	**Balance**				

注:根据第四次全国经济普查结果对2018及之前年度数据进行了修订。
Note:Based on the results of the fourth national economic census, the data of 2018 and previous years are revised.

6-8 分市州单位GDP能耗降低率
Reduction Rate of Energy Consumption per Unit GDP by Cities and Prefectures

地 区	Regions	2016年单位GDP能耗比2015年降低 (±%) 2016year Unit GDP energy consumption lower than in 2015	2017年单位GDP能耗比2016年降低 (±%) 2017year Unit GDP energy consumption lower than in 2016	2018年单位GDP能耗比2017年降低 (±%) 2018year Unit GDP energy consumption lower than in 2017	2019年单位GDP能耗比2018年降低 (±%) 2019year Unit GDP energy consumption lower than in 2018
全 省	**Total**	**-5.02**	**-5.62**	**-4.40**	**-3.41**
武汉市	Wuhan	-4.64	-4.85	-4.88	-3.31
黄石市	Huangshi	-6.48	-4.97	-3.77	-2.48
十堰市	Shiyan	-7.29	-7.07	-6.45	-4.26
宜昌市	Yichang	-7.19	-4.77	-4.52	-4.25
襄阳市	Xiangyang	-4.75	-5.20	-4.71	-4.80
鄂州市	Ezhou	-4.32	-8.05	-4.89	-4.54
荆门市	Jingmen	-5.66	-4.35	-5.20	-3.22
孝感市	Xiaogan	-4.80	-5.06	-5.73	-1.20
荆州市	Jingzhou	-4.07	-4.67	-3.06	-6.86
黄冈市	Huanggang	-4.54	-5.62	-4.06	-0.79
咸宁市	Xianning	5.39	0.98	-3.55	-3.70
随州市	Suizhou	-4.24	-4.28	6.44	-3.09
恩施州	Enshi	-3.38	-4.13	-2.58	-3.19
仙桃市	Xiantao	-4.91	-4.05	-4.57	-4.13
潜江市	Qianjiang	-7.52	-9.20	-5.03	-4.51
天门市	Tianmen	-4.84	-4.94	-4.94	-4.15
神农架	Shennongjia	-8.43	-2.55	-2.04	-0.32

注：表中数据根据第四次全国经济普查结果修订核算。
Note:The data in the table are revised according to the results of the fourth national economic census.

主要统计指标解释

能源生产总量 指一定时期内,一次能源生产量的总和。该指标是观察能源生产水平、规模、构成和发展速度的总量指标。一次能源生产量包括原煤、原油、天然气、水电、核能及其他动力能(如风能、地热能等)发电量,不包括低热值燃料生产量、生物质能、太阳能等的利用和由一次能源加工转换而成的二次能源产量。

能源消费总量 指一定区域内(国家或地区)国民经济各行业和居民家庭在一定时期消费的各种能源的总和。能源消费总量分为三部分,即终端能源消费量、能源加工转换损失量和能源损失量。

(1)终端能源消费量:指一定时期内地区各行业和居民生活消费的各种能源在扣除了用于加工转换二次能源消费量和损失量以后的数量。

(2)能源加工转换损失量:指一定时期内地区投入加工转换的各种能源数量之和与产出各种能源产品之和的差额。该指标是观察能源在加工转换过程中损失量变化的指标。

(3)能源损失量:指一定时期内,能源在输送、分配、储存过程中发生的损失和由客观原因造成的各种损失量,不包括各种气体能源放空、放散量。

单位国内生产总值能耗 指一定时期内,一个国家或地区每生产一个单位的国内生产总值所消耗的能源。计算公式为:

$$单位国内生产总值能耗=\frac{能源消费总量}{国内生产总值}$$

Explanatory Notes on Main Statistical Indicators

Total Energy Production refers to the total production of primary energy by all energy producing enterprises in a given period of time. It is a comprehensive indicator to show the capacity, scale, composition and development of energy production. The production of primary energy includes that of coal, crude oil, natural gas, hydro–power and electricity generated by nuclear energy and other means such as wind power and geothermal power. However, it excludes the production of fuels of low calorific value, bio–energy, solar energy and the secondary energy converted from the primary energy.

Total Domestic Energy Consumption refers to the total consumption of energy of various kinds by material production sectors, non material production sectors and households in a given period of time. It is a comprehensive indicator to show the scale, composition and development of energy consumption. The total energy consumption includes that of coal, crude oil and their products, natural gas and electricity, However, it excludes the consumption of fuel of low calorific value, bio–energy and solar energy. Total domestic energy consumption can be divided into three parts: final energy consumption, loss during the process of energy conversion, and energy loss.

(1)Final Energy Consumption: It refers to the total energy consumption by material production sectors, non material production sectors and households in a given period of time, but excludes the consumption in conversion of the primary energy into the secondary energy and the loss in the process of energy conversion.

(2)Loss During the Process of Energy Conversion: It refers to the total input of various kinds of energy for conversion, minus the total output of various kinds of energy in a given period of time. It is an indicator to show the loss that occurs during the process of energy conversion.

(3)Energy Loss: It refers to the total of the loss of energy during the course of energy transport, distribution and storage and the loss caused by any objective reason in a given period of time. The loss of various kinds of gas due to gas discharges and stocktaking is excluded.

Energy Consumption per Unit of GDP refers to the energy consumption per unit of gross domestic production in a country or the gross region production in a region in the same reference period. The formula is:

Energy Consumption per Unit of GDP = Total Energy Consumption / Gross Domestic Production

7 财政和金融

Government Finance and Banking

资料整理人员：金　花

财政和金融

GOVERNMENT FINANCE AND BANKING

2019

地方一般公共预算收入	Local Public Financial Revenue(100 million yuan)	3388.57 (亿元)
地方一般公共预算支出	Local Public Financial Expenditure(100 million yuan)	7970.21 (亿元)
金融机构(含外资)人民币存款年末余额	Balance of RMB Deposits of Financial Organizations (including Foreign Funded Enterprises) By the End of the year(100 million yuan)	59747.70 (亿元)
#住户存款	#People's Savings Deposit	29804.55 (亿元)
金融机构(含外资)人民币贷款年末余额	Balance of RMB Loans of Financial Organizations (including Foreign Funded Enterprises) By the End of the year(100 million yuan)	50663.96 (亿元)

一般公共预算收入与一般公共预算支出(亿元)

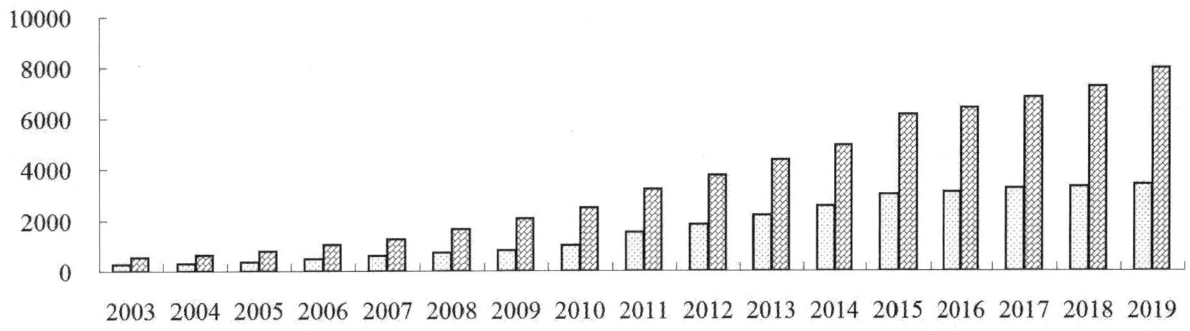

一般公共预算收入与一般公共预算支出(亿元)
Local Budgetary Revenue and Expenditure(100 million yuan)

年份(Year)	2003	2004	2005	2006	2007	2008	2009	2010	2011	2012	2013	2014	2015	2016	2017	2018	2019
一般公共预算收入 (Local Public Financial Revenue)	260	311	376	476	590	711	815	1011	1527	1823	2191	2567	3006	3102	3248	3307.08	3388.57
一般公共预算支出 (Local Public Financial Expenditure)	540	646	779	1047	1274	1650	2091	2501	3215	3760	4372	4934	6133	6423	6832	7258.27	7970.21

7-1 历年地方财政收支额及指数
Amount and Indices of Local Financial Revenue and Expenditure over the Years

单位:亿元 (100 million yuan)

年份 Year	财政总收入 Total fiscal revenue	地方一般公共预算收入 Local Public Financial Revenue	地方一般公共预算支出 Local Public Financial Expenditure	指数(上年=100) Index (previous year=100)	
				收入 Revenue	支出 Expenditure
1952	3.81	3.81	1.96	100.0	100.0
1957	6.27	6.27	3.55	109.8	96.7
1965	11.26	11.26	6.85	97.4	105.2
1970	15.20	15.20	15.73	170.6	158.1
1975	24.05	24.05	17.52	139.5	103.9
1978	31.38	31.38	29.98	149.0	148.6
1980	34.01	34.01	26.53	107.6	94.5
1985	50.26	50.26	43.60	119.3	137.5
1990	77.85	77.85	84.82	100.8	106.1
1995	180.57	99.69	162.43	128.7	118.4
1996	216.68	124.51	197.44	124.9	121.6
1997	246.35	139.89	223.70	112.4	113.3
1998	284.44	168.95	280.12	120.8	125.2
1999	314.91	194.44	336.46	115.1	120.1
2000	343.98	214.35	368.77	110.2	109.6
2001	374.15	231.94	484.40	108.2	131.4
2002	435.50	243.44	511.39	105.0	105.6
2003	483.90	259.76	540.44	106.7	105.7
2004	589.65	310.45	646.29	119.5	119.6
2005	727.61	375.52	778.72	121.0	120.5
2006	901.17	476.08	1047.00	126.8	134.5
2007	1115.47	590.36	1274.27	124.0	121.7
2008	1338.75	710.85	1650.28	120.4	129.5
2009	1541.55	814.87	2090.92	114.6	126.7
2010	1918.94	1011.23	2501.40	124.1	119.7
2011	2639.81	1526.91	3214.74	151.0	128.5
2012	3115.63	1823.05	3759.79	119.4	117.0
2013	3566.89	2191.22	4371.65	120.2	116.3
2014	4096.00	2566.90	4934.15	117.1	112.9
2015	4705.00	3005.53	6132.84	117.1	124.3
2016	4974.00	3102.06	6422.98	107.3	104.7
2017	5441.42	3248.44	6831.74	108.4	105.9
2018	5684.85	3307.08	7258.27	101.8	106.2
2019	5787.04	3388.57	7970.21	102.5	109.8

7-2 财政收支
Financial Revenue and Expenditure

单位:亿元 (100 million yuan)

指标	Item	2016	2017	2018	2019
地方一般公共预算收入	**Local Public Financial Revenue**	**3102.06**	**3248.44**	**3307.08**	**3388.57**
#税收收入	Revenue	2122.93	2247.60	2463.52	2530.82
#增值税	#Taxes on Value Added	563.33	493.75	937.57	975.87
营业税	Run Taxes	374.23	366.92		
企业所得税	Enterprise Income Taxes	299.12	349.40	394.37	407.05
个人所得税	Individual Income Taxes	92.98	121.94	135.87	98.23
城市维护建设税	Taxes on City Maintenance and Construction	143.48	162.73	181.87	179.97
房产税	Real Estate Taxews	59.70	82.67	89.31	100.67
耕地占用税	Taxes on Use of Cultivated Land	115.60	106.37	105.47	98.71
地方一般公共预算支出	**Local Public Financial Expenditure**	**6422.98**	**6831.74**	**7258.27**	**7970.21**
1.一般公共服务	General Public Service	639.60	726.84	739.21	795.05
2.外交	Foreign Affairs				
3.国防	National Defence	3.55		4.61	5.83
4.公共安全	Public Security	352.73	402.14	428.99	452.92
5.教育	Education	1047.37	1114.57	1065.64	1147.1
6.科学技术	Science and Technology	190.11	236.37	268.49	319.28
7.文化体育与传媒	Culture, Sports and Media	96.61	92.32	113.15	148.53
8.社会保障和就业	Social Security and Employment	978.82	1109.41	1172.00	1267.01
9.医疗卫生与计划生育	Medical Care and family planning	588.90	633.91	575.74	601.82
10.节能环保	Environmental Protecction	145.64	151.27	211.30	282.13
11.城乡社区	Community Service in Urban and Rural Community	588.47	745.62	848.56	924.62
12.农林水	Water Affairs of Agriculture and Forestry	704.59	650.95	785.55	828.21
13.交通运输	Transportation	391.79	272.05	370.64	429.39
14.其他支出	Others	694.78	696.29	674.39	768.32

7-3 财政收入占地区生产总值的比重

Percentage of Local Financial Revenue to GDP

年份 Year	地方一般公共预算收入(亿元) Local Public Financial Revenue (100 million yuan)	地区生产总值(亿元) Gross Domestic Product (100 million yuan)	一般公共预算收入占地区生产总值的比重(%) Percentage of Local Financial Revenue to GDP (%)
1980	26.53	199.38	13.31
1985	43.50	396.26	10.98
1986	58.04	442.04	13.13
1987	60.98	517.77	11.78
1988	68.66	626.52	10.96
1989	79.07	717.08	11.03
1990	84.82	824.38	10.29
1991	95.09	913.38	10.41
1992	94.14	1088.39	8.65
1993	115.07	1325.83	8.68
1994	77.46	1700.92	4.55
1995	99.69	2109.38	4.73
1996	124.51	2499.77	4.98
1997	139.89	2856.47	4.90
1998	168.95	3114.02	5.43
1999	194.44	3229.29	6.02
2000	214.35	3545.39	6.05
2001	231.94	3880.53	5.98
2002	243.44	4212.82	5.78
2003	259.76	4757.45	5.46
2004	310.45	5664.15	5.48
2005	375.52	6631.65	5.66
2006	476.08	7670.83	6.21
2007	590.36	9396.62	6.28
2008	710.85	11413.87	6.23
2009	814.87	13082.03	6.23
2010	1011.23	16114.59	6.28
2011	1526.91	19815.57	7.71
2012	1823.05	22479.66	8.11
2013	2191.22	25064.92	8.74
2014	2566.90	27693.04	9.27
2015	3005.53	29882.83	10.06
2016	3102.06	32665.38	9.50
2017	3248.44	35478.09	9.16
2018	3307.08	39366.55	8.40
2019	3388.57	45828.31	7.40

7-4 市州一般公共预算收入
Local Public Financial Revenue of Cities and Prefecture

单位:亿元 (100 million yuan)

市州	Municipalities	2005	2009	2010	2011	2012	2013	2014	2015	2016	2017	2018	2019
全　省	**The Total**	**375.52**	**814.87**	**1011.23**	**1526.91**	**1823.05**	**2191.22**	**2566.90**	**3005.53**	**3102.06**	**3248.44**	**3307.08**	**3388.57**
省　级	Provinial	94.59	184.06	206.78	188.67	130.07	126.27	133.16	155.96	169.23	231.33	144.27	143.95
武汉市	Wuhan	138.82	316.07	390.19	673.26	828.58	978.52	1101.02	1245.63	1322.10	1402.93	1528.70	1564.12
黄石市	Huangshi	11.96	26.03	34.10	53.84	65.64	78.36	89.38	100.53	105.47	111.09	117.02	119.55
十堰市	Shiyan	11.37	25.76	43.77	66.71	76.93	73.53	85.77	93.38	100.27	107.66	113.30	119.96
荆州市	Jingzhou	12.05	22.36	27.60	44.33	56.76	71.95	88.17	103.95	115.45	122.50	134.31	139.42
宜昌市	Yichang	22.53	54.94	70.24	113.98	153.25	206.31	271.51	339.10	300.04	242.08	237.24	240.79
襄阳市	Xiangyang	18.40	37.02	51.01	97.41	139.85	191.53	249.24	339.10	320.70	314.91	295.52	300.24
鄂州市	Ezhou	4.93	13.02	15.66	26.31	33.02	38.43	42.74	47.17	52.91	58.33	57.93	60.05
荆门市	Jingmen	9.34	18.14	23.25	39.39	50.69	59.84	69.82	80.43	91.73	101.25	105.76	110.48
孝感市	Xiaogan	10.78	26.97	34.20	51.58	69.50	89.05	107.22	122.77	129.23	131.95	130.19	135.53
黄冈市	Huanggang	13.14	32.17	38.98	51.61	62.92	79.98	96.04	112.82	119.52	133.33	139.24	141.40
咸宁市	Xianning	7.43	18.14	23.34	35.56	45.82	58.71	70.76	80.12	83.34	87.70	91.32	94.62
恩施自治州	Enshi	8.35	18.28	22.16	31.89	40.43	50.05	57.82	67.23	71.91	74.93	80.21	80.65
随州市	Suizhou	4.25	7.60	9.53	17.07	22.99	29.67	36.68	43.34	45.55	48.60	47.38	49.10
仙桃市	Xiantao	2.81	5.05	7.35	13.13	17.14	21.00	24.16	27.69	29.08	30.90	33.35	34.63
天门市	Tianmen	1.37	3.53	4.71	7.90	11.00	15.02	17.35	19.59	17.97	19.25	20.40	21.36
潜江市	Qianjiang	3.02	4.86	7.25	12.50	16.02	20.00	22.69	22.85	23.32	25.09	25.84	27.50
神农架林区	Shennongjia	0.42	0.87	1.10	1.77	2.44	3.00	3.37	3.86	4.25	4.63	5.10	5.22

7-5 市州一般公共预算支出
Local Public Financial Expenditure of Cities and Prefecture

单位:亿元 (100 million yuan)

市州	Municipalities	2005	2009	2010	2011	2012	2013	2014	2015	2016	2017	2018	2019
全　省	**The Total**	**778.70**	**2090.92**	**2501.40**	**3214.74**	**3759.79**	**4371.65**	**4934.15**	**6132.84**	**6422.98**	**6831.74**	**7258.27**	**7970.21**
省　级	Provinial	205.75	258.00	273.40	378.50	449.69	484.45	661.60	893.13	758.76	822.87	789.90	713.80
武汉市	Wuhan	176.88	503.64	583.55	765.04	885.55	1122.88	1175.10	1338.05	1524.68	1728.28	1929.54	2238.16
黄石市	Huangshi	23.47	80.85	102.56	128.69	140.43	150.79	152.97	225.94	224.10	224.27	246.50	265.37
十堰市	Shiyan	33.42	118.50	146.98	185.09	207.75	231.42	258.87	307.65	323.70	341.35	374.02	406.95
荆州市	Jingzhou	39.51	130.35	163.15	197.18	226.83	255.92	276.29	346.48	384.71	406.23	433.18	489.57
宜昌市	Yichang	47.63	156.50	196.51	241.13	297.45	364.44	439.92	537.53	531.97	493.77	503.58	596.99
襄阳市	Xiangyang	49.19	148.16	184.92	248.14	313.97	364.87	437.93	584.50	624.12	666.99	670.97	729.68
鄂州市	Ezhou	10.38	35.67	43.01	56.66	62.69	70.87	75.65	86.80	100.24	116.37	121.67	124.95
荆门市	Jingmen	24.58	81.66	95.46	125.34	142.20	158.79	178.96	225.90	246.09	267.52	269.31	293.68
孝感市	Xiaogan	32.50	109.79	133.58	172.61	201.79	227.90	253.18	290.38	356.87	360.06	382.52	408.84
黄冈市	Huanggang	44.40	155.09	188.13	225.54	278.92	305.16	344.66	401.03	439.87	454.48	482.59	535.34
咸宁市	Xianning	21.41	84.97	100.02	127.07	143.03	158.14	176.97	190.85	216.15	226.10	248.34	280.27
恩施自治州	Enshi	32.12	102.25	129.79	160.14	179.69	216.69	216.32	332.59	320.24	339.25	391.76	446.04
随州市	Suizhou	14.11	46.11	57.23	72.32	85.55	100.04	103.70	153.10	148.32	149.70	154.14	157.98
仙桃市	Xiantao	8.29	26.25	32.91	42.34	47.71	50.08	59.56	69.30	74.58	78.93	90.67	92.82
天门市	Tianmen	6.22	23.44	28.27	38.51	41.84	46.53	54.36	64.73	67.96	74.02	78.38	88.65
潜江市	Qianjiang	6.99	23.03	28.60	37.68	42.01	46.80	51.27	64.11	63.54	61.76	70.10	77.21
神农架林区	Shennongjia	1.86	6.66	13.33	12.76	12.69	15.88	16.84	20.78	17.08	19.76	21.10	23.92

7-6 金融机构(含外资)人民币存款年末余额
Balance of RMB Deposits in Financial Organizations (including Foreign Investment) at Year-end

单位:亿元 (100 million yuan)

指标	Item	2019
各项存款	**Deposits**	59747.70
(一)境内存款	**Domestic Deposits**	59709.67
1.住户存款	Household Deposits	29804.55
(1)活期存款	Demand Deposits	10376.55
(2)定期及其他存款	Regular and Other Deposits	19428.00
2.非金融企业存款	Non Financial Enterprise Deposits	17446.03
(1)活期存款	Demand Deposits	9323.33
(2)定期及其他存款	Regular and Other Deposits	8122.70
3.广义政府存款	General Government Deposits	10866.36
(1)财政性存款	Public Financial Deposits	1608.27
(2)机关团体存款	Bank Deposits	9258.08
4.非银行业金融机构存款	Non Banking Financial Institutions Deposits	1592.74
(二)境外存款	**Offshore Deposits**	38.03

7-7 金融机构(含外资)人民币贷款年末余额
Balance of RMB Loans in Financial Organizations (including Foreign Investment) at Year-end

单位:亿元 (100 million yuan)

指标	Item	2019
各项贷款	**Loans**	50663.96
(一)境内贷款	**Domestil Loans**	50659.47
1.住户贷款	Household Loans	16584.11
(1)短期贷款	Short-term Loans	2031.57
消费贷款	Consumer Loans	1060.97
经营贷款	Operating Loans	970.60
(2)中长期贷款	Medium-term and Long-term Loans	14552.54
消费贷款	Consumer Loans	12634.88
经营贷款	Operating Loans	1917.66
2.非金融企业及机关团体贷款	Non Financial Enterprise and Institution Loans	34075.24
(1)短期贷款	Short-term Loans	6981.19
(2)中长期贷款	Medium and Long Term Loans	23255.66
(3)票据融资	Bill Financing	2440.82
(4)融资租赁	Loans for Accomodation and Rent	1372.27
(5)各项垫款	Money Advanced Payment for Others	25.31
3.非银行业金融机构贷款	Non Banking Financial Institution Loans	0.12
(二)境外贷款	**Foreign Loans**	4.49

7-8 保险业务主要指标
Major Indicators of Insurance Business

项 目		Item		2016	2017	2018	2019
一、保险密度	(元/人)	Density of Insurance	(yuan/person)	1787.19	2281.89	2485.93	2916.43
二、保险深度	(%)	Depth of Insurance	(%)	3.26	3.69	3.74	3.77
三、保费收入	(亿元)	Premium	(100 million yuan)	1051.00	1346.77	1470.92	1728.57
(一)财产保险		Property Insurnce		263.22	308.53	351.97	397.85
1.财产险		Property Insurnce		13.65	14.37	16.41	17.83
2.机动车辆保险		Machine Driving Cars Insurnce		219.76	249.85	272.56	299.16
3.责任险		Responsibility Insurance		10.75	12.95	17.74	23.65
4.信用保证险		Credit Guarantee Insurance		5.27	12.59	22.97	29.44
5.其它		Others		13.79	18.77	22.29	27.77
(二)人身保险		Life Insurance		788.54	1038.24	1118.95	1330.72
1.人身意外伤害保险		Accident Insurance		30.13	35.45	39.90	43.73
团体保险		Group Insurance		11.69	12.59	13.33	14.95
个人保险		Individual Insurance		18.44	22.86	26.58	28.78
2.健康险		Healthy Insurance		128.41	172.72	238.28	312.03
团体保险		Group Insurance		30.75	39.47	55.02	74.64
个人保险		Individual Insurance		97.66	133.25	183.26	237.39
3.寿险		Personal Insurance		630.00	830.07	840.76	974.95
团体保险		Group Insurance		0.74	0.79	0.72	1.14
个人保险		Individual Insurance		629.27	829.28	840.04	973.81
四、各项赔款和给付	(亿元)	Claim and Payment	(100 million yuan)	372.36	406.47	466.67	512.26
(一)财产保险		Property Insurnce		141.80	153.30	182.35	210.43
1.财产险		Property Insurnce		8.81	6.24	6.64	7.97
2.机动车辆保险		Machine Driving Cars Insurnce		114.11	127.06	145.36	156.22
3.责任险		Responsibility Insurance		5.35	6.56	8.46	12.47
4.信用保证险		Credit Guarantee Insurance		2.80	2.42	6.03	14.07
5.其它		Others		10.73	11.02	15.86	19.71
(二)人身保险		Life Insurance		230.55	253.18	284.32	301.82
1.人身意外伤害保险		Accident Insurance		6.98	8.84	10.51	12.53
团体保险		Group Insurance		3.67	4.37	4.76	5.56
个人保险		Individual Insurance		3.31	4.46	5.76	6.97
2.健康险		Healthy Insurance		38.41	52.70	79.01	110.84
团体保险		Group Insurance		24.69	31.79	48.49	66.49
个人保险		Individual Insurance		13.72	20.91	30.52	44.35
3.寿险		Personal Insurance		185.16	191.64	194.80	178.45
团体保险		Group Insurance		8.27	8.77	7.90	5.40
个人保险		Individual Insurance		176.89	182.87	186.90	173.05

注:本表采用数据均为保险业新口径数据。
Note:Data from this table are based on the new standard.

主要统计指标解释

财政总收入 指地方一般预算收入与上划中央税收收入之和。

公共财政收入 是指各级政府为履行职能，按照国家法律、法规规定收取的纳入一般预算管理的各项税收及非税收入总和。主要包括：

(1)各项税收：包括国内增值税、国内消费税、进口货物增值税和消费税、出口货物退增值税和消费税、营业税、企业所得税、个人所得税、资源税、城市维护建设税、房产税、印花税、城镇土地使用税、土地增值税、车船税、船舶吨税、车辆购置税、关税、耕地占用税、契税、烟叶税等。

(2)非税收入：包括专项收入、行政事业性收费、罚没收入和其他收入。

公共财政支出 国家财政将筹集起来的资金进行分配使用，以满足经济建设和各项事业的需要。主要包括：

(1)一般公共服务：指政府提供基本公共管理与服务的支出，包括人大事务、政协事务、政府办公厅(室)及相关机构事务、发展与改革事务、统计信息事务、财政事务、税收事务、审计事务、海关事务、人力资源事务、纪检监察事务、人口与计划生育事务、商贸事务、知识产权事务、工商行政管理事务、国土资源事务、海洋管理事务、测绘事务、地震事务、气象事务、民族事务、宗教事务、港澳台侨事务、档案事务、共产党事务、民主党派事务及工商联事务、群众团体事务、彩票事务等。

(2)外交：指政府外交事务支出，包括外交行政管理、驻外机构、对外援助、国际组织、对外合作与交流、边界勘界联检等方面的支出。

(3)国防：指政府用于国防方面的支出，包括用于现役部队、预备役部队、民兵、国防科研事业、专项工程、国防动员等方面的支出。

(4)公共安全：指政府维护社会公共安全方面的支出，包括武装警察、公安、国家安全、检察、法院、司法行政、监狱、劳教、国家保密、缉私警察等。

(5)教育：指政府教育事务支出，包括教育行政管理、学前教育、小学教育、初中教育、普通高中教育、普通高等教育、初等职业教育、中专教育、技校教育、职业高中教育、高等职业教育、广播电视教育、留学生教育、特殊教育、干部继续教育、教育机关服务等。

(6)科学技术：指用于科学技术方面的支出，包括科学技术管理事务、基础研究、应用研究、技术研究与开发、科技条件与服务、社会科学、科学技术普及、科技交流与合作等。

(7)文化教育与传媒：指政府在文化、文物、体育、广播影视、新闻出版等方面的支出。

(8)社会保障和就业：指政府在社会保障与就业方面的支出，包括社会保障和就业管理事务、民政管理事务、财政对社会保险基金的补助、补充全国社会保障基金、行政事业单位离退休、企业改革补助、就业补助、抚恤、退役安置、社会福利、残疾人事业、城市居民最低生活保障、其他城镇社会救济、农村社会救济、自然灾害生活救助、红十字事务等。

(9)医疗卫生：指政府医疗卫生方面的支出，包括医疗卫生管理事务支出、医疗服务支出、医疗保障支出、疾病预防控制支出、卫生监督支出、妇幼保健支出、农村卫生支出等。

(10)节能环保：指政府环境保护支出，包括环境保护管理事务支出、环境监测与监察支出、污染治理支出、自然生态保护支出、天然林保护工程支出、退耕还林支出、风沙荒漠治理支出、退牧还草支出、已垦草原退耕还草、能源节约利用、污染减排、可再生能源和资源综合利用等支出。

(11)城乡社区事务：指政府城乡社区事务支出，包括城乡社区管理事务支出、城乡社区规划与管理支出、城乡社区公共设施支出、城乡社区住宅支出、城乡社区环境卫生支出、建设市场管理与监督支出等。

(12)农林水事务：指政府农林水事务支出，包括农业支出、林业支出、水利支出、扶贫支出、农业综合开发支出等。

(13)交通运输:指政府交通运输和邮政业方面的支出,包括公路运输支出、水路运输支出、铁路运输支出、民用航空运输支出、邮政业支出等。

信贷资金 指金融机构以信用方式积聚和分配的货币资金。金融机构信贷资金的来源有各项存款、金融债券发行、应付及暂收款、对国际金融机构负债、流通中货币、各项准备、所有者权益和其他项目等;信贷资金的运用有各项贷款、有价证券及投资、应收及预付款、委托投资、金银占款、外汇占款、库存现金、财政借款及在国际金融机构中的资产等。

存款 指企业、机关、团体或居民根据资金必须收回的原则,把货币资金存入银行或其他信贷机构保管并取得一定利息的一种信用活动形式。根据存款对象或性质的不同可划分为企业存款、财政存款、机关团体存款、基本建设存款、储蓄存款、农村存款、委托存款、其他存款等科目。它是银行信贷资金的主要来源。

贷款 指银行或其他信贷机构根据资金必须归还的原则,按一定利率,为企业、个人等提供资金的一种信用活动形式。我国银行贷款分为短期贷款、中期流动资金贷款、中长期贷款、信托贷款、融资租赁、委托贷款、票据融资、各项垫款等。

保险公司 在中国境内的、经过保险监督管理部门批准设立,并依法登记注册的各类商业保险公司。

保险金额 指保险人承担赔偿或者给付保险金责任的最高限额。

保费 指投保人为取得保险人在约定范围内所承担赔偿责任而支付给保险人的费用。

赔款 指保险人根据保险合同的规定,向被保险人支付的赔偿保险责任损失的金额。

给付 包括死伤医疗给付和满期给付。死伤医疗给付是指保险人根据人寿保险及长期健康保险合同的规定,因被保险人在保险期内发生保险责任范围内的保险事故支付给被保险人(或受益人)的金额。满期给付是指被保险人生存期满,保险人按人寿保险合同规定支付给被保险人的满期保险金额。

Explanatory Notes on Main Statistical Indicators

Total income refers to the local fiscal revenue and the general budget tax revenue and central planning. Public Financial revenue is to perform its functions in accordance with national laws and regulations collected into the general budget of the revenue management and non-tax revenues combined. Public Financial Expenditure refers to the distribution and use of the funds the government finances has risen, so as to meet the needs of economic construction and various causes. It includes the following main items:

(1) Expenditure for general public services: It refers to the spending on the basic public management and services which provided by governments, including the expense on affairs of People' s Congress, affairs of People' s Political Consultative Conference, affairs of government general office and relative institutions, affairs of development and reform, affairs of statistics, affairs of finance, affairs of taxation, affairs of audit, affairs of customs, affairs of human resources and social security, affairs of discipline inspection and supervision, affairs of population and family planning, affairs of commerce and trade, affairs of intellectual property, affairs of administration for industry and commerce, affairs of land and resources, affairs of oceanic administration, affairs of surveying and mapping, affairs of earthquake, ethnic affairs, religious affairs, affairs of Hong Kong, Macao, Taiwan, and Overseas Chinese, affairs of archives administration, affairs of Chinese Communist Party, affairs of democratic parties and federation of industry and commerce, affairs of mass organization, and affairs of lottery, etc.

(2) Expenditure for foreign affairs: It refers to the spending of government on foreign affairs, including the expense on administration of foreign affairs, missions overseas, external assistance, international organizations, foreign cooperation and communication, surveying and joint inspection on borderline, etc.

(3) Expenditure for national defence: It refers to the spending of government on national defence, including the expense on active force, reserve force, militia, scientific research on national defence, special projects, mobilization of national defence, etc.

(4) Expenditure for public security: It refers to the spending of government on maintaining social and public security, including the expense on armed police force, public security, state security, prosecution, courts, justice, prison, labour education and rehabilitation, protection of state secrecy, anti-smuggling police, etc.

(5) Expenditure for education: It refers to the spending of government on education, including the expense on the administration of education, pre-primary education, primary education, secondary education, high school education, regular higher education, primary vocational education, secondary vocational education, technical school education, vocational high school education and higher vocational education, radio and television education, student abroad education, special education, on the job training of cadres, education authorities services, etc.

(6) Expenditure for science and technology: It refers to the spending of government on science and technology (S&T), including the expense on the administration of S&T, basic research, applied research, research and development, conditions and services of S&T, popularization of social science, science and technology, exchanges and cooperation of S&T, etc.

(7) Expenditure for culture, sport and media: It refers to the spending of government on culture, cultural heritage, sports, radio, film, television, press and publication, etc.

(8) Expenditure for social safety net and employment effort: It refers to the spending of government on social safety net and employment, including the expense on administration of social safety net and employment, civil affairs, budgetary subsidy on the social insurance funds, subsidy on National Social Security Fund, retirees of administrative units and institutions, subsidy on enterprise reform, subsidy on employment effort, pension, placement of ex-serviceman, social welfare, the handicapped undertakings, the system of cost of living allowances for urban residents, other urban social relief, rural social relief, living relief of natural disasters, affairs of Red Cross Society, etc.

(9) Expenditure for medical and health care: It refers to the spending of government on medical and health care, including the expense on administration of medical and health care, medical services, health care, disease prevention and control, health inspection and supervision, women and children's health, rural health care, etc.

(10) Expenditure for environment protection: It refers to the spending of government on environment protection, including the expense on administration of environment protection, environment monitoring and supervision, pollution control, natural ecology protection, project of virgin forests protection, reforesting farmland, controlling the sources of dust storms, returning pastureland to grassland, returning pastureland to grassland, returning cultivated land to grassland, energy conservation, emissions reduction, comprehensive utilization of renewable energy and resources, etc.

(11) Expenditure for urban and rural community affairs: It refers to the spending of government on urban and rural community affairs, including the expense on administration of urban and rural community, planning and management of urban and rural community, public facilities of urban and rural community, housing of urban and rural community, sanitation of urban and rural community, management and supervision on the construction market, etc.

(12) Expenditure for agriculture, forestry and water conservancy: It refers to the spending of government on agriculture, forestry and water conservancy, including the expense on agriculture, forestry, water conservancy, poverty alleviation, comprehensive agricultural development, etc.

(13) Expenditure for transportation: It refers to the spending of government on transportation and postal services, including the expense on road transportation, waterway transportation, railway transportation, civil aviation transportation, and postal services.

Credit Funds refer to the funds issued as loans by banking institutions. The sources of credit funds of the banking institutions included deposits, issue of financial bonds, account-payable and temporary gathering, liabilities to international financial institutions, currency in circulation, various reserves, owners' rights and interests and other items. The credit funds can be used in forms of loans, securities and investment, account receivable and advance payment, entrusted investment, gold, foreign exchange, cash on hand, government debt and assets in the international financial institutions.

Deposit is a form of credit by which enterprises, institutions, organizations or households can put money into banks and other credit institutions for safekeeping and interest earning under the principle of free withdrawal. According to different depositors, deposits are divided into enterprise deposits, treasury deposits, deposits of government agencies and organizations, capital construction deposits, savings deposits, rural saving deposits, entrusted deposits and other deposits. Deposits are major sources of the credit funds of banks.

Loan is a form of credit by which banks and other credit institutions provide funds at certain interest rate to enterprises and individuals in the light of the principle of unconditional repayment. Loans from Chinese banks include circulating capital loans, fixed assets loans, loans to urban and rural individuals engaged in industrial and commercial business and agricultural loans.

Insurance Companies refer to commercial insurance companies of various forms registered by law and established in China with the approval of insurance regulatory agencies.

Amount Insured refers to the maximum that the insurant will get for the claim of the case insured.

Premium is the fee paid by the insurant to the insurer to obtain the obligation of compensation from the insurance within the agreed terms.

Settled Claim is the compensation paid by the insurer to the insurant in accordance with the insurance contract.

Payment includes payment for death, injury or medical treatment and mature payment. Payment for death, injury or medical treatment refers to the money paid to the insurant (or the beneficiary) in accordance with the life or health insurance contract when the insurant encounters accidents within the insured period covered in the contract. Mature payment refers to the mature payment to the insurant in accordance with the life insurance contract at the end of the insured period.

8 价　格

Price

资料整理人员：阳　夏　熊承煦　肖　强　潘　路

8-1 物价总指数(2019)
General Price Indices (2019)

基 期	Base Period	商品零售价格总指数 General Rtail Price Index	居民消费价格总指数 General Consumption Price Index
以1950年价格为100	The Price of 1950 Equals 100	692.1	1123.5
以1952年价格为100	The Price of 1952 Equals 100	613.8	988.4
以1957年价格为100	The Price of 1957 Equals 100	555.7	876.1
以1965年价格为100	The Price of 1965 Equals 100	497.9	770.9
以1970年价格为100	The Price of 1970 Equals 100	501.8	773.8
以1975年价格为100	The Price of 1975 Equals 100	502.5	766.2
以1978年价格为100	The Price of 1978 Equals 100	498.5	763.4
以1980年价格为100	The Price of 1980 Equals 100	470.0	697.0
以1985年价格为100	The Price of 1985 Equals 100	409.8	586.0
以1990年价格为100	The Price of 1990 Equals 100	254.2	369.5
以1995年价格为100	The Price of 1995 Equals 100	136.2	173.8
以2000年价格为100	The Price of 2000 Equals 100	138.7	161.8
以2005年价格为100	The Price of 2005 Equals 100	133.7	146.6
以2010年价格为100	The Price of 2010 Equals 100	117.5	126.4
以2015年价格为100	The Price of 2015 Equals 100	105.1	109.1
以上年价格为100	The Price of Last Year Equals 100	102.6	103.1

8-2 各市、县物价指数(2019)
General Price Indices of Cities and Counties (2019)

(上年=100) (preceding year = 100)

地 区	Region	居民消费价格指数 Consumer Price Index	商品零售价格指数 Retail Price Index	农业生产资料价格指数 Agricultural Production Material Price Index
湖北省	**Hubei**	**103.1**	**102.6**	**103.0**
武汉市	Wuhan	103.2	102.5	
黄石市	Huangshi	102.8	102.9	
十堰市	Shiyan	103.1	103.4	
竹山县	Zhushan	102.9	103.0	102.2
宜昌市	Yichang	102.7	102.7	
宜都市	Yidu	103.8	103.6	107.4
襄阳市	Xiangyang	102.4	102.3	
老河口市	Laohekou	103.2	103.3	108.2
鄂州市	Ezhou	102.7	101.7	
荆门市	Jingmen	103.4	103.0	
孝感市	Xiaogan	103.3	102.1	
大悟县	Dawu	102.6	102.5	101.4
荆州市	Jingzhou	103.2	101.6	
洪湖市	Honghu	103.3	102.8	102.7
黄冈市	Huanggang	103.5	102.9	
浠水县	Xishui	103.3	102.1	104.1
麻城市	Macheng	104.1	102.3	102.1
咸宁市	Xianning	102.7	102.2	
崇阳县	Chongyang	102.6	101.7	104.1
随州市	Suizhou	103.2	101.8	
恩施市	Enshi	103.1	101.9	
天门市	Tianmen	102.4	102.3	101.3

8-3 全省居民消费、商品零售价格分类指数(2019)
Provincial Consumer Price Indices and Retail Price Indices by Category (2019)

(上年=100) (preceding year=100)

类　　别	Item	全　省 Provincial Indices	城　市 Urban Indices	农　村 Rural Indices
居民消费价格总指数	**General Consumer Price Index**	**103.1**	**103.0**	**103.2**
*服务价格指数	Service Price Index	102.1	102.0	102.5
一、食品烟酒	Food Tobacco and Alcohol	107.0	106.9	107.2
二、衣着	Clothing	101.6	102.0	100.5
三、居住	Residence	101.9	101.7	102.4
四、生活用品及服务	Daily Necessities and Services	100.4	100.3	100.5
五、交通和通信	Transportation and Communication	99.3	99.7	98.5
六、教育文化和娱乐	Education,Culture and Recreation	102.5	102.7	102.0
七、医疗保健	Medicine	101.8	101.0	103.6
八、其他用品和服务	Other Supplies and Services	102.6	102.7	102.3
商品零售价格总指数	**General Price Index**	**102.6**	**102.6**	**102.6**
一、食品	Foods	108.7	108.6	109.2
二、饮料、烟酒	Beverage, Tobacco and Liquor	101.1	101.1	101.0
三、服装、鞋帽	Garments, Shoes and Hats	101.5	101.8	100.0
四、纺织品	Texiles	101.3	101.0	102.2
五、家用电器及音像器材	Household Electric Appliance and Stereo	97.3	97.0	98.8
六、文化办公用品	Stationery and Business Articles	98.2	97.9	100.4
七、日用品	Daily Use Articles	100.4	100.3	100.9
八、体育娱乐用品	Sports and Receation Articles	100.8	100.9	100.2
九、交通、通信用品	Transportation and Communication Articles	99.9	100.0	98.8
十、家具	Furniture	101.7	101.9	100.2
十一、化妆品	Cosmetics	101.9	102.0	101.4
十二、金银饰品	Gold and Silver Jewelery	107.7	108.0	105.4
十三、中西药品及医疗保健用品	Chinese Traditional Medicine, Western Medicines and Health Care Appliances	103.5	103.4	103.8
十四、书报杂志及电子出版物	Books, Newspaper, Magzines and Electronic Publications	106.8	106.9	106.2
十五、燃料	Fuels	98.2	98.3	97.8
十六、建筑材料及五金电料	Building and Decoration Materials	100.8	100.7	101.4
农业生产资料价格指数	**General Price Index of Means of Agricultural**	**103.0**		

8-4 工业生产者出厂价格指数
Producer Price Indices for Industrial Products

分 类	Group Name	上年=100 preceding year=100	1990年=100 1990=100	
		2019	2018	2019
总指数	**General Indices**	**100.2**	**291.06**	**291.64**
一、按轻重工业分	Grouped by Light Industry and Heavy Industry			
1.轻工业	Light Industry	100.1	234.35	234.56
以农产品为原料	Using Farm Products as Raw Material	100.3	266.14	266.99
以非农产品为原料	Using Non-Farm Products as Raw Material	99.0	159.52	157.88
2.重工业	Heavy Industry	100.3	347.32	348.35
采 掘	Mining and Quarrying	106.2	726.34	771.34
原 料	Raw Material	98.1	529.55	519.45
加 工	Processing	100.6	204.82	206.01
二、按两大部类分	Grouped by Two Sectors			
1.生产资料	Means of Production	99.9	338.34	337.95
采 掘	Mining and Quarrying	106.2	725.75	770.71
原 料	Raw Material	97.6	432.73	422.28
加 工	Processing	100.1	215.99	216.22
2.生活资料	Consumer Goods	101.0	210.84	212.94
食 品	Foods	101.2	282.03	285.36
衣 着	Clothing	100.1	237.15	237.49
一般日用品	Daily Use Articles	102.3	210.52	215.45
耐用消费品	Durable Consumer Goods	99.7	63.34	63.13

8-5 原材料、燃料、动力购进价格指数
Purchasing Price Indices for Raw Materials, Fuels and Power

分　类	Group Name	上年=100 preceding year=100	1990年=100 1990=100	
		2019	2018	2019
总指数	**General Index**	**99.3**	**429.65**	**426.64**
燃料、动力类	Fuel Powers	96.3	711.03	685.02
黑色金属材料类	Ferrous Metal	100.4	365.94	367.48
有色金属材料类	Non-ferrous Metal	97.9	357.04	349.42
化工原材料类	Chemical Materials	95.8	234.63	224.68
木材及纸浆类	Timber and Pulp	95.3	212.37	202.31
建筑材料及非金属矿类	Construction Materials and Non-Metal Mining Industry	104.6	350.58	366.61
其它工业原材料及半成品类	Other Industrial Raw Materials and Semi-Finished Products	100.2	186.88	187.25
农副产品类	Farm and Sideline Products	103.8	439.26	455.95
纺织原料类	Textile Raw Materials	99.1	214.61	212.66

8-6 固定资产投资价格指数
Price Indices for Investment in Fixed Assets

分类	Name of Group	上年=100 preceding year=100	1990年=100 1990=100
		2019	2019
总指数	**Total Indices**	**104.0**	**354.0**
建筑安装工程	Construction and Installation	104.4	422.1
设备、工器具	Equipment and Devices	100.5	181.1
其他费用	Others	105.7	415.9

主要统计指标解释

居民消费价格指数 是反映一定时期内城乡居民所购买的生活消费品价格和服务项目价格变动趋势和程度的相对数，是对城市居民消费价格指数和农村居民消费价格指数进行综合汇总计算的结果。该指数可以观察和分析消费品的零售价格和服务价格变动对城乡居民实际生活费支出的影响程度。

城市居民消费价格指数 是反映一定时期内城市居民家庭所购买的生活消费品价格和服务项目价格变动趋势和程度的相对数。该指数可以观察和分析消费品的零售价格和服务项目价格变动对城镇职工货币工资的影响，作为研究职工生活和确定工资政策的依据。

农村居民消费价格指数 是反映一定时期内农村居民家庭所购买的生活消费品价格和服务项目价格变动趋势和程度的相对数。该指数可以观察农村消费品的零售价格和服务项目价格变动对农村居民生活消费支出的影响，直接反映农民生活水平的实际变化情况，为分析和研究农村居民生活问题提供依据。

商品零售价格指数 是反映一定时期内城乡商品零售价格变动趋势和程度的相对数。商品零售价格的变动直接影响到城乡居民的生活支出和国家的财政收入，影响居民购买力和市场供需的平衡，影响到消费与积累的比例关系。因此，该指数可以从一个侧面对上述经济活动进行观察和分析。

农业生产资料价格指数 指反映一定时期内农业生产资料价格变动趋势和程度的相对数。农业生产资料价格指数分为小农具、饲料、产品畜、役畜、半机械化农具、机械化农具、化学肥料、农药及农药械、农机用油、其他农业生产资料十大类。其编制目的是了解农业生产中物质资料投入价格的变动状况，服务于国民经济核算。1994年以前，农业生产资料价格指数仅仅是商品零售价格指数的一个类别，此后，从商品零售价格指数中分离出来，单独编制。

农产品生产者价格指数 是反映一定时期内，农产品生产者出售农产品价格水平变动趋势及幅度的相对数。该指数可以客观反映全国农产品生产价格水平和结构变动情况，满足农业与国民经济核算需要。其中某代表品生产价格指数是通过对全部有出售该产品行为的调查单位的个体指数进行几何平均求得的，类价格指数是通过对其所属的类（或代表品）的价格指数进行加权平均求得的。季度累计价格指数的计算方法与分季指数的计算方法相同。

工业生产者出厂价格指数 是反映一定时期内全部工业产品出厂价格总水平的变动趋势和程度的相对数，包括工业企业售给本企业以外所有单位的各种产品和直接售给居民用于生活消费的产品。该指数可以观察出厂价格变动对工业总产值及增加值的影响。

工业生产者购进价格指数 是反映工业企业作为生产投入，而从物资交易市场和能源、原材料生产企业购买原材料、燃料和动力产品时，所支付的价格水平变动趋势和程度的统计指标，是扣除工业企业物质消耗成本中的价格变动影响的重要依据。

目前，我国编制的原材料、燃料和动力购进价格指数所调查的产品包括燃料动力、黑色金属、有色金属、化工、建材等九大类的近1800种产品。

固定资产投资价格指数 是反映一定时期内固定资产投资品及项目的价格变动趋势和程度的相对数。固定资产投资额是由建筑安装工程投资完成额、设备工器具购置投资完成额和其他费用投资完成额三部分组成的。编制固定资产投资价格指数应首先分别编制上述三部分投资的价格指数，然后采用加权算术平均法求出固定资产投资价格总指数。

该指数可以准确地反映固定资产投资中涉及的各类投资品和取费项目价格变动趋势和变动幅度，消除按现价计算的固定资产投资指标中的价格变动因素，真实地反映固定资产投资的规模、速度、结构和效益，为国家科学地制定、检查固定资产投资计划并提高宏观调控水平，为完善国民经济核算体系提供科学的、可靠的依据。

房地产价格指数 是反映一定时期内房地产价格变动趋势和程度的相对数，包括新建住宅销售价格指数、二手住宅销售价格指数。

Explanatory Notes on Main Statistical Indicators

Consumer Price Indices reflect the trend and degree of changes in prices of consumer goods and services purchased by urban and rural households during a given period. It can be used to observe and analyze the impact of price changes in consumer goods and services on wages (in monetary terms) of urban and rural staff and workers, and provide basis for policy–making concerning the living cost and wages of staff and workers.

Urban Consumer Price Indices reflect the trend and degree of changes in prices of consumer goods and services purchased by urban households during a given period. It can be used to observe the impact of change in retail prices of consumer goods and service prices in urban areas on the wage of urban workers' money. It provides basis for analysis and research on condition of life in urban areas.

Rural Consumer Price Indices reflect the trend and degree of changes in prices of consumer goods and services purchased by rural households during a given period. It can be used to observe the impact of change in retail prices of consumer goods and service prices in rural areas on living expenditure of rural households, and to show the changes in the living standard of peasants. It provides basis for analysis and research on condition of life in rural areas.

Retail Price Indices reflect the trend and degree of change in retail prices of commodities during a given period. The change in retail prices of commodities directly affect the living expenditure of urban and rural residents, government revenue, purchasing power of residents and the equilibrium of market supply and demand, and the ratio of consumption to accumulation. Therefore, the retail price indices are useful to analyze the changes of the above economic activities.

Price Indices of Means of Agricultural Production reflect the trend and degree of changes in prices of means of agricultural production during a given period. Price indices of means of agricultural production are composed of 10 categories including small farm tools, feeds, domestic animals for meat, draught domestic animals, semi–mechanized farm machinery, mechanized farm machinery, chemical fertilizers, pesticides and spraying machinery, fuels for farm machinery and other means of agricultural production. Compilation of these indices helps to understand the changes in prices of input into agricultural production and facilitate the compilation of national account statistics. Before 1994, price indices of means of agricultural production was a sub–category in the in the retail price indices of commodities, and it has been compiled separately since 1994.

Indices of Producers' Prices for Farm Products reflect the trend and degree of changes in producers' prices received by farmers when they sell farm products during a given period. These indices depict the change in the level and structure of producers' prices of farm products of the country and meet the needs of agriculture statistics and national account statistics. The producers' price index of a given product is calculated through geometrical mean of individual indices of all surveyed units who sell such product, and the indices of a product category is obtained through weighted mean of price indices of all products in the category. Method for calculating accumulative quarterly indices is the same as for calculating the distinctive quarterly indices.

Producer Price Indices for Industrial Producers reflect the trend and degree of changes in general ex–factory prices of all industrial products during a given period, including sales of industrial products by an industrial enterprise to all units outside the enterprise, as well as sales of consumer goods to residents. It can be used to analyze the impact of ex–factory prices on gross output value and value–added of the industrial sector.

Purchasing Price Indices for Industrial Producers reflect changes in the level and degree of prices paid by industrial enterprises when they purchase production input such as raw materials, fuels and power from the market or from other energy or raw materials producing enterprises. These indices provide important basis for measuring the material consumption of industrial enterprises after removing influence of price changes.

At present, close to 1,800 products in 9 categories, including fuels and power, ferrous metals, non-ferrous metals, chemicals, building materials, are covered in China for the survey to produce indices of purchasing prices of raw materials, fuels and power.

Price Indices of Investment in Fixed Assets reflect the trend and degree of changes in prices of investment goods and projects in fixed assets during a given period. The investment in fixed assets consists of three components, namely the investment in construction and installation, the investment in purchases of equipment and instrument, and the investment in other items. Price indices of investment in fixed assets are calculated as the weighted arithmetic mean of the price indices of the three components of investment in fixed assets.

Removing the factor of price change in the aggregates of investment at current prices, this indicator shows the changes in the prices of commodities and fees involved in the investment of fixed assets, and can be used to observe the actual size, growth, structure, and efficiency of investment in fixed assets and provides reliable and scientific data for government planning, management, decision-making, and further improving the current national accounting system.

Price Indices for Real Estate reflect the trend and degree of changes in prices of real estate during a given period, including sales price indices of new houses, sales price indices of second-hand housing.

9 居民生活

People's Livelihood

资料整理人员：盛　坤　孙胜男　程文懿

9-1 居民生活水平情况
People's Living Standard

项目	Item	单位	unit	2005	2010	2017	2018	2019
一、城乡就业	Employment							
每一农村劳动力负担人数	Average Person Supported by a Rural Laborer	人	person	1.34	1.27	1.40	1.46	1.46
每一城镇就业者负担人数	Average Person Supported by a Urban Laborer	人	person	1.96	2.01	1.89	1.87	1.88
城镇登记失业率	The Rate of Registered Unemployment	%	percentage	4.33	4.18	2.59	2.55	2.44
二、城乡居民收入	Revenue							
农村居民人均可支配收入	Net Income of Rural Residents Per Capita	元	yuan	3099.00	5832.00	13812.09	14977.82	16390.86
农村居民人均可支配收入指数(1990=100)	Indices of Net Income of Rural Residents Per Capita (1990=100)	%	percentage	461.80	869.24	2058.29	2232.01	2443.00
城镇居民人均可支配收入	Annual Disposable Income of Urban Residents	元	yuan	8786.00	16058.00	31889.42	34454.63	37601.36
城镇居民人均可支配收入指数(1990=100)	Indices of Net Annual Disposable Income of Urban Residents (1990=100)	%	percentage	615.80	1125.45	2233.80	2413.49	2635.35
国有职工平均工资	Average Wages of Staff and Workers in State-Owned Units	元	yuan	14774	35981	78423	85712	91665
三、城乡居民人平消费水平	Consumption Level							
农村居民	Rural Residents	元	yuan	2503	4758	13090	16296	
城镇居民	Urban Residents	元	yuan	8051	13576	28121	31018	
四、储蓄	Savings							
城乡居民人平储蓄存款余额	Balance of Saving Deposits of Rural and Urban Residents Per Capita	元	yuan	7929	17216	40744	44531	50329
五、平均每人居住面积								
城市(大、中)	Floor Area of Housing Per Capita Municipalities (Large and Medium-sized)	平方米	sq.m	29.90	33.20	45.07	44.97	46.31
农村	Rural Areas	平方米	sq.m	36.05	40.99	58.71	57.76	58.68
六、交通	Transportations							
城镇每百户拥有汽车	Cars Ouned Per 100	辆	set		5.53	25.18	36.34	37.33
七、文化	Culture							
每百人每天有报纸	Newspaper Owned Per 100 Persons Every Day	份	unit	8.89	8.70	4.94	4.16	3.41
每人每年有图书、杂志	Books and Magazines Owned Per Capita Anuually	册	unit	8.99	9.90	6.32	6.54	6.53
八、教育	Education							
学龄儿童入学率	Emrollment Ratio of School-Age Children	%	percentsge	99.65	99.96	100.00	100.00	100.00
每万人口有大学生数	Number of University Students Per 10000 Persons	人	person	167.91	226.58	237.01	242.68	252.75
九、卫生	Health Care							
每千人有医院病床数	Number of Hospital-Beds Owned By Per 1000 Person	张	unit	2.31	3.26	6.36	6.65	6.86
每千人有医生	Number of Doctors Owned By Per 1000 Persons	人	person	1.49	1.62	2.50	2.57	2.62

注：1.平均每人居住面积中，城市(大、中)从2002年起为建筑面积，以前年份为居住面积。

2.2014年起使用城乡一体化住户收支与生活状况调查数据，与之前的分城镇和农村住户调查的范围、方法、指标口径有所不同(此后相关表同)。

Notes: a)Of Average Housing Areas, it refers to Construction Area of Municipalities (large and medium-sized)areas.since 2002, before2002, it refers to living areas.

b)The integrated household income and expenditure survey has been used since 2014, including both urban and rural households. The coverage , methodology and definitionsused in the survey are different from those used for the separate urban and rural household survey prior to 2014.

9-2 居民消费水平
People's Consumption Level

年份 year	居民消费 (亿元) People's Censurption (100 million yuan)	农村居民 rural residernts	城镇居民 wrban residernts	居民消费水平 (元) level of consumption	农村居民 rural residernts	城镇居民 wrban residernts
1982	126.75	90.67	36.08	266	227	462
1983	141.49	101.17	40.32	293	251	502
1984	172.19	120.41	51.78	352	300	592
1985	203.23	129.78	73.45	411	328	738
1986	247.13	158.31	88.82	493	402	825
1987	271.22	172.47	98.75	533	434	891
1988	328.82	204.21	124.61	638	509	1092
1989	398.09	255.09	143.00	762	630	1218
1990	434.62	273.27	161.35	813	659	1341
1991	475.85	286.08	189.77	869	674	1541
1992	546.61	301.60	245.01	986	706	1926
1993	694.49	357.14	337.35	1236	831	2554
1994	845.15	413.40	431.75	1486	964	3086
1995	1095.97	504.12	591.85	1908	1183	3989
1996	1346.74	594.80	751.94	2323	1396	4892
1997	1438.12	614.90	823.22	2459	1441	5208
1998	1518.87	610.20	908.67	2579	1427	5632
1999	1507.12	558.43	948.69	2545	1302	5802
2000	1594.07	559.11	1034.96	2680	1302	6250
2001	1767.37	585.41	1181.96	2962	1365	7042
2002	1951.54	606.80	1344.74	3263	1418	7899
2003	2188.04	637.70	1550.34	3853	1926	6547
2004	2452.62	700.77	1751.85	4309	2134	7277
2005	2785.42	815.32	1970.10	4883	2503	8051
2006	3154.40	912.15	2242.25	5533	2832	9041
2007	3709.69	1051.82	2657.87	6513	3300	10593
2008	4225.38	1217.95	3007.43	7406	3864	11780
2009	4456.31	1277.72	3178.59	7791	4137	12080
2010	5136.78	1419.65	3717.13	8977	4758	13576
2011	6241.95	1597.69	4644.26	10873	5653	15935
2012	7085.46	1830.83	5254.63	12283	6705	17296
2013	8053.82	2064.74	5989.08	13912	7755	19156
2014	9124.48	2292.06	6832.42	15712	8788	21355
2015	10167.87	2434.73	7733.14	17429	9542	23561
2016	11379.23	2709.89	8669.34	19391	10860	25703
2017	12914.48	3185.97	9728.51	21913	13090	28121
2018	14832.97	3871.33	10961.64	25100	16296	31018

9-3 居民消费水平指数
Indices of People's Consumption Level

(1978年=100)

年份 year	居民消费 (%) People's Censurption (%)	农村居民 rural residernts	城镇居民 wrban residernts	居民消费水平 (%) level of consumption(%)	农村居民 rural residernts	城镇居民 wrban residernts
1982	156.2	169.2	132.3	149.0	164.2	111.5
1983	172.2	186.6	145.4	162.1	179.7	119.0
1984	196.6	205.4	181.4	183.3	198.7	136.6
1985	218.4	212.2	233.3	201.1	208.2	154.2
1986	253.2	247.7	267.4	229.7	244.3	163.5
1987	263.0	255.1	282.4	235.4	249.4	167.4
1988	268.8	257.1	295.6	237.8	248.6	170.4
1989	278.8	273.6	292.7	243.0	262.6	163.9
1990	290.5	281.2	312.9	247.6	263.3	170.8
1991	275.4	257.6	314.1	229.3	235.7	167.6
1992	281.7	254.0	339.6	231.8	230.5	175.3
1993	338.3	276.9	460.8	274.7	250.1	229.1
1994	380.3	292.4	553.4	304.9	264.6	259.6
1995	421.7	303.5	653.0	334.8	276.3	288.9
1996	474.9	340.2	737.9	373.6	310.0	315.2
1997	499.1	342.9	802.9	389.3	311.8	333.1
1998	549.5	354.6	927.3	425.5	321.8	377.1
1999	571.5	356.0	989.4	440.0	322.1	397.1
2000	599.5	361.0	1062.6	459.8	326.0	420.9
2001	661.3	377.2	1206.1	505.8	341.3	471.0
2002	738.6	391.9	1394.3	564.0	355.3	537.0
2003	807.3	393.9	1578.3	614.7	359.2	595.0
2004	868.7	405.3	1726.7	659.6	372.5	640.2
2005	963.4	458.4	1899.3	729.5	425.0	692.7
2006	1074.5	502.7	2133.2	814.1	471.3	767.5
2007	1191.6	556.8	2366.7	903.7	527.9	841.9
2008	1280.1	599.2	2540.8	969.7	574.4	888.2
2009	1353.2	630.8	2690.5	1022.0	616.9	913.1
2010	1508.6	675.9	3046.2	1138.5	684.1	993.5
2011	1723.1	710.1	3586.1	1295.7	758.7	1098.8
2012	1898.9	785.5	3946.9	1421.3	868.7	1160.3
2013	2107.4	862.9	4395.3	1572.0	979.0	1255.4
2014	2343.1	940.2	4920.1	1741.8	1088.6	1373.4
2015	2577.9	984.0	5499.9	1907.2	1164.9	1497.1
2016	2844.6	1075.3	6087.3	2092.2	1301.1	1612.3
2017	3166.0	1248.4	6683.9	2318.2	1549.7	1725.2
2018	3511.1	1418.2	7357.7	2563.9	1803.8	1859.8

9-4 城镇居民家庭基本情况

年份 Year	调查户数 (户) Number of Households Surveyed (household)	平均每户家庭人口 (人) Average Number of people Per Household (person)	平均每户就业人口 (人) Number of Employees Per Household (person)	每一就业者负担人数 (人) Average Persons Supported by a Labor (person)
1963	240	5.30	1.63	3.25
1964	299	5.36	1.61	3.33
1965	370	5.22	1.60	3.26
1980	571	4.20	2.32	1.81
1985	1658	3.84	2.15	1.79
1987	1900	3.73	2.12	1.76
1988	1950	3.61	2.07	1.74
1989	1990	3.52	2.05	1.72
1990	1990	3.47	2.04	1.70
1991	1990	3.45	2.04	1.69
1992	1940	3.36	2.02	1.66
1993	1890	3.29	1.98	1.66
1994	1330	3.23	1.95	1.66
1995	1330	3.22	1.92	1.68
1996	1390	3.24	1.95	1.66
1997	1790	3.23	1.89	1.71
1998	1640	3.19	1.90	1.68
1999	1540	3.15	1.86	1.69
2000	1540	3.14	1.81	1.73
2001	1540	3.10	1.77	1.75
2002	1600	3.07	1.64	1.87
2003	1600	3.06	1.68	1.82
2004	1700	3.03	1.65	1.83
2005	1800	2.98	1.52	1.96
2006	1800	2.96	1.55	1.91
2007	1850	2.95	1.59	1.86
2008	1900	2.96	1.50	1.97
2009	1900	2.94	1.48	1.99
2010	1900	2.93	1.46	2.01
2011	1900	2.90	1.47	1.97
2012	1900	2.89	1.48	1.95
2013	1718	2.77	1.53	1.81
2014	3060	2.85	1.59	1.79
2015	3073	2.85	1.53	1.86
2016	3053	2.86	1.52	1.88
2017	3031	2.84	1.51	1.89
2018	3489	3.00	1.60	1.87
2019	3409	3.01	1.60	1.88

注：1.2002年方法制度重新修订,部分指标有所变化:原"平均每人居住面积"改为"平均每人建筑总面积";原"平均每人实际收入"改为"平均每人总收入";原"平均每人实际支出"改为"平均每人总支出"。

2.2014年起使用城乡一体化住户收支与生活状况调查数据,与之前的分城镇和农村住户调查的范围、方法、指标口径有所不同(此后相关表同)。

3.2014年起为城镇常住居民人均可支配收入,与2014年以前不同。

Basic Conditions of Urban Households

平均每户就业面(%) Percentage of Employed Persons Per Household (%)	平均每人 Per Capita		平均每人 Per Capita			平均每人建筑面积(平方米) Average Living Floor Space Per Cappita (sq.m)
	总收入(元) Actual Income (yuan)	*可支配收入(元) Disposable Income (yuan)	总支出(元) Actual Expenditures (yuan)	消费性支出 Living Expenditures	*食品 Food	
30.75	238.1	238.1	237.2	218.4	133.9	
30.04	232.9	232.9	228.3	211.7	122.7	
30.65	224.3	224.3	218.8	204.4	118.0	3.3
55.24	413.7	413.7	394.2	369.3	210.6	5.1
55.99	713.3	704.2	693.1	644.2	324.5	7.9
56.84	960.6	951.8	919.1	836.1	443.2	8.4
57.34	1136.4	1128.1	1153.1	1058.8	538.9	8.9
58.24	1271.6	1262.6	1250.0	1130.7	607.0	9.1
58.79	1437.1	1427.2	1349.4	1220.3	652.4	9.8
59.13	1603.7	1592.9	1538.2	1380.2	717.4	9.6
60.12	1886.4	1874.2	1799.9	1577.7	799.0	9.9
60.18	2453.5	2438.7	2358.1	2097.6	941.5	10.5
60.37	3360.0	3346.0	3588.6	2733.1	1307.1	11.1
59.63	4031.9	4016.7	3977.3	3433.8	1680.6	11.9
60.19	4367.0	4350.2	4290.6	3713.5	1731.4	11.8
58.51	4693.8	4673.2	4549.7	3855.6	1773.6	12.8
59.56	4849.4	4826.4	4903.1	4074.4	1787.7	12.7
59.04	5234.5	5212.8	5333.8	4340.6	1783.4	13.2
57.64	5542.6	5524.5	5643.6	4644.5	1779.4	13.9
57.10	5888.7	5856.0	5774.8	4804.8	1799.4	15.2
53.42	7142.2	6789.0	7159.7	5608.9	2087.8	26.2
54.90	7745.8	7322.0	7551.1	5963.3	2279.6	26.3
54.46	8522.1	8022.8	8076.1	6398.5	2516.2	27.3
51.01	9395.1	8786.0	8582.8	6737.0	2625.4	29.9
52.36	10533.3	9803.0	9839.7	7397.0	2868.4	31.0
53.90	12421.8	11485.0	11476.7	8701.0	3456.0	32.3
50.68	14174.3	13153.0	12471.0	9478.0	3996.0	32.0
50.34	15698.0	14367.0	13868.0	10294.0	4160.5	32.8
49.83	17572.8	16058.4	15612.3	11451.0	4429.3	33.2
50.69	20193.3	18373.9	18123.4	13163.8	5363.7	35.5
51.21	22903.9	20839.6	20107.1	14496.0	5837.9	35.8
55.23	25180.5	22906.4	20419.5	15749.5	6259.2	38.8
55.73	27538.9	24852.3	23175.1	16681.4	3688.3	41.9
53.69	30057.4	27051.5	24798.4	18192.3	3897.6	43.2
53.23	32239.8	29385.8	27376.3	20040.0	4262.6	44.5
52.97	34972.3	31889.4	28784.6	21275.6	4244.0	45.1
52.32	38860.2	34454.6	35600.7	23995.9	3883.4	45.0
53.10	42207.9	37601.4	40544.4	26421.8	4154.2	46.3

Note: a)" Per Capita Living Space (sq.m)" in the above table was changed into "Per Capita Living Floor Space(sq.m)";"Per Capita Actual Income(yuan)"into; "Per Capita Actual Expenditures(yuan)" into "Per Capita Total Expenditures(yuan)';owing to the changes of items in the reversion of 2002 mearurement system.

b)The integrated household income and expenditure survey has been used since 2014, including both urban and rural households. The coverage , methodology and definitions used in the survey are different from those used for the separate urban and rural household survey prior to 2014.

c)The concept is Per Capita Disposable Income of Rural Permanent Residents since 2014 ,different from that before 2014.

9-5 城镇居民家庭收支情况(2019)

单位：元

项目	Item	总计 Total
调查户数(户)	Households Surveyed	3409
比重(%)	Ratio	100.00
平均每户家庭人口(人)	Average Number of Residents Per Household	3.01
平均每户离退休人口(人)	Average Number of Retirees Per Household	0.44
平均每一就业者负担人数(人)	Average Persons supported by a Urban Labor	1.88
平均每户就业面(%)	Average Employment Rate Per Household	53.10
平均每人总收入	Per Capita Total Income	42207.91
#可支配收入	Disposable Income	37601.36
平均每人借贷收入	Income of Loans Per Capita	2587.85
#提取储蓄存款	Savings Withdrawn	443.96
平均每人借贷支出	Expenditures of Loans Per Capita	4907.41
#存入储蓄款	Money Saved	30.52
平均每人总支出	Total Expenditure Per Capita	40544.41
#消费性支出	Consumption Expenditure	26421.77
一、食品烟酒	Food Cigarettes and Wine	7334.30
食品	Food	4154.21
谷物	Grain	753.77
薯类	Patato	40.06
豆类	Bean	60.52
食用油	Edible Oil	142.98
蔬菜和食用菌	Vegetable and Edible Fungi	545.92
肉类	Meat	873.70
禽类	Poultry	198.28
水产品	Aquatic Products	370.82
蛋类	Egg	103.66
奶类	Milk	261.08
干鲜瓜果类	Fruits and Processed Products	457.59
糖果糕点类	Sweet	143.19
其他食品	Others	202.63
烟酒	Cigarettes and Wine	927.13
饮料	Drink	118.35
饮食服务	Food Service	2134.61
二、衣着	Clothing	1886.72
衣类	Clothing	1606.12
鞋类	Shoes	280.60
三、居住	Residence	5929.36
租赁房房租	Rent	212.78
住房维修及管理	Management	901.80
水电燃料及其他	Water and Power	821.60
自有住房折算租金	Converted Rent of Zts Own	3993.18
四、生活用品及服务	Household Facilities Articles and Services	1868.99
家具及室内装饰品	Furniture	298.28
家用器具	Appliances	704.67
家用纺织品	Drygoods	110.36
家庭日用杂品	Commodity	357.01
个人用品	Personal Helongings	333.08
家庭服务	Households Service	65.59
五、交通通信	Transport and Communication	3283.90
交通	Transport	2579.35
通信	Communication	704.55
六、教育文化娱乐	Education Culture and Recreation	2966.97
教育	Education	1921.44
文化娱乐用品	Cultural Recreation Articals	374.10
文化娱乐服务	Cultural Recreation Services	671.43
七、医疗保健	Medicine and Medical Service	2471.35
医疗器具及药品	medical apparatus and instruments	597.22
医疗服务	Medical Service	1874.13
八、其他用品和服务	Miscellaneous Goods and Services	680.18
其他用品	Goods	369.10
其他服务	Services	311.08

注：2014年起城镇居民消费居住支出中自有住房折算租金指现住房为自有住房的住户为自身消费提供住房服务的折算价值，属于实物消费，不包括在现金消费支出中。

Income and Consumption Expenditure of Urban Households (2019)

(yuan)

低收入户 Low Income Households	中低收入户 Lower Middle Income Households	中等收入户 Middle Income Households	中高收入户 Upper Middle Income Households	高收入户 High Income Households
682	682	682	682	682
20.01	20.01	20.01	20.01	20.01
3.38	3.41	3.06	2.71	2.47
0.16	0.33	0.55	0.62	0.52
1.97	1.91	1.89	1.90	1.72
50.73	52.36	52.82	52.73	58.14
15037.17	24752.30	37329.48	50691.43	101600.00
9674.91	22223.62	32852.20	46955.71	93933.26
1129.42	397.69	972.04	502.79	12182.86
854.95	219.99	461.09	118.11	538.15
551.64	807.21	2467.36	2248.53	22980.55
6.42	9.91	69.87	13.63	62.94
23460.97	24243.84	34677.49	42109.42	93332.39
14886.38	18089.87	23399.04	31418.66	52562.61
4288.20	5409.56	7213.92	8800.55	12816.46
2675.02	3285.31	4195.01	5033.37	6405.65
372.12	430.11	596.70	768.81	1931.18
32.46	38.45	41.22	46.43	44.21
48.18	53.76	64.73	73.02	67.78
142.05	136.64	146.03	151.10	140.17
335.77	456.79	600.83	723.93	693.86
612.84	735.61	953.88	1075.89	1102.63
132.00	190.67	213.04	238.12	237.65
208.90	284.88	395.41	504.90	535.44
80.33	95.41	107.58	118.06	126.61
215.82	203.98	257.70	331.61	329.46
258.57	363.93	464.08	585.48	715.17
88.42	112.96	140.24	192.80	209.98
147.55	182.11	213.56	223.22	271.53
507.84	577.09	741.22	975.19	2193.72
73.64	94.06	111.14	134.70	205.98
1031.71	1453.11	2166.55	2657.29	4011.11
895.70	1348.15	1646.13	2182.21	4008.76
739.13	1110.33	1367.48	1839.21	3562.47
156.56	237.82	278.64	343.00	446.29
2860.72	3584.50	5230.98	8207.59	11847.54
117.04	149.54	206.54	297.82	347.63
461.57	380.63	803.09	1497.17	1705.20
488.61	589.38	794.32	927.63	1531.89
1793.50	2464.95	3427.03	5484.97	8262.83
752.18	1037.97	1133.13	1454.89	6023.41
161.42	319.40	251.42	296.61	521.24
96.03	91.91	124.16	171.80	3775.39
69.12	82.35	106.83	134.81	184.52
209.03	269.68	290.52	375.98	751.25
166.89	249.24	312.79	411.39	621.37
49.70	25.39	47.40	64.31	169.64
2181.59	2426.85	2403.41	3849.50	6519.27
1763.20	1884.81	1769.54	2971.13	5291.62
418.39	542.03	633.87	878.38	1227.66
1831.92	2329.11	2478.96	3188.14	5831.22
1463.69	1769.74	1654.34	1915.63	3124.10
215.36	256.66	269.20	442.30	818.85
152.87	302.71	555.42	830.21	1888.27
1820.25	1625.35	2831.57	2948.80	3584.39
293.52	372.51	779.20	721.96	968.68
1526.73	1252.84	2052.36	2226.84	2615.70
255.82	328.39	460.95	786.97	1931.56
130.65	156.51	257.10	472.31	1029.89
125.17	171.88	203.85	314.66	901.67

Note: Home ownership conversion in urban household residence consumption expenditure in 2014,refers to a resident who lives on a self-owned house now, provides housing service the conversion value for their own consumption. It belongs to material consumption, not included in cash consumption expenditure.

9-6 城镇居民家庭平均每百户年末耐用品拥有量(2019)

品名		Item		总平均 Total Average	低收入户 Low Income Households
摩托车	(辆)	Motorcycles	unit	37.18	62.20
助力车	(辆)	Auxiliary Drving Bikes	unit	40.29	45.97
家用汽车	(辆)	Cars for Household Use	unit	37.33	28.75
洗衣机	(台)	Washing Machins	unit	98.61	93.84
电冰箱	(台)	Refrigerators	unit	106.32	104.73
彩色电视机	(台)	Color TV Sets	unit	122.88	122.10
家用电脑	(台)	Computers	unit	72.37	51.89
照相机	(架)	Cameras	unit	15.75	4.71
中高档乐器	(件)	Medium and High-Grade Musical Instruments	unit	7.27	1.88
微波炉	(台)	Microwave Stove	unit	45.86	23.89
空调器	(台)	Air Conditioners	unit	168.39	125.20
热水器	(台)	Showers	unit	103.22	96.39
洗碗机	(台)	Dishwasher	unit	1.91	1.08
健身器材	(件)	Health Care Instruments	unit	6.69	2.79
固定电话	(部)	Fixed telephone	set	10.07	6.45
移动电话	(部)	Mobile Phones	set	261.31	270.02
空气净化器(含新风系统)	(台)		unit	5.52	1.12

Main Durable Goods Owned per 100 Urban Households (2019)

中低收入户 Lower Middle Income Households	中等收入户 Middle Income Households	中高收入户 Upper Middle Income Households	高收入户 High Income Households
48.16	37.01	20.96	17.62
48.91	42.62	36.36	27.60
32.79	34.00	39.18	51.89
99.38	99.66	99.94	100.25
106.74	107.29	105.16	107.67
120.96	116.84	122.85	131.65
64.01	69.56	81.42	94.94
6.86	10.84	20.07	36.24
4.13	6.44	9.12	14.79
36.62	48.29	54.14	66.32
149.59	160.15	185.36	221.57
105.11	103.61	101.99	108.99
1.69	1.02	1.68	4.06
6.13	4.74	8.65	11.13
7.35	11.42	13.24	11.90
279.64	264.52	252.13	240.23
2.27	4.10	6.61	13.48

9-7 城镇居民家庭房屋居住分布情况
Housing Distribution of Urban Households

分　组	Group	各组户数占总户数比重(%) Percentage of Household in Each Group of the Total Households				
		2015	2016	2017	2018	2019
总　计	Total	3073.0	3053.0	3031.0	3488.7	3409.4
一、房屋产权	Building Property Right					
租赁公房	Leased Pubilc Houses	4.6	3.4	3.4	2.8	2.1
租赁私房	Leased Private Houses	6.4	5.4	5.0	3.9	3.0
原有私房	Original Private Houses	28.9	30.7	30.4	41.1	43.2
房改私房	Private Houses	23.5	22.3	22.4	11.5	39.1
商品房	Commercial Houses	28.9	29.6	30.6	39.3	11.0
借用房	Borrowed	0.9	1.0	1.3	0.8	0.8
其他	Others	6.8	7.6	6.8	0.6	0.7
二、住宅样式	Housing Pattens					
单栋住宅	Sole-Unit Houses	34.3	36.0	36.3	35.5	37.0
四居室	Four-Room Houses	3.7	3.7	3.8	3.5	3.6
三居室	Three-Room Houses	26.5	24.7	24.4	29.4	30.0
二居室	Two-Room Houses	26.7	27.9	28.0	26.1	24.7
一居室	One-Room Houses	6.4	5.6	5.6	4.6	4.0
普通楼房	Ordinary Houses					
平房及其他	Bungalow and Others	2.5	2.1	1.9	0.8	0.7
三、用水情况	Waters					
独用自来水	Private Tap Water	95.0	95.8	95.6	92.3	92.6
公用自来水	Public Tap Water					
井、河水	Water from Rivers and Wells	4.1	3.7	3.7	5.1	5.1
其他	Others	0.9	0.6	0.6	2.6	2.3
四、卫生设备	Sanitary Faciities					
无卫生设备	Have not	2.6	1.6	1.3	1.7	
独立卫生设备	Independent Health Facilities	90.7	94.1	94.4	97.8	98.5
公用卫生设备	Public Health Facilities	6.7	4.3	4.2	0.5	1.5
五、取暖设备	Warming Facilities					
无取暖设备	Have not	37.3	37.5	36.8	36.3	34.4
空调设备	Air Conditioner					
暖　气	Heater					
其　他	Others	62.7	62.5	63.2	63.7	65.6
六、燃料使用情况	Fuel Material Usage Conditions					
煤	Coal	2.2	0.9	0.8	0.2	0.0
罐装液化石油气	LPG cylinders	30.5	46.5	44.4	31.7	33.6
管道液化石油气	LPG Pipeline	1.6	2.0	2.1	2.3	1.4
管道煤气	Piped Coal Gas	1.6	1.1	0.9	1.3	0.9
管道天然气	Gas pipeline	22.4	38.1	39.9	50.5	52.6
其　他	Others	41.8	11.4	11.9	14.0	11.4
七、通信设备使用情况	Telecommunication Facilities Usage Conditions					
1.每百户固定电话	Per 100 fixed telephone	33.9	28.7	27.1	13.2	10.1
2.每百户移动电话	Mobile Phones Per 100 Households	223.1	233.5	234.6	261.3	261.3

注：2014年起住宅样式为四居室的数据包含四居室及以上单元房的占比。
Note: The data refers to four bedroom and above for four bedroom units since 2014.

9-8 农民家庭基本情况
Basic Conditions of Rural Households

年份	调查户数 Number of Households Surveyed	常住人口(人) Permanent Residents (person)	平均每户常住人口(人) Average Permanent Residents Per Households (person)	平均每户整半劳动力(人) Average Full-Time and Part-Time Labors Per Household (person)	平均每个劳动力负担人口(人) Average Person Supported by Each Labor (person)
1982	948	5364	5.66	2.73	2.08
1983	1470	8267	5.62	2.99	1.88
1984	1510	8317	5.51	3.02	1.83
1985	3300	16473	5.07	2.98	1.71
1986	3300	16432	4.98	2.96	1.68
1987	3300	16195	4.91	2.94	1.67
1988	3300	15966	4.84	2.93	1.65
1989	3300	15567	4.72	2.86	1.65
1990	3300	15411	4.67	2.84	1.65
1991	3300	15094	4.57	2.66	1.72
1992	3300	14900	4.52	2.63	1.71
1993	3300	14651	4.44	2.65	1.67
1994	3300	14466	4.38	2.72	1.61
1995	3300	14447	4.38	2.77	1.58
1996	3300	14053	4.26	2.75	1.55
1997	3200	13453	4.2	2.64	1.60
1998	3200	13239	4.14	2.62	1.58
1999	3200	13082	4.09	2.63	1.55
2000	3300	13557	4.11	2.76	1.49
2001	3300	13490	4.09	2.75	1.49
2002	3300	13420	4.07	2.78	1.46
2003	3300	13385	4.06	2.86	1.42
2004	3300	13356	4.05	2.92	1.39
2005	3300	13228	4.01	2.99	1.34
2006	3300	13259	4.02	3.03	1.34
2007	3300	13186	4	3.06	1.30
2008	3300	13163	3.99	3.08	1.29
2009	3300	13151	3.99	3.12	1.28
2010	3300	13123	3.98	3.14	1.27
2011	3300	13120	3.98	3.12	1.27
2012	3300	13140	3.98	3.12	1.28
2013	2096	7921	3.78	2.88	1.31
2014	2522	7233	2.87	2.03	1.41
2015	2540	7309	2.88	2.04	1.41
2016	2549	7360	2.89	2.05	1.41
2017	2538	7287	2.87	2.06	1.40
2018	2140	6594	3.08	2.1	1.46
2019	2220	6838	3.08	2.12	1.46

注：1.2014年起使用城乡一体化住户收支与生活状况调查数据,与之前的分城镇和农村住户调查的范围、方法、指标口径有所不同(此后相关表同)。
2.2014年起农民人均纯收入改为农村常住居民人均可支配收入。

Note: a)The integrated household income and expenditure survey has been used since 2014 , including both urban and rural households. The coverage , methodology and definitions used in the survey are different from those used for the separate urban and rural household survey prior to 2014.(Related tables the same ever since).

b)Per Capita Income of Rural Households has been changed into Per Capita Disposable Income of Rural Permanent Residents since 2014.

9–8 续表 1 continued

年 份 year	平均每户经营耕地面积(亩) Space of Cultivation land Per Household (mu)	平均每户年末拥有生产性固定资产原值(元) Value of Production Fixed Assets Per Household (yuan)	平均每户年内新建购房屋面积(平方米) Floor Space of Rooms Newly Built Per Household (sq.m)	平均每人年末使用房屋面积(平方米) Lving Space Per Capita (sq.m)
1982	0.57	159.2	5.36	16.45
1983	8.95	389.97	5.65	18.04
1984	8.66	530.2	6.7	19.03
1985	7.6	557.86	8.24	21.18
1986	7.48	610.47	8.45	22.63
1987	7.31	672.87	7.79	23.5
1988	7.04	759.61	4.9	24.15
1989	6.95	819.53	5.5	25.1
1990	6.79	861.91	6.2	25.73
1991	6.58	1068.45	4.56	27.33
1992	6.47	1146.94	4.07	27.94
1993	6.36	1281.66	3.75	25.8
1994	6.69	1542.58	3.91	25.22
1995	6.73	1775.57	4.66	25.92
1996	6.82	2291.6	4.25	26.58
1997	6.56	2688.67	4.98	27.99
1998	6.08	2604.21	4.74	28.38
1999	6.08	2543.61	4.19	29.87
2000	5.93	2482.02	3.48	30.11
2001	5.94	2773.52	2.98	31.19
2002	6.01	2953.37	4.65	31.55
2003	6.03	2989.82	4.01	32.44
2004	6.15	3046.47	2.82	33.68
2005	6.15	4121.2	3.88	36.05
2006	6.12	4297.19	4.22	36.77
2007	6.41	4996	3.36	37.96
2008	6.36	5434.99	5.9	39.04
2009	6.51	6368.83	4.4	40.11
2010	6.73	7078.46	5.05	40.99
2011	6.44	9636.11	7.88	44.24
2012	6.8	10813.13	5.46	44.98
2013	7.08	13839.73	6.06	41.84
2014	6.97	12048.41	5.81	54.78
2015	7.9	12226.49	4.08	55.61
2016	8.24	12709.63	2.51	57.67
2017	8.1	13287.33	2.85	58.71
2018	7.3	17213.25	3.19	57.76
2019	7.3	16299.52		58.68

9–8 续表 2 continued

年 份	平均每户年末使用房屋价值(元) Value of Per Households Living Space (yuan)	平均每人总收入(元) Total Income Per Capita (yuan)	平均每人纯收入(元) Net Income Per Capita (yuan)	平均每人生活消费支出(元) Living Expenditures Per Capita (yuan)
1982	1261.51	311.51	286.07	226.96
1983	1688.93	405.14	299.24	252.47
1984	1786.54	525.86	392.29	305.03
1985	2068.78	569.74	421.24	334.63
1986	2319.44	605.67	445.13	373.53
1987	2514.22	638.64	460.66	408.69
1988	2751.40	710.47	497.84	450.62
1989	3095.15	820.70	571.84	540.13
1990	3545.50	957.01	670.80	607.58
1991	4661.58	936.57	626.92	615.40
1992	4885.77	1015.62	677.82	611.84
1993	5004.02	1135.77	783.18	722.09
1994	5887.81	1690.49	1170.06	1012.95
1995	6729.46	2184.20	1511.22	1245.10
1996	10050.26	2642.45	1863.62	1630.41
1997	11432.61	2913.16	2102.20	1660.13
1998	12966.45	2917.66	2172.24	1699.43
1999	13654.80	2871.62	2217.08	1572.90
2000	13717.28	3008.13	2268.50	1555.61
2001	16007.50	3124.10	2352.16	1649.18
2002	16581.94	3239.81	2444.06	1745.63
2003	19010.48	3378.80	2566.76	1801.63
2004	20254.50	3826.27	2890.01	2088.98
2005	24815.99	4221.81	3099.20	2430.19
2006	27772.00	4580.79	3419.35	2732.46
2007	31696.83	5365.78	3997.48	3090.00
2008	36250.27	6266.27	4656.38	3652.57
2009	41493.01	6663.13	5035.26	3725.40
2010	47606.56	7699.27	5832.27	4090.78
2011	61870.37	9387.20	6897.92	5010.74
2012	77338.15	10525.66	7851.71	5726.73
2013	101314.51	11896.06	8866.95	6279.52
2014	110492.00	14836.14	10849.06	8680.93
2015	125534.00	15819.16	11843.89	9803.15
2016	145244.08	16807.81	12724.97	10938.30
2017	148155.46	17927.34	13812.09	11632.51
2018	181945.74	20158.66	14977.82	13946.26
2019	191268.89	22524.84	16390.86	15328.02

9-9 农民家庭年人均纯收入(可支配收入)及构成

Annual Per Capita Net Income (Disposable Income) and Composition of Rural Households

单位：元 (yuan)

指标	Item	2005	2009	2010	2011	2012	2013	2014	2015	2016	2017	2018	2019
全年总收入	Total Revenue	4221.81	6663.13	7699.27	9387.20	10525.66	11896.06	14836.14	15819.16	16807.81	17927.34	20158.66	22524.84
全年纯收入	Annual Net Income	3099.20	5035.26	5832.27	6897.92	7851.71	8866.95	10849.06	11843.89	12724.97	13812.09	14977.82	16390.86
工资性收入	Money Wage	941.64	1900.54	2186.11	2703.05	3189.84	3648.20	3298.61	3682.91	4023.04	4389.58	4886.79	5352.90
家庭经营纯收入	House Business Revenue	2049.04	2828.53	3234.94	3731.34	4123.49	4616.55	5009.34	5281.41	5534.01	5963.95	6270.85	6807.69
转移性收入	Transfer Income	91.71	247.81	304.30	379.08	472.51	518.07	2415.66	2718.79	3009.32	3292.77	3634.24	4019.61
财产性收入	Property Income	16.81	58.37	106.92	84.45	65.87	84.13	125.44	160.78	158.60	165.79	185.94	210.66
比重(纯收入=100)	Ratio (net income = 100)												
工资性收入	Money Wage	30.38	37.74	37.48	39.19	40.63	41.14	30.40	31.10	31.62	31.78	32.63	32.66
家庭经营纯收入	House Business Revenue	66.12	56.17	55.47	54.09	52.52	52.06	46.17	44.59	43.49	43.18	41.87	41.53
转移性收入	Transfer Income	2.96	4.92	5.22	5.50	6.02	5.84	22.27	22.96	23.65	23.84	1.24	1.29
财产性收入	Property Income	0.54	1.16	1.83	1.22	0.84	0.95	1.16	1.35	1.25	1.20	24.26	24.52

注：2014年起为农村常住居民人均可支配收入、工资性收入、家庭经营净收入、财产净收入、转移净收入。

Note: It has been Per Capita Disposable Income of Rural Permanent Residents, Money Wage, House Business Revenue. Property Income, Transfer Income since 2014.

9-10 农民家庭年人均纯收入(可支配收入)分组

Annual Grouping of Per Capita Net Income (Disposable Income)of Rural Households

单位：户 (household)

指标	Item	2005	2007	2008	2009	2010	2011	2012	2013	2014	2015	2016	2017	2018	2019
调查户总计	Total Households Surveyed	3300	3300	3300	3300	3300	3300	3300	2096	2522	2540	2549	2538	2140	2220
2000元以下	Below 2000 yuan	710	508	414	411	257	233	155	48	70	69	70	59	80	68
2000–3000元	2000–3000 yuan	787	659	519	478	365	295	197	83	57	51	35	58	29	15
3000–4000元	3000–4000 yuan	684	660	559	492	419	313	289	127	118	85	71	61	67	46
4000–5000元	4000–5000 yuan	479	510	510	460	469	373	286	170	139	147	117	79	71	61
5000元以上	5000 yuan and Over	640	969	1298	1459	1790	2086	2373	1668						
5000–10000元	5000–10000 yuan									814	796	689	648	546	462
10000–15000元	10000–15000 yuan									661	612	621	589	518	499
15000–20000元	15000–20000 yuan									353	349	386	400	331	383
20000元以上	20000 yuan and Over									311	431	561	644	498	686

注：2014年起为农村常住居民人均可支配收入分组。

Note: It has been Rural Permanent Grouped by Per Capita Disposable Income since 2014.

9-11 农民家庭年人均经营总收入
Annual Per Capita Total Business Income of Rural Households

单位：元 (yuan)

指标	Item	2012	2013	2014	2015	2016	2017	2018	2019
家庭经营总收入	Total Income of Family Business	6718.36	7022.00	8699.22	8928.74	9242.06	9625.59	10927.48	12299.81
农业收入	Farming	4056.77	4049.41	4663.10	4927.80	4875.69	4887.51	4011.98	4346.83
林业收入	Forestry	88.49	140.80	272.35	292.41	345.81	271.17	99.46	105.77
牧业收入	Animal Husbandry	1044.46	1077.50	1610.39	1235.80	1199.91	1242.35	1694.16	1951.14
渔业收入	Fishery	423.50	403.93	476.41	696.02	654.65	846.48	1381.42	1642.34
工业收入	Industry	144.59	60.66	204.82	160.40	167.05	167.68	354.24	288.86
建筑业收入	Construction	177.49	307.83	188.27	110.67	261.24	359.50	546.40	900.20
交通运输邮电业收入	Transportation, Post Services	322.49	328.76	353.50	461.56	472.43	551.38	490.88	530.99
批零贸易餐饮业收入	Wholesales, Retail Sales and Catering	317.95	401.46	572.30	646.44	886.04	887.31	1864.94	2011.22
社会服务和文教卫生业收入	Social Services and Public Health Services	113.54	177.96	211.73	189.00	141.72	137.63	167.96	205.32
农林牧渔服务业收入	Agriculture and forestry services			133.44	171.08	189.94	222.58	254.81	262.25
其他家庭经营收入	Other Family Revenue	26.87	10.54	12.93	37.56	47.59	51.99	61.23	54.89

9-12 农民家庭年人均生产支出
Annual Per Capita Production Expenditures of Rural Households

单位：元 (yuan)

指标	Item	2011	2012	2013	2014	2015	2016	2017	2018	2019
一、家庭经营费用支出	Expenditures of Family Business	2199.08	2402.73	2408.72	3413.49	3366.25	3412.31	3349.56	4277.95	5134.74
农业生产支出	Agricultural Expenditures	1029.67	1076.28	1049.49	1329.35	1566.04	1535.20	1387.20	1105.56	1288.39
林业生产支出	Forestry Expenditures	16.65	16.33	19.52	27.68	23.91	126.05	25.67	13.86	31.88
牧业生产支出	Animal Husbandary Expenditures	593.09	693.65	753.88	1279.08	923.32	765.09	795.14	1222.16	1459.20
渔业生产支出	Fishery Expenditures	216.01	230.50	174.04	217.63	366.77	276.83	420.32	663.93	833.36
工业生产支出	Industrial Expenditures	54.66	84.17	28.31	78.83	57.14	81.29	54.87	150.34	171.19
建筑业支出	Construction Expenditures	61.78	54.28	120.30	158.47	43.86	143.14	218.87	110.29	313.12
交通运输邮电业支出	Expenditures of Transportation and Post Services	107.32	120.00	81.99	74.77	136.61	114.81	132.11	79.25	87.42
批零贸易餐饮业支出	Expenditures of Wholesales, Retail Sales and Catering	90.88	100.13	82.03	166.42	175.88	276.11	215.23	832.21	802.40
社会服务和文教卫生业支出	Expenditures of Social Services and Public Health Services	19.82	20.52	69.33	39.98	18.10	25.19	16.19	18.19	46.11
农林牧渔服务业支出	Agriculture and forestry services				36.77	44.08	60.89	74.14	67.38	85.44
其他家庭经营支出	Other Family Expenditures	9.22	6.85	2.19	4.51	10.54	7.70	9.82	14.78	16.24
二、购置住房、生产性固定资产支出	Purchase of Housing, the Productive Expenditure of Fixed Assets	231.28	240.00	315.23	876.97	1244.33	862.13	762.17	1098.59	1293.24
三、税费支出	Expenditures of Taxation	9.28	11.09							

9-13 农民家庭年人均生活消费支出
Annual Per Capita Living Consumption Expenditure of Rural Households

单位：元 (yuan)

指标	Item	2011	2012	2013	2014	2015	2016	2017	2018	2019
全年总支出	Total Annual Expenditures	7971.52	8923.73	9477.33	16775.27	18257.83	19372.81	19739.32	23946.03	26484.28
生活消费支出	Living Expenditures	5010.74	5726.73	6279.52	8680.93	9803.15	10938.30	11632.51	13946.26	15328.02
一、食品消费	Food Consumption	1954.62	2154.01	2308.45	2724.10	2952.69	3295.30	3332.38	3928.22	4163.70
主食	Grain	334.56	350.86	334.10	440.21	446.36	466.19	486.50	478.65	501.05
副食	Non-Staple Food	859.31	969.20	1037.53	1401.57	1539.65	1734.74	1663.16	1885.15	2004.27
其他食品	Others	480.38	542.32	514.98	691.15	744.25	828.79	862.39	947.36	1003.67
在外饮食	Travelling Catering Service	273.91	282.94	393.63	191.17	222.44	265.57	320.34	617.06	654.71
二、衣着消费	Clothing Consumption	272.12	316.41	347.67	495.73	549.14	568.71	626.40	783.07	825.71
三、居住消费	Residence Consumption	1086.86	1206.16	1415.73	1944.56	2150.27	2407.90	2512.27	2954.25	3277.95
住房	Housing	918.61	973.60	1013.20	1523.05	1693.72	1931.67	2047.55	2516.83	2750.42
电费	Electricity Fees	85.04	112.57	138.37	209.40	230.15	248.22	254.18	256.19	310.50
燃料	Fuel	55.28	91.16	197.33	115.15	116.80	107.37	113.77	104.71	122.61
四、家庭设备用品及服务	Familty facilities and Services	359.57	397.86	425.00	574.31	599.92	669.01	706.20	852.22	839.58
耐用消费品	Durable Consumer Goods	230.49	238.55	249.85	298.95	298.90	328.12	343.23	414.88	385.84
日用杂品	Daily Necessities	116.88	142.41	164.10	260.06	286.12	320.73	338.53	410.01	430.71
五、交通通讯消费	Transportation and Telecommunication Fees	414.36	496.10	605.95	816.43	1218.42	1381.37	1384.68	1933.05	2228.83
交通工具	Transportation	186.09	235.85	324.51	378.07	743.70	835.55	826.12	1310.21	1592.14
通讯工具	Telecommunication	33.04	39.84	45.85	76.43	89.87	94.07	116.12	136.61	118.35
交通、邮电服务费	Transport, Postal Services	195.23	220.41	235.48	361.94	384.85	451.76	442.44	486.24	518.35
六、教育文化娱乐	Culture, Education and Receation	341.87	394.63	407.42	1010.19	1118.15	1156.60	1330.67	1551.43	1807.64
文教娱乐用品	Cultural, Educational and Receational Articles	94.96	107.87	104.20	122.61	156.33	145.88	164.33	205.32	222.93
学杂费	School Fees	139.02	136.21	159.18	98.51	90.58	93.95	85.73	147.41	183.61
技术培训费	Technical Training	10.43	12.85	28.88	20.89	36.57	51.56	74.32	116.35	128.92
一揽子教育服务费	Education Service Charge				661.05	712.83	693.66	761.58	823.98	989.45
文体休闲娱乐费	Sports Recreation Fee	17.44	23.05	35.58	62.47	78.67	76.99	102.87	111.71	110.78
七、医疗保健消费	Medicine and Medical Services Fees	438.20	591.87	624.40	907.33	985.09	1213.47	1438.32	1588.03	1921.78
医疗保健用品	Health Care Supplies	102.19	117.28	127.71	200.10	225.14	269.73	303.46	382.47	375.22
医疗保健服务费	Health Care Service Fees	336.01	474.59	496.69	707.22	759.94	943.74	1134.86	1205.57	1546.56
八、其他商品和服务	Other Commdities and Services	143.14	169.68	144.90	208.28	229.48	245.94	301.59	355.99	262.83

9-14 农民家庭年人均现金收支
Annual Per Capita Cash Revenue and Expenditure of Rural Households

单位：元 (yuan)

指 标	Item	2012	2013	2014	2015	2016	2017	2018	2019
期内现金收入合计	Total Cash Income at Year-End	9337.04	10819.88	13243.58	13958.40	15145.85	16228.97	18888.95	21154.30
一、工资性现金收入	Cash Income By Wages	3186.99	3858.97	3282.57	3663.96	4000.55	4370.51	4866.90	5328.80
二、家庭经营现金收入	Cash Income By Family Business	5546.68	5959.60	7328.03	7336.22	7921.93	8318.33	10084.50	11390.05
农业	Farm Products	3096.78	3179.27	3614.71	3658.73	3873.47	3751.74	3304.21	3690.44
林业	Forestry Products	88.34	142.91	163.40	172.04	241.80	224.36	77.18	78.48
牧业	Animal husbandary Products	837.81	891.19	1404.35	1039.15	995.89	1128.45	1596.84	1738.25
渔业	Fishery Products	418.62	395.83	468.59	689.58	644.76	835.71	1365.82	1629.16
工业	Industry Products	144.59	60.66	204.82	160.40	167.05	167.68	354.24	288.86
建筑业	Building Industry	177.49	307.83	188.27	110.67	261.24	359.50	546.40	900.20
交通运输邮电业	Transportation and Post Service	322.49	328.76	353.50	461.56	472.43	551.38	490.88	530.99
批零贸易餐饮业	Retail Sales and Catering	317.95	401.46	572.30	646.44	886.04	887.31	1864.94	2011.22
社会服务和文教卫生业	Social services and educational sector	113.54	177.96	211.73	189.00	141.72	137.63	167.96	205.32
农林牧渔服务业	Agriculture and forestry services			133.44	171.08	189.94	222.58	254.81	262.25
其他家庭经营收入	Cash Income of Other	26.87	10.54	12.93	37.56	47.59	51.99	61.23	54.89
三、转移性现金收入	Transfer Cash Income	544.46	902.05	2497.66	2791.31	3053.31	3361.28	3738.76	226.18
四、财产性现金收入	Property Cash Income	58.91	99.26	135.33	166.91	170.07	178.85	198.80	4209.27
期内现金支出合计	Total Cash Expenditures at Year-End	8149.22	8563.81	14688.88	15923.32	16677.01	17014.59	21165.56	23472.02
一、家庭经营费用现金支出	Cash Expenditures By Family Business	2285.75	2243.66	3249.87	3222.08	3290.04	3230.71	4143.15	5019.04
购买化肥	Fertilizers Purchases	374.44	396.06	456.72	515.12	482.81	411.64	319.30	422.11
购买农药	Purchases of Farm Chemical	129.82	112.80	140.48	142.26	154.19	149.47	137.07	144.28
购买农用薄膜	Purchase of Agricultural Film	6.31	4.80	7.94	8.01	8.65	7.26	4.01	3.90
二、购买住房、生产性固定资产支出	Purchase of Housing, the Productive Expenditure	240.00	315.23	876.97	1244.33	862.13	762.17	1098.59	1293.24
三、税费现金支出	Cash Expenditures of Taxations	10.85							
四、生活消费现金支出	Cash Expenditures of Living Consumption	5070.68	5531.07	6738.17	7612.82	8364.76	9026.62	11300.60	12431.46
五、转移性现金支出	Transfer Cash Expenditures	530.85	471.72	287.31	321.74	363.36	440.55	511.35	626.33
六、财产性现金支出	Property Cash Expenditures	11.10	2.13	8.67	6.12	11.47	13.06	12.86	15.52

9-15 农民家庭年人均出售主要农副产品情况
Annual Per Capita Selling of Farm and Sideline Products of Rural Households

单位：千克

品 名	Item	2005	2009	2010	2011	2012	2013	2014	2015	2016	2017	2018	2019
粮食	Grain	383.48	422.65	447.78	451.98	489.22	591.56	770.96	888.88	982.69	960.01	924.51	938.02
小麦	Wheat	54.25	62.01	75.44	86.70	91.93	79.55	111.05	129.72	151.98	138.05	128.72	112.16
稻谷	Paddy	302.70	320.27	331.71	302.69	329.15	432.85	528.86	588.64	656.03	684.99	674.81	671.05
棉花	Cotton	55.95	76.43	55.03	88.30	93.94	72.29	48.98	30.33	19.31	23.01	18.98	15.24
油料	Oil Producer	77.73	77.04	72.15	60.91	58.57	73.99	77.34	52.15	45.97	40.04	38.21	53.04
糖料	Sugar	5.47	4.48	6.43	0.16	0.17	2.16	2.08	2.21	3.43	1.80	0.13	
烟草	Tobacco	2.34	2.92	2.77	2.97	3.82	7.89	7.07	14.35	13.67	7.37	2.76	5.20
蔬菜	Vegetable	135.09	133.11	139.41	137.62	143.53	99.54	134.68	163.39	125.98	181.69	152.25	155.06
瓜类	Melon	14.21	19.07	19.69	17.40	17.60	40.74	33.63	10.12	15.49	20.49	7.60	31.69
水果	Fruits	69.54	99.70	78.09	66.13	109.87	62.86	111.30	97.70	93.46	109.78	104.67	137.01
茶叶	Tea	1.24	1.29	1.95	4.17	8.08	5.02	5.01	7.55	8.39	8.00	7.61	8.07
猪肉	Pork	29.70	28.70	30.92	22.91	25.68	28.51	58.86	41.76	32.19	40.52	30.98	27.82
家禽	Poultry	4.47	7.29	8.38	2.28	2.80	1.65	8.63	4.26	3.61	1.99	13.26	9.84
蛋类	Eggs	11.98	10.94	11.19	10.33	13.01	16.54	29.12	14.59	13.58	19.47	78.07	85.04
水产品	Aquatic Products	28.59	42.12	38.70	43.09	43.25	39.61	40.65	68.30	62.48	72.54	77.75	116.76

9-16 农民家庭主要生活用品购买量
Purchases of Articles for Main Daily Necessities of Rural Households

品 名	Item		2009	2011	2012	2013	2014	2015	2016	2017	2018	2019
粮食	(千克/人) Grain	(Kg/person)	29.46	42.35	44.45	38.34	44.06	47.43	49.61	50.47	61.25	68.59
植物油	(千克/人) Edible Vegetable Oil	(Kg/person)	3.61	5.20	5.70	5.11	7.41	8.07	7.88	7.50	7.38	9.22
动物油	(千克/人) Edible Animal Oil	(Kg/person)	0.33	0.43	0.39	0.27	0.47	0.49	0.42	0.44	0.40	0.39
蔬菜	(千克/人) Vegetables	(Kg/person)	17.73	19.40	18.27	16.51	25.95	27.28	31.31	33.07	44.99	41.61
猪肉	(千克/人) Pork	(Kg/person)	7.43	8.38	8.71	8.76	13.13	14.32	13.80	14.74	18.35	15.61
牛羊肉	(千克/人) Beef and Mutton	(Kg/person)	0.51	0.56	0.47	0.54	0.85	1.04	1.14	1.22	1.38	1.54
家禽	(千克/人) Poultry	(Kg/person)	1.17	1.26	1.24	0.97	2.40	2.46	2.95	2.58	3.60	4.60
鲜蛋	(千克/人) Fresh Eggs	(Kg/person)	1.30	1.85	2.20		2.83	4.32	4.16	3.77	3.81	4.39
鲜活鱼类	(千克/人) Fresh Fish	(Kg/person)	6.99	7.11	7.06		9.58	10.13	10.31	9.30	11.14	12.72
卷烟	(盒/人) Tobacco	(pack/person)	27.50	31.12	31.42	26.93	41.00	40.03	40.62	38.60	36.79	38.82
酒	(千克/人) Wine	(Kg/person)	10.72	11.37	11.06	10.06	14.24	12.76	11.78	10.72	8.88	7.70
水果	(千克/人) Fruits	(Kg/person)	6.22	6.87	8.27		17.63	19.69	23.07	25.35	30.07	27.97
服装	(件/人) Clothing	(piece/person)	1.95	2.46	2.52							
鞋类	(双/人) Footwear	(Two/person)	1.36	1.39	1.80		2.10	2.37	2.35	2.23	2.11	2.09
水泥	(千克/人) Cement	(Kg/person)	150.72	236.88	149.81							
钢材	(千克/人) Steel	(Kg/person)	10.21	13.85	9.72							
生活用煤	(千克/人) Coal	(Kg/person)	19.70	14.77	13.18		14.84	15.18	18.06	18.18	10.85	14.81
电视机	(台/百户) TV Sets	(set/100 households)	3.70	6.67	6.48	5.76	5.31	7.17	6.39	5.66	6.38	5.69
洗衣机	(台/百户) Washing Machine	(set/100 households)	3.21	6.09	5.09	4.44	4.93	4.35	4.48	4.29	4.92	4.20
电风扇	(台/百户) Electric Fans	(set/100 households)	10.52	10.79	13.67							
电冰箱	(台/百户) Refrigerators	(set/100 households)	7.00	8.30	7.12	6.16	6.03	6.61	6.62	5.62	7.26	6.57
自行车(含电动)	(辆/百户) Bycicle	(set/100 households)	4.67	7.18	7.30	6.54	6.99	6.27	5.63	5.37	6.90	6.39
摩托车	(辆/百户) Motocycle	(set/100 households)	3.88	6.09	5.30	3.91	3.65	3.51	3.18	2.99	4.13	3.05
热水器	(台/百户) Shower	(set/100 households)	4.36	6.18	5.70	3.58	2.75	3.20	3.19	2.66	4.05	4.58
电话机	(部/百户) Telephone Sets	(set/100 households)	3.36	3.41	2.76	1.86	1.03	1.37	0.83	0.99	0.88	0.49
手机	(部/百户) Mobile Phones	(set/100 households)	18.92	25.39	28.00	33.40	39.75	39.44	34.97	31.79	30.82	26.95

9-17 农民家庭年人均主要食品消费量
Annual Per Capita Major Foods' Consumption of Rural Households

单位：千克 (Kg)

品　名	Item	2009	2011	2012	2013	2014	2015	2016	2017	2018	2019
一、粮食	Grain	178.37	162.86	151.06	125.59	153.08	152.05	137.15	136.85	136.07	147.01
#小麦	Wheat	17.60	17.41	15.55	10.17	16.74	17.90	14.74	15.70	16.60	18.11
稻谷	Paddy	146.13	135.87	126.67	104.27	121.21	118.83	107.22	106.54	103.38	112.62
豆类	Bean	3.22	2.53	1.97	3.85	7.25	7.86	8.72	7.70	9.20	9.85
二、蔬菜及菜制品	Fresh Vegetables and	137.51	131.68	119.33	88.16	118.03	123.06	123.22	113.01	113.78	118.58
鲜菜	Fresh Vegetables	136.22	130.67	118.25	86.56	116.30	121.40	121.10	111.36	111.49	116.26
三、油脂类	Oil and Fats	5.49	8.17	10.39	11.05	29.71	16.04	15.52	14.10	12.27	14.08
植物油	Edible Vegetable Oil	5.13	7.71	9.93	10.61	29.02	15.24	14.89	13.51	11.86	13.61
动物油	Edible Animal Oil	0.36	0.46	0.47	0.43	0.70	0.79	0.62	0.58	0.41	0.46
四、肉禽及其制品	Meat and Processed Products	22.79	22.90	22.80	22.91	29.82	31.20	29.15	27.52	31.54	24.31
猪肉	Pork	17.98	17.40	17.63	18.11	23.12	24.12	21.43	20.29	23.44	20.90
牛羊肉	Beef and Mutton	0.57	0.65	0.53	0.63	0.93	1.14	1.26	1.28	1.41	1.55
家禽	Poultry	2.91	3.23	2.94	2.87	4.19	4.27	4.60	4.00	4.70	5.97
五、蛋类及蛋制品	Eggs and Processed Products	4.47	5.03	5.02	4.68	6.65	8.31	8.08	7.26	6.61	7.43
六、奶及奶制品	Milk and Dariy Products	1.22	1.55	1.67	2.11	3.53	3.58	4.12	3.70	4.17	4.32
七、水产品	Aquatic Products	8.33	8.38	8.54	7.93	11.10	11.75	12.15	11.09	13.12	14.90
鱼类	Fish	7.93	8.03	8.09	7.58	10.55	10.97	11.20	10.06	11.98	13.48
八、干鲜瓜果	Fresh and Dry	15.70	16.38	16.83	13.33	20.74	22.42	26.28	28.68	34.02	32.93
九、酒类	Liquor and Drinks	10.77	11.40	11.12	10.08	14.25	12.78	11.85	10.81	8.92	7.80
白酒	Wine Spirit	3.70	3.69	3.52	3.65	5.82	5.51	5.22	5.27	4.43	3.40
啤酒	Beer	7.01	7.67	7.53	6.41	8.41	7.24	6.58	5.52	4.48	4.37

9-18 农民家庭每百户主要耐用消费品拥有量
Main Durable Goods Owned per 100 Rural Households

品名		Item		2009	2011	2012	2013	2014	2015	2016	2017	2018	2019
彩电	(台)	Color TV Set	(unit)	109.18	114.36	116.24	114.35	116.50	118.46	120.09	121.73	121.00	121.26
照相机	(架)	Camera	(unit)	2.64	3.55	3.64	5.24	4.89	3.84	2.97	3.72	2.57	2.65
洗衣机	(台)	Washing Machine	(unit)	47.97	57.09	62.42	53.79	57.94	65.02	73.13	75.52	84.52	86.52
电冰箱	(台)	Refrigerator	(unit)	51.48	73.73	80.18	75.82	79.53	84.75	93.01	95.81	102.11	104.93
摩托车	(辆)	Motocycle	(unit)	64.12	72.33	74.76	68.84	76.52	77.87	78.47	80.16	82.24	83.19
摄像机	(台)	Videorecorder	(unit)	0.70	1.42	1.52	0.62	0.50	0.44	0.37			
抽油烟机	(台)	Ventilator	(unit)	10.03	13.70	15.82	10.94	13.59	14.89	14.86	17.35	30.39	32.24
空调机	(台)	Air Conditioner	(unit)	18.36	28.58	33.15	33.05	37.79	43.49	56.47	62.65	86.25	88.14
热水器	(台)	Shower	(unit)	32.00	48.24	55.91	52.16	58.01	61.71	68.63	71.21	84.74	87.17
电话机	(部)	Telephone Set	(set)	55.70	41.94	40.06	31.44	37.15	27.43	20.71	19.49	9.79	7.62
移动电话	(部)	Moblile Phone	(set)	152.27	204.82	215.06	211.52	223.46	232.18	236.26	238.70	268.13	270.85
家用计算机	(台)	PC	(unit)	7.39	15.58	19.73	22.14	25.72	26.23	27.04	27.94	31.92	33.61

9-19 市、州农民年人均纯收入(可支配收入)
Annual Per Capita Net Income of Rural Household of Cities and Prefectures

单位：元 (yuan)

地区	Item	农村居民人均纯收入							农村常住居民人均可支配收入						
		2007	2008	2009	2010	2011	2012	2013	2013	2014	2015	2016	2017	2018	2019
全省	**Province**	**3997**	**4656**	**5035**	**5832**	**6898**	**7852**	**8867**	**9692**	**10849**	**11844**	**12725**	**13812**	**14978**	**16391**
武汉市	Wuhan	5371	6349	7161	8295	9814	11190	12713	14390	16160	17722	19152	20887	22652	24776
黄石市	Huangshi	3742	4374	4811	5524	6487	7477	8492	9781	10957	12004	12925	13972	15125	16516
十堰市	Shiyan	2490	2841	3110	3499	4044	4566	5226	6212	7046	7779	8514	9373	10295	11378
宜昌市	Yichang	4022	4686	5186	5980	7055	8046	9121	10458	11837	12990	14057	15253	16514	18134
襄阳市	Xiangyang	4114	4880	5440	6365	7549	8684	9785	11176	12534	13650	14762	16005	17305	18933
鄂州市	Ezhou	4393	5096	5718	6645	7909	9072	10210	11309	12692	13812	14813	16168	17609	19313
荆门市	Jingmen	4652	5332	5956	6951	8248	9387	10615	12082	13481	14716	15811	17167	18776	20556
孝感市	Xiaogan	3915	4636	5131	5943	7029	7988	9023	10360	11597	12655	13554	14744	15988	17510
荆州市	Jingzhou	4140	4889	5464	6453	7664	8710	9909	11280	12625	13728	14707	15962	17300	18893
黄冈市	Huanggang	3295	3744	4130	4634	5438	6142	6966	8385	9388	10252	11076	12116	13238	14490
咸宁市	Xianning	3737	4411	4873	5606	6588	7505	8480	9709	10891	11940	12812	13925	15116	16591
随州市	Suizhou	4177	4967	5457	6279	7427	8419	9490	10702	11984	13022	14077	15268	16538	18094
恩施自治州	Enshi	2143	2519	2810	3255	3939	4571	5235	6364	7194	7969	8728	9588	10524	11620
仙桃市	Xiantao	4695	5248	5856	6807	8006	9076	10365	11809	13193	14422	15462	16736	18177	19891
潜江市	Qianjiang	4378	4929	5531	6486	7684	8785	10017	11448	12862	14076	15113	16397	17797	19494
天门市	Tianmen	4207	4761	5326	6207	7407	8507	9608	10809	12086	13178	14107	15367	16598	18138
神农架林区	Shennongjia	2850	3330	3707	4083	4640	5110	5677	6305	6920	7578	8342	9205	10091	11171

注：2013年前分城镇和农村开展住户调查，指标为农民人均纯收入。2014年起使用城乡一体化住户收支与生活状况调查数据，指标改为农村常住居民人均可支配收入。

Note: Urban and rural household surveys are separate prior to 2013,the concept is Per Capita Net Income of Rural Households, The data from an integrated household income and expenditure survey has been used since 2014 , the concept was changed into Per Capita Disposable Income of Rural Permanent Residents.

主要统计指标解释

一、城镇住户调查(到2012年)

城镇家庭人口 指居住在一起,经济上合在一起共同生活的家庭成员。凡计算为家庭人口的成员其全部收支都包括在本家庭中。

城镇就业面 指就业人口占家庭人口的百分比。

城镇就业者负担人数 指家庭人口与就业人口之比。

城镇家庭总收入 指家庭成员得到的工资性收入、经营净收入、财产性收入、转移性收入之和,不包括出售财物收入和借贷收入。

城镇居民家庭可支配收入 指家庭成员得到可用于最终消费支出和其它非义务性支出以及储蓄的总和,即居民家庭可以用来自由支配的收入。它是家庭总收入扣除交纳的个人所得税、个人交纳的社会保障支出以及记账补贴后的收入。计算公式为:

城镇居民家庭可支配收入=家庭总收入-交纳所得税-个人交纳的社会保障支出-记帐补贴

城镇家庭总支出 指家庭除借贷支出以外的全部实际支出。包括现金消费支出、财产性支出、转移性支出、社会保障支出、购房与建房支出。

城镇家庭现金消费支出 指家庭用于日常生活的全部现金支出,包括食品、衣着、家庭设备及用品、交通通信、文教娱乐、医疗保健、其他等八大类支出。

城镇家庭服务性消费支出 指家庭用于支付社会提供的各种文化和生活方面的非商品性服务费用。

城镇家庭收入分组方法 是将所有调查户依户人均可支配收入由低到高排队,按10%,10%,20%,20%,20%,10%,10%的比例依次分成:最低收入户、较低收入户、中等偏下收入户、中等收入户、中等偏上收入户、高收入户、最高收入户等七组。总体中最低5%的户为困难户。

恩格尔系数 指食品支出在现金消费支出中所占的比例。计算公式为:

$$\text{恩格尔系数}=\frac{\text{食品支出}}{\text{现金消费支出}}\times 100\%$$

二、农村住户调查(到2012年)

农村住户 指农村常住户。农村常住户指长期(一年以上)居住在乡镇(不包括城关镇)行政管理区域内的住户,以及长期居住在城关镇所辖行政村范围内的农村住户。户口不在本地而在本地居住一年及以上的住户也包括在本地农村常住户范围内;有本地户口,但举家外出谋生一年以上的住户,无论是否保留承包耕地都不包括在本地农村住户范围内。

常住人口 指全年经常在家或在家居住6个月以上,而且经济和生活与本户连成一体的人口。外出从业人员在外居住时间虽然在6个月以上,但收入主要带回家中,经济与本户连为一体,仍视为家庭常住人口;在家居住,生活和本户连成一体的国家职工、退休人员也为家庭常住人口。但是现役军人、中专及以上(走读生除外)的在校学生、以及常年在外(不包括探亲、看病等)且已有稳定的职业与居住场所的外出从业人员,不算家庭常住人口。家庭常住人口主要作为计算农村住户平均每人收入、消费和积累水平及分析家庭人口状况的依据。

整、半劳动力 整劳动力指男子18周岁到50周岁,女子18周岁到45周岁;半劳动力指男子16周岁到17周岁,51周岁到60周岁;女子16周岁到17周岁,46周岁到55周岁,同时具有劳动能力的人。虽然在劳动年龄之内,但已丧失劳动能力的人,不应算为劳动力;超过劳动年龄,但能经常参加劳动,计入半劳动力数内。常住人口中的职工,若这些职工为劳动力,就包括在本户的整半劳动力中。

总收入 指调查期内农村住户和住户成员从各种来源渠道得到的收入总和。按收入的性质划分为工资性收入、家庭经营收入、财产性收入和转移性收入。

工资性收入 指农村住户成员受雇于单位或个人,靠出卖劳动而获得的收入。

家庭经营收入 指农村住户以家庭为生产经营单位进行生产筹划和管理而获得的收入。农村住户家庭经营活动按行业划分为农业、林业、牧业、渔业、工业、建筑业、交通运输业邮电业、批发和零售贸易餐饮业、社会服务业、文教卫生业和其他家庭经营。

财产性收入 指金融资产或有形非生产性资产的所有者向其他机构单位提供资金或将有形非生产性资产供其支配,作为回报而从中获得的收入。

转移性收入 指农村住户和住户成员无须付出任何对应物而获得的货物、服务、资金或资产所有权等,不包括无偿提供的用于固定资本形成的资金。一般情况下,是指农村住户在二次分配中的所有收入。

现金收入 指农村住户和住户成员在调查期内得到以现金形态表现的收入。按来源分成工资性收入、家庭经营现金收入、财产性收入、转移性收入。

农村居民家庭纯收入 指农村住户当年从各个来源得到的总收入相应地扣除所发生的费用后的收入总和。计算方法:

农村居民家庭纯收入=总收入-家庭经营费用支出-税费支出-生产性固定资产折旧-赠送农村内部亲支

纯收入主要用于再生产投入和当年生活消费支出,也可用于储蓄和各种非义务性支出。"农民人均纯收入"按人口平均的纯收入水平,反映的是一个地区农村居民的平均收入水平。

总支出 指农村住户用于生产、生活和再分配的全部支出。包括家庭经营费用支出、购置生产性固定资产支出、税费支出、消费支出、财产性支出和转移性支出。

三、一体化住户调查

从2012年四季度起,国家统计局对分别进行的城乡住户调查实施了一体化改革,统一了城乡居民收入指标名称、分类和统计标准,建立了城乡统一的一体化住户调查《住户收支与生活状况调查》,并据此获得全国居民有关数据。

居民可支配收入 居民可支配收入指居民可用于最终消费支出和储蓄的总和,即居民可用于自由支配的收入。既包括现金收入、也包括实物收入。按照收入的来源,可支配收入包含四项,分别为:工资性收入、经营性净收入、转移性净收入和财产性净收入。

居民消费支出 居民消费支出是指居民用于满足家庭日常生活消费需要的全部支出,既包括现金消费支出,也包括实物消费支出。消费支出可划分为食品烟酒、衣着、居住、生活用品及服务、交通和通信、教育文化和娱乐、医疗保健以及其他用品及服务八大类。

Explanatory Notes on Main Statistical Indicators

Ⅰ.Urban Households(to the year of 2012)

Population of Urban Households refer to members of the household living and sharing economically together. All income and expenditure of the population of the household are included in the income and expenditure of the household.

Proportion of Urban Employment referto the proportion of employed population to the population of urban households.

Number of Dependents per Urban Employee refers to the ratio between number of persons in urban households and the number of dependents.

Total Income of Urban Households refers to the sum of wage and salary, net business income, income from properties, and income from transfers of members of the households, excluding income from selling of properties and income from borrowings.

Disposable Income of Urban Households refers to the actual income at the disposal of members of the households which can be used for final consumption, other non-compulsory expenditure and savings. This equals to total income minus income tax, personal contribution to social security and sample household subsidy for keeping diaries. Following formula is used:

Disposable income = total household income – income tax – personal contribution to social security – sample household subsidy for keeping diaries

Total Expenditure of Urban Households refer to all expenditure of the households except expenditure on leading. It includes expenditure on consumption, on purchasing or building houses, on transfers, on properties and on social security.

Consumption Expenditure of Urban Households refers to total expenditure of the sample households for consumption in daily life, including expenditure on eight categories such as food, clothing, household appliances and services, health care and medical services, transport and communications, recreation, education and cultural services, housing, miscellaneous goods and services.

Expenditure of Urban Households on Consumption of Services refers to expenditure of households on services of various kinds provided by the society.

Urban Households by Income Group All households in the sample are grouped, by per capita disposable income of the household, into groups of lowest income, low income, lower middle income, middle income, upper middle income, high income and highest income, each group consisting of 10%, 10%, 20%, 20%, 20%, 10% and 10% of all households respectively. The lowest 5% of households are also referred to as poor households.

Engel Coefficient refers to the percentage of expenditure on food in the total consumption expenditure, using the following formula:

Engel Coefficient = (expenditure on food / total living consumption expenditure) x 100%

Ⅱ. Rural Households(to the year of 2012)

Rural Households refer to resident households in rural areas. Resident households in rural areas are the households residing for more than one year in the areas under the jurisdiction of administration of township governments (excluding county towns), and in the areas under the jurisdiction of administration of villages in county towns. Migrated households residing in the current addresses for over one year with their household registration in other places are included in the resident households of their current addresses. For households with their household registration in one place but all members of the households moving away for living in another place for over one year, they will not be included in the rural households of the area where they are registered, irrespective of whether they still keep their contracted land.

Resident Population refers to population staying at home permanently or for over 6 months during a year and sharing life economically with the household. Members of the household staying away from the household for over 6 months but keeping a close economic relation with the household by sending the majority of income to the household are regarded as resident population of the household. Government staff and workers or retirees living as close members of the household are also considered as resident population. However, servicemen, students of secondary technical schools or schools of higher education and persons with stable jobs and residence outside the household (excluding those visiting relatives or seeking medical service) are not included as resident population of the household. Resident population is used in calculating income, consumption, accumulation on per capita basis of rural households and in analyzing composition of rural households.

Full/Semi Labor Force Full labor force refers to persons capable of work, aged 18–50 for males and 18–45 for females. Semi labor force refers to persons capable of work, aged 16–17 and 51–60 for males and 16–17 and 46–55 for females. Persons at their working ages but not capable of work are not to be included as labor force. Persons not at working ages but participating regularly in work are included in semi labor force. For staff and workers as resident population of the household, they are included as full or semi labor force of the household if they are in the labor force.

Total Income refers to the sum of income earned from various sources by the rural households and their members during the reference period, and is classified as income from wages and salaries, income from household operations, income from properties and income from transfers.

Income from Wages and Salaries refers to income from labor earned by the members of rural households employed by other units or individuals.

Income from Household Operations refers to income by the rural households as units of production and operations. Operations by rural households are classified by economic activities as agriculture, forestry, animal husbandry, fishery, manufacturing, construction, transportation, post and telecommunications, wholesale, retail and catering, social service, culture, education, health, and other household operations.

Income from Properties refers to the income received as returns by owners of financial assets or tangible non-productive assets by providing capitals or tangible non-productive assets to other institutional units.

Income from Transfers refers to the receipt by rural households and their members of goods, services, capitals or rights of assets without giving or repaying accordingly, excluding capitals provided to them for the formation of fixed assets. In general, it refers to all income received by rural households through redistribution.

Cash Income refers to income received by rural households and their members in the form of cash during the reference period. It is classified, by source of income, into income from wages and salaries, cash income from household operations, income from properties and income from transfers.

Net Income refers to the total income of rural households from all sources minus all corresponding expenses. The formula for calculation is as follows:

Net income = total income – taxes and fees paid – household operation expenses – taxes and fees depreciation of fixed assets for production – subsidy for participating in household survey – gifts to non-rural relatives

Net income is mainly used as input for reproduction and as consumption expenditure of the year, and also used for savings and non-compulsory expenses of various forms. "Per capital net income of farmers" is the level of net income averaged by population which reflects the average income level of rural households in a given area.

Total Expenditure refers to total expenses of rural households on production, consumption and redistribution, including expenditure on household operations, on purchase of productive fixed assets, depreciation of productive fixed assets, taxes and fees, expenses on household consumption, expenses on properties and expenses on transfers.

Ⅲ. Integrated Household Survey

In the fourth quarter of 2012, the NBS launched its reform on the household survey programin order to produceaggregates with the same concepts and definitions for urban and rural population. This new survey program is an integrated one whereas there had existed two separate household surveys for the urban and rural households. The reform took a number of measures, including the integration of concepts, classifications and standards, which provided a basis for producing data covering all households. The new survey includes the following indicators:

Disposable Income of Households has a national coverage comparable between urban and rural households, and refers to the kind ofincome that households call have at them disposal. It includes income both in cash and in kind from four categories: income from wages and salaries, cash income from household operations, income from properties and income from transfers.

Consumption Expenditure of Households has anational coverage comparable between urban and rural households, and refers to the all the expenditures of households for consumption in daily life. It includes expenditure in cash and in kind on eight categories: food; clothing; housing; household appliances and services; transport and communications; education, cultural and recreational activities; and medical care. The expenditure on housing also includes rents, water, electricity, fuels and imputed rents Of owner—occupied dwellings.

10 城市概况

City Overview

资料整理人员：程文懿

10–1 主要城市土地面积、人口情况(2019)
Land Area and Populations of Major Cities (2019)

城市	Municipalities	土地面积(平方公里) Land Area (sq.km)	常住人口(万人) Resident Population (10 000 persons)	当年出生人口(人) Births (persons)	当年死亡人口(人) Deaths (persons)	人口密度(人/平方公里) Population Desity (person/sq.km)
武汉	Wuhan Municipality	8569	1121.20	114610	51221	1308.44
黄石	Huangshi Municipality	4583	247.54	32763	11757	540.13
十堰	Shiyan Municipality	23666	339.80	39712	24272	143.58
宜昌	Yichang Municipality	21230	413.79	29330	27123	194.91
襄阳	Xiangyang Municipality	19728	568.00	57314	38291	287.92
鄂州	Ezhou Municipality	1596	105.97	10221	6762	663.97
荆门	Jingmen Municipality	12404	289.75	20824	15354	233.59
孝感	Xiaogan Municipality	8904	492.10	52029	23666	552.67
荆州	Jingzhou Municipality	14242	557.01	58227	32706	391.10
黄冈	Huanggang Municipality	17457	633.30	81866	40186	362.78
咸宁	Xianning Municipality	9752	254.84	38897	14094	261.32
随州	Suizhou Municipality	9614	222.10	27597	13449	231.02

10–2 主要城市就业情况(2019)
Employment of Major Cities (2019)

单位：人 (persons)

城市	Municipalities	从业人数期末人数(城镇) Employment (year-end)	从业人员按三次产业分 Employment Grouped by Type of Industry：第一产业 Primary Industry	第二产业 Secondary Industry	第三产业 Tertiary Industry	#城镇私营和个体人数 #Employment in Private Enterprises and Self-employed Individuals of Urban Areas
武汉	Wuhan Municipality	2144215	3708	864667	1275840	2595600
黄石	Huangshi Municipality	299740	820	159547	139373	914538
十堰	Shiyan Municipality	693072	7818	319267	365987	580268
宜昌	Yichang Municipality	834008	10572	418434	405002	1106421
襄阳	Xiangyang Municipality	1114801	32672	559875	522254	518273
鄂州	Ezhou Municipality	233356	297	151060	81999	129665
荆门	Jingmen Municipality	413504	2318	213612	197574	466822
孝感	Xiaogan Municipality	839803	7066	435958	396779	706570
荆州	Jingzhou Municipality	377372	14126	141886	221360	1612794
黄冈	Huanggang Municipality	791195	15480	451307	324408	286076
咸宁	Xianning Municipality	210396	421	65555	144420	
随州	Suizhou Municipality	133644	459	55283	77902	818483

10-3 主要城市地区生产总值及指数(2019)
Gross Domestic Products and Indices of Major Cities (2019)

城 市	Municipalities	地区生产总值 (亿元) Gross Domestic Product (100 million yuan)	(当年价格) 第一产业 Primary Industry	第二产业 Secondary Industry	第三产业 Tertiary Industry	人均地区生产总值 (元) Per Capita GDP(yuan)
武汉	Wuhan Municipality	16223.00	378.99	5988.88	9855.34	145545
黄石	Huangshi Municipality	1767.00	103.82	900.38	762.99	71511
十堰	Shiyan Municipality	2013.00	171.46	884.18	957.08	59163
宜昌	Yichang Municipality	4461.00	416.05	2054.15	1990.62	107830
襄阳	Xiangyang Municipality	4813.00	449.25	2329.24	2034.35	84815
鄂州	Ezhou Municipality	1140.00	100.49	550.30	489.28	106678
荆门	Jingmen Municipality	2034.00	242.89	961.50	829.38	70203
孝感	Xiaogan Municipality	2301.00	310.37	983.30	1007.73	46772
荆州	Jingzhou Municipality	2516.00	434.58	933.77	1148.13	45097
黄冈	Huanggang Municipality	2323.00	403.01	876.56	1043.16	36685
咸宁	Xianning Municipality	1595.00	200.00	704.90	690.08	62650
随州	Suizhou Municipality	1162.00	156.22	544.08	461.93	52380

10-4 主要城市固定资产投资(2019)
Investment in Fixed Assets of Major Cities (2019)

城市	Municipalities	固定资产投资增速(%) Growth Rate of Fixed Assert Investment(%)	新增固定资产 (亿元) Newly Increased Fixed Assets (100 million yuan)	商品房屋销售额(亿元) Commercial Housing Sales (100 million yuan)	#住宅 #Residential Buildings	待售面积 (万平方米) Area of Sale (10 000 sq.m)
武汉	Wuhan Municipality	9.8	2016.03	4751.24	4125.07	192.29
黄石	Huangshi Municipality	12.6	403.64	222.55	213.23	34.06
十堰	Shiyan Municipality	11.8	34.20	150.52	134.01	172.61
宜昌	Yichang Municipality	12.1	1184.20	361.44	343.51	104.39
襄阳	Xiangyang Municipality	12.1	1287.81	436.41	412.38	112.64
鄂州	Ezhou Municipality	12.2	302.95	123.32	121.68	3.48
荆门	Jingmen Municipality	12.0	101.91	190.15	165.20	150.29
孝感	Xiaogan Municipality	12.3	65.91	209.16	201.31	103.27
荆州	Jingzhou Municipality	11.7	464.91	274.87	252.73	78.03
黄冈	Huanggang Municipality	11.3	643.98	265.16	253.11	183.26
咸宁	Xianning Municipality	11.7	549.34	221.02	186.64	131.55
随州	Suizhou Municipality	11.3	351.15	108.41	99.12	11.08

10-5 主要城市规模以上工业基本情况(2019)

Basic Statistics on Industry above Designated Size of Major Cities (2019)

单位: 亿元 (100 million yuan)

城市	Municipalities	工业企业单位数(个) Number of Industrial Enterprises (unit)	资产总计 Total Assets	利润总额 Total Profits
武汉	Wuhan Municipalities	2890	16324.48	867.20
黄石	Huangshi Municipalities	711	2113.77	44.37
十堰	Shiyan Municipalities	948	2306.72	86.43
宜昌	Yichang Municipalities	1288	4966.50	233.43
襄阳	Xiangyang Municipalities	1655	3627.86	185.58
鄂州	Ezhou Municipalities	509	747.84	99.28
荆门	Jingmen Municipalities	998	1892.71	56.26
孝感	Xiaogan Municipalities	1157	1536.61	22.67
荆州	Jingzhou Municipalities	1174	1997.77	55.23
黄冈	Huanggang Municipalities	1365	1390.84	8.36
咸宁	Xianning Municipalities	964	1111.50	44.20
随州	Suizhou Municipalities	694	837.80	23.80

10-6 主要城市规上工业经济效益情况(2019)

Economic Efficiency of Industry above Designated Size of Major Cities (2019)

(%)

城市	Municipalities	企业亏损面 Loss Making Rate of Enterprises	资产负债率 Assets Liability Ratio	成本费用利润率 Ratio of Profits to Industrial Cost	产品销售率 Proportion of Products Sold
武汉	Wuhan Municipalities	16.2	53.54	6.67	97.70
黄石	Huangshi Municipalities	14.9	56.32	6.59	97.48
十堰	Shiyan Municipalities	9.9	67.43	6.43	96.91
宜昌	Yichang Municipalities	5.9	50.50	12.86	95.93
襄阳	Xiangyang Municipalities	6.8	51.51	7.32	96.86
鄂州	Ezhou Municipalities	9.1	53.48	7.68	96.57
荆门	Jingmen Municipalities	7.6	45.93	6.37	96.59
孝感	Xiaogan Municipalities	6.8	49.27	5.15	97.64
荆州	Jingzhou Municipalities	8.5	45.60	6.84	96.43
黄冈	Huanggang Municipalities	7.7	52.17	6.66	96.26
咸宁	Xianning Municipalities	5.5	42.03	8.87	97.79
随州	Suizhou Municipalities	3.1	45.26	11.08	97.11

10-7 主要城市财政收支(2019)
Government Revenue and Expenditures of Major Cities (2019)

单位：亿元 (100 million yuan)

城市	Municipalities	公共财政收入 The public finance income	#各项税收 #Taxes	公共财政支出 The public finance expenditures	#社会保障和就业支出 #Subsides Expenditures for Social Security	#城乡社区事务支出 #Expenditures for City Maintenance
武汉	Wuhan Municipality	1564.12	1320.34	2237.10	340.80	451.60
黄石	Huangshi Municipality	119.55	83.88	265.68	52.07	22.42
十堰	Shiyan Municipality	119.96	86.19	406.95	62.11	16.53
宜昌	Yichang Municipality	240.79	166.92	596.99	83.32	76.53
襄阳	Xiangyang Municipality	300.24	201.67	729.68	101.93	173.32
鄂州	Ezhou Municipality	60.05	43.97	125.31	20.41	20.31
荆门	Jingmen Municipality	110.48	81.84	293.68	45.86	24.75
孝感	Xiaogan Municipality	135.53	101.97	408.84	69.49	27.40
荆州	Jingzhou Municipality	139.42	99.23	489.57	96.92	33.43
黄冈	Huanggang Municipality	141.40	100.02	534.34	90.78	23.39
咸宁	Xianning Municipality	94.62	66.71	280.27	38.86	11.90
随州	Suizhou Municipality	49.10	37.67	157.98	28.76	9.04

10-8 主要城市金融机构存贷款余额(2019)
Deposits and Loans Balance of Banking Institutions of Major Cities (2019)

单位：亿元 (100 million yuan)

城市	Municipalities	年末金融机构人民币各项存款余额 Deposit Balance	#居民储蓄存款 #Savings Deposits from Residents	年末金融机构人民币各项贷款余额 Loans Balance
武汉	Wuhan Municipality	27980.43	8992.96	30569.52
黄石	Huangshi Municipality	1875.12	1075.91	1379.73
十堰	Shiyan Municipality	2533.56	1643.74	1520.41
宜昌	Yichang Municipality	3863.12	2250.23	3525.50
襄阳	Xiangyang Municipality	3786.57	2640.81	2502.18
鄂州	Ezhou Municipality	772.14	444.09	596.60
荆门	Jingmen Municipality	2159.69	1467.45	1255.26
孝感	Xiaogan Municipality	2594.32	1844.23	1376.53
荆州	Jingzhou Municipality	3395.27	2376.59	1902.62
黄冈	Huanggang Municipality	3605.89	2574.33	1859.50
咸宁	Xianning Municipality	1594.70	951.14	1107.48
随州	Suizhou Municipality	1465.23	1050.15	767.46

10-9 主要城市贸易、外经情况(2019)

Domestic Trade and Foreign Economy of Major Cities (2019)

城市	Municipalities	社会消费品零售总额(亿元) Total Retail Sales of consumer Goods (100 million yuan)	进出口总额(亿元) Total Import and Export (USD 100 million)	进口 Imports	出口 Exports	当年实际使用外资金额(亿美元) ActualForeign Direct Investment (USD 100 million)
武汉	Wuhan Municipality	7774.49	2440.20	1077.90	1362.30	123.09
黄石	Huangshi Municipality	898.27	40.50	20.07	20.44	2.18
十堰	Shiyan Municipality	1193.01	61.90	2.91	58.99	0.87
宜昌	Yichang Municipality	1665.00	220.60	25.60	195.00	3.02
襄阳	Xiangyang Municipality	1862.84	227.30	30.20	197.10	9.58
鄂州	Ezhou Municipality	421.86	6.80	4.07	2.73	0.44
荆门	Jingmen Municipality	917.06	96.40	33.50	62.90	4.93
孝感	Xiaogan Municipality	1213.16	100.40	15.20	85.20	3.86
荆州	Jingzhou Municipality	1671.47	118.47	23.36	95.11	0.50
黄冈	Huanggang Municipality	1332.78	70.70	5.10	65.60	0.58
咸宁	Xianning Municipality	623.10	62.78	6.91	55.88	0.37
随州	Suizhou Municipality	654.64	61.70	2.80	58.90	1.67

10-10 主要城市邮电、电力情况(2019)

Postal and Telecommunication Services and Electricity in Major Cities (2019)

城市	Municipalities	邮电业务收入(亿元) Revenue from Posts and Telecommunication Services(100 million yuan)	固定电话用户(万户) Telephones (10 000 Subscribers)	移动电话用户(万户) Mobile Telephones (10 000 Subscribers)	国际互联网用户(万户) Internet Service (10 000 Subscribers)	全年用电量(亿千瓦小时) Electricity Consumption (100 million kWh)	#城乡居民生活用电 #Urban and Rural Residents Electricity Consumption
武汉	Wuhan Municipality	290.61	157.70	1577.20	532.00	615.46	126.20
黄石	Huangshi Municipality	61.09	21.66	241.82	75.25	148.32	19.00
十堰	Shiyan Municipality	23.49	20.29	313.40	139.15	103.13	20.78
宜昌	Yichang Municipality	36.39	36.30	416.20	141.37	234.05	28.17
襄阳	Xiangyang Municipality	23.49	20.29	313.40	139.15	103.13	20.78
鄂州	Ezhou Municipality	13.37	8.13	97.50	37.69	73.82	8.88
荆门	Jingmen Municipality	25.89	19.36	242.66	82.58	109.53	17.31
孝感	Xiaogan Municipality	37.20	29.71	352.44	93.65	145.84	30.83
荆州	Jingzhou Municipality	49.58	37.91	480.01	145.67	145.15	38.40
黄冈	Huanggang Municipality	41.72	40.42	504.81	182.58	139.78	37.22
咸宁	Xianning Municipality	22.46	29.16	247.85	79.31	97.30	20.32
随州	Suizhou Municipality	17.82	10.79	193.19	56.89	45.96	13.16

10-11 主要城市居民收支情况(2019)
Income and Expenditure of Major Urban Households (2019)

单位:元 (yuan)

城市	Municipalities	城镇常住居民人均可支配收入 Per Capita Disposable Income of Urban Residents	城镇常住居民人均消费性支出 Per Capita Living Expenditure of Urban Residents	城镇人均住房建筑面积(平方米) Per Capita Housing Construction Area of Urban (sq.m)
武汉	Wuhan Municipality	51706	34005	38.25
黄石	Huangshi Municipality	38725	24962	38.50
十堰	Shiyan Municipality	33577	21642	37.78
宜昌	Yichang Municipality	38463	24296	46.10
襄阳	Xiangyang Municipality	37297	22248	56.00
鄂州	Ezhou Municipality	34541	21211	47.00
荆门	Jingmen Municipality	36805	24895	34.90
孝感	Xiaogan Municipality	35695	24751	42.80
荆州	Jingzhou Municipality	35910	22848	49.33
黄冈	Huanggang Municipality	31812	23426	41.69
咸宁	Xianning Municipality	33191	22606	45.89
随州	Suizhou Municipality	31961	20752	51.00

10-12 主要城市居民消费支出、价格(2019)
Consumption Expenditures and Price of Major Urban Households (2019)

单位:元 (yuan)

城市	Municipalities	城镇常住居民人均消费性支出 Per Capita Living Expenditures for Consumption of Urban Residents				居民消费价格指数(上年=100) Consumer Price Index (preceding year=100)
		#医疗保健 #Medicine and Medicine and Medical Service	#交通和通讯 #Transport and Telecom-munication	#娱乐、教育、文化服务 #Recreation,Education and Cultural Services	#居住 #Residence	
武汉	Wuhan Municipality	2532	3820	3827	9187	103.2
黄石	Huangshi Municipality	2247	2667	3417	3879	102.8
十堰	Shiyan Municipality	1662	2808	2909	3763	103.1
宜昌	Yichang Municipality	2285	2831	2645	5443	102.7
襄阳	Xiangyang Municipality	1746	2859	2369	4487	102.4
鄂州	Ezhou Municipality	1939	1796	2293	3568	102.7
荆门	Jingmen Municipality	2685	2103	3275	4405	103.4
孝感	Xiaogan Municipality	1683	2450	3094	2500	103.3
荆州	Jingzhou Municipality	1779	2958	2700	4673	103.2
黄冈	Huanggang Municipality	1677	2063	2731	2549	103.5
咸宁	Xianning Municipality	2294	2550	3074	4804	102.7
随州	Suizhou Municipality	1663	2215	2560	3604	103.2

10-13 主要城市文教、科技、卫生情况(2019)
Culture and Education, Science and Technology, Public Health of Major Cities (2019)

城市	Municipalities	普通本专科在校学生数(万人) Number of Students Enrolled in Institutions of Higher Education (10 000 persons)	公共图书馆图书总藏量(万册) Total Volume of Collection of Public Libraries (10 000 volumes)	医疗卫生机构数(个) Number of Health Care Institutions (unit)	医疗卫生机构床位数(万张) Number of Beds In Health Care Intitutions (10 000 units)	执业(助理)医师(万人) Practioner Doctors (Assitant) (10 000 persons)
武汉	Wuhan Municipality	100.69	896.80	6497	9.64	4.13
黄石	Huangshi Municipality	4.75	182.00	1443	1.78	0.65
十堰	Shiyan Municipality	6.01	161.22	2772	3.06	1.03
宜昌	Yichang Municipality	6.00	363.42	2664	2.91	1.15
襄阳	Xiangyang Municipality	6.01	161.22	2772	3.06	1.03
鄂州	Ezhou Municipality	1.58	107.00	490	0.57	0.22
荆门	Jingmen Municipality	1.87	112.69	1923	1.89	0.73
孝感	Xiaogan Municipality	3.64	171.55	2311	2.56	0.97
荆州	Jingzhou Municipality	9.26	138.20	3155	3.27	1.26
黄冈	Huanggang Municipality	4.12	306.84	3854	3.82	1.23
咸宁	Xianning Municipality	3.30	129.09	1345	1.58	0.71
随州	Suizhou Municipality	0.75	41.50	1330	1.23	0.52

主要统计指标解释

商品房销售额 指房地产开发企业本年出售商品房屋的合同总价款(即双方签署的正式买卖合同中所确定的合同总价)。该指标与商品房销售面积同口径。

城镇私营和个体就业人员 城镇私营就业人员指在工商管理部门注册登记,其经营地址设在县城关镇(含县城关镇)以上的私营企业就业人员,包括私营企业投资者和雇工。城镇个体就业人员指在工商管理部门注册登记,并持有城镇户口或在城镇长期居住,经批准从事个体工商经营的就业人员,包括个体经营者和在个体工商户劳动的家庭帮工和雇工。

医疗卫生机构 指从卫生(卫生计生)行政部门取得《医疗机构执业许可证》、《中医诊所备案证》、《计划生育技术服务许可证》,或从民政、工商行政、机构编制管理部门取得法人单位登记证书,为社会提供医疗服务、公共卫生服务或从事医学科研和医学在职培训等工作的单位。医疗卫生机构包括医院、基层医疗卫生机构、专业公共卫生机构、其他医疗卫生机构。

Explanatory Notes on Main Statistical Indicators

Value of Commercialized Housing Sold refers to the total contracted value (i.e. value of sales/purchase for selling/purchase of commercialized housing as designated in the contract signed by both sides) received from the sales of the buildings by real estate development companies during the reference time. This indicator has the same coverage as the area of commercialized housing sold.

Persons Employed in Private Enterprises and Self-Employed Individuals in Urban Areas Persons employed in private enterprises refer to the persons employed in the private enterprises which have been registered at the departments of industrial and commercial administration for which the business operation are situated at a county town (i.e. a town where the county government is located), or at urban areas with administrative hierarchy higher than a county town. The self-employed individuals in urban areas refer to persons who hold the certificates of residence in urban areas or have resided in the urban areas for a long time and have been registered at the departments of industrial and commercial administration and approved to be engaged in individual industrial or commercial business, including self-employed persons as well as helpers and hired laborers who work in individual households.

Medical and Health Care Institutions refer to the units which have been qualified the Certification of Health Care Institution, filing certificate of traditional Chinese medicine clinic, certification of family planning technical service by the administration of public health (family planning), or qualified the Certification of Corporate Unit by the civil affairs, administration for industry and commerce, commission office for public sector reform, and engaging in medical health care services, public health services, or medicine research and on-job training, etc., including: hospitals, health care institutions at grass-root level, specialized public health institutions, and other medical and health care institutions.

11 资源和环境

Resources and Environment

资料整理人员：康世华

11-1 “三废”排放和处理综合利用情况

Comprehensive Utilization Situation of "Three Wastes" Discharge and Treatment

分类	Item	2014	2015	2016	2017	2018
一、废水排放总量 (万吨)	Total Volume of Waste Water Discharged (10 000 ton)	301703	313785	274787	272694	269605
工业废水排放总量	Total Volume of Industrial Waste Water Discharged	81657	80817	49090	44158	45849
二、工业废气排放量 (亿标立方米)	Total Volume of Waste Gas Discharged (100 million cu.m)	21702	23643	29519	20176	24241
三、废气中污染物排放量 (万吨)	Pollutants Discharged in Waste Gas (10 000 ton)					
二氧化硫	Sulfur Dioxide	58.38	55.14	28.56	22.01	17.70
#工业二氧化硫	#Industrial Sulfur Dioxide	50.62	47.07	18.55	11.61	9.13
烟粉尘	Soot and Dust	50.40	44.69	27.58	18.80	15.85
四 、工业固体废物产生量 (万吨)	Volume of Industrial Solid Wastes Producced (10 000 ton)	8006	7750	7109	8112	8472
已处置的	Teated	1701	2078	1494	1021	636
已综合利用的	Utilized In a Comprehensive Way	6139	5253	4332	4812	5599
已贮存的	Stored	221	488	1505	2624	2582
工业固体废物排放量	Volume of Industrial Solid Wastes Emission	0.46	0.50	0.22	0.58	0.25
五、工业锅炉数 (台)	Total Number of Boiler (unit)	2617	3107	2694	2407	2293
工业锅炉蒸吨数 (蒸吨)	Steam Tons of Boiler (steam ton)	87176	83972	81870	100748	93046
六、工业炉窑 (座)	Number of Industrial Kiln Stove (unit)	2262	2157	1589	1667	2078

11-2 工业污染治理情况

项　　目		Item	Unit	1990	1995	2000
一、汇总工业企业单位数	(个)	Total Number of Industrial Enterprises	(unit)	991	613	583
二、污染治理项目本年投资来源合计	(万元)	Total Resource of Investment in Pollutant Treatment Projects	(10 000 yuan)	18051	27433	85238
国家预算内资金		State Budgetary Funds		5568	3540	962
其　他		Others		1372	7966	61881
三、污染治理项目本年完成投资合计	(万元)	Total Investment in Pollutant Treatment Projects	(10 000 yuan)			85238
治理废水		Waste Water		5637	12042	45653
治理废气		Waste Gas		9891	9164	26668
治理固体废物		Solid Waste		1371	5293	6072
治理噪声		Noise Abatement		534	583	644
其　他		Others		618	351	6201
四、本年施工项目数	(个)	Projects Carried Out in This Year	(unit)	1545	939	851
治理废水		Waste Water		450	305	384
治理废气		Waste Gas		758	367	361
治理固体废物		Solid Waste		119	121	27
治理噪声		Noise Abatement		139	109	31
其　他		Others		79	37	48
五、本年竣工项目	(个)	Projects Completed in This Year	(unit)	1312	832	692
治理废水		Waste Water		353	256	316
治理废气		Waste Gas		662	339	286
治理固体废物		Solid Waste		99	96	22
治理噪声		Noise Abatement		126	106	26
其　他		Others		72	35	42

Statistics on Treatment of Industrial Pollution

2005	2009	2010	2011	2012	2013	2014	2015	2016	2017	2018
336	225	159	232	171	147	152	161	305	302	201
148097	281332	277416	153812	154496	251745	262884	157944	169061	188536	137427
7591	5602	3892	7216	4128	3667	1890	1035	631	38	265
133121	271638	271631	145306	149693	247868	258817	155917	167800	188472	137162
148097	281332	277416	153812	154496	251745	262884	157944	169061	174632	137434
48068	54002	35627	84573	35868	15873	18409	26067	39707	31296	22807
40008	213918	197293	47920	80510	216673	230712	120301	98518	124206	88293
11408	5970	9580	10505	3565	1720	2762	1375	8475	5542	828
440	675	867	1081	1114	52	104	275	367	637	1172
48173	6768	34050	9734	33439	17427	10896	9927	21994	1219	24335
473	318	226	364	136	113	127	199	302	233	187
191	126	98	158	43	28	38	63	99	52	34
176	132	74	122	56	59	78	96	151	141	112
15	11	13	17	7	3	2	7	21	2	3
20	11	12	18	8	1	4	5	4	2	6
71	38	29	49	22	22	5	28	27	36	32
428	273	195	331	117	148	134	146	238	164	128
174	108	84	143	42	42	37	41	80	30	20
160	111	64	112	49	83	88	73	116	108	81
11	10	10	16	7	3	1	4	17	2	2
18	9	10	18	6		3	5	4	2	5
65	35	27	42	13	20	5	23	21	22	20

11-3 工业企业废水处理设施情况
Statistics on Industrial Waste Water Treatment Facilities

项 目	Item	2000	2005	2010	2013	2014	2015	2016	2017	2018
汇总企业单位数 (个)	Total Number of Enterprises (unit)	2172	2313	2643	3590	3911	4555	4198	3834	3775
治理设施数量 (套)	Number of Treatment Facilities	2120	2163	2093	2084	2238	2562	1942	2109	2139
处理能力 (万吨/日)	Treatment Capacity(10 000 ton/day)		912	1037	1029	1043	1052	566	625	629
运行费用 (万元)	Operation Fees (10 000 yuan)	46651	77931	137920	168277	232869	224053	195593	249534	273845

主要统计指标解释

工业废水排放量 指经过企业厂区所有排放口排到企业外部的工业废水量。包括生产废水、外排的直接冷却水、超标排放的矿井地下水和与工业废水混排的厂区生活污水,不包括外排的间接冷却水(清污不分流的间接冷却水应计算在内)。

工业废水排放达标量 指报告期内废水中各项污染物指标都达到国家或地方排放标准的外排工业废水量,包括未经处理外排达标的,经废水处理设施处理后达标排放的,以及经污水处理厂处理后达标排放的。

工业废水排放达标率 指工业废水排放达标量占工业废水排放量的百分率,计算公式为:

$$工业废水排放达标率=\frac{工业废水排放达标量}{工业废水排放量}\times 100\%$$

工业废气排放量 指报告期内企业厂区内燃料燃烧和生产工艺过程中产生的各种排入大气的含有污染物的气体的总量,以标准状态(273K,101325Pa)计算。测算公式为:

工业废气排放量 = 燃料燃烧过程中废气排放量 + 生产工艺过程中废气排放量

工业烟尘排放量 指企业厂区内燃料燃烧过程中产生的烟气中夹带的颗粒物排放量。

工业粉尘排放量 指企业在生产工艺过程中排放的能在空气中悬浮一定时间的固体颗粒物排放量。如钢铁企业的耐火材料粉尘、焦化企业的筛焦系统粉尘、烧结机的粉尘、石灰窑的粉尘、建材企业的水泥粉尘等。不包括电厂排入大气的烟尘。

工业固体废物产生量 指报告期内企业在生产过程中产生的固体状、半固体状和高浓度液体状废弃物的总量,包括危险废物、冶炼废渣、粉煤灰、炉渣、煤矸石、尾矿、放射性废物和其他废物等;不包括矿山开采的剥离废石和掘进废石(煤矸石和呈酸性或碱性的废石除外)。酸性或碱性废石指采掘的废石其流经水、雨淋水的pH值小于4或pH值大于10.5者。

工业固体废物综合利用量 指报告期内企业通过回收、加工、循环、交换等方式,从固体废物中提取或者使其转化为可以利用的资源、能源和其他原材料的固体废物量(包括当年利用往年的工业固体废物贮存量),如用作农业肥料、生产建筑材料、筑路等。综合利用量由原产生固体废物的单位统计。

工业固体废物综合利用率 指工业固体废物综合利用量占工业固体废物产生量(包括综合利用往年贮存量)的百分率。计算公式为:

$$工业固体废物综合利用率=\frac{工业固体废物综合利用量}{工业固体废物产生量+综合利用往年贮存量}\times 100\%$$

生活垃圾无害化处理率 指报告期生活垃圾无害化处理量与生活垃圾产生量比率。在统计上,由于生活垃圾产生量不易取得,可用清运量代替。计算公式为:

$$生活垃圾无害化处理率=\frac{生活垃圾无害化处理量}{生活垃圾产生量}\times 100\%$$

Explanatory Notes on Main Statistical Indicators

Waste Water Discharged by Industry refers to the volume of waste water discharged by industrial enterprises through all their outlets, including waste water from production process, directly cooled water, groundwater from mining wells which does not meet discharge standards and sewage from households mixed with waste water produced by industrial activities, but excluding indirectly cooled water discharged (It should be included if the discharge is not separated with waste water).

Industrial Waste Water Meeting Discharge Standard srefers to volume of industrial waste water discharge which, with or without treatment, reaches national or local standards with regard to all pollutants.

Ratio of Industrial Waste Water Meeting Discharge Standard srefers to percentage of industrial waste water meeting discharge standards over total industrial waste water discharge. It is calculated as:

Ratio of industrial waste water meeting discharge standards = industrial waste water meeting discharge standards / total industrial waste water discharge × 100%

Industrial Waste Air Emission refers to discharge into atmosphere of waste air containing pollutants generated from fuel burning and production process in enterprises within a given period of time. It is calculated at standard status (273K, 101325Pa) as:

Industrial waste air emission = emission through fuel burning + emission through production process

Industrial Soot Emission refers to volume of soot in smoke emitted in process of fuel burning in premises of enterprises.

Industrial Dust Emission refers to volume of dust emitted by production process of enterprises and suspended in the air for a given period of time, including dust from refractory material of iron and steel works, dust from coke–screening systems and sintering machines of coke plants, dust from lime kilns and dust from cement production in building material enterprises, but excluding soot and dust emitted from power plants.

Industrial Solid Wastes Produced refers to total volume of solid, semi–solid and high concentration liquid residues produced by industrial enterprises from production process in a given period of time, including hazardous wastes, slag, coal ash, gangue, tailings, radioactive residues and other wastes, but excluding stones stripped or dug out in mining (gangue and acid or alkaline stones not included). A stone is acid or alkaline depending on the pH value of the water below 4 or above 10.5 when the stone is in, or soaked by, the water.

Industrial Solid Wastes Utilized refers to volume of solid wastes from which useful materials can be extracted or which can be converted into usable resources, energy or other materials by means of reclamation, processing, recycling and exchange (including utilizing in the year the stocks of industrial solid wastes of the previous year). Examples of such utilizations include fertilizers, building materials and road materials. The information shall be collected by the producing units of the wastes.

Ratio of Industrial Solid Wastes Utilized refers to the percentage of industrial solid wastes utilized over industrial solid wastes produced (including stocks of the previous years). It is calculated as:

Ratio of industrial solid wastes utilized = volume of industrial solid wastes utilized / (industrial solid wastes produced + stock of previous years) × 100%

Ratio of Consumption Wastes Treated refers to consumption wastes treated over that produced. In practical statistics, as it is difficult to estimate, the volume of consumption wastes produced is replaced with that transported. It is calculated as:

Ratio of consumption wastes treated = consumption wastes treated / consumption wastes produced × 100%

12 农业

Agriculture

资料整理人员：周 真 雷 迪

12-1 农村基层组织和农业基本情况
Basic Conditions of Rural Grassroots Units and Agriculture

指标	Item	2000	2005	2010	2015	2017	2018	2019
农村组织情况(个)	**Rural Units (unit)**							
乡个数	Township	476	217	201	168	165	163	162
镇个数	Town Governments	853	737	742	761	761	762	760
村委会个数	Village Committees	32400	26678	26018	25343	24312	23571	23202
村民小组个数	Villager Group	259250	212587	209598	208546	206739	205059	203005
农业生产条件	**AgriculturalProductionConditions**							
年末实有耕地面积(千公顷)	Cultivated Areas (Year-End) (1 000 hectares)			5312.28	5255.00	5235.91	5235.40	
农业机械总动力(万千瓦)	Total Agricultural Machinery Power (10 000 kW)	1414.00	2057.37	2796.99	4465.51	4335.47	4424.59	4515.73
化肥施用量 (万吨)	Consumption of Chemical Fertilizers (10 000 tons)	247.08	285.83	350.77	333.87	317.93	295.82	273.89
农村用电量(亿千瓦小时)	Electricity Consumed in Rural Areas (100 million kWh)	60.86	70.09	109.78	149.10	156.57	165.21	178.55
农作物播种面积(千公顷)	**Total Sown Area of Farm Crops** (1000 hectares)							
总播种面积	Total Sown Area	7584.07	7391.30	7383.59	7986.30	7956.13	7952.90	7815.89
其中:粮食	Grain Crops	4156.20	4068.15	4139.12	4784.38	4852.99	4847.01	4608.60
棉花	Cotton Crops	318.07	360.95	482.37	267.62	204.80	159.26	162.83
油料	Oil-Bearing Crops	1503.44	1460.20	1390.30	1389.39	1291.33	1255.82	1278.60
#油菜籽	Rapeseed	1158.94	1178.65	1089.43	1070.11	971.17	932.97	938.31
花生	Peanuts	193.42	171.71	198.50	221.65	230.53	232.60	243.62
甘蔗	Sugarcane	22.17	9.95	7.04	6.30	6.57	6.45	6.48
烤烟	Flue-Cured Tobacco	48.10	43.68	39.36	39.60	36.62	33.63	30.38
主要农产品产量(万吨)	**Volume of Major Agricultural** Products (10 000 tons)							
其中:粮食	Grain Crops	2218.49	2177.38	2304.26	2914.75	2846.12	2839.47	2724.98
棉花	Cotton Crops	30.43	37.50	47.41	30.08	18.40	14.93	14.36
油料	Oil-Bearing Crops	269.98	293.90	302.28	316.71	307.69	302.48	313.95
#油菜籽	Rapeseed	192.40	219.15	220.35	226.02	213.17	205.31	211.35
花生	Peanuts	53.46	60.19	66.64	73.21	78.37	80.67	85.71
肉类产量	Output of Meat	271.19	342.63	383.48	443.66	435.35	430.95	349.20
水产品产量	Output of Aquatic Products	234.34	318.21	353.09	455.80	465.42	458.40	469.54

注:主要农产品播种面积、产量2007年-2017年数据依据第三次全国农业普查结果进行了修订。
Note: Statistics of major farm products output of 2007-2017 is adjusted according to the Third Agricultural Census.

12-2 农林牧渔业总产值
Gross Output Value of Farming, Forestry, Animal Husbandry and Fishery

单位:亿元　　当年价格　　(At current price, 100 million yuan)

年 份 Year	农林牧渔业总产值 Gross Output Value of FFAF	农业 Farming	林业 Foresty	畜牧业 Animal Husbandry	渔业 Fishery	农林牧渔专业及辅助业活动 Service Industry for Farming, Forestry, Animal husbandry and Fishery
1949	10.72	7.22	0.69	0.97	0.10	
1952	16.59	12.08	0.79	1.48	0.18	
1957	28.59	20.55	1.46	3.81	0.46	
1962	33.66	26.52	1.71	3.61	0.46	
1965	47.48	37.44	1.98	6.02	0.51	
1970	51.27	40.62	2.07	6.41	0.92	
1975	74.68					
1978	84.46					
1979	109.85					
1980	94.95	64.70	7.28	17.29	1.46	
1985	192.32	129.61	8.15	39.08	8.18	
1986	219.10	146.79	8.75	43.86	10.77	
1987	249.68	160.13	9.97	54.86	14.19	
1988	297.51	175.12	10.98	80.80	18.83	
1989	335.04	198.56	11.75	91.47	20.66	
1990	402.23	252.92	14.15	98.04	23.88	
1991	405.04	247.01	16.81	102.19	25.06	
1992	435.42	265.53	17.36	110.37	27.59	
1993	501.17	301.99	22.39	134.02	42.77	
1994	786.84	481.82	26.47	219.53	59.01	
1995	988.53	612.12	28.33	268.09	79.98	
1996	1140.76	670.27	33.62	337.02	99.86	
1997	1243.68	711.91	37.33	381.40	113.04	
1998	1222.58	688.06	41.29	371.37	121.86	
1999	1126.10	645.98	40.86	311.43	127.83	
2000	1125.64	615.74	40.24	338.77	130.89	
2001	1172.82	658.26	27.11	352.63	134.82	
2002	1203.30	671.20	28.33	354.84	148.93	
2003	1342.09	733.36	34.78	383.71	170.43	
2004	1695.44	921.59	31.78	514.52	205.68	21.87
2005	1775.58	932.15	37.30	545.40	236.49	24.24
2006	1842.20	995.46	40.50	487.09	221.42	97.73
2007	2281.21	1147.31	41.86	678.27	310.83	102.90
2008	2900.59	1385.21	49.69	985.51	372.98	107.20
2009	2924.66	1490.91	57.67	851.62	413.14	111.30
2010	3407.64	1883.22	65.37	883.09	458.58	117.40
2011	4110.16	2244.55	86.10	1137.84	508.80	132.90
2012	4542.16	2416.35	100.10	1244.29	626.20	155.22
2013	4920.13	2585.15	122.00	1286.55	748.40	178.03
2014	5162.94	2651.16	157.00	1301.06	844.20	209.53
2015	5387.13	2674.07	180.60	1354.28	922.77	255.42
2016	5863.98	2794.79	203.43	1527.29	1030.01	308.46
2017	6129.72	2962.49	213.26	1478.10	1089.08	386.79
2018	6207.83	3033.76	235.23	1386.53	1105.95	446.36
2019	6681.85	3257.85	258.47	1521.49	1152.68	491.36

注:农林牧渔业总产值2007年-2017年数据依据第三次全国农业普查结果进行了修订。

Note: Gross output value of farm,forestry,animal husbandry and fishery of 2007-2017 is adjusted according to the Third Agricultural Census.

12-3 农、林、牧、渔业总产值指数(上年=100)
Indices of Gross Output Value of Farming, Forestry, Animal Husbandry and Fishery (preceding year=100)

单位:% 上年=100 (preceding year=100)

年份 Year	合计 Total	农业 Farming	林业 Forestry	畜牧业 Animal Husbandry	渔业 Fishery	农林牧渔专业及辅助性活动 Service Industry for Farming, Forestry, Animal husbandry and Fishery
1978	104.00	103.10	104.90	107.60	94.20	
1980	88.80	83.70	102.80	108.10	111.30	
1985	106.30	101.70	103.00	127.80	133.30	
1986	103.40	100.60	98.50	107.30	129.80	
1987	102.70	101.20	104.50	101.00	120.10	
1988	97.20	93.90	90.60	105.40	105.60	
1989	105.00	104.50	101.60	105.20	108.30	
1990	107.10	108.40	106.00	104.90	106.70	
1991	100.70	97.66	118.80	104.23	104.94	
1992	107.50	107.50	103.27	108.00	110.10	
1993	115.10	113.73	128.97	121.43	155.02	
1994	157.00	159.55	118.27	163.80	137.93	
1995	125.63	127.04	106.99	122.12	135.54	
1996	115.40	109.50	118.67	125.71	124.87	
1997	109.02	106.21	111.04	113.17	113.20	
1998	98.30	96.65	110.61	97.37	107.80	
1999	92.11	93.88	98.95	83.86	104.90	
2000	99.96	95.32	98.48	108.78	102.39	
2001	104.19	106.91	67.37	104.09	103.00	
2002	102.60	101.97	104.50	100.63	110.47	
2003	111.53	109.26	122.77	108.14	114.44	
2004	126.33	125.67	91.37	134.09	120.68	
2005	104.73	101.15	117.37	106.00	114.98	110.84
2006	105.37	109.29	108.58	96.04	109.87	116.05
2007	103.90	104.15	99.50	102.90	105.10	105.40
2008	106.20	102.80	105.00	110.00	112.00	102.00
2009	105.40	104.05	107.60	106.90	107.20	101.80
2010	104.50	103.40	117.50	105.30	105.80	101.50
2011	104.40	106.11	109.90	101.20	102.10	106.90
2012	105.60	103.65	108.10	107.70	108.80	106.60
2013	105.60	104.70	110.70	104.50	108.70	112.60
2014	105.60	103.22	123.30	105.90	107.20	119.20
2015	105.40	104.69	121.50	101.65	106.07	122.87
2016	104.90	104.90	112.00	99.00	108.34	118.70
2017	105.00	104.60	110.10	102.60	102.70	123.50
2018	103.40	103.80	109.10	102.50	99.80	111.20
2019	103.47	103.92	109.73	97.13	106.65	108.37

注:农林牧渔业总产值2007年-2017年数据依据第三次全国农业普查结果进行了修订。

Note: Gross output value of farm,forestry ,animal husbandry and fishery of 2007-2017 is adjusted according to the Third Agricultural Census.

12-4 农、林、牧、渔业总产值指数(1978年=100)

Indices of Gross Output Value of Farming, Forestry, Animal Husbandry and Fishery (year of 1978 =100)

单位:%　　1978年=100　　(year 1978 =100)

年份 Year	合计 Total	农业 Farming	林业 Forestry	牧业 Animal Husbandry	渔业 Fishery
1980	97.3	91.4	104.7	127.9	121.5
1985	157.7	142.4	114.0	206.2	338.6
1987	167.5	145.0	117.3	282.7	527.8
1988	162.9	136.1	106.3	285.5	557.3
1989	171.0	142.3	108.0	301.0	603.6
1990	183.1	154.2	114.5	315.7	644.0
1991	181.7	147.7	125.9	334.0	631.8
1992	194.4	158.7	120.1	360.7	689.3
1993	207.4	168.0	129.5	410.9	936.1
1994	227.8	175.0	152.0	461.7	1203.0
1995	259.9	195.3	156.0	535.1	1530.2
1996	277.6	198.0	168.5	611.1	1732.0
1997	304.0	213.4	179.3	671.6	2007.4
1998	307.3	209.1	204.6	682.3	2164.0
1999	309.5	220.2	196.7	627.9	2270.0
2000	318.1	226.3	194.2	650.4	2324.5
2001	327.6	238.7	141.6	669.6	2382.4
2002	334.2	233.1	145.9	700.2	2677.3
2003	351.8	237.2	167.2	730.8	2824.4
2004	374.7	257.9	153.9	760.8	2979.6
2005	392.4	260.9	180.6	806.4	3425.9
2006	171.8	137.9	58.7	502.2	2214.2
2007	178.5	143.6	58.4	516.8	2327.1
2008	189.6	147.7	61.3	568.4	2606.4
2009	199.8	153.6	66.0	607.7	2794.0

12-4 续表 continued

单位:% 1978年=100 (year 1978 =100)

年份 Year	合计 Total	农业 Farming	林业 Forestry	牧业 Animal Husbandry	渔业 Fishery
2010	208.8	158.9	77.5	639.9	2956.1
2011	218.0	168.6	85.2	647.5	3018.2
2012	230.2	174.7	92.1	697.4	3283.8
2013	243.1	183.0	102.0	728.8	3569.5
2014	256.7	188.8	125.7	771.8	3826.5
2015	270.6	197.7	152.8	784.5	4058.9
2016	283.8	207.4	171.1	776.7	4397.5
2017	298.0	216.9	188.4	796.9	4516.3
2018	308.2	225.2	205.6	816.7	4507.0
2019	318.9	234.0	225.6	793.2	4806.9

注:农林牧渔业总产值、增加值2007年-2017年数据依据第三次全国农业普查结果进行了修订。
Note: Grass output value of farm,forestry ,animal husbandry and fishery of 2007-2017 is adjusted according to the Third Agricultural Census.

12-5 农、林、牧、渔业增加值(2019) Value Added of Farming, Forestry, Animal Husbandry and Fishery (2019)

单位:亿元 (100 million yuan)

项 目	Item	合计 Total	农业 Farming	林业 Forestry	牧业 Animal Husbandry	渔业 Fishery	农林牧渔服务业 Service Industry for Farming, Forestry,Animal husbandry and Fishery
一、总产值(现价)	Gross Output Value(current price)	6681.85	3257.85	258.47	1521.49	1152.68	491.36
二、中间消耗	Intermedium-Consumption	2667.85	1100.55	117.14	713.27	450.44	286.45
三、增加值	Value-Added	4014.00	2157.30	141.33	808.22	702.24	204.91

12-6 农作物播种面积

单位:千公顷

年 份 Year	总播种面积 Total Sown Areas	粮食作物 Grain Crops	小麦 Wheat	稻谷 Rice	薯类 Tubers	玉米 Corn	大豆 Soybean	经济作物 Economic Crops
1978	7931.05	5544.78	1122.28	2894.63	427.23	403.14	173.43	2386.27
1980	7477.06	5352.04	1292.29	2708.22	387.46	406.91	138.94	2125.02
1985	7331.71	5108.25	1331.42	2538.57	354.01	374.17	134.64	2223.46
1990	7361.14	5200.01	1352.10	2636.47	391.90	386.11	164.65	2161.13
1991	7423.92	5194.50	1347.53	2622.79	402.38	395.19	150.61	2229.42
1992	7183.83	4955.35	1287.91	2537.49	392.59	376.18	140.23	2228.48
1993	7125.47	4812.05	1271.23	2377.82	384.33	365.96	181.69	2313.42
1994	7181.43	4797.95	1225.60	2373.26	203.39	373.02	201.52	2383.48
1995	7431.71	4776.65	1179.93	2408.66	397.65	393.77	188.01	2655.06
1996	7579.01	4880.28	1230.14	2448.58	419.53	405.07	174.71	2698.73
1997	7739.21	4944.66	1276.52	2467.51	415.74	400.30	182.51	2794.55
1998	7695.98	4737.15	1212.08	2244.74	431.02	442.84	201.32	2958.83
1999	7788.66	4673.11	1074.43	2284.98	448.72	460.82	207.01	3115.55
2000	7584.07	4156.20	845.10	1995.29	467.61	424.10	224.75	3427.87
2001	7488.99	4015.73	735.85	1953.77	237.75	401.11	218.01	3473.26
2002	7281.61	3816.08	679.02	1888.75	430.61	384.04	217.82	3465.53
2003	7153.24	3572.74	603.43	1808.75	208.56	349.81	196.47	3580.50
2004	7225.13	3817.89	605.08	2084.02	403.79	357.49	186.05	3407.24
2005	7391.30	4068.05	730.61	2162.39	397.75	428.79	179.79	3323.25
2006	7100.59	3902.27	1016.93	1975.07	218.67	431.93	118.40	3198.32
2007	6993.69	4032.18	1099.41	2027.17	217.51	444.55	117.20	2961.51
2008	7132.86	3891.72	1006.35	1956.92	212.20	488.24	115.60	3241.14
2009	7330.17	4072.96	1001.98	2093.62	230.05	536.46	111.36	3257.20
2010	7380.25	4135.78	1011.70	2087.84	260.83	572.53	109.94	3244.47
2011	7457.92	4191.52	1028.32	2081.07	283.93	603.37	108.12	3266.40
2012	7687.83	4294.51	1084.08	2086.42	275.94	663.58	105.67	3393.32
2013	7734.78	4416.60	1117.11	2202.55	272.53	653.43	103.27	3318.17
2014	7794.75	4522.12	1099.38	2201.79	274.15	745.72	136.79	3272.64
2015	7986.31	4784.38	1122.15	2383.35	276.80	813.53	144.40	3201.92
2016	7908.50	4816.14	1140.67	2358.67	276.35	797.33	202.25	3092.36
2017	7956.13	4852.99	1153.21	2368.07	282.72	794.78	212.34	3103.14
2018	7952.90	4847.01	1104.96	2390.99	308.13	781.20	219.77	3105.89
2019	7815.89	4608.60	1017.74	2286.75	322.47	727.53	211.72	3207.29

注:2007年—2017年数据依据第三次全国农业普查结果进行了修订。

Sown Areas of Farm Crops

(1 000 hectares)

棉花 Cotton	油菜籽 Rape-Seed	花生 Peanuts	芝麻 Sesame	黄红麻 Jute and Ambary	甘蔗 Sugar-cane	甜菜 Beet-Roots	烤烟 Flue-Cured Tobacco
593.19	165.27	34.14	102.71	8.39	2.31	0.13	24.75
591.67	175.75	40.76	113.51	12.17	1.49	0.12	9.69
464.97	361.42	65.94	173.31	94.17	7.85	0.08	37.67
455.92	744.31	63.75	126.85	27.33	8.07	0.01	46.35
461.55	610.10	61.59	128.17	20.42	8.47	0.02	56.83
507.19	534.41	64.73	126.32	18.15	10.64	0.02	72.76
486.06	522.14	79.70	127.24	22.41	15.00	0.03	64.32
497.58	615.87	86.97	114.77	11.70	15.73		38.69
502.03	838.82	91.91	110.04	10.83	15.97	0.03	41.16
474.38	855.26	90.82	107.72	8.59	16.59		51.92
480.56	829.80	95.20	107.35	10.10	18.00		70.99
431.58	887.01	121.48	113.62	7.94	19.97		48.47
310.70	1003.64	143.87	127.14	4.30	23.34		48.32
318.07	1158.94	193.42	143.82	3.14	22.17		48.10
346.65	1118.06	210.06	129.93	2.65	18.88		40.43
286.37	1155.25	206.04	138.88	5.13	19.18		42.90
355.02	1174.63	201.11	124.00	2.97	17.24		39.45
408.30	1186.10	173.03	111.20	1.36	10.01		39.94
360.95	1178.65	171.71	102.52	0.98	9.95		43.68
496.40	1001.20	140.10	97.24	0.69	3.70		32.13
514.84	912.69	139.45	88.14	0.53	3.48		32.42
544.31	1056.00	180.24	87.79	0.41	6.19		45.97
461.74	1112.36	190.41	91.45	0.26	9.36		54.42
482.37	1089.43	198.50	82.46	0.07	7.04		39.36
491.61	1055.39	203.96	77.28	0.06	6.60		45.61
476.29	1062.61	257.57	74.28	0.05	6.37		49.40
419.11	1098.94	217.77	69.06	0.04	5.95		46.69
348.13	1101.62	218.37	71.50	0.02	5.83		36.53
267.62	1070.11	221.65	66.75	0.02	6.30		39.60
204.96	983.62	232.14	64.31	0.04	6.42	0.02	40.89
204.80	971.17	230.53	62.69	0.03	6.57	0.02	36.62
159.26	932.97	232.60	67.87	0.01	6.45	0.02	33.63
162.83	938.31	243.62	77.22	0.01	6.48		30.38

Note: Statistics of 2007−2017 is adjusted according to the Third Agricultural Census.

12-7 主要农作物播种面积和产量(2019)
Sown Areas and Output of Major Farm Crops (2019)

指 标	Item	播种面积(千公顷) Sown Areas (1 000 hectares)	总产量(万吨) Total Output(10000 ton)
农作物总播种面积	**Total Sown Areas of Farm Crops**	7815.89	—
粮食作物总计	**Total Grain**	4608.60	2724.98
夏粮	Summer Grain	1253.75	457.00
小麦	Wheat	1017.74	390.68
大麦	Barley	7.65	2.43
秋粮	Autumn Grain	3354.86	2267.98
稻谷	Rice	2286.75	1877.06
#中稻	#Semilate Rice	1977.02	1678.05
双季晚稻	Late Double- crop Rice	167.20	114.76
薯类	Tubers	322.47	106.43
玉米	Corn	727.53	307.22
高粱	Sorghum	4.31	1.58
大豆	Soybeans	211.72	34.60
绿豆	#Green Beans	6.27	0.82
经济作物(全口径)	**Economic Crops**	3207.29	—
棉花	Cotton	162.83	14.36
油料	Oil-Bearing Crops	1278.60	313.95
#花生	#Peanuts	243.62	85.71
油菜籽	Rapeseed	938.31	211.35
芝麻	Sesame	77.22	12.92
麻类	Hemp Crops	2.66	0.70
#黄红麻	#Jute	0.01	0.003
苎麻	Ramie	2.57	0.67
糖料	Sugar Crops	6.48	27.90
#甘蔗	#Sugarcane	6.48	27.90
烟叶	Tobacco Crops	35.72	6.31
中草药材	Crude Drugs	239.80	—
蔬菜及食用菌	#Vegetable	1257.94	4086.71
瓜果类	Melon and Fruits	96.91	349.19
其他农作物	Others	126.35	—

注: 2007-2017年数据依据第三次全国农业普查结果进行了修订。
Note: Statistics of 2007-2017 is adjusted according to the Third Agricultural Census.

12-8 主要农产品产量
Output of Major Farm Products

单位:万吨 (10 000 ton)

年 份 Year	粮 食 Grain	夏 粮 Summer Grain	秋 粮 Autumn Grain	棉 花 Cotton	油 料 Oil Bearing Crops	花 生 Peanuts	油菜籽 Rapeseed
1949	578.13	101.85	476.28	5.74	13.37	3.17	4.12
1952	747.54	148.81	598.73	12.17	22.34	4.56	7.09
1957	986.08	180.87	805.21	21.02	25.26	11.23	4.86
1962	960.41	246.34	714.07	14.22	18.30	3.81	4.29
1965	1241.34	255.01	986.33	38.29	22.32	5.15	6.76
1970	1268.67	187.06	1081.62	29.64	14.93	4.82	3.94
1975	1561.51	230.10	1331.41	40.61	21.44	5.12	10.65
1978	1725.60	315.04	1410.56	36.67	23.71	4.90	10.72
1980	1536.43	341.32	1195.11	31.63	20.58	5.85	11.59
1985	2216.13	429.58	1786.56	49.22	72.98	13.52	41.14
1990	2475.03	474.96	2000.07	51.73	95.75	12.79	70.90
1991	2244.10	476.20	1767.90	49.11	106.29	11.44	83.75
1992	2426.60	450.90	2022.83	60.99	99.74	15.72	70.86
1993	2325.70	471.87	1853.85	42.50	111.74	20.68	78.35
1994	2422.10	472.70	1949.40	45.00	137.77	24.81	98.07
1995	2463.84	447.20	2016.64	58.60	189.44	27.28	146.24
1996	2484.40	465.24	2019.16	43.01	181.82	30.77	134.88
1997	2634.40	542.60	2091.80	58.09	195.47	31.24	147.53
1998	2475.79	501.69	1974.10	32.50	216.69	42.87	154.76
1999	2451.88	392.71	2059.17	28.15	228.27	48.15	159.97
2000	2218.49	322.39	1896.10	30.43	269.98	53.46	192.40
2001	2138.49	319.14	1819.35	37.35	279.45	63.99	194.79
2002	2047.00	232.27	1841.73	32.26	245.29	72.25	151.40
2003	1921.02	255.65	1665.37	32.50	272.72	68.37	187.10
2004	2100.12	271.24	1828.96	39.54	314.38	63.19	235.12
2005	2177.38	302.49	1874.89	37.50	293.90	60.19	219.15
2006	2099.10	369.08	1730.02	55.20	254.45	48.40	191.83
2007	2139.07	409.86	1729.21	55.80	252.78	49.01	190.71
2008	2145.47	382.28	1763.19	49.98	279.20	50.24	209.17
2009	2291.05	392.08	1898.97	48.22	306.83	64.21	227.13
2010	2304.26	411.90	1892.36	47.41	302.28	66.64	220.35
2011	2407.45	415.67	1991.78	52.90	293.13	71.67	206.02
2012	2485.14	437.75	2047.39	53.53	305.13	78.16	212.15
2013	2586.21	490.08	2096.13	46.36	315.57	72.21	227.90
2014	2658.26	493.82	2164.44	36.30	321.18	73.83	230.86
2015	2914.75	493.09	2421.66	30.08	316.71	73.21	226.02
2016	2796.35	497.59	2298.76	19.00	305.15	77.98	211.14
2017	2846.12	488.25	2357.87	18.40	307.69	78.37	213.17
2018	2839.47	467.60	2371.87	14.93	302.48	80.67	205.31
2019	2724.98	457.00	2267.98	14.36	313.95	85.71	211.35

注:2007年-2017年数据依据第三次全国农业普查结果进行了修订。
Note: Statistics of 2007-2017 is adjusted according to the Third Agricultural Census.

12-9 人均占有主要农产品产量
Per Capita Output of Major Farm Products

单位:千克/人 (kg/person)

年 份 Year	粮 食 Grain	棉 花 Cotton	油 料 Oil Bearing Crops	猪、牛、羊肉 Output of Pork, Beef and Mutton	水产品 Output of Aquatic Products
1952	275	4.5	8.2		2.9
1957	327	7.0	8.4		4.0
1962	302	4.4	5.8		2.3
1965	359	11.1	6.4		3.3
1970	319	7.5	3.8		2.8
1975	357	9.3	4.9		2.6
1978	379	8.1	5.2		2.4
1980	330	6.8	4.4	11.9	2.9
1985	452	10.0	14.9	20.7	7.6
1990	467	9.8	18.1	27.7	13.4
1991	415	8.9	19.6	29.0	12.9
1992	443	11.1	18.2	31.9	14.9
1993	416	7.6	20.0	35.3	18.1
1994	431	8.0	24.5	41.8	23.0
1995	429	10.2	33.0	48.6	26.3
1996	428	7.4	31.4	40.4	30.1
1997	450	9.9	33.4	44.4	34.6
1998	419	5.5	36.7	44.2	37.0
1999	413	5.0	38.4	44.8	38.6
2000	372	5.1	45.3	45.5	39.3
2001	358	6.3	46.8	48.3	40.5
2002	342	5.4	41.0	49.4	45.4
2003	316	6.5	45.5	51.4	47.8
2004	349	6.6	52.3	54.1	50.2
2005	361	6.2	48.7	56.8	52.8
2006	365	7.4	46.2	42.0	46.7
2007	376	9.8	44.4	45.2	49.1
2008	376	8.8	48.9	50.4	54.9
2009	401	8.4	53.7	53.8	59.1
2010	403	8.3	52.8	55.3	61.7
2011	419	9.2	51.1	55.9	62.1
2012	431	9.3	52.9	60.8	67.4
2013	447	8.0	54.5	63.3	70.9
2014	458	6.3	55.3	65.2	74.6
2015	500	5.2	54.3	63.8	78.1
2016	477	3.2	52.0	62.0	80.2
2017	483	3.1	52.2	61.9	79.0
2018	481	2.5	51.2	60.7	77.6
2019	460	2.4	53.0	45.4	79.3

注:按全省常住人口计算的人均占有量。
Note: The data is caculated by resident population.

12-10 蚕、茶、果生产情况

Statistics on Production of Silkworm Cocoons, Tea and Fruits

指 标	Item	1995	2000	2005	2010	2015	2017	2018	2019
蚕茧产量 (万吨)	Silkworm Cocoons (10 000 tons)	2.24	1.22	1.07	0.68	0.62	0.44	0.40	0.38
茶叶产量 (万吨)	Tea (10 000 tons)	3.90	6.37	8.50	16.36	26.13	30.33	32.98	35.25
#红茶	Red Tea	0.12		0.65	1.51	2.97	3.42	3.34	3.70
绿茶	Green Tea	3.05	5.15	6.72	13.59	19.06	21.12	23.54	24.12
其他茶	Others			0.18	0.30	0.28	0.65	0.64	0.83
园林水果产量(万吨)	Garden fruit production (10 000 tons)	114.70	215.68	260.79	446.81	646.94	621.25	655.46	661.04
#苹果	#Apples	3.21	3.02	1.24	0.99	1.39	1.24	0.97	0.79
柑桔	Citrus	58.14	94.62	146.26	320.41	490.92	465.90	488.05	478.22
梨	Pears	26.02		46.80	44.35	42.52	37.49	37.31	40.37
葡萄	Grapes			4.97	11.82	21.40	24.18	27.88	29.81
桃子	Peaches	14.59	30.87	46.88	52.87	68.16	70.78	77.27	86.54
猕猴桃	Kiwi fruit			0.85	1.42	5.04	6.79	7.42	8.42
红枣	Dates			2.02	2.79	3.63	3.10	3.26	3.07
柿子	Persimmons			4.77	4.51	5.14	4.69	5.16	5.01
茶园面积(千公顷)	Area of Tea Plantations (1 000 hectares)	113.39	121.02	138.43	195.08	261.50	283.31	321.50	347.71
#当年采摘面积	#Pick Area	7.42		101.62	142.21	188.02	202.90	232.68	264.79
果园(千公顷)	Area of Orchards (1 000 hectares)	199.80	233.93	265.05	343.72	338.28	345.82	366.17	380.86
#苹果园	#Apples	13.66	8.98	3.30	1.51	0.97	1.33	1.03	0.96
柑桔园	Citrus	98.39	99.13	143.15	220.04	218.95	217.77	227.23	232.76
梨园	Pears	35.42	33.49	35.90	29.59	24.06	22.91	23.88	24.53
葡萄园	Grapes			4.77	5.22	10.27	14.19	15.47	15.70

注:2007-2017年数据依据第三次全国农业普查结果进行了修订。

Note: Statistics of 2007-2017 is adjusted according to the Third Agricultural Census.

12-11 林业生产情况
Statistics on Production of Forestry

单位：公顷 (hectare)

指标名称	Item	2017	2018	2019
造林面积	Build Forestry Areas	199831	181597	199645
用材林	Material Forests	79368	65479	57976
经济林	Economic Forests	41091	39446	42924
防护林	Windbreak Forests	74127	74612	97026
薪炭林	Firewood Forests	2300	1609	1107
特种用途林	Forests for Soecial Puppse	2945	451	612
更新造林	Updateing Areas	4004	4098	5913
四旁(零星)植树(万株)	Planting	14577	11404	
育苗面积	Raise Seedlings Areas	42808	42105	
主要林产品产量(吨)	Output of Forestry Products (ton)			
生漆	Lacquer	3217	2664	
油桐籽	Tung-Oil Seeds	21593	21400	
乌桕籽	Tea-oil Seeds	11701	10234	
油茶籽	Tallow Seeds	146879	194836	209419
五倍子	Gallnut	2826	2767	
棕片	palm pieces	3044	3014	
松脂	Turpentine	42665	13280	
竹笋干	Bamboo Shoots	22154	16547	19891
核桃	Walnut	121800	123487	122401
板栗	Chestnut	434780	405495	390281
花椒	Pepper	1916	1940	
八角	Star anise	59	124	
食用菌	Edible fungi	183932	193714	
木材采伐量(万立方米)	Output of Timber Cut(10 000 cu.m)	348.6	368	534
竹材采伐量(万根)	Output of Bamboo Cut (10 000 cu.m)	3825.9	3744	3724.5

注:1.林业数据来源于林业部门。

Note: Statistics of forestry sources from the Department of Forestry of Hubei Province.

12-12 畜牧业生产情况
Statistics on Production of Livestock

指 标	Item	2000	2005	2010	2015	2017	2018	2019
牲畜年末存栏头数 (万头)	**(10 000 heads)**							
大牲畜	Large Animals	431.50	384.32	266.08	226.93	238.46	241.53	243.55
牛	Cattles and Buffalloes	428.38	382.14	264.78	226.31	238.00	241.09	243.15
马	Horses	1.83	1.58	0.83	0.43	0.33	0.35	0.33
驴	Donkeys	0.98	0.44	0.34	0.15	0.11	0.07	0.06
骡	Mules	0.30	0.16	0.12	0.03	0.02	0.02	0.02
猪	Hogs	2132.79	2289.05	2526.60	2613.15	2578.53	2521.80	1617.86
羊 (万只)	Sheep (10 000 heads)	224.80	337.66	414.96	501.14	543.53	546.79	553.35
畜产品产量 (万头)	**Livestock Products (10 000heads)**							
猪牛羊出栏头数	Hogs, Sheep and Goats	3023.96	3841.82	4536.52	5269.97	5160.31	5081.06	3914.69
当年肉猪出栏头数	Hogs	2714.44	3345.18	3905.44	4566.00	4448.02	4363.50	3189.24
当年出售和自宰的肉用牛	Ox by Sold and Killed	104.26	115.49	104.86	111.49	107.90	108.33	109.52
当年出售和自宰的肉用羊(万只)	Sheep by Slod and Killed (10 000heads)	205.26	381.15	526.22	592.48	604.40	609.23	615.93
肉类总产量 (万吨)	**Output of Meat (10 000 tons)**	271.19	342.63	383.48	443.66	435.35	430.95	349.20
猪肉	Pork	215.84	271.23	292.91	346.83	339.29	333.18	242.95
牛肉	Beef	13.80	16.91	15.07	16.03	15.76	15.82	15.99
羊肉	Mutton	3.04	6.00	8.36	9.48	9.67	9.75	9.85
禽肉	Poultry	38.51	48.49	66.34	69.92	69.61	71.35	79.48
其他畜禽产品产量 (吨)	**Others (tons)**							
牛奶产量	Milk Cow	56400	122223	111324	134071	127577	128100	133800
绵羊毛产量	Sheep's Wool	34.57	4	3.13	7.16	7.90	9.00	9.00
山羊毛产量	Goats' Wool	52.17	16.00	8.21	32.67	9.25	48.00	48.00
蜂蜜	Cashmere	9187	7890	10832	31532	27750	23434	22914
禽蛋 (万吨)	Poultry Eggs (10 000 tons)	102.56	121.25	133.68	168.37	168.17	171.53	178.75

注:畜牧业2007-2017年数据依据第三次全国农业普查结果进行了修订。
Note: Statistics of Livestock is adjusted according to the Third Agricultural Census.

12-13 水产品产量
Output of Aquatic Products

指 标	Item	2000	2005	2010	2015	2017	2018	2019
水产品产量 (万吨)	**Output of Aquatic Products (10 000 tons)**	**234.34**	**318.03**	**353.00**	**455.89**	**465.42**	**458.40**	**469.54**
#鱼类产量	Fish	219.88	277.82	308.42	379.60	369.53	348.86	349.08
虾蟹产量	Shrimp, Prawn and Crab	7.51	7.71	35.93	67.38	86.90	101.69	112.60
贝类产量	Shell Fish	5.38	1.13	4.32	2.74	2.25	0.92	0.80
其它类产量	Others	1.58		3.66	5.37	6.74	6.93	7.06
养殖产量	Artificially Cultivated	194.84	274.45	321.56	435.99	436.13	440.30	432.54
#精养鱼池	Intensive fish culture pond						303.16	308.29
稻田养虾	Shrimp farming in rice paddies						67.30	78.89
捕捞产量	Captured	39.50	43.58	31.44	19.10	29.30	18.11	16.18
鱼苗产量 (亿尾)	Young Fry (100 million tons)	444.01	521.39	750.00	1020.00	1165	1184	1192
鱼种产量 (万吨)	Advanced Fry (10 000 tons)	38.79	54.04	82.03	128.16	111.33	105.14	103.82
投放鱼种量 (万吨)	Volume of Advanced Fry (10 000 tons)	40.16	57.08	80.74	115.64	107.47	99.64	95.26
水产养殖面积(千公顷)	**Aquatic Raised Areas (1 000 hectares)**							
池 塘	Ponds	291.10	339.57	340.40	484.17	531.17	535.15	532.56
#精养鱼池	Intensive fish culture pond						390.91	397.91
稻 田	Paddy				257.84	334.89	393.50	460.51
#稻田养虾	Shrimp farming in rice paddies						381.46	448.59

注:数据来源于省水产局,2012-2017年数据依据第三次全国农业普查结果进行了修订。

Note: Data sources from the Fisheries Bureau of Bubei Province. Statistics of 2012-2017 is adjusted according to the Third Agricultural Census.

12-14 农业现代化情况
Statistics on Agricultural Modernization

单位：千公顷

指 标	Item	2000	2005	2010	2015	2017	2018	2019
农业机械化情况	**Statistics on Agricultural Machinery**							
机耕面积	Areas Ploughed by Tractors	1969.55	2015.93	4517.14	6036.19	5929.27	6099.78	5983.54
机播面积	Seeded Areas by Tractors	255.69	233.66	815.61	2335.23	2685.64	3049.25	3099.30
机械植保面积	Plant Protection Area by Tractors	2426.95	2848.66	4074.38	4850.88	4934.92	5002.67	5071.48
机械收获面积	Harvest Area by Tractors	643.65	1407.62	2780.52	4233.67	4360.01	4589.12	4539.20
农村电气化情况	**Electrification of Rural Area**							
农村用电量 (亿千瓦小时)	Electricity Consumed in Rural Area (100 million kWh)	60.86	70.09	109.78	149.1	156.57	165.21	178.55
农用物资使用情况	**Used Agricultural Product Material**							
化肥施用量(折纯量) (万吨)	Consumption of Chemical Fertilizers (10 000 tons)	247.08	285.83	350.77	333.87	317.93	295.82	273.89
每亩耕地施用化肥(折纯量)(千克)	Per Mu Consumption of Chemical Fertilizers (kg)			44.02	42.36	40.48	37.64	
农用塑料薄膜使用量 (万吨)	Used Plastic Film (10 000 tons)		5.46	6.38	7.13	6.59	6.36	5.88
农用柴油使用量 (万吨)	Used Diesel Oil (10 000 tons)	107.81	41.31	58.29	65.61	66.31	65.10	63.54
农药使用量 (万吨)	Used Agricultural Chemical Insecticides (10 000 tons)	11.54	11.02	14	12.07	10.96	10.33	9.70
农田水利情况	**Irrigation and Water Conservancy**							
耕地灌溉面积	Irrigation Area of Cultivated Land			2522.47	2899.15	2919.17	2931.90	2968.99
占耕地面积的比重(%)	Share of Caltivated Area (%)			47.5	55.2	55.8	56.0	

12-15 主要农业机械
Major Agricultural Machinery

年 份 Year	农业机械总动力 (万千瓦) Total Power of Agricultural Machinery(1000 kW)	农用大中型拖拉机 (万台) Large and Medium Agricultural Tractors(10 000 units)	农用小型及手扶拖拉机(万台) Mini and Walking Agricultural Tractors (10 000 units)	农用水泵 (万台) Agricultual Water Pump(10 000 units)	联合收割机 (台) Combine Hearvesters (unit)
1978	616.07	2.80	7.75	21.22	425
1980	772.53	3.60	10.90	23.70	602
1985	910.94	5.72	14.62	21.06	479
1990	1099.62	8.60	17.70	24.30	2335
1991	1120.92	8.60	18.30	24.10	455
1992	1120.90	8.45	17.92	23.98	390
1993	1108.99	7.89	16.99	23.95	345
1994	1136.13	7.38	15.72	24.37	346
1995	1174.34	7.12	15.47	26.56	312
1996	1222.20	7.03	16.47	27.62	553
1997	1276.04	7.11	18.50	28.76	1521
1998	1325.90	7.13	20.60	29.59	2338
1999	1363.70	7.03	22.67	32.57	2559
2000	1414.00	6.82	23.63	35.47	2704
2001	1469.24	6.58	24.88	40.46	3363
2002	1557.40	6.64	26.68	43.89	5722
2003	1661.70	6.59	28.23	45.63	6708
2004	1768.60	6.83	32.09	50.82	10585
2005	2057.37	7.66	48.39	55.92	16085
2006	2263.15	8.50	55.69	71.42	22407
2007	2551.08	9.30	74.12	82.70	29803
2008	2796.99	10.42	85.23	87.73	34983
2009	3057.24	11.85	90.84	87.70	41904
2010	3371.00	12.71	99.10	85.40	50509
2011	3571.23	13.08	106.48	89.48	58398
2012	3842.16	13.84	111.56	103.30	66860
2013	4081.05	14.94	114.12	105.63	73808
2014	4292.90	15.85	112.98	110.60	81410
2015	4468.12	16.84	113.81	110.13	88704
2016	4187.75	18.18	114.67	110.97	95747
2017	4335.47	18.97	115.12	111.38	99432
2018	4424.59	16.15	115.87	108.96	102197
2019	4515.73	17.22	114.94	116.91	106069

注:2018年调整了农用拖拉机大中小型划分方法。
Note: The classification method of large, medium and small agricultural tractors was adjusted in 2018.

12-16 市、州农、林、牧、渔业总产值及指数

Gross Output Value and Its Indices of Farming, Forestry, Animal Husbandry and Fishery of Cities and Prefectures

市、州	Municipalities and Prefecrures	绝对数(亿元) Absolute Number (100 milion yuan)		指数(%) Indices (%)	
		2018	2019	2018	2019
全 省	**Province**	**6207.83**	**6681.85**	**103.4**	**103.5**
武汉市	Wuhan	619.74	653.17	103.3	103.3
黄石市	Huangshi	164.13	177.91	103.4	103.7
十堰市	Shiyan	276.13	299.73	103.5	103.6
宜昌市	Yichang	666.62	719.19	103.5	103.6
襄阳市	Xiangyang	727.35	789.95	103.7	103.6
鄂州市	Ezhou	162.10	173.15	103.3	103.6
荆门市	Jingmen	401.20	431.87	103.4	103.5
孝感市	Xiaogan	504.22	545.99	103.5	103.5
荆州市	Jingzhou	711.42	766.45	103.6	103.6
黄冈市	Huanggang	662.36	710.61	103.5	103.5
咸宁市	Xianning	329.49	352.74	103.5	103.6
随州市	Suizhou	257.93	280.84	103.3	103.6
恩施州	Enshi	302.83	329.14	103.5	103.7
仙桃市	Xiaotao	146.20	155.67	103.3	103.4
潜江市	Qianjiang	131.58	141.73	103.5	103.6
天门市	Tianmen	140.76	149.64	103.4	103.5
神农架	Shennongjia	3.77	4.08	103.5	103.8

注：本表数据依据第三次全国农业普查结果进行了修订。
Note: Statistics of this table is adjusted accordng the Third Agricultural Census.

12-17 市、州农、林、牧、渔业产值(现价)(2019)

Gross Output Value of Farming, Forestry, Animal Husbandry and Fishery of Cities and Prefectures (At Current Prices)(2019)

单位:亿元 (100 million yuan)

市、州	Municipalities and Prefecrures	合计 Total	农业 Farming	林业 Forestry	牧业 Animal Husbandry	渔业 Fishery	农林牧渔专业及辅助性活动 Professional and Ancillary Service for Farming, Forestry, Animal husbandry and Fishery
全省	**Province**	**6681.85**	**3257.85**	**258.47**	**1521.49**	**1152.68**	**491.36**
武汉市	Wuhan	653.17	411.15	13.53	73.98	103.10	51.41
黄石市	Huangshi	177.91	71.02	9.58	34.28	53.63	9.40
十堰市	Shiyan	299.73	167.12	30.53	76.42	17.29	8.37
宜昌市	Yichang	719.19	430.70	25.92	164.91	45.94	51.72
襄阳市	Xiangyang	789.95	391.87	20.64	271.64	46.91	58.89
鄂州市	Ezhou	173.15	39.94	3.85	31.45	89.30	8.61
荆门市	Jingmen	431.87	193.89	9.71	96.28	94.47	37.52
孝感市	Xiaogan	545.99	247.97	18.41	140.50	99.55	39.56
荆州市	Jingzhou	766.45	320.04	15.14	126.13	239.43	65.71
黄冈市	Huanggang	710.61	313.18	38.99	179.02	123.41	56.00
咸宁市	Xianning	352.74	179.39	25.08	63.85	58.03	26.38
随州市	Suizhou	280.84	131.59	14.99	91.30	19.91	23.06
恩施州	Enshi	329.14	180.19	24.81	100.50	1.32	22.33
仙桃市	Xiaotao	155.67	53.11	1.62	22.07	71.86	7.01
潜江市	Qianjiang	141.73	56.15	2.60	23.88	47.41	11.69
天门市	Tianmen	149.64	67.96	2.55	24.42	41.08	13.63
神农架	Shennongjia	4.08	2.57	0.54	0.85	0.04	0.08

12-18 市、州农、林、牧、渔业中间消耗(2019)

Intermediate-Consumption of Farming, Forestry, Animal Husbandry and Fishery of Cities and Prefectures (2019)

单位:亿元 (100 million yuan)

市、州	Municipalities and Prefecrures	合计 Total	农业 Farming	林业 Forestry	牧业 Animal Husbandry	渔业 Fishery	农林牧渔专业及辅助性活动 Professional and Ancillary Service for Farming, Forestry,Animal husbandry and Fishery
全省	**Province**	**2667.85**	**1100.55**	**117.14**	**713.27**	**450.44**	**286.45**
武汉市	Wuhan	253.31	141.40	5.85	34.85	40.67	30.53
黄石市	Huangshi	70.02	24.70	3.94	15.36	20.69	5.33
十堰市	Shiyan	124.71	61.12	14.94	37.08	6.77	4.80
宜昌市	Yichang	281.05	142.97	12.52	77.66	18.25	29.63
襄阳市	Xiangyang	316.73	127.38	8.57	127.72	18.15	34.91
鄂州市	Ezhou	69.20	13.81	1.62	14.52	34.10	5.15
荆门市	Jingmen	173.63	65.21	4.01	44.92	37.32	22.17
孝感市	Xiaogan	218.61	82.00	8.71	65.74	39.61	22.55
荆州市	Jingzhou	305.24	106.22	6.96	59.04	93.94	39.08
黄冈市	Huanggang	284.00	101.93	18.07	83.40	48.20	32.41
咸宁市	Xianning	141.30	63.74	10.91	29.55	22.16	14.95
随州市	Suizhou	114.60	44.94	6.41	42.63	7.58	13.04
恩施州	Enshi	138.64	66.14	11.35	47.87	0.51	12.77
仙桃市	Xiaotao	60.24	17.19	0.76	10.29	27.90	4.09
潜江市	Qianjiang	56.17	18.62	1.22	10.90	18.47	6.96
天门市	Tianmen	58.72	22.15	1.09	11.36	16.09	8.04
神农架	Shennongjia	1.68	1.02	0.21	0.38	0.02	0.05

12-19 市、州农、林、牧、渔业增加值(2019)

Value Added of Farming, Forestry, Animal Husbandry and Fishery of Cities and Prefectures (2019)

单位:亿元 (100 million yuan)

市、州	Municipalities and Prefecrures	合计 Total	农业 Farming	林业 Forestry	牧业 Animal Husbandry	渔业 Fishery	农林牧渔专业及辅助性活动 Professional and Ancillary Service for Farming, Forestry,Animal husbandry and Fishery
全省	**Province**	**4014.00**	**2157.30**	**141.33**	**808.22**	**702.24**	**204.91**
武汉市	Wuhan	399.86	269.75	7.68	39.13	62.44	20.88
黄石市	Huangshi	107.89	46.32	5.63	18.93	32.94	4.08
十堰市	Shiyan	175.03	106.00	15.59	39.34	10.52	3.57
宜昌市	Yichang	438.14	287.73	13.39	87.25	27.69	22.09
襄阳市	Xiangyang	473.22	264.49	12.08	143.93	28.76	23.98
鄂州市	Ezhou	103.96	26.13	2.23	16.93	55.20	3.46
荆门市	Jingmen	258.24	128.68	5.70	51.36	57.15	15.35
孝感市	Xiaogan	327.38	165.97	9.70	74.76	59.94	17.01
荆州市	Jingzhou	461.21	213.82	8.18	67.09	145.49	26.63
黄冈市	Huanggang	426.60	211.26	20.91	95.62	75.22	23.59
咸宁市	Xianning	211.44	115.65	14.18	34.30	35.88	11.43
随州市	Suizhou	166.24	86.65	8.58	48.67	12.33	10.02
恩施州	Enshi	190.50	114.05	13.45	52.63	0.81	9.56
仙桃市	Xiaotao	95.43	35.92	0.86	11.78	43.96	2.91
潜江市	Qianjiang	85.55	37.54	1.38	12.97	28.93	4.73
天门市	Tianmen	90.91	45.82	1.46	13.06	24.98	5.59
神农架	Shennongjia	2.40	1.55	0.33	0.46	0.03	0.03

12-20 市、州耕地面积(2018)

Cultivated Area of Cities and Prefectures(2018)

单位:公顷 (hm²)

市、州	Municipalities and Prefecrures	耕地 Cultivated land	水田 Paddy Field	水浇地 Irrigated Land	旱地 Dry Land
全 省	**Province**	**5235395**	**2647870**	**479411**	**2108114**
武汉市	Wuhan	293857	139783	84117	69957
黄石市	Huangshi	117297	63743	1196	52358
十堰市	Shiyan	239317	45055	2905	191357
宜昌市	Yichang	347355	122680	18040	206635
襄阳市	Xiangyang	703432	259801	11147	432484
鄂州市	Ezhou	55289	25743	16367	13180
荆门市	Jingmen	501773	324148	8588	169037
孝感市	Xiaogan	439275	277101	57870	104303
荆州市	Jingzhou	682706	435123	225768	21816
黄冈市	Huanggang	532728	349428	16124	167176
咸宁市	Xianning	200830	130628	17075	53127
随州市	Suizhou	253609	178309	5242	70058
恩施州	Enshi	451653	107301	312	344039
仙桃市	Xiantao	119424	61193	4750	53481
潜江市	Qianjiang	122230	62168	5261	54801
天门市	Tianmen	167344	65626	4379	97339
神农架	Shennongjia	7277	40	272	6965

注:本表数据来源于自然资源厅。

Note: Statistics of this table Sources from the Department of Land and Reaources of Hubei Province.

12-21 市、州农作物总播种面积

Total Sown Areas of Farm Crops of Cities and Prefectures

单位:千公顷

市、州	Municipalities and Prefecrures	2018	粮食作物 Total Grain	2019	粮食作物 Total Grain
全 省	**Province**	**7952.90**	**4847.01**	**7815.89**	**4608.60**
武汉市	Wuhan	409.04	150.78	406.84	143.05
黄石市	Huangshi	174.14	91.18	174.40	87.84
十堰市	Shiyan	405.38	218.78	408.92	209.80
宜昌市	Yichang	587.83	324.01	596.11	314.58
襄阳市	Xiangyang	1051.13	830.15	1022.92	781.67
鄂州市	Ezhou	93.18	43.42	91.64	41.19
荆门市	Jingmen	661.30	476.75	654.55	459.02
孝感市	Xiaogan	581.48	360.45	570.93	344.95
荆州市	Jingzhou	1090.12	737.99	1061.24	702.28
黄冈市	Huanggang	814.98	411.64	810.16	391.09
咸宁市	Xianning	424.83	204.71	420.79	194.45
随州市	Suizhou	319.74	227.81	287.20	192.44
恩施自治州	Enshi	726.57	375.60	711.33	367.20
仙桃市	Xiantao	219.40	119.93	216.75	115.93
潜江市	Qianjiang	148.79	103.52	141.70	99.81
天门市	Tianmen	234.99	164.22	230.18	157.40
神农架林区	Shennongjia	10.00	6.07	10.24	5.90

12-22 市、州主要农作物产量(2019)
Output of Major Farm Crops of Cities and Prefectures (2019)

单位：万吨 (10 000tons)

市、州	Municipalities and Prefecrures	粮食 Grain	稻谷 Rice	小麦 Wheat	玉米 Corn	薯类 Tubers	大豆 Soybean	棉花 Cotton
全省	**Province**	**2724.98**	**1877.06**	**390.68**	**307.22**	**106.43**	**34.60**	**14.36**
武汉市	Wuhan	88.60	75.01	2.76	8.04	1.07	1.48	1.07
黄石市	Huangshi	53.83	46.43	2.11	2.74	2.04	0.35	0.37
十堰市	Shiyan	81.18	21.82	16.91	26.53	11.86	2.51	0.01
宜昌市	Yichang	151.05	66.35	12.89	49.60	19.26	1.74	0.81
襄阳市	Xiangyang	467.08	184.36	184.72	88.82	7.12	0.97	0.89
鄂州市	Ezhou	25.38	21.58	1.80	0.81	0.37	0.33	0.47
荆门市	Jingmen	286.46	217.95	38.97	23.54	0.95	4.91	0.49
孝感市	Xiaogan	231.23	201.73	22.37	4.93	1.16	0.83	0.90
荆州市	Jingzhou	451.18	375.64	50.81	15.45	0.68	7.35	3.80
黄冈市	Huanggang	268.63	245.01	11.04	4.78	5.09	2.45	2.50
咸宁市	Xianning	116.46	99.30	1.78	6.79	7.17	1.08	0.39
随州市	Suizhou	142.47	121.33	13.00	5.60	2.08	0.25	0.46
恩施州	Enshi	146.32	35.35	0.49	60.34	45.40	3.56	
仙桃市	Xiaotao	72.31	56.99	6.97	5.94	0.44	1.62	1.06
潜江市	Qianjiang	59.57	48.48	8.12	1.01	0.39	1.51	0.15
天门市	Tianmen	81.17	59.64	15.86	1.34	0.70	3.61	0.99
神农架	Shennongjia	2.07	0.08	0.08	0.96	0.67	0.06	

12–22 续表 continued

单位：万吨 (10 000tons)

市、州	Municipalities and Prefecrures	油料 Oil Bearing Crops	花生 Peanuts	油菜籽 Rapeseed	芝麻 Sesame	麻类 Hemp Crops	苎麻 Ramie	糖类 Sugar Crops	甘蔗 Crane	烟叶 Tobacoo Crops	烤烟 Tobacco
全省	**Province**	**313.95**	**85.71**	**211.35**	**12.92**	**0.70**	**0.67**	**27.90**	**27.90**	**6.31**	**5.23**
武汉市	Wuhan	13.41	4.48	7.51	1.42			1.93	1.93		
黄石市	Huangshi	11.01	1.63	7.62	1.72	0.29	0.29	0.60	0.60		
十堰市	Shiyan	15.93	5.38	8.63	1.79	0.01	0.00	1.58	1.58	1.03	1.03
宜昌市	Yichang	21.03	3.44	17.25	0.33			0.11	0.11	0.70	0.58
襄阳市	Xiangyang	35.70	23.52	8.73	2.37			0.79	0.79	0.59	0.58
鄂州市	Ezhou	4.32	0.80	2.72	0.05			0.60	0.60		
荆门市	Jingmen	31.75	6.43	24.65	0.67			1.09	1.09	0.001	
孝感市	Xiaogan	22.73	8.13	14.09	0.51	0.004	0.004	1.80	1.80		
荆州市	Jingzhou	43.30	0.65	41.46	1.19	0.01	0.01	3.63	3.63		
黄冈市	Huanggang	48.21	16.75	30.03	1.20	0.31	0.29	3.44	3.44		
咸宁市	Xianning	16.74	3.50	12.26	0.60	0.08	0.08	7.65	7.65		
随州市	Suizhou	9.92	3.95	4.82	0.11			0.21	0.21		
恩施州	Enshi	12.11	2.17	9.60	0.04					3.99	3.04
仙桃市	Xiaotao	12.37	0.41	11.41	0.56			3.34	3.34		
潜江市	Qianjiang	4.11	0.61	3.33	0.17			0.57	0.57		
天门市	Tianmen	11.27	3.88	7.23	0.17			0.56	0.56		
神农架	Shennongjia	0.03		0.02							

12-23 市、州大牲畜、羊、猪年末存栏、出栏、肉产量(2019)
Statistics on Live Animals, Sheep, Hogs in Stock/out of Stock at Year-end and Output of Meat of Cities and Prefectures(2019)

市、州	Municipalities and Prefecrures	牛存栏(万只) Cattles and Bufflaoes	羊存栏 (万只) Sheep in Stock (10 000 heads)	家禽存笼 (万只) Poultry stockpile (10 000 heads)	年末生猪存栏 (万头) Hogs in Stock at Year-end(10 000 heads)
全省	**Province**	**243.15**	**553.35**	**36214.91**	**1617.86**
武汉市	Wuhan	6.03	3.22	1776.95	86.28
黄石市	Huangshi	3.27	4.05	858.69	39.23
十堰市	Shiyan	20.17	80.14	1196.11	69.47
宜昌市	Yichang	10.06	101.99	1511.46	231.58
襄阳市	Xiangyang	50.15	95.50	7837.18	202.28
鄂州市	Ezhou	0.69	0.28	460.22	29.76
荆门市	Jingmen	11.46	33.13	2476.55	115.87
孝感市	Xiaogan	24.08	20.22	4988.73	117.96
荆州市	Jingzhou	4.32	9.28	3411.18	140.37
黄冈市	Huanggang	59.27	78.49	5435.26	157.85
咸宁市	Xianning	11.78	22.55	1215.08	96.08
随州市	Suizhou	17.41	38.40	2479.73	75.34
恩施州	Enshi	19.02	61.84	832.49	179.08
仙桃市	Xiaotao	0.28	0.23	479.45	20.94
潜江市	Qianjiang	1.13	0.92	470.97	25.27
天门市	Tianmen	3.67	1.11	760.78	28.99
神农架	Shennongjia	0.37	2.02	24.08	1.50

12-23 续表 continued

市、州 Municipalities and Prefecrures	年内出栏肉猪(万头) Hogs out of Stock at Year-end (10 000 heads)	年内出栏羊(万只) Sheep out of Stock at Year-end (10 000 heads)	出笼禽(万只) Poultry out of Stock at Year-end (10 000 heads)	猪肉产量(万吨) Output of pork Meat (10 000 tons)	牛肉产量(万吨) beef	羊肉(万吨) muttom	禽蛋产量(万吨) Output of Eggs (10 000 tons)
全省 Province	**3189.24**	**615.93**	**59394.01**	**242.95**	**15.99**	**9.85**	**178.75**
武汉市 Wuhan	168.61	3.55	4088.50	12.84	0.33	0.06	9.33
黄石市 Huangshi	76.66	4.08	2294.53	5.84	0.13	0.07	4.70
十堰市 Shiyan	135.76	83.31	2778.64	10.34	0.85	0.93	6.25
宜昌市 Yichang	425.09	123.39	2942.95	32.38	0.79	1.95	6.42
襄阳市 Xiangyang	395.31	131.54	7152.42	30.11	5.17	2.62	36.22
鄂州市 Ezhou	59.90	1.20	1019.51	4.57	0.14	0.02	3.77
荆门市 Jingmen	261.62	44.68	4313.88	19.93	1.24	0.77	11.86
孝感市 Xiaogan	231.58	20.29	9646.73	17.64	1.03	0.32	25.55
荆州市 Jingzhou	297.77	13.70	6390.12	22.68	0.35	0.14	16.99
黄冈市 Huanggang	308.48	62.28	4976.23	23.50	3.39	1.08	28.11
咸宁市 Xianning	187.77	16.19	3231.33	14.30	0.19	0.35	4.61
随州市 Suizhou	147.23	44.60	6681.85	11.21	0.89	0.54	13.06
恩施州 Enshi	317.76	62.03	1126.20	24.20	0.96	0.93	3.98
仙桃市 Xiaotao	53.66	0.45	713.61	4.10	0.09	0.00	1.78
潜江市 Qianjiang	55.96	1.85	988.18	4.27	0.22	0.03	2.41
天门市 Tianmen	63.14	0.98	1018.23	4.82	0.20	0.01	3.68
神农架 Shennongjia	2.93	1.83	31.10	0.22	0.02	0.04	0.03

12-24 市、州主要土特产品产量(2019)
Output of Main Native Products of Cities and Prefectures (2019)

市、州	Municipalities and Prefecrures	茶叶(万吨) Tea (10 000 tons)	蚕茧(吨) Silkworm Coccons (ton)	桑蚕茧 Mulbeery Silkworm Coccons	园林水果(万吨) Fruits (10 000 tons)	桃子 Peaches	柑橘 Citrus	苹果 Apples
全省	**Province**	35.25	3769	3630	661.04	86.54	478.22	0.79
武汉市	Wuhan	0.26			14.13	4.65	3.35	0.03
黄石市	Huangshi	0.11	475	475	7.76	0.85	5.16	0.02
十堰市	Shiyan	1.55	676	676	28.18	1.19	23.90	0.04
宜昌市	Yichang	9.33	321	321	377.11	3.81	365.45	0.10
襄阳市	Xiangyang	1.00	442	442	51.47	39.90	3.14	0.18
鄂州市	Ezhou	0.02			3.69	0.32	2.40	
荆门市	Jingmen	0.03			39.52	6.56	12.77	
孝感市	Xiaogan	0.85			16.30	8.64	2.28	0.10
荆州市	Jingzhou	0.03			45.99	2.23	29.01	
黄冈市	Huanggang	3.84	1685	1685	7.33	2.71	2.34	0.06
咸宁市	Xianning	5.86			9.11	1.24	4.27	0.01
随州市	Suizhou	0.32	139		15.55	10.92	0.65	0.08
恩施州	Enshi	12.05	31	31	35.46	1.28	22.34	0.18
仙桃市	Xiaotao				1.67	0.43	0.53	
潜江市	Qianjiang				5.88	1.43	0.29	
天门市	Tianmen				1.84	0.38	0.35	
神农架	Shennongjia	0.01			0.04	0.01		

12-25 市、州人平粮、棉、油、肉、水产品生产水平(2019)
Per Capita Production Level of Grain, Cotton, Oil, Meat and Aquatic Products of Cities and Prefectures (2019)

单位:千克 (kg)

市、州	Municipalities and Prefecrures	粮食 Grain	棉花 Cotton	油料 Oil Bearing Crops	猪肉 Pork	水产品 AquaticProducts	禽蛋 Eggs
按常住人口平均	**Average of Total Population**						
全省	Province	460.15	2.43	53.01	41.03	79.29	30.18
武汉市	Wuhan	79.49	0.96	12.03	11.52	39.69	8.37
黄石市	Huangshi	217.84	1.50	44.55	23.63	84.48	19.00
十堰市	Shiyan	238.61	0.02	46.83	30.39	16.42	18.38
宜昌市	Xiangyang	365.12	1.97	50.84	78.27	43.05	15.52
襄阳市	Ezhou	823.12	1.58	62.91	53.06	34.26	63.83
鄂州市	Jingmen	237.47	4.37	40.41	42.76	270.71	35.25
荆门市	Xiaogan	988.82	1.68	109.60	68.80	161.45	40.95
孝感市	Jingzhou	469.94	1.83	46.19	35.85	84.30	51.92
荆州市	Yichang	808.54	6.81	77.59	40.64	201.09	30.45
黄冈市	Huanggang	424.28	3.95	76.15	37.12	72.46	44.40
咸宁市	Xianning	457.45	1.52	65.77	56.17	85.74	18.11
随州市	Suizhou	642.09	2.09	44.70	50.52	38.17	58.87
恩施州	Enshi	432.39		35.78	71.51	0.75	11.76
仙桃市	Xiaotao	634.24	9.29	108.51	35.96	258.47	15.58
潜江市	Tianmen	616.60	1.59	42.59	44.20	147.62	24.94
天门市	Qianjiang	644.30	7.84	89.48	38.26	95.50	29.23
神农架	Shennongjia	270.29		3.40	29.22	0.94	3.66

12-26 市、州农业机械、用电、化肥、水利情况(2019)
Agricultural Machinery, Electricity Consumption, Chemical Fertilizers and Irrigation of Cities and Prefectures (2019)

市、州	Municipalities and Prefecrures	农业机械总动力(万千瓦特) Total Power of Agricultural Machinery (10 000kW)	当年实际机耕面积(千公顷) Actual Sown Areas (1 000 hectares)	农村用电量(万千瓦小时) Rural Electricity Consumption (1 000kW/h)	化肥施用量(折纯量)(万吨) Consumption of Chemical Fertilizers (pure) (10 000tons)	耕地灌溉面积(千公顷) Irrigation Area of Cultivated Land (1 000 hectares)
全省	**Province**	**4515.73**	**5983.54**	**1785529.11**	**273.89**	**2968.99**
武汉市	Wuhan	237.72	258.02	144889.00	11.08	168.19
黄石市	Huangshi	122.84	113.86	115100.00	4.69	73.15
十堰市	Shiyan	180.55	279.18	74856.00	9.23	60.34
宜昌市	Yichang	310.55	424.84	115727.00	30.11	164.52
襄阳市	Xiangyang	680.84	938.54	173974.10	35.60	312.93
鄂州市	Ezhou	57.04	57.33	59606.00	6.96	54.53
荆门市	Jingmen	494.27	557.85	127673.00	28.41	243.02
孝感市	Xiaogan	272.49	416.51	169317.00	18.09	358.23
荆州市	Jingzhou	648.04	880.08	272241.00	30.50	573.30
黄冈市	Huanggang	376.29	684.94	216164.42	31.09	322.05
咸宁市	Xianning	190.12	281.45	50053.69	11.07	126.57
随州市	Suizhou	223.33	219.36	53627.00	15.17	110.73
恩施自治州	Enshi	243.73	338.13	64304.10	24.14	105.70
仙桃市	Xiaotao	146.18	173.10	62560.36	5.28	113.53
潜江市	Qianjiang	150.01	125.84	49447.58	5.02	73.28
天门市	Tianmen	170.04	229.52	34113.86	7.06	108.18
神农架林区	Shennongjia	11.70	5.00	1875.00	0.38	0.73

主要统计指标解释

农林牧渔业总产值　指以货币表现的农、林、牧、渔业全部产品和对农林牧渔业生产活动进行的各种支持性服务活动的价值总量，它反映一定时期内农林牧渔业生产总规模和总成果。1957年以前的农林牧渔业总产值中包括了厩肥和农民自给性手工业(如农民自制衣服、鞋、袜，自己从事粮食初步加工等)。1958年及以后，林业中增加了村及村以下竹木采伐产值；牧业中取消了厩肥产值；副业中取消了农民自给性手工业产值，增加了村及村以下办的工业产值；渔业中增加了海洋捕捞水产品产值。1980年及以后，在副业中增加了农民家庭兼营工业商品部分的产值。从1984年起村及村以下工业产值划归工业。从1993年起取消副业，将野生动物的捕猎划入牧业，野生植物采集和农民家庭兼营商品性工业划归农业。从2003年起，执行新的国民经济行业分类标准，农林牧渔业总产值中包括了农林牧渔服务业产值。林业中增加了森林采运业产值。农业中取消了家庭兼营商品性工业产值，将野生林产品的采集划归林业。第一次农业普查以后，由于畜牧业产品年报数据与普查数据之间存在一定的差距，国家统计局农调总队对畜牧业年报数据与普查数据进行衔接，对畜牧业产值进行相应调整。

农林牧渔业总产值的计算方法通常是按农、林、牧、渔业产品及其副产品的产量分别乘以各自单位产品价格求得；少数生产周期较长，当年没有产品或产品产量不易统计的，则采用间接方法匡算其产值；然后将四业产品产值相加即为农林牧渔业总产值。

粮食产量　指全社会的产量。包括国有经济经营的、集体统一经营的和农民家庭经营的粮食产量，还包括工矿企业办的农场和其他生产单位的产量。粮食除包括稻谷、小麦、玉米、高粱、谷子及其他杂粮外，还包括薯类和豆类。其产量计算方法，豆类按去豆荚后的干豆计算；薯类(包括甘薯和马铃薯，不包括芋头和木薯)1963年以前按每4公斤鲜薯折1公斤粮食计算，从1964年开始改为按5公斤鲜薯折1公斤粮食计算。城市郊区作为蔬菜的薯类(如马铃薯等)按鲜品计算，并且不作粮食统计。其他粮食一律按脱粒后的原粮计算。1989年以前全国粮食产量数据主要靠全面报表取得，1989年开始使用抽样调查数据。

棉花产量　指全社会的产量。包括春播棉和夏播棉。产量按皮棉计算。不包括木棉。

油料产量　指全部油料作物的生产量。包括花生、油菜籽、芝麻、向日葵籽、胡麻籽(亚麻籽)和其他油料。不包括大豆、木本油料和野生油料。花生以带壳干花生计算。

水产品产量　指人工养殖的水产品和天然生长的水产品的捕捞量。包括海水的鱼类、虾蟹类、贝类和藻类以及内陆水域的鱼类、虾蟹类和贝类，不包括淡水生植物。水产品产量是通过各级水产和统计部门逐级上报取得数据。1995年及以前，贝类中牡蛎按鲜肉计算；蚶、蛤、蛏按5斤鲜品折1斤计算。1996年以后则统一按鲜品计算。

猪、牛、羊肉产量　指当年出栏并已屠宰、除去头蹄下水后带骨肉(即胴体重)的重量。包括全社会范围内的产量。1996年前为各级逐级上报数据。1996年第一次农业普查以后，由于畜牧业产品年报数据与普查数据之间存在一定的差距，国家统计局农调总队对畜牧业年报数据与普查数据进行衔接。1999年以后，国家统计局开展了猪、牛、羊、禽等主要畜禽品种的抽样调查，并用抽样数据作为国家定案数据使用。未开展抽样调查的品种，仍使用各级统计部门逐级上报数据。

期初(末)畜禽存栏头(只)数　指报告期初(末)农村各种合作经济组织和国营农场、农民个人、机关、团体、学校、工矿企业、部队等单位以及城镇居民饲养的大牲畜、猪、羊、家禽等畜禽的存栏数。数据上报方式及数据调整情况同猪、牛、羊肉产量。

常用耕地　是指耕地总资源中专门种植农作物并经常进行耕种、能够正常收获的土地。包括当年实际耕种的熟地；弃耕、休闲不满三年，随时可以复耕的地；开荒利用三年以上的土地。在统计口径上包括南方小于1米、北方小于2米宽的沟、渠、路和田埂。不包括临时种植农作物的坡度在25度以上的陡坡地;在河套、湖畔、库区临时开发的成片或零星土地;也不包括已列为国家和省(区、市)退耕计划但临时耕种的土地。常用耕地是国家需要重点保护的耕地,是反映我国农业综合生产能力的一个重要指标。

农作物播种面积 指实际播种或移植有农作物的面积。凡是实际种植有农作物的面积,不论种植在耕地上还是种植在非耕地上,均包括在农作物播种面积中。在播种季节基本结束后,因遭灾而重新改种和补种的农作物面积,也包括在内。它是反映我国耕地面积利用情况的一个重要指标。目前,农作物播种面积主要包括粮食、棉花、油料、糖料、麻类、烟叶、蔬菜和瓜类、药材和其他农作物九大类。

有效灌溉面积 指具有一定的水源,地块比较平整,灌溉工程或设备已经配套,在一般年景下,当年能够进行正常灌溉的耕地面积。在一般情况下,有效灌溉面积应等于灌溉工程或设备已经配备,能够进行正常灌溉的水田和水浇地面积之和。它是反映我国耕地抗旱能力的一个重要指标。

农用化肥施用量 指本年内实际用于农业生产的化肥数量,包括氮肥、磷肥、钾肥和复合肥。化肥施用量要求按折纯量计算数量。折纯量是指把氮肥、磷肥、钾肥分别按含氮、含五氧化二磷、含氧化钾的百分之百成份进行折算后的数量。复合肥按其所含主要成分折算。公式为:

折纯量=实物量×某种化肥有效成份含量的百分比

农业机械总动力 指主要用于农、林、牧、渔业的各种动力机械的动力总和。包括耕作机械、排灌机械、收获机械、农用运输机械、植物保护机械、牧业机械、林业机械、渔业机械和其他农业机械〔内燃机按引擎马力折成瓦(特)计算、电动机按功率折成瓦(特)计算〕。不包括专门用于乡、镇、村、组办工业、基本建设、非农业运输、科学试验和教学等非农业生产方面用的动力机械与作业机械。这个指标的统计数据主要来源于农机部门。

乡村从业人员 指乡村人口中劳动年龄在16周岁以上实际参加生产经营活动并取得实物或货币收入的人员,包括劳动年龄内经常参加劳动的人员,也包括超过劳动年龄但经常参加劳动的人员,但不包括户口在家的在外学生、现役军人和丧失劳动能力的人,也不包括待业人员和家务劳动者。从业人员按从事主业时间最长(时间相同按收入)分为农林牧渔业从业人员、工业从业人员、建筑业从业人员、交通运输业、仓储及邮电通信业从业人员、批零贸易业、餐饮业从业人员、其他非农行业从业人员。

Explanatory Notes on Main Statistical Indicators

Gross Output Value of Agriculture, Forestry, Animal Husbandry and Fishery refers to the total value of products of farming, forestry, animal husbandry and fishery, and total value of services rendered to support farming, forestry, animal husbandry and fishery activities. It reflects the total scale and results of agricultural production during a given period. Prior to 1957, Chinas gross agricultural output value included barnyard manure and handicraft products for self-consumption (clothes, shoes, stockings, and initial grain processing undertaken by peasants). Since 1958, cutting and felling of bamboo and trees by villages and other cooperative organizations under villages have been included in forestry; value of barnyard manure has been excluded from animal husbandry; self consumed handicrafts has been excluded from sideline occupations, while the output value of industries run by villages and cooperative organizations under village had been included in sideline occupations and the output value of fish catches by motor fishing boats has been added to fishery. Since 1980, the value of handicraft products made for sale by individuals in households had been added to sideline occupations. Since 1984, industries run by villages and under villages have been included in the sector of industry. Since 1993, the subdivision of sideline occupations has been canceled, and the hunting of wild animals has been classified into animal husbandry, and the gathering of wild plants and commodity industry run by rural household have been included in farming. A new industrial classification of economic activities was introduced in 2003. Under the new classification, value of services to farming, forestry, animal husbandry and fishery is included in the gross output value of agriculture, value of wood felling and transport is included in forestry, value of industrial output by rural households is not included in agriculture, and the collection of wild forest products is taken from agriculture and included in the forestry. The first agriculture census of China revealed some discrepancy between the production of animal products from the annual reports and that from the census. Efforts were made by the Rural Socio-economic Survey Organization of NBS to adjust the output value of animal husbandry to make the figures from the annual reports consistent with the census data.

Gross output value of agriculture is obtained by first multiplying the output of each product or by product by its price, resulting in the output value of each single item. For a small number of products, annual output of which is not available or difficult to get due to the long production (growing) process involved, the output value is estimated through an indirect approach. The sum of output value of all products of farming, forestry, animal husbandry and fishery is then equal to the gross output value of agriculture.

Grain Output refers to the total output in the whole country including grains produced by state farms, collective units, rural households, as well as by farms affiliated to industrial and mining enterprises and other production units. Grain includes rice, wheat, corn, sorghum, millet and other miscellaneous grains as well as tubers and bean. Output of beans refers to dry beans without pods. The output of tubers (sweet potatoes and potatoes, not including taros and cassava) was converted into that of grain at the ratio 4:1, i.e. 4 kilograms of fresh tubers was equivalent to 1 kilogram of grain up to 1963. Since 1964 the ratio for conversion has been 5:1. Tubers supplied as vegetables (such as potatoes) in cities and suburbs are calculated as fresh vegetables and their output is not included in the output of grain. Output of all other grains refers to husked grain. Data on grain production before 1989 were obtained through Comprehensive Statistical Reporting System. Since 1989, data from sample surveys are used.

Cotton Output refers to the cotton production in the whole country including cotton sown in spring and in autumn. Output is measured as the weight of ginned cotton. Ceiba is not included.

Output of Oil-bearing Crops refers to the total production of oil-bearing crops of various kinds, including peanuts, (dry, in shell) rapeseeds, sesame, sunflower seeds, flax seeds, and other oil-bearing crops. Soybeans, oil-bearing woody plants, and wild oil-bearing crops are not included.

Output of Aquatic Products refers to catches of both artificially cultured and naturally grown aquatic products, including fish, shrimps, crabs and shellfish in sea and inland water as well as seaweed. Freshwater plants are not included. Data on output of aquatic products are reported by aquatic product and statistical agencies level by level. Before 1995, among the shellfish, the oyster was counted as fresh meat; 5 kilograms of ark shell, clams and frogs are equivalent to 1 kilogram of fresh aquatic products; they are all counted as fresh aquatic products since 1996.

Output of Pork, Beef, and Mutton refers to the meat of slaughtered hogs, cattle, sheep and goats with head, feet, and offal taken away. Data refers to the production of the whole country. The first agriculture census of China in 1996 revealed some discrepancy between the production of animal products from the annual reports and that from the census. Efforts were made by the Rural Socio-economic Survey Organization of NBS to adjust the output value of animal husbandry to make the figures from the annual reports consistent with the census data. Since 1999, NBS conducted sample survey for the major animal husbandry products, such as hogs, cattle, sheep and goats and fowls, and the data from sample surveys are used as national finalized data. Those products, which are not covered by the sample survey, are still reported by statistical agencies level by level.

Number of Livestock or Poultry in Stock at Beginning (or End) refers to the total number of large animals, pigs, sheep, fowls, etc. raised by rural cooperative organizations, state farms, rural individuals, government agencies, schools, industrial and mining enterprises, army, and urban residents at the beginning (or end) of the reference period. Data reporting system and data adjustment are the same as that in the output of pork, beef and mutton.

Regularly Cultivated Land refers to farmland among the total land resources, which is exclusively used for farming and is under regular cultivation with harvest in normal years. Included are currently cultivated land, land that has been abandoned or put in idle for less than 3 years and could be re–used for cultivation at any time, and new–claimed land that has been put into cultivation for more than 3 years. According to statistical coverage, it includes the gouges, dykes, roads and ridges of field with 1 meter wide in Southern areas and 2 meters wide in Northern areas. Excluded under this category are steep slope land over 25 degrees under temporary cultivation, land (large or small plots) that is claimed along river bends, lake sides or banks of reservoirs, as well as land that has been designated under the "Green for Grain" programme of the state and provincial governments but is still temporarily under cultivation. The regularly cultivated land is the key protection land of the nation, an important indicator reflecting the comprehensive productivity of agriculture of China.

Sown Area of Crops refers to area of land sown or transplanted with crops regardless of being in cultivated area or non–cultivated area. Area of land re–sown due to natural disasters is also included. This is an important indicator that can reflect the utilization condition of the cultivated land in China. At present, the sown area of crops mainly include the following 9 categories of crops: grain, cotton, oil–bearing crops, sugar crops, fiber crops, Tobacco, Vegetables and melons, medicinal materials and other farm crops.

Irrigated Area refers to areas that are effectively irrigated, i.e. level land, which has water source and complete sets of irrigation facilities to lift and move adequate water for irrigation purpose under normal conditions. Under normal conditions, irrigated area is the sum of watered fields and irrigated fields where irrigation systems or equipment have been installed for regular irrigation purpose. This important indicator reflects drought resistance capacity of the cultivated land in China.

Consumption of Chemical Fertilizers in Agriculture refers to the quantity of chemical fertilizers applied in agriculture in the year, including nitrogenous fertilizer, phosphate fertilizer, potash fertilizer, and compound fertilizer. The consumption of chemical fertilizers is required in calculation to convert the gross weight into weight containing 100% effective component (e.g. 100% nitrogen content in nitrogenous fertilizer, 100% phosphorous pent oxide contents in phosphate fertilizer, 100% potassium oxide contents in potash fertilizer). Compound fertilizer is converted with its major component. The formula is :

Volume of effective component= physical quantity x effective component of certain chemical fertilizer (%)

Total Power of Farm Machinery refers to total mechanical power of machinery used in farming, forestry, animal husbandry, and fishery, including ploughing, irrigation and drainage, harvesting, transport, plant protection, stock breeding, forestry and fishery. The power of internal combustion engines is required to convert horsepower into watts and the power of electric motors is required to be converted into watts. Machinery employed for non–agricultural purposes, such as the machines used in township run and village–run industry, construction, non–agricultural transport, scientific experiments and teaching, is excluded. Data are mainly from agricultural machinery agencies.

Rural Employed Persons refer to rural labor forces aged over 16 years old who are engaged in real production and management activities and receive payment in kind or wages, including those covered within the age frame and regularly participating in production activities, and those who are out of the range of age frame and also participating in production activities regularly. Excluding students studying in other places with their permanent residence registered in local areas, servicemen and persons incapable of working; also excluding those who are waiting for jobs and those engaged in household work. Persons employed are classified as persons engaged in agriculture, forestry, animal husbandry or fishery activities; persons engaged in industrial activities; persons engaged in construction activities; persons engaged in transport, storage and telecommunications activities; persons engaged in whole sales and retail sales trade and catering activities; and persons engaged in other non–agriculture activities, depending upon the longest period of employment in major activities (or using income indicator when period of employment is the same).

13 工 业

Industry

资料整理人员：魏燕子　刘洪韬　高　媛

工 业

Industry
2019

规模以上工业企业	Industrial Enterprises Above Designated Size		
工业总产值(现价)	Total Output Value (at current price)	47572.06	(亿元)
#轻工业	Light Industry	16352.06	(亿元)
重工业	Heavy Industry	31220.00	(亿元)
#大型企业	Large Scale Enterprises	14877.30	(亿元)
中型企业	Medium Scale Enterprises	9853.75	(亿元)
资产总计	Total Assets	42530.89	(亿元)
负债合计	Total Liability	22178.45	(亿元)
营业收入	Business Revenue	45461.08	(亿元)
利税总额	Total Profits and Taxes	5274.52	(亿元)
从业人员年平均人数	Annually Average number of Employment	335.87	(万人)

规模以上工业总产值构成(%)
Composition of Industry above desginated size

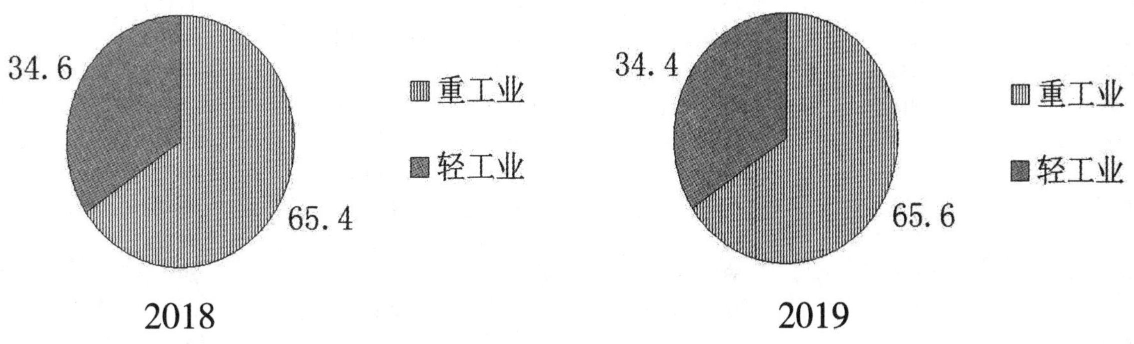

2018　　2019

规模以上工业增加值(上年=100)

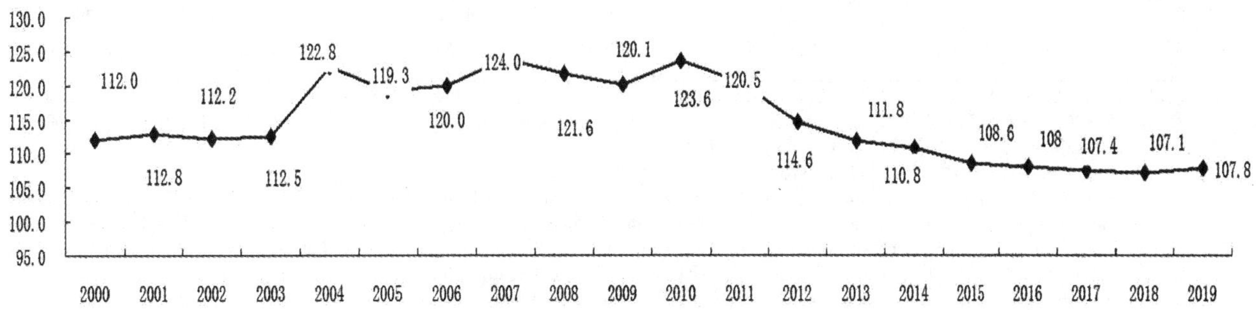

13-1 工业发展基本情况
Basic Situation of Industrial Development

年份 Year	工业企业单位数(个) Number of Industrial Enterprises (unit)	轻工业 Light industry	重工业 Heavy industry	工业总产值(当年价)(亿元) Total Output Value (currentprice) (100 million yuan)	轻工业 Light industry	重工业 Heavy industry
1979	16073	10100	5973	220.82	93.45	107.37
1985	25011	15309	9702	467.22	216.47	250.75
1986	27697	16890	10807	538.28	256.06	282.22
1987	26294	15528	10766	659.19	315.49	343.70
1988	26016	15279	10737	834.84	405.13	429.71
1989	25999	15035	10964	976.93	463.35	513.58
1990	25913	14885	11028	1008.20	476.76	531.44
1991	25204	14317	10887	1136.02	531.26	604.76
1992	23985	13428	10557	1373.66	605.11	768.55
1993	22600	11958	10642	1992.31	770.20	1222.11
1994	23275	12096	11179	3024.72	1360.78	1663.94
1995	27815	14827	12988	3697.91	1870.12	1827.79
1996	25986	13618	12368	4836.33	2470.90	2365.43
1997	24498	12723	11775	5977.00	3158.47	2818.53
1998	7399	3581	3818	6731.31	3534.67	3196.64
1999	6874	3308	3566	2831.70	1109.92	1721.78
2000	6282	3026	3256	3064.43	1177.24	1887.18
2001	6197	2981	3216	3239.51	1194.90	2044.61
2002	6183	2947	3236	3589.26	1184.78	2404.48
2003	6271	2789	3482	3631.29	1192.46	2438.82
2004	6232	2632	3600	4960.25	1180.07	3780.17
2005	6813	2953	3860	6066.96	1503.00	4563.95
2006	7546	3272	4274	7454.07	1898.34	5555.73
2007	8996	3808	5188	9601.52	2492.88	7108.64
2008	12067	4806	7261	13454.94	3344.80	10110.14
2009	14027	5515	8512	15567.02	4234.52	11332.50
2010	16106	6326	9780	21623.12	5935.78	15687.33
2011	10633	4347	6286	28072.73	8370.27	19702.45
2012	12441	5012	7429	33450.66	10941.70	22508.95
2013	14650	5855	8795	39208.98	13405.24	25803.74
2014	15957	6453	9504	43393.87	15378.14	28015.73
2015	16413	6646	9767	45809.57	16810.65	28998.91
2016	16296	6680	9616	48766.71	18027.68	30739.04
2017	15097	6100	8997	45642.59	15630.86	30011.74
2018	15222	6272	8950	45765.33	15817.24	29948.09
2019	15520	6230	9290	47572.06	16352.06	31220.00

注：1.本表规模以上工业1997年及以前统计范围为乡及乡以上工业。1998-2006年为全部国有工业及年销售收入500万元以上非国有工业企业;2007年-2010年为主营业务收入500万元以上工业企业。2011年起为主营业务收入2000万元及以上的工业法人企业。(下表同)

2."国有及国有控股经济"一栏,1998年以前统计范围为国有工业。

3.2017年行业小类码按照《国民经济行业分类》(GB/T4754-2017)填写。(下表同)

Note: 1.The scopes of industrial statistics are all township and above town industrial enterprises before 1998.The scopes are all state-owned industrial enterprises and non-state-owned industrial enterprise with revenue from principal business over 5 million yuan from 1998 to 2006.For 2007 to 2010, the scopes are all industrial enterprices with revenue from principal business over 5 million yuan.From 2011,the scopes are all industrial enterprises with revenue from principal business over 20 millon yuan.The same applies to the talbe following.

2."State-owned and state-controlled economy"a column,prior to 1998 statistics the range of state-owned industries.

3.Accordring to GB/T4754-2017,the small classes code of industries are filled in the table from 2017.The same applies to the talbe following.

13-1 续表 continued

单位: 亿元 (100 million yuan)

年份 Year	主营业务收入(亿元) Main business income (100 million yuan)	利润总额(亿元) Total profits (100 million yuan)	利税总额(亿元) Total profits and taxes (100 million yuan)	职工人数(万人) Number of employees (1000 persons)
1979	163.52	20.70	34.19	161.98
1985	381.43	43.64	80.82	306.83
1986	438.95	40.22	82.14	333.63
1987	526.95	48.54	96.16	343.43
1988	654.72	58.85	117.28	356.43
1989	706.99	50.99	112.12	360.88
1990	705.97	26.73	88.40	358.65
1991	800.01	31.79	103.46	367.41
1992	1041.66	43.19	127.15	357.74
1993	1500.71	67.00	167.92	357.97
1994	1690.94	74.06	190.29	381.45
1995	2066.38	52.26	181.57	379.84
1996	2305.57	43.93	181.41	369.80
1997	2681.36	57.71	221.53	362.50
1998	2433.92	44.71	195.96	274.43
1999	2602.26	68.82	232.24	250.07
2000	2870.36	106.47	293.58	230.36
2001	3043.82	134.49	335.36	212.48
2002	3378.31	175.60	404.23	205.82
2003	3993.99	194.40	444.96	198.60
2004	4832.43	270.98	559.28	176.70
2005	5962.54	371.84	727.48	188.30
2006	7314.81	454.00	897.19	190.85
2007	9390.43	647.85	1229.16	200.35
2008	13081.90	909.03	1761.47	235.90
2009	15331.62	1092.47	1987.88	272.39
2010	21151.56	1668.55	2950.08	294.97
2011	27072.02	1864.46	3093.57	279.59
2012	32325.95	2046.28	3528.80	311.13
2013	38183.39	2475.07	4451.87	346.29
2014	41401.49	2402.63	4465.72	359.45
2015	43179.21	2456.00	4599.15	352.64
2016	45850.64	2713.46	4754.74	339.51
2017	43210.52	2608.03	4603.47	309.78
2018	43515.86	3752.76	6542.53	315.55
2019	44492.00	3049.57	5274.52	335.87

13-2 规模以上工业企业单位数和产销总值(2019)

单位:亿元

项 目	Item	企业单位数(个) Number of Enterprises (unit)
总 计	**Total**	**15520**
一、按登记注册类型分组:	**Grouped by Type of Registration**	
内资企业	Inner Funded Enterprises	14779
国有企业	State Owned Enterprises	98
中央企业	Central Enterprises	35
地方企业	Local Enterprises	63
集体企业	Collective-owned Enterprise	48
股份合作企业	Share Holding Cooperative Enterprises	4
联营企业	Joint Owned Enterprise	3
国有联营企业	State Joint Ownership	
集体联营企业	Collective Joint Ownership	1
国有与集体联营企业	Joint State- Collective Ownership	1
其他联营企业	Other Joint Owned Enterprise	1
有限责任公司	Responsibility Co. Ltd	3997
国有独资公司	State Solely Funded Co.	137
其他有限责任公司	Others	3860
股份有限公司	Share Holding Co.Ltd.	814
私营企业	Private - owned enterprises	9806
私营独资企业	Solely Private - owned enterprises	171
私营合伙企业	Private Joint Venture	29
私营有限责任公司	Private Responsibility Co. Ltd	8900
私营股份有限公司	Private Share Holding Co.Ltd.	706
其他企业	Others	9
港、澳、台商投资企业	Hongkong, Macao and Taiwan Funded Enterprises	285
合资经营企业(港或澳、台资)	Joint Venture with Hongkong, Macao and Taiwan	116
合作经营企业(港或澳、台资)	Cooperate with Hongkong, Macao and Taiwan Funded	
港澳台商独资经营企业	Enterprises Solely Funded by Hongkong, Macao and Taiwan Businessmen	148
港澳台商投资股份有限公司	Share Holding Co.Ltd. With Hongkong, Macao and Taiwan Investment	10
其他港澳台商投资企业	Other Hongkong, Macao and Taiwan Funded Enterprises	11
外商投资企业	Foreign Funded Enterprises	456
中外合资经营企业	Sino - Foreign Joint Funded Enterprises	230
中外合作经营企业	Sino - Foreign Cooperative Funded Enterprises	4
外资企业	Foreign Solely Funded Enterprises	201
外商投资股份有限公司	Foreign Funded Share Holding Co.Ltd.	11
其他外商投资企业	Other Foreign Funded Enterprises	10
二、在总计中:亏损企业	**Of the Total: enterprises running under deficit**	**1435**
在总计中:国有控股企业	Of the Total: State-Owned Share Holding Enterprises	773
在总计中:轻工业	Of the Total: Light Industry	6230
重工业	Heavy Industry	9290
在总计中:大型企业	Of the Total: Large Scale Enterprises	309
中型企业	Medium Scale Enterprises	1498
小型企业	Small Enterprises	13713

Number of Industrial Enterprises above Designated Size and Gross Production and Sales(2019)

工业总产值（当年价格） Total Output Value (current price)	资产总计 Total Assets	流动资产合计 Circulating Funds	应收帐款 Accounts Received	固定资产净额 NBV of Fixed Assets
47572.06	**42530.89**	**19878.13**	**5004.26**	**12233.10**
40036.24	36450.97	16702.00	4250.00	10389.02
1602.60	2681.58	872.91	188.40	1372.37
1474.38	2482.53	761.62	143.50	1317.62
128.21	199.05	111.29	44.91	54.76
71.84	45.24	26.54	8.94	12.50
1.90	2.38	1.92	0.74	0.17
1.56	0.83	0.51	0.22	0.08
0.58	0.12	0.03	0.03	
0.22	0.54	0.43	0.18	0.08
0.76	0.17	0.04	0.02	
13987.31	15230.34	7482.86	1956.63	3994.19
2542.42	3660.24	1657.84	278.60	1051.51
11444.89	11570.10	5825.03	1678.03	2942.67
4710.05	9100.05	3774.91	808.84	2149.92
19649.46	9386.42	4540.17	1285.35	2859.16
353.04	133.77	70.90	7.88	38.29
42.16	13.40	4.67	1.23	4.93
17718.74	8311.37	4012.87	1163.45	2560.08
1535.53	927.88	451.74	112.78	255.86
11.52	4.13	2.18	0.88	0.63
2094.13	1940.66	923.60	244.75	664.96
1117.31	1115.56	570.02	138.31	294.65
841.14	669.92	282.72	88.85	307.20
39.43	57.31	12.03	6.63	37.23
96.24	97.88	58.83	10.96	25.88
5441.69	4139.26	2252.54	509.52	1179.12
4312.91	3228.09	1704.40	297.76	920.10
22.97	22.79	9.31	1.55	10.84
1018.64	803.05	482.81	191.98	227.26
46.86	36.14	19.95	6.59	11.54
40.32	49.19	36.07	11.64	9.38
4330.89	**8262.43**	**2782.66**	**470.93**	**2985.60**
11722.96	19408.01	7910.42	1567.06	5825.98
16352.06	9706.18	5265.90	1082.05	2648.65
31220.00	32824.71	14612.24	3922.22	9584.45
14877.30	19631.69	8628.35	1723.96	5728.91
9853.75	8884.44	4421.51	1232.72	2374.24
22841.02	14014.76	6828.27	2047.58	4129.95

13-2 续表 1 continued

单位: 亿元

项 目	Item	固定资产原价 Original Price of Fixed Assets
总 计	**Total**	**25092.16**
一、按登记注册类型分组:	**Grouped by Type of Registration**	
内资企业	Inner Funded Enterprises	21544.89
国有企业	State Owned Enterprises	2823.97
中央企业	Central Enterprises	2724.20
地方企业	Local Enterprises	99.77
集体企业	Collective-owned Enterprise	23.87
股份合作企业	Share Holding Cooperative Enterprises	0.46
联营企业	Joint Owned Enterprise	0.47
国有联营企业	State Joint Ownership	
集体联营企业	Collective Joint Ownership	0.06
国有与集体联营企业	Joint State- Collective Ownership	0.41
其他联营企业	Other Joint Owned Enterprise	
有限责任公司	Responsibility Co. Ltd	8070.01
国有独资公司	State Solely Funded Co.	2535.69
其他有限责任公司	Others	5534.32
股份有限公司	Share Holding Co.Ltd.	4310.74
私营企业	Private - owned enterprises	6313.88
私营独资企业	Solely Private - owned enterprises	101.18
私营合伙企业	Private Joint Venture	9.58
私营有限责任公司	Private Responsibility Co. Ltd	5673.07
私营股份有限公司	Private Share Holding Co.Ltd.	530.04
其他企业	Others	1.49
港、澳、台商投资企业	Hongkong, Macao and Taiwan Funded Enterprises	1156.00
合资经营企业(港或澳、台资)	Joint Venture with Hongkong, Macao and Taiwan	531.25
合作经营企业(港或澳、台资)	Cooperate with Hongkong, Macao and Taiwan Funded	
港澳台商独资经营企业	Enterprises Solely Funded by Hongkong, Macao and Taiwan Businessmen	539.64
港澳台商投资股份有限公司	Share Holding Co.Ltd. With Hongkong, Macao and Taiwan Investment	42.85
其他港澳台商投资企业	Other Hongkong, Macao and Taiwan Funded Enterprises	42
外商投资企业	Foreign Funded Enterprises	2391.27
中外合资经营企业	Sino - Foreign Joint Funded Enterprises	1834.37
中外合作经营企业	Sino - Foreign Cooperative Funded Enterprises	31.56
外资企业	Foreign Solely Funded Enterprises	469.99
外商投资股份有限公司	Foreign Funded Share Holding Co.Ltd.	23.76
其他外商投资企业	Other Foreign Funded Enterprises	32
二、在总计中:亏损企业	**Of the Total: enterprises running under deficit**	**6651.20**
在总计中:国有控股企业	Of the Total: State-Owned Share Holding Enterprises	12276.11
在总计中:轻工业	Of the Total: Light Industry	5607.60
重工业	Heavy Industry	19484.56
在总计中:大型企业	Of the Total: Large Scale Enterprises	11856.10
中型企业	Medium Scale Enterprises	5124.60
小型企业	Small Enterprises	8111.47

(100 million Yuan)

累计折旧 Accumulated Depreciation	负债合计 Total Liability	流动负债合计 Total Circulating Liability	应付账款 Account Payable
12195.02	**22178.45**	**16644.75**	**5312.27**
10549.01	18637.85	13504.28	4126.02
1448.22	1777.17	1376.78	488.60
1403.38	1648.68	1311.08	473.09
44.85	128.49	65.69	15.51
11.71	28.60	13.15	3.31
0.27	1.89	1.75	0.35
0.36	0.48	0.39	0.21
0.03	0.08		
0.33	0.34	0.34	0.18
	0.06	0.05	0.03
3735.17	8630.22	6487.68	2026.99
1462.02	2073.60	1513.45	463.96
2273.15	6556.62	4974.23	1563.03
2136.52	3905.09	2407.40	659.90
3216.41	4292.82	3215.62	946.31
57.16	59.13	46.39	3.49
3.42	4.59	2.93	1.02
2895.97	3812.57	2852.05	842.47
259.87	416.52	314.24	99.33
0.35	1.58	1.52	0.35
481.51	964.89	786.33	274.74
231.62	571.51	485.54	175.61
228.44	308.76	246.33	79.17
5.36	38.35	16.45	5.34
16.10	46.26	38.01	14.61
1164.50	2575.71	2354.14	911.51
891.22	2079.63	1917.55	726.18
20.72	10.74	8.51	1.07
220.26	438.20	390.30	170.11
10.14	14.59	11.80	5.78
22.16	32.55	25.98	8.36
3350.06	**5161.25**	**3703.90**	**1138.03**
6091.42	10556.48	7661.93	2326.14
2813.52	4395.49	3457.51	916.18
9381.50	17782.96	13187.23	4396.10
6079.75	10587.56	8013.68	2747.97
2484.72	4678.04	3644.97	1060.03
3630.55	6912.85	4986.09	1504.28

13–2 续表 2 continued

单位:亿元

项 目	Item	所有者权益合计 Total Rights of Owners
总　　计	**Total**	**20299.32**
一、按登记注册类型分组:	**Grouped by Type of Registration**	
内资企业	Inner Funded Enterprises	17760.31
国有企业	State Owned Enterprises	904.41
中央企业	Central Enterprises	833.85
地方企业	Local Enterprises	70.55
集体企业	Collective–owned Enterprise	16.49
股份合作企业	Share Holding Cooperative Enterprises	0.49
联营企业	Joint Owned Enterprise	0.35
国有联营企业	State Joint Ownership	
集体联营企业	Collective Joint Ownership	0.03
国有与集体联营企业	Joint State– Collective Ownership	0.21
其他联营企业	Other Joint Owned Enterprise	0.11
有限责任公司	Responsibility Co. Ltd	6594.26
国有独资公司	State Solely Funded Co.	1586.64
其他有限责任公司	Others	5007.62
股份有限公司	Share Holding Co.Ltd.	5187.90
私营企业	Private – owned enterprises	5053.86
私营独资企业	Solely Private – owned enterprises	73.47
私营合伙企业	Private Joint Venture	8.81
私营有限责任公司	Private Responsibility Co. Ltd	4461.73
私营股份有限公司	Private Share Holding Co.Ltd.	509.86
其他企业	Others	2.55
港、澳、台商投资企业	Hongkong, Macao and Taiwan Funded Enterprises	975.82
合资经营企业(港或澳、台资)	Joint Venture with Hongkong, Macao and Taiwan	544.11
合作经营企业(港或澳、台资)	Cooperate with Hongkong, Macao and Taiwan Funded	
港澳台商独资经营企业	Enterprises Solely Funded by Hongkong, Macao and Taiwan Businessmen	361.13
港澳台商投资股份有限公司	Share Holding Co.Ltd. With Hongkong, Macao and Taiwan Investment	18.95
其他港澳台商投资企业	Other Hongkong, Macao and Taiwan Funded Enterprises	51.62
外商投资企业	Foreign Funded Enterprises	1563.19
中外合资经营企业	Sino – Foreign Joint Funded Enterprises	1148.46
中外合作经营企业	Sino – Foreign Cooperative Funded Enterprises	12.06
外资企业	Foreign Solely Funded Enterprises	364.48
外商投资股份有限公司	Foreign Funded Share Holding Co.Ltd.	21.56
其他外商投资企业	Other Foreign Funded Enterprises	16.64
二、在总计中:亏损企业	**Of the Total: enterprises running under deficit**	**3100.66**
在总计中:国有控股企业	Of the Total: State–Owned Share Holding Enterprises	8852.44
在总计中:轻工业	Of the Total: Light Industry	5280.81
重工业	Heavy Industry	15018.51
在总计中:大型企业	Of the Total: Large Scale Enterprises	9044.13
中型企业	Medium Scale Enterprises	4209.19
小型企业	Small Enterprises	7045.99

(100 million Yuan)

实收资本 Assets Recevied	国家资本 National Assets	集体资本 Collective Assets	法人资本 Corperative Assets	个人资本 Individual Assets	港澳台资本 Assets from Hongkong, Macao and Taiwan Funded Enterprises	外商资本 Total Rights of the Owners Foreign Assets
8894.20	**1707.53**	**178.60**	**4442.14**	**1806.96**	**185.18**	**449.48**
7607.92	1416.71	161.20	4150.51	1769.80	20.03	39.55
624.25	34.34	0.71	587.42	1.48		0.31
597.76	16.28		581.03	0.15		0.31
26.48	18.06	0.71	6.39	1.33		
6.04	0.01	4.44	0.62	0.97		
0.12		0.06	0.07			
0.17		0.09	0.05	0.03		
0.01		0.01				
0.14		0.08	0.05			
0.03				0.03		
3459.08	856.92	69.60	2041.37	402.39	17.54	30.95
606.94	220.82		373.30	6.56		
2852.14	636.10	69.60	1668.07	395.82	17.54	30.95
1113.77	496.71	54.45	241.01	311.83		7.58
2403.60	28.74	31.86	1279.92	1052.28	2.49	0.71
16.13			5.61	10.07	0.46	
4.14		0.03	1.44	2.68		
2195.41	21.56	23.31	1201.75	938.55	2.03	0.61
187.91	7.17	8.51	71.13	100.99		0.10
0.87			0.05	0.83		
417.90	73.58	4.15	136.17	9.29	145.47	46.27
176.33	44.34	2.84	67.53	4.75	35.88	20.79
208.89	29.24	1.31	54.01	4.42	96.40	23.50
14.64			14.22	0.12	0.19	0.10
18.05			0.41		12.99	1.88
868.39	217.25	13.25	155.46	27.86	19.68	363.65
650.64	205.28	13.01	131.15	18.12	16.15	197.88
9.90	4.82		0.15			4.93
179.61	2.15	0.24	14.94	9.69	3.53	147.55
16.29			5.48	0.05		10.08
11.96	5.00		3.75			3.21
2372.03	**322.47**	**40.79**	**1623.66**	**160.46**	**46.44**	**93.10**
3738.60	1529.26	31.61	1798.80	156.79	1.47	147.91
1809.45	115.55	47.66	762.58	644.86	106.63	114.24
7084.76	1591.99	130.94	3679.56	1162.09	78.55	335.23
2997.81	969.67	25.97	1354.54	300.21	65.95	211.55
2076.81	318.45	47.68	1213.53	307.68	51.11	122.58
3819.58	419.42	104.95	1874.06	1199.06	68.11	115.34

13-2 续表 3 continued

单位:亿元

项 目	Ite5	营业收入 Business Revenue
总　计	**Total**	**45461.08**
一、按登记注册类型分组:	**Grouped by Type of Registration**	
内资企业	Inner Funded Enterprises	38135.13
国有企业	State Owned Enterprises	1557.09
中央企业	Central Enterprises	1442.54
地方企业	Local Enterprises	114.55
集体企业	Collective-owned Enterprise	72.54
股份合作企业	Share Holding Cooperative Enterprises	1.93
联营企业	Joint Owned Enterprise	1.35
国有联营企业	State Joint Ownership	
集体联营企业	Collective Joint Ownership	0.39
国有与集体联营企业	Joint State- Collective Ownership	0.23
其他联营企业	Other Joint Owned Enterprise	0.74
有限责任公司	Responsibility Co. Ltd	13810.96
国有独资公司	State Solely Funded Co.	2677.79
其他有限责任公司	Others	11133.17
股份有限公司	Share Holding Co.Ltd.	4606.33
私营企业	Private - owned enterprises	18073.86
私营独资企业	Solely Private - owned enterprises	332.36
私营合伙企业	Private Joint Venture	42.24
私营有限责任公司	Private Responsibility Co. Ltd	16280.58
私营股份有限公司	Private Share Holding Co.Ltd.	1418.68
其他企业	Others	11.07
港、澳、台商投资企业	Hongkong, Macao and Taiwan Funded Enterprises	2131.35
合资经营企业(港或澳、台资)	Joint Venture with Hongkong, Macao and Taiwan	1170.27
合作经营企业(港或澳、台资)	Cooperate with Hongkong, Macao and Taiwan Funded	
港澳台商独资经营企业	Enterprises Solely Funded by Hongkong,	828.14
港澳台商投资股份有限公司	Share Holding Co.Ltd. With Hongkong, Macao and Taiwan Investment	38.49
其他港澳台商投资企业	Other Hongkong, Macao and Taiwan Funded Enterprises	94.44
外商投资企业	Foreign Funded Enterprises	5194.60
中外合资经营企业	Sino - Foreign Joint Funded Enterprises	4064.40
中外合作经营企业	Sino - Foreign Cooperative Funded Enterprises	23.02
外资企业	Foreign Solely Funded Enterprises	1022.97
外商投资股份有限公司	Foreign Funded Share Holding Co.Ltd.	44.33
其他外商投资企业	Other Foreign Funded Enterprises	39.88
二、在总计中:亏损企业	**Of the Total: enterprises running under deficit**	**4132.62**
在总计中:国有控股企业	Of the Total: State-Owned Share Holding Enterprises	11659.35
在总计中:轻工业	Of the Total: Light Industry	15281.29
重工业	Heavy Industry	30179.79
在总计中:大型企业	Of the Total: Large Scale Enterprises	14943.04
中型企业	Medium Scale Enterprises	9251.94
小型企业	Small Enterprises	21266.10

(100 million Yuan)

主营业务收入 Revenue of Major Business	营业成本 Operating Costs	税金及附加 Tax	销售费用 Selling Expenses
44492.00	**37730.71**	**1000.71**	**1349.14**
37429.34	31723.11	818.11	1094.57
1545.14	1472.85	7.87	7.19
1435.32	1379.31	5.04	3.38
109.82	93.54	2.83	3.80
71.62	61.65	1.33	1.07
1.92	1.49	0.01	0.14
1.35	1.36	0.01	0.02
0.39	0.36		
0.23	0.33		
0.74	0.67	0.01	0.02
13326.61	11254.25	547.64	396.71
2544.62	1887.22	446.17	36.04
10781.99	9367.03	101.47	360.67
4485.73	3573.54	107.16	164.87
17985.90	15349.79	153.88	524.23
332.22	272.43	4.95	13.47
42.23	34.46	0.78	1.28
16203.91	13856.14	137.29	464.59
1407.54	1186.76	10.86	44.89
11.07	8.17	0.20	0.34
1972.33	1741.13	12.50	104.71
1072.06	937.53	7.94	77.48
768.84	704.48	3.78	20.76
38.42	34.52	0.14	1.30
93.01	64.60	0.65	5.17
5090.33	4266.47	170.10	149.86
3995.06	3321.40	163.30	116.67
22.77	19.15	0.15	0.59
989.67	863.00	5.84	29.51
43.48	33.05	0.38	1.85
39.36	29.87	0.41	1.25
3835.11	**3873.15**	**48.13**	**73.85**
11316.41	9253.92	699.18	262.66
15075.59	12199.22	575.25	636.24
29416.41	25531.49	425.46	712.90
14290.37	11991.45	755.53	428.27
9068.38	7727.21	73.65	305.16
21133.25	18012.05	171.53	615.70

13-2 续表 4 continued

单位: 亿元

项 目	Item	管理费用 Management Expenses
总 计	**Total**	**1616.40**
一、按登记注册类型分组:	**Grouped by Type of Registration**	
内资企业	Inner Funded Enterprises	1363.36
国有企业	State Owned Enterprises	48.78
中央企业	Central Enterprises	42.33
地方企业	Local Enterprises	6.44
集体企业	Collective-owned Enterprise	3.77
股份合作企业	Share Holding Cooperative Enterprises	0.22
联营企业	Joint Owned Enterprise	0.08
国有联营企业	State Joint Ownership	
集体联营企业	Collective Joint Ownership	
国有与集体联营企业	Joint State- Collective Ownership	0.06
其他联营企业	Other Joint Owned Enterprise	0.02
有限责任公司	Responsibility Co. Ltd	505.32
国有独资公司	State Solely Funded Co.	114.43
其他有限责任公司	Others	390.89
股份有限公司	Share Holding Co.Ltd.	183.92
私营企业	Private - owned enterprises	620.83
私营独资企业	Solely Private - owned enterprises	11.67
私营合伙企业	Private Joint Venture	1.56
私营有限责任公司	Private Responsibility Co. Ltd	554.42
私营股份有限公司	Private Share Holding Co.Ltd.	53.18
其他企业	Others	0.44
港、澳、台商投资企业	Hongkong, Macao and Taiwan Funded Enterprises	62.86
合资经营企业(港或澳、台资)	Joint Venture with Hongkong, Macao and Taiwan	33.47
合作经营企业(港或澳、台资)	Cooperate with Hongkong, Macao and Taiwan Funded	
港澳台商独资经营企业	Enterprises Solely Funded by Hongkong, Macao and Taiwan usinessmen	26.33
港澳台商投资股份有限公司	Share Holding Co.Ltd. With Hongkong,	0.45
其他港澳台商投资企业	Other Hongkong, Macao and Taiwan Funded Enterprises	3
外商投资企业	Foreign Funded Enterprises	190.19
中外合资经营企业	Sino - Foreign Joint Funded Enterprises	143.86
中外合作经营企业	Sino - Foreign Cooperative Funded Enterprises	0.71
外资企业	Foreign Solely Funded Enterprises	41.76
外商投资股份有限公司	Foreign Funded Share Holding Co.Ltd.	1.57
其他外商投资企业	Other Foreign Funded Enterprises	2
二、在总计中:亏损企业	**Of the Total: enterprises running under deficit**	**196.11**
在总计中:国有控股企业	Of the Total: State-Owned Share Holding Enterprises	439.72
在总计中:轻工业	Of the Total: Light Industry	544.78
重工业	Heavy Industry	1071.62
在总计中:大型企业	Of the Total: Large Scale Enterprises	487.87
中型企业	Medium Scale Enterprises	342.76
小型企业	Small Enterprises	785.77

(100 million Yuan)

财务费用 Financial Expenses	利息收入 Interest Income	利息费用 Interest Expenses	投资收益 Investment Income
414.84	**74.40**	**392.10**	**280.91**
394.15	40.88	341.43	265.51
18.67	1.20	18.17	2.73
16.85	1.11	16.87	2.77
1.82	0.08	1.30	–0.04
0.23	0.01	0.17	0.05
0.01			
0.01			
0.01			
131.23	22.24	134.62	66.44
26.88	5.89	31.14	53.35
104.35	16.35	103.49	13.09
68.05	13.61	83.71	191.95
175.84	3.82	104.73	4.34
4.81	0.09	2.27	0.01
0.55		0.28	
154.27	3.27	90.44	4.12
16.22	0.46	11.75	0.21
0.10		0.01	
11.28	22.45	32.55	4.62
4.86	21.36	26.27	2.14
5.03	0.39	4.38	2.47
1.24	0.01	1.13	
0.14	0.69	0.76	
9.41	11.08	18.12	10.78
3.86	10.71	12.90	9.53
0.12	–0.03	0.17	
5.23	0.29	4.78	1.19
0.25	0.06	0.26	
–0.05	0.05	0.01	0.07
74.75	**8.42**	**72.09**	**6.31**
128.09	34.10	163.82	239.13
128.67	10.87	94.99	25.30
286.17	63.54	297.10	255.61
115.35	54.68	173.49	236.66
91.83	10.50	81.81	22.15
207.66	9.22	136.80	22.10

13-2 续表 5 continued

单位: 亿元

项 目	Item	其他收益 Other Income
总 计	**Total**	**142.12**
一、按登记注册类型分组:	**Grouped by Type of Registration**	
内资企业	Inner Funded Enterprises	118.58
国有企业	State Owned Enterprises	4.26
中央企业	Central Enterprises	4.18
地方企业	Local Enterprises	0.08
集体企业	Collective-owned Enterprise	
股份合作企业	Share Holding Cooperative Enterprises	
联营企业	Joint Owned Enterprise	
国有联营企业	State Joint Ownership	
集体联营企业	Collective Joint Ownership	
国有与集体联营企业	Joint State- Collective Ownership	
其他联营企业	Other Joint Owned Enterprise	
有限责任公司	Responsibility Co. Ltd	72.85
国有独资公司	State Solely Funded Co.	10.73
其他有限责任公司	Others	62.12
股份有限公司	Share Holding Co.Ltd.	21.73
私营企业	Private - owned enterprises	19.73
私营独资企业	Solely Private - owned enterprises	
私营合伙企业	Private Joint Venture	
私营有限责任公司	Private Responsibility Co. Ltd	17.55
私营股份有限公司	Private Share Holding Co.Ltd.	2.18
其他企业	Others	
港、澳、台商投资企业	Hongkong, Macao and Taiwan Funded Enterprises	6.83
合资经营企业(港或澳、台资)	Joint Venture with Hongkong, Macao and Taiwan	2.33
合作经营企业(港或澳、台资)	Cooperate with Hongkong, Macao and Taiwan Funded	
港澳台商独资经营企业	Enterprises Solely Funded by Hongkong,	3.70
港澳台商投资股份有限公司	Share Holding Co.Ltd. With Hongkong, Macao and Taiwan Investment	
其他港澳台商投资企业	Other Hongkong, Macao and Taiwan Funded Enterprises	0.80
外商投资企业	Foreign Funded Enterprises	16.72
中外合资经营企业	Sino - Foreign Joint Funded Enterprises	16.12
中外合作经营企业	Sino - Foreign Cooperative Funded Enterprises	0.01
外资企业	Foreign Solely Funded Enterprises	0.48
外商投资股份有限公司	Foreign Funded Share Holding Co.Ltd.	0.01
其他外商投资企业	Other Foreign Funded Enterprises	0.09
二、在总计中:亏损企业	**Of the Total: enterprises running under deficit**	**23.77**
在总计中:国有控股企业	Of the Total: State-Owned Share Holding Enterprises	64.66
在总计中:轻工业	Of the Total: Light Industry	22.86
重工业	Heavy Industry	119.26
在总计中:大型企业	Of the Total: Large Scale Enterprises	66.44
中型企业	Medium Scale Enterprises	42.72
小型企业	Small Enterprises	32.96

(100 million Yuan)

营业利润 Operating Profits	营业外收入 Non-operating Income	营业外支出 Non-operating Expenses	利润总额 Total Profits	所得税费用 Income Tax	亏损企业 亏损总额 Total Loss of Enterprises Running under Deficit
2995.99	**109.00**	**66.75**	**3049.57**	**391.01**	**256.04**
2482.66	92.74	57.90	2528.83	277.62	176.88
-6.50	3.52	1.79	-4.78	1.71	23.18
-11.97	3.11	1.69	-10.55	1.49	22.69
5.47	0.41	0.10	5.78	0.22	0.49
4.18	0.35	0.09	4.44	0.21	0.41
0.05	0.03	0.04	0.05		0.01
-0.14	0.02		-0.12		0.15
0.02			0.02		
-0.16	0.02		-0.15		0.15
0.01			0.01		
802.74	41.95	26.70	818.01	134.67	96.60
185.46	10.62	8.06	188.03	46.27	5.95
617.28	31.33	18.64	629.98	88.40	90.66
581.56	13.75	11.59	586.50	74.35	27.16
1100.01	33.12	17.68	1123.98	66.67	29.37
19.98	0.16	0.26	19.88	1.33	0.13
3.61		0.10	3.52	0.37	
987.54	29.42	16.24	1009.24	57.84	28.30
88.88	3.54	1.09	91.34	7.14	0.93
0.76			0.76		
173.57	6.00	3.76	175.81	30.85	11.33
86.79	3.30	1.48	88.61	13.28	3.82
65.84	2.43	1.17	67.11	12.73	5.83
-0.19	0.14	0.01	-0.07	0.26	1.65
21	0.12	1.09	20.16	4.59	0.04
339.76	10.26	5.09	344.93	82.54	67.82
272.23	5.93	2.49	275.67	69.07	48.16
2.21	0.18	0.10	2.29	0.61	0.01
53.13	3.93	1.72	55.35	11.08	17.49
6.58	0.13	0.11	6.60	1.05	0.67
6	0.09	0.68	5.01	0.72	1.49
-263.07	**19.55**	**12.52**	**-256.04**	**6.00**	**256.04**
845.90	30.36	19.25	857.01	186.19	147.44
1081.88	38.43	20.53	1099.78	121.66	41.81
1914.11	70.56	46.21	1949.80	269.34	214.23
1086.42	36.89	28.26	1095.05	197.67	98.73
598.24	29.53	13.97	616.58	87.35	75.84
1311.32	42.57	24.52	1337.94	105.98	81.47

13-2 续表6 continued

单位: 亿元

项 目	Item	利税总额 Total Profits and Taxes
总　　计	**Total**	**5274.52**
一、按登记注册类型分组:	**Grouped by Type of Registration**	
内资企业	Inner Funded Enterprises	4387.87
国有企业	State Owned Enterprises	35.72
中央企业	Central Enterprises	24.19
地方企业	Local Enterprises	11.53
集体企业	Collective-owned Enterprise	8.49
股份合作企业	Share Holding Cooperative Enterprises	0.16
联营企业	Joint Owned Enterprise	-0.08
国有联营企业	State Joint Ownership	
集体联营企业	Collective Joint Ownership	0.03
国有与集体联营企业	Joint State- Collective Ownership	-0.14
其他联营企业	Other Joint Owned Enterprise	0.02
有限责任公司	Responsibility Co. Ltd	1727.90
国有独资公司	State Solely Funded Co.	749.39
其他有限责任公司	Others	978.51
股份有限公司	Share Holding Co.Ltd.	847.95
私营企业	Private - owned enterprises	1766.55
私营独资企业	Solely Private - owned enterprises	34.73
私营合伙企业	Private Joint Venture	5.68
私营有限责任公司	Private Responsibility Co. Ltd	1588.30
私营股份有限公司	Private Share Holding Co.Ltd.	137.83
其他企业	Others	1.19
港、澳、台商投资企业	Hongkong, Macao and Taiwan Funded Enterprises	245.15
合资经营企业(港或澳、台资)	Joint Venture with Hongkong, Macao and Taiwan	121.90
合作经营企业(港或澳、台资)	Cooperate with Hongkong, Macao and Taiwan Funded	
港澳台商独资经营企业	Enterprises Solely Funded by Hongkong, Macao and Taiwan Businessmen	98.27
港澳台商投资股份有限公司	Share Holding Co.Ltd. With Hongkong, Macao and Taiwan Investment	0.30
其他港澳台商投资企业	Other Hongkong, Macao and Taiwan Funded Enterprises	25
外商投资企业	Foreign Funded Enterprises	641.50
中外合资经营企业	Sino - Foreign Joint Funded Enterprises	542.80
中外合作经营企业	Sino - Foreign Cooperative Funded Enterprises	3.04
外资企业	Foreign Solely Funded Enterprises	80.95
外商投资股份有限公司	Foreign Funded Share Holding Co.Ltd.	7.92
其他外商投资企业	Other Foreign Funded Enterprises	7
二、在总计中:亏损企业	**Of the Total: enterprises running under deficit**	**-148.42**
在总计中:国有控股企业	Of the Total: State-Owned Share Holding Enterprises	1902.90
在总计中:轻工业	Of the Total: Light Industry	2153.61
重工业	Heavy Industry	3120.91
在总计中:大型企业	Of the Total: Large Scale Enterprises	2262.64
中型企业	Medium Scale Enterprises	940.09
小型企业	Small Enterprises	2071.79

(100 million Yuan)

应交税金及附加 Tax and Extra Charges	本年应付职工薪酬 Wages Welfarism payable This Year	本年应交增值税 Value Added Payable of the Current Year	全部从业人员年平均人数(万人) Average Number of Empolyment of the Current Year (10000 persons)
2615.95	**2963.12**	**1224.23**	**335.87**
2136.66	2540.86	1040.93	301.19
42.21	163.72	32.62	9.94
36.24	153.69	29.70	8.74
5.97	10.03	2.92	1.20
4.27	4.74	2.73	0.76
0.11	0.22	0.10	0.04
0.04	0.11	0.02	0.04
0.01	0.01	0.01	
0.01	0.03	0.01	0.02
0.01	0.07		0.01
1044.56	977.29	362.25	86.62
607.63	212.44	115.20	12.03
436.93	764.86	247.05	74.59
335.79	386.43	154.28	32.26
709.25	1007.92	488.69	171.48
16.18	13.08	9.91	1.81
2.53	1.85	1.38	0.20
636.90	910.44	441.77	159.05
53.64	82.54	35.63	10.42
0.43	0.44	0.24	0.07
100.19	146.48	56.84	14.52
46.57	82.55	25.35	7.84
43.90	57.37	27.39	6.08
0.62	1.13	0.23	0.15
9.10	5.43	3.87	0.44
379.10	275.78	126.47	20.16
336.20	185.18	103.83	11.93
1.36	1.35	0.60	0.07
36.68	81.56	19.75	7.57
2.37	3.83	0.93	0.30
2.49	3.87	1.35	0.28
113.62	**402.76**	**59.49**	**35.33**
1232.08	921.92	346.71	59.08
1175.50	945.98	478.59	160.73
1440.46	2017.14	745.65	175.14
1365.26	1095.34	412.06	82.34
410.86	748.21	249.85	77.03
839.83	1119.57	562.32	176.50

13-2 续表7 continued

单位:亿元

项 目	Item	企业单位数(个) Number of Enterprises (unit)
按行业分	**Grouped by sector**	
采矿业	**Mining and Qarrying**	**400**
煤炭开采和洗选业	Coal Mining and Processing	8
石油和天然气开采业	Petroleum and Natural Gas Extraction	1
黑色金属矿采选业	Ferrous Metals Mining and Processing	34
有色金属矿采选业	Non-ferrous Metals Mining and Processing	24
非金属矿采选业	Non-metal Minerals Mining and Processing	327
开采辅助活动	Mining Auxiliary Activities	4
其他采矿业	Other Minerals Mining and Processing	2
制造业	**Manufacturing**	**14696**
农副食品加工业	Food Processing	1476
食品制造业	Food Production	358
酒、饮料和精制茶制造业	Wine,Beverage and Refined Tea Production	409
烟草制品业	Tobacco Processing	7
纺织业	Textile Industry	887
纺织服装、服饰业	Textile,Garments, and Fashion Industry	466
皮革、毛皮、羽毛及其制品和制鞋业	Leather, Furs,Down and Related Products	159
木材加工和木、竹、藤、棕、草制品业	Timber Processing, Wood, Bamboo, Cane, Palm and Sraw Products	280
家具制造业	Furniture Manufacturing	151
造纸和纸制品业	Papermaking and Paper Products	197
印刷和记录媒介复制业	Printing and Record Processing	323
文教、工美、体育和娱乐用品制造业	Stationery, Education and Sports Goods	257
石油加工、炼焦和核燃料加工业	Petroleum Processing, Coking Products and Nuclear Fuel Processing	47
化学原料和化学制品制造业	Raw Chemical Material and Chemical Products	949
医药制造业	Medical and pharmaceutical Products	416
化学纤维制造业	Chemical Fibers	20
橡胶和塑料制品业	Rubber and plastic products	578
非金属矿物制品业	Nonmetal Material Products	1977
黑色金属冶炼和压延加工业	Smelting and Pressing of Ferrous Metals	101
有色金属冶炼和压延加工业	Smelting and Pressing of Nonferrous Metals	157
金属制品业	Metal Products	856
通用设备制造业	Ordinary Machinery Manufacturing	702
专用设备制造业	Special Purpose Equipment Manufacturing	742
汽车制造业	Motor manufacturing	1548
铁路、船舶、航空航天和其他运输设备制造业	Railway,Watercraft,Aviation and other Transporlation Equipment manufacturing	151
电气机械和器材制造业	Electric Machinery and Equipment	698
计算机、通信和其他电子设备制造业	Telecommunication Computer,Equipment and Other Electronic Equipment Manufacturing	452
仪器仪表制造业	Instruments and Meters, Manufacturing	163
其他制造业	Other Manufacturing	46
废弃资源综合利用业	Waste Comprehensive Vtilization of Resources Industry	98
金属制品、机械和设备修理业	Metal products,Machinery and Equipment Repairing	25
电力、燃气及水的生产和供应业	**Electric Power, Gas and Water Production and Supply**	**424**
电力、热力生产和供应业	Electric Power, Steam and Hot Water Production and Supply	237
燃气生产和供应业	Gas Production and Supply	79
水的生产和供应业	Tap Water Production and Supply	108

(100 million Yuan)

工业总产值(当年价格) Total Output Value(current price)	资产总计 Total Assets	流动资产合计 Circulating Funds	应收帐款净额 Accounts Received	固定资产净额 NBV of Fixed Assets
895.14	**887.83**	**342.78**	**127.66**	**280.14**
7.17	7.57	3.73	1.09	2.08
37.06	252.62	55.89	46.87	103.65
140.77	116.56	48.74	21.71	38.20
46.08	51.64	24.60	2.68	15.74
553.74	385.21	179.45	45.42	85.63
84.65	67.54	25.92	6.62	34.73
25.67	6.69	4.45	3.27	0.11
44339.86	**35660.96**	**18803.91**	**4684.82**	**8342.87**
3982.05	1574.60	761.74	150.66	506.57
1039.04	623.06	299.49	71.67	194.09
1167.31	1138.85	742.88	57.80	233.48
673.99	581.67	451.49	50.47	76.02
2200.06	934.13	412.94	87.71	350.61
888.84	372.50	180.47	35.95	118.77
272.75	90.65	48.75	12.06	23.19
436.21	289.07	128.38	20.71	93.93
239.19	202.99	86.17	14.36	72.44
571.77	458.42	195.03	44.47	153.71
641.26	369.81	214.89	75.87	96.37
568.04	372.73	231.07	26.38	90.77
547.95	206.19	75.74	14.78	84.93
3801.58	3207.63	1189.18	220.12	959.46
1276.13	1304.70	668.31	139.85	323.62
60.82	41.71	20.02	3.94	13.26
1098.10	560.36	289.50	72.21	155.52
3576.89	2152.30	1012.49	349.66	728.76
2130.45	2474.05	861.57	77.78	839.74
882.96	367.55	193.30	27.80	117.78
1822.49	1190.08	733.21	215.40	268.33
1490.12	1112.58	640.77	198.53	237.43
1326.30	1145.14	780.47	240.65	215.17
7247.53	7217.37	4274.51	972.97	1119.85
650.55	1239.55	768.25	154.05	214.76
2258.18	1688.52	1108.70	460.35	316.50
2577.05	4036.00	2018.94	773.72	596.90
280.54	214.97	146.53	50.38	38.97
86.60	66.79	45.63	6.35	13.82
445.90	355.74	172.07	40.44	74.56
99.21	71.25	51.42	17.73	13.56
2337.06	**5982.09**	**731.43**	**191.78**	**3610.10**
2050.96	5235.78	455.04	136.27	3367.25
182.58	248.64	93.51	11.75	95.51
103.52	497.67	182.88	43.76	147.34

13-2 续表 8 continued

单位: 亿元

项 目	Item	固定资产原价 Original Price of Fixed Assets
按行业分	**Grouped by sector**	
采矿业	**Mining and Qarrying**	**697.10**
煤炭开采和洗选业	Coal Mining and Processing	3.59
石油和天然气开采业	Petroleum and Natural Gas Extraction	325.37
黑色金属矿采选业	Ferrous Metals Mining and Processing	90.89
有色金属矿采选业	Non-ferrous Metals Mining and Processing	32.15
非金属矿采选业	Non-metal Minerals Mining and Processing	169.67
开采辅助活动	Mining Auxiliary Activities	75.22
其他采矿业	Other Minerals Mining and Processing	0.21
制造业	**Manufacturing**	**17682.93**
农副食品加工业	Food Processing	1107.27
食品制造业	Food Production	377.19
酒、饮料和精制茶制造业	Wine,Beverage and Refined Tea Production	437.26
烟草制品业	Tobacco Processing	131.57
纺织业	Textile Industry	861.20
纺织服装、服饰业	Textile,Garments, and Fashion Industry	257.41
皮革、毛皮、羽毛及其制品和制鞋业	Leather, Furs,Down and Related Products	87.13
木材加工和木、竹、藤、棕、草制品业	Timber Processing, Wood, Bamboo, Cane, Palm and Sraw Products	164.43
家具制造业	Furniture Manufacturing	105.93
造纸和纸制品业	Papermaking and Paper Products	248.88
印刷和记录媒介复制业	Printing and Record Processing	224.22
文教、工美、体育和娱乐用品制造业	Stationery, Education and Sports Goods	263.11
石油加工、炼焦和核燃料加工业	Petroleum Processing, Coking Products and Nuclear Fuel Processing	181.07
化学原料和化学制品制造业	Raw Chemical Material and Chemical Products	2255.35
医药制造业	Medical and pharmaceutical Products	602.76
化学纤维制造业	Chemical Fibers	40.16
橡胶和塑料制品业	Rubber and Plastic Products	355.56
非金属矿物制品业	Nonmetal Material Products	1393.88
黑色金属冶炼和压延加工业	Smelting and Pressing of Ferrous Metals	2079.28
有色金属冶炼和压延加工业	Smelting and Pressing of Nonferrous Metals	222.51
金属制品业	Metal Products	552.18
通用设备制造业	Ordinary Machinery Manufacturing	546.62
专用设备制造业	Special Purpose Equipment Manufacturing	455.44
汽车制造业	Motor manufacturing	2283.73
铁路、船舶、航空航天和其他运输设备制造业	Railway,Watercraft,Aviation and other Transporlation Equipment manufacturing	369.32
电气机械和器材制造业	Electric Machinery and Equipment	621.28
计算机、通信和其他电子设备制造业	Telecommunication Computer,Equipment and Other Electronic Equipment Manufacturing	1190.18
仪器仪表制造业	Instruments and Meters, Manufacturing	83.13
其他制造业	Other Manufacturing	31.82
废弃资源综合利用业	Waste Comprehensive Vtilization of Resources Industry	120.94
金属制品、机械和设备修理业	Metal products,Machinery and Equipment Repairing	32.12
电力、燃气及水的生产和供应业	**Electric Power, Gas and Water Production and Supply**	**6712.14**
电力、热力生产和供应业	Electric Power, Steam and Hot Water Production and Supply	6297.65
燃气生产和供应业	Gas Production and Supply	160.82
水的生产和供应业	Tap Water Production and Supply	253.67

(100 million Yuan)

累计折旧 Accumulated Depreciation	负债合计 Total Liability	流动负债合计 Total Circulating Liability	应付账款 Account Payable
409.06	**481.09**	**332.81**	**77.44**
1.47	5.26	5.25	2.93
221.72	128.93	73.91	12.29
50.24	72.07	56.89	11.24
16.04	19.15	15.10	1.99
81.97	204.83	137.79	32.33
37.52	45.10	43.79	16.66
0.10	5.75	0.08	
8759.03	**18428.17**	**14585.14**	**4843.78**
548.74	635.81	496.72	116.44
179.36	281.21	232.52	75.41
190.95	587.21	528.58	68.25
74.83	204.24	202.35	74.96
512.78	395.53	302.48	67.00
129.71	164.53	125.84	26.53
54.31	40.80	31.40	12.48
81.08	144.00	78.03	17.37
35.64	73.87	45.51	19.59
83.57	267.70	195.70	51.03
118.47	172.06	141.24	49.37
173.10	216.74	82.16	20.87
94.50	128.59	104.04	22.32
1299.93	1577.18	1149.44	287.29
267.91	553.85	451.70	80.38
26.40	21.19	16.89	4.97
193.75	239.71	186.04	53.15
625.84	914.76	732.51	271.83
1240.47	1446.64	1156.26	322.26
99.21	235.53	175.72	38.53
250.94	656.92	479.64	124.19
279.56	580.31	463.99	144.19
222.43	662.84	515.61	176.18
1088.97	3904.36	3283.04	1348.94
145.47	827.00	683.48	250.99
266.52	926.59	746.41	307.18
358.69	2184.12	1656.36	738.57
42.30	112.52	94.20	32.40
17.13	40.10	37.86	8.03
34.48	189.34	158.59	17.43
21.99	42.92	30.83	15.65
3026.97	**3269.22**	**1726.79**	**391.06**
2879.17	2824.12	1438.46	332.20
42.37	157.92	145.90	35.72
105.43	287.18	142.43	23.14

13-2 续表 9 continued

单位:亿元

项 目	Item	所有者权益合计 Total Rights of Owners
按行业分	**Grouped by sector**	
采矿业	**Mining and Qarrying**	**406.01**
煤炭开采和洗选业	Coal Mining and Processing	2.32
石油和天然气开采业	Petroleum and Natural Gas Extraction	123.69
黑色金属矿采选业	Ferrous Metals Mining and Processing	44.00
有色金属矿采选业	Non-ferrous Metals Mining and Processing	32.50
非金属矿采选业	Non-metal Minerals Mining and Processing	180.12
开采辅助活动	Mining Auxiliary Activities	22.45
其他采矿业	Other Minerals Mining and Processing	0.93
制造业	Manufacturing	17180.29
农副食品加工业	Food Processing	935.34
食品制造业	Food Production	338.60
酒、饮料和精制茶制造业	Wine,Beverage and Refined Tea Production	551.64
烟草制品业	Tobacco Processing	377.43
纺织业	Textile Industry	530.05
纺织服装、服饰业	Textile,Garments, and Fashion Industry	201.84
皮革、毛皮、羽毛及其制品和制鞋业	Leather, Furs,Down and Related Products	49.85
木材加工和木、竹、藤、棕、草制品业	Timber Processing, Wood, Bamboo, Cane, Palm and Sraw Products	144.94
家具制造业	Furniture Manufacturing	129.12
造纸和纸制品业	Papermaking and Paper Products	189.77
印刷和记录媒介复制业	Printing and Record Processing	197.70
文教、工美、体育和娱乐用品制造业	Stationery, Education and Sports Goods	154.90
石油加工、炼焦和核燃料加工业	Petroleum Processing, Coking Products and Nuclear Fuel Processing	77.34
化学原料和化学制品制造业	Raw Chemical Material and Chemical Products	1626.34
医药制造业	Medical and pharmaceutical Products	747.94
化学纤维制造业	Chemical Fibers	20.15
橡胶和塑料制品业	Rubber and plastic products	320.30
非金属矿物制品业	Nonmetal Material Products	1234.56
黑色金属冶炼和压延加工业	Smelting and Pressing of Ferrous Metals	1021.24
有色金属冶炼和压延加工业	Smelting and Pressing of Nonferrous Metals	131.83
金属制品业	Metal Products	529.81
通用设备制造业	Ordinary Machinery Manufacturing	530.22
专用设备制造业	Special Purpose Equipment Manufacturing	481.27
汽车制造业	Motor manufacturing	3309.59
铁路、船舶、航空航天和其他运输设备制造业	Railway,Watercraft,Aviation and other Transporlation Equipment manufacturing	412.20
电气机械和器材制造业	Electric Machinery and Equipment	761.66
计算机、通信和其他电子设备制造业	Telecommunication Computer,Equipment and	1851.12
仪器仪表制造业	Instruments and Meters, Manufacturing	102.41
其他制造业	Other Manufacturing	26.69
废弃资源综合利用业	Waste Comprehensive Vtilization of Resources Industry	166.11
金属制品、机械和设备修理业	Metal products,Machinery and Equipment Repairing	28.33
电力、燃气及水的生产和供应业	**Electric Power, Gas and Water Production and Supply**	**2713.04**
电力、热力生产和供应业	Electric Power, Steam and Hot Water Production and Supply	2411.83
燃气生产和供应业	Gas Production and Supply	90.72
水的生产和供应业	Tap Water Production and Supply	210.49

(100 million Yuan)

所有者权益合计 Total Rights of Owners						
实收资本 Assets Recevied	国家资本 National Assets	集体资本 Collective Assets	法人资本 Corperative Assets	个人资本 Individual Assets	港澳台资本 Assets from Hongkong, Macao and Taiwan Funded Enterprises	外商资本 Total Rights of the Owners Foreign Assets
127.12	**49.08**	**5.06**	**34.26**	**38.45**	**0.26**	
2.04			1.32	0.72		
37.24	30.91	0.56	2.16	3.61		
6.52	3.81	0.11	1.07	1.27	0.26	
67.05	2.79	4.39	27.18	32.68		
14.07	11.54		2.53			
0.20	0.03			0.17		
7452.87	1206.49	154.85	3696.32	1665.06	174.67	431.20
322.98	8.38	7.42	119.38	158.75	11.10	17.14
112.19	8.13	0.87	41.84	45.20	2.61	13.45
152.49	9.40	3.02	44.86	45.04	23.96	23.46
31.35	29.90	1.05	0.40			
203.43	10.73	7.31	93.50	83.33	2.60	5.93
80.41	5.86	0.55	33.53	36.74	3.28	0.45
25.32	1.87		4.91	10.08	4.27	4.20
54.25	0.72	3.06	22.41	27.91		0.13
74.95	0.07	0.02	59.45	15.28	0.13	
115.08	0.07	1.96	76.47	22.94	6.58	7.00
73.04	6.49	1.08	28.90	33.67	1.71	1.20
66.15	0.48	1.96	20.98	30.24	11.19	1.30
87.71	71.29	0.10	10.00	3.74	1.19	
567.34	142.02	22.13	247.25	121.44	5.63	28.03
236.13	22.15	10.32	101.17	59.94	30.19	6.22
13.18		0.01	3.52	1.39	1.71	6.55
120.81	1.70	7.31	45.33	56.36	2.38	0.90
508.97	33.78	10.66	215.02	218.36	8.93	21.67
472.52	131.47	0.27	302.63	32.63	1.22	1.30
73.03	33.33	0.11	8.58	16.79		14.22
249.78	32.71	1.49	125.80	82.42	6.22	1.10
596.12	37.98	14.21	461.99	68.96	4.71	7.86
224.67	34.66	5.64	96.74	75.59	0.46	11.35
1021.34	368.22	32.59	197.02	136.38	12.58	186.13
223.18	28.74	1.23	174.96	9.36	0.65	1.23
324.60	14.24	13.69	151.43	101.94	2.46	35.78
1244.68	161.86	3.29	940.64	76.07	28.18	34.45
39.18	2.01	0.70	23.48	12.70	0.02	0.14
8.67	0.15	0.01	6.66	1.84		0.01
118.75	5.35	2.16	31.27	78.96	0.71	
10.57	2.73	0.63	6.20	1.01		
1314.22	**451.95**	**18.70**	**711.56**	**103.44**	**10.25**	**18.31**
1205.90	414.03	10.16	674.04	88.75	8.48	10.43
46.00	9.74	4.95	23.42	3.33	1.77	2.79
62.32	28.18	3.59	14.10	11.36		5.09

13-2 续表 10 continued

单位: 亿元

项 目	Item	营业收入 Business Revenue
按行业分	**Grouped by sector**	
采矿业	**Mining and Qarrying**	**859.36**
煤炭开采和洗选业	Coal Mining and Processing	**6.98**
石油和天然气开采业	Petroleum and Natural Gas Extraction	70.05
黑色金属矿采选业	Ferrous Metals Mining and Processing	129.99
有色金属矿采选业	Non-ferrous Metals Mining and Processing	43.05
非金属矿采选业	Non-metal Minerals Mining and Processing	491.38
开采辅助活动	Mining Auxiliary Activities	92.29
其他采矿业	Other Minerals Mining and Processing	25.62
制造业	**Manufacturing**	**42235.73**
农副食品加工业	Food Processing	3677.10
食品制造业	Food Production	1015.09
酒、饮料和精制茶制造业	Wine,Beverage and Refined Tea Production	997.65
烟草制品业	Tobacco Processing	775.05
纺织业	Textile Industry	2059.42
纺织服装、服饰业	Textile,Garments, and Fashion Industry	839.26
皮革、毛皮、羽毛及其制品和制鞋业	Leather, Furs,Down and Related Products	257.07
木材加工和木、竹、藤、棕、草制品业	Timber Processing, Wood, Bamboo, Cane, Palm and Sraw Products	403.62
家具制造业	Furniture Manufacturing	220.12
造纸和纸制品业	Papermaking and Paper Products	521.86
印刷和记录媒介复制业	Printing and Record Processing	583.37
文教、工美、体育和娱乐用品制造业	Stationery, Education and Sports Goods	520.00
石油加工、炼焦和核燃料加工业	Petroleum Processing, Coking Products and Nuclear Fuel Processing	684.01
化学原料和化学制品制造业	Raw Chemical Material and Chemical Products	3575.17
医药制造业	Medical and pharmaceutical Products	1197.12
化学纤维制造业	Chemical Fibers	55.55
橡胶和塑料制品业	Rubber and plastic products	1017.19
非金属矿物制品业	Nonmetal Material Products	3419.26
黑色金属冶炼和压延加工业	Smelting and Pressing of Ferrous Metals	2315.34
有色金属冶炼和压延加工业	Smelting and Pressing of Nonferrous Metals	876.26
金属制品业	Metal Products	1737.71
通用设备制造业	Ordinary Machinery Manufacturing	1399.70
专用设备制造业	Special Purpose Equipment Manufacturing	1287.96
汽车制造业	Motor manufacturing	6818.32
铁路、船舶、航空航天和其他运输设备制造业	Railway,Watercraft,Aviation and other Transporlation Equipment manufacturing	588.07
电气机械和器材制造业	Electric Machinery and Equipment	2120.69
计算机、通信和其他电子设备制造业	Telecommunication Computer,Equipment and Other Electronic Equipment Manufacturing	2437.42
仪器仪表制造业	Instruments and Meters, Manufacturing	249.02
其他制造业	Other Manufacturing	81.21
废弃资源综合利用业	Waste Comprehensive Vtilization of Resources Industry	419.83
金属制品、机械和设备修理业	Metal products,Machinery and Equipment Repairing	86.29
电力、燃气及水的生产和供应业	**Electric Power, Gas and Water Production and Supply**	**2366.02**
电力、热力生产和供应业	Electric Power, Steam and Hot Water Production and Supply	2067.28
燃气生产和供应业	Gas Production and Supply	187.91
水的生产和供应业	Tap Water Production and Supply	110.83

主营业务收入 Revenue of Major Business	营业成本 Business Cost	税金及附加 Tax	销售费用 Selling Expenses
822.08	**698.71**	**19.33**	**26.87**
6.97	**5.97**	**0.16**	**0.14**
37.36	59.40	2.72	0.82
128.88	105.95	2.10	4.47
41.84	27.58	0.96	0.50
489.85	389.49	12.77	20.24
91.56	86.49	0.29	0.06
25.62	23.83	0.33	0.64
41352.97	**35083.37**	**965.52**	**1306.74**
3666.29	3181.57	27.70	99.21
1005.47	834.64	6.75	50.99
971.17	708.58	31.32	73.66
722.89	208.96	434.39	11.10
2051.92	1768.85	18.61	62.11
837.86	720.61	6.98	27.08
256.58	225.48	1.73	4.27
401.19	347.69	4.68	10.32
219.50	182.80	2.97	7.25
517.56	449.15	3.04	19.60
579.64	481.95	5.65	19.38
519.01	443.09	5.85	14.23
496.18	569.98	87.81	3.58
3523.46	2973.78	103.55	102.01
1167.98	795.41	10.18	160.44
51.47	50.08	0.46	1.39
1010.81	859.71	7.38	29.84
3406.17	2780.58	33.18	114.72
2139.34	2106.26	10.72	17.09
839.45	766.58	4.51	5.85
1718.24	1499.66	10.91	49.88
1386.38	1182.69	10.76	45.22
1277.15	1073.57	8.32	44.57
6707.50	5694.34	96.36	186.14
581.95	521.04	3.41	8.66
2055.33	1806.66	13.71	59.49
2409.20	2125.16	9.11	58.86
248.09	194.76	1.66	11.73
80.94	70.18	0.35	1.49
418.05	385.03	3.11	5.53
86.20	74.53	0.36	1.05
2316.95	**1948.61**	**15.86**	**15.53**
2030.46	1702.25	14.16	1.85
183.16	157.80	0.59	6.77
103.33	88.56	1.11	6.91

13-2 续表 11 continued

单位:亿元

项 目	Item	管理费用 Management Expenses
按行业分	**Grouped by sector**	
采矿业	**Mining and Qarrying**	**44.23**
煤炭开采和洗选业	Coal Mining and Processing	0.38
石油和天然气开采业	Petroleum and Natural Gas Extraction	9.13
黑色金属矿采选业	Ferrous Metals Mining and Processing	8.00
有色金属矿采选业	Non-ferrous Metals Mining and Processing	3.20
非金属矿采选业	Non-metal Minerals Mining and Processing	20.40
开采辅助活动	Mining Auxiliary Activities	2.55
其他采矿业	Other Minerals Mining and Processing	0.57
制造业	**Manufacturing**	**1514.68**
农副食品加工业	Food Processing	95.94
食品制造业	Food Production	38.21
酒、饮料和精制茶制造业	Wine,Beverage and Refined Tea Production	44.36
烟草制品业	Tobacco Processing	20.25
纺织业	Textile Industry	73.60
纺织服装、服饰业	Textile,Garments, and Fashion Industry	31.62
皮革、毛皮、羽毛及其制品和制鞋业	Leather, Furs,Down and Related Products	9.18
木材加工和木、竹、藤、棕、草制品业	Timber Processing, Wood, Bamboo, Cane, Palm and Sraw Products	12.70
家具制造业	Furniture Manufacturing	8.37
造纸和纸制品业	Papermaking and Paper Products	17.72
印刷和记录媒介复制业	Printing and Record Processing	24.25
文教、工美、体育和娱乐用品制造业	Stationery, Education and Sports Goods	18.73
石油加工、炼焦和核燃料加工业	Petroleum Processing, Coking Products and Nuclear Fuel Processing	6.51
化学原料和化学制品制造业	Raw Chemical Material and Chemical Products	126.67
医药制造业	Medical and pharmaceutical Products	71.59
化学纤维制造业	Chemical Fibers	1.78
橡胶和塑料制品业	Rubber and plastic products	38.97
非金属矿物制品业	Nonmetal Material Products	120.83
黑色金属冶炼和压延加工业	Smelting and Pressing of Ferrous Metals	68.79
有色金属冶炼和压延加工业	Smelting and Pressing of Nonferrous Metals	14.15
金属制品业	Metal Products	62.97
通用设备制造业	Ordinary Machinery Manufacturing	63.29
专用设备制造业	Special Purpose Equipment Manufacturing	56.71
汽车制造业	Motor manufacturing	282.18
铁路、船舶、航空航天和其他运输设备制造业	Railway,Watercraft,Aviation and other Transporlation Equipment manufacturing	33.72
电气机械和器材制造业	Electric Machinery and Equipment	70.69
计算机、通信和其他电子设备制造业	Telecommunication Computer,Equipment and Other Electronic Equipment Manufacturing	67.86
仪器仪表制造业	Instruments and Meters, Manufacturing	15.95
其他制造业	Other Manufacturing	3.96
废弃资源综合利用业	Waste Comprehensive Vtilization of Resources Industry	9.50
金属制品、机械和设备修理业	Metal products,Machinery and Equipment Repairing	3.63
电力、燃气及水的生产和供应业	**Electric Power, Gas and Water Production and Supply**	**57.52**
电力、热力生产和供应业	Electric Power, Steam and Hot Water Production and Supply	42.24
燃气生产和供应业	Gas Production and Supply	5.59
水的生产和供应业	Tap Water Production and Supply	9.69

(100 million Yuan)

财务费用 Financial Expenses	利息收入 Interest Income	利息费用 Interest Expenses	投资收益 Investment Income
12.61	**0.48**	**9.98**	**0.25**
0.03		0.03	
2.77	0.10	2.86	
2.19	0.03	2.12	
0.17	0.08	0.22	0.07
6.88	0.11	4.12	0.17
0.53	0.16	0.63	0.01
0.04			
320.74	**71.65**	**304.86**	**246.96**
29.32	0.78	21.32	2.34
4.80	2.15	4.86	3.08
10.31	1.85	8.57	2.78
-2.05	1.41	0.03	6.50
28.06	0.27	13.82	2.55
6.93	0.16	4.67	1.51
1.00	0.21	0.68	
4.69	0.04	3.12	0.01
1.67	0.07	1.16	0.07
6.69	0.47	5.72	0.23
4.50		3.35	0.25
5.16	0.05	3.04	0.11
1.80	0.69	2.38	-0.03
32.61	0.78	34.64	5.64
11.25	2.12	12.07	5.51
0.48		0.43	-0.02
9.91	0.63	7.28	0.60
31.45	1.37	17.46	6.09
20.47	3.93	23.14	44.06
6.81	0.60	6.17	-18.79
15.71	1.83	11.05	0.04
12.81	0.98	10.19	1.13
12.99	1.02	10.58	2.41
22.40	21.43	34.87	158.80
7.66	2.18	7.83	1.89
13.17	1.38	11.26	1.40
10.26	24.92	36.60	14.76
2.38	0.14	1.86	0.72
0.06	0.12	0.21	
6.12	0.06	5.22	3.32
1.32	0.01	1.28	
81.46	**2.27**	**77.25**	**33.68**
74.97	1.85	71.48	31.66
2.51	-0.01	2.28	0.77
3.98	0.43	3.49	1.25

13-2 续表 12 continued

单位: 亿元

项 目	Item	资产减值损失 Assets Devaluation
按行业分	**Grouped by sector**	
采矿业	**Mining and Qarrying**	**0.86**
煤炭开采和洗选业	Coal Mining and Processing	
石油和天然气开采业	Petroleum and Natural Gas Extraction	0.09
黑色金属矿采选业	Ferrous Metals Mining and Processing	0.41
有色金属矿采选业	Non-ferrous Metals Mining and Processing	0.24
非金属矿采选业	Non-metal Minerals Mining and Processing	0.13
开采辅助活动	Mining Auxiliary Activities	-0.01
其他采矿业	Other Minerals Mining and Processing	
制造业	**Manufacturing**	**99.49**
农副食品加工业	Food Processing	8.85
食品制造业	Food Production	0.38
酒、饮料和精制茶制造业	Wine,Beverage and Refined Tea Production	6.58
烟草制品业	Tobacco Processing	-0.04
纺织业	Textile Industry	0.18
纺织服装、服饰业	Textile,Garments, and Fashion Industry	-0.08
皮革、毛皮、羽毛及其制品和制鞋业	Leather, Furs,Down and Related Products	0.01
木材加工和木、竹、藤、棕、草制品业	Timber Processing, Wood, Bamboo, Cane, Palm and Sraw Products	1.08
家具制造业	Furniture Manufacturing	0.01
造纸和纸制品业	Papermaking and Paper Products	0.50
印刷和记录媒介复制业	Printing and Record Processing	0.17
文教、工美、体育和娱乐用品制造业	Stationery, Education and Sports Goods	0.57
石油加工、炼焦和核燃料加工业	Petroleum Processing, Coking Products and Nuclear Fuel Processing	0.04
化学原料和化学制品制造业	Raw Chemical Material and Chemical Products	7.21
医药制造业	Medical and pharmaceutical Products	2.17
化学纤维制造业	Chemical Fibers	0.11
橡胶和塑料制品业	Rubber and plastic products	0.63
非金属矿物制品业	Nonmetal Material Products	2.31
黑色金属冶炼和压延加工业	Smelting and Pressing of Ferrous Metals	6.58
有色金属冶炼和压延加工业	Smelting and Pressing of Nonferrous Metals	-0.18
金属制品业	Metal Products	-0.01
通用设备制造业	Ordinary Machinery Manufacturing	1.49
专用设备制造业	Special Purpose Equipment Manufacturing	1.79
汽车制造业	Motor manufacturing	26.09
铁路、船舶、航空航天和其他运输设备制造业	Railway,Watercraft,Aviation and other Transporlation Equipment manufacturing	9.41
电气机械和器材制造业	Electric Machinery and Equipment	1.18
计算机、通信和其他电子设备制造业	Telecommunication Computer,Equipment and Other Electronic Equipment Manufacturing	21.54
仪器仪表制造业	Instruments and Meters, Manufacturing	0.33
其他制造业	Other Manufacturing	0.03
废弃资源综合利用业	Waste Comprehensive Vtilization of Resources Industry	0.50
金属制品、机械和设备修理业	Metal products,Machinery and Equipment Repairing	0.06
电力、燃气及水的生产和供应业	**Electric Power, Gas and Water Production and Supply**	**2.90**
电力、热力生产和供应业	Electric Power, Steam and Hot Water Production and Supply	2.24
燃气生产和供应业	Gas Production and Supply	0.33
水的生产和供应业	Tap Water Production and Supply	0.33

(100 million Yuan)

公允价值变动收益 Profit and Loss Arising from Fair Value Changes	资产处置收益 Income from Disposal of Assets	其他收益 Other Income	营业利润 Operating Profits	营业外收入 Non-operating Income	营业外支出 Non-operating Expense	利润总额 Total Profits	所得税费用 Income Tax	亏损企业亏损总额 Total Loss of Enterprises Running
0.07	**0.02**	**1.37**	**53.38**	**1.25**	**2.68**	**51.95**	**7.91**	**7.89**
0.15			0.45		0.01	0.44	0.02	0.07
	-0.04	0.28	-6.51	0.51	0.55	-6.55	2.07	6.55
		0.61	7.29	0.03	0.20	7.13	0.97	0.25
			10.06	0.20	0.19	10.07	1.67	0.06
-0.08	-0.02	0.18	39.58	0.42	1.70	38.30	2.55	0.96
	0.08	0.30	2.29	0.09	0.03	2.34	0.63	
			0.22			0.22		
-26.69	**-2.27**	**136.98**	**2661.58**	**100.37**	**59.26**	**2714.02**	**320.36**	**231.41**
0.07	-0.01	1.99	220.97	7.25	2.78	225.44	8.91	3.85
-0.45	0.02	1.75	75.02	2.12	1.23	75.94	7.42	1.45
-5.84	-0.21	2.72	115.14	7.31	5.57	116.88	20.54	8.96
		0.03	106.55	2.52	0.77	108.30	31.90	0.12
-0.31	-0.02	1.58	100.20	2.19	0.83	101.55	7.09	3.19
0.50	0.03	0.36	46.12	0.83	0.70	46.22	2.00	0.86
	-0.14		13.38	0.46	0.07	13.77	0.51	0.39
	0.02	0.23	20.30	0.70	0.32	20.67	1.25	0.68
		0.90	16.43	0.39	0.04	16.78	1.28	0.21
	0.08	1.15	21.85	5.13	1.36	25.62	3.76	3.75
0.11	-0.74	1.16	41.00	1.50	1.26	41.24	3.67	1.52
0.09	0.09	0.28	29.39	0.39	0.52	29.26	1.42	0.20
		0.02	5.42	0.35	0.45	5.32	1.27	2.15
0.02	3.04	5.73	195.82	8.46	8.08	196.22	23.47	25.44
0.29	0.12	4.23	134.19	3.47	3.00	134.66	16.44	8.65
0.01		0.10	0.62	0.14	0.04	0.73	0.05	0.97
	0.93	2.51	65.12	1.85	0.98	65.99	4.68	1.09
0.13	-0.16	7.30	323.82	6.98	8.69	322.17	36.16	4.84
-2.13	9.58	4.33	85.14	7.48	7.18	93.69	11.81	2.76
-15.73	-22.90	2.16	16.37	2.01	1.21	17.17	0.51	1.94
	2.20	2.44	86.20	3.46	1.06	88.60	8.33	7.15
-0.56	0.74	3.15	68.66	3.95	1.84	70.77	3.75	4.44
-0.32	0.07	3.45	68.35	2.93	0.63	73.44	5.28	5.15
0.39	3.05	23.52	565.10	11.78	6.27	570.62	85.11	61.26
-0.16	1.47	6.71	2.03	2.47	0.88	3.62	2.19	19.02
-3.01	0.94	10.82	120.18	4.56	1.67	123.08	15.06	7.67
1.71	0.33	37.34	77.41	6.29	1.20	82.49	12.27	47.61
-0.75	-0.45	2.67	16.60	1.08	0.23	17.43	2.56	3.94
	0.03	0.01	3.69	0.22	0.14	3.76	0.16	0.04
-0.75	-0.38	8.34	16.93	1.90	0.16	18.91	1.17	1.70
			3.58	0.20	0.10	3.68	0.34	0.41
3.01	**1.39**	**3.75**	**281.02**	**7.37**	**4.84**	**283.58**	**62.73**	**16.70**
2.92	1.10	3.08	264.07	4.52	4.18	264.42	57.02	9.36
0.02		0.13	14.89	0.52	0.39	15.03	3.74	2.61
0.07	0.29	0.54	2.06	2.33	0.27	4.13	1.97	4.73

13-2 续表13 continued

单位: 亿元

项 目	Item	利税总额 Total Profits
按行业分	**Grouped by sector**	
采矿业	**Mining and Qarrying**	**99.08**
煤炭开采和洗选业	Coal Mining and Processing	0.87
石油和天然气开采业	Petroleum and Natural Gas Extraction	-0.72
黑色金属矿采选业	Ferrous Metals Mining and Processing	14.29
有色金属矿采选业	Non-ferrous Metals Mining and Processing	13.34
非金属矿采选业	Non-metal Minerals Mining and Processing	67.21
开采辅助活动	Mining Auxiliary Activities	3.34
其他采矿业	Other Minerals Mining and Processing	0.75
制造业	**Manufacturing**	**4776.61**
农副食品加工业	Food Processing	330.07
食品制造业	Food Production	112.04
酒、饮料和精制茶制造业	Wine,Beverage and Refined Tea Production	183.27
烟草制品业	Tobacco Processing	628.02
纺织业	Textile Industry	171.96
纺织服装、服饰业	Textile,Garments, and Fashion Industry	76.43
皮革、毛皮、羽毛及其制品和制鞋业	Leather, Furs,Down and Related Products	24.74
木材加工和木、竹、藤、棕、草制品业	Timber Processing, Wood, Bamboo, Cane, Palm and Sraw Products	34.93
家具制造业	Furniture Manufacturing	26.37
造纸和纸制品业	Papermaking and Paper Products	45.32
印刷和记录媒介复制业	Printing and Record Processing	64.67
文教、工美、体育和娱乐用品制造业	Stationery, Education and Sports Goods	47.71
石油加工、炼焦和核燃料加工业	Petroleum Processing, Coking Products and Nuclear Fuel Processing	105.43
化学原料和化学制品制造业	Raw Chemical Material and Chemical Products	377.98
医药制造业	Medical and pharmaceutical Products	192.83
化学纤维制造业	Chemical Fibers	2.07
橡胶和塑料制品业	Rubber and plastic products	99.32
非金属矿物制品业	Nonmetal Material Products	464.61
黑色金属冶炼和压延加工业	Smelting and Pressing of Ferrous Metals	138.99
有色金属冶炼和压延加工业	Smelting and Pressing of Nonferrous Metals	38.46
金属制品业	Metal Products	146.98
通用设备制造业	Ordinary Machinery Manufacturing	117.47
专用设备制造业	Special Purpose Equipment Manufacturing	112.49
汽车制造业	Motor manufacturing	843.22
铁路、船舶、航空航天和其他运输设备制造业	Railway,Watercraft,Aviation and other Transporlation Equipment manufacturing	17.60
电气机械和器材制造业	Electric Machinery and Equipment	177.62
计算机、通信和其他电子设备制造业	Telecommunication Computer,Equipment and Other Electronic Equipment Manufacturing	116.28
仪器仪表制造业	Instruments and Meters, Manufacturing	26.83
其他制造业	Other Manufacturing	5.66
废弃资源综合利用业	Waste Comprehensive Vtilization of Resources Industry	41.88
金属制品、机械和设备修理业	Metal products,Machinery and Equipment Repairing	5.36
电力、燃气及水的生产和供应业	**Electric Power, Gas and Water Production and Supply**	**398.82**
电力、热力生产和供应业	Electric Power, Steam and Hot Water Production and Supply	371.39
燃气生产和供应业	Gas Production and Supply	18.61
水的生产和供应业	Tap Water Production and Supply	8.82

(100 million Yuan)

应交税金及附加 Tax and Extra Charges	本年应付职工薪酬 Wages Welfarism Payable this year	本年应交增值税 Value Added Payable of the	全部从业人员年平均人数(万人) Average Number of Empolyment of the Current Year
55.05	**73.14**	**27.80**	**6.48**
0.45	1.05	0.27	0.11
7.90	19.83	3.11	1.08
8.13	15.05	5.06	1.31
4.94	4.80	2.31	0.50
31.46	21.01	16.13	2.90
1.63	10.43	0.71	0.51
0.54	0.97	0.21	0.07
2382.95	**2673.19**	**1097.04**	**318.23**
113.55	138.08	76.94	17.02
43.52	60.18	29.35	7.68
86.93	64.91	35.07	7.01
551.62	26.06	85.33	0.73
77.50	159.17	51.80	67.42
32.21	74.94	23.23	12.27
11.48	19.44	9.25	3.15
15.51	20.86	9.58	3.46
10.87	18.08	6.62	2.24
23.45	26.73	16.66	3.32
27.10	53.87	17.78	5.15
19.86	31.21	12.59	4.15
101.38	10.19	12.30	0.71
205.23	178.27	78.21	18.07
74.61	109.25	47.98	11.24
1.39	4.14	0.88	0.57
38.00	58.96	25.94	7.60
178.60	201.33	109.26	22.15
57.11	144.15	34.58	7.84
21.79	42.15	16.77	3.73
66.72	112.03	47.47	11.97
50.46	104.97	35.95	10.43
44.33	107.81	30.73	10.42
357.71	442.90	176.25	36.76
16.17	52.19	10.56	6.20
69.61	137.52	40.83	13.22
46.06	216.52	24.67	17.92
11.96	28.46	7.74	2.86
2.06	6.06	1.55	0.68
24.14	12.28	19.85	1.29
2.02	10.48	1.32	0.97
177.97	**216.83**	**99.38**	**11.13**
163.99	183.86	92.81	8.04
7.32	10.74	2.99	0.98
6.66	22.23	3.58	2.11

13-3 国有控股工业企业单位数和主要经济指标 (2019)

单位: 亿元

项 目	Item	企业单位数（个）Number of Enterprises (unit)
总　　计	**Total**	**773**
在总计中:	Of the Total	
亏损企业	Enterprises running under Deficit	147
在总计中:	Of the Total:	
中央企业	Central Enterprises	279
地方企业	Local Enterprises	494
在总计中:	Of the Total:	
轻工业	Light Industry	150
重工业	Heavy Industry	623
在总计中:	Of the Total:	
大型企业	Large Scale Enterprises	109
中型企业	Medium Scale Enterprises	186
小型企业	Small Enterprises	478
按行业分	Grouped by sector	
采矿业	**Mining and Qarrying**	**23**
煤炭开采和洗选业	Coal Mining and Processing	1
石油和天然气开采业	Petroleum and Natural Gas Extraction	1
黑色金属矿采选业	Ferrous Metals Mining and Processing	4
有色金属矿采选业	Non-ferrous Metals Mining and Processing	2
非金属矿采选业	Non-metal Minerals Mining and Processing	12
开采辅助活动	Mining Auxiliary Activities	3
其他采矿业	Other Minerals Mining and Processing	
制造业	**Manufacturing**	**563**
农副食品加工业	Food Processing	32
食品制造业	Food Production	11
酒、饮料和精制茶制造业	Wine,Beverage and Refined Tea Production	12
烟草制品业	Tobacco Processing	6
纺织业	Textile Industry	13
纺织服装、服饰业	Textile,Garments, and Fashion Industry	11
皮革、毛皮、羽毛及其制品和制鞋业	Leather, Furs,Down and Related Products	
木材加工和木、竹、藤、棕、草制品业	Timber Processing, Wood, Bamboo, Cane, Palm and Saraw Products	5
家具制造业	Furniture Manufacturing	
造纸和纸制品业	Papermaking and Paper Products	2
印刷和记录媒介复制业	Printing and Record Processing	15
文教、工美、体育和娱乐用品制造业	Stationery, Education and Sports Goods	2
石油加工、炼焦和核燃料加工业	Petroleum Processing, Coking Products and Nuclear Fuel Processing	6
化学原料和化学制品制造业	Raw Chemical Material and Chemical Products	47
医药制造业	Medical and pharmaceutical Products	21
化学纤维制造业	Chemical Fibers	
橡胶和塑料制品业	Rubber and plastic products	6
非金属矿物制品业	Nonmetal Material Products	55
黑色金属冶炼和压延加工业	Smelting and Pressing of Ferrous Metals	11
有色金属冶炼和压延加工业	Smelting and Pressing of Nonferrous Metals	6
金属制品业	Metal Products	28
通用设备制造业	Ordinary Machinery Manufacturing	30
专用设备制造业	Special Purpose Equipment Manufacturing	27
汽车制造业	Motor manufacturing	83
铁路、船舶、航空航天和其他运输设备制造业	Railway,Watercraft,Aviation and other Transporlation Equipment nufacturing	40
电气机械和器材制造业	Electric Machinery and Equipment	36
计算机、通信和其他电子设备制造业	Telecommunication Computer,Equipment and Other Electronic quipment Manufacturing	31
仪器仪表制造业	Instruments and Meters, Manufacturing	16
其他制造业	Other Manufacturing	2
废弃资源综合利用业	Waste Comprehensive Vtilization of Resources Industry	5
金属制品、机械和设备修理业	Metal products,Machinery and Equipment Repairing	4
电力、燃气及水的生产和供应业	**Electric Power, Gas and Water Production and Supply**	**187**
电力、热力生产和供应业	Electric Power, Steam and Hot Water Production and Supply	113
燃气生产和供应业	Gas Production and Supply	12
水的生产和供应业	Tap Water Production and Supply	62

Number and Main Economic Indicators of State-Holding Industrial Enterprises(2019)

(100 million yuan)

工业总产值(当年价格) Total Output Value (current price)	资产总计 Total Assets	流动资产合计 Circulating Funds	固定资产净额 NBV of Fixed Assets	固定资产原价 Original Value of Fixed Assets	营业收入 Revenue	全部从业人员年平均人数(万人) Average Number of Empolyment of the Curreat Year (10 000 Persons)
11722.96	**19408.01**	**7910.42**	**5825.98**	**12276.11**	**11659.35**	**59.08**
2554.59	5096.68	1304.39	2261.42	5504.68	2419.39	15.79
8921.03	13967.83	5642.18	4631.17	9673.15	8826.10	36.58
2801.93	5440.19	2268.24	1194.81	2602.96	2833.25	22.51
1471.31	1360.21	903.09	224.83	446.42	1582.91	6.58
10251.65	18047.80	7007.33	5601.15	11829.68	10076.43	52.50
8990.42	14795.65	5886.81	4406.98	9466.44	8927.46	42.32
1638.89	2718.10	1239.46	659.60	1547.16	1606.39	10.66
1093.65	1894.26	784.15	759.40	1262.51	1125.50	6.10
208.27	**417.95**	**127.13**	**169.72**	**476.50**	**241.48**	**2.37**
0.47	2.31	1.84	0.36	0.89	0.52	0.04
37.06	252.62	55.89	103.65	325.37	70.05	1.08
61.50	55.91	26.86	18.97	51.42	54.63	0.46
11.29	21.15	8.20	5.34	14.93	11.35	0.19
13.56	18.94	8.88	6.69	8.83	12.93	0.09
84.39	67.02	25.46	34.71	75.06	92.00	0.51
9544.45	**13872.22**	**7302.18**	**2465.87**	**5738.36**	**9408.97**	**47.36**
155.70	33.87	18.27	7.95	26.17	150.64	0.37
82.41	106.36	53.96	19.31	32.19	100.58	0.78
36.52	37.12	20.00	7.72	19.00	26.84	0.42
673.79	579.65	451.26	74.85	129.71	774.82	0.72
42.46	57.13	29.78	16.35	28.42	42.95	0.57
17.82	36.26	22.77	3.86	12.36	16.47	0.78
7.71	8.47	4.01	1.46	2.31	6.92	0.11
12.07	12.22	2.67	8.36	14.88	13.32	0.05
56.76	58.26	45.20	10.13	28.08	59.81	0.32
1.47	3.26	1.43	1.67	2.24	1.57	0.02
321.42	110.65	23.64	53.05	116.52	301.00	0.33
1028.85	1413.76	402.79	395.29	826.72	1030.67	3.98
93.70	184.24	86.62	42.38	67.99	96.63	0.90
63.19	45.79	23.86	4.88	8.65	48.71	0.30
242.60	276.01	120.00	105.63	175.47	249.95	1.53
1231.51	1914.02	613.08	658.32	1773.30	1266.82	4.75
464.54	215.65	114.37	70.80	142.78	486.63	1.28
291.30	366.23	254.31	56.72	107.08	282.08	2.13
110.92	251.30	160.90	44.00	86.87	102.23	1.60
180.62	267.36	209.07	39.88	82.25	183.48	1.37
2799.65	4330.01	2658.23	392.71	976.64	2596.42	11.48
480.01	1130.53	701.50	192.84	324.83	434.15	4.57
359.03	467.61	317.87	61.89	134.14	378.99	2.11
688.50	1820.84	865.62	166.61	567.48	656.21	5.55
45.90	77.78	51.92	15.73	27.03	44.43	0.71
25.74	37.92	29.11	7.17	12.70	26.93	0.21
14.68	10.70	4.74	3.53	4.94	14.64	0.07
15.58	19.22	15.20	2.78	7.61	15.08	0.35
1970.25	**5117.82**	**481.11**	**3190.39**	**6061.27**	**2008.91**	**9.35**
1824.40	4614.44	311.00	3025.30	5776.20	1851.68	7.36
86.26	107.76	25.34	47.05	89.14	86.99	0.38
59.59	395.62	144.77	118.04	195.93	70.24	1.61

13-4 集体工业企业单位数和主要经济指标(2019)

单位:亿元

项 目	Item	企业单位数(个) Number of Enterprises (unit)
总 计	**Total**	**48**
在总计中:	Of the Total:	
亏损企业	Enterprises running under Deficit	5
在总计中:	Of the Total:	
轻工业	Light Industry	12
重工业	Heavy Industry	36
在总计中:	Of the Total:	
大型企业	Large Scale Enterprises	
中型企业	Medium Scale Enterprises	7
小型企业	Small Enterprises	41
按行业分	Grouped by sector	
采矿业	**Mining and Qarrying**	**13**
煤炭开采和洗选业	Coal Mining and Processing	
石油和天然气开采业	Petroleum and Natural Gas Extraction	
黑色金属矿采选业	Ferrous Metals Mining and Processing	4
有色金属矿采选业	Non-ferrous Metals Mining and Processing	
非金属矿采选业	Non-metal Minerals Mining and Processing	9
开采辅助活动	Mining Auxiliary Activities	
其他采矿业	Other Minerals Mining and Processing	
制造业	**Manufacturing**	**31**
农副食品加工业	Food Processing	
食品制造业	Food Production	
酒、饮料和精制茶制造业	Wine,Beverage and Refined Tea Production	2
烟草制品业	Tobacco Processing	
纺织业	Textile Industry	
纺织服装、服饰业	Textile,Garments, and Fashion Industry	3
皮革、毛皮、羽毛及其制品和制鞋业	Leather, Furs,Down and Related Products	
木材加工和木、竹、藤、棕、草制品业	Timber Processing, Wood, Bamboo, Cane, and Nuclear Fuel Processing	
家具制造业	Furniture Manufacturing	
造纸和纸制品业	Papermaking and Paper Products	
印刷和记录媒介复制业	Printing and Record Processing	2
文教、工美、体育和娱乐用品制造业	Stationery, Education and Sports Goods	
石油加工、炼焦和核燃料加工业	Petroleum Processing, Coking Products and Nuclear Fuel Processing	
化学原料和化学制品制造业	Raw Chemical Material and Chemical Products	1
医药制造业	Medical and pharmaceutical Products	1
化学纤维制造业	Chemical Fibers	
橡胶和塑料制品业	Rubber and plastic products	4
非金属矿物制品业	Nonmetal Material Products	5
黑色金属冶炼和压延加工业	Smelting and Pressing of Ferrous Metals	1
有色金属冶炼和压延加工业	Smelting and Pressing of Nonferrous Metals	2
金属制品业	Metal Products	1
通用设备制造业	Ordinary Machinery Manufacturing	1
专用设备制造业	Special Purpose Equipment Manufacturing	
汽车制造业	Motor manufacturing	3
铁路、船舶、航空航天和其他运输设备制造业	Railway,Watercraft,Aviation and other Transporlation Equipment manufacturing	2
电气机械和器材制造业	Electric Machinery and Equipment	
计算机、通信和其他电子设备制造业	Telecommunication Computer,Equipment and Other Electronic Equipment Manufacturing	
仪器仪表制造业	Instruments and Meters, Manufacturing	
其他制造业	Other Manufacturing	
废弃资源综合利用业	Waste Comprehensive Vtilization of Resources Industry	2
金属制品、机械和设备修理业	Metal products,Machinery and Equipment Repairing	1
电力、燃气及水的生产和供应业	**Electric Power, Gas and Water Production and Supply**	**4**
电力、热力生产和供应业	Electric Power, Steam and Hot Water Production and Supply	
燃气生产和供应业	Gas Production and Supply	
水的生产和供应业	Tap Water Production and Supply	4

Number and Main Economic Indicators of Collective-Owned Industrial Enterprises(2019)

(100 million yuan)

工业总产值(当年价格) Total Output Value(current price)	资产总计 Total Assets	流动资产合计 Circulating Funds	固定资产净额 NBV of Fixed Assets	固定资产原价 Original Value of Fixed Assets	营业收入 Revenue	全部从业人员年平均人数(万人) Average Number of Empolyment of the Curreat Year (10 000 Persons)
71.84	**45.24**	**26.54**	**12.50**	**23.87**	**72.54**	**0.76**
6.10	17.03	9.56	5.87	7.84	5.48	0.10
14.60	4.05	2.64	0.98	1.63	13.35	0.16
57.25	41.20	23.89	11.53	22.24	59.20	0.59
20.64	22.05	13.07	7.56	12.24	21.78	0.36
51.20	23.19	13.46	4.94	11.62	50.76	0.40
30.67	**10.72**	**5.14**	**4**	**8.93**	**29.97**	**0.23**
17.62	4.3	2.7	1.85	3.78	17.51	0.1
13.05	6.42	2.44	2.15	5.15	12.46	0.13
37.36	**20.3**	**13.48**	**3.14**	**8.42**	**39.82**	**0.47**
1.39	0.35	0.13	0.14	0.24	1.38	0.03
1.54	0.85	0.7	0.06	0.2	1.57	0.04
4.23	0.64	0.27	0.27	0.33	4.13	0.02
0.54	0.23	0.15			0.54	
0.97	0.2	0.03	0.17	0.19	0.14	0.01
6.47	2	1.51	0.34	0.67	6.13	0.08
8.58	6.45	5.38	0.93	3.35	10.29	0.05
3.25	2.2	0.83	0.38	1.03	3.24	0.03
1.66	0.78	0.61		0.01	1.62	0.01
0.74	0.85	0.67	0.13	0.39	0.59	0.01
1.22	0.56	0.3	0.06	0.15	1	0.05
3.63	0.7	0.51	0.07	0.36	3.36	0.03
1.27	1.02	0.63	0.15	0.28	1.26	0.01
1.65	2.95	1.32	0.41	1.07	4.36	0.09
0.22	0.52	0.44	0.03	0.15	0.21	0.01
3.8	**14.21**	**7.91**	**5.39**	**6.53**	**2.75**	**0.06**
3.8	14.21	7.91	5.39	6.53	2.75	0.06

13-5 外商投资和港澳台商投资工业企业单位数和主要经济指标(2019)

单位: 亿元

项 目	Item	企业单位数(个) Number of Enterprises (unit)
总计	**Total**	**741**
在总计中:	Of the Total:	
亏损企业	Enterprises running under Deficit	138
在总计中:	Of the Total:	
港、澳、台商投资企业	Hongkong, Macao and Taiwan Funded Enterprises	285
合资经营企业(港或澳、台资)	Joint Venture with Hongkong, Macao and Taiwan	116
合作经营企业(港或澳、台资)	Cooperate with Hongkong, Macao and Taiwan Funded	
港澳台商独资经营企业	Enterprises Solely Funded by Hongkong, Macao and Taiwan Businessmen	148
港澳台商投资股份有限公司	Share Holding Co.Ltd.With Hongkong,Macao and Taiwan Businessmen	10
其他港澳台投资	Othes	11
外商投资企业	Foreign Funded Enterprises	456
中外合资经营企业	Sino - Foreign Joint Funded Enterprises	230
中外合作经营企业	Sino - Foreign Cooperative Funded Enterprises	4
外资企业	Foreign Solely Funded Enterprises	201
外商投资股份有限公司	Foreign Funded Share Holding Co.Ltd.	11
其他外商投资	Othes	10
在总计中:	Of the Total:	
国有控股企业	State-Owned Share Holding Enterprises	48
在总计中:	Of the Total:	
轻工业	Light Industry	274
重工业	Heavy Industry	467
在总计中:	Of the Total:	
大型企业	Large Scale Enterprises	66
中型企业	Medium Scale Enterprises	187
小型企业	Small Enterprises	488
按行业分	Grouped by sector	
采矿业	**Mining and Qarrying**	**2**
煤炭开采和洗选业	Coal Mining and Processing	
石油和天然气开采业	Petroleum and Natural Gas Extraction	
黑色金属矿采选业	Ferrous Metals Mining and Processing	1
有色金属矿采选业	Non-ferrous Metals Mining and Processing	1
非金属矿采选业	Non-metal Minerals Mining and Processing	
开采辅助活动	Mining Auxiliary Activities	
其他采矿业	Other Minerals Mining and Processing	

Number and Main Economic Indicators of Industrial Enterprises with Hong Kong, Macao, Taiwan and Foreign Funds(2019)

(100 million yuan)

工业总产值(当年价格) Total Output Value (current price)	资产总计 Total Assets	流动资产合计 Circulating Funds	固定资产净额 Total Fixed Assets	固定资产原价 Original Value of Fixed Assets	营业收入 Revenue	全部从业人员年平均人数(万人) Average Number of Empolyment of the Curreat Year (10 000 Persons)
7535.82	**6079.92**	**3176.13**	**1844.08**	**3547.28**	**7325.95**	**34.68**
440.04	819.43	261.53	381.23	760.82	483.83	4.75
2094.13	1940.66	923.60	664.96	1156.00	2131.35	14.52
1117.31	1115.56	570.02	294.65	531.25	1170.27	7.84
841.14	669.92	282.72	307.20	539.64	828.14	6.08
39.43	57.31	12.03	37.23	42.85	38.49	0.15
96.24	97.88	58.83	25.88	42.26	94.44	0.44
5441.69	4139.26	2252.54	1179.12	2391.27	5194.60	20.16
4312.91	3228.09	1704.40	920.10	1834.37	4064.40	11.93
22.97	22.79	9.31	10.84	31.56	23.02	0.07
1018.64	803.05	482.81	227.26	469.99	1022.97	7.57
46.86	36.14	19.95	11.54	23.76	44.33	0.30
40.32	49.19	36.07	9.38	31.60	39.88	0.28
2762.27	2222.94	1233.08	551.54	1207.85	2556.41	6.11
1732.01	1315.28	708.23	404.98	760.46	1662.44	13.19
5803.81	4764.64	2467.91	1439.10	2786.82	5663.51	21.48
4663.53	3408.98	1806.93	945.87	1919.63	4557.02	18.18
1621.08	1460.26	793.34	457.59	813.22	1558.68	10.13
1251.21	1210.69	575.87	440.62	814.43	1210.26	6.36
0.61	**9.46**	**1.4**	**0.13**	**0.39**	**1.12**	**0.06**
	8.45	0.63			0.4	0.01
0.61	1.01	0.77	0.13	0.39	0.72	0.05

13-5 续表1 continued

单位: 亿元

项 目	Item	企业单位数(个) Number of Enterprises (unit)
制造业	**Manufacturing**	**686**
农副食品加工业	Food Processing	36
食品制造业	Food Production	23
酒、饮料和精制茶制造业	Wine,Beverage and Refined Tea Production	25
烟草制品业	Tobacco Processing	
纺织业	Textile Industry	40
纺织服装、服饰业	Textile,Garments, and Fashion Industry	25
皮革、毛皮、羽毛及其制品和制鞋业	Leather, Furs,Down and Related Products	12
木材加工和木、竹、藤、棕、草制品业	Timber Processing, Wood, Bamboo, Cane, Palm and Sraw Products	4
家具制造业	Furniture Manufacturing	2
造纸和纸制品业	Papermaking and Paper Products	12
印刷和记录媒介复制业	Printing and Record Processing	9
文教、工美、体育和娱乐用品制造业	Stationery, Education and Sports Goods	16
石油加工、炼焦和核燃料加工业	Petroleum Processing, Coking Products and Nuclear Fuel Processing	3
化学原料和化学制品制造业	Raw Chemical Material and Chemical Products	41
医药制造业	Medical and pharmaceutical Products	31
化学纤维制造业	Chemical Fibers	2
橡胶和塑料制品业	Rubber and plastic products	15
非金属矿物制品业	Nonmetal Material Products	36
黑色金属冶炼和压延加工业	Smelting and Pressing of Ferrous Metals	8
有色金属冶炼和压延加工业	Smelting and Pressing of Nonferrous Metals	1
金属制品业	Metal Products	16
通用设备制造业	Ordinary Machinery Manufacturing	33
专用设备制造业	Special Purpose Equipment Manufacturing	21
汽车制造业	Motor manufacturing	187
铁路、船舶、航空航天和其他运输设备制造业	Railway,Watercraft,Aviation and other Transporlation Equipment manufacturing	7
电气机械和器材制造业	Electric Machinery and Equipment	37
计算机、通信和其他电子设备制造业	Telecommunication Computer,Equipment and Other Electronic Equipment Manufacturing	37
仪器仪表制造业	Instruments and Meters, Manufacturing	5
其他制造业	Other Manufacturing	
废弃资源综合利用业	Waste Comprehensive Vtilization of Resources Industry	2
金属制品、机械和设备修理业	Metal products,Machinery and Equipment Repairing	
电力、燃气及水的生产和供应业	**Electric Power, Gas and Water Production and Supply**	**53**
电力、热力生产和供应业	Electric Power, Steam and Hot Water Production and Supply	21
燃气生产和供应业	Gas Production and Supply	27
水的生产和供应业	Tap Water Production and Supply	5

(100 million yuan)

工业总产值(当年价格) Total Output Value (current price)	资产总计 Total Assets	流动资产合计 Circulating Funds	固定资产净额 Total Fixed Assets	固定资产原价 Original Value of Fixed Assets	营业收入 Revenue	全部从业人员年平均人数(万人) Average Number of Empolyment of the Curreat Year (10 000 Persons)
7263.12	**5612.38**	**3055.15**	**1584.02**	**3126.75**	**7039.78**	**33.71**
288.46	164.56	98.94	48.32	74.84	285	1.01
146.4	87.12	42.69	32.53	75.92	131.16	1.16
221.52	167.37	82.22	56.59	137.57	205.02	1.29
126.81	55.5	25.16	22.7	49.55	121.71	1.48
50.16	40.11	26.13	10.13	17.72	48.17	1.05
32.12	18.83	8.55	7.16	14.65	28.5	1.12
6.54	2.76	0.79	0.64	1.3	6.26	0.09
3.69	1.83	0.94	0.69	1.05	1.78	0.03
134.9	172.41	69.95	81.2	110.54	133.22	0.65
36.95	25.15	20.02	2.84	12.52	32.95	0.25
81.55	54.65	36.07	14.99	37.54	81.2	0.67
61.52	32.45	15.44	12.55	24.16	55.09	0.07
670.28	489.02	144.52	221.18	412.77	665.73	1.35
289	350.43	178.18	80.97	140.55	285.66	2.5
20.55	11.03	5.55	4.95	11.71	15.87	0.08
33.1	27.3	16.67	7.65	12.44	32.95	0.26
170.78	192.06	86.72	81.11	165.99	167.25	1.3
267.72	279.12	117.3	95.27	154.08	419.05	0.79
2.64	0.76	0.43	0.07	0.09	2.57	0.01
55.26	44.19	15.61	16.01	36.1	54.85	0.31
84.94	86.19	58.91	18.88	33.97	82.1	0.79
87.86	93.11	67.51	20.66	32.25	79.1	1.1
3513.66	2637.31	1571.15	611.38	1306.66	3304.09	10.67
17.48	18.66	16.02	2.31	5.42	17.91	0.2
386.55	212.55	140.92	59.66	127.66	374.62	2.31
457.57	342.82	204.69	73.28	129.19	392.29	3.09
3.62	4.72	3.87	0.27	0.47	4.05	0.07
11.49	0.37	0.2	0.03	0.04	11.63	0.01
272.08	**458.08**	**119.63**	**259.93**	**420.13**	**285.08**	**0.92**
156.84	299.34	66.66	188.09	324.17	163.23	0.16
107.3	123.38	44.04	61.88	84.52	113.86	0.59
7.94	35.36	8.93	9.96	11.44	7.99	0.17

13-6 私营工业企业单位数和主要经济指标(2019)

单位:亿元

项 目	Item	企业单位数(个) Number of Enterprises (unit)
总计	**Total**	**9806**
在总计中:	Of the Total:	
亏损企业	Enterprises running under Deficit	649
在总计中:	Of the Total:	
轻工业	Light Industry	4261
重工业	Heavy Industry	5545
在总计中:	Of the Total:	
大型企业	Large Scale Enterprises	71
中型企业	Medium Scale Enterprises	670
小型企业	Small Enterprises	9065
按行业分	Grouped by sector	
采矿业	**Mining and Qarrying**	**268**
煤炭开采和洗选业	Coal Mining and Processing	7
石油和天然气开采业	Petroleum and Natural Gas Extraction	
黑色金属矿采选业	Ferrous Metals Mining and Processing	15
有色金属矿采选业	Non-ferrous Metals Mining and Processing	12
非金属矿采选业	Non-metal Minerals Mining and Processing	233
开采辅助活动	Mining Auxiliary Activities	1
其他采矿业	Other Minerals Mining and Processing	
制造业	**Manufacturing**	**9438**
农副食品加工业	Food Processing	1062
食品制造业	Food Production	212
酒、饮料和精制茶制造业	Wine,Beverage and Refined Tea Production	246
烟草制品业	Tobacco Processing	
纺织业	Textile Industry	666
纺织服装、服饰业	Textile,Garments, and Fashion Industry	336
皮革、毛皮、羽毛及其制品和制鞋业	Leather, Furs,Down and Related Products	133
木材加工和木、竹、藤、棕、草制品业	Timber Processing, Wood, Bamboo, Cane, Palm and Sraw Products	205
家具制造业	Furniture Manufacturing	115
造纸和纸制品业	Papermaking and Paper Products	138
印刷和记录媒介复制业	Printing and Record Processing	205
文教、工美、体育和娱乐用品制造业	Stationery, Education and Sports Goods	189
石油加工、炼焦和核燃料加工业	Petroleum Processing, Coking Products and Nuclear Fuel Processing	24
化学原料和化学制品制造业	Raw Chemical Material and Chemical Products	578
医药制造业	Medical and pharmaceutical Products	218
化学纤维制造业	Chemical Fibers	12
橡胶和塑料制品业	Rubber and plastic products	406
非金属矿物制品业	Nonmetal Material Products	1437
黑色金属冶炼和压延加工业	Smelting and Pressing of Ferrous Metals	52
有色金属冶炼和压延加工业	Smelting and Pressing of Nonferrous Metals	110
金属制品业	Metal Products	581
通用设备制造业	Ordinary Machinery Manufacturing	423
专用设备制造业	Special Purpose Equipment Manufacturing	417
汽车制造业	Motor manufacturing	841
铁路、船舶、航空航天和其他运输设备制造业	Railway,Watercraft,Aviation and other Transporlation Equipment manufacturing	67
电气机械和器材制造业	Electric Machinery and Equipment	376
计算机、通信和其他电子设备制造业	Telecommunication Computer,Equipment and Other Electronic Equipment Manufacturing	212
仪器仪表制造业	Instruments and Meters, Manufacturing	74
其他制造业	Other Manufacturing	33
废弃资源综合利用业	Waste Comprehensive Vtilization of Resources Industry	60
金属制品、机械和设备修理业	Metal products,Machinery and Equipment Repairing	10
电力、燃气及水的生产和供应业	**Electric Power, Gas and Water Production and Supply**	**100**
电力、热力生产和供应业	Electric Power, Steam and Hot Water Production and Supply	59
燃气生产和供应业	Gas Production and Supply	20
水的生产和供应业	Tap Water Production and Supply	21

Number and Main Economic Indicators of Private Industrial Enterprises(2019)

(100 million yuan)

工业总产值 (当年价格) Total Output Value (current price)	资产总计 Total Assets	流动资产合计 Circulating Funds	固定资产净额 NBV of Fixed Assets	固定资产原价 Original Value of Fixed Assets	营业收入 Revenue	全部从业人员年平均人数(万人) Average Number of Empolyment of the Curreat Year(10 000 Persons)
19649.46	**9386.42**	**4540.17**	**2859.16**	**6313.88**	**18073.86**	**171.48**
771.83	893.84	473.10	195.32	342.39	604.87	7.68
9108.55	4048.96	1888.47	1343.62	3049.40	8389.61	109.77
10540.91	5337.46	2651.70	1515.53	3264.48	9684.25	61.71
1375.07	800.51	432.56	236.27	465.84	1293.28	10.83
3679.91	1981.34	963.59	683.38	1645.37	3331.77	33.24
14594.48	6604.57	3144.03	1939.51	4202.67	13448.81	127.41
453.95	**238**	**98.49**	**63.24**	**130.37**	**401.21**	**2.21**
6.69	5.26	1.88	1.72	2.7	6.46	0.07
32.23	23.67	8.78	5.68	11.38	28.1	0.19
21.73	17.12	8	6.77	11.74	21.37	0.16
393.04	191.43	79.37	49.05	104.39	344.99	1.79
0.26	0.52	0.46	0.02	0.16	0.29	
19107.55	**8928.2**	**4379.63**	**2692.57**	**6023.54**	**17591.69**	**168.67**
2618.65	993.34	461	329.08	715.55	2424.7	11.15
484.27	263.08	114.07	92.25	178.36	463.45	3.32
457.05	256.19	125.46	80.63	134.02	419.34	2.71
1560.31	591.05	253.38	233.23	610.19	1455.68	60.46
618.86	230.69	94.67	86.66	189.72	585.37	7.89
221.72	65.93	37.55	14.21	68.33	211.26	1.76
281.66	133.18	50.45	36.32	84.4	256.95	2.02
180.98	144.22	58.09	53.9	81.19	168.9	1.54
345.9	152.04	72.85	51.38	98.89	313.45	1.92
374	178.57	90.6	50.22	123.7	326.92	2.95
354.25	158.6	58.78	62.59	182.94	321.3	2.56
25.34	14.59	7.5	4.48	5.49	23.02	0.1
1559.39	723.17	293.36	226.06	706	1390.14	6.94
440.12	326.29	165.71	96.31	210.69	388.64	3.74
28.82	12.45	5.72	4.41	15.73	28.22	0.16
738.64	323.93	164.89	96.47	243.48	694.54	5.01
2353.95	1124.88	529.59	376.28	715.99	2236.51	14.1
380.93	159	65.32	54.29	83.97	379.31	1.38
260.37	97.98	50.82	31.03	54.28	245.79	1.5
988.55	453.08	265.53	113	249.5	929.23	6.26
880.56	407.68	214.87	111.53	297.49	824.85	5.04
608.2	335.32	191.18	74.36	212.73	569.82	4.6
1671.78	955.86	514.88	221.1	401.16	1492.3	10.78
119.57	45.34	22.72	13.28	27.97	104.2	1.04
731.43	398.08	242.69	81.46	155.28	633.2	4.45
492.09	232.84	139.66	61.97	100.29	411.51	3.53
112.43	53.77	35.24	8.89	20.62	85.95	0.8
37.65	18.23	10.15	4.22	8.61	32.86	0.27
154.81	70.34	39.17	18.63	32.69	149.43	0.49
25.27	8.48	3.73	4.33	14.28	24.85	0.2
87.97	**220.22**	**62.04**	**103.34**	**159.97**	**80.95**	**0.56**
54.18	172.98	41	88.84	119.85	47.63	0.28
13.35	23.36	12.8	5.65	9.36	14.06	0.1
20.44	23.88	8.24	8.85	30.76	19.26	0.18

13-7 大中型工业企业单位数和产销总值（2019）

单位: 亿元

项 目	Item	企业单位数(个) Number of Enterprises(unit)
总 计	Total	1807
一、按登记注册类型分组:	Grouped by Type of Registration	
内资企业	Inner Funded Enterprises	1554
国有企业	State Owned Enterprises	38
中央企业	Central Enterprises	25
地方企业	Local Enterprises	13
集体企业	Collective-owned Enterprise	7
股份合作企业	Share Holding Cooperative Enterprises	
联营企业	Joint Owned Enterprise	
国有联营企业	State Joint Ownership	
集体联营企业	Collective Joint Ownership	
国有与集体联营企业	Joint State- Collective Ownership	
其他联营企业	Other Joint Owned Enterprise	
有限责任公司	Responsibility Co. Ltd	578
国有独资公司	State Solely Funded Co.	47
其他有限责任公司	Others	531
股份有限公司	Share Holding Co.Ltd.	190
私营企业	Private - owned enterprises	741
私营独资企业	Solely Private - owned enterprises	6
私营合作企业	Private Joint Venture	
私营有限责任公司	Private Responsibility Co. Ltd	667
私营股份有限公司	Private Share Holding Co.Ltd.	68
其他企业	Others	
港、澳、台商投资企业	Hongkong, Macao and Taiwan Funded Enterprises	115
合资经营企业(港或澳、台资)	Joint Venture with Hongkong, Macao and Taiwan	54
合作经营企业(港或澳、台资)	Cooperate with Hongkong, Macao and Taiwan Funded	
港澳台商独资经营企业	Enterprises Solely Funded by Hongkong, Macao and Taiwan Businessmen	53
港澳台商投资股份有限公司	Share Holding Co.Ltd. With Hongkong, Macao and Taiwan Investment	2
其他港澳台投资	Others	6
外商投资企业	Foreign Funded Enterprises	138
中外合资经营企业	Sino - Foreign Joint Funded Enterprises	72
中外合作经营企业	Sino - Foreign Cooperative Funded Enterprises	
外资企业	Foreign Solely Funded Enterprises	58
外商投资股份有限公司	Foreign Funded Share Holding Co.Ltd.	5
其他外商投资	Others	3
二、在总计中:亏损企业	Of the Total: enterprises running under deficit	178
在总计中:国有控股企业	Of the Total: State-Owned Share Holding Enterprises	295
在总计中:轻工业	Of the Total: Light Industry	843
重工业	Heavy Industry	964
在总计中:大型企业	Of the Total: Large Scale Enterprises	309
中型企业	Medium Scale Enterprises	1498

Number and Gross production and Sales of Large and Medium-sized Industrial Enterprises (2019)

(100 million yuan)

工业总产值(当年价格) Total Output Value (current price)	资产总计 Total Assets	流动资产合计 Circulating Funds	固定资产净额 NBV of Fixed Assets	固定资产原价 Original Value of Fixed Assets	营业收入 Revenue	全部从业人员年平均人数(万人) Average Number of Empolyment of the Curreat Year(10 000 Persons)
24731.05	**28516.14**	**13049.86**	**8103**	**16980.70**	**24194.98**	**159.37**
18446.43	23646.90	10449.60	6700	14247.86	18079.29	131.05
1521.10	2547.52	808.87	1324	2729.64	1477.23	9.08
1444.41	2429.13	728.26	1301	2690.85	1411.80	8.52
76.69	118.39	80.61	23	38.80	65.43	0.57
20.64	22.05	13.07	8	12.24	21.78	0.36
8232.86	10307.39	5077.68	2523	5547.20	8375.92	52.19
2375.75	3365.49	1528.36	945	2376.54	2519.04	10.89
5857.11	6941.90	3549.32	1578	3170.65	5856.88	41.29
3616.84	7988.09	3153.83	1926	3847.55	3579.31	25.35
5054.98	2781.85	1396.15	920	2111.21	4625.05	44.07
74.84	61.73	44.53	16	30.68	74.51	0.26
4439.77	2325.58	1159.81	782	1839.63	4041.27	39.27
540.37	394.53	191.81	122	240.91	509.27	4.54
1698.97	1516.70	757.57	461	818.73	1756.56	12.63
971.50	993.02	512.67	252	449.20	1044.70	7.12
603.66	377.11	178.32	148	289.26	589.84	4.99
32.12	52.24	9.37	36	40.49	31.82	0.11
91.70	94.34	57.22	25	39.79	90.21	0.41
4585.64	3352.53	1842.69	943	1914.11	4359.13	15.69
3837.03	2771.05	1484.32	782	1560.06	3603.31	9.58
681.61	519.92	315.25	147	310.41	692.04	5.67
37.14	22.50	13.17	6	15.90	34.08	0.24
29.86	39.07	29.95	7	27.73	29.70	0.20
3259.85	**6045.88**	**1710.96**	**2400**	**5738.65**	**3159.97**	**22.85**
10629.31	17513.75	7126.27	5067	11013.60	10533.85	52.98
7254.77	5299.41	3090.19	1359	2823.10	6927.56	59.27
17476.27	23216.72	9959.67	6744	14157.59	17267.42	100.10
14877.30	19631.69	8628.35	5729	11856.10	14943.04	82.34
9853.75	8884.44	4421.51	2374.24	5124.6	9251.94	77.03

13-7 续表1 continued

单位: 亿元

项 目	Item	企业单位数（个） Number of Enterprises (unit)
按行业分	**Grouped by sector**	
采矿业	**Mining and Qarrying**	**30**
煤炭开采和洗选业	Coal Mining and Processing	1
石油和天然气开采业	Petroleum and Natural Gas Extraction	1
黑色金属矿采选业	Ferrous Metals Mining and Processing	8
有色金属矿采选业	Non-ferrous Metals Mining and Processing	6
非金属矿采选业	Non-metal Minerals Mining and Processing	10
开采辅助活动	Mining Auxiliary Activities	3
其他采矿业	Other Minerals Mining and Processing	1
制造业	**Manufacturing**	**1728**
农副食品加工业	Food Processing	99
食品制造业	Food Production	59
酒、饮料和精制茶制造业	Wine,Beverage and Refined Tea Production	50
烟草制品业	Tobacco Processing	2
纺织业	Textile Industry	194
纺织服装、服饰业	Textile,Garments, and Fashion Industry	105
皮革、毛皮、羽毛及其制品和制鞋业	Leather, Furs,Down and Related Products	16
木材加工和木、竹、藤、棕、草制品业	Timber Processing, Wood, Bamboo, Cane, Palm and Sraw Products	18
家具制造业	Furniture Manufacturing	13
造纸和纸制品业	Papermaking and Paper Products	31
印刷和记录媒介复制业	Printing and Record Processing	35
文教、工美、体育和娱乐用品制造业	Stationery, Education and Sports Goods	29
石油加工、炼焦和核燃料加工业	Petroleum Processing, Coking Products and Nuclear Fuel Processing	4
化学原料和化学制品制造业	Raw Chemical Material and Chemical Products	113
医药制造业	Medical and pharmaceutical Products	74
化学纤维制造业	Chemical Fibers	2
橡胶和塑料制品业	Rubber and plastic products	54
非金属矿物制品业	Nonmetal Material Products	124
黑色金属冶炼和压延加工业	Smelting and Pressing of Ferrous Metals	27
有色金属冶炼和压延加工业	Smelting and Pressing of Nonferrous Metals	26
金属制品业	Metal Products	53
通用设备制造业	Ordinary Machinery Manufacturing	66
专用设备制造业	Special Purpose Equipment Manufacturing	60
汽车制造业	Motor manufacturing	216
铁路、船舶、航空航天和其他运输设备制造业	Railway,Watercraft,Aviation and other Transporlation Equipment manufacturing	30
电气机械和器材制造业	Electric Machinery and Equipment	87
计算机、通信和其他电子设备制造业	Telecommunication Computer,Equipment and Other Electronic Equipment Manufacturing	103
仪器仪表制造业	Instruments and Meters, Manufacturing	20
其他制造业	Other Manufacturing	3
废弃资源综合利用业	Waste Comprehensive Vtilization of Resources Industry	7
金属制品、机械和设备修理业	Metal products,Machinery and Equipment Repairing	8
电力、燃气及水的生产和供应业	**Electric Power, Gas and Water Production and Supply**	**49**
电力、热力生产和供应业	Electric Power, Steam and Hot Water Production and Supply	25
燃气生产和供应业	Gas Production and Supply	6
水的生产和供应业	Tap Water Production and Supply	18

(100 million yuan)

工业总产值(当年价格) Total Output Value (current price)	资产总计 Total Assets	流动资产合计 Circulating Funds	固定资产净额 NBV of Fixed Assets	固定资产原价 Original Value of Fixed Assets	营业收入 Revenue	全部从业人员年平均人数(万人) Average Number of Empolyment of the Curreat Year(10 000 Persons)
308.00	**485.84**	**171.81**	**182.90**	**516.78**	**334.49**	**3.46**
0.47	2.31	1.84	0.36	0.89	0.52	0.04
37.06	252.62	55.89	103.65	325.37	70.05	1.08
90.79	74.85	35.19	30.13	74.71	84.23	0.98
21.58	28.73	14.29	6.75	18.88	19.14	0.32
48.29	54.23	34.69	7.19	21.66	43.13	0.47
84.39	67.02	25.46	34.71	75.06	92.00	0.51
25.42	6.08	4.45	0.11	0.21	25.42	0.06
22625.40	**23703.74**	**12513.50**	**5264.08**	**11270.23**	**22039.79**	**147.72**
1061.79	432.91	217.06	145.52	365.65	956.41	5.97
519.87	373.69	186.99	113.37	235.44	523.43	4.49
616.72	847.46	622.14	129.31	263.77	548.93	3.91
653.14	543.20	419.73	71.08	120.87	757.29	0.66
993.02	495.46	221.06	194.25	459.38	954.98	12.18
422.91	213.07	107.21	79.17	151.78	406.89	6.87
52.80	35.27	17.19	11.10	30.49	48.17	1.96
83.72	108.09	53.29	43.78	58.28	75.80	1.16
59.90	62.18	25.07	26.05	33.93	54.63	0.81
333.04	330.09	134.06	116.05	171.18	294.36	1.80
234.99	159.33	107.23	35.06	90.27	207.92	1.99
189.65	93.31	51.96	31.78	81.45	172.98	1.60
476.53	162.68	50.46	72.33	155.76	610.44	0.47
2056.14	2216.51	768.92	695.49	1457.89	1976.60	10.58
727.02	827.39	422.45	205.28	386.54	710.73	6.97
24.89	18.18	9.14	5.47	18.64	19.74	0.36
323.33	230.98	123.59	59.03	132.15	310.73	2.93
794.66	715.78	311.11	268.79	519.94	767.55	7.01
1884.06	2370.79	799.67	816.27	2037.76	2082.91	7.08
485.35	251.26	124.96	90.26	177.69	481.58	2.68
512.75	522.49	338.29	111.36	241.72	510.84	4.63
425.14	577.95	327.88	118.87	263.07	407.02	4.41
468.87	541.97	397.88	98.53	229.41	483.44	4.68
5059.44	5732.91	3392.25	811.20	1741.05	4762.72	23.10
484.29	1081.95	667.09	190.42	324.96	430.47	4.83
1302.83	993.74	678.57	176.87	354.66	1218.53	7.44
1958.55	3330.11	1676.68	465.28	1005.34	1866.01	13.90
101.60	120.28	81.57	25.87	52.82	100.24	1.58
29.65	41.01	30.82	7.79	14.58	30.82	0.33
230.01	215.37	107.98	36.70	65.22	219.42	0.58
58.74	58.33	41.20	11.75	28.54	48.21	0.76
1797.65	**4326.55**	**364.55**	**2656.18**	**5193.70**	**1820.69**	**8.20**
1690.16	3938.48	220.85	2536.65	5001.94	1702.77	6.66
72.18	80.10	25.89	41.86	57.83	73.50	0.43
35.31	307.97	117.81	77.67	133.93	44.42	1.11

13-8 规模以上工业企业生产能力(2019)
Production Capacity of Industrial Enterprises above Designated Size (2019)

产品名称		Item		年初生产能力 Capacity at the Beginning of the Year	年末生产能力 Capacity at the End of the Year
原煤	万吨	Coal	10000 ton	48.8	61
天然原油	万吨	Crude Petroleum Oil	10000 ton	54.9	54
卷烟	万支	Cigarettes	10000 pieces	1930	2090.5
棉纺锭/纺纱量	万锭/万吨	Knitting Spindle/Capacity	10000 spindle/10000 ton	717.6	714.8
气流纺锭/纺纱量	万头/万吨	Air Spindle/Capacity	10000 spindle/10000 ton	26.8	27.3
棉布织机/布	万台/亿米	Cotton Loom/Cloth	10000 piece/hundred million meters	44.9	43.6
原油加工能力/原油加工量	万吨/万吨	Crude Oil Processing pacity	10000 ton/10000 ton	1650	1745
焦炭	万吨	Coke	10000 ton	941	903
烧碱(折100%)	万吨	Caustic Soda (100%)	10000 ton	99.3	101.3
碳化钙(电石,折 300升/千克)	万吨	Calcium Carbide (300 L/kg)	10000 ton	33.5	33.8
农用氮、磷、钾化学肥料总计(折纯)	万吨	Chemical Fertilizers	10000 ton	821.4	863.5
初级形态塑料	万吨	Primary Plastic	10000 ton	217.6	228.8
化学纤维	万吨	Chemical Fiber	10000 ton	34.5	34.2
硅酸盐水泥熟料	万吨	Portland Cement Clinker	10000 ton	6997.2	7088.2
水泥	万吨	Cement	10000 ton	14224.5	14318
平板玻璃	万重量箱	Plain Glass	10000 weight case	10767	10933
生铁	万吨	Pig Ion	10000 ton	2706.7	2603.9
粗钢	万吨	Crude Steel	10000 ton	3944	3899
钢材	万吨	Rolled Steel	10000 ton	4240.9	4368.2
铁合金	万吨	Ferroalloy	10000 ton	33.7	35.9
原铝(电解铝)	万吨	Electrolyzed Aluminum	10000 ton	12.1	11.5
金属切削机床	万台	Metal-cutting Machine Tools	10000 pieces	2.4	2.1
汽车	万辆	Automobile	10000 unit	266.1	303
其中:基本型乘用车(轿车)	万辆	Cars	10000 unit	205.4	238.2
家用电冰箱	万台	Home Refrigerators	10000 pieces	550	600
房间空气调节器	万台	Air Conditioners	10000 pieces	1812.3	2032.7
微型计算机设备	万台	computers	10000 pieces	1602.7	1863.4
移动通信手持机(手机)	万台	Mobile Phones	10000 pieces	7859.2	8223.1
发电设备容量总计/发电量	万千瓦/万千瓦小时	Generating Capacity	10000 kwh	6607.9	6960.8
其中:火电设备容量/发电量		Thermal Power	10000 kwh	2642.4	2943.9
水电设备容量/发电量		Hydropower	10000 kwh	3431.3	3429.5
风电设备容量/发电量		Wind Power	10000 kwh	264.9	288.8

13-9 规模以上工业主要产品产量(2019)
Main Products' Output of Industry above Designated Size (2019)

名 称	计量单位	Name	Measurement	产品产量
原煤	吨	Original Coal	ton	385272.11
#无烟煤	吨	Anthracite	ton	
一般烟煤	吨	General Bituminous Coal	ton	
洗精煤	吨	Cleaned Coal	ton	0.00
天然原油	吨	Natural Oil	ton	536230.00
天然气	万立方米	Natural Gas	10000 cu.m	48930.00
铁矿石原矿	吨	Iron Ore	ton	16003020.00
铜金属含量	吨	Copper	ton	80135.30
锌金属含量	吨	Zinc	ton	6902.00
钨精矿折合量(折三氧化钨65%)	吨	Tungsten Concentrate Equivalent Amount	ton	838.36
钼精矿折合量(折纯钼45%)	吨	Molybdenum Concentrate Equivalent Amount	ton	140.00
磷矿石(折含五氧化二磷30%)	吨	Phosphate Rock (30% of Phosphorus Pentoxide)	ton	37321263.76
原盐	吨	Crude Salt	ton	4273479.00
小麦粉	吨	Wheat Flour	ton	2660320.86
大米	吨	Rice	ton	29056510.86
饲料	吨	Feed	ton	15382507.93
#配合饲料	吨	Compoud Feed	ton	7988026.57
混合饲料	吨	Mixed feed	ton	2571769.63
精制食用植物油	吨	Refined Edible Vegetable oil	ton	3491580.99
鲜、冷藏肉	吨	Fresh and Chilled Meat	ton	1210330.10
冷冻水产品	吨	Frozen Seafood	ton	682229.85
糖果	吨	Candy	ton	340265.21
速冻米面食品	吨	Frozen Rice\Flour Food	ton	86178.23
方便面	吨	Instant Noodles	ton	208736.00
乳制品	吨	Dairy Products	ton	983270.04
#液体乳	吨	Liquid Dairies	ton	861706.39
乳粉	吨	Milk Powder	ton	6729.00
罐头	吨	Can	ton	740307.38
酱油	吨	Soy Sauce	ton	76708.00
冷冻饮品	吨	Frozen Drinks	ton	174312.47
食品添加剂	吨	Food Additives	ton	624607.82
发酵酒精(折96度,商品量)	千升	Fermentation of Alcohol	kl	258131.00
饮料酒	千升	Alcoholic Beverage	kl	2796927.49
#白酒(折65度,商品量)	千升	Liquor (of 65 degrees, the amount of goods)	kl	629973.34
啤酒	千升	Beer	kl	1282379.09
葡萄酒	千升	Wine	kl	1436.14
饮料	吨	Drinks	ton	12521391.37

13-9 续表1 continued

名 称	计量单位	name		产品产量
#碳酸饮料类(汽水)	吨	Carbonated Beverages (soft drinks)	ton	1140958.93
包装饮用水类	吨	Packaging of Drinking Water	ton	4085796.76
果汁和蔬菜汁饮料类	吨	Fruit Juice and Vegetable Juice	ton	779721.10
精制茶	吨	Refined Tea	ton	432200.05
卷烟	万支	Cigarette	10000 pieces	12737740.00
纱	吨	Yarn	ton	3221197.71
#棉纱	吨	Cotton Yarn	ton	1924500.11
棉混纺纱	吨	Cotton Blended Yarn	ton	567872.83
化学纤维纱	吨	Chemical Fiber Yarn	ton	728824.77
布	万米	Fabric	10000 meters	571510.24
#棉布	万米	Cotton	10000 meters	447741.69
棉混纺布	万米	Cotton Blended Cloth	10000 meters	84223.79
化学纤维短纤布	万米	Chemical-Fiber Cloth	10000 meters	39393.76
印染布	万米	Dyed Cloth	10000 meters	39249.81
亚麻布(含亚麻≥55%)	万米	Linen Fabric (containing linen≥ 55%)	10000 meters	428.50
苎麻布(含苎麻≥55%)	万米	Ramie fabric (containing linen ≥ 55%)	10000 meters	1366.00
蚕丝	吨	Silk	ton	505.69
蚕丝被	万条	Silk Quilt	10000 pieces	144.47
无纺布(无纺织物)	吨	Non-woven Fabric	ton	671783.85
服装	万件	Clothing	10000 pieces	121034.57
#梭织服装	万件	Tated Garments	10000 pieces	97923.58
#羽绒服	万件	Down Jacket	10000 pieces	1075.89
西服套装	万件	Western-style	10000 pieces	1888.60
衬衫	万件	Shirt	10000 pieces	1203.41
针织服装	万件	Knitted Garments	10000 pieces	23110.99
天然毛皮服装	万件	Leather Clothes	piece	107.57
皮革鞋靴	万双	Leather Footwear	10000 pairs	3818.19
人造板	立方米	Artificial Board	cu.m	11489800.87
#胶合板	立方米	Plywood	cu.m	3479259.58
纤维板	立方米	FibreBoard	cu.m	5260966.64
刨花板	立方米	Shaving Board	cu.m	377802.00
人造板表面装饰板	平方米	Artificial Board for Surface Decoration	sq.m	14233446.96
复合木地板	平方米	Composite Wood Flooring	cu.m	66201346.80
家具	件	Furniture	piece	13471872.00
#木质家具	件	Wood Furniture	piece	5422542.00
金属家具	件	Metal Furniture	piece	989066.00
软体家具	件	Upholstered Furniture	piece	561875.00

13-9 续表2 continued

名 称	计量单位	name		产品产量
纸浆(原生浆及废纸浆)	吨	Pulp (original pulp and waste paper pulp)	ton	338240.48
机制纸及纸板(外购原纸加工除外)	吨	Machine Made Paper and PaperBoard (excludingprocessing outsourcing base paper)	ton	4158252.26
#未涂布印刷书写用纸	吨	Uncoating Writing Paper	ton	407463.68
#新闻纸	吨	Newsprint	ton	5872.00
卫生用纸原纸	吨	Toilet Paper	ton	85849.54
箱纸板	吨	Case Board	ton	52178.85
纸制品	吨	Paper Products	ton	5706389.19
#瓦楞纸箱	吨	Corrugated Case	ton	2172506.00
单色印刷品	令	Monochrome Print	ream	7335486.85
多色印刷品	对开色令	Multi-color Print	folio color ream	33199055.76
原油加工量	吨	Crude Oil Processing Capacity	ton	15099310.68
汽油	吨	Gasoline	ton	4024732.02
煤油	吨	Kerosene	ton	1490617.33
柴油	吨	Diesel Fuel	ton	4659387.04
润滑油	吨	Lubricating Oil	ton	82398.68
燃料油	吨	Fuel Oil	ton	70593.14
石脑油	吨	Naphtha	ton	1452705.00
溶剂油	吨	Megilp	ton	0.00
液化石油气	吨	LPG	ton	668136.80
石油焦	吨	Petroleum Coke	ton	998256.14
石油沥青	吨	Petroleum Pitch	ton	189403.50
焦炭	吨	Coke	ton	8341211.00
硫酸(折100%)	吨	Sulfuric Acid (100% discount)	ton	8489214.77
盐酸(氯化氢,含量31%)	吨	Hydrochloric Acid (hydrogen chloride, 31%)	ton	484056.00
浓硝酸(折100%)	吨	Concentrated Nitric Acid (100% discount)	ton	6346.74
烧碱(折100%)	吨	Caustic Soda (100% discount)	ton	800092.00
#离子膜法烧碱(折100%)	吨	Ionic Membrane Method(100% discount)	ton	613000.00
纯碱(碳酸钠)	吨	Soda Ash (sodium carbonate)	ton	1640750.46
乙烯	吨		ton	900250.57
丙烯	吨		ton	449568.22
纯苯	吨		ton	199323.50
精甲醇	吨	Refined Methanol	ton	502363.93
合成氨(无水氨)	吨	Anhydrous Amonia	ton	3452046.59
农用氮、磷、钾化学肥料总计(折纯)	吨	Agricultural Nitrogen, Phosphorus and Potassium	ton	5583190.17
#氮肥(折含N100%)	吨	N (of N 100%)	ton	2430105.25
#尿素(折含N100%)	吨	Urea (of N 100%)	ton	715730.21

13-9 续表3 continued

名 称	计量单位	name		产品产量
磷肥(折五氧化二磷100 %)	吨	P (of 100% phosphorus pentoxide)	ton	2793900.78
磷酸一铵(实物量)	吨	MAP (physical quantity)	ton	7926455.78
磷酸二铵(实物量)	吨	DAP (physical quantity)	ton	4723410.30
化学农药原药(折有效成分100%)	吨	Chemical Pesticide Active Compound	ton	184756.45
#杀虫剂原药	吨	Pesticide Active Compound	ton	11679.00
除草剂原药	吨	Herbicide Active Compound	ton	137562.53
涂料	吨	Paint	ton	2629399.78
初级形态的塑料	吨	Primary Form Plastic	ton	2025054.14
#聚丙烯树脂	吨	Polypropylene Resin	ton	724398.91
聚氯乙烯树脂	吨	PVC Resin	ton	211264.00
聚苯乙烯树脂	吨	Polystyrene Resin	ton	32377.00
ABS树脂	吨	ABS Resin	ton	36699.00
合成橡胶	吨	Synthetic Rubber	ton	15026.19
化学试剂	吨	Chemical Reagent	ton	1617458.60
合成洗涤剂	吨	Synthetic Detergent	ton	234519.61
化学药品原药	吨	Original Drug Chemicals	ton	198229.55
中成药	吨	Chinese Patent Medicine	ton	320848.39
化学纤维用浆粕	吨	Chemical Fiber Pulp	ton	38491.53
化学纤维	吨	Chemical Fiber	ton	265155.67
#人造纤维(纤维素纤维)	吨	Artificid Fiber	ton	106155.00
#粘胶短纤维	吨	Fibranne	ton	82506.00
粘胶纤维长丝	吨	Viscose Filament	ton	15503.00
合成纤维	吨	Synthetic Fiber	ton	159000.67
#涤纶纤维	吨	Polyester Fiber	ton	100271.76
丙纶纤维	吨	Polypropylene Fiber	ton	46064.00
橡胶轮胎外胎	条	Rubber Cover Tyre	piece	7488334.00
#子午线轮胎外胎	条	Radial Tire	piece	5543687.00
塑料制品	吨	Plastic Products	ton	5262324.64
#塑料薄膜	吨	Plastic Film	ton	467987.11
#农用薄膜	吨	Agricultural Film	ton	36447.00
泡沫塑料	吨	Foam	ton	114703.08
塑料人造革、合成革	吨	Plastic Leather and Synthetic Leather	ton	12299.65
日用塑料制品	吨	Household Plastic Products	ton	672803.93
硅酸盐水泥熟料	吨	Cement Clinker	ton	63789434.08
#窑外分解窑水泥熟料	吨	Cement Kiln Clinker	ton	48314637.02
水泥	吨	Cement	ton	116228445.25
#强度等级42.5水泥(含R型)	吨	Strength Grade 42.5 Cement (including R-type)	ton	38187959.50

13-9 续表4 continued

名 称	计量单位	name		产品产量
强度等级52.5水泥(含R型)	吨	Strength Grade 52.5 Cement (including R-type)	ton	1246400.50
商品混凝土	立方米	Concrete	cu.m	109172857.23
水泥混凝土排水管	千米	Concrete Drainage Pipe	km	5193.43
水泥混凝土压力管	千米	Concrete Pressure Pipe	km	324.10
水泥混凝土电杆	根	Cement Concrete Pole	piece	1252675.00
预应力混凝土桩	米	Prestressed Concrete Pile	meter	19582209.50
石膏板	万平方米	Gypsum Board	10000 sq.m	37550.98
砖	万块	Brick	10000 pieces	5584054.50
瓦	万片	Tile	10000 pieces	147564.00
瓷质砖	平方米	Porcelain Tile	sq.m	247063220.11
陶质砖	平方米	Ceramic Tile	sq.m	62124432.86
天然大理石建筑板材	平方米	Natural Marble Building Boards	sq.m	29836976.97
天然花岗石建筑板材	平方米	Natural Granite Building Boards	sq.m	179958438.01
沥青和改性沥青防水卷材	平方米	Asphalt and Modified Bitumen Sheet	sq.m	151031836.76
平板玻璃	重量箱	Plate Glass	weight case	102994379.53
钢化玻璃	平方米	Tempered Glass	sq.m	29128455.45
夹层玻璃	平方米	Laminated Glass	sq.m	4905674.61
中空玻璃	平方米	Insulating Glass	sq.m	8625891.23
日用玻璃制品	吨	Daily Glass Products	ton	1015711.64
玻璃包装容器	吨	Glass Containers	ton	835573.31
玻璃纤维纱	吨	Glass Fiber Yarn	ton	6240.00
纤维增强塑料制品	吨	Fiber Reinforced Plastic Products	ton	24703.37
卫生陶瓷制品	件	Sanitary Ceramic Products	piece	14531929.00
耐火材料制品	吨	Refractory Products	ton	2927138.61
石墨及炭素制品	吨	Graphite and Carbon Products	ton	378542.74
生铁	吨	Pig Iron	ton	27651618.00
粗钢	吨	Crude Steel	ton	36115062.72
铸铁件	吨	Iron Casting	ton	3675924.86
铸钢件	吨	Steel Casting	ton	563064.42
钢材	吨	Steel	ton	37715781.48
#铁道用钢材	吨	Railway Steel	ton	627618.00
#重轨	吨	Heavy Rail	ton	627618.00
大型型钢	吨	Large-scale Steel	ton	223605.00
中小型型钢	吨	Small and Medium Scale Steel	ton	1347108.00
棒材	吨	Bar	ton	2461994.17
钢筋	吨	Steel Bar	ton	9542889.91
线材(盘条)	吨	Wire (coil)	ton	3184194.85

13-9 续表5 continued

名 称	计量单位	name		产品产量
特厚板	吨	Special Plate	ton	292689.00
厚钢板	吨	Thick Steel Plate	ton	560298.00
中板	吨	Middle Plate	ton	1229508.00
热轧薄板	吨	Hot-rolled Sheet	ton	57759.00
冷轧薄板	吨	Cold-rolled Sheet	ton	1056875.65
中厚宽钢带	吨	Thick Wide Strip	ton	4721661.00
热轧薄宽钢带	吨	Hot-rolled Thin Wide Strip	ton	2678083.26
冷轧薄宽钢带	吨	Cold-rolled Wide Strip	ton	2021480.65
热轧窄钢带	吨	Hot-rolled Narrow Strip	ton	528672.29
冷轧窄钢带	吨	Cold-rolled Narrow Strip	ton	36725.00
镀层板(带)	吨	Coated Plate	ton	2951570.58
涂层板(带)	吨	Coated Plate	ton	984124.29
铁合金	吨	Ferroallory	ton	248628.61
十种有色金属	吨	10 Kinds of Nonferrous Metals	ton	858399.29
#精炼铜(电解铜)	吨	Refined Copper (electrolytic copper)	ton	536035.00
铅	吨	Lead	ton	234473.00
原铝(电解铝)	吨	Electrolytic Aluminum	ton	69032.56
黄金	千克	Gold	kg	11747.60
白银(银锭)	千克	Silver (silver bullion)	kg	1237026.93
铝合金	吨	Aluminum Alloy	ton	164726.73
铜材	吨	Copper	ton	350728.28
铝材	吨	Aluminum	ton	1190184.46
金属切削工具	万件	Metal Cutting Tools	10000 pieces	29450.15
钢丝	吨	Wire	ton	109263.98
钢丝绳	吨	Wire Rope	ton	47978.00
钢绞线	吨	Strand	ton	162376.03
锻件	吨	Forge Piece	ton	321729.70
粉末冶金零件	吨	Powder Metallurgy	ton	10863.00
工业锅炉	蒸发量吨	Industrial Boiler	ton	3213.00
发动机	千瓦	Engine	kw	155836539.00
#汽车用发动机	千瓦	Automotive Engine	kw	155836539.00
电站用汽轮机	千瓦	Power Plant Steam Turbine	kw	1332000.00
电站水轮机	千瓦	Turbine	kw	22710.00
金属切削机床	台	Metal Cutting Machine	piece	10517.00
#数控金属切削机床	台	CNC Metal Cutting Machine	piece	5734.00
金属成形机床	台	Metal Forming Machine	piece	12409.00
#数控金属成形机床(数控锻压设备)	台	CNC Metal Forming Machine	piece	1354.00

13-9 续表6 continued

名 称	计量单位	name		产品产量
铸造机械	台	Foundry Machinery	piece	55186.00
电焊机	台	Electric Welding Machine	piece	446.03
机床数控装置	套	Machine Digital Control Device	piece	4048.00
起重机	吨	Crane	piece	54492.16
电动车辆(电动叉车)	台	Electric Vehicles (electric forklift)	piece	36693.00
输送机械(输送机和提升机)	吨	Transportation Machinery (conveyors and elevators)	ton	93052.58
泵	台	Pump	piece	672779.00
#真空泵	台	Vacuum Pump	piece	16167.00
气体压缩机	台	Gas Compressor	piece	65657486.00
#制冷设备用压缩机	台	Refrigeration Equipment with Compressor	piece	65651591.00
阀门	吨	Valve	ton	67625.08
液压元件	件	Hydraulic Components	piece	1108285.00
气动元件	件	Pneumatic components	piece	354818.00
滚动轴承	万套	Roller	10000 pieces	14352.27
齿轮	吨	Gear	ton	223355.38
风机	台	Fans	piece	148717.00
包装专用设备	台	Special Equipment Package	piece	7245.00
金属密封件	万件	Metal Sealing Element	10000 pieces	6584.43
金属紧固件	吨	Metal Fastenings	ton	329243.20
弹簧	吨	Spring	ton	98321.51
减速机	台	Reducer	piece	299449.00
矿山专用设备	吨	Mining Special Equipment	ton	403806.72
混凝土机械	台	Concrete Machinery	piece	1190.00
金属冶炼设备	吨	Metal Smelting Equipment	ton	22388.00
金属轧制设备	吨	Metal Rolling Equipment	ton	15061.90
炼油、化工生产专用设备	吨	Oil Refining and Chemical Production Special	ton	88546.50
塑料加工专用设备	台	Plastics Processing Special Equipment	piece	908.00
模具	套	Mold	piece	456271.00
农产品初加工机械	台	Equipment for Agricultural Products Pretreating	piece	40605.00
饲料生产专用设备	台	Equipment for Feed Production	piece	2557.00
小型拖拉机	台	Small Tractor	piece	1327.00
收获机械	台	Harvesting Machinery	piece	34.00
收获后处理机械	台	Post-harvesting Processing Machinery	piece	84995.00
环境污染防治专用设备	台(套)	Equipment for Environmental Pollution Control	piece	17804.00
#大气污染防治设备	台(套)	Air Pollution Control Equipment	piece	10816.00
水质污染防治设备	台(套)	Water Pollution Control Equipment	piece	6100.00

13-9 续表7 continued

名 称	计量单位	name		产品产量
固体废弃物处理设备	台(套)	Solid Waste Handling Equipment	piece	504.00
工业机器人	套	Industrial Robot	piece	10440.00
汽车	辆	Car	piece	2239661.00
#基本型乘用车(轿车)	辆	Passenger Vehicles	piece	962749.00
#1升<排量≤1.6升	辆	1.0 Liter < Displacement ≤ 1.6 Liter	piece	395743.00
1.6升<排量≤2.0升	辆	1.6 Liter < Displacement ≤ 2.0 Liter	piece	366977.00
多功能乘用车(MPV)	辆	MPV	piece	99271.00
运动型多用途乘用车(SUV)	辆	SUV	piece	665861.00
客车	辆	Bus	piece	42288.00
#中型客车(7米<车长≤10米)	辆	Medium Passenger Bus(7 m<car length≤10 m)	piece	1798.00
轻型客车(车长≤7米)	辆	Light buses (car length≤ 7 m)	piece	40490.00
载货汽车	辆	Lorry	piece	419088.00
#新能源汽车	辆	New Energy Vehicles	piece	60554.00
改装汽车	辆	Modified Cars	piece	278018.00
低速载货汽车	辆	Low Speed Truck	piece	8853.00
铁路货车	辆	Railway Wagon	piece	11444.00
城市轨道车辆	辆	Railway Wagon	piece	421.00
民用钢质船舶	载重吨	Civil Steel Ships	ton	682094.00
电动自行车	辆	Electric Bicycle	piece	387261.00
发电机组(发电设备)	千瓦	Generating Units (power equipment)	kw	1203117.00
#水轮发电机组	千瓦	Generator Group	kw	15000.00
汽轮发电机	千瓦	Turbonator	kw	1168500.00
交流电动机	千瓦	AC Motors	kw	2368663.08
变压器	千伏安	Transformer	kva	30882014.00
互感器	台	Mutual Inductor	kva	458780.00
高压开关板	面	High-voltage Switch Board	piece	50076.00
低压开关板	面	Low-voltage Switch Board	piece	9050277.00
高压开关设备(11万伏以上)	台	High Voltage Switchgear (11 KV and above)	piece	104210.00
通信及电子网络用电缆	对千米	Communication and Electronic Networks Cables	km	1320770.00
电力电缆	千米	Power Cable	km	1639481.26
光纤	千米	Optical Fiber	km	43312987.79
光缆	芯千米	Optical Cable	km	60550595.49
绝缘制品	吨	Insulation Products	ton	94465.65
锂离子电池	只(自然只)	Li-ion Battery	piece	1085879762.00
铅酸蓄电池	千伏安时	Lead-acid Battery	kvah	40527637.88
碱性蓄电池	只(自然只)	Alkaline Battery	piece	4499000.00

13-9 续表8 continued

名 称	计量单位	name		产品产量
原电池及原电池组(非扣式)	万只	Primary Cells and Primary Batteries	10000 pieces	8239.86
太阳能电池	千瓦	Solar Battery	kw	921479.16
家用电冰箱	台	Household Refrigerator	piece	5398509.00
家用冷柜(家用冷冻箱)	台	Household Refrigerator (household freezers)	piece	1842477.00
房间空气调节器	台	Room Air Conditioners	piece	21109316.00
家用吸排油烟机	台	Home Ventilator	piece	9669.00
家用电热水器	台	Water Heater	piece	2615929.00
家用燃气灶具	台	Kitchen Range	piece	1131015.00
太阳能热水器	平方米	Solar Water Heater	sq.m	31916.00
电光源	万只	Light Sources	10000 pieces	63910.33
#白炽灯泡	万只	Incandescent Bulb	10000 pieces	8168.55
荧光灯	万只	Fluorescent Lamp	10000 pieces	10054.75
灯具及照明装置	套(台、个)	Lamps and Lighting Fittings	pieces	34585598.00
电子计算机整机	台	Computers	pieces	12998681.00
#微型计算机设备	台	Micro-computer Equipment	pieces	12702399.00
#平板电脑	台	Tablet PC	pieces	8693477.00
显示器	台	Monitor	pieces	15193826.00
移动通信手持机(手机)	台	Mobile Handset (cell phone)	pieces	39199501.00
#智能手机	台	Intelligent Mobile Phone	pieces	33575018.00
半导体分立器件	万只	Semiconductor Discrete Devices	10000 pieces	975110.36
集成电路圆片	万片	IC Wafer	10000 pieces	30.22
光电子器件	万只(片、套)	Optoelectronic Devices	10000 pieces	78093.07
#发光二极管(LED)	万只	Light-emitting Diode (LED)	10000 pieces	539979.40
电子元件	万只	Electronic Component	10000 pieces	1797005.71
印制电路板	平方米	Printed Board	sq.m	10884411.71
工业自动调节仪表与控制系统	台(套)	Automatic Adjustment and Control System	piece	420726.00
电工仪器仪表	台	Electric Instrument	piece	7178388.00
分析仪器及装置	台(套)	Analytical Instrument	piece	1716.00
汽车仪器仪表	台	Car Instrument	piece	625670.00
光学仪器	台(个)	Optical Instrument	piece	228677.00
发电量	万千瓦小时	Power Generation	10000 kwh	28964022.70
#火力发电量	万千瓦小时	Thermal Capacity	10000 kwh	14688196.12
水力发电量	万千瓦小时	Hydroelectricity	10000 kwh	14668385.64
风力发电量	万千瓦小时	Wind Power Capacity	10000 kwh	589534.84
煤气生产量	万立方米	Coal Gas	10000 cu.m	4132195.83
自来水生产量	万立方米	Water Production	10000 cu.m	392380.96

13-10 规模以上工业企业主要经济效益指标(2019)

项 目	Item	企业亏损面(%) Enterprises deficit (%)
总 计	**Total**	**9.2**
一、按登记注册类型分组:	**Grouped by Type of Registration**	
内资企业	Inner Funded Enterprises	8.8
国有企业	State Owned Enterprises	20.4
中央企业	Central Enterprises	17.1
地方企业	Local Enterprises	22.2
集体企业	Collective-owned Enterprise	10.4
股份合作企业	Share Holding Cooperative Enterprises	25.0
联营企业	Joint Owned Enterprise	33.3
国有联营企业	State Joint Ownership	
集体联营企业	Collective Joint Ownership	
国有与集体联营企业	Joint State- Collective Ownership	100.0
其他联营企业	Other Joint Owned Enterprise	
有限责任公司	Responsibility Co. Ltd	13.2
国有独资公司	State Solely Funded Co.	16.8
其他有限责任公司	Others	13.1
股份有限公司	Share Holding Co.Ltd.	11.3
私营企业	Private - owned enterprises	6.6
私营独资企业	Solely Private - owned enterprises	1.2
私营合伙企业	Private Joint Venture	3.4
私营有限责任公司	Private Responsibility Co. Ltd	6.8
私营股份有限公司	Private Share Holding Co.Ltd.	5.4
其他企业	Others	
港、澳、台商投资企业	Hongkong, Macao and Taiwan Funded Enterprises	17.9
合资经营企业(港或澳、台资)	Joint Venture with Hongkong, Macao and Taiwan	19.0
合作经营企业(港或澳、台资)	Cooperate with Hongkong, Macao and Taiwan Funded	
港澳台商独资经营企业	Enterprises Solely Funded by Hongkong, Macao and Taiwan Businessmen	16.9
港澳台商投资股份有限公司	Share Holding Co.Ltd. With Hongkong, Macao and Taiwan Investment	20.0
其他港澳台商投资企业	Others	18.2
外商投资企业	Foreign Funded Enterprises	19.1
中外合资经营企业	Sino - Foreign Joint Funded Enterprises	17.0
中外合作经营企业	Sino - Foreign Cooperative Funded Enterprises	25.0
外资企业	Foreign Solely Funded Enterprises	21.4
外商投资股份有限公司	Foreign Funded Share Holding Co.Ltd.	18.2
其他外商投资企业	Others	20.0
二、在总计中:亏损企业	**Of the Total: enterprises running under deficit**	**100.0**
在总计中:国有控股企业	Of the Total: State-Owned Share Holding Enterprises	19.0
在总计中:轻工业	Of the Total: Light Industry	7.4
重工业	Heavy Industry	10.5
在总计中:大型企业	Of the Total: Large Scale Enterprises	10.0
中型企业	Medium Scale Enterprises	9.8
小型企业	Small Enterprises	9.2

Main Economic Efficiency Indicators of Industrial Enterprises above Designated Size (2019)

总资产贡献率(%) Contributing Ratie of Tatal Assets(%)	资产负债率(%) Assets Liability Ratio(%)	流动资产周转率(次/年) Current Asset Tuinover (Times/year)	成本费用利润率(%) Ratio of Riofits to Industrial Cost(%)
13.15	**52.15**	**2.29**	**7.30**
12.86	51.13	2.28	7.20
1.97	66.27	1.78	-0.31
1.61	66.41	1.89	-0.73
6.40	64.55	1.03	5.44
19.14	63.22	2.73	6.62
6.70	79.29	1.00	2.42
-9.58	57.91	2.68	-8.28
29.25	70.49	12.04	5.29
-24.01	61.80	0.53	-37.90
9.60	37.22	16.50	0.72
12.08	56.66	1.85	6.53
21.16	56.65	1.62	8.89
9.21	56.67	1.91	6.05
10.09	42.91	1.22	14.19
19.90	45.73	3.98	6.68
27.60	44.21	4.69	6.47
44.42	34.29	9.04	9.29
20.16	45.87	4.06	6.66
16.07	44.89	3.14	6.93
29.08	38.32	5.07	8.39
13.15	49.72	2.31	9.01
11.37	51.23	2.05	8.23
15.27	46.09	2.93	8.78
2.49	66.93	3.20	-0.18
25.28	47.26	1.61	27.48
15.67	62.23	2.31	7.38
16.88	64.42	2.38	7.60
14.23	47.10	2.47	11.13
10.64	54.57	2.12	5.79
22.46	40.37	2.22	17.74
13.70	66.18	1.11	14.70
-1.03	**62.47**	**1.49**	**-5.93**
10.47	54.39	1.47	8.28
23.05	45.29	2.90	8.06
10.22	54.18	2.07	6.94
12.13	53.93	1.73	8.22
11.38	52.65	2.09	7.15
15.69	49.33	3.11	6.76

13-10 续表 continued

项 目	Item	企业亏损面(%) Enterprises Deficit(%)
按行业分	**Grouped by sector**	
采矿业	**Mining and Qarrying**	**7.5**
煤炭开采和洗选业	Coal Mining and Processing	25.0
石油和天然气开采业	Petroleum and Natural Gas Extraction	100.0
黑色金属矿采选业	Ferrous Metals Mining and Processing	14.7
有色金属矿采选业	Non-ferrous Metals Mining and Processing	8.3
非金属矿采选业	Non-metal Minerals Mining and Processing	5.8
开采辅助活动	Mining Auxiliary Activities	25.0
其他采矿业	Other Minerals Mining and Processing	
制造业	**Manufacturing**	**9.0**
农副食品加工业	Food Processing	5.8
食品制造业	Food Production	8.1
酒、饮料和精制茶制造业	Wine,Beverage and Refined Tea Production	6.4
烟草制品业	Tobacco Processing	14.3
纺织业	Textile Industry	7.6
纺织服装、服饰业	Textile,Garments, and Fashion Industry	7.3
皮革、毛皮、羽毛及其制品和制鞋业	Leather, Furs,Down and Related Products	6.9
木材加工和木、竹、藤、棕、草制品业	Timber Processing, Wood, Bamboo, Cane, Palm and Sraw Products	5.4
家具制造业	Furniture Manufacturing	3.3
造纸和纸制品业	Papermaking and Paper Products	13.7
印刷和记录媒介复制业	Printing and Record Processing	9.0
文教、工美、体育和娱乐用品制造业	Stationery, Education and Sports Goods	3.5
石油加工、炼焦和核燃料加工业	Petroleum Processing, Coking Products and Nuclear Fuel Processing	17.0
化学原料和化学制品制造业	Raw Chemical Material and Chemical Products	9.8
医药制造业	Medical and pharmaceutical Products	11.5
化学纤维制造业	Chemical Fibers	25.0
橡胶和塑料制品业	Rubber and plastic products	3.8
非金属矿物制品业	Nonmetal Material Products	5.7
黑色金属冶炼和压延加工业	Smelting and Pressing of Ferrous Metals	12.9
有色金属冶炼和压延加工业	Smelting and Pressing of Nonferrous Metals	17.8
金属制品业	Metal Products	7.9
通用设备制造业	Ordinary Machinery Manufacturing	8.7
专用设备制造业	Special Purpose Equipment Manufacturing	7.3
汽车制造业	Motor manufacturing	15.1
铁路、船舶、航空航天和其他运输设备制造业	Railway,Watercraft,Aviation and other Transporlation Equipment manufacturing	12.6
电气机械和器材制造业	Electric Machinery and Equipment	13.8
计算机、通信和其他电子设备制造业	Telecommunication Computer,Equipment and Other Electronic Equipment Manufacturing	18.4
仪器仪表制造业	Instruments and Meters, Manufacturing	11.0
其他制造业	Other Manufacturing	6.5
废弃资源综合利用业	Waste Comprehensive Vtilization of Resources Industry	16.3
金属制品、机械和设备修理业	Metal products,Machinery and Equipment Repairing	24.0
电力、燃气及水的生产和供应业	**Electric Power, Gas and Water Production and Supply**	**18.9**
电力、热力生产和供应业	Electric Power, Steam and Hot Water Production and Supply	21.9
燃气生产和供应业	Gas Production and Supply	6.3
水的生产和供应业	Tap Water Production and Supply	21.3

总资产贡献率(%) Contributing Ratie of Tatal Assets(%)	资产负债率(%) Assets Liability Ratio(%)	流动资产周转率(次/年) Current Asset Tuinover (Times/year)	成本费用利润率(%) Ratio of Riofits to Industrial Cost(%)
12.23	**54.19**	**2.51**	**6.60**
11.85	69.42	1.87	6.79
0.81	51.04	1.25	-8.85
14.05	61.83	2.67	5.90
26.12	37.08	1.75	31.60
18.49	53.17	2.74	8.72
5.63	66.77	3.56	2.60
11.29	86.05	5.76	0.86
14.05	**51.68**	**2.25**	**6.98**
22.27	40.38	4.83	6.58
18.42	45.13	3.39	8.10
16.68	51.56	1.34	13.85
107.73	35.11	1.72	45.00
19.86	42.34	4.99	5.22
21.73	44.17	4.65	5.86
27.82	45.01	5.27	5.69
13.15	49.81	3.14	5.47
13.53	36.39	2.55	8.32
11.03	58.40	2.68	5.15
18.39	46.53	2.71	7.67
13.60	58.15	2.25	6.04
51.95	62.37	9.03	0.90
12.84	49.17	3.01	5.98
15.54	42.45	1.79	12.60
5.99	50.80	2.77	1.34
18.91	42.78	3.51	6.96
22.33	42.50	3.38	10.48
6.39	58.47	2.69	4.14
11.98	64.08	4.53	2.15
13.12	55.20	2.37	5.38
11.39	52.16	2.18	5.35
10.66	57.88	1.65	6.04
11.87	54.10	1.60	9.04
1.88	66.72	0.77	0.62
11.10	54.88	1.91	6.17
3.17	54.12	1.21	3.46
13.28	52.34	1.70	7.49
8.62	60.03	1.78	4.88
13.22	53.23	2.44	4.61
9.31	60.24	1.68	4.47
7.92	**54.65**	**3.23**	**13.45**
8.42	53.94	4.54	14.49
8.41	63.51	2.01	8.69
2.39	57.70	0.61	3.77

13-11 规模以上工业企业产销总值及主要经济指标(分地区)(2019)

单位: 亿元

地区	Region	企业单位数(个) Number of Enterprises(unit)	亏损企业 Enterprises Running under Deficit
全省	Province	15520	1435
武汉	Wuhan	2903	470
黄石	Huangshi	712	106
十堰	Shiyan	948	94
宜昌	Yichang	1293	76
襄阳	Xiangyang	1662	113
鄂州	Ezhou	481	44
荆门	Jingmen	998	76
孝感	Xiaogan	1168	80
荆州	Jingzhou	1176	100
黄冈	Huanggang	1264	97
咸宁	Xianning	964	53
随州	Suizhou	686	21
恩施	Enshi	279	44
仙桃	Xiantao	423	28
潜江	Qianjiang	253	11
天门	Tianmen	299	17
神农架	Shennongjia	11	5

Gross production and Sales and Main Economic Indicators of Industrial Enterprises above Designated Size (By Regions) (2019)

(100 million yuan)

资产总计 Total Assets	流动资产合计 Circulating Funds	应收帐款净额 Accounts Receivable
42530.89	19878.13	5004.26
17252.72	8677.21	2203.35
2131.07	1207.35	173.83
2306.79	1367.05	344.43
5079.86	1424.17	279.41
3789.88	1998.21	665.70
747.84	313.81	85.85
1892.71	782.96	171.33
1647.26	740.28	189.01
2011.79	1027.82	264.23
1354.90	592.55	160.19
1111.50	480.16	114.59
849.29	363.70	106.81
403.01	116.74	29.20
621.81	261.98	80.62
822.93	288.87	92.11
467.13	218.19	43.16
40.41	17.10	0.45

13-11 续表 1 continued

单位: 亿元

地区	Region	固定资产净额 Total Fixed Assets	固定资产原价 Original Price of Fixed Assets
全省	Province	12233.10	25092.16
武汉	Wuhan	4118.01	8759.77
黄石	Huangshi	529.85	954.57
十堰	Shiyan	431.97	773.24
宜昌	Yichang	1909.31	3497.86
襄阳	Xiangyang	1027.03	1845.35
鄂州	Ezhou	301.30	583.59
荆门	Jingmen	675.74	1276.05
孝感	Xiaogan	665.73	2297.77
荆州	Jingzhou	492.27	1170.36
黄冈	Huanggang	419.04	697.10
咸宁	Xianning	328.70	562.57
随州	Suizhou	289.16	443.94
恩施	Enshi	228.27	420.75
仙桃	Xiantao	246.58	459.77
潜江	Qianjiang	368.20	771.00
天门	Tianmen	190.08	561.13
神农架	Shennongjia	11.87	17.33

累计折旧 Accumulated	负债合计 Total Liability	流动负债合计 Total Circulating Liability	应付账款 Aaounts Payable	所有者权益合计 Total Rights of Owners
12195.02	22178.45	16644.75	5312.27	20299.32
4337.51	9237.18	7166.90	2794.74	8009.63
397.76	1200.17	1004.95	198.46	930.75
312.01	1555.52	1294.64	404.57	751.27
1549.06	2565.38	1501.23	318.89	2514.48
765.37	1952.11	1525.80	500.90	1820.43
264.96	399.97	328.19	79.23	337.23
526.24	869.28	651.05	128.75	1023.43
1690.67	811.58	493.94	140.40	835.67
643.86	917.46	772.59	216.20	1091.19
231.33	706.90	533.62	144.00	647.64
214.63	467.20	347.90	103.08	640.49
134.32	384.39	241.42	68.67	464.91
177.74	223.87	146.81	22.24	179.14
184.08	301.36	238.43	71.19	319.47
395.24	355.98	250.98	70.27	466.95
364.77	200.83	130.50	47.32	255.50
5.47	29.27	15.80	3.37	11.14

13-11 续表 2 continued

单位: 亿元

地区	Region	所有者权益合计 Total Rights of Owners	
		实收资本 Assets Recevied	国家资本 National Assets
全省	Province	8894.20	1707.53
武汉	Wuhan	4084.92	698.80
黄石	Huangshi	355.51	129.90
十堰	Shiyan	403.09	162.81
宜昌	Yichang	711.92	199.88
襄阳	Xiangyang	599.73	121.47
鄂州	Ezhou	220.81	99.61
荆门	Jingmen	401.01	66.95
孝感	Xiaogan	357.15	47.40
荆州	Jingzhou	377.60	43.28
黄冈	Huanggang	350.18	29.78
咸宁	Xianning	252.89	8.44
随州	Suizhou	233.44	27.00
恩施	Enshi	111.08	57.01
仙桃	Xiantao	103.27	4.80
潜江	Qianjiang	199.29	9.43
天门	Tianmen	128.52	0.90
神农架	Shennongjia	3.81	0.08

(100 million Yuan)

集体资本 Collective Assets	法人资本 Corperative Assets	个人资本 Individual Assets	港澳台资本 Assets from Hongkong, Macao and Taiwan	外商资本 Foreign Assets	营业成本 Cost
178.60	4442.14	1806.96	185.18	449.48	37730.71
31.35	2636.04	319.29	77.59	226.04	11553.57
12.88	88.33	63.28	31.08	30.04	1743.42
20.28	106.14	62.21	1.64	50.02	1717.67
21.30	242.09	213.47	12.89	16.03	2812.32
18.17	243.47	150.49	11.24	35.73	5070.76
7.71	71.60	36.76	0.79	1.34	1168.61
7.41	147.59	168.84	0.77	9.45	2754.36
4.40	138.76	139.15	14.19	13.25	2392.85
9.72	110.05	182.64	5.57	26.34	1843.34
6.24	150.12	143.91	11.60	8.54	1288.74
6.41	110.29	112.44	11.62	3.59	1578.08
20.41	74.40	107.63	0.50	3.50	1155.37
4.11	24.11	24.96	0.89		127.12
3.06	40.70	27.32	3.10	24.30	875.84
3.70	160.96	24.05	0.70	0.46	850.42
1.04	96.01	28.70	1.02	0.86	793.85
0.42	1.49	1.82			4.39

13-11 续表 3 continued

单位: 亿元

地区	Region	税金及附加 Tax of Business	销售费用 Selling Expenses
全省	Province	1000.71	1349.14
武汉	Wuhan	643.97	413.76
黄石	Huangshi	18.01	53.27
十堰	Shiyan	16.53	66.70
宜昌	Yichang	35.06	145.38
襄阳	Xiangyang	37.62	135.58
鄂州	Ezhou	9.86	48.29
荆门	Jingmen	104.27	95.46
孝感	Xiaogan	33.00	87.88
荆州	Jingzhou	15.95	62.06
黄冈	Huanggang	11.42	39.33
咸宁	Xianning	15.43	50.32
随州	Suizhou	10.08	44.72
恩施	Enshi	1.75	6.24
仙桃	Xiantao	7.29	51.20
潜江	Qianjiang	36.64	16.46
天门	Tianmen	2.99	32.25
神农架	Shennongjia	0.86	0.23

(100 million Yuan)

管理费用 Management Expense	财务费用 Financial Expenses	利息费用 Interest Expenses	其他收益 Other Income	投资收益 Investment Income	营业利润 Operating Profits
1616.40	414.84	392.10	142.12	280.91	2995.99
527.91	67.17	110.27	81.77	221.77	841.11
56.33	17.77	19.06	2.59	−15.91	123.41
79.93	16.86	17.67	8.08	12.53	121.17
126.54	73.14	74.09	10.17	39.74	413.68
223.28	42.38	32.56	13.12	8.49	400.79
55.92	10.33	7.60	0.55	1.16	91.82
100.82	28.87	23.06	4.44	5.27	190.27
102.25	36.51	16.16	3.14	2.20	130.68
64.97	22.92	18.91	1.78	3.73	131.53
46.48	15.30	11.79	7.31	0.40	92.96
50.91	18.79	12.18	6.43	0.34	149.74
46.29	18.45	10.45	1.33	0.70	140.50
9.09	7.28	5.99	0.27	0.76	19.56
55.13	11.61	8.45	0.21	−0.38	60.16
27.50	8.29	6.51	0.73	−0.05	38.01
42.52	17.86	16.11	0.20	0.08	49.41
0.52	1.29	1.22		0.07	1.18

13-11 续表 4 continued

单位: 亿元

地区	Region	营业外收入 Non-operating Income	营业外支出 Non-operating Expense	利润总额 Total Profits	所得税费用 Income Tax	亏损企业亏损总额 Total Loss of Enterprises Running under Deficit
全省	Province	109.00	66.75	3049.57	391.01	256.04
武汉	Wuhan	34.16	19.07	856.53	157.82	142.21
黄石	Huangshi	6.73	5.38	124.76	21.71	10.58
十堰	Shiyan	4.60	2.45	123.32	11.15	10.17
宜昌	Yichang	13.81	12.55	414.94	62.17	18.68
襄阳	Xiangyang	9.82	8.58	404.82	38.87	14.79
鄂州	Ezhou	2.22	3.01	99.28	6.33	1.87
荆门	Jingmen	4.65	3.21	191.69	14.14	4.70
孝感	Xiaogan	8.02	1.90	136.81	8.88	11.79
荆州	Jingzhou	8.93	2.00	138.46	17.40	12.29
黄冈	Huanggang	3.66	2.84	93.78	9.01	6.98
咸宁	Xianning	5.17	2.69	152.22	16.11	3.07
随州	Suizhou	2.09	1.10	141.50	5.04	1.82
恩施	Enshi	1.23	0.61	20.17	3.09	1.70
仙桃	Xiantao	2.36	0.37	62.16	8.34	5.90
潜江	Qianjiang	1.29	0.76	38.54	4.53	8.31
天门	Tianmen	0.18	0.17	49.41	5.96	0.62
神农架	Shennongjia	0.08	0.08	1.19	0.45	0.55

(100 million Yuan)

利税总额 Total Profits and Taxes	应交税金及附加 Tax alafor Business	本年应付工资薪酬 Wases Welfarism Payable This Year	本年应交增值税 Value Added Payable of the Current Year	全部从业人员年平均人数(万人) Average Number of Empolyment of the Current Year (10000 persons)
5274.52	2615.95	2963.12	1224.23	335.87
1871.14	1172.43	948.23	370.64	73.02
181.54	78.49	129.43	38.77	14.80
191.53	79.36	143.38	51.68	14.65
573.99	221.22	203.17	124.00	71.58
585.60	219.64	393.18	143.16	31.80
149.81	56.86	156.02	40.66	8.04
373.12	195.58	121.27	77.17	15.67
256.17	128.24	158.28	86.36	20.19
219.50	98.43	165.05	65.08	18.57
143.10	58.34	111.81	37.90	15.75
214.05	77.94	94.90	46.41	11.97
207.06	70.60	63.99	55.48	9.05
29.27	12.19	17.26	7.35	2.18
102.96	49.14	100.11	33.51	12.04
102.51	68.51	84.72	27.34	6.82
70.47	27.02	71.61	18.07	9.64
2.70	1.97	0.71	0.66	0.09

13-12　分市州规模以上工业企业主要经济效益指标(2019)

单位:%

地 区	Item	企业亏损面 Loss Making Rate of Enterprises	总资产贡献率 Contributing Rate of Total Assets
全省	Province	9.2	13.15
武汉市	Wuhan	16.2	11.18
黄石市	Huangshi	14.9	9.22
十堰市	Shiyan	9.9	8.83
宜昌市	Yichang	5.9	12.75
襄阳市	Xiangyang	6.8	16.23
鄂州市	Ezhou	9.1	20.99
荆门市	Jingmen	7.6	20.89
孝感市	Xiaogan	6.8	16.43
荆州市	Jingzhou	8.5	11.74
黄冈市	Huanggang	7.7	11.42
咸宁市	Xianning	5.5	20.26
随州市	Suizhou	3.1	25.52
恩施市	Enshi	15.8	8.75
仙桃市	Xiantao	6.6	17.87
潜江市	Qianjiang	4.3	13.14
天门市	Tianmen	5.7	18.53
神农架林区	Shennongjia	45.5	9.70

Main Economic Efficiency Indicators of Industrial Enterprises above Designated Size by Region (2019)

资产负债率 Assets Liability Ratio	流动资产周转率(次/年) Current Asset Turnover(Times/Year)	成本费用利润率 Ratio of Profits to Industrial Cost
52.15	2.29	7.30
53.54	1.62	6.67
56.32	1.73	6.59
67.43	1.49	6.43
50.50	2.54	12.86
51.51	2.98	7.32
53.48	4.47	7.68
45.93	4.22	6.37
49.27	3.82	5.15
45.60	2.11	6.84
52.17	2.54	6.66
42.03	3.91	8.87
45.26	3.92	11.08
55.55	1.46	13.43
48.46	4.07	6.22
43.26	3.42	4.21
42.99	4.30	5.57
72.44	0.49	18.43

主要统计指标解释

工业 指从事自然资源的开采，对采掘品和农产品进行加工和再加工的物质生产部门。具体包括：(1)对自然资源的开采，如采矿、晒盐等(但不包括禽兽捕猎和水产捕捞)；(2)对农副产品的加工、再加工，如粮油加工、食品加工、缫丝、纺织、制革等；(3)对采掘品的加工、再加工，如炼铁、炼钢、化工生产、石油加工、机器制造、木材加工等，以及电力、自来水、煤气的生产和供应等；(4)对工业品的修理、翻新，如机器设备的修理、交通运输工具(如汽车)的修理等。

工业统计调查单位为独立核算法人工业企业。

独立核算法人工业企业指从事工业生产经营活动的单位。独立核算法人工业企业应同时具备以下条件：①依法成立，有自己的名称、组织机构和场所，能够承担民事责任；②独立拥有和使用资产，承担负债，有权与其他单位签订合同；③独立核算盈亏，并能够编制资产负债表。

本年鉴中涉及的企业登记注册类型：

国有及国有控股企业 指国有企业加上国有控股企业。国有企业(即原全民所有制工业或国营工业)指企业全部资产归国家所有，并按《中华人民共和国企业法人登记管理条例》规定登记注册的非公司制的经济组织。包括国有企业、国有独资公司和国有联营企业。1957年以前的公私合营和私营工业，后均改造为国营工业，1992年改为国有工业，这部分工业的资料不单独分列时，均包括在国有企业内。国有控股企业是对混合所有制经济的企业进行的“国有控股”分类。它是指这些企业的全部资产中国有资产(股份)相对其他所有者中的任何一个所有者占资(股)最多的企业。该分组反映了国有经济控股情况。

集体企业 指企业资产归集体所有，并按《中华人民共和国企业法人登记管理条例》规定登记注册的经济组织。是社会主义公有制经济的组成部分。包括城乡所有使用集体投资举办的企业，以及部分个人通过集资自愿放弃所有权并依法经工商行政管理机关认定为集体所有制的企业。

股份合作企业 指以合作制为基础，由企业职工共同出资入股，吸收一定比例的社会资产投资组建，实行自主经营，自负盈亏，共同劳动，民主管理，按劳分配与按股分红相结合的一种集体经济组织。

联营企业 指两个及两个以上相同或不同所有制性质的企业法人或事业单位法人，按自愿、平等、互利的原则，共同投资组成的经济组织。联营企业包括：

国有联营企业指国有企业与国有企业间的联营；

集体联营企业指集体企业与集体企业间的联营；

国有与集体联营企业指国有企业与集体企业间的联营。

有限责任公司 指根据《中华人民共和国公司登记管理条例》规定登记注册，由两个以上，五十个以下的股东共同出资，每个股东以其所认缴的出资额对公司承担有限责任，公司以其全部资产对其债务承担责任的经济组织。

有限责任公司包括国有独资公司以及其他有限责任公司。

股份有限公司 指根据《中华人民共和国企业法人登记管理条例》规定登记注册，其全部注册资本由等额股份构成并通过发行股票筹集资本，股东以其认购的股份对公司承担有限责任，公司以其全部资产对其债务承担责任的经济组织。

私营企业 指由自然人投资设立或由自然人控股，以雇佣劳动为基础的营利性经济组织。包括按照《公司法》、《合伙企业法》、《私营企业暂行条例》规定登记注册的私营有限责任公司、私营股份有限公司、私营合伙企业和私营独资企业。

港、澳、台商投资企业 指企业注册登记类型中的港、澳、台资合资、合作、独资经营企业和股份有限公司之和。

外商投资企业 指企业注册登记类型中的中外合资、合作经营企业、外资企业和外商投资股份有限公司之和。

“三资”企业系指港、澳、台商投资企业和外资企业的简称。

轻工业 指主要提供生活消费品和制作手工工具的工业。按其所使用的原料不同，可分为两大类：(1)以农产品为原料的轻工业,是指直接或间接以农产品为基本原料的轻工业。主要包括食品制造、饮料制造、烟草加工、纺织、缝纫、皮革和毛皮制作、造纸以及印刷等工业;(2)以非农产品为原料的轻工业,是指以工业品为原料的轻工业。主要包括文教体育用品、化学药品制造、合成纤维制造、日用化学制品、日用玻璃制品、日用金属制品、手工工具制造、医疗器械制造、文化和办公用机械制造等工业。

重工业 指为国民经济各部门提供物质技术基础的主要生产资料的工业。按其生产性质和产品用途,可以分为下列三类:(1)采掘(伐)工业,是指对自然资源的开采,包括石油开采、煤炭开采、金属矿开采、非金属矿开采等工业;(2)原材料工业,指向国民经济各部门提供基本材料、动力和燃料的工业。包括金属冶炼及加工、炼焦及焦炭、化学、化工原料、水泥、人造板以及电力、石油和煤炭加工等工业;(3)加工工业,是指对工业原材料进行再加工制造的工业。包括装备国民经济各部门的机械设备制造工业、金属结构、水泥制品等工业,以及为农业提供的生产资料如化肥、农药等工业。

根据上述划分原则,修理业中以重工业产品为修理作业对象的划为重工业,反之划为轻工业。

工业总产值

(1)定义:

工业总产值是以货币形式表现的,工业企业在一定时期内生产的工业最终产品或提供工业性劳务活动的总价值量。它反映一定时间内工业生产的总规模和总水平。

(2)计算原则:

工业生产的原则,即凡是企业在报告期生产的经检验合格的产品,不管是否在报告期销售,均包括在内。

最终产品的原则,即凡是计入工业总产值的产品,必须是本企业生产的经检验合格的,不需要再进行任何加工的最终产品。如果企业有中间产品(半成品)对外销售,则对外销售的中间产品应视为企业的最终产品。

工厂法原则,即工业总产值是以工业企业作为基本计算(核算)单位,即按企业的最终产品计算工业总产值。按这种方法计算的工业总产值,不允许同一产品价值在企业内部重复计算,不能把企业内部各个车间(分厂)生产的成果相加,但允许企业间的重复计算。

(3)内容及计算方法:

1995年全国工业普查对工业总产值(原规定)的内容及计算原则和方法做了某些修订,修订后的工业总产值(新规定)包括三项内容:即本期生产成品价值、对外加工费收入、在制品半成品期末期初差额价值三部分。

本期生产成品价值:指企业本期生产,并在报告期内不再进行加工,经检验、包装入库的全部工业成品(半成品)价值合计,包括企业生产的自制设备及提供给本企业在建工程、其他非工业部门和福利部门等单位使用的成品价值。本期生产成品价值为按自备原材料生产的产品的数量乘以本期不含增值税(销项税额)的产品实际销售平均单价计算;会计核算中按成本价格转帐的自制设备和自产自用的成品,按成本价格计算生产成品价值。生产成品价值中不包括用定货者来料加工的成品(半成品)价值。

对外加工费收入:指企业在报告期内完成的对外承接的工业品加工(包括用定货者来料加工产品)的加工费收入和对外工业修理作业所取得的加工费收入。对外加工费收入按不含增值税(销项税额)的价格计算,可根据会计"产品销售收入"科目的有关资料取得。

对于本企业对内非工业部门提供的加工修理、设备安装的劳务收入,如果企业会计核算基础较好,能取得这部分资料,而且这部分价值所占比重较大,应包括在对外加工费收入中。

自制半成品在制品期末期初差额价值:指企业报告期在制品期末减期初的差额价值,本指标一般可以从会计核算资料中取得。如果会计产品成本核算中不计算半成品、在制品的成本,则总产值中也不包括这部分价值,反之则包括。

(4)工业总产值统计范围变化和计算方法修订情况:

1984年以前工业总产值不包括村办工业,村办工业总产值划归农业。1984年以后工业总产值包括村办工业。

1995年工业普查对工业总产值计算方法做了修订,即从1995年始按新修订(新规定)方法计算工业总产值。新规定与原规定的区别如下:

全价与加工费的计算原则不同:新规定为凡自备原材料,不论其生产繁简程度如何,一律按全价计算工业总产值;凡来料加工,允许按加工费计算工业总产值。原规定则视生产加工的繁简程度不同,规定哪些行业按全价,哪些行业按加工费计算工业总产值。

自制半成品、在产品期末期初差额价值的计算原则不同:新规定要求,凡会计产品成本核算时计算了成本的差额价值,总产值中就应包括,否则可不包括;原规定则按生产周期六个月的界限区分,凡生产周期六个月以上的企业,总产值计算中应包括这部分差额价值,否则可不包括。

计算价格不同:新规定按不含增值税(销项税额)的价格计算;原规定则按含增值税(销项税额)的价格计算。

工业增加值 指工业企业在报告期内以货币表现的工业生产活动的最终成果。

工业增加值有两种计算方法:一是生产法,即工业总产出减去工业中间投入加上应交增值税;二是收入法,即从收入的角度出发,根据生产要素在生产过程中应得到的收入份额计算,具体构成项目有固定资产折旧、劳动者报酬、生产税净额、营业盈余,这种方法也称要素分配法。本年鉴中的工业增加值是以生产法计算的。

生产法工业增加值的计算方法为:

工业增加值=工业总产出-工业中间投入+应交增值税

(1)工业总产出:指工业企业在一定时期内工业生产活动的总成果。工业总产出包括:成品生产价值,对外加工费收入,自制半成品、在产品期末期初差额价值。1995年后用新规定计算的工业总产值代替。

(2)工业中间投入:指工业企业在工业生产活动中消耗的外购物质产品和对外支付的服务费用。服务费用包括支付给物质生产部门(工业、农业、批发零售贸易业、建筑业、运输邮电业)的服务费用和支付给非物质生产部门(如保险、金融、文化教育、科学研究、医疗卫生、行政管理等)的服务费用。工业中间投入的确定须遵循以下原则:必须从外部购入的,并已计入工业总产出的产品和服务价值;必须是本期投入生产,并一次性消耗掉(包括本期摊销的低值易耗品等)的产品和服务价值。

工业中间投入包括直接材料费用、制造费用中的工业中间投入、管理费用中的工业中间投入、销售费用中的工业中间投入和利息支出五部分。

资产总计 指企业拥有或控制的能以货币计量的经济资源,包括各种财产、债权和其他权利。资产按流动性分为流动资产、长期投资、固定资产、无形资产、递延资产和其他资产。该指标根据企业会计"资产负债表"中"资产总计"项目的期末数增列。

流动资产 指企业可以在一年内或者超过一年的一个生产周期内变现或者耗用的资产,包括现金及各种存款、短期投资,应收及预付款项、存货等。

流动资产平均余额 指企业在报告期内全部流动资产的平均余额。

固定资产原价 指企业在建造、购置、安装、改建、扩建、技术改造某项固定资产时所支出的全部货币总额。它一般包括买价、包装费、运杂费和安装费等。

固定资产净值年平均余额 指固定资产净值在报告期内余额的平均数。计算公式为:

$$\text{固定资产净值年平均余额}=\frac{\text{1至12月各月月初、月末固定资产净值之和}}{24}$$

该指标根据"资产负债表"中"固定资产原价"、"累计折旧"指标的期初、期末数计算填列。

固定资产净值指固定资产原价减去历年已提折旧额后的净额。计算公式为:

固定资产净值=固定资产原价-累计折旧

负债合计 指企业所承担的能以货币计量,将以资产或劳务偿付的债务,偿还形式包括货币、资产或提供劳务。负债一般按偿还期长短分为流动负债和长期负债。根据会计"资产负债表"中"负债合计"的年末数填列。

所有者权益 指企业投资人对企业净资产的所有权。企业净资产等于企业全部资产减去全部负债后的余额,包括企业投资人对企业的最初投入的实际到位的资产及资本公积金、盈余公积金和未分配利润。所有者权益合计数小于零,表示企业资不抵债。

主营业务收入 指会计"利润表"中对应指标的本年累计数。未执行2001年《企业会计制度》的企业,用"产品销售收入"的本期累计数代替。

主营业务成本 指会计"利润表"中对应指标的本年累计数。未执行2001年《企业会计制度》的企业,用"产品销售成本"的本期累计数代替。

主营业务税金及附加 指会计"利润表"中对应指标的本年累计数。未执行2001年《企业会计制度》的企业，用"产品销售税金及附加"的本期累计数代替。

利润总额 指企业生产经营活动的最终成果，是企业在一定时期内实现的盈亏相抵后的利润总额(亏损以"-"号表示)，它等于营业利润加上补贴收入加上投资收益加上营业外净收入再加上以前年度损益调整。

本年应交增值税 指企业在报告期内应交纳的增值税额。它等于本年销项税额加上出口退税加上进项税额转出数减去本年进项税额。小规模纳税企业直接按全年计税销售额乘以征收率计算取得。

从业人员平均人数 是指报告期内每天拥有的从业人员人数。其计算公式为：

$$季平均人数=\frac{季内各月平均人数之和}{3}$$

$$月平均人数=\frac{报告月内每天实有人数之和}{报告月日历日数}$$

$$年平均人数=\frac{年内各月平均人数之和}{12}$$

总资产贡献率 反映企业全部资产的获利能力，是企业经营业绩和管理水平的集中体现，是评价和考核企业盈利能力的核心指标。计算公式为：

$$总资产贡献率(\%)=\frac{利润总额+税金总额+利息支出}{资产总计}\times 100\%$$

公式中：税金总额为产品销售税金及附加与应交增值税之和；平均资产总额为期初期末资产之和的算术平均值。

资产负债率 该指标既反映企业经营风险的大小，也反映企业利用债权人提供的资金从事经营活动的能力。计算公式为：

$$资产负债率(\%)=\frac{负债总额}{资产总额}\times 100\%$$

资产与负债均为报告期期末数。

流动资产周转次数 指一定时期内流动资产完成的周转次数，反映投入工业企业流动资金的周转速度。计算公式为：

$$流动资产周转资转次数=\frac{营业收入}{流动资产合计}$$

公式中：全部流动资产平均余额为期初和期末的流动资产之和的算术平均值。

成本费用利润率 反映企业投入的生产成本及费用的经济效益，同时也反映企业降低成本所取得的经济效益。计算公式为：

$$成本费用利润率(\%)=\frac{利润总额}{成本费用总额}\times 100\%$$

公式中：成本费用总额为产品销售成本、销售费用、管理费用、财务费用之和。

全员劳动生产率 该指标反映企业的生产效率和劳动投入的经济效益。计算公式为：

$$全员劳动生产率(元/人)=\frac{工业增加值}{全部从业人员平均人数}$$

产品销售率 该指标反映工业产品已实现销售的程度，是分析工业产销衔接情况，研究工业产品满足社会需求的指标。计算公式为：

$$产品销售率(\%)=\frac{工业销售产值}{工业总产值（现价）}\times 100\%$$

Explanatory Notes on Main Statistical Indicators

Industry refers to the material production sector which is engaged in extraction of natural resources and processing and reprocessing of minerals and agricultural products, including (1) extraction of natural resources, such as mining, salt production (but not including hunting and fishing); (2) processing and reprocessing of farm and sideline produces, such as rice husking, flour milling, wine making, oil pressing, silk reeling, spinning and weaving, and leather making; (3) manufacture of industrial products, such as steel making, iron smelting, chemicals manufacturing, petroleum processing, machine building, timber processing; water and gas production and electricity generation and supply; (4)repairing of industrial products such as the repairing of machinery and means of transport (including cars).

Units of industrial statistics survey corporate industrial enterprises with independent accounting system.

Corporate industrial enterprises with independent accounting system refer to enterprises engaging in industrial production activities, which meet the following requirements: (1)They are established legally, having their own names, organizations, location, able to take civil liability; (2)They possess and use their assets independently, assume liabilities, and are entitled to sign contracts with other units; (3)They are financially independent and compile their own balance sheets.

Enterprises covered in the industrial statistics in the Yearbook include following categories by their registration:

State-owned and State-holding Enterprises refer to state-owned enterprises plus state-holding enterprises. State-owned enterprises (originally known as state-run enterprises with ownership by the whole society) are non-corporate economic entities registered in accordance with the Regulation of the People's Republic of China on the Management of Registration of Legal Enterprises, where all assets are owned by the state. Included in this category are state-owned enterprises, state-funded corporations and state-owned joint-operation enterprises. Joint state-private industries and private industries, which existed before 1957, were transformed into state-run industries since 1957, and into state-owned industries after 1992. Statistics on those enterprises are included in the state-owned industries instead of grouping them separately. State-holding enterprises is a sub-classification of enterprises with mixed ownership, referring to enterprises where the percentage of state assets (or shares by the state) is larger than any other single share holder of the same enterprise. This sub-classification illustrates the control of the state over a particular industry.

Collective-owned Enterprises refer to economic entities registered in accordance with the Regulation of the People's Republic of China on the Management of Registration of Legal Enterprises, where assets are owned by collectively. Collective enterprises constitute an integral part of the socialist economy with public ownership. They include urban and rural enterprises invested by collectives, and some enterprises registered in industrial and commercial administration agency as collective units where funds are pulled together by individuals who voluntarily give up their right of ownership.

Share-holding Cooperative Enterprises refer to economic units set up on cooperative basis, with funding partly from members of the enterprise and partly from outside investment, where the operation and management is decided by the members who also participate in the production, and the distribution of income is based both on work (labour input) and on shares (capital input).

Joint-operation enterprises refer to economic units that are established by joint investment by two or more corporate enterprises or institutions of the same or different types of ownership on voluntary, equal and mutual-beneficial basis. They include:

a) state-owned joint-operation enterprises (joint operation between state-owned enterprises);

b) collective joint-operation enterprises (joint operation between collective enterprises; and

c) state-collective joint-operation enterprises (joint operation between state and collective enterprises).

Limited Liability Corporations refer to economic units registered in accordance with the Regulation of the People's Republic of China on the Management of Registration of Corporations, with capitals from 2 to 49 investors, each investor bears limited liability to the corporation depending on his/her holding of shares, and the corporation bears liability to its debt to the maximum of its total assets.

Share-holding Corporations Ltd. refer to economic units registered in accordance with the Regulation of the People's Republic of China on the Management of Registration of Corporate Enterprises, with total registered capitals divided into equal shares and raised through issuing stocks. Each investor bears limited liability to the corporation depending on the holding of shares, and the corporation bears liability to its debt to the maximum of its total assets.

Private Enterprises refer to economic units invested or controlled (by holding the majority of the shares) by natural persons who hire labours for profit–making activities. Included in this category are private limited liability corporations, private share–holding corporations Ltd., private partnership enterprises and private sole investment enterprises registered in accordance with the Corporation Law, Partnership Enterprise Law and Tentative Regulation on Private Enterprises.

Enterprises with Funds from Hong Kong, Macao and Taiwan refers to all industrial enterprises registered as the joint–venture, cooperative, sole (exclusive) investment industrial enterprises and limited liability corporations with funds from Hong Kong, Macao and Taiwan.

Foreign Funded Enterprises refers to all industrial enterprises registered as the joint–venture, cooperative, sole (exclusive) investment industrial enterprises and limited liability corporations with foreign funds.

Enterprise with Hong Kong, Macao, Taiwan and foreign fund refer to all the enterpries with funds from Hong Kong Macao and Taiwan and foreign funded enterprises.

Light Industry refers to the industry that produces consumer goods and hand tools. It consists of two categories, depending on the materials used:

(1) Industries using farm products as raw materials. These are branches of light industry which directly or indirectly use farm products as basic raw materials, including the manufacture of food and beverages, tobacco processing, textile, clothing, fur and leather manufacturing, paper making, printing, etc.

(2) Industries using non farm products as raw materials. These are branches of light industry which use manufactured goods as raw materials, including the manufacture of cultural, educational articles and sports goods, chemicals, synthetic fiber, chemical products for daily use, glass products for daily use, metal products for daily use, hand tools, medical apparatus and instruments, and the manufacture of cultural and clerical machinery.

Heavy Industry refers to the industry which produces capital goods, and provides various sectors of the national economy with necessary material and technical basis. It consists of the following three branches according to the purpose of production or the use of products:

(1) Mining, quarrying and logging industry refers to the industry that extracts natural resources, including extraction of petroleum, coal, metal and non–metal ores.

(2) Raw materials industry refers to the industry that provides various sectors of the national economy with raw materials, fuels and power. It includes smelting and processing of metals, coking and coke chemistry, chemical materials and building materials such as cement, plywood, and power, petroleum refining and coal dressing.

(3) Manufacturing industry refers to the industry that processes raw materials. It includes machine–building industry which equips sectors of the national economy, industries of metal structure and cement products, industries producing means of agricultural production, such as chemical fertilizers and pesticides.

According to the above principle of classification, the repairing trades, which are engaged primarily in repairing products of heavy industry are classified into heavy industry while these engaged in repairing products of light industry are classified into light industry.

Gross Industrial Output Value

(1) Definition: Gross industrial output value is the total volume of final industrial products produced and industrial services provided during a given period. It reflects the total achievements and overall scale of industrial production during a given period.

(2) Principles for calculation:

Statistics on industrial production follow the principle that all products produced by the enterprises and accepted during the reference period are to be included no matter whether they are sold or not during the reference period.

Determination of final products follow the principle that all products that are included in the calculation of grow industrial output value are the final products of the enterprise which have been accepted through quality check and require no further processing. If an enterprise has intermediate (semi–finished) products to sell, these intermediate products are considered as the final products of the enterprise.

Gross industrial output value is calculated following the principle of factory approach, i.e. industrial enterprise is used as the basic accounting unit in calculating the gross industrial output value. By this approach, value of the same product is not to be double counted, and the output value of different workshops (branch factories) should not be added. However, this approach does not exclude the possibility of double counting between enterprises.

(3) Content and calculation method: The old definition of gross industrial output value was modified during the national industrial census in 1995. The revised (new) definition of gross industrial output value consists of 3 components: value of the finished products during the reference period, income from external processing, and value of change in semi–finished products at the end and at the beginning of the reference period.

Value of the finished products during the reference period: refers to the value of all finished (semi–finished) industrial products that are produced during the reference period without the need for further processing, checked for acceptance, packed and put into the warehouse of the enterprise, including the value of own–produced equipment and the value of products provided to the projects under construction of the enterprise, and to other non–industrial or welfare units. Value of finished products during the reference period is calculated by the quantity of products produced using own materials multiplied by the average unit prices at which products are sold (excluding value–added tax). Own–produced equipment and products produced for own use are value at cost prices as in the case of enterprise accounting. Value of finished products does not include the value of finished products (semi–finished products) that are produced using the materials from the clients who make the orders.

Income from external processing: refers to income from contracted external processing of industrial products (including processing of industrial products using materials from the clients), and the income from industrial repairing work provided to other units. Income from external processing is calculated using information from the item "products sales income" in the enterprise accounting at the prices excluding value–added tax.

For income from services such as processing, repairing and installation of equipment provided to non–industrial units within the enterprise, if the accounting work of the enterprise is good enough to separate it from other records, and the share of such services is significant, it should also be included in the income from external processing.

Value of change in semi–finished products at the end and at the beginning of the reference period: refers to the value of change in semi–finished products at the end and at the beginning of the reference period, which generally can be obtained from accounting records of enterprises. If the enterprise accounting excludes the cost of semi–finished products, then it should not be included in the gross industrial output value, and vice versa.

(4) Changes in the coverage and method of calculation of gross industrial output value

Prior to 1984, the value of rural industry run by villages was classified into agriculture instead of industry. Since 1984, it has been included in the gross industrial output value. Method of calculation for the gross industrial output value was modified in the industrial census in 1995. The difference in the new method as compared with the old one is outlined below:

Principle in using full value vs. processing fee: The new method stipulates that all products produced using own materials are to be calculated with full value in reporting the gross industrial output value irrespective of sophistication of production, and for external processing, it allows calculation using processing fee. In the old method, however, the use of full value or processing fee was determined by the degree of sophistication of production in different branches of industries.

Principle in determining the value of change in semi–finished products: The new method requires that value of the change in semi–finished products should be included in the gross industrial output value if it is included in the accounting record of the enterprise, otherwise it should not be included. By the old method, it is determined by the type of enterprises in terms of production cycle. If the production cycle is over 6 months, the value of change in semi–finished products is included in the gross industrial output value, otherwise it is excluded.

Difference in prices: The new method uses prices excluding value–added tax in the calculation of gross industrial output value, while the old method used prices including value–added tax.

Value–added of Industry refers to the final results of industrial production of industrial enterprises in money terms during the reference period.

Industrial value–added can be calculated by two approaches: the production approach, i.e. gross industrial output value minus intermediate input plus value–added tax, and the income approach, i.e. income for various factors used in the course of production, including depreciation of fixed assets, remuneration of labourers, net of production tax, and operating surplus. Value–added of industry in the Yearbook is calculated by production approach as following:

Value–added of industry = gross industrial output industrial intermediate input + value–added tax

(1) Gross industrial output: refers to the total achievements of industrial production during a given period. Gross industrial output includes value of finished products, income from external processing, and value of change in semi–finished products at the end and at the beginning of the reference period. Since 1995, it was substituted by the gross industrial output value by new method.

(2) Industrial intermediate input: refers to purchased goods and paid services consumed during the industrial production of enterprises. Fees paid for services include fees paid for the services provided by material production sectors (industry, agriculture, wholesale and retail trade, construction, transport, post and telecommunications) and by non–material production sectors (insurance, banking, culture, education, scientific research, health and medical care, public administration, etc.). The determination of industrial intermediate input follows the principle that the goods and services must be purchased from outside and included in the gross industrial output, and that the goods and services are inputted into production and consumed (include low–value consumables) during the reference period.

Industrial intermediate input includes 5 components, namely direct consumption of materials, industrial intermediate input in manufacturing cost, industrial intermediate input in management cost, industrial intermediate input in marketing cost and expenditure on interest.

Total Assets refer to all economic resources, in monetary terms, that is owned or controlled by enterprises, including properties, creditors equity and other economic rights of all forms. Classified by the degree of equitability, total assets include circulating assets, long–term investment, fixed assets, intangible assets and deferred assets, and other assets. Data on this indicator can be obtained by the year–end figures of total assets in the Assets and Liability Table of accounting records of enterprises.

Working Capitals refer to capitals that an enterprise can cash or use during one year or one production cycle that may exceeds one year, including cash and savings deposits of various forms, short–term investment, money receivable and prepaid money, inventories, etc.

Annual Average Value of Working Capitals refers to the average value of all working capitals of the enterprise during the reference period.

Original Value of Fixed Assets refers to the total value, in monetary terms, that an enterprise spent on fixed assets, through construction, purchase, installation, transformation, expansion or technical upgrading. Generally, it covers cost of purchase, packing, transportation and installation, etc.

Annual Average of Net Value of Fixed Assets refer to average of the net value of fixed assets during the reference period, calculated with the following formula:

Annual Average of Net Value of Fixed Assets = sum of net value of fixed assets at the beginning and at the end of each month from January to December / 24.

Information on this indicator can be obtained from the beginning and ending figures of the original value of fixed assets and cumulative depreciation from the Assets and Liability Table of enterprises.

Net value of fixed assets refers to the original value of fixed assets minus depreciation over the years, i.e.:

Net value of fixed assets = original value of fixed assets cumulative depreciation

Total Liabilities refer to payable liabilities of enterprises that have to repay in terms of money, assets or labour services. In terms of payment, it can be divided into liquid liabilities and long–term liabilities. Data on this item is obtained from the ending figures on total liabilities from theAssets and Liability Table from the enterprises.

Owner's Equity refers to the ownership of net assets of enterprise by its investors. The net assets equal the total assets minus total liabilities of the enterprise, including the actual assets invested into the enterprise by investors, accumulation of capitals and operating surplus and non–distributed profits. The enterprise's assets is less than its liabilities if the sum of owner's equity is smaller than zero.

Revenue from Principal Business refers to the annual accumulation of corresponding item in the "profit table" of the accountant. For enterprises that do not follow the 2001 Enterprise Accounting Standards, the year–end accumulation of revenue from the sales of products is used as a substitute.

Cost of Principal Business refers to the annual accumulation of corresponding item in the "profit table" of the accountant. For enterprises that do not follow the 2001 Enterprise Accounting Standards, the year–end accumulation of cost for the sales of products is used as a substitute.

Tax and Extra Charges from Principal Business refer to the annual accumulation of corresponding item in the "profit table" of the accountant. For enterprises that do not follow the 2001 Enterprise Accounting Standards, the year–end accumulation of tax and extra charges from the sales of products is used as a substitute.

Total Profits refer to the final achievements of production and operation of the enterprises, represented by the total profits after deducting losses (loss is expressed by the negative figure). It is the sum of profits from operation, income from subsidies, investment earnings, net income from activities other than operation, and adjustment of profits and losses of previous years.

Value–added Tax Payable refers to the amount of the value–added tax which should be paid by the enterprises during the reference period. It is the sum of tax on sales, export rebate, and transferred tax on purchases of the current year, minus the tax on purchases of the current year. Value–added tax payable of small–size enterprises is determined by the taxable sales of the year multiplied by the tax rate.

Average Annual Number of Employed Persons Employed persons refer to all those who are employed in enterprises and receive remunerations therefrom, including currently working employees, retirees who are re–employed, teachers of local–run schools, as well as foreigners, staff from Hong Kong, Macao and Taiwan, part–time employees and persons with second job who are employed by the enterprise, and employees of other units temporarily working in the enterprises, but excluding former employees who left the enterprise with their employment records still kept by the enterprises.

Average number of employed persons refers to the number of employees everyday during the reference period, calculated with the following formula:

Monthly average number = sum of actual employees everyday in reference month/number of calendar dates in reference month

Quarterly average number = sum of monthly average number in reference quarter/3

Annual average number = sum of monthly average number in reference year/12

Ratio of Profits, Taxes and Interests to Average Assets reflects the profit–making capability of all assets of the enterprise and is a key indicator manifesting the performance and management and evaluating the profit–making potential of the enterprise. It is cal–

culated as follows:

Ratio of Profits, Taxes and Interests to Average Assets (%) = [(total profits + total taxes + interest payment) / average assets] × 100%

In the above formula, total taxes is the sum of tax and extra charges on the sales of products and value–added tax payable; and average assets is the arithmetic mean of the sum of beginning assets and ending assets.

Ratio of Debts to Assets reflect both the operation risk and the capability of the enterprise in making use of the capital from the creditors. It is calculated as follows:

Ratio of Debts to Assets (%) = (total debts / total assets) × 100%

Both assets and debts are figures at the end of the reference period.

Turnover of Working Capitals refers to the number of times of turnover of working capital in a given period of time, which reflects the speed of the turnover of working capital of industrial enterprises, and is calculated as follows:

Turnover of Working Capital=(sales revenue of products) / (average balance of total working capital)

In the above formula, average balance of total working capital refers to the arithmetic mean of the sum of working capital at the beginning and at the end of the reference period.

Ratio of Profits to Total Industrial Costs refers to the ratio of profits realized in a given period to the total costs in the same period, which reflects the economic efficiency of input cost and is calculated as follows:

Ratio of Profits to Total Industrial Cost (%)=(total profits/ total costs) × 100%

Total costs in the above formula is the sum of cost of products sold, marketing cost, management cost and financial cost.

Overall Labour Productivity is an indicator reflecting the production efficiency of an enterprise and the economic efficiency of its labour input, calculated by the formula:

Overall Labour Productivity (yuan/person) = industrial value–added / average of all persons engaged

Sales Ratio of Products is an indicator reflecting the actual sale of industrial products, analyzing the production–selling and supply–demand relations. It is calculated as:

Sales Ratio of Products (%) = value of industrial sales / gross industrial output value (current prices) * 100%

14 建筑业

Construction

资料整理人员：樊喜珍

14-1 建筑业企业概况
Basic Statistics on Construction Enterprises

项目 Item	总计 Total	国有及控股 State-Owned	地方 Local - Owned	中央 Central- Owned	其他经济 Others
企业单位个数(个) Number of Enterprises (unit)					
1995	912	323	277	46	50
1996	1696	403	250	53	95
1997	1761	429	378	51	125
1998	1838	433	379	54	199
1999	2120	491	432	59	332
2000	2070	488	440	48	409
2001	1661	393	350	43	459
2002	1625	363	327	36	782
2003	1808	558	488	70	906
2004	2357	433	378	55	2566
2005	2114	524	448	76	1322
2006	2238	320	279	41	1695
2007	2516	449	383	66	1876
2008	2975	440	374	66	2374
2009	2878	396	331	65	2330
2010	2845	388	334	54	2315
2011	2640	376	330	46	2134
2012	2952	390	335	55	2440
2013	3376	399	334	66	2879
2014	3217	386	324	62	2741
2015	3346	384	323	61	2875
2016	3534	389	325	64	3145
2017	3873	391	329	62	3482
2018	4196	375	316	59	3821
2019	4565	367	304	63	4198
职工平均人数(万人) Average Staff and Workers (10000 persons)					
1995	57.28	38.05	18.86	19.19	2.61
1996	76.51	36.83	18.58	18.25	3.48
1997	76.09	36.36	18.60	17.76	3.77
1998	82.63	38.22	19.22	19.00	5.59
1999	85.72	39.57	22.57	17.00	9.46
2000	82.76	36.58	21.73	14.83	10.82
2001	83.11	36.16	19.99	16.44	17.65
2002	93.50	34.20	21.25	12.95	35.80
2003	108.82	50.20	30.72	19.48	41.64
2004	105.30	44.40	28.10	16.30	48.70
2005	110.09	41.70	22.85	18.85	56.79
2006	114.25	27.26	15.18	12.08	76.71
2007	136.14	39.73	19.52	20.21	86.97
2008	137.61	38.51	18.40	20.11	92.49
2009	146.02	41.68	18.76	22.92	97.12
2010	170.71	54.40	22.31	32.09	110.74
2011	141.88	42.61	15.06	27.55	94.49
2012	169.33	50.83	15.10	35.73	114.29
2013	174.18	40.50	14.83	25.67	130.64
2014	206.37	49.04	19.48	29.56	153.98
2015	232.85	55.21	19.07	36.14	174.45
2016	269.17	61.15	17.25	43.91	208.02
2017	254.74	60.35	18.57	41.78	194.39
2018	254.34	55.78	14.55	41.23	198.56
2019	251.25	57.36	18.02	39.34	193.89

14-1 续表 1 continued

项 目 Item	总 计 Total	国有及国有控股 State-Owned	地 方 Local - Owned	中 央 Central- Owned	其他经济 Others
建筑业总产值(亿元) Gross Output Value of Construction Enterprises (100 million yuan)					
1995	227.41	178.51	58.96	119.55	15.19
1996	284.43	187.00	60.83	126.17	18.29
1997	305.97	199.53	63.59	135.94	21.75
1998	343.65	223.80	73.98	149.82	26.70
1999	399.02	246.58	88.07	158.51	45.13
2000	454.35	266.03	106.76	159.27	64.86
2001	529.02	279.39	112.32	167.07	131.93
2002	639.11	301.93	143.90	158.03	238.29
2003	876.26	535.71	227.72	307.99	257.56
2004	1114.33	676.45	285.29	391.16	370.63
2005	1349.32	776.70	268.77	507.92	502.71
2006	1667.00	545.64	184.87	360.77	1048.92
2007	2110.80	1065.26	234.03	831.23	976.85
2008	2710.80	1333.87	241.63	1092.24	1319.41
2009	3421.89	1621.66	191.86	1429.80	1722.37
2010	4344.39	2287.08	414.78	1872.30	1996.10
2011	5586.45	2934.99	501.47	2433.52	2566.42
2012	7040.65	3428.40	627.89	2800.51	3478.70
2013	8465.50	3933.36	757.54	3175.82	4465.39
2014	10059.59	4755.30	921.65	3833.65	5232.75
2015	10591.71	4695.04	1072.67	3622.37	5825.87
2016	11862.40.	5549.57	1071.13	4478.43	6312.83
2017	13391.23	6350.70	1325.65	5025.05	7040.53
2018	15133.87	6737.91	1205.66	5532.25	8395.96
2019	16979.59	8058.87	1713.24	6345.63	8920.72
施工房屋面积(万平方米) Floor Space of Buildings Under Construction (10000 sq.m)					
1995	3284.30	2122.80	1185.20	937.60	293.90
1996	4548.80	2224.60	1203.30	1021.30	315.80
1997	4604.20	2330.60	1226.90	1103.70	388.30
1998	5310.00	2488.80	1288.80	1200.00	573.70
1999	5797.00	2703.40	1578.40	1125.00	764.20
2000	6256.50	2889.10	1564.50	1324.60	919.20
2001	6662.59	2792.50	1480.20	1312.30	1817.10
2002	7215.88	2836.00	1452.00	1384.00	2637.90
2003	8933.44	3817.50	2102.60	1714.90	3541.10
2004	11772.31	5089.10	2522.60	2566.50	5334.30
2005	12091.16	4568.90	1993.30	2575.60	6257.50
2006	14478.24	3811.18	1016.18	2795.00	9545.40
2007	16679.70	5503.80	1666.40	3837.40	10139.80
2008	18376.50	5703.90	1060.40	4643.50	11920.60
2009	20499.30	5672.40	522.50	5149.90	14027.50
2010	25046.70	6752.80	968.80	5784.00	17660.30
2011	31023.80	9209.70	1549.00	7660.70	21031.70
2012	39112.20	10747.20	1661.70	9085.50	27459.10
2013	48937.96	14424.51	1734.33	12690.18	33914.19
2014	62227.88	22903.06	2137.75	20765.31	38763.33
2015	62195.32	21339.76	2258.52	19081.24	40349.12
2016	72759.57	32325.74	3165.63	29160.12	40433.82
2017	79257.69	35888.37	3085.28	32803.09	43369.32
2018	88238.10	39202.58	3151.11	36051.47	49035.52
2019	92042.23	43717.24	3845.39	39871.85	48324.99

14-1 续表 2 continued

项 目 Item	总 计 Total	国有控股 State-Owned	地 方 Local - Owned	中 央 Central- Owned	其他经济 Others
竣工房屋面积(万平方米) Floor Space of Buildings Completed (10000 sq.m)					
1995	1175.90	622.20	466.90	155.30	69.40
1996	1880.70	653.30	501.30	152.00	103.90
1997	1982.30	765.30	522.10	243.20	92.50
1998	2374.00	836.00	624.00	212.00	239.40
1999	2873.00	1023.10	776.10	247.00	365.60
2000	3150.10	1096.30	836.10	260.20	481.80
2001	3673.40	1237.00	828.30	408.70	1102.30
2002	4146.60	1261.80	889.30	372.50	1738.80
2003	4840.80	1578.80	1143.40	435.40	2268.30
2004	6647.10	2561.30	1563.20	998.10	3265.30
2005	6896.90	2125.60	923.70	1201.90	3979.80
2006	7376.20	1137.10	450.40	686.70	5560.30
2007	8425.00	1620.90	858.60	762.30	5895.30
2008	9256.10	1386.00	537.90	848.10	7394.00
2009	10280.70	1587.10	255.90	1331.20	8198.90
2010	12813.40	2185.70	364.50	1821.20	10174.90
2011	16468.10	2593.00	600.00	1993.00	13274.20
2012	20395.20	1938.00	649.80	1288.30	17751.90
2013	22773.70	2278.00	571.70	1706.30	20077.10
2014	24867.30	2393.00	1105.00	1288.00	22165.10
2015	26825.20	3717.00	908.50	2808.50	22719.00
2016	28599.93	4714.59	772.76	3941.82	23885.34
2017	30836.86	5596.78	854.54	4742.24	25240.08
2018	32691.00	5336.02	508.38	4827.64	27354.98
2019	33907.92	8228.57	842.09	7386.48	25679.35
房屋建筑面积竣工率(%) Rate of Floor Space of Buildings Completed (%)					
1995	35.80	41.20	39.40	16.60	23.60
1996	41.30	29.40	41.70	14.90	32.90
1997	43.10	32.70	42.60	22.00	23.80
1998	44.70	33.60	48.40	17.70	41.70
1999	49.60	37.80	49.20	22.00	47.80
2000	50.30	37.90	53.40	19.60	52.40
2001	55.10	44.30	56.00	31.10	60.70
2002	57.50	44.50	61.20	26.90	65.90
2003	54.20	41.30	51.10	25.40	64.10
2004	56.50	50.30	62.00	38.90	61.20
2005	57.00	46.50	46.30	46.70	63.60
2006	50.90	29.80	44.30	24.60	58.30
2007	50.50	29.50	51.50	19.90	58.10
2008	50.40	24.30	50.70	18.30	62.00
2009	50.20	28.00	49.00	25.80	58.40
2010	51.20	32.40	37.60	31.50	57.60
2011	53.10	28.20	38.70	26.00	63.10
2012	52.10	18.00	39.10	14.20	64.60
2013	46.50	15.80	33.00	13.40	59.20
2014	40.00	10.40	51.70	6.20	57.20
2015	43.10	17.40	40.20	14.70	56.30
2016	39.31	14.58	24.41	13.52	59.07
2017	38.91	15.59	27.70	14.46	58.20
2018	37.05	13.61	16.13	13.39	55.79
2019	36.84	18.82	21.90	18.53	53.14

注：本表资料包括施工总承包和专业承包企业，不含劳务分包企业(下同)。

Note:In this table, the data including general contract and specilized contract enterprises under construction, excluding labor divided contract (the same as the following tables)

14-2 按登记注册类型分的企业数及合同情况(2019)

单位:亿元

指标名称	Item	有工作量的建筑业企业个数(个) Number of Construction Enterprises with Work (unit)
总计	**Total**	**4565**
其中:国有及国有控股企业	State-owned and State-holding Enterprises	367
一、按登记注册类型分组	Grouped by Status of Registration	
内资企业	**Domestic Funded Enterprises**	**4556**
国有企业	State-owned Enterprises	126
集体企业	Collective-owned Enterprises	64
股份合作企业	Cooperative Enterprises	3
联营企业	Joint Ownership Enterprises	2
国有联营企业	State Joint Ownership Enterprises	
集体联营企业	Collective Joint Ownership Enterprises	2
国有与集体联营企业	Joint State-collective Enterprises	
其他联营企业	Other Joint Ownership Enterprises	
有限责任公司	Limited Liability Corporations	1568
国有独资公司	State Sole Funded Corporations	69
其他有限责任公司	Other Limited Liability Corporations	1499
股份有限公司	Share-holding Corporations Ltd.	132
私营企业	Private Enterprises	2658
私营独资企业	Private-funded Enterprises	13
私营合伙企业	Private Partnership Enterprises	
私营有限责任公司	Private Limited Liability Corporations	2554
私营股份有限公司	Private Share-holding Corporations Ltd.	91
其他企业	Other Enterprises	3
港、澳、台商投资企业	**Enterprises with Funds from Hong Kong,Macao and Taiwan**	**5**
合资经营企业(港或澳、台资)	Joint-venture Enterprises	4
合作经营企业(港或澳、台资)	Cooperative Enterprises	
港、澳、台商独资经营企业	Enterprises with Sole Fund	1
港、澳、台商投资股份有限公司	Share-holding Corporations Ltd.	
其他港澳台投资	Other Enterprises with Funds from Hong Kong,Macao and Taiwan	
外商投资企业	**Foreign Funded Enterprises**	**4**
中外合资经营企业	Joint-venture Enterprises	4
中外合作经营企业	Cooperative Enterprises	
外资企业	Enterprises with Sole Fund	
外商投资股份有限公司	Share-holding Corporations Ltd.	
其他外商投资	Other Foreign Funded Enterprises	

Number of Enterprises and Contract Status by Registration Status（2019）

(100 million yuan)

合同情况(亿元) Condition on Contracts(100 million yuan)		
签订的合同额 Total Value of Contracts	1.上年结转合同额 Value from Contracts Signedin Last Year	2.本年新签合同额 Value from New Contracts Signed in This Year
39715.89	**19501.83**	**20214.06**
26826.13	15076.47	11749.66
39613.39	**19470.91**	**20142.48**
549.53	171.66	377.87
87.13	14.90	72.23
13.67	4.39	9.28
0.69	0.29	0.39
0.69	0.29	0.39
31664.11	16738.15	14925.95
12819.00	8150.41	4668.59
18845.11	8587.75	10257.36
1444.70	690.89	753.82
5852.00	1849.51	4002.48
10.41	2.55	7.86
5482.45	1734.59	3747.86
359.14	112.38	246.76
1.56	1.10	0.46
2.79	**0.60**	**2.20**
2.79	0.59	2.20
0.01	0.01	0.00
99.71	**30.33**	**69.39**
99.71	30.33	69.39

14-3　按登记注册类型分的建筑业总产值(2019)

单位:亿元

指标名称	Item	建筑业总产值 Total Output Value
总计	**Total**	**16979.59**
其中:国有及国有控股企业	State-owned and State-holding Enterprises	8058.87
一、按登记注册类型分组	Grouped by Status of Registration	
内资企业	**Domestic Funded Enterprises**	**16920.51**
国有企业	State-owned Enterprises	337.95
集体企业	Collective-owned Enterprises	73.24
股份合作企业	Cooperative Enterprises	8.31
联营企业	Joint Ownership Enterprises	0.58
国有联营企业	State Joint Ownership Enterprises	
集体联营企业	Collective Joint Ownership Enterprises	0.58
国有与集体联营企业	Joint State-collective Enterprises	
其他联营企业	Other Joint Ownership Enterprises	
有限责任公司	Limited Liability Corporations	11448.12
国有独资公司	State Sole Funded Corporations	3082.54
其他有限责任公司	Other Limited Liability Corporations	8365.58
股份有限公司	Share-holding Corporations Ltd.	822.24
私营企业	Private Enterprises	4229.38
私营独资企业	Private-funded Enterprises	8.56
私营合伙企业	Private Partnership Enterprises	
私营有限责任公司	Private Limited Liability Corporations	3922.76
私营股份有限公司	Private Share-holding Corporations Ltd.	298.06
其他企业	Other Enterprises	0.69
港、澳、台商投资企业	**Enterprises with Funds from Hong Kong,Macao and Taiwan**	**1.42**
合资经营企业(港或澳、台资)	Joint-venture Enterprises	1.41
合作经营企业(港或澳、台资)	Cooperative Enterprises	
港、澳、台商独资经营企业	Enterprises with Sole Fund	0.01
港、澳、台商投资股份有限公司	Share-holding Corporations Ltd.	
外商投资企业	**Foreign Funded Enterprises**	**57.66**
中外合资经营企业	Joint-venture Enterprises	57.66
外资企业	Enterprises with Sole Fund	
外商投资股份有限公司	Share-holding Corporations Ltd.	
其他外商投资	Other Foreign Funded Enterprises	

Total Output Value of Construction by Status of Registration(2019)

(100 million yuan)

其中:装饰装修产值 Output Value of Decoration	其中:在外省完成的产值 Output Value Completed in Other Provinces	建筑工程产值 Output Value of Construction	安装工程产值 Output Vaule of Installation	其他产值 Others
570.46	**6402.63**	**15118.83**	**1317.83**	**542.93**
65.29	5152.98	7303.63	499.08	256.16
565.33	**6381.40**	**15059.81**	**1317.78**	**542.92**
0.81	17.99	310.50	4.59	22.86
0.72	0.24	62.60	10.41	0.23
0.00	0.00	8.31	0.00	0.00
0.04	0.00	0.58	0.00	0.00
0.04	0.00	0.58	0.00	0.00
315.22	5640.10	10143.54	957.15	347.43
3.26	2216.38	2780.47	199.40	102.67
311.96	3423.72	7363.07	757.75	244.77
8.88	126.08	710.35	86.92	24.96
239.64	596.46	3823.35	258.60	147.43
0.06	0.36	8.29	0.26	0.00
231.03	543.58	3549.19	246.30	127.27
8.55	52.53	265.86	12.03	20.16
0.02	0.54	0.58	0.11	0.00
0.33	**0.00**	**1.36**	**0.04**	**0.01**
0.33	0.00	1.36	0.04	0.01
0.00	0.00	0.01	0.00	0.00
4.81	**21.23**	**57.66**	**0.00**	**0.00**
4.81	21.23	57.66	0.00	0.00

14-4 按隶属关系和资质等级分的建筑业总产值构成(2019)

单位:亿元

指标名称	Item	建筑业总产值 Total Output Value
总计	**Total**	**16979.59**
一、按隶属关系分组	**Grouped by Jurisdiction of Management**	
中央	Centre	6345.63
地方	Province (Autonomous Region、Municipality)	4114.77
其他	Others	6519.18
二、按企业资质等级分组	**Grouped by Qualification Criteria**	
企业资质等级(施工总承包)	General Contracting	16118.42
特级	Special Grade	6583.48
一级	First Grade	6404.10
二级	Second Grade	2022.22
三级及以下	Third Grade and Below	1108.62
企业资质等级(专业总承包)	Professional Contraction Construction	861.17
一级	First Grade	565.67
二级	Second Grade	169.68
三级及以下	Third Grade and Below	125.82

Composition of Total Output Value of Construction Enterprises by Affiliation and Qualification Criteria(2019)

(100 million yuan)

其中:装饰装修产值 Output Value of Decoration	其中:在外省完成的产值 Output Value Completed in Other Provinces	建筑工程产值 Output Value of Construction	安装工程产值 Output Vaule of Installation	其他产值 Others
570.46	**6402.63**	**15118.83**	**1317.83**	**542.93**
32.19	4806.98	5746.47	381.80	217.36
102.33	485.33	3659.59	357.30	97.88
435.95	1110.33	5712.77	578.72	227.69
432.86	6242.53	14522.29	1112.48	483.65
47.68	4254.18	6084.96	305.99	192.52
289.16	1809.19	5718.95	534.27	150.89
51.06	130.52	1754.95	188.74	78.53
44.97	48.65	963.43	83.48	61.72
137.60	160.10	596.54	205.35	59.27
111.54	133.28	420.41	110.05	35.21
20.68	12.12	96.16	60.34	13.18
5.38	14.71	79.98	34.96	10.88

14-5 按登记注册类型分的建筑业企业完成房屋建筑竣工面积(2019)

单位:万平方米

指标名称	Item	合计 Total	住宅房屋 Residential Buildings
总计	**Total**	**33907.92**	**22135.76**
其中:国有及国有控股企业	State-owned and State-holding Enterprises	8228.57	4259.63
按登记注册类型分组	Grouped by Status of Registration		
内资企业	**Domestic Funded Enterprises**	**33819.53**	**22078.53**
国有企业	State-owned Enterprises	128.65	67.55
集体企业	Collective-owned Enterprises	338.16	224.54
股份合作企业	Cooperative Enterprises	0.61	0.61
联营企业	Joint Ownership Enterprises	5.18	2.74
国有联营企业	State Joint Ownership Enterprises		
集体联营企业	Collective Joint Ownership Enterprises	5.18	2.74
国有与集体联营企业	Joint State-collective Enterprises		
其他联营企业	Other Joint Ownership Enterprises		
有限责任公司	Limited Liability Corporations	20254.27	12282.14
国有独资公司	State Sole Funded Corporations	3653.87	1740.42
其他有限责任公司	Other Limited Liability Corporations	16600.39	10541.72
股份有限公司	Share-holding Corporations Ltd.	1365.86	777.34
私营企业	Private Enterprises	11726.24	8723.62
私营独资企业	Private-funded Enterprises	61.87	45.80
私营合伙企业	Private Partnership Enterprises		
私营有限责任公司	Private Limited Liability Corporations	11118.61	8269.78
私营股份有限公司	Private Share-holding Corporations Ltd.	545.76	408.03
其他企业	Other Enterprises	0.57	0
港、澳、台商投资企业	**Enterprises with Funds from Hong Kong,Macao and Taiwan**	**2.29**	**0**
合资经营企业(港或澳、台资)	Joint-venture Enterprises	2.29	0
合作经营企业(港或澳、台资)	Cooperative Enterprises		
港、澳、台商独资经营企业	Enterprises with Sole Fund	0.00	0
港、澳、台商投资股份有限公司	Share-holding Corporations Ltd.		
外商投资企业	**Foreign Funded Enterprises**	**86.11**	**57.23**
中外合资经营企业	Joint-venture Enterprises	86.11	57.23
中外合作经营企业	Cooperative Enterprises		
外资企业	Enterprises with Sole Fund		
外商投资股份有限公司	Share-holding Corporations Ltd.		
其他外商投资	Other Foreign Funded Enterprises		

Completed Floor Space of Buildings Constructed by Construction Enterprises by Registration Status (2019)

(10 000sq.m)

商业及服务用房屋 Houses for Business and Service	办公用房屋 Office Buildings	科研、教育、医疗用房屋 Houses for Scientific Research、Education and Medical Treatment	文化、体育、娱乐用房屋 Houses for Culture、Sports and Entertainment	厂房及建筑物 Workshop and Buildings	仓库 Storage	其他未列明的房屋建筑物* Others
3648.14	**1749.44**	**1600.13**	**387.27**	**3236.76**	**242.80**	**907.61**
1702.95	448.88	401.39	93.15	678.90	160.99	482.68
3647.76	**1735.91**	**1592.91**	**387.27**	**3234.96**	**242.80**	**899.39**
4.82	25.39	20.64	0.31	7.32	1.83	0.78
37.79	11.89	7.16	0.68	50.30	3.43	2.37
0.00	0.00	0.00	0.00	0.00	0.00	0.00
0.00	1.10	0.10	0.00	0.69	0.00	0.56
0.00	1.10	0.10	0.00	0.69	0.00	0.56
2882.86	909.12	1218.95	320.41	1807.42	184.25	649.12
743.45	127.53	134.72	42.71	384.06	95.03	385.94
2139.40	781.58	1084.22	277.69	1423.37	89.23	263.18
187.83	90.81	145.43	24.41	105.75	14.97	19.32
534.47	697.60	200.63	41.46	1263.22	38.32	226.92
1.98	1.01	1.97	0.00	7.60	0.00	3.50
512.01	616.76	196.36	41.46	1233.58	38.32	210.34
20.48	79.83	2.30	0.00	22.03	0.00	13.08
0.00	0.00	0.00	0.00	0.26	0.00	0.31
0.38	**0.00**	**0.00**	**0.00**	**1.81**	**0.00**	**0.10**
0.38	0.00	0.00	0.00	1.81	0.00	0.10
0.00	0.00	0.00	0.00	0.00	0.00	0.00
0.00	**13.54**	**7.22**	**0.00**	**0.00**	**0.00**	**8.12**
0.00	13.54	7.22	0.00	0.00	0.00	8.12

14-6 按隶属关系和资质等级分的建筑业企业工程完成情况(2019)

指标名称	Item	房屋建筑施工面积 Floor Space of Buildings under Construcion
一、按隶属关系分组	**Grouped by Jurisdiction of Management**	
中央	Centre	39871.85
地方	Province (Autonomous Region、Municipality)	20581.21
其他	Others	31589.17
四、按企业资质等级分组	**Grouped by Qualification Criteria**	
企业资质等级(施工总承包)	Enterprises Qualification Criteria (General Contracting)	91088.23
特级	Special Grade	50029.61
一级	First Grade	24958.52
二级	Second Grade	11636.03
三级及以下	Third Grade and Below	4464.07
企业资质等级(专业总承包)	Enterprises Qualification Criteria (Professional Contraction Construction)	954.01
一级	First Grade	542.59
二级	Second Grade	132.66
三级及以下	Third Grade and Below	278.76

Project Completion Situation of Construction Enterprises by Affiliation and Qualification Criteria(2019)

本年新开工面积 Floor Space of New Construction This Year	房屋建筑竣工面积 Floor Space of Buildings Completed	住宅房屋 Residential Buildings	商业及服务用房屋 Houses forBusiness Use
9096.62	7386.48	3880.13	1662.15
10690.67	9727.35	5928.32	1020.05
18271.33	16794.10	12327.31	965.94
37528.93	33467.37	21989.81	3481.98
16353.65	13416.13	7477.98	2209.37
12929.33	11834.68	8886.66	841.82
5389.58	5323.81	3722.75	281.39
2856.37	2892.74	1902.43	149.40
529.69	440.55	145.95	166.17
295.00	230.13	35.00	110.34
82.45	44.09	15.95	16.28
152.24	166.33	95.00	39.55

14-7 分市州建筑业企业生产情况(2019)
Statistics on Production of Construction Enterprises by Cities and Prefectures(2019)

单位:亿元 (100 million yuan)

项目	Item	建筑业总产值 Total Output Value of Construction Industry	建筑工程产值 Output Value of Construction Projects	安装工程产值 Output Value of Installation Projects	其他产值 Output Value of Other Projects	竣工产值 Output Value of Projects Completed
湖北省	**Hubei**	**16979.59**	**15118.83**	**1317.83**	**542.93**	**8058.03**
武汉市	Wuhan	10375.93	9194.73	834.01	347.19	4462.26
黄石市	Huangshi	490.17	445.08	25.93	19.16	281.96
十堰市	Shiyan	534.68	496.60	26.42	11.65	194.34
宜昌市	Yichang	1295.67	1175.62	89.15	30.90	484.67
襄阳市	Xiangyang	1133.24	1007.76	104.14	21.34	613.06
鄂州市	Ezhou	205.32	169.57	27.22	8.53	91.20
荆门市	Jingmen	190.56	171.44	13.18	5.93	122.78
孝感市	Xiaogan	480.81	395.55	64.04	21.22	310.96
荆州市	Jingzhou	298.77	270.63	16.01	12.12	180.01
黄冈市	Huanggang	1067.94	989.18	58.61	20.15	732.37
咸宁市	Xianning	219.05	203.53	10.44	5.09	149.90
随州市	Suizhou	135.18	123.28	2.33	9.57	87.94
恩施州	Enshi	122.66	114.59	4.38	3.68	68.27
仙桃市	Xiantao	133.42	117.81	6.95	8.66	88.56
潜江市	Qianjiang	146.46	124.81	17.17	4.47	95.90
天门市	Tianmen	142.03	112.36	17.52	12.16	87.18
神农架	Shennongjia	7.71	6.29	0.32	1.09	6.70

14-8 分市州建筑业企业工程完成情况(2019)

Project Completion Situation of Construction Enterprises by Cities and Prefectures(2019)

单位:万平方米 (10 000 sq.m)

项 目	Item	房屋建筑施工面积 Floor Space of Housing Construction	本年新开工面积 Beginning projects in This Year	房屋建筑竣工面积 Floor Space of Housing Projects Completed	#住 宅 Residential Buildings	#办公用房 Office Buildings
湖北省	**Hubei**	**92042.23**	**38058.62**	**33907.92**	**22135.76**	**1749.44**
武汉市	Wuhan	60105.01	20594.74	17498.37	10662.96	836.72
黄石市	Huangshi	2590.42	1393.36	1442.73	965.61	50.47
十堰市	Shiyan	1565.73	807.76	760.58	551.03	9.86
宜昌市	Yichang	4926.77	2110.48	1844.78	1294.52	78.07
襄阳市	Xiangyang	5659.99	2077.58	1996.76	1410.79	79.43
鄂州市	Ezhou	772.78	379.27	454.83	314.12	5.99
荆门市	Jingmen	1006.22	593.87	526.01	371.27	46.81
孝感市	Xiaogan	2665.87	1917.51	1562.05	986.34	102.30
荆州市	Jingzhou	1481.53	725.51	677.58	460.52	18.08
黄冈市	Huanggang	6906.93	4938.02	4610.17	3361.41	381.25
咸宁市	Xianning	1000.37	698.85	738.62	551.02	43.21
随州市	Suizhou	1044.68	663.83	521.02	390.20	29.25
恩施州	Enshi	630.13	295.73	268.69	153.05	18.47
仙桃市	Xiantao	576.94	360.58	422.34	322.48	21.27
潜江市	Qianjiang	420.23	50.51	163.67	49.02	3.87
天门市	Tianmen	672.28	439.51	410.05	287.66	23.88
神农架	Shennongjia	16.34	11.51	9.66	3.75	0.52

主要统计指标解释

建筑业统计单位 指从事房屋、构筑物建造和设备安装活动的法人企业。建筑业法人企业应具有建筑业资质并能够独立核算，同时其应具备以下条件：①依法成立，有自己的名称、组织机构和场所，能够承担民事责任；②独立拥有和使用资产，承担负债，有权与其他单位签订合同；③独立核算盈亏，能够编制资产负债表。

建筑业总产值 是以货币形式表现的建筑业企业在一定时期内生产的建筑业产品和提供的服务的总和。建筑业总产值包括：

(1)建筑工程产值：指列入建筑工程预算内的各种工程价值。

(2)安装工程产值：指设备安装工程价值，不包括被安装设备本身的价值。

(3)其他产值：建筑业总产值中除建筑工程、安装工程以外的产值。包括房屋构筑物修理产值、非标准设备制造产值、总包企业向分包企业收取的管理费以及不能明确划分的施工活动所完成的产值。

a.房屋构筑物修理产值：指房屋和构筑物修理所完成的产值，但不包括被修理房屋、构筑物本身价值和生产设备的修理产值。

b.非标准设备制造产值：指加工制造没有定型的非标准生产设备的加工费和原材料价值(如化工厂、炼油厂用的各种罐、槽，矿井生产统一使用的各种漏斗、三角槽、阀门等)以及附属加工厂为本企业承建工程制作的非标准设备的价值。

建筑业增加值 指建筑业企业在报告期内以货币形式表现的建筑业生产经营活动的最终成果。

从2004年第一次全国经济普查开始，建筑业现价增加值按生产法和分配法(收入法)两种方法计算，以收入法的计算结果为准，即从收入的角度出发，根据生产要素在生产过程中应得的收入份额计算。具体计算方法：经济普查年度建筑业增加值按照《经济普查年度GDP核算方案》计算，非经济普查年度建筑业增加值按照《非经济普查年度GDP核算方案》计算。

房屋建筑施工面积 指在报告期内施过工的全部房屋建筑面积，包括本期新开工的房屋面积、上期施工跨入本期继续施工的房屋面积、上期停缓建在本期恢复施工的房屋面积、本期竣工的房屋面积及本期施工后又停缓建的房屋面积。

房屋建筑竣工面积 指在报告期内房屋建筑按照设计要求全部完工，达到了使用条件，经验收鉴定合格，正式移交使用单位的房屋建筑面积。

Explanatory Notes on Main Statistical Indicators

Statistical Unit in Construction refers to corporate enterprise engaged in the construction of buildings and structures and in the installation of equipment. A corporate construction enterprise should have qualification certificates with independent accounting system, and should meet the following 3 requirements: a) being set up in line with relevant legal basis, having its full name, organization and location, and capable of taking civil liabilities; b) independently possessing and using its assets and assuming its liabilities, and entitled to sign contracts with other institutions; and c) making independent accounts of its profits and losses, and capable of compiling its own balance sheet.

Gross Output Value of Construction refers to total of construction products and services, expressed in money terms, produced or rendered by construction and installation enterprises during a given period of time. It includes:

(1) Output value of construction projects, that is the value of projects covered by the project budgets;

(2) Output value of installation projects, that is the value of the installation of equipment, (excluding the value of the equipment to be

installed);

(3) Output value of others, that is the output value of construction industry excluding that of construction projects and installation projects. It includes: output value of repair of buildings and structures; output value of non–standard equipment manufacturing; overhead expenses received by contracted enterprises to the sub–contracted enterprises and the completed output value of construction activities that have no clear definition.

a. Output value of repair of buildings and structures, that is the value created through the repairs of buildings or structures, but does not include the value of buildings or structures being repaired and the value of the repair of production equipment;

b. Output value of manufactured non–standard equipment, that is the value of non–standard production equipment including raw materials and manufacturing cost made for the construction project (i.e., chemical plant; kettles or tanks used by refineries; various fillers, triangle tanks, valves used by mines), and the output value of equipment manufactured by subsidiary workshops.

Value–added of Construction refers to the final result of the activities of production and management of construction industry in monetary terms in the reference period.

Starting from the 2004 economic census, value–added of construction is calculated by both production approach and income approach, with the income approach as the final approach, where the calculation is based on the share of production factor in the production process. Specifically, value–added of construction for census years is calculated in accordance with the Programme of Compilation of GDP and National Accounts for the Year of Economic Census, and value–added of construction for other years is calculated in accordance with the Programme of Compilation of GDP and National Accounts for the Non Economic Census Years.

Floor Space of Buildings Under Construction refers to floor space of buildings under construction during the reference period, including newly started buildings, buildings started earlier and continued during the reference period, and buildings suspended earlier but restarted during the reference period, buildings completed during the reference period, and buildings under construction and then suspended during the reference period.

Floor Space of Buildings Completed refers to the floor space of buildings that are completed in the reference period in accordance with the requirements of the design, up to the standard for putting them into use, and have been checked and accepted by concerned departments as qualified ones.

15 交通运输、邮电

Transport, Postal and Telecommunication Services

资料整理人员：赵静洁

交通运输、邮电
Transport, Postal and Telecommunication Services
2019

客运量	Passenger Capacity of The Whole Society	88926.43	(万人)
#公路	Public Road	69584.36	(万人)
货运量	Volume of Freight Traffic	188143.15	(万吨)
#公路	Public Road	143548.61	(万吨)
邮电业务总量	Business Volume of Post and Telecommunications	3824.44	(亿元)
#函件	Letters	6530.42	(万件)
年末固定电话用户	Fixed Telephone Subscribers at Year-end	518.93	(万户)
年末移动电话用户	Mobile Telephone Subscribers at Year-end	5688.02	(万户)

全 社 会 客 货 运 量
Passenger Capactity of The Whole Society

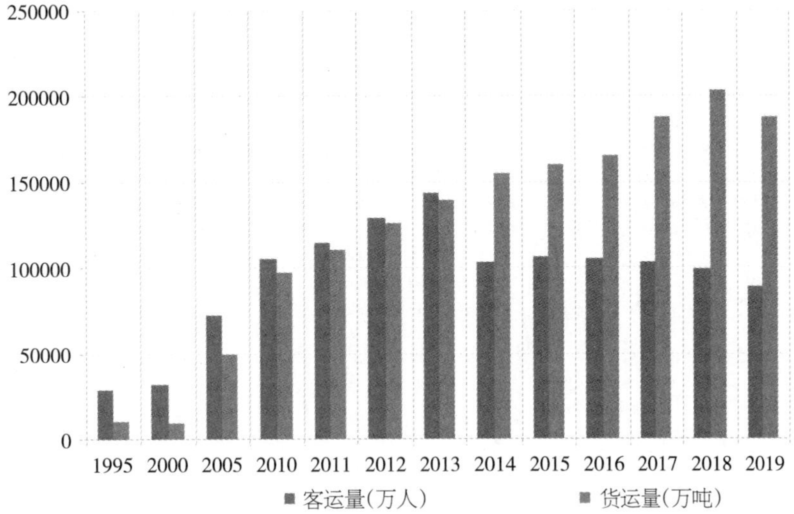

附:客货运量

Passenger Capacity of The Whole Society

年份 Year	客运量(万人) Passenger Capacity (10 000 persons)	货运量(万吨) volume of freight traffic (10 000 tons)
1995	28508	10174
2000	31593	9345
2005	71892	49924
2010	105132	96938
2012	129511	126195
2013	143100	139740
2014	103672	154736
2015	104694	156357
2016	105813	165125
2017	103549	187638
2018	98720	203704
2019	88926	188143

注:1.2014年因公路运输统计方法调整,数据与前期不可比(下同)。
2.2017年因运输调整统计方法,数据与前期不可比(下同)。
3.2019年因公路运输统计方法调整,数据与前期不可比(下同)。

Note:1.From 2014, due to the statistics method of road transport has been adjusted, the data can not be compared with the previous period(the same below).
2.From 2017,due to the statistics method of transportation has been adjusted, the data can not be compared with the previous(the same below).
3.From 2019, due to the statistics method of road transport has been adjusted, the data can not be compared with the previous period(the same below).

15-1 交通运输业基本情况

指标		1995	2000	2005	2010
运输线路长度	(公里)				
铁路营业里程		1940	2025	2758	3032
公路总里程		48728	57850	91131	206212
#等级公路里程		30910	48062	76075	187812
#高速公路			569	1649	3674
一级公路		641	611	1092	2210
二级公路		4967	7911	15225	16159
内河航道里程		8969	8309	8988	8988
客运量总计	(万人)	28508.20	31593.00	71892.00	105415.50
铁路		2300.00	3469.00	4615.00	7281.30
公路		24315.00	27184.00	66183.00	96873.00
水运		1745.00	679.00	601.00	375.80
民用航空		150.00	261.00	494.00	885.40
旅客周转量	(亿人公里)	285.29	398.32	803.90	1262.26
货运量总计	(万吨)	10173.62	9345.19	49923.52	97006.94
铁路		3986.00	3857.00	8491.00	10145.60
公路		2600.00	2228.00	33481.00	71020.00
水运		3585.00	3255.00	7944.00	15832.00
货物周转量	(亿吨公里)	776.44	831.64	1682.48	3370.37
民用车辆拥有量	(万辆)			393.90	761.11
民用汽车拥有量		34.89	47.55	103.04	224.60
载客汽车		14.96	24.69	53.40	151.51
载货汽车		18.61	21.72	30.96	53.29
营运汽车				20.33	36.60
私人汽车			41.72	59.66	165.39
民用运输船舶拥有量	(艘)		5905	5362	5502
机动船			4188	4158	4634
驳船			1717	1204	868
港口货物吞吐量	(万吨)		4113.46	13992.51	18782.67

注:1.2014年因公路运输统计方法调整,数据与前期不可比(下同)。
2.2017年因运输调整统计方法,数据与前期不可比(下同)。
3.2019年因公路运输统计方法调整,数据与前期不可比(下同)。
4.2019年因港口货物吞吐量统计方法调整,数据与前期不可比(下同)。

Basic Conditions of Transport

2014	2015	2016	2017	2018	2019
4059	4062	4140	4216	4341	5165
236932	252980	260179	269484	275039	289029
224184	240936	249819	259591	265912	281422
5096	6204	6204	6252	6367	6860
3344	5231	5460	5874	6093	6465
18033	21555	22005	22712	23179	23936
9066	9066	9066	9066	9067	9067
103671.80	104693.75	105813.14	103549.03	98719.70	88926.43
14302.70	15083.90	15855.30	14876.60	15700.40	17216.06
87804.00	87953.26	88220.89	86772.19	80989.51	69584.36
533.80	574.46	572.22	624.63	647.79	631.63
1031.30	1082.13	1164.73	1275.61	1382.00	1494.37
1458.24	1490.81	1521.05	1365.87	1348.98	1386.79
154735.73	156356.93	165124.84	187637.83	203703.74	188143.15
7681.30	6579.00	6744.20	3773.40	4116.40	5479.90
116280.00	115800.30	122654.50	147710.51	163145.18	143548.61
30765.00	33968.00	35715.80	36143.90	36431.99	39104.66
5798.12	5908.40	6159.90	6276.67	6605.49	6133.74
1042.36	959.35	902.95	1008.15	1081.82	1174.57
439.39	504.36	593.33	683.42	775.70	864.10
345.84	424.70	515.17	601.48	683.57	762.34
72.73	70.16	69.71	74.32	84.35	93.48
42.95	55.25	51.92	52.50	57.32	61.93
300.61	433.90	524.16	609.12	693.95	775.25
4744	4357	4010	3595	3278	3366
4500	4155	3857	3466	3172	3270
244	202	153	129	106	96
28969.15	32949.52	35191.90	36903.31	34620.55	30660.74

Note:1.From 2014, due to the statistics method of road transport has been adjusted, the data can not be compared with the previous period(the same below).
2.From 2017, due to the statistics method of transportation has been adjusted, the data can not be compared with the previous(the same below).
3.From 2019, due to the statistics method of road transport has been adjusted, the data can not be compared with the previous period(the same below).
4.From 2019, due to the statistics method of port handling capacity has been adjusted, the data can not be compared with the previous period(the same below).

15-2 客运量

Passenger Traffic

单位：万人 (10 000 persons)

年份 Year	总计 Total	铁路 Railway	公路 Highway	水运 Waterway	民用航空 Civil Aviation
1978	12009.20	2854.00	7429.00	1722.00	4.20
1980	16629.26	3217.00	11282.00	2123.00	7.26
1985	28178.22	3353.00	22378.00	2433.00	14.22
1990	32145.93	2107.00	27333.00	2693.00	12.93
1991	33982.62	2016.00	29279.00	2654.00	33.62
1992	34726.00	2077.00	29635.00	2894.00	120.00
1993	30152.00	2265.00	25116.00	2665.00	106.00
1994	29607.00	2358.00	24819.00	2210.00	120.00
1995	28508.20	2300.00	24315.00	1743.00	150.00
1996	29045.40	2248.00	25180.00	1449.00	168.00
1997	29503.08	2127.00	25684.00	1538.00	154.08
1998	28208.00	2218.00	24540.00	1306.00	144.00
1999	29360.14	2545.00	25596.00	1080.00	139.14
2000	63306.00	3469.00	58897.00	679.00	261.00
2001	62696.00	3632.00	58018.00	767.00	279.00
2002	63382.00	3813.00	58623.00	638.00	308.00
2003	62880.00	3602.00	58371.00	573.00	334.42
2004	68167.00	4072.00	63127.00	522.00	446.11
2005	71892.00	4615.00	66183.00	601.00	494.00
2006	75440.00	4850.00	69335.00	706.00	549.00
2007	84088.00	5125.00	77514.00	736.00	712.70
2008	89720.00	6027.00	82532.00	388.00	774.00
2009	96219.00	6440.00	88703.00	371.00	705.00
2010	105415.50	7281.30	96873.00	375.80	885.40
2011	114736.92	8503.80	104971.00	347.60	914.52
2012	129510.90	9764.90	118369.00	443.50	933.50
2013	143100.28	12101.80	129533.75	528.00	936.73
2014	103671.40	14302.70	87804.00	533.80	1031.30
2015	104693.73	15083.90	87953.26	574.46	1082.13
2016	105813.14	15855.30	88220.89	572.22	1164.73
2017	103549.03	14876.60	86772.19	624.63	1275.61
2018	98719.70	15700.40	80989.51	647.79	1382.00
2019	88926.43	17216.06	69584.36	631.63	1494.37

注：1.2014年因公路运输统计方法调整，数据与前期不可比(下同)。
2.2017年因铁路运输调整统计方法，数据与前期不可比(下同)。
3.2019年因公路运输统计方法调整，数据与前期不可比(下同)。

Note:1.From 2014, due to the statistics method of has been adjusted, the data can not be compared with the previous period(the same below).
2.From 2017,due to the statistics method of railway transportation has been adjusted, the data can not be compared with the previous(the same below).
3.From 2019, due to the statistics method of road transport has been adjusted, the data can not be compared with the previous period(the same below).

15-3 旅客周转量
Passenger-Kilometers

单位：亿人公里 (100 million passenger-km)

年份 Year	总计 Total	铁路 Railway	公路 Highway	水运 Waterway	民用航空 Civil Aviation
1978	69.38	30.72	24.85	13.54	0.17
1980	95.88	41.79	36.20	17.52	0.37
1985	185.25	84.00	81.33	19.40	0.52
1990	225.85	82.83	112.83	29.28	0.91
1991	257.68	98.09	126.70	30.19	2.70
1992	286.35	104.89	135.61	34.72	11.13
1993	281.28	113.60	123.64	33.50	10.54
1994	283.98	121.91	121.40	28.71	11.96
1995	285.29	129.47	117.76	22.71	15.35
1996	285.04	121.17	124.97	21.09	17.81
1997	282.53	118.62	123.39	24.14	16.38
1998	278.66	126.68	118.51	18.79	14.68
1999	300.38	146.54	124.46	14.09	15.29
2000	563.78	232.00	297.46	8.84	25.48
2001	574.24	248.00	293.35	5.87	27.02
2002	633.69	283.00	317.02	3.60	30.07
2003	617.68	271.00	309.00	4.00	33.68
2004	703.95	322.80	334.00	3.20	43.95
2005	803.90	389.40	358.00	4.20	52.30
2006	847.42	408.10	374.80	5.10	59.42
2007	947.71	440.80	423.80	5.30	77.81
2008	1077.68	474.01	522.57	2.30	78.80
2009	1096.31	466.70	562.34	2.49	64.78
2010	1262.26	528.90	631.39	2.92	99.05
2011	1444.66	639.15	700.06	2.49	102.97
2012	1576.00	663.60	804.07	2.94	106.36
2013	1761.10	756.40	892.25	3.14	109.31
2014	1458.24	854.40	483.89	2.85	120.10
2015	1490.81	869.30	489.29	3.32	128.90
2016	1521.05	895.80	487.33	3.35	134.57
2017	1365.87	734.70	482.27	4.06	144.84
2018	1348.98	731.80	453.44	4.74	159.00
2019	1386.79	803.51	392.09	4.76	186.43

15-4 货运量
Freight Traffic

单位：万吨 (10 000 tons)

年份 Year	总计 Total	铁路 Railway	公路 Highway	水运 Waterway	*内河 Inland Waterway	*海运 Seashipping
1978	10199	3513	3556	3130		
1980	8420	3211	2199	3110		
1985	11059	2659	3852	3463		
1990	10916	3901	2941	3784		
1991	11217	3957	2999	3996		
1992	11565	4018	2828	4364		
1993	11184	4029	2734	4248		
1994	10663	3964	2666	3641		
1995	10174	3986	2600	3585		
1996	9928	3779	2537	3268		
1997	9389	3882	2280	3119		
1998	10154	3999	2009	4040		
1999	10517	3964	2141	4313		
2000	40949	6558	27863	6270	6202	68
2001	41476	7094	29851	4275	4198	77
2002	42064	7400	28777	5630	5390	240
2003	44661	7825	30348	6195	5830	365
2004	47073	7872	31584	7259	6823	436
2005	50317	8491	33481	7944	7466	478
2006	52885	8990	35361	8242	7679	536
2007	58523	9728	39568	9027	7765	1262
2008	75778	10202	52759	12681	8182	4499
2009	82714	9839	59563	13305	8108	5197
2010	97007	10145	71020	15832	9916	6082
2011	110168	10059	82741	17358	10817	6536
2012	125392	9177	97136	19070	11836	7275
2013	139740	9010	108824	21897	13575	8042
2014	154736	7681	116280	30765	21152	8476
2015	156357	6579	115800	33968	27564	6226
2016	165125	6744	122655	35716	29898	5728
2017	187638	3773	147711	36144	30482	5537
2018	203704	4116	163145	36432	31110	5322
2019	188143	5480	143549	39105	31526	7579

15-5 货物周转量
Freight Ton-Kilometers

单位：亿吨公里 (100 million ton-km)

年份 Year	总计 Total	铁路 Railway	公路 Highway	水运 Waterway	#内河 Inland Waterway	#海运 Seashipping
1978	281.09	191.72	9.22	80.15		
1980	326.85	206.14	9.85	110.85		
1985	507.57	320.37	16.59	169.94		
1990	670.53	415.17	14.72	235.04		
1991	720.23	455.00	14.67	245.41		
1992	757.00	461.81	13.89	272.70		
1993	753.52	477.64	11.99	259.90		
1994	743.21	505.57	10.23	222.32		
1995	776.44	544.40	9.62	222.20		
1996	775.79	552.32	9.93	208.05		
1997	725.34	501.77	8.72	212.21		
1998	696.62	465.81	7.59	220.63		
1999	696.27	457.70	8.25	227.76		
2000	1156.57	618.37	227.16	305.29	295.07	10.22
2001	1097.60	634.90	218.97	237.31	226.15	11.16
2002	1212.82	680.00	211.49	313.60	271.30	42.29
2003	1313.13	703.80	224.00	377.00	315.38	61.61
2004	1485.76	781.83	235.60	461.08	395.75	65.33
2005	1689.86	987.60	251.00	443.20	391.05	105.00
2006	1730.93	1021.40	266.10	437.90	379.81	58.10
2007	1902.17	1138.20	302.09	458.00	361.93	95.83
2008	2699.97	1096.90	789.37	810.46	416.17	394.29
2009	2808.46	1032.40	930.10	845.18	402.82	442.36
2010	3370.37	1144.60	1079.13	1145.52	547.77	470.00
2011	4044.45	1226.80	1277.71	1538.83	625.26	609.61
2012	4693.61	1194.10	1565.45	1590.65	740.76	683.36
2013	4883.01	1195.70	1818.18	1868.08	946.02	756.69
2014	5798.12	1109.10	2340.56	2347.32	1347.07	891.82
2015	5908.40	995.70	2380.62	2530.91	1851.27	618.02
2016	6159.90	971.50	2506.85	2680.34	2040.82	600.69
2017	6276.67	744.80	2741.91	2788.80	2143.64	585.12
2018	6605.49	798.80	2955.53	2850.00	2222.91	627.08
2019	6133.74	938.73	2268.11	2925.55	2158.62	766.93

15-6 全省民用车辆拥有量(2019)
Number of Civil Vehicles Owned in the Province(2019)

单位：辆 (unit)

指标	Item	总计 Total	营运 Working	非营运 Non-Working
合计	**Total**	**11745699**	**750195**	**10981698**
汽车	Civil Vehicles	8640983	619308	8007869
载客汽车	Passenger Vehicles	7623437	163990	7445641
#大型	Lage Scale	61550	41851	13253
中型	Medium Scale	27683	9978	10345
小型	Small Scale	7516481	112160	7404321
#轿车	Cars	4530368	106330	4424038
载货汽车	Trucks	934813	437615	497198
#重型	Heavy Scale	238996	222458	16538
中型	Medium Scale	58071	49003	9068
轻型	Light Scale	637454	166119	471335
#普通载货	Ordinary Trucks	410417	62932	347485
其他汽车	Other Vehicles	82733	17703	65030
#三轮汽车	Tricycle Motocars	5253	573	4680
低速货车	Low Speed Vehicles	25145	9766	15379
摩托车	Motorear	3030786	58009	2972777
#普通	Ordinary Motor	2992227	57997	2934230
轻便	Light Motor	38559	12	38547
挂车	Freight Trailers	73862	72835	1027
其他类型车	Other Motor Vehicles	28	3	25

注：本表“其他汽车”中，包括三轮和四轮农用运输车。

Note:Tricycles and four-wheel farming vehicles are inclued in“Other Vehicles”

15-7 私人车辆拥有量
Possession of Private Vehicles

单位：辆 (unit)

指标	Item	2000	2005	2010	2015	2016	2017	2018	2019
私人汽车	Private Vehicles	475500	596601	1653948	4338967	5241602	6091207	6939463	7752483
载客汽车	Passenger Vehicles	245500	297095	1153728	3796713	4704592	5543501	6333079	7082548
#大型	#Lage Scale	29200	3312	2939	770	650	432	385	360
#轿车	#Cars		177650	773727	2414210	2938643	3387453	3827327	4249714
载货汽车	Ordinary Trucks	211400	135352	327509	473513	478375	498195	558088	620493
#重型	#Heavy Scale		8766	33281	59388	63829	65158	76314	87219
其它汽车	Others		164154	172711	68741	58635	49511	48296	49442
摩托车	Motors	1241000	2853113	4971619	4501871	3046392	3188833	2989016	3012446
挂车	Freight Trailers	4400	1714	6467	11405	12684	15037	17863	24246

15-8 水路运输工具拥有量(2019)
Possession of Waterway Transport Vehicles(2019)

指标	Item	机动船 Power Boat	客船 Passenger Ship	货船 Cargo Ship	拖船 Tugboat
数量 (艘)	Quantity (ship)	3270	339	2875	56
总载重量 (吨)	Total Carrying Capacity (tonage)	7224953	559	7224394	
净载重量 (吨)	Net Load (tonage)	7076475	559	7075916	
载客量 (客位)	Passenger Carrying Capacity (person)	34747	34747		
标准箱位	TEU	3783		3783	
功率 (千瓦)	Power (kw)	1846820	90233	1713981	42606

15-9 分市、州公路旅客运输完成情况(2019)
Completion of Highway Passenger Transportation by Cities and Prefectures(2019)

地区	Region	客运量(万人) Passenger Traffic (10,000 person)	旅客周转量(万人公里) Turnover Volume of Passenger Traffic (100 million passenger-km)
武汉市	Wuhan	4883	434716
黄石市	Huangshi	2629	163272
十堰市	Shiyan	3278	298436
宜昌市	Yichang	9483	483235
襄阳市	Xiangyang	9568	471954
鄂州市	Ezhou	1481	89063
荆门市	Jingmen	1834	124146
孝感市	Xiaogan	5796	255933
荆州市	Jingzhou	5591	292542
黄冈市	Huanggang	7883	400273
咸宁市	Xianning	5011	287464
随州市	Suizhou	2304	138212
恩施自治州	Enshi	3910	236806
仙桃市	Xiantao	1919	74963
潜江市	Qianjiang	1333	56731
天门市	Tianmen	2111	91369
神农架林区	Shennongjia	572	21810

15-10 邮电业务基本情况
Basic Conditions of Postal and Telecommunication Services

指标	Item	2005	2010	2015	2018	2019
邮电业务总量 (亿元)	**Business Volume of Postal and Telecommunicaion (100 million yuan)**	**373.63**	**1028.09**	**962.66**	**2380.51**	**3824.44**
邮政业务总量	Business Volume of Postal Services	23.40	55.71	137.41	345.24	458.51
电信业务总量	Business Volume of Telecommunication Services	350.20	972.38	825.25	2035.27	3365.93
函件 (亿件)	Letters (100 million pcs)	1.30	1.00	0.68	0.74	0.65
包裹 (万件)	Package (10 000 pcs)	320.00	210.10	105.80	61.51	54.91
快递业务量 (万件)	Pieces of Express Mail Services (10 000 pcs)	685.30	5476.60	50847.30	135307.74	168499.77
报刊期发数 (万份)	Issue of Newspapers and Magzines (10 000 pcs)	643.00	557.00	587.00	391.30	371.90
年末固定电话用户 (万户)	Number of Fixed Telephone Subscribers at Year-end (10 000 subscribers)	1236.00	1026.40	872.50	568.91	518.93
年末移动电话用户 (万户)	Number of Mobile Telephone Subscribers at Year-end (10 000 subscribers)	1401.00	3454.70	4650.60	5569.79	5688.02
互联网宽带接入用户 (万户)	Broadband Users (10 000 subscribers)	128.00	459.40	983.50	1480.73	1708.32
年末城市宽带用户 (万户)	Urban Broadband Users at Year-end (10 000 subscribers)			703.70	1074.17	1208.57
年末农村宽带用户 (万户)	Rural Broadband Users at Year-end (10 000 subscribers)			154.90	406.56	499.75
邮路总长度(单程) (公里)	Length of Postal Routes(One Way) (km)		57483	163136	262100	265400
邮路线路总条数 (条)	Postal Routes (unit)		411	767	863	1683
农村投递线路条数 (条)	Rural Delivery Routes (unit)		4198	3562	3635	3634
农村投递线路长度(单程) (公里)	Rural Delivery Routes(One Way) (km)		194656	205502	187782	187419
移动电话交换机容量 (万户)	Capacity of Mobile Telephone Swicthboard (10 000 units)		5862.70	8748.70	8502.30	9043.50
互联网宽带接入端口 (万个)	Broadband Subscribers Port of Internet (10 000 ports)			1600.30	3001.35	3062.28
长途光缆线路长度 (万公里)	Length of Long-Distance Optical Cable Lines (10 000 km)		2.70	3.14	3.22	3.08

注：1.邮电业务总量统计口径2011年发生变化，与以前各年份不可比。
2.2017年2月，工信部调整了统计口径，2017年电信行业数据与2016年及以往年度电信行业数据不可比。
3.2019年邮路线路总条数统计口径有调整，与以往各年份不可比。

Note: 1.Note:The statistic on total volume of post and telecommunication have been reconfigured from 2011.Datas of other year can not compare with the data of 2011.
2.In February 2017, the Ministry of Industry and Information Technology adjusted its statistical calibre. The 2017 telecommunications industry data is not comparable with the 2016 and previous years 'telecommunications industry data.
3.Form 2019, due to the statistics method of Postal Routes has been adjusted, the data can not be compared with the previous period.

15-11 邮电通信水平
Postal and Telecommunication Services Available

指标	Item	2005	2010	2014	2015	2017	2018	2019
每百人平均函件量	Annual Average Number of Letters Mailed per 100 persons	228.0	174.7	114.8	115.5	114.9	125.7	110.3
(件/百人)	(unit/100 person)							
每百人平均订阅报刊量	Annual Average Number of Newspaper and Magazine Subscribed per 100 persons	977.9	962.7	1247.8	1211.8	1145.0	1129.5	1095.7
(份/百人)	(unit/100 person)							
每百人平均包裹	Annual Average Number of Package per 100 persons	5.6	3.4	2.4	1.8	1.2	1.0	0.9
(件/百人)	(unit/100 person)							
电话普及率	Popularization Rate of Telephone per 100 persons	43.9	78.3	94.8	94.4	95.8	103.7	104.9
(部/百人)	(unit/100 person)							
移动电话普及率	Popularization Rate of Mobile Telephone per 100 persons	23.3	60.4	79.2	79.5	84.6	94.1	96.1
(部/百人)	(unit/100 person)							

主要统计指标解释

铁路营业里程 又称营业长度(包括正式营业和临时营业里程),指办理客货运输业务的铁路正线总长度。凡是全线或部分建成双线及以上的线路,以第一线的实际长度计算;复线、站线、段管线、岔线和特殊用途线以及不计算运费的联络线都不计算营业里程。该指标可以反映铁路运输业基础设施的发展水平,也是计算客货周转量、运输密度和机车车辆运用效率等指标的基础资料。

公路总里程 指在一定时期内实际达到《公路工程[WTBZ]技术标准JTJ01-88》规定的等级公路,并经公路主管部门正式验收交付使用的公路里程数。包括大中城市的郊区公路以及通过小城镇街道部分的公路里程和桥梁、渡口的长度,不包括大中城市的街道、厂矿、林区生产用道和农业生产用道的里程。两条或多条公路共同经由同一路段,只计算一次,不得重复计算里程长度。该指标可以反映公路建设的发展规模,也是计算运输网密度等指标的基础资料。

内河航道里程 也称内河通航里程,指在一定时期内,能通航运输船舶及排筏的天然河流、湖泊水库、运河及通航渠道的长度。包括全年季节性通航累计三个月以上的航道,不包括仅供零散流放竹、木排的河道。该指标可以反映内河水运网的规模、水平和发展情况。

货(客)运量 指在一定时期内,各种运输工具实际运送的货物(旅客)数量。该指标是反映运输业为国民经济和人民生活服务的数量指标,也是制定和检查运输生产计划、研究运输发展规模和速度的重要指标。货运按吨计算,客运按人计算。货物不论运输距离长短、货物类别,均按实际重量统计。旅客不论行程远近或票价多少,均按一人一次客运量统计;半价票、小孩票也按一人统计。

货物(旅客)周转量 指在一定时期内,由各种运输工具运送的货物(旅客)数量与其相应运输距离的乘积之总和。该指标可以反映运输业生产的总成果,也是编制和检查运输生产计划,计算运输效率、劳动生产率以及核算运输单位成本的主要基础资料。计算货物周转量通常按发出站与到达站之间的最短距离,也就是计费距离计算。计算公式为:

货物(旅客)周转量=Σ(货物(旅客)运输量×运输距离)

民用汽车拥有量 指报告期末,在公安交通管理部门按照《机动车注册登记工作规范》,已注册登记领有民用车辆牌照的全部汽车数量。汽车拥有量统计的主要分类:根据汽车结构分为载客汽车、载货汽车及其他汽车;根据汽车所有者不同分为个人(私人)汽车、单位汽车;根据汽车的使用性质分为营运汽车、非营运汽车;根据汽车大小规格不同载客汽车分为大型、中型、小型和微型,载货汽车分为重型、中型、轻型和微型。

邮电业务总量 指以货币形式表示的邮政、电信通信企业为社会提供各类邮政、电信通信服务的总数量。计算方法为各类业务的实物量分别乘以相应的不变单价,求出各类业务的货币量加总求得。没有不变单价的业务按其业务收入直接相加。

年末固定电话用户 指接入本地电信运营商固定电话网上的电话用户。包括:住宅用户、单位用户、公用电话用户等。

年末移动电话用户 指通过移动电话交换机进入移动电话网、占用移动电话号码的各类电话用户。包括签约用户和智能网预付费用户。一个移动电话号码统计为一户。

Explanatory Notes on Main Statistical Indicators

Length of Railways in Operation refers to the total length of the trunk line under passenger and freight transportation (including both full operation and temporary operation). The calculation is based on the actual length of the first line even if this line has a full or partial double track or more tracks, excluding double tracks, station sidings, tracks under the charge of stations, branch lines, special-purpose lines and the non-payable connecting lines. The length of railways in operation is an important indicator to show the development of the infrastructure for the railway transport, and also the essential data to calculate volume of passenger freight transport, traffic density and utilization efficiency of the locomotives and carriages.

Length of Highways refers to the length of highways which are built in conformity with the grades specified by the highway engineering standard formulated by the Ministry of Communications, and have been formally checked and accepted by the departments of highways and put into use. The length of highways includes that of the suburb highways at large and medium-sized cities, highways passing through streets at small cities and towns, and also the length of bridges and ferries. It does not include the length of streets in big and medium-sized cities and highways built for the production purpose at factories, mines, forest areas and agricultural areas. If two or more highways go the same section of the way, the length of the section is only calculated for once and no duplication is allowed. The length of highways is an important indicator to show the development of the highway construction and to provide essential information to calculate the transport network density.

Length of Navigable Inland Waterways it is an indicator reflecting the size and development of inland water network, it refers to the length of the natural rivers, lakes, reservoirs, canals, and ditches open to navigation during a given period, which enables the transport by ships and rafts. It includes the channels open to navigation for over an accumulative 3 months in a year, yet this does not include the river courses, which are only used to float odd logs and bamboo rafts. This indicator can reflect the scale, level and development situation of the inland waterway network.

Freight (Passenger) Traffic refers to the volume of freight (passenger) transported with various means. Freight transport is calculated in tons and passenger traffic is calculated in the number of persons. Despite the type of freight and traveling distance, the freight transport is calculated in the actual weight of the goods: and despite the traveling distance and ticket price, the passenger traffic is calculated by the principle that one person can be counted only once in one travel. The passengers who travel with a half price ticket or a child ticket is also calculated as one person. The freight (passenger) traffic provides a quantitative measure to show how the transport industry serves the national economy and people, and is also an important indicator for planning the transport industry and for studying the development scale and speed of the transport industry.

Freight Ton-kilometers (Passenger-kilometers) refer to the sum of the products of the volume of transported cargo (passengers) multiplying by the transport distance. It is an important indicator to reflect the achievement of transportation industry. Normally, the shortest distance between the departure station and the destination station (i.e., the payable distance) is the basis to calculate the freight ton-kilometers. This is an important indicator to show the total results of the transport industry, to prepare and examine the transport plan and to measure the efficiency, the labour productivity and the unit cost of transport.

The formula is as follows:

Freight ton-kilometers (passenger-kilometers) = $\sum$ {freight (passenger) traffic × distance of transportation}

Possession of Civil Motor Vehicles refer to the total numbers of vehicles that are registered and received vehicles license tags according to the Work Standard for Motor Vehicles Registration formulated by transport management office under department of public security at the end of reference period. They are divided into following categories according to the structure of motor vehicles: passenger vehicles, trucks and others; and private vehicles and vehicles for units use according to ownerships; working vehicles and non-working vehicles according to kind of usage; large passenger vehicles, medium passenger vehicles, small passenger vehicles and mini passenger vehicle, heavy trucks, light–heavy trucks, light trucks and mini trucks according to sizes of vehicles.

Business Volume of Postal and Telecommunications refers to the total amount of postal and telecommunication services, expressed in value terms, provided by the post and telecommunications departments for society. Business volume of post and telecommunications is the sum of each service in kind multiplying with its correspondent unit price(constant price).Business without constant price add their business revenue directly.

Number of Fixed Telephone Subscribers at Year–end refers to the persons who own mobile telephone numbers and are connected with the mobile telephone communication network through the mobile telephone switchboards, including contracted subscribers and pre–paid subscribers for intelligent network. One mobile telephone is taken as a subscriber.

Number of Mobile Telephone Subscribers at Year–end refers to subscribers that are connected to the local telecommunication service provider through fix line network, including household subscribers, institutional subscribers and public telephones.

16 国内贸易

Domestic Trade

资料整理人员：朱　莉　王　芳

国 内 贸 易

Domestic Trade
2019

社会消费品零售总额	Total Retail Sales of Consumer Goods	22722.31	(亿元)
商品零售额	Retail Sales	19909.72	(亿元)
餐饮收入额	Food and Beverage Revenue	2812.59	(亿元)

社会消费品零售总额(亿元)
Total Retail Sales of Consumer Goods(100 million yuan)

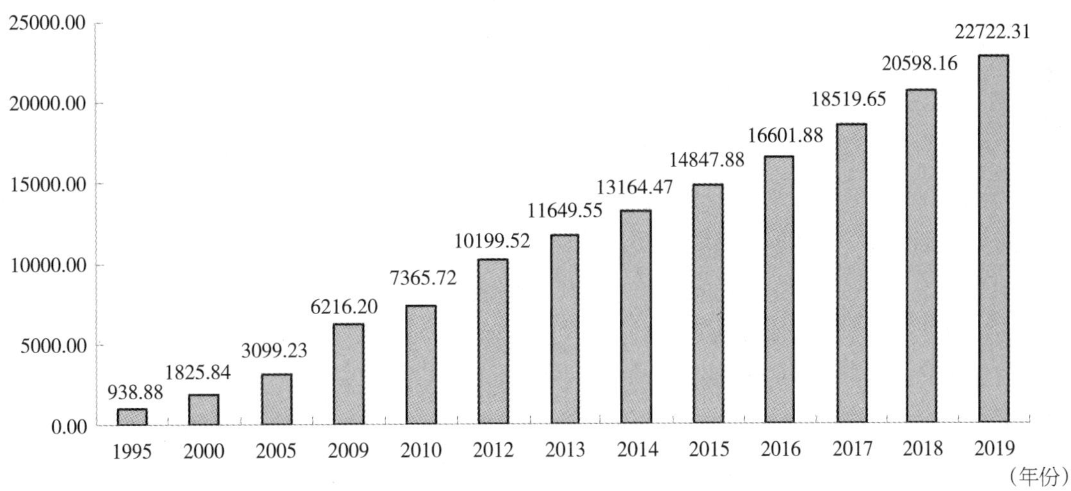

社会消费品零售总额(亿元)
Total Retail Sales of Consumer Goods(100 million yuan)

年份 year	1995	2000	2005	2009	2010	2012	2013	2014	2015	2016	2017	2018	2019
社会消费品零售总额 Total Retail Sales of Consumer Goods	938.88	1825.84	3099.23	6216.20	7365.72	10199.52	11649.55	13164.47	14847.88	16601.88	18519.65	20598.16	22722.31

注:1995年及以后社会消费品零售总额根据2018年经济普查数据调整。
Note:Since 1995,the total retail sales of consumer goods were readjusted according to the data of general economic survey.

16-1 按地区分社会消费品零售总额
Total Retail Sales of Consumer Goods by Region

单位:亿元 (100 million yuan)

年份 Year	零售额 Total Retail Sales of Consumer Goods	市 City	县 County	县以下 Below County Level
1978	59.84	19.24	16.56	24.04
1980	81.91	28.98	17.01	35.92
1985	181.17	75.26	31.64	74.17
1990	326.36	166.44	45.62	114.3
1991	362.26	190.65	50.04	121.57
1992	411.52	221.59	55.04	134.89
1993	522.67	294.56	69.05	159.05
1994	727.41	413.71	102.25	211.44
1995	938.88	543.89	128.73	266.26
1996	1157.35	695.38	131.60	330.37
1997	1362.42	812.56	148.47	401.39
1998	1503.98	909.75	158.45	435.78
1999	1645.96	1037.75	153.64	454.57
2000	1825.84	1151.48	181.27	493.08
2001	2020.53	1296.20	198.67	525.66
2002	2183.80	1466.37	205.82	511.61
2003	2425.08	1610.79	223.90	590.39
2004	2711.28	2105.44	284.86	320.99
2005	3099.23	2160.36	290.04	648.83
2006	3601.89	2528.90	338.91	734.07
2007	4294.36	3014.43	410.45	869.48
2008	5346.00	3753.37	514.16	1078.46
2009	6216.20	4328.55	615.30	1272.35
2010	7365.72	(城镇)6235.18	(城区)5282.73	(乡村)1130.53
2011	8792.13	(城镇)7453.26	(城区)6216.18	(乡村)1338.87
2012	10199.52	(城镇)8680.56	(城区)7139.30	(乡村)1518.96
2013	11649.55	(城镇)9855.37	(城区)7624.26	(乡村)1794.18
2014	13164.47	(城镇)11170.41	(城区)8632.97	(乡村)1994.06
2015	14847.88	(城镇)12588.85	(城区)9636.71	(乡村)2259.03
2016	16601.88	(城镇)14088.49	(城区)10685.95	(乡村)2513.39
2017	18519.65	(城镇)15729.03	(城区)11825.29	(乡村)2790.62
2018	20598.16	(城镇)17501.70	(城区)13035.36	(乡村)3096.45
2019	22722.31	(城镇)19311.04	(城区)14245.87	(乡村)3411.27

注:1.1996 年及以后社会消费品零售总额及各分组指标中不含售给城乡居民生活用住房的零售额。
2.1992年及以后社会消费品零售总额及各分组指标根据2018年经济普查数据调整。
3.2010 年起采用国家新制定的城乡划分标准:城镇(其中:城区)、乡村

Note:a)Since 1996, the residential house was exclued in the total retail sales of consumer goods and all the targets by groups.
b)Since 1992,the total retail sales of consumer goods and all the targets by groups were readjusted according to the data of general economic survey.
c)Since 2010, a new towm and country division national standard is applied:town(including urban area), country.

16-2 分市、州社会消费品零售总额

Total Retail Sales of Consumer Goods by Cities and Prefectures

单位:亿元 (100 million yuan)

地区	Region	2012	2013	2014	2015	2016	2017	2018	2019
全省	**Province**	**10199.52**	**11649.55**	**13164.47**	**14847.88**	**16601.88**	**18519.65**	**20598.16**	**22722.31**
武汉	Wuhan	3703.08	4205.74	4788.39	5301.82	5843.66	6493.24	7169.70	7774.49
黄石	Huangshi	473.52	532.70	587.52	655.70	735.40	827.02	921.34	1026.38
十堰	Shiyan	494.33	566.76	628.05	729.39	832.28	948.85	1064.33	1193.01
宜昌	Yichang	779.84	911.85	996.47	1116.42	1273.20	1373.13	1530.34	1710.43
襄阳	Xiangyang	858.82	999.11	1085.03	1217.73	1388.75	1562.75	1747.86	1955.18
鄂州	Ezhou	198.87	226.55	248.34	280.74	321.05	365.01	411.03	455.72
荆门	Jingmen	375.17	430.14	479.37	570.52	649.14	732.09	822.03	917.06
孝感	Xiaogan	576.62	659.22	728.20	836.10	929.39	1030.35	1148.46	1278.66
荆州	Jingzhou	751.47	860.84	957.74	1075.99	1208.61	1350.77	1505.48	1671.47
黄冈	Huanggang	614.27	703.67	785.51	961.70	1068.03	1197.65	1334.86	1470.72
咸宁	Xianning	321.42	369.10	407.38	449.69	499.03	566.02	634.74	708.40
随州	Suizhou	323.58	344.47	384.21	430.64	482.68	535.80	595.24	654.64
恩施	Enshi	212.07	247.11	440.80	491.03	553.63	620.94	689.59	763.78
仙桃	Xiantao	191.90	221.05	248.80	281.60	315.40	355.37	398.74	445.25
潜江	Qianjiang	141.74	161.90	166.42	185.92	208.38	233.20	260.54	291.35
天门	Tianmen	176.42	202.27	224.31	248.66	277.47	309.82	344.33	384.96
神农架	Shennongjia	6.39	7.07	7.96	14.23	15.77	17.64	19.56	20.83

注:1.本表各市、州数据包含了"其他"部分的全口径数据;

2.以上数据根据经济普查的结果进行了调整。

Note:a)"Others " was included in the total retail sales of consumer goods in the form.

b)Total was adjusted accoding to the economic census data.

16-3 批发和零售业连锁经营情况
Basic Conditions of Wholesale and Retail Sale Chain Stores Industries

指标名称		Item		合计 Total		直营店 Direct Sales Store		加盟店 League Store	
				2018	2019	2018	2019	2018	2019
一、门店总数	(个)	Number of Stores	(unit)	10667	12177	7967	8581	2700	3596
其中:批发业	(个)	Number of Stores	(unit)	828	858	456	495	372	363
零售业	(个)	Number of Stores	(unit)	9839	11319	7511	8086	2328	3233
二、零售营业面积	(百平方米)	Floor Space of Retail Business	(100 sq.m)	73091	69419	71067	66752	2024	2666
其中:批发业	(百平方米)	Floor Space of Retail Business	(100 sq.m)	3538	4175	2854	3491	684	684
零售业	(百平方米)	Floor Space of Retail Business	(100 sq.m)	69553	65244	68213	63261	1340	1982
三、从业人员	(人)	Person Engaged	(person)	127942	126744	121531	119268	6411	7476
其中:批发业	(个)	Person Engaged	(person)	6965	7904	6071	7058	894	846
零售业	(人)	Person Engaged	(person)	120977	118840	115460	112210	5517	6630
四、商品购进总额	(亿元)	Total Value of Commodities Purchased	(100 000 000 yuan)	1931.39	1978.23	1903.80	1942.82	27.59	35.40
#统一配送商品购进额		#Total Purchasing Value		1037.48	1200.32	1030.14	1191.04	7.34	9.29
#自有配送中心配送商品购进额		#Commodities Purchased From Dispatching Center		764.68	797.62	757.87	788.69	6.81	8.94
#非自有配送中心配送商品购进额		#Commodities Purchased From Nondispatching Center		102.66	103.07	102.45	102.91	0.21	0.16
五、商品销售额	(亿元)	Sales Amount	(100 000 000 yuan)	2196.59	2195.76	2164.06	2149.96	32.54	45.80
#零售额		#Retail Sales		1798.56	1816.22	1788.86	1801.29	9.70	14.93

16-4 住宿和餐饮业连锁经营情况
Basic Conditions of Hotels and Catering Services Chain Stores Industries

指标名称	Item	合计 Total		直营店 Direct Sales Store		加盟店 League Store	
		2018	2019	2018	2019	2018	2019
一、门店总数 (个)	Number of Stores (unit)	1403	1666	1402	1646	1	20
二、餐饮营业面积 (百平方米)	Floor Space of Restaurant Business (100 sq.m)	6342	5405	6342	5353		52
三、从业人员 (人)	Person Engaged (person)	45017	34726	44995	34027	22	699
四、客房数 (间)	Number of Hotel Rooms (unit)	7145	6733	7083	6671	62	62
五、床位数 (个)	Number of Beds (unit)	9146	9155	9048	9057	98	98
六、餐位数 (位)	Restaurant Seating Capacity	137006	136987	137006	135657		1330
七、商品购进总额 (万元)	Total Value of Commodities Purchased (10 000 yuan)	259148	274764	259146	271296	2	3468
#统一配送商品购进额	#Total Purchasing Value	213550	220334	213548	216866	2	3468
#自有配送中心配送商品购进额	#Commodities Purchased From Dispatching Center	112058	106302	112056	106300	2	2
非自有配送中心配送商品购进额	#Commodities Purchased From Nondispatching Center	58827	55565	58827	55565		
八、营业额 (万元)	Turnover (10 000 yuan)	833032	930715	832779	920843	254	9872
#餐费收入	Meals Revenue	780006	877763	780006	868145		9618
#商品销售额	Merchandise Sales	12006	15240	12004	15238	2	2

16-5 按登记注册类型分限额以上批发零售业基本情况(2019)

Basic Conditions of Enterprises above Designated Size of Wholesale and Retail Trade by Registration Type(2019)

登记注册类型	Type of Registration	法人企业数(个) Number of Corperations (unit)	年末从业人数(人) Person Engaged at Year-end (person)	零售营业面积(万平方米) Floor Space of Retail Business (10 000 sq.m)
总计	**Total**	**8451**	**503151**	**2177.8**
一、批发业	**Wholesales**	**3425**	**202030**	**466.5**
按登记注册类型分组	**Grouped by Registration Type**			
内资	**Domestic Funded Enterprises**	**3371**	**182405**	**440.9**
国有	State-owned Enterprises	51	13624	9.1
集体	Collective-owned Enterprises	14	288	1.2
股份合作	Cooperative Enterprises	2	122	0.4
联营企业	Joint Ownership Enterprises	1	225	
国有联营	State Joint Ownership Enterprises			
集体联营	Collective Joint Ownership Enterprises	1	225	
国有与集体联营	Joint State-collective Enterprises			
其他联营	Other Joint Ownership Enterprises			
有限责任公司	Limited Liability Corporations	1138	65758	173.5
国有独资公司	State Sole Funded Corporations	27	4625	18.3
其他有限责任公司	Other Limited Liability Corporations	1111	61133	155.3
股份有限公司	Share-holding Corporations Ltd.	87	43006	26.6
私营企业	Private Enterprises	2030	57043	225.8
私营独资	Private-funded Enterprises	44	758	2.3
私营合伙	Private Partnership Enterprises	5	128	0.9
私营有限责任公司	Private Limited Liability Corporations	1936	54052	219.8
私营股份有限公司	Private Share-holding Corporations Ltd.	45	2105	2.9
其他	Other Enterprises	48	2339	4.3
港澳台商投资企业	**Enterprises with Funds from Hongkong, Macao and Taiwan**	**28**	**11493**	**3.1**
合资经营	Joint-venture Enterprises	5	453	0.0
合作经营	Cooperative Enterprises			
独资经营	Enterprises with Sole Investment	22	10645	3.1
投资股份有限公司	Share-holding Corporations Ltd.	1	395	
外商投资企业	**Foreign Funded Enterprises**	**26**	**8132**	**22.6**
中外合资经营	Sino-foreign Joint-venture Enterprises	14	3095	21.5
外资企业	Enterprises with Sole Foreign Investment	10	4897	1.0
外商投资股份有限公司	Share-holding Co. Ltd. with Foreign Investment			
其他外资企业	Other Enterprises with Sole Foreign Investment	2	140	

16-5 续表 continued

登记注册类型	Type of Registration	法人企业数(个) Number of Corperations (unit)	年末从业人数(人) Person Engaged at Year-end (person)	零售营业面积(万平方米) Floor Space of Retail Business (10 000 sq.m)
二、零售业	**Retail Trade**	**5026**	**301121**	**1711.3**
按登记注册类型分组	**Grouped by Registration Type**			
内资	**Domestic Funded Enterprises**	**4974**	**279172**	**1597.6**
国有	State-owned Enterprises	70	3277	22.5
集体	Collective-owned Enterprises	50	7572	37.4
股份合作	Cooperative Enterprises	5	157	0.5
联营企业	Joint Ownership Enterprises	3	340	0.6
国有联营	State Joint Ownership Enterprises			
集体联营	Collective Joint Ownership Enterprises	1	285	0.5
国有与集体联营	Joint State-collective Enterprises	1	48	0.0
其他联营	Other Joint Ownership Enterprises	1	7	0.0
有限责任公司	Limited Liability Corporations	1392	102226	545.2
国有独资公司	State Sole Funded Corporations	11	2054	11.9
其他有限责任公司	Other Limited Liability Corporations	1381	100172	533.3
股份有限公司	Share-holding Corporations Ltd.	88	46950	385.6
私营企业	Private Enterprises	3350	117963	605.3
私营独资	Private-funded Enterprises	359	6293	31.5
私营合伙	Private Partnership Enterprises	24	358	1.6
私营有限责任公司	Private Limited Liability Corporations	2902	99049	525.5
私营股份有限公司	Private Share-holding Corporations Ltd.	65	12263	46.7
其他	Other Enterprises	16	687	0.5
港澳台商投资企业	**Enterprises with Funds from Hongkong, Macao and Taiwan**	**33**	**10849**	**48.3**
合资经营	Joint-venture Enterprises	7	1607	13.3
合作经营	Cooperative Enterprises			
独资经营	Enterprises with Sole Investment	24	8946	33.9
其他港澳台投资企业	Other Enterprises with Funds from Hongkong, Macao and Taiwan	2	296	1.1
外商投资企业	**Foreign Funded Enterprises**	**19**	**11100**	**65.4**
中外合资经营	Sino-foreign Joint-venture Enterprises	3	114	0.1
中外合作经营	Sino-foreign Cooperative Enterprises			
外资企业	Enterprises with Sole Foreign Investment	15	10771	65.2
外商投资股份有限公司	Share-holding Co. Ltd. with Foreign Investment	1	215	0.1

16-6 按国民经济行业限额以上批发零售业基本情况(2019)
Basic Conditions of Enterprises above Designated Size of Wholesale and Retail Trade by Sector(2019)

项目	Item	法人企业数(个) Number of Corperations (unit)	年末从业人数(人) Person Engaged at Year-end (person)	零售营业面积(万平方米) Floor Space of Retail Business (10 000 sq.m)
总计	**Total**	**8451**	**503151**	**2177.79**
一、批发业	**Wholesales**	**3425**	**202030**	**466.51**
农、林、牧、渔产品批发业	Wholesales of Agriculture, Forestry, Animal Husbandry and Fishery Products	264	7996	99.02
食品、饮料及烟草制品批发业	Wholesales of Foods, Beverage and Tobacco	570	51620	90.21
米、面制品及食用油批发业	Wholesales of Rice, Noodles and Edible Oil	96	4832	8.06
烟草制品批发业	Wholesales of Tobacco	23	11695	0.45
纺织、服装及家庭用品批发业	Wholesales of Textile Products, Garments and Household Articles	183	14145	12.81
服装批发业	Wholesales of Garments	49	5155	6.31
家用视听设备批发业	Wholesales of Household Audio-visual Equipment	16	1835	1.01
文化、体育用品及器材批发业	Wholesales of Cultural and Sports Goods and Equipments	65	6859	16.88
医药及医疗器材批发业	Wholesales of Medicnes and Medical Appliances	563	56178	45.16
矿产品、建材及化工产品批发业	Wholesales of Mineral Products, Building Materials and Chemical Products	1155	47046	163.63
煤炭及制品批发业	Wholesales of Coal and Coal-made Products	120	1992	3.82
石油及制品批发业	Wholesales of Petroleum Products	133	24966	92.87
非金属矿及制品批发	Wholesales of Non-metal and Non-metal Mines	46	1216	2.08
金属及金属矿批发业	Wholesales of Metal and Metal Mines	328	5724	5.94
建材批发业	Wholesales of Construction Materials	228	4892	39.21
化肥批发业	Wholesales of Chemical Fertilizers	92	4252	15.28
机械设备、五金产品及电子产品批发	Wholesales of Machinery Equipment, Hardware, and Electronic Products	534	16243	31.82
汽车及零配件批发业	Wholesales of Cars and Spare Parts	174	4952	10.56
计算机、软件及辅助设备批发业	Wholesales of Computers, Softwares and Assisted Equipments	32	1405	0.34
贸易经纪与代理	Trade Agent	7	101	
其他批发业	Other Wholesales	84	1842	6.98
二、零售业	**Retail Sales**	**5026**	**301121**	**1711.28**
综合零售业	Retail Sales of Department	797	134917	866.29
百货零售业	Department Stores	420	45135	468.48
超级市场零售业	Supermarkets	276	83914	358.23
食品、饮料及烟草制品专门零售业	Monopoly Retail of Foods, Beverage and Tobacco	534	20916	59.69
纺织、服装及日用品专门零售业	Monopoly Retail of Textile, Garments, and Daily Used Articles	244	14967	61.69
服装零售业	Retail Sales of Garments	131	9194	50.75
文化、体育用品及器材专门零售业	Monopoly Retail of Cultural, Sports Products and Equipments	201	6376	26.47
体育用品及器材零售业	Retail Sales of Sports Goods and Equipment	5	125	0.62
图书报刊零售业	Retail Sales of Books, Newspapers and Periodicals	23	1441	4.44
医药及医疗器材专门零售业	Monopoly Retail of Medicine and Medical Appliances	231	24262	62.98
汽车、摩托车、零配件和燃料及其他动力销售	Monopoly Retail of Cars, Motorcycle, Spare Parts, Fuel and Other Power	1491	57031	369.15
汽车新车零售业	Retail Sales of New Cars	1105	43819	258.33
机动车燃油零售业	Retail Sales of Motor Vehicles Fuels	224	10104	80.37
家用电器及电子产品专门零售业	Monopoly Retail of Home Appliances and Electronic Products	734	24400	139.87
家用视听设备零售业	Retail Sales of Home Audio-visual Equipment	316	9184	56.18
计算机、软件及辅助设备零售业	Retail Sales of Computers, Softwares and Assisted Equipments	138	3365	3.94
通信设备零售业	Retail Sales of Communication Equipments	64	4245	7.38
五金、家具及室内装修材料专门零售业	Monopoly Retail of Hardware, Furnitures and Decorative Materials	371	8044	79.58
货摊、无店铺及其他零售业	Retail Sales of Stalls、Storeless and Others	423	10208	45.55
互联网零售	Retail on the Internet	290	7030	13.26

16-7 按登记注册类型分限额以上住宿和餐饮业基本情况(2019)
Basic Conditions of Enterprises above Designated Size in Hotels and Catering Services by Registration Type(2019)

项目	Item	法人企业数(个) Number of Corperations (unit)	年末从业人数(人) Person Engaged at Year-end (person)	餐饮营业面积(万平方米) Floor Space of Catering Business (10 000 sq.m)
一、住宿业	**Hotel Trade**	**917**	**55138**	**346.89**
按登记注册类型分组	**Grouped by Registration Type**			
内资	**Domestic Funded Enterprises**	**897**	**51014**	**332.44**
国有	State-owned Enterprises	23	1689	11.35
集体	Collective-owned Enterprises	9	878	5.22
股份合作	Cooperative Enterprises			
联营企业	Joint Ownership Enterprises	1	167	0.07
国有联营	State Joint Ownership Enterprises	1	167	0.07
集体联营	Collective Joint Ownership Enterprises			
国有与集体联营	Joint State-collective Enterprises			
其他联营	Other Joint Ownership Enterprises			
有限责任公司	Limited Liability Corporations	285	20905	120.21
国有独资公司	State Sole Funded Corporations	11	1139	7.04
其他有限责任公司	Other Limited Liability Corporations	274	19766	113.17
股份有限公司	Share-holding Corporations Ltd.	20	2014	14.59
私营企业	Private Enterprises	559	25361	181.00
私营独资	Private-funded Enterprises	34	859	3.63
私营合伙	Private Partnership Enterprises	9	265	0.80
私营有限责任公司	Private Limited Liability Corporations	508	23934	174.97
私营股份有限公司	Private Share-holding Corporations Ltd.	8	303	1.61
其他	Other Enterprises			
港澳台商投资企业	**Enterprises with Funds from Hongkong, Macao and Taiwan**	**13**	**2831**	**9.15**
合资经营	Joint-venture Enterprises	2	390	2.99
合作经营	Cooperative Enterprises	1	317	0.24
独资经营	Enterprises with Sole Investment	6	1244	3.26
投资股份有限公司	Share-holding Co. Ltd. With Investment	3	695	1.98
外商投资企业	**Foreign Funded Enterprises**	**7**	**1293**	**5.31**
中外合资经营	Sino-foreign Joint-venture Enterprises	2	617	2.32
中外合作经营	Sino-foreign Cooperative Enterprises			
外资企业	Enterprises with Sole Foreign Investment	3	350	1.28
外商投资股份有限公司	Share-holding Co. Ltd. with Foreign Investment	2	326	1.72
二、餐饮业	**Catering Trade**	**1492**	**101226**	**373.19**
按登记注册类型分组	**Grouped by Registration Type**			
内资	**Domestic Funded Enterprises**	**1470**	**76975**	**338.22**
国有	State-owned Enterprises	8	402	3.66
集体	Collective-owned Enterprises	2	92	0.21
股份合作	Cooperative Enterprises			
联营企业	Joint Ownership Enterprises	1	138	0.50
国有联营	State Joint Ownership Enterprises			
集体联营	Collective Joint Ownership Enterprises	1	138	0.50
国有与集体联营	Joint State-collective Enterprises			
其他联营	Other Joint Ownership Enterprises			
有限责任公司	Limited Liability Corporations	306	19319	84.35
国有独资公司	State Sole Funded Corporations	2	1214	0.83
其他有限责任公司	Other Limited Liability Corporations	304	18105	83.53
股份有限公司	Share-holding Corporations Ltd.	19	4244	8.00
私营企业	Private Enterprises	1133	52660	240.48
私营独资	Private-funded Enterprises	192	3878	21.37
私营合伙	Private Partnership Enterprises	12	327	1.67
私营有限责任公司	Private Limited Liability Corporations	911	47721	198.00
私营股份有限公司	Private Share-holding Corporations Ltd.	18	734	19.45
其他	Other Enterprises	1	120	1.00
港澳台商投资企业	**Enterprises with Funds from Hongkong, Macao and Taiwan**	**12**	**19456**	**30.25**
合资经营	Joint-venture Enterprises	2	235	1.05
合作经营	Cooperative Enterprises			
独资经营	Enterprises with Sole Investment	10	19221	29.20
投资股份有限公司	Share-holding Co. Ltd. With Investment			
外商投资企业	**Foreign Funded Enterprises**	**10**	**4795**	**4.73**
中外合资经营	Sino-foreign Joint-venture Enterprises	1	546	0.81
外资企业	Enterprises with Sole Foreign Investment	9	4249	3.92
外商投资股份有限公司	Share-holding Co. Ltd. with Foreign Investment			
其他外商投资企业	Other Enterprises with Sole Foreign Investment			

16-8 按国民经济行业限额以上住宿和餐饮业基本情况(2019)
Basic Conditions of Enterprises above Designated Size of Hotels and Catering Services by Sector(2019)

行业	Item	法人企业数(个) Number of Corperations (unit)	年末从业人数(人) Person Engaged at Year-end (person)	餐饮营业面积(万平方米) Floor Space of Catering Business (10 000 sq.m)
总计	**Total**	**2409**	**156364**	**720.09**
一、住宿业	**Hotel**	**917**	**55138**	**346.89**
按国民经济行业分组	Grouped by Sector			
旅游饭店	Tourist Hotel	402	34702	203.99
一般旅馆	Regular Hotel	474	18107	114.93
民宿服务	B&B Service	2	23	0.15
其他住宿服务	Other Accomodation Service	39	2306	27.82
二、餐饮业	**Catering**	**1492**	**101226**	**373.19**
按国民经济行业分组	Grouped by Sector			
正餐服务	Dinner	1442	74109	335.24
快餐服务	Fast Food	23	18713	28.84
饮料及冷饮服务	Beverage and Cold Drink Services	8	4017	4.21
餐饮配送及外卖送餐服务	Catering Distribution and Takeaway Service	14	4240	3.72
其他餐饮业	Others	5	147	1.19

16-9 按国民经济行业分限额以上住宿和餐饮业经营情况(2019) Business Conditions of Enterprises above Designated Size of Hotels and Catering Services by Sector(2019)

行业	Item	营业额(亿元) Turnover (100 million yuan)	客房收入 Revnue from Guest Rooms	餐费收入 Revenue from Catering Bills	商品销售收入 Revenue from Commodity Sales	其他收入 Revenue from Others	年末住宿和餐饮企业拥有床位数(万个) Number of Beds owned by Hotels and Catering Enterprises at Year-end (10 000 units)	年末住宿和餐饮企业拥有餐位数(万位) Number of Seats owned by Hotels and Catering Enterprises at Year-end (10 000 units)
总计	**Total**	**435.31**	**102.23**	**307.62**	**12.77**	**12.70**	**27.62**	**99.45**
一、住宿业	**Hotel**	**135.22**	**77.38**	**46.37**	**2.76**	**8.71**	**21.10**	**24.52**
按国民经济行业分组	Grouped by Sector							
旅游饭店	Tourist Hotel	84.39	44.52	31.04	1.47	7.36	12.69	16.73
一般旅馆	Regular Hotel	46.64	30.41	13.88	1.23	1.13	7.67	7.00
民宿服务	B&B Service	0.10	0.08	0.01	0.00		0.02	0.00
其他住宿业	Other Accomodation Service	4.10	2.37	1.44	0.06	0.21	0.73	0.79
二、餐饮业	**Catering**	**300.09**	**24.85**	**261.25**	**10.01**	**3.99**	**6.52**	**74.93**
按国民经济行业分组	Grouped by Sector							
正餐服务	Dinner	218.19	24.85	181.61	8.47	3.27	6.52	63.06
快餐服务	Fast Food	52.06		51.65	0.01	0.40		6.05
饮料及冷饮服务	Beverage and Cold Drink Services	20.10		18.46	1.43	0.21		2.60
餐饮配送及外卖送餐服务	Catering Distribution and Takeaway Service	9.47		9.26	0.09	0.11		3.09
其他餐饮业	Others	0.27		0.27	0.00	0.00		0.13

16-10 按登记注册类型分限额以上住宿和餐饮业经营情况(2019)

单位:亿元

项 目	Item	营业额 Turnover	客房收入 Revnue from Guest Rooms
总计	**Total**	**435.31**	**102.23**
一、住宿业	**Hotels**	**135.22**	**77.38**
按登记注册类型分组	**Grouped by Registration Type**		
内资	**Domestic Funded Enterprises**	**124.63**	**71.49**
国有	State-Owned Enterprises	3.47	1.48
集体	Collective-owned Enterprises	2.76	1.30
股份合作	Cooperative Enterprises		
联营企业	Joint Ownership Enterprises	0.23	0.11
国有联营	State Joint Ownership Enterprises	0.23	0.11
集体联营	Collective Joint Ownership Enterprises		
国有与集体联营	Joint State-collective Enterprises		
其他联营	Other Joint Ownership Enterprises		
有限责任公司	Limited Liability Corporations	47.66	26.93
国有独资公司	State Sole Funded Corporations	2.64	1.17
其他有限责任公司	Other Limited Liability Corporations	45.03	25.76
股份有限公司	Share-holding Corporations Ltd.	3.76	2.06
私营企业	Private Enterprises	66.73	39.61
私营独资	Private-funded Enterprises	3.65	2.83
私营合伙	Private Partnership Enterprises	0.87	0.47
私营有限责任公司	Private Limited Liability Corporations	61.38	35.72
私营股份有限公司	Private Share-holding Corporations Ltd.	0.83	0.59
其他	Other Enterprises		
港澳台商投资企业	**Enterprises with Funds from Hongkong, Macao and Taiwan**	**7.48**	**4.24**
合资经营	Joint-venture Enterprises	1.55	0.67
合作经营	Cooperative Enterprises	0.86	0.51
独资经营	Enterprises with Sole Investment	2.96	1.74
投资股份有限公司	Share-holding Co. Ltd. With Investment	1.85	1.19
外商投资企业	**Foreign Funded Enterprises**	**3.11**	**1.64**
中外合资经营	Sino-Foreign Joint-venture Enterprises	1.47	0.70
外资企业	Enterprises with Sole Foreign Investment	0.86	0.41
外商投资股份有限公司	Share-holding Co. Ltd. with Foreign Investment	0.79	0.53
其他外商投资企业	Other Foreign Founded Enterprises		
二、餐饮业	**Catering**	**300.09**	**24.85**
按登记注册类型分组	**Grouped by Registration Type**		
内资	**Domestic Funded Enterprises**	**225.55**	**24.64**
国有	State-Owned Enterprises	0.99	0.34
集体	Collective-owned Enterprises	0.49	0.00
股份合作	Cooperative Enterprises		
联营企业	Joint Ownership Enterprises	0.40	
国有联营	State Joint Ownership Enterprises		
集体联营	Collective Joint Ownership Enterprises	0.40	
国有与集体联营	Joint State-collective Enterprises		
其他联营	Other Joint Ownership Enterprises		
有限责任公司	Limited Liability Corporations	56.91	6.14
国有独资公司	State Sole Funded Corporations	2.78	
其他有限责任公司	Other Limited Liability Corporations	54.13	6.14
股份有限公司	Share-holding Corporations Ltd.	11.50	0.38
私营企业	Private Enterprises	155.01	17.72
私营独资	Private-funded Enterprises	24.04	2.60
私营合伙	Private Partnership Enterprises	1.02	0.12
私营有限责任公司	Private Limited Liability Corporations	128.32	14.69
私营股份有限公司	Private Share-holding Corporations Ltd.	1.62	0.32
其他	Other Enterprises	0.25	0.05
港澳台商投资企业	**Enterprises with Funds from Hongkong, Macao and Taiwan**	**63.36**	**0.17**
合资经营	Joint-venture Enterprises	0.30	0.06
合作经营	Cooperative Enterprises		
独资经营	Enterprises with Sole Investment	63.06	0.11
投资股份有限公司	Share-holding Co. Ltd. With Investment		
外商投资企业	**Foreign Funded Enterprises**	**11.18**	**0.04**
中外合资经营	Sino-Foreign Joint-venture Enterprises	1.02	
外资企业	Enterprises with Sole Foreign Investment	10.17	0.04

Business Conditions of Enterprises above Designated Size of Hotels and Catering Services by Registration Type(2019)

(100 million yuan)

餐费收入 Revenue from Catering Bills	商品销售收入 Revenue from Commodity Sales	其他收入 Revenue from Others	年末床位数 (万个) Number of Beds at Year-end (10 000 units)	年末餐位数 (万位) Number of Seats at Year-end (10 000 units)
307.62	**12.77**	**12.70**	**27.62**	**99.45**
46.37	**2.76**	**8.71**	**21.10**	**24.52**
42.40	**2.71**	**8.02**	**20.32**	**23.50**
1.73	0.04	0.23	0.40	0.87
1.30	0.03	0.14	0.23	0.51
0.10		0.01	0.03	0.04
0.10		0.01	0.03	0.04
15.37	1.00	4.36	8.55	7.75
0.77	0.21	0.48	0.32	0.54
14.60	0.80	3.87	8.23	7.21
1.25	0.12	0.33	0.58	0.81
22.65	1.51	2.96	10.52	13.52
0.66	0.13	0.03	0.44	0.40
0.40	0.00	0.00	0.10	0.04
21.36	1.38	2.92	9.82	12.78
0.23	0.01	0.00	0.16	0.30
2.80	**0.00**	**0.44**	**0.48**	**0.61**
0.88	0.00	0.00	0.07	0.04
0.33		0.02	0.04	0.14
0.91		0.31	0.24	0.20
0.56		0.10	0.11	0.19
1.17	**0.05**	**0.25**	**0.30**	**0.41**
0.64	0.02	0.10	0.10	0.12
0.33	0.03	0.09	0.11	0.18
0.20	0.01	0.06	0.10	0.11
261.25	**10.01**	**3.99**	**6.52**	**74.93**
188.92	**8.59**	**3.39**	**6.43**	**64.84**
0.48	0.01	0.16	0.07	0.25
0.49	0.00		0.01	0.02
0.40				0.32
0.40				0.32
46.77	2.67	1.33	1.68	17.00
1.53	1.26			0.23
45.25	1.41	1.33	1.68	16.77
10.78	0.27	0.06	0.13	3.99
129.94	5.51	1.83	4.49	43.23
20.16	1.21	0.08	0.39	4.20
0.90	0.00	0.00	0.04	0.28
107.59	4.30	1.75	3.95	37.96
1.29	0.01	0.00	0.11	0.79
0.06	0.14		0.05	0.03
61.20	**1.41**	**0.58**	**0.08**	**8.37**
0.12		0.13	0.04	0.09
61.08	1.41	0.45	0.04	8.28
11.12	**0.00**	**0.02**	**0.02**	**1.72**
1.02				0.43
10.11	0.00	0.02	0.02	1.29

16-11 按登记注册类型分限额以上批发和零售业商品购、销、存总额(2019)
Total Purchases, Sales and Stock of Enterprises above Designated Size of Wholesale and Retail Trades by Registration Type(2019)

单位:亿元 (100 million yuan)

项目	Item	购进总额 Total Purchasing Value	销售总额 Total Sales Value	批发 Whole-sales	零售 Retail Sales	年末库存总额 Total Value of Inventory at Year-end
总计	**Total**	**17832.79**	**20460.40**	**13604.32**	**6856.09**	**1087.85**
一、批发业	**Wholesales**	**12462.60**	**14194.68**	**13215.68**	**979.01**	**691.38**
按登记注册类型分组	**Grouped by Registration Type**					
内资	**Domestic Funded Enterprises**	**11305.10**	**12776.07**	**12009.87**	**766.20**	**634.56**
国有	State-owned Enterprises	517.51	808.84	787.54	21.30	36.65
集体	Collective-owned Enterprises	7.59	9.69	6.66	3.03	0.20
股份合作	Cooperative Enterprises	0.74	0.81	0.40	0.41	0.04
联营企业	Joint Ownership Enterprises	0.24	0.66	0.66		0.04
国有联营	State Joint Ownership Enterprises					
集体联营	Collective Joint Ownership Enterprises	0.24	0.66	0.66		0.04
国有与集体联营	Joint State-collective Enterprises					
其他联营	Other Joint Ownership Enterprises					
有限责任公司	Limited Liability Corporations	6395.28	6994.58	6586.58	408.00	304.40
国有独资公司	State Sole Funded Corporations	617.91	644.57	609.15	35.42	15.52
其他有限责任公司	Other Limited Liability Corporations	5777.36	6350.01	5977.44	372.58	288.87
股份有限公司	Share-holding Corporations Ltd.	2096.85	2245.00	2170.36	74.64	174.51
私营企业	Private Enterprises	2245.47	2659.27	2417.92	241.35	117.19
私营独资	Private-funded Enterprises	30.50	39.28	28.79	10.49	0.61
私营合伙	Private Partnership Enterprises	2.26	2.78	2.01	0.77	0.03
私营有限责任公司	Private Limited Liability Corporations	2161.52	2557.10	2336.83	220.26	114.07
私营股份有限公司	Private Share-holding Corporations Ltd.	51.19	60.12	50.29	9.83	2.48
其他	Other Enterprises	41.42	57.22	39.75	17.47	1.53
港澳台商投资企业	**Enterprises with Funds from Hongkong, Macao and Taiwan**	**498.14**	**686.88**	**658.12**	**28.76**	**17.13**
合资经营	Joint-venture Enterprises	19.91	22.14	21.90	0.24	1.84
合作经营	Cooperative Enterprises					
独资经营	Enterprises with Sole Investment	471.12	654.77	626.25	28.52	13.34
投资股份有限公司	Share-holding Corporations Ltd.	7.12	9.98	9.98		1.96
外商投资企业	**Foreign Funded Enterprises**	**659.35**	**731.73**	**547.68**	**184.04**	**39.69**
中外合资经营	Sino-foreign Joint-venture Enterprises	457.51	499.73	433.90	65.83	24.44
外资企业	Enterprises with Sole Foreign Investment	198.59	228.18	109.97	118.21	15.22
外商投资股份有限公司	Share-holding Co. Ltd. with Foreign Investment					
其他外资企业	Other Enterprises with Sole Foreign Investment	3.25	3.81	3.81		0.02
二、零售业	**Retail Trade**	**5370.20**	**6265.72**	**388.64**	**5877.08**	**396.47**
按登记注册类型分组	**Grouped by Registration Type**					
内资	**Domestic Funded Enterprises**	**4941.38**	**5762.34**	**318.85**	**5443.50**	**377.43**
国有	State-owned Enterprises	60.06	90.04	9.65	80.38	2.08
集体	Collective-owned Enterprises	83.30	94.83	2.24	92.59	7.24
股份合作	Cooperative Enterprises	1.31	2.47	0.52	1.95	0.06
联营企业	Joint Ownership Enterprises	43.37	47.02	0.12	46.90	0.22
国有联营	State Joint Ownership Enterprises					
集体联营	Collective Joint Ownership Enterprises	41.34	44.60		44.60	0.22
国有与集体联营	Joint State-collective Enterprises	1.84	2.18		2.18	0.00
其他联营	Other Joint Ownership Enterprises	0.19	0.24	0.12	0.12	0.00
有限责任公司	Limited Liability Corporations	2057.30	2439.24	118.51	2320.73	158.30
国有独资公司	State Sole Funded Corporations	61.28	88.76	26.32	62.44	2.63
其他有限责任公司	Other Limited Liability Corporations	1996.02	2350.48	92.19	2258.29	155.67
股份有限公司	Share-holding Corporations Ltd.	1062.25	1106.94	69.26	1037.68	66.73
私营企业	Private Enterprises	1628.18	1975.00	117.63	1857.37	142.72
私营独资	Private-funded Enterprises	115.27	132.43	2.32	130.11	3.79
私营合伙	Private Partnership Enterprises	4.43	4.92	0.05	4.87	0.17
私营有限责任公司	Private Limited Liability Corporations	1445.96	1750.92	103.59	1647.33	133.47
私营股份有限公司	Private Share-holding Corporations Ltd.	62.52	86.73	11.67	75.06	5.29
其他	Other Enterprises	5.60	6.81	0.91	5.90	0.09
港澳台商投资企业	**Enterprises with Funds from Hongkong, Macao and Taiwan**	**196.16**	**254.54**	**1.11**	**253.43**	**9.01**
合资经营	Joint-venture Enterprises	8.87	22.85		22.85	0.59
合作经营	Cooperative Enterprises					
独资经营	Enterprises with Sole Investment	185.93	229.69	1.11	228.58	8.22
其他港澳台投资企业	Other Enterprises with Funds from Hongkong, Macao and Taiwan	1.36	2.01		2.01	0.20
外商投资企业	**Foreign Funded Enterprises**	**232.66**	**248.83**	**68.68**	**180.15**	**10.03**
中外合资经营	Sino-foreign Joint-venture Enterprises	1.67	1.98	0.09	1.90	0.33
中外合作经营	Sino-foreign Cooperative Enterprises					
外资企业	Enterprises with Sole Foreign Investment	229.64	245.73	68.52	177.21	9.69
外商投资股份有限公司	Share-holding Co. Ltd. with Foreign Investment	1.35	1.11	0.07	1.04	0.01

16-12 按国民经济行业分限额以上批发和零售业商品购、销、存总额(2019)
Total Purchases, Sales and Stock of Enterprises above Designated Size of Wholesale and Retail Trade by Sector(2019)

单位:亿元 (100 million yuan)

行业	Item	购进总额 Total Purchasing Value	销售总额 Total Sales Value	批发 Whole sales	零售 Retail Sales	年末库存总额 Total Value of Inventory at Year-end
总计	**Total**	**17832.79**	**20460.40**	**13604.32**	**6856.09**	**1087.85**
一、批发业	**Wholesales**	**12462.60**	**14194.68**	**13215.68**	**979.01**	**691.38**
农、林、牧、渔产品批发业	Wholesales of Agriculture, Forestry, Animal Husbandry and Fishery Products	427.65	495.75	434.34	61.41	64.50
食品、饮料及烟草制品批发业	Wholesales of Foods, Beverage and Tobacco	1504.21	2099.66	1882.89	216.77	105.97
米、面制品及食用油批发业	Wholesales of Rice, Noodles and Edible Oil	158.90	216.23	181.26	34.97	8.31
烟草制品批发业	Wholesales of Tobacco	488.65	766.48	757.06	9.42	30.04
纺织、服装及家庭用品批发业	Wholesales of Textile Products, Garments and Household Articles	354.52	417.00	286.38	130.62	37.16
服装批发业	Wholesales of Garments	132.57	167.53	51.90	115.63	10.02
家用视听设备批发业	Wholesales of Household Audio-visual Equipment	77.17	78.82	75.13	3.69	10.14
文化、体育用品及器材批发业	Wholesales of Cultural and Sports Goods and Equipments	234.19	254.51	223.87	30.64	18.60
医药及医疗器材批发业	Wholesales of Medicnes and Medical Appliances	2051.19	2385.55	2324.97	60.58	212.44
矿产品、建材及化工产品批发业	Wholesales of Mineral Products, Building Materials and Chemical Products	6512.17	7018.99	6649.72	369.27	173.58
煤炭及制品批发业	Wholesales of Coal and Coal-made Products	354.82	389.06	335.65	53.41	6.40
石油及制品批发业	Wholesales of Petroleum Products	3435.20	3573.47	3347.67	225.80	86.01
非金属矿及制品批发	Wholesales of Non-metal and Non-metal Mines	43.12	45.54	43.81	1.73	3.69
金属及金属矿批发业	Wholesales of Metal and Metal Mines	1739.08	1848.75	1803.48	45.27	50.64
建材批发业	Wholesales of Construction Materials	202.92	241.63	215.94	25.69	7.27
化肥批发业	Wholesales of Chemical Fertilizers	266.88	273.77	270.03	3.74	11.42
机械设备、五金产品及电子产品批发	Wholesales of Machinery Equipment, Hardware, and Electronic Products	1276.34	1392.75	1293.64	99.11	73.30
汽车及零配件批发业	Wholesales of Cars and Spare Parts	588.13	644.81	601.09	43.72	49.26
计算机、软件及辅助设备批发业	Wholesales of Computers, Softwares and Assisted Equipments	330.99	332.38	330.35	2.03	2.50
贸易经纪与代理	Trade Agent	8.11	11.33	11.33		0.26
其他批发业	Other Wholesales	94.21	119.16	108.55	10.61	5.55
二、零售业	**Retail Sales**	**5370.20**	**6265.72**	**388.64**	**5877.08**	**396.47**
综合零售业	Retail Sales of Department	1614.51	1807.86	69.43	1738.43	119.28
百货零售业	Department Stores	841.77	933.38	29.09	904.29	56.98
超级市场零售业	Supermarkets	706.37	793.14	22.42	770.72	57.76
食品、饮料及烟草制品专门零售业	Monopoly Retail of Foods, Beverage and Tobacco	308.63	367.39	32.81	334.58	15.60
纺织、服装及日用品专门零售业	Monopoly Retail of Textile, Garments, and Daily Used Articles	105.69	151.27	15.62	135.65	21.09
服装零售业	Retail Sales of Garments	66.97	95.42	5.34	90.08	11.44
文化、体育用品及器材专门零售业	Monopoly Retail of Cultural, Sports Products and Equipments	58.22	86.82	8.90	77.92	11.55
体育用品及器材零售业	Retail Sales of Sports Goods and Equipment	3.86	4.21		4.21	0.13
图书报刊零售业	Retail Sales of Books, Newspapers and Periodicals	10.87	11.52	0.67	10.86	2.92
医药及医疗器材专门零售业	Monopoly Retail of Medicine and Medical Appliances	133.95	178.65	16.39	162.26	18.18
汽车、摩托车、零配件和燃料及其他动力销售	Monopoly Retail of Cars, Motorcycle, Spare Parts, Fuel and Other Power	1707.43	2046.45	117.69	1928.75	143.15
汽车新车零售业	Retail Sales of New Cars	1295.33	1525.72	41.79	1483.93	132.65
机动车燃油零售业	Retail Sales of Motor Vehicles Fuels	358.13	453.36	68.78	384.58	6.87
家用电器及电子产品专门零售业	Monopoly Retail of Home Appliances and Electronic Products	480.61	525.93	112.85	413.09	38.45
家用视听设备零售业	Retail Sales of Home Audio-visual Equipment	122.38	145.16	10.62	134.55	9.74
计算机、软件及辅助设备零售业	Retail Sales of Computers, Softwares and Assisted Equipments	37.35	46.32	3.60	42.73	2.48
通信设备零售业	Retail Sales of Communication Equipments	142.92	153.46	71.90	81.56	1.96
五金、家具及室内装修材料专门零售业	Monopoly Retail of Hardware, Furnitures and Decorative Materials	205.42	243.16	8.26	234.90	15.31
货摊、无店铺及其他零售业	Retail Sales of Stalls、Storeless and Others	755.73	858.19	6.68	851.51	13.87
互联网零售	Retail on the Internet	711.80	803.98	2.64	801.34	11.79

16-13　限额以上批发和零售业企业资产及负债(2019)
Assets and Liabilities of Enterprises above Designated Size of Wholesale and Retail Trade(2019)

单位:亿元　　(100 million yuan)

项目	Item	流动资产合计 Total Circulating Funds	固定资产原价 Original Price of Fixed Assets	资产总计 Total Assets	负债合计 Total Liabilities	所有者权益合计 Total Creditor's Equity
总计	**Total**	**5878.37**	**1449.86**	**8026.84**	**5751.06**	**2261.59**
一、批发业	**Wholesales**	**4401.55**	**787.32**	**5657.19**	**4118.86**	**1529.28**
1.按登记注册类型分组	**Grouped by Registration Type**					
内资	**Domestic Funded Enterprises**	**3835.26**	**745.44**	**4981.00**	**3554.60**	**1417.34**
国有	State-owned Enterprises	170.83	68.54	219.97	90.18	129.79
集体	Collective-owned Enterprises	1.75	0.64	2.61	1.35	1.05
股份合作	Cooperative Enterprises	0.08	0.05	0.11	0.05	0.05
联营企业	Joint Ownership Enterprises	0.30	0.00	0.31	0.02	0.29
国有联营	State Joint Ownership Enterprises					
集体联营	Collective Joint Ownership Enterprises	0.30	0.00	0.31	0.02	0.29
国有与集体联营	Joint State-collective Enterprises					
其他联营	Other Joint Ownership Enterprises					
有限责任公司	Limited Liability Corporations	2216.41	288.05	2769.55	2170.89	593.48
国有独资公司	State Sole Funded Corporations	202.37	22.41	311.33	244.11	67.22
其他有限责任公司	Other Limited Liability Corporations	2014.04	265.64	2458.22	1926.78	526.26
股份有限公司	Share-holding Corporations Ltd.	714.69	250.44	1069.30	698.83	369.92
私营企业	Private Enterprises	724.97	130.41	903.84	587.75	312.98
私营独资	Private-funded Enterprises	4.06	2.55	6.13	3.43	2.68
私营合伙	Private Partnership Enterprises	0.11	0.16	0.25	0.23	0.03
私营有限责任公司	Private Limited Liability Corporations	695.57	121.40	865.83	567.93	294.81
私营股份有限公司	Private Share-holding Corporations Ltd.	25.23	6.30	31.63	16.17	15.46
其他	Other Enterprises	6.23	7.31	15.30	5.53	9.77
港澳台商投资企业	**Enterprises with Funds from Hongkong, Macao and Taiwan**	**410.03**	**13.12**	**472.87**	**350.99**	**121.88**
合资经营	Joint-venture Enterprises	101.42	0.49	119.61	95.49	24.12
合作经营	Cooperative Enterprises					
独资经营	Enterprises with Sole Investment	292.00	9.96	327.46	243.12	84.34
投资股份有限公司	Share-holding Co. Ltd. With Investment	16.61	2.67	25.80	12.38	13.42
外商投资企业	**Foreign Funded Enterprises**	**156.25**	**28.77**	**203.32**	**213.27**	**-9.94**
中外合资经营	Sino-foreign Joint-venture Enterprises	88.70	23.71	131.84	155.93	-24.08
外资企业	Enterprises with Sole Foreign Investment	58.31	4.93	61.96	47.76	14.20
外商投资股份有限公司	Share-holding Co. Ltd. with Foreign Investment					
其他外资企业	Other Enterprises with Sole Foreign Investment	9.25	0.13	9.52	9.58	-0.06
2.按国民经济行业分组	**Grouped by Sector**					
农、林、牧、渔产品批发业	Wholesales of Agriculture, Forestry, Animal Husbandry and Fishery Products	194.46	39.18	251.93	175.91	75.92
食品、饮料及烟草制品批发业	Wholesales of Foods, Beverage and Tobacco	797.23	164.76	978.36	600.43	377.27
米、面制品及食用油批发业	Wholesales of Rice, Noodles and Edible Oil	85.41	21.51	126.01	71.63	54.37
烟草制品批发业	Wholesales of Tobacco	159.91	61.35	200.72	75.52	125.20
纺织、服装及家庭用品批发业	Wholesales of Textile Products, Garments and Household Articles	150.37	10.14	162.57	137.99	24.38
服装批发业	Wholesales of Garments	35.86	4.24	40.05	32.52	7.53
家用视听设备批发业	Wholesales of Household Audio-visual Equipment	56.25	0.43	57.37	55.36	2.00
文化、体育用品及器材批发业	Wholesales of Cultural and Sports Goods and Equipments	189.93	16.96	214.33	159.52	54.79
医药及医疗器材批发业	Wholesales of Medicnes and Medical Appliances	1367.52	96.27	1595.43	1143.48	451.76
矿产品、建材及化工产品批发业	Wholesales of Mineral Products, Building Materials and Chemical Products	1114.32	419.49	1768.81	1262.98	498.88
煤炭及制品批发业	Wholesales of Coal and Coal-made Products	87.52	11.80	109.61	62.99	46.15
石油及制品批发业	Wholesales of Petroleum Products	286.62	344.65	718.40	472.01	241.38
非金属及金属矿批发业	Wholesales of Non-metellic Mineral and Metal Industry	33.00	2.89	69.71	63.38	6.34
金属及金属矿批发业	Wholesales of Metal and Metal Mines	466.93	24.33	527.01	406.30	119.58
建材批发业	Wholesales of Construction Materials	67.13	12.76	85.13	52.78	32.09
化肥批发业	Wholesales of Chemical Fertilizers	62.54	9.89	75.37	57.85	17.51
机械设备、五金产品及电子产品批发	Wholesales of Machinery Equipment, Hardware and Electronic Products	558.64	32.95	649.14	612.71	35.78
汽车及零配件批发业	Wholesales of Cars and Spare Parts	266.75	11.43	315.28	292.98	21.93
计算机、软件及辅助设备批发业	Wholesales of Computers, Softwares and Assisted Equipments	161.08	0.86	162.37	145.41	16.93
贸易经纪与代理	Trade Agent	3.22	0.70	3.40	2.51	0.89
其他批发业	Other Wholesales	25.86	6.88	33.23	23.32	9.60

16-13 续表 continued

单位:亿元 (100 million yuan)

项 目	Item	流动资产合计 Total Circulating Funds	固定资产原价 Original Price of Fixed Assets	资产总计 Total Assets	负债合计 Total Liabilities	所有者权益合计 Total Creditor's Equity
二、零售业	**Retail Trade**	**1476.82**	**662.54**	**2369.65**	**1632.20**	**732.32**
1.按登记注册类型分组	**Grouped by Registration Type**					
内资	**Domestic Funded Enterprises**	**1327.25**	**602.49**	**2153.85**	**1465.25**	**683.47**
国有	State-owned Enterprises	10.12	15.52	29.22	17.58	11.59
集体	Collective-owned Enterprises	9.07	6.15	14.76	9.42	5.30
股份合作	Cooperative Enterprises	0.19	0.95	0.89	0.49	0.41
联营企业	Joint Ownership Enterprises	1.11	0.56	1.51	0.65	0.86
国有联营	State Joint Ownership Enterprises					
集体联营	Collective Joint Ownership Enterprises	0.69	0.39	0.88	0.27	0.61
国有与集体联营	Joint State-collective Enterprises	0.05	0.02	0.06	0.02	0.04
其他联营	Other Joint Ownership Enterprises	0.37	0.15	0.57	0.36	0.21
有限责任公司	Limited Liability Corporations	614.32	205.76	886.85	637.87	247.85
国有独资公司	State Sole Funded Corporations	6.50	18.12	37.20	24.63	12.56
其他有限责任公司	Other Limited Liability Corporations	607.82	187.64	849.65	613.24	235.29
股份有限公司	Share-holding Corporations Ltd.	159.60	200.50	462.90	306.83	156.07
私营企业	Private Enterprises	530.81	170.19	753.01	489.88	259.21
私营独资	Private-funded Enterprises	14.27	15.73	29.27	8.78	19.97
私营合伙	Private Partnership Enterprises	0.44	0.65	0.93	0.27	0.66
私营有限责任公司	Private Limited Liability Corporations	489.82	133.23	668.69	449.94	215.54
私营股份有限公司	Private Share-holding Corporations Ltd.	26.29	20.58	54.11	30.89	23.03
其他	Other Enterprises	2.03	2.84	4.72	2.53	2.19
港澳台商投资企业	**Enterprises with Funds from Hongkong, Macao and Taiwan**	**64.34**	**26.03**	**88.23**	**68.98**	**19.25**
合资经营	Joint-venture Enterprises	6.27	9.79	15.32	11.28	4.04
合作经营	Cooperative Enterprises					
独资经营	Enterprises with Sole Investment	57.76	15.69	72.39	57.26	15.13
其他港澳台投资企业	Other Enterprises with Funds from Hongkong, Macao and Taiwan	0.30	0.55	0.52	0.44	0.07
外商投资企业	**Foreign Funded Enterprises**	**85.24**	**34.02**	**127.57**	**97.97**	**29.60**
中外合资经营	Sino-foreign Joint-venture Enterprises	2.27	1.71	3.23	1.27	1.96
中外合作经营	Sino-foreign Cooperative Enterprises					
外资企业	Enterprises with Sole Foreign Investment	82.28	32.22	123.62	96.53	27.10
外商投资股份有限公司	Share-holding Co. Ltd. with Foreign Investment	0.68	0.10	0.72	0.17	0.55
2.按国民经济行业分组	**Grouped by Sector**					
综合零售业	Retail Sales of Department	368.20	312.18	804.37	533.17	270.71
百货零售业	Department Stores	216.55	175.04	497.94	327.01	170.53
超级市场零售业	Supermarkets	129.76	132.37	278.86	182.62	96.11
食品、饮料及烟草制品专门零售业	Monopoly Retail of Foods, Beverage and Tobacco	122.15	31.99	165.19	87.31	77.59
纺织、服装及日用品专门零售业	Monopoly Retail of Textile, Garments,and Daily Used Articles	75.84	22.00	101.42	66.19	34.99
服装零售业	Retail Sales of Garments	40.98	17.72	62.18	45.37	16.65
文化、体育用品及器材专门零售业	Monopoly Retail of Cultural, Sports Products and Equipments	35.30	11.80	47.47	32.62	14.62
体育用品及器材零售业	Retail Sales of Sports Goods and Equipment	0.35	0.32	0.44	1.65	-1.22
图书报刊零售业	Retail Sales of Books, Newspapers and Periodicals	9.62	4.78	14.06	8.38	5.66
医药及医疗器材专门零售业	Monopoly Retail of Medicine and Medical Appliances	69.59	17.14	91.66	70.52	21.11
汽车、摩托车、零配件和燃料及其他动力销售	Monopoly Retail of Cars, Motorcycle, Spare Parts, Fuel and Other Power	452.03	179.65	706.95	532.63	172.14
汽车新车零售业	Retail Sales of New Cars	386.74	90.30	509.58	382.39	126.26
机动车燃油零售业	Retail Sales of Motor Vehicles Fuels	45.56	80.26	167.12	134.26	31.68
家用电器及电子产品专门零售业	Monopoly Retail of Home Appliances and Electronic Products	143.28	41.52	186.48	114.35	71.18
家用视听设备零售业	Retail Sales of Home Audio-visual Equipment	32.10	13.10	47.07	26.50	20.48
计算机、软件及辅助设备零售业	Retail Sales of Computers, Softwares and Assisted Equipments	16.22	2.46	18.99	9.55	9.41
通信设备零售业	Retail Sales of Communication Equipments	35.35	1.52	37.26	31.86	5.39
五金、家具及室内装修材料专门零售业	Monopoly Retail of Hardware, Furnitures and Decorative Materials	67.99	18.73	91.77	58.77	32.61
货摊、无店铺及其他零售业	Retail Sales of Stalls ,Storeless and Others	142.43	27.54	174.34	136.63	37.35
互联网零售	Retail on the Internet	127.21	10.40	138.75	118.51	20.12

16-14 限额以上批发和零售业企业主要财务指标(2019)
Main Financial Indicators of Enterprises above Designated Size of Wholesale and Retail Trade(2019)

单位:亿元 (100 million yuan)

项目	Item	营业收入 Revenue of Business	营业成本 Cost of Business	其他业务利润 Profits of Other Business	利润总额 Total Profits
总计	**Total**	**17807.03**	**16037.10**	**73.95**	**482.54**
一、批发业	**Wholesales**	**12558.06**	**11480.78**	**22.97**	**329.54**
1.按登记注册类型分组	**Grouped by Registration Type**				
内资	**Domestic Funded Enterprises**	**11271.35**	**10380.14**	**4.94**	**297.38**
国有	State-owned Enterprises	682.00	484.11	0.58	78.13
集体	Collective-owned Enterprises	8.84	7.78		0.41
股份合作	Cooperative Enterprises	0.69	0.52		0.07
联营企业	Joint Ownership Enterprises	0.60	0.57	0.00	0.03
国有联营	State Joint Ownership Enterprises				
集体联营	Collective Joint Ownership Enterprises	0.60	0.57	0.00	0.03
国有与集体联营	Joint State-collective Enterprises				
其他联营	Other Joint Ownership Enterprises				
有限责任公司	Limited Liability Corporations	6163.64	5846.73	6.15	119.47
国有独资公司	State Sole Funded Corporations	576.93	560.50	0.13	9.46
其他有限责任公司	Other Limited Liability Corporations	5586.72	5286.23	6.02	110.01
股份有限公司	Share-holding Corporations Ltd.	1990.05	1854.40	-2.76	26.26
私营企业	Private Enterprises	2373.50	2142.91	0.97	69.09
私营独资	Private-funded Enterprises	35.58	31.65		2.01
私营合伙	Private Partnership Enterprises	2.67	2.34		0.24
私营有限责任公司	Private Limited Liability Corporations	2281.23	2060.57	0.98	64.61
私营股份有限公司	Private Share-holding Corporations Ltd.	54.03	48.34	-0.01	2.23
其他	Other Enterprises	52.02	43.12		3.92
港澳台商投资企业	**Enterprises with Funds from Hongkong, Macao and Taiwan**	**604.36**	**465.46**	**0.42**	**44.28**
合资经营	Joint-venture Enterprises	21.37	18.58	0.00	0.05
合作经营	Cooperative Enterprises				
独资经营	Enterprises with Sole Investment	574.13	439.97	0.41	43.68
投资股份有限公司	Share-holding Co. Ltd. With Investment	8.87	6.91		0.55
外商投资企业	**Foreign Funded Enterprises**	**682.35**	**635.18**	**17.62**	**-12.12**
中外合资经营	Sino-foreign Joint-venture Enterprises	452.16	436.16	-0.02	-14.23
外资企业	Enterprises with Sole Foreign Investment	226.87	196.16	17.63	2.07
外商投资股份有限公司	Share-holding Co. Ltd. with Foreign Investment				
其他外资企业	Other Enterprises with Sole Foreign Investment	3.32	2.86	0.01	0.04
2.按国民经济行业分组	**Grouped by Sector**				
农、林、牧、渔产品批发业	Wholesales of Agriculture, Forestry, Animal Husbandry and Fishery Products	429.60	399.32	-10.09	17.52
食品、饮料及烟草制品批发业	Wholesales of Foods, Beverage and Tobacco	1800.11	1351.43	0.81	173.47
米、面制品及食用油批发业	Wholesales of Rice, Noodles and Edible Oil	200.69	185.44	0.05	3.96
烟草制品批发业	Wholesales of Tobacco	642.03	446.00	0.44	78.14
纺织、服装及家庭用品批发业	Wholesales of Textile Products, Garments and Household Articles	396.26	345.35	17.96	8.58
服装批发业	Wholesales of Garments	169.33	143.21	17.43	2.84
家用视听设备批发业	Wholesales of Household Audio-visual Equipment	69.74	65.19	0.00	0.56
文化、体育用品及器材批发业	Wholesales of Cultural and Sports Goods and Equipments	221.58	187.27	0.81	9.98
医药及医疗器材批发业	Wholesales of Medicnes and Medical Appliances	2099.94	1873.40	5.95	68.84
矿产品、建材及化工产品批发业	Wholesales of Mineral Products, Building Materials and Chemical Products	6217.81	6000.59	6.67	53.31
煤炭及制品批发业	Wholesales of Coal and Coal-made Products	349.37	326.81	0.20	8.74
石油及制品批发业	Wholesales of Petroleum Products	3187.71	3097.62	4.34	12.35
非金属及金属矿批发业	Wholesales of Non-metellic Mineral and Metal Industry	42.14	37.50	0.61	0.13
金属及金属矿批发业	Wholesales of Metal and Metal Mines	1601.38	1561.86	0.92	9.92
建材批发业	Wholesales of Construction Materials	216.80	198.62	0.01	5.66
化肥批发业	Wholesales of Chemical Fertilizers	252.26	238.05	0.57	4.39
机械设备、五金产品及电子产品批发	Wholesales of Machinery Equipment, Hardware and Electronic Products	1274.24	1214.21	0.77	-5.64
汽车及零配件批发业	Wholesales of Cars and Spare Parts	579.11	555.09	0.29	-8.53
计算机、软件及辅助设备批发业	Wholesales of Computers, Softwares and Assisted Equipments	321.28	317.46	0.00	0.18
贸易经纪与代理	Trade Agent	10.56	9.93		0.14
其他批发业	Other Wholesales	107.95	99.26	0.10	3.34

16-14 续表 continued

单位:亿元 (100 million yuan)

项目	Item	营业收入 Revenue of Business	营业成本 Cost of Business	其他业务利润 Profits of Other usiness	利润总额 Total Profits
二、零售业	**Retail Trade**	**5248.97**	**4556.33**	**50.98**	**153.00**
1.按登记注册类型分组	**Grouped by Registration Type**				
内资	**Domestic Funded Enterprises**	**4785.27**	**4165.18**	**28.85**	**136.20**
国有	State-owned Enterprises	84.37	75.01	0.08	2.54
集体	Collective-owned Enterprises	75.55	67.23	0.74	2.65
股份合作	Cooperative Enterprises	1.95	1.35	0.02	0.05
联营企业	Joint Ownership Enterprises	45.80	41.26		2.18
国有联营	State Joint Ownership Enterprises				
集体联营	Collective Joint Ownership Enterprises	43.50	39.22		2.16
国有与集体联营	Joint State-collective Enterprises	2.07	1.84		0.00
其他联营	Other Joint Ownership Enterprises	0.24	0.19		0.02
有限责任公司	Limited Liability Corporations	2142.50	1895.38	9.78	48.96
国有独资公司	State Sole Funded Corporations	89.42	84.56		-0.40
其他有限责任公司	Other Limited Liability Corporations	2053.08	1810.82	9.78	49.36
股份有限公司	Share-holding Corporations Ltd.	637.34	537.57	13.08	16.49
私营企业	Private Enterprises	1791.42	1542.53	5.16	62.55
私营独资	Private-funded Enterprises	122.24	100.54	0.18	10.39
私营合伙	Private Partnership Enterprises	4.29	3.52	0.00	0.28
私营有限责任公司	Private Limited Liability Corporations	1585.06	1370.59	4.47	49.02
私营股份有限公司	Private Share-holding Corporations Ltd.	79.83	67.89	0.50	2.85
其他	Other Enterprises	6.34	4.84	0.00	0.78
港澳台商投资企业	**Enterprises with Funds from Hongkong, Macao and Taiwan**	**242.47**	**201.86**	**19.37**	**11.57**
合资经营	Joint-venture Enterprises	15.75	12.84	0.32	0.28
合作经营	Cooperative Enterprises				
独资经营	Enterprises with Sole Investment	224.76	187.47	19.05	11.37
其他港澳台投资企业	Other Enterprises with Funds from Hongkong, Macao and Taiwan	1.97	1.56		-0.08
外商投资企业	**Foreign Funded Enterprises**	**221.23**	**189.28**	**2.76**	**5.22**
中外合资经营	Sino-foreign Joint-venture Enterprises	1.87	0.51	0.24	0.25
中外合作经营	Sino-foreign Cooperative Enterprises				
外资企业	Enterprises with Sole Foreign Investment	218.37	188.15	2.52	4.91
外商投资股份有限公司	Share-holding Co. Ltd. with Foreign Investment	0.99	0.62	0.00	0.07
2.按国民经济行业分组	**Grouped by Sector**				
综合零售业	Retail Sales of Department	1306.03	1054.61	38.85	58.96
百货零售业	Department Stores	657.09	528.16	23.95	41.43
超级市场零售业	Supermarkets	574.67	463.25	14.50	16.94
食品、饮料及烟草制品专门零售业	Monopoly Retail of Foods, Beverage and Tobacco	296.49	232.96	2.89	23.56
纺织、服装及日用品专门零售业	Monopoly Retail of Textile, Garments,and Daily Used Articles	136.85	107.07	0.89	1.93
服装零售业	Retail Sales of Garments	85.29	66.18	0.65	-0.74
文化、体育用品及器材专门零售业	Monopoly Retail of Cultural, Sports Products and Equipments	77.46	62.31	0.41	4.19
体育用品及器材零售业	Retail Sales of Sports Goods and Equipment	3.75	3.44	0.00	0.21
图书报刊零售业	Retail Sales of Books, Newspapers and Periodicals	10.64	8.02	0.24	0.68
医药及医疗器材专门零售业	Monopoly Retail of Medicine and Medical Appliances	162.19	130.16	0.62	4.00
汽车、摩托车、零配件和燃料及其他动力销售	Monopoly Retail of Cars, Motorcycle, Spare Parts, Fuel and Other Power	1837.47	1697.53	5.32	24.48
汽车新车零售业	Retail Sales of New Cars	1377.07	1274.27	4.65	18.18
机动车燃油零售业	Retail Sales of Motor Vehicles Fuels	398.54	371.47	0.55	3.46
家用电器及电子产品专门零售业	Monopoly Retail of Home Appliances and Electronic Products	469.82	407.19	0.94	16.22
家用视听设备零售业	Retail Sales of Home Audio-visual Equipment	132.65	111.72	0.30	6.60
计算机、软件及辅助设备零售业	Retail Sales of Computers, Softwares and Assisted Equipments	43.67	36.29	0.12	3.13
通信设备零售业	Retail Sales of Communication Equipments	136.05	126.65	0.04	1.27
五金、家具及室内装修材料专门零售业	Monopoly Retail of Hardware, Furnitures and Decorative Materials	220.61	192.70	0.25	10.68
货摊、无店铺及其他零售业	Retail Sales of Stalls ,Storeless and Others	742.05	671.80	0.83	8.98
互联网零售	Retail on the Internet	689.59	629.08	0.19	5.65

16-15 限额以上餐饮业企业资产及负债(2019)
Assets and Liabilities of Enterprises above Designated Size of Catering Services(2019)

单位:亿元 (100 million yuan)

项目	Item	流动资产合计 Total Circulating Funds	固定资产原价 Original Price of Fixed Assets	资产总计 Total Assets	负债合计 Total Liabilities	所有者权益合计 Total Creditor's Equity
总计	**Total**	**123.99**	**129.56**	**283.30**	**195.71**	**83.49**
1.按国民经济行业分组	**Grouped by Sector**					
正餐服务	Dinner	110.73	117.21	249.28	177.81	67.39
快餐服务	Fast Food	2.95	9.37	16.74	11.74	4.98
饮料及冷饮服务	Beverage and Cold Drink Services	7.20	2.34	12.44	4.34	8.10
餐饮配送及外卖送餐服务	Catering Distribution and Takeaway Service	3.03	0.44	4.59	1.73	2.86
其他餐饮业	Others	0.08	0.20	0.25	0.08	0.16
2.按登记注册类型分组	**Grouped by Registration Type**					
内资	**Domestic Funded Enterprises**	**109.81**	**113.96**	**247.96**	**175.01**	**68.86**
国有	State-Owned Enterprises	0.51	0.44	0.94	0.41	0.33
集体	Collective-owned Enterprises	5.36	0.15	7.47	6.10	1.37
股份合作	Cooperative Enterprises					
联营企业	Joint Ownership Enterprises	1.54	1.59	2.56	0.53	2.03
国有联营	State Joint Ownership Enterprises					
集体联营	Collective Joint Ownership Enterprises	1.54	1.59	2.56	0.53	2.03
国有与集体联营	Joint State-collective Enterprises					
其他联营	Other Joint Ownership Enterprises					
有限责任公司	Limited Liability Corporations	22.28	30.13	53.71	41.01	12.09
国有独资公司	State Sole Funded Corporations	1.52	0.92	2.27	1.71	0.56
其他有限责任公司	Other Limited Liability Corporations	20.76	29.21	51.44	39.30	11.53
股份有限公司	Share-holding Corporations Ltd.	4.60	3.41	9.39	3.22	5.12
私营企业	Private Enterprises	75.45	77.69	173.27	123.38	47.64
私营独资	Private-funded Enterprises	4.11	7.50	11.07	3.90	7.09
私营合伙	Private Partnership Enterprises	0.37	0.34	0.93	0.20	0.73
私营有限责任公司	Private Limited Liability Corporations	69.65	68.76	158.27	116.78	39.44
私营股份有限公司	Private Share-holding Corporations Ltd.	1.32	1.10	3.00	2.51	0.38
其他	Other Enterprises	0.07	0.55	0.63	0.36	0.27
港澳台商投资企业	**Enterprises with Funds from Hongkong, Macao and Taiwan**	**10.72**	**14.15**	**30.00**	**17.97**	**12.03**
合资经营	Joint-venture Enterprises	1.09	1.97	2.62	3.74	-1.12
合作经营	Cooperative Enterprises					
独资经营	Enterprises with Sole Investment	9.63	12.17	27.38	14.23	13.14
投资股份有限公司	Share-holding Co. Ltd. With Investment					
外商投资企业	**Foreign Funded Enterprises**	**3.47**	**1.45**	**5.34**	**2.73**	**2.61**
中外合资经营	Sino-Foreign Joint-venture Enterprises	0.35	0.36	0.36	0.24	0.11
外资企业	Enterprises with Sole Foreign Investment	3.12	1.09	4.98	2.49	2.49
外商投资股份有限公司	Share-holding Co. Ltd. with Foreign Investment					
其他外商投资企业	Other Enterprises with Sole Foreign Investment					

16-16 限额以上餐饮业企业主要财务指标(2019)

Main Financial Indicators of Enterprises above Designated Size of Catering Services(2019)

单位:亿元 (100 million yuan)

项 目	Item	营业收入 Revenue of Business	营业成本 Cost of Business	其他业务利润 Profits of Other Business	利润总额 Total Profits
总计	**Total**	**282.28**	**164.29**	**0.72**	**20.95**
1.按国民经济行业分组	**Grouped by Sector**				
正餐服务	Dinner	204.57	124.71	0.69	14.96
快餐服务	Fast Food	49.29	25.46	0.03	2.40
饮料及冷饮服务	Beverage and Cold Drink Services	19.00	7.05		3.16
餐饮配送及外卖送餐服务	Catering Distribution and Takeaway Service	9.18	6.92	0.00	0.42
其他餐饮业	Others	0.24	0.16	0.00	0.01
2.按登记注册类型分组	**Grouped by Registration Type**				
内资	**Domestic Funded Enterprises**	**211.64**	**133.18**	**0.72**	**13.88**
国有	State-Owned Enterprises	0.97	0.36	0.00	0.00
集体	Collective-owned Enterprises	0.46	0.44		-0.03
股份合作	Cooperative Enterprises				
联营企业	Joint Ownership Enterprises	0.40	0.35		-0.10
国有联营	State Joint Ownership Enterprises				
集体联营	Collective Joint Ownership Enterprises	0.40	0.35		-0.10
国有与集体联营	Joint State-collective Enterprises				
其他联营	Other Joint Ownership Enterprises				
有限责任公司	Limited Liability Corporations	53.52	33.88	0.22	1.85
国有独资公司	State Sole Funded Corporations	2.39	2.10		-0.04
其他有限责任公司	Other Limited Liability Corporations	51.13	31.79	0.22	1.89
股份有限公司	Share-holding Corporations Ltd.	10.76	7.45	0.00	0.52
私营企业	Private Enterprises	145.29	90.51	0.50	11.62
私营独资	Private-funded Enterprises	22.37	16.68	0.01	3.04
私营合伙	Private Partnership Enterprises	1.06	0.73		0.09
私营有限责任公司	Private Limited Liability Corporations	120.31	72.22	0.48	8.44
私营股份有限公司	Private Share-holding Corporations Ltd.	1.55	0.88	0.00	0.06
其他	Other Enterprises	0.25	0.20		0.00
港澳台商投资企业	**Enterprises with Funds from Hongkong, Macao and Taiwan**	**59.69**	**26.06**		**5.80**
合资经营	Joint-venture Enterprises	0.30	0.07		-0.07
合作经营	Cooperative Enterprises				
独资经营	Enterprises with Sole Investment	59.40	25.98		5.87
投资股份有限公司	Share-holding Co. Ltd. With Investment				
外商投资企业	**Foreign Funded Enterprises**	**10.94**	**5.05**	**0.00**	**1.28**
中外合资经营	Sino-Foreign Joint-venture Enterprises	0.96	0.83		0.07
外资企业	Enterprises with Sole Foreign Investment	9.99	4.22	0.00	1.21
外商投资股份有限公司	Share-holding Co. Ltd. with Foreign Investment				
其他外商投资企业	Other Enterprises with Sole Foreign Investment				

16-17 限额以上住宿业企业资产及负债(2019)
Assets and Liabilities of Enterprises above Designated Size of Hotels Services(2019)

单位:亿元 (100 million yuan)

项目	Item	流动资产合计 Total Circulating Funds	固定资产原价 Original Price of Fixed	资产总计 Total Assets	负债合计 Total Liabilities	所有者权益合计 Total Creditor's Equity
总计	**Total**	**95.34**	**218.84**	**302.12**	**211.29**	**90.39**
1.按国民经济行业分组	**Grouped by Sector**					
旅游饭店	Tourist Hotel	67.40	170.92	226.48	161.51	64.68
一般旅馆	Regular Hotel	24.09	41.55	64.37	42.96	21.27
民宿服务	B&B Service	0.02	0.07	0.10	0.04	0.06
其他住宿业	Other Accomodation Service	3.83	6.30	11.17	6.79	4.38
2.按登记注册类型分组	**Grouped by Registration Type**					
内资	**Domestic Funded Enterprises**	**88.88**	**195.92**	**276.54**	**190.15**	**85.85**
国有	State-Owned Enterprises	2.30	4.62	5.42	2.70	2.66
集体	Collective-owned Enterprises	2.52	6.78	5.63	2.65	2.99
股份合作	Cooperative Enterprises					
联营企业	Joint Ownership Enterprises	0.17	0.11	0.65	0.87	-0.22
国有联营	State Joint Ownership Enterprises	0.17	0.11	0.65	0.87	-0.22
集体联营	Collective Joint Ownership Enterprises					
国有与集体联营	Joint State-collective Enterprises					
其他联营	Other Joint Ownership Enterprises					
有限责任公司	Limited Liability Corporations	39.87	77.80	121.33	88.13	33.16
国有独资公司	State Sole Funded Corporations	1.90	11.33	19.00	7.65	11.35
其他有限责任公司	Other Limited Liability Corporations	37.97	66.47	102.33	80.48	21.81
股份有限公司	Share-holding Corporations Ltd.	4.26	10.92	19.13	9.87	9.22
私营企业	Private Enterprises	39.77	95.68	124.38	85.93	38.04
私营独资	Private-funded Enterprises	1.03	1.90	3.02	1.46	1.56
私营合伙	Private Partnership Enterprises	0.26	0.47	0.81	0.37	0.45
私营有限责任公司	Private Limited Liability Corporations	37.93	92.57	118.66	83.05	35.20
私营股份有限公司	Private Share-holding Corporations Ltd.	0.54	0.74	1.89	1.05	0.84
其他	Other Enterprises					
港澳台商投资企业	**Enterprises with Funds from Hongkong, Macao and Taiwan**	**3.43**	**6.44**	**10.88**	**9.28**	**1.72**
合资经营	Joint-venture Enterprises	1.50	0.83	3.44	2.57	0.86
合作经营	Cooperative Enterprises	0.21	0.41	0.34	0.30	0.05
独资经营	Enterprises with Sole Investment	0.65	2.15	4.34	3.61	0.83
投资股份有限公司	Share-holding Co. Ltd. With Investment	1.02	3.04	2.70	2.65	0.04
外商投资企业	**Foreign Funded Enterprises**	**3.03**	**16.48**	**14.69**	**11.87**	**2.82**
中外合资经营	Sino-foreign Joint-venture Enterprises	2.13	8.04	8.40	4.27	4.13
外资企业	Enterprises with Sole Foreign Investment	0.73	2.67	2.88	2.86	0.02
外商投资股份有限公司	Share-holding Co. Ltd. with Foreign Investment	0.17	5.77	3.41	4.74	-1.33
其他外商投资企业	Other Enterprises with Sole Foreign Investment					

16-18 限额以上住宿业企业主要财务指标(2019)
Main Financial Indicators of Enterprises above Designated Size of Hotels Services(2019)

单位:亿元 (100 million yuan)

项目	Item	营业收入 Revenue of Business	营业成本 Cost of Business	其他业务利润 Profits of Other Business	利润总额 Total Profits
总计	**Total**	**128.20**	**57.59**	**1.06**	**3.72**
1.按国民经济行业分组	**Grouped by Sector**				
旅游饭店	Tourist Hotel	80.59	33.92	0.60	1.52
一般旅馆	Regular Hotel	43.59	21.94	0.45	2.14
民宿服务	B&B Service	0.09	0.04		0.01
其他住宿业	Other Accomodation Service	3.92	1.69	0.01	0.05
2.按登记注册类型分组	**Grouped by Registration Type**				
内资	**Domestic Funded Enterprises**	**118.23**	**54.25**	**1.05**	**3.87**
国有	State-Owned Enterprises	3.22	1.15	0.02	0.47
集体	Collective-owned Enterprises	2.71	1.43	0.01	0.10
股份合作	Cooperative Enterprises				
联营企业	Joint Ownership Enterprises	0.22	0.15		0.00
国有联营	State Joint Ownership Enterprises	0.22	0.15		0.00
集体联营	Collective Joint Ownership Enterprises				
国有与集体联营	Joint State-collective Enterprises				
其他联营	Other Joint Ownership Enterprises				
有限责任公司	Limited Liability Corporations	45.19	19.95	0.54	-0.81
国有独资公司	State Sole Funded Corporations	2.52	1.28	0.01	-0.10
其他有限责任公司	Other Limited Liability Corporations	42.68	18.67	0.53	-0.71
股份有限公司	Share-holding Corporations Ltd.	3.55	0.96	0.02	-0.21
私营企业	Private Enterprises	63.34	30.61	0.47	4.33
私营独资	Private-funded Enterprises	3.39	2.47	0.00	0.26
私营合伙	Private Partnership Enterprises	0.82	0.57		0.06
私营有限责任公司	Private Limited Liability Corporations	58.27	27.35	0.46	3.98
私营股份有限公司	Private Share-holding Corporations Ltd.	0.86	0.22	0.00	0.03
其他	Other Enterprises				
港澳台商投资企业	**Enterprises with Funds from Hongkong, Macao and Taiwan**	**7.00**	**2.60**	**0.01**	**-0.11**
合资经营	Joint-venture Enterprises	1.48	0.65	0.01	0.03
合作经营	Cooperative Enterprises	0.81	0.37		-0.12
独资经营	Enterprises with Sole Investment	2.70	0.73	0.00	-0.01
投资股份有限公司	Share-holding Co. Ltd. With Investment	1.75	0.78		0.01
外商投资企业	**Foreign Funded Enterprises**	**2.97**	**0.75**		**-0.04**
中外合资经营	Sino-foreign Joint-venture Enterprises	1.43	0.19		0.00
外资企业	Enterprises with Sole Foreign Investment	0.77	0.44		0.02
外商投资股份有限公司	Share-holding Co. Ltd. with Foreign Investment	0.77	0.11		-0.06
其他外商投资企业	Other Enterprises with Sole Foreign Investment				

16-19 亿元以上商品交易市场基本情况(2019)
Basic Statistics on Commodity Exchange Markets of Transaction Value over 100 Million Yuan(2019)

市场	Market	市场数量(个) Number of Markets (unit)	摊位数(个) Number of Booths (unit)	营业面积(万平方米) Operating Area (10 000 sq.m)	成交额(亿元) Turnover (100 million yuan)
总计	**Total**	**120**	**86802**	**688.71**	**2308.80**
综合市场	**Integrated Markets**	**37**	**27146**	**209.31**	**694.30**
综合贸易市场	Integrated Trade Markets	37	27146	209.31	694.30
生产资料综合市场	Production Comprehensive Market	2	6577	108.00	313.39
工业消费品综合市场	Industrial Consumable Comprehensive Markets	6	5936	44.25	59.20
农产品综合市场	Farm Produce Comprehensive Markets	17	7920	31.10	171.48
其他综合市场	Other Comprehensive Markets	12	6713	25.97	150.24
专业市场	**Special Markets**	**83**	**59656**	**479.39**	**1614.50**
生产资料市场	Production Markets	15	5543	79.77	443.28
农业生产用具市场	Agricultural Production Equipment Markets				
农用生产资料市场	Agricultural Production Markets				
煤炭市场	Coal and Charcoal Markets				
木材市场	Wood Markets				
建材市场	Building Material Markets	10	3389	50.73	79.99
化工材料及制品市场	Chemical Materials and Products Markets				
金属材料市场	Metal Materials Markets	5	2154	29.04	363.30
机械设备市场	Mechanical Equipments Markets				
其他生产资料市场	Others				
农产品市场	Farm Produce Markets	16	10674	81.05	410.68
粮油市场	Grain and Oil Markets	1	403	3.15	2.56
肉禽蛋市场	Meat, Poultry and Eggs Markets				
水产品市场	Aquatic Products Markets	4	4307	38.67	247.53
蔬菜市场	Vegetables Markets	3	521	5.32	6.99
干鲜果品市场	Dried and Fresh Melons and Fruits Markets	4	4157	25.53	141.42
棉麻土畜、烟叶市场	Cotton, Local & Livestock Products, and Tobacco Markets				
其他农产品市场	Others	4	1286	8.39	12.18
食品、饮料及烟酒市场	Food, Beverages, Tobacco and Liquor Markets	5	3831	9.12	69.75
食品饮料市场	Food and Beverages Markets	1	351	1.05	5.08
茶叶市场	Tea Markets	2	1320	0.74	18.66
烟酒市场	Tobacco and Liquor Markets				
其他食品饮料及烟酒市场	Others	2	2160	7.32	46.00
纺织、服装、鞋帽市场	Textiles, Clothing, Shoes and Hats Markets	18	24991	124.22	127.93
布料及纺织品市场	Cloth and Textiles Markets	2	235	1.07	2.01
服装市场	Clothing Markets	12	11762	65.85	87.64
鞋帽市场	Shoes and Hats Markets	2	720	5.00	4.36
其他纺织服装鞋帽市场	Others	2	12274	52.30	33.91
日用品及文化用品市场	Daily Use Articles and Cultural Goods Markets	3	1101	10.17	57.10

16-19 续表 continued

市场	Market	市场数量(个) Number of Markets (unit)	摊位数(个) Number of Booths (unit)	营业面积(万平方米) Operating Area (10 000 sq.m)	成交额(亿元) Turnover (100 million yuan)
小商品市场	Merchandise Markets	1	326	0.40	3.19
箱包市场	Luggage Markets				
玩具市场	Toys Markets				
文具市场	Stationary Markets				
图书、报刊杂志市场	Books, Newspapers and Magazines Markets				
音像制品及电子出版物市场	Video Products and E-journal Markets				
体育用品市场	Sports Markets				
其他日用品及文化用品市场	Others	2	775	9.77	53.91
黄金、珠宝、玉器等首饰市场	Gold, Jewelry, Jade Markets				
电器、通讯器材、电子设备市场	Electrical Appliances, Communication Appliances and Electronical Appliances Markets	2	701	3.30	19.34
家电市场	Household Appliances Markets	2	701	3.30	19.34
通讯器材市场	Communication Appliances Markets				
照相、摄像器材市场	Cameras and Video Equipments Markets				
计算机及辅助设备市场					
其他电器、通讯器材、电子设备市场	Others				
医药、医疗用品及器材市场	Medicine, Medical Materials and Medical Instruments Markets				
中药材市场	Chinese Medicine Markets				
其他医药、医疗用品及器材市场	Others				
家具、五金及装饰材料市场	Furniture, Hardware and Decoration Materials Markets	19	9877	121.87	216.29
家具市场	Furniture Markets	4	829	13.20	8.02
装饰材料市场	Decoration Materials Markets	12	5165	93.88	186.93
灯具市场	Lamps Markets				
厨具、盥洗设备市场	Kitchen Utensils, Washing Equipments Markets				
五金材料市场	Hardware Materials Markets	3	3883	14.78	21.34
其他装修市场	Others				
汽车、摩托车及零配件市场	Cars, Motorcycles and Spare Parts Markets	5	2938	49.90	270.14
汽车市场	Cars Markets	4	938	23.90	99.94
摩托车市场	Motorcycles Markets				
机动车零配件市场	Vehicle Spare Parts Markets	1	2000	26.00	170.20
花、鸟、鱼、虫市场	Flower, Bird, Fish and Insects Markets				
花卉市场	Flower Markets				
鸟市场	Bird Markets				
观赏鱼市场	Fish Markets				
其他花鸟鱼虫市场	Others				
旧货市场	Second Hand Markets				
古玩、古董、字画市场	Antiques,Calligraphy and Painting Markets				
邮票、硬币市场	Stamps and Coins Markets				
其他旧货市场	Others				
其他专业市场	Others				

主要统计指标解释

社会消费品零售总额 指企业(单位、个体户)通过交易直接售给个人、社会集团非生产、非经营用的实物商品金额,以及提供餐饮服务所取得的收入金额。个人包括城乡居民和入境人员,社会集团包括机关、社会团体、部队、学校、企事业单位、居委会或村委会等。

批发业 指向其他批发或零售单位(含个体经营者)及其他企事业单位、机关团体等批量销售生活用品、生产资料的活动,以及从事进出口贸易和贸易经纪与代理的活动,包括拥有货物所有权,并以本单位(公司)的名义进行交易活动,也包括不拥有货物的所有权,收取佣金的商品代理、商品代售活动;还包括各类商品批发市场中固定摊位的批发活动,以及以销售为目的的收购活动。

零售业 指百货商店、超级市场、专门零售商店、品牌专卖店、售货摊等主要面向最终消费者(如居民等)的销售活动,以互联网、邮政、电话、售货机等方式的销售活动,还包括在同一地点,后面加工生产,前面销售的店铺(如面包房);谷物、种子、饲料、牲畜、矿产品、生产用原料、化工原料、农用化工产品、机械设备(乘用车、计算机及通信设备除外)等生产资料的销售不作为零售活动;多数零售商对其销售的货物拥有所有权,但有些则是充当委托人的代理人,进行委托销售或以收取佣金的方式进行销售。

批发和零售业商品购进、销售、库存额 指各种登记注册类型的批发和零售业企业(单位)以本企业(单位)为总体的,从国内、国外市场购进的商品总价,销售和出口的商品总价,库存的商品总价等情况。该指标可以反映商品流转过程中商品的购进、销售、库存之间的比例关系和存在的问题。

商品购进额 指从本企业以外的单位和个人购进(包括从国外直接进口)作为转卖或加工后转卖的商品金额(含增值税)。商品购进包括:(1)从工农业生产者、批发和零售业企业、住宿和餐饮业企业、出版社或报社的出版发行部门和其他服务业企业购进的商品;(2)从机关团体、社会团体购进的商品;(3)从海关、市场管理部门购进的缉私和没收的商品;(4)从居民收购的废旧商品等。不包括:(1)企业为本单位自身经营用,不是作为转卖而购进的商品,如材料物资、包装物、低值易耗品、办公用品等;(2)未通过买卖行为而收入的商品,如接受其他部门移交的商品、借入的商品、收入代其他单位保管的商品、其他单位赠送的样品、加工回收的成品等;(3)经本单位介绍,由买卖双方直接结算,本单位只收取手续费的业务;(4)销售退回和买方拒付货款的商品;(5)商品溢余;(6)期货交易商品。

商品销售额 指对本单位以外的单位和个人出售的商品金额(包括售给本单位消费用的商品,含增值税)。商品销售包括:(1)售给个人和社会集团消费用的商品;(2)售给农业、工业、建筑业、服务业等国民经济各行业用于生产、经营用的商品,包括售予批发和零售业作为转卖或加工后转卖的商品;(3)对国(境)外直接出口的商品。商品销售不包括:(1)未通过买卖行为付出的商品,如因机构变动移交给其他企业单位的商品、借出的商品、归还受其他单位委托代保管的商品、付出的加工原料和赠送给其他单位的样品等;(2)促销返券所销售的、不计入营业收入的商品;(3)经本单位介绍,由买卖双方直接结算,本单位只收取手续费的业务;(4)未发生所有权转移的商品预付卡销售,如加油卡;(5)汽车维修、电话卡销售等服务性经济活动;(6)购货退回的商品;(7)商品损耗和损失;(8)出售本单位自用的废旧物资;(9)期货交易商品;(10)自来水供应企业、电力企业、天然气供应企业提供的水、电、气。

商品库存额 对于批发和零售业法人单位和个体经营户,是指报告期末取得所有权的全部商品金额(含增值税);对于批发和零售业产业活动单位,是指报告期末实际在库且归属法人具有所有权的全部商品金额(含增值税)。库存商品包括:(1)存放在本单位(如门市部、批发站、采购站、经营处)的仓库、货场、货柜和货架中的商品;(2)挑选、整理、包装中的商品;(3)已记入购进而尚未运到本单位的商品,即发货单或银行承兑凭证已到而货未到的商品;(4)寄放他处的商品,如因购货方拒绝付款而暂时存在购货方的商品;(5)委托其他单位代销(未作销售或调出)尚未售出的商品;(6)代其他单位购进尚未交付的商品。不包括:所有权不属于本单位的商品;委托外单位加工的商品;外贸企业代理其他单位从国外进口,尚未付给订货单位的商品;代国家储备部门保管的商品。

住宿业 指为旅行者提供短期留宿场所的活动，有些单位只提供住宿，也有些单位提供住宿、饮食、商务、娱乐一体的服务，不包括主要按月或按年长期出租房屋住所的活动。

餐饮业 指通过即时制作加工、商业销售和服务性劳动等，向消费者提供食品和消费场所及设施的服务。

营业额 指住宿和餐饮业单位在经营活动中，因提供服务或销售商品等取得的全部收入（含增值税），收入主要来源于提供客房、餐费服务、商品销售和其他服务，如商务服务。不包括多产业法人企业附营的其他行业产业活动单位的餐费收入、商品销售收入等各项收入。其中，客房收入指住宿和餐饮业单位在经营活动中因提供住宿服务取得的收入（含增值税）。不包括多产业法人企业附营的其他行业产业活动单位的客房收入。餐费收入指本单位为顾客提供就餐服务取得的收入（含增值税）。包括：经烹饪、调制加工后出售的各种食品，如主食、炒菜、凉拌菜等的收入。不包括多产业法人企业附营的其他行业产业活动单位的餐费收入。

连锁总店（总部） 指负责连锁企业资源（商号、商誉、经营模式、服务标准、管理模式等等）的开发、配置、控制或使用等功能的企业核心管理机构。连锁经营是指经营同类商品或服务，使用统一商号的若干店铺，在同一总店（总部）的管理下，采取统一采购或特许经营等方式，实现规模效益的组织形式，包括直营连锁、特许连锁和自愿连锁三种形式。其中，直营连锁是指连锁店铺由连锁公司全资或控股开设，在总部的直接控制下，开展统一经营的连锁经营形式；特许连锁是指拥有注册商标、企业标志、专利、专有技术等经营资源的企业（特许人），以合同形式将其拥有的经营资源许可其他经营者（被特许人）使用，被特许人按合同约定在统一的经营模式下开展经营，并向特许人支付特许经营费用的连锁经营形式；自愿连锁是指若干个店铺或企业自愿组合起来，在不改变各自资产所有权关系的情况下，以同一个品牌形象面对消费者，以共同进货为纽带开展的连锁经营形式。

亿元以上商品交易市场 指年成交额在亿元及以上的商品交易市场。商品交易市场是指经有关部门和组织批准设立，有固定场所、设施，有经营管理部门和监管人员，若干市场经营者入内，常年或实际开业三个月以上，集中、公开、独立地进行生活消费品、生产资料等现货商品交易以及提供相关服务的交易场所，包括各类消费品市场、生产资料市场等。

Explanatory Notes on Main Statistical Indicators

Total Retail Sales of Consumer Goods refer to the amount obtained by enterprises (units, self-employed individuals) through direct sales of non-production and non-business physical commodity to individuals, social institutions, and revenue from providing catering services. Individuals include rural and urban households, population from abroad, social institutions include government agencies, social organizations, military units, schools, institutions, neighborhood (village) committees.

Wholesale Trade refers to the activities of selling wholesale commodities for daily use and capital goods to enterprises of wholesale and retail trades (including self-employed individuals) and other enterprises, institutions and government organs and organizations, and the activities of engaging in import and export and acting as a trade agent. The wholesaler may have the ownership of the commodities for wholesale and trade in the name of its own (a company), and the wholesaler can act as commission agent or commodity broker without the ownership of commodities. Also included are the wholesale activities at the fixed stalls in wholesale market and the acquisition for sales purpose.

Retail Trade refers to the activities of department store, supermarket, franchised store, brand store, retail stall and on-the-spot-making-selling store selling commodities to the final consumers (residents) by any means including internet, post, telephone, sales machine. It also includes shops with sales and production located in the same places (such as bakeries). Retail trade excludes the activities of sales of capital goods such as grain, seed, feed, livestock, mineral products, raw material for production, industrial chemicals, chemical products for agricultural use, machine and equipment (excluding vehicles, computers and communication equipment). Most retailers have the ownership of commodities to sell, but some are acting as agents or brokers to make transactions for a commission.

Purchase, Sales and Stock of Commodities by Wholesale and Retail Trades refer to the total volume of commodities purchased, total volume of sales and exports, and the stock of commodities by wholesale and retail enterprises (establishments) of different status of registration from domestic and overseas markets. This indicator reflects the relationship among purchase, sales and stock of commodities in the circulation of goods and reveals the existing problems.

Total Purchases of Commodities refer to the total value of purchases of commodities by enterprises (establishments) from other establishments or individuals (including direct import from abroad) for the purpose of re–selling, either with or without further processing of the commodities purchased. The commodities include: (1) commodities purchased from agricultural and industrial producer, wholesaler, retailer, publishing house and other enterprises,institutions and individual operators of service business; (2) commodities purchased from institutions and government departments; (3) confiscated goods purchased from the customs authorities or market management agencies; (4) second–hand goods and wastes purchased from residents; The commodities exclude (1) commodities purchased by enterprises (establishments) for use in their own business operation, commodities obtained without buying or selling procedures such as materials, consumable goods of low value, office appliance, etc. (2) received goods without trading, such as goods handed over from others, borrowed goods, preserved goods for others, donated goods from others, processed and retrieved goods, etc. (3) goods of direct settlement between buyer and seller with handling fees introduced by others, (4) goods returned or refused to pay by the buyer, (5) excessive goods, (6)futures trading commodities.

Total Sales of Commodities refer to value of commodities sold by the establishments to other establishments and individuals (including goods sold for self–consumption, including the value–added tax). The commodities include: (1) commodities sold to individuals and social groups for their consumption; (2) commodities sold to establishments in all industries for their production and operation, including agriculture, industry, construction, and catering services including commodities sold to wholesale and retail establishments for re–selling, with or without further processing; and (3) commodities for direct export to abroad. Excluded are (1) extended commodities without trading, such as goods handed over to other enterprises and institutions because of the change of organizations, lent goods, returned goods preserved for others, extended processing materials and samples donated to others;(2) commodities sold in shopping coupon promotion and not included in sales revenue;(3) goods of direct settlement between buyer and seller with handling fees introduced by others;(4) sales of prepaid cards without transfer of ownership, such as fuel cards ;(5) service economic activities such as vehicle maintenance and telephone card sales; (6) goods returned after purchase; (7) damaged and spoiled goods;(8) waste and used goods of self–use; (9) commodities traded in futures;(10) water, electricity and gas provided by water supply enterprises, power enterprises and natural gas supply enterprises.

Total Stock of Commodities For the legal entities and self–employed individuals engaged in wholesale and retail trade, it refers to total value (including VAT) of commodities possessed at the end of the reference period; and for wholesale and retail establishments, it refers to the value (including VAT) of all commodities actually in stock and owned by their legal persons at the end of reference period. The commodities in stock includes: (1) commodities located in storage, garages, counters, and shelves of operating places of wholesale and retail trades (such as sale stores, wholesale centres, procurement stations and operating offices); (2) commodities in the process of being selected, sorted, and packed; (3) commodities not arrived but recorded as purchase in the account, i.e. commodities not arrived but payment receipts for the commodities from the sellers or the banks arrived; (4) commodities deposited in other places rather than places mentioned above, for instance: commodities in the hold of purchasers temporarily due to the refusal of payment; (5) commodities entrusted to other units to sell but not sold yet; (6) commodities purchased for other units but not delivered yet. Commodities not included as stock are those not owned by the enterprises (units), commodities on commission for processing, imported commodities of agency of foreign trade enterprise but not yet delivered to ordering units and finally those put in stock on behalf of the state reserves units.

Hotel Services refer to the accommodation services provided to visitors. Some units may provide only accommodation while others provide a combination of accommodation, meals, business services and/or recreational facilities. It excludes activities related to the provision of long-term primary residences in facilities such as apartments typically leased on a monthly or annual basis.

Catering Services refer to the activities of providing foods, serving locations and facilities to customers through instant processing, commercial sales and service-type labor.

Business Revenue refers to total revenue (including VAT) of hotels and catering services received from providing services or selling commodities through business activities, income comes mainly from providing hotels, catering services, selling of commodities and other services, such as commodity services.It does not include revenue such as meal fees,selling of commodities of other industrial units affiliated with multi industrial legal entities.Income from hotels refers to income(including VAT) of hotels and catering services by providing lodging services through business activities.Income from catering services refers to income (including VAT) from providing catering services,including selling of cooked or prepared foods,such as staple food,cooked dishes,or cold dishes.It does not include meal fees of other industrial units affiliated with multi industrial legal entities.

Chain Head Stores (headquarter) refer to the core leading stores responsible for development, allocation, administration and utilization of resources (name of stores, brand of stores, operation model, service standard, management way, etc.) of chain stores. Chain stores refers to the stores engaged in providing homogeneous commodities or services, with the central leadership of head store (headquarters) and guided by common policies, conduct centralized purchase and distributed selling of commodities, in order to gain better efficiency through standardized operation. The chain stores include regular chain stores, franchise chain stores and voluntary chain stores.

Regular Chain store refers to chain stores that are invested or controlled by the headquarters. They operate under direct and unified management from the headquarters.

Franchise chain store refers to the chain stores (franchisees) which are franchised with operation resources such as trade marks, names, patent and operation know-how by the franchisors in form of contract and pay the operation fees to the franchisors.

Voluntary chain store refers to the stores operate jointly on the voluntary bases while maintaining their status of independent legal entities with full ownership of their assets. They sell goods of same brand from same channel of resource to the consumers.

Large Commodity Markets with Transaction Value over 100 Million Yuan refer to the commodity markets with an annual transaction at and above 100 million. The commodity market refers to the markets approved and managed by related departments, where there are fixed sites, facilities, managers and administration offices, where there are a certain number of traders to operate for three month and above or all the year, where the commodities including the articles for daily consumption and capital goods and services are traded in a centralized, independent and open way. Such market includes markets of daily goods and market of capital goods, etc.

17 科技和教育

Science, Technology and Education

资料整理人员：谢　涛　余佑玲

17-1 科技活动基本情况
Basic Statistics on Scientific and Technological Activities

项目	Item	2010	2015	2016	2017	2018	2019
R&D人员 (人)	R & D Personels	142683	220977	218322	235263	257427	285507
R&D经费内部支出 (万元)	Inner Expenditures of R & D Funds (10 000 yuan)	2637885	5617415	6000422	7006253	8220501	9578823
基础研究	Basic Research	102494	230593	258642	279435	305641	432337
应用研究	Practical Research	472497	705635	738875	897664	1081924	1193805
实验发展	Experiment Development	2062893	4681187	5002905	5829155	6832936	7952681

17-2 科技活动项目、成果与机构情况
Basic Statistics on Scientific and Technical Projects, Achievement and Institutions

项目	Item	2015	2016	2017	2018	2019
发表科技论文 (篇)	Scientific Research Papers Published (piece)	93190	92176	94556	101559	102385
出版科技专著数 (种)	Scientific and Techincal Books Published (kind)	2827	3014	3022	3085	2828
科技项目(课题)数 (个)	Number of Scientific Projects (unit)	56218	58613	63305	70663	82700
科技项目经费支出 (万元)	Expenses for Scientific Projects (10 000 yuan)	4504527	4930193	6560914	7150914	8871831
科学研究与开发机构数 (个)	Number of Scientific Research Institutions and Development Organizations (unit)	2245	2158	2340	2679	3675
科研机构R&D人员数 (人)	R & D Staff (person)	75338	69351	76297	86062	100760
科研机构R&D内部支出 (万元)	Inner Expenditures of R & D Funds (10 000 yuan)	2111784	2014238	2228424	3702437	4547728
科研机构年末仪器设备资产原价 (万元)	Original Price of Fixed Assets of Scientific Research Institutions and Organizations at Year-end (10 000 yuan)	2635298	2793709	3698655	4163826	5234410

17-3 政府部门所属科学研究与开发机构科技活动情况
Basic Statistics on State-Owned Research and Development Institutions

项目	Item	机构(个) Number of Institutions (unit)	科技活动人员 (person) Persons Engaged (person)	大学本科及以上学历 Bachelor's Degrees and Above	#R&D人员 Research and Development Persons	科技活动收入(万元) Revenue (10 000 yuan)	#政府拨款 Government Appropriations
2016年总计	**Total of 2016**	**213**	**8630**	**6604**	**6878**	**556491**	**369793**
一、自然科学和技术领域	Natural Science and Technology	196	7721	5838	6419	522869	340391
县级政府部门属	Department of County	105	827	191	88	15643	5922
市、州级政府部门属	Department of Cities and Prefecture	45	1299	832	552	40567	25706
省政府部门属	Department of Province	34	2367	1963	1305	167140	87741
国务院部门属	Department of State Council	12	3228	2852	4474	299517	221021
#中科院武汉分院属	#Chinese Academy of Science Wuhan Branch	6	1660	1532	3456	143244	123345
二、社会、人文科学领域	Sosiety and Humanity	8	349	275	256	14476	14284
2017年总计	**Total of 2017**	**196**	**8336**	**6660**	**6925**	**601867**	**405210**
一、自然科学和技术领域	Natural Science and Technology	181	7460	5872	6498	572968	380729
县级政府部门属	Department of County	96	725	168	98	15716	5903
市、州级政府部门属	Department of Cities and Prefecture	49	1416	906	604	49557	29462
省政府部门属	Department of Province	38	2881	2525	1700	214987	114533
国务院部门属	Department of State Council	13	3314	3061	4523	321608	255314
#中科院武汉分院属	#Chinese Academy of Science Wuhan Branch	7	1772	1653	3547	159915	138045
二、社会、人文科学领域	Sosiety and Humanity	6	335	289	283	11362	11261
2018年总计	**Total of 2018**	**176**	**8747**	**7080**	**7324**	**613235**	**409953**
一、自然科学和技术领域	Natural Science and Technology	163	8034	6437	7064	586029	386926
县级政府部门属	Department of County	86	606	151	133	21239	6352
市、州级政府部门属	Department of Cities and Prefecture	38	1357	887	570	48294	31002
省政府部门属	Department of Province	27	2790	2295	1762	196148	107648
国务院部门属	Department of State Council	12	3281	3104	4599	320348	241925
#中科院武汉分院属	#Chinese Academy of Science Wuhan Branch	6	1712	1592	3636	168347	141934
二、社会、人文科学领域	Sosiety and Humanity	5	307	267	233	13695	12611
2019年总计	**Total of 2019**	**144**	**9166**	**7715**	**7378**	**586195**	**404084**
一、自然科学和技术领域	Natural Science and Technology	132	8404	7015	7088	559699	381365
县级政府部门属	Department of County	58	444	143	85	4661	4518
市、州级政府部门属	Department of Cities and Prefecture	35	1424	1050	588	43696	28822
省政府部门属	Department of Province	27	3194	2764	1973	191070	114526
国务院部门属	Department of State Council	12	3342	3058	4442	320272	233499
#中科院武汉分院属	#Chinese Academy of Science Wuhan Branch	6	1792	1595	3402	165982	136781
二、社会、人文科学领域	Sosiety and Humanity	4	249	223	228	9515	9479

17-3 续表 continued

项目	Item	经费支出(万元) Expenditures (10 000 yuan)	#科技经费支出 Expenditure on Science & Technology	#R&D经费内部支出 Inner Expenditure of R & D	研究课题数(个) Number of Projects	课题经费投入(万元) Investment on Subject Study (10 000 Yuan)	参加课题组(人年) Number of Persons Engaged in Subjects Study (person/year)
2016年总计	**Total of 2016**	**512891**	**393131**	**226536**	**4411**	**209941**	**6054**
一、自然科学和技术领域	Natural Science and Technology	484537	372076	216617	4249	204030	5614
县级政府部门属	Department of County	16483	6198	393	30	610	97
市、州级政府部门属	Department of Cities and Prefecture	37568	24841	6714	220	5232	544
省政府部门属	Department of Province	143463	89492	31381	912	27974	1321
国务院部门属	Department of State Council	287022	251543	178129	3087	170212	3653
#中科院武汉分院属	#Chinese Academy of Science Wuhan Branch	133984	118371	113700	1930	87436	2228
二、社会、人文科学领域	Sosiety and Humanity	13195	9722	6880	74	4379	249
2017年总计	**Total of 2017**	**557544**	**432622**	**252554**	**4372**	**216130**	**6258**
一、自然科学和技术领域	Natural Science and Technology	529758	408102	240941	4136	212735	5812
县级政府部门属	Department of County	16101	5943	392	33	708	97
市、州级政府部门属	Department of Cities and Prefecture	44334	36451	8887	223	4733	675
省政府部门属	Department of Province	188790	128464	40141	760	27260	1719
国务院部门属	Department of State Council	308320	261764	203135	3356	183429	3766
#中科院武汉分院属	#Chinese Academy of Science Wuhan Branch	151043	126304	120939	1968	90818	2305
二、社会、人文科学领域	Sosiety and Humanity	11354	10501	9153	101	646	276
2018年总计	**Total of 2018**	**558237**	**457738**	**284470**	**4768**	**231693**	**7056**
一、自然科学和技术领域	Natural Science and Technology	532000	435384	275149	4620	229425	6688
县级政府部门属	Department of County	21671	6407	1402	68	2065	188
市、州级政府部门属	Department of Cities and Prefecture	42862	37172	13274	185	7511	584
省政府部门属	Department of Province	176773	133686	58414	833	27668	1974
国务院部门属	Department of State Council	290693	258120	202059	3534	192181	3942
#中科院武汉分院属	#Chinese Academy of Science Wuhan Branch	153315	139524	134301	1994	107938	2400
二、社会、人文科学领域	Sosiety and Humanity	13749	11614	8785	114	810	175
2019年总计	**Total of 2019**	**597671**	**528659**	**333979**	**5086**	**255656**	**6738**
一、自然科学和技术领域	Natural Science and Technology	569198	505384	323647	4888	251776	6383
县级政府部门属	Department of County	6821	4571	819	37	1054	90
市、州级政府部门属	Department of Cities and Prefecture	47031	42114	13009	214	7563	467
省政府部门属	Department of Province	199161	164768	72039	898	31141	1830
国务院部门属	Department of State Council	316183	293751	237780	3739	212018	3996
#中科院武汉分院属	#Chinese Academy of Science Wuhan Branch	173397	161080	154309	2179	11834	2525
二、社会、人文科学领域	Sosiety and Humanity	11166	8980	8384	87	530	174

17-4 科学情报文献机构情况
Statistics on Scientific Intelligence Literature Organizations

项目	Item	2000	2005	2010	2015	2016	2017	2018	2019
机构 (个)	Institutions (unit)	14	12	11	9	9	9	8	8
职工总数 (人)	Total Number of Employees (person)	564	546	553	513	586	566	429	531
从事科技活动人员	Persons engaged in Scientific Activities	511	456	512	465	560	541	406	513
#大学本科及以上学历	#Bachelor's degrees and Above	337	306	347	386	491	499	376	477
经费收入总额 (万元)	Funds (10 000 yuan)	2629	6677	8706	14573	19145	17537	13497	19384
#政府拨款	#Government Appropriations	1679	5210	6009	11840	15117	13221	10416	13240
经费支出总额 (万元)	Expendtitures (10 000 yuan)	2340	6778	7955	12348	15158	16432	12488	17308
#劳务费	#Service Charge	970	1179	2668	4210	6228	7988	6103	9351

17-5 高等院校科技活动情况
Statistics on Scientific and Technological Activities of Institutions of Higher Education

项目	Item	2018			2019		
		合计 Total	自然科学和技术领域 Natural Science and Technology	社会、人文科学领域 Sosiety and Humanity	合计 Total	自然科学和技术领域 Natural Science and Technology	社会、人文科学领域 Sosiety and Humanity
科学研究与开发机构数 (个)	Institutions of Research and Development (unit)	759	529	260	846	549	297
科技活动人员数 (人)	Number of Personels in Scientific and Technical Activities (person)	92937	59737	33200	96192	61544	34648
研究与发展经费内部支出 (万元)	Inner Expenditures of Research and Development (10 000 yuan)	720743	633982	86761	1046914	945119	101795
研究课题数 (个)	Number of Research Projects (unit)	59232	35676	23556	65388	40959	24429
项目(课题)经费投入 (万元)	Funds Invested in Research Projects (10 000 yuan)	862796	802476	60320	1005805	932982	72823
项目(课题)参加人员折合全时当量 (人年)	Number of Persons Engaged in Projects (person-year)	19822	14378	5444	22305	16234	6071

17-6 大中型工业企业科技活动情况

Statistics on Research and Development Activities of Largeand Medium-Sized Industrial Enterprises

单位:万元 (10 000 yuan)

项目	Item	2010	2015	2016	2017	2018	2019
大中型企业个数 (个)	Large and Medium Enterprises (unit)	1421	2204	2175	2024	1936	1814
有R&D活动的企业数 (个)	Number of Enterprises with Scientific Activities (unit)	559	717	776	833	896	978
研究与试验发展人员数 (人)	Persons Engaged in Research and Development (person)	64329	105848	105525	106304	109777	105616
企业办研发机构数 (个)	Number of Research and Development Organizations Opened by Enterprises (unit)	457	534	479	492	622	727
R&D项目数 (个)	Numbqer of R&D Projects (unit)	4602	4954	5554	6605	6864	8076
全部R&D项目经费支出 (万元)	Expenses for Development Projects (10 000 yuan)	1193793	2627715	2786500	3405456	3203595	3978954
研究与发展经费支出 (万元)	Expenditures for Research and Development (10 000 yuan)	1429050	3272348	3347523	3412053	3586924	3933177
新产品开发费支出 (万元)	Expenditures for Developing New Products (10 000 yuan)	1760964	2856350	3056850	3337557	3927504	9643198
技术改造经费支出 (万元)	Expenditures for Technical Innovation (10 000 yuan)	1326521	835034	487186	657675	784592	984980
技术引进经费支出 (万元)	Expenditures for Technology Introduction (10 000 yuan)	190418	147979	141254	154477	95897	46184
消化吸收经费支出 (万元)	Expenditures for Technology Utilization (10 000 yuan)	29408	16046	15780	13501	11245	763
购买国内技术经费支出 (万元)	Expenditures for Purchasing Domestic Technology (10 000 yuan)	21561	50314	23891	22937	24707	38721

17-7 有科技活动的规模以上工业企业主要分组指标

指标	Item	有R&D活动企业(个) Number of Enterprises with R & D Activities (unit)	
		2018	2019
总计	**Total**	3803	4877
一、按登记注册类型分	**Grouped by Type of Registration**		
内资企业	Domestic-funded Enterprises	3597	4655
国有企业	State-owned Enterprises	10	21
集体企业	Collective-owned Enterprises	3	4
股份合作企业	Cooperative Enterprises	2	2
联营企业	Associated Enterprises		
有限责任公司	Limited Liability Companies	1103	1339
股份有限公司	Share Holding Co., Ltd	372	416
私营企业	Private Enterprises	2107	2873
其他企业	Others		
港、澳、台商投资企业	Hongkong, Maco and Taiwan-invested Enterprises	86	84
合资经营企业(港或澳、台资)	Joint Ventures (Hongkong, Maco or Taiwan Invested Enterprises)	47	42
合作经营企业(港或澳、台资)	Cooperative Ventures(Hongkong, Maco or Taiwan Invested Enterprises)		
港、澳、台商独资经营企业	Enterprises Solely Funded by hongkong, Maco and Taiwan Businessmen	34	36
港、澳、台商投资股份有限公司	Hongkong, Maco and Taiwan Funded Share Holding Co.Ltd.	3	4
其他港澳台投资企业	Other Hongkong, Maco and Taiwan Funded Share Holding Co., Ltd.	2	2
外商投资企业	Foreign-invested Enterprises	120	138
中外合资经营企业	Sino-Foreign Joint Ventures	74	85
中外合作经营企业	Sino-Foreign Contractual Joint Ventures		1
外资企业	Foreign Funded Enterprises	37	45
外商投资股份有限公司	Foreign Funded Share Holding Co., Ltd.	5	3
其他外商投资企业	Other Enterprises Invested by Foreign Businessmen	4	4
二、按行业分	**Grouped by Sector**		
煤炭开采和洗选业	Coal Mining and Processing		
石油和天然气开采业	Petroleum and Natural Gas Extraction	1	1
黑色金属矿采选业	Ferrous Metals Mining and Processing	9	11
有色金属矿采选业	Non-ferrous Metals Mining and Processing	1	3
非金属矿采选业	Non-metal Minerals Mining and Processing	30	64
开采辅助活动	Mining Auxiliary	1	2
其他采矿业	Other Mining		
农副食品加工业	Primary Products and Food Processing Industry	254	319

Major Indicators of Industrial Enterprises above Designated Size with Research and Development Activities

有研发机构的企业(个) Number of Enterprises with R & D Units (unit)		R&D人员合计(人) R & D Personels (person)		R&D经费支出(万元) Funding for R & D Expenditure (10 000 yuan)		新产品开发经费支出(万元) Funding for New Product Development Expenditures (10 000 yuan)		新产品销售收入(万元) Revenue of New Product Sales (10 000 yuan)	
2018	2019	2018	2019	2018	2019	2018	2019	2018	2019
1318	2012	167053	175724	5255194	5865143	5854098	6909409	88629723	97076662
1238	1905	146426	158762	4633014	5200825	4990161	5985985	75682411	83068323
7	13	3903	2843	70368	106094	84565	117121	334063	936364
2	1	69	78	1633	4183	712	2584	270	1182
		45	30	524	509			4424	
399	564	57382	59915	1923503	2210512	2119383	2671060	29344947	32789943
161	229	32820	31439	1257236	1155240	1175647	1290381	14989289	14804894
669	1097	52207	64457	1379751	1724288	1609855	1904494	31009419	34526729
	1						345		9211
32	46	9302	5652	254460	160967	312238	230297	3404677	3427777
19	27	7416	4123	174546	105928	212885	150067	2252771	2103751
12	18	1637	1322	72327	38160	85464	59448	953111	1082847
		62	146	3041	15193	6997	17025	54923	52405
1	1	187	61	4546	1686	6893	3757	143872	188774
48	61	11325	11310	367720	503351	551698	693128	9542635	10580562
32	37	7044	6423	259809	363942	412470	478262	7530086	8045904
	1		45		574		574		
13	21	3555	3887	62384	75156	78965	121149	1308047	1210317
1		384	100	39018	2152	56004	3817	575569	3406
2	2	342	855	6509	61527	4259	89325	128932	1320935
1	1	765	679	4521	16533	4070	6842	100	778293
3	3	172	215	4637	3711	430	1877	7915	13338
1	1	117	198	2026	3394		149	96437	96811
10	29	553	1189	24299	50368	3493	13013	144087	225381
	1	260	262	3116	2607	2157	4229		
						232			
86	135	6717	6492	199829	200605	205551	226874	5527756	6131864

17-7 续表 continued

指 标	Item	有R&D活动企业(个) Number of Enterprises with R & D Activities (unit)	
		2018	2019
食品制造业	Food Production	91	119
酒、饮料和精制茶制造业	Beverage Production	85	128
烟草制品业	Tabacco Processing	4	5
纺织业	Textile Industry	132	201
纺织服装、服饰业	Textile Wearing Apparel and Accessaries	34	63
皮革、毛皮、羽毛及其制品和制鞋业	Leather, Fur, Feather and Related Products	28	36
木材加工及木、竹、藤、棕、草制品业	Timber Processing and Wood, Bamboo, Rattan, Palm and Sraw Products	38	58
家具制造业	Furniture Manufacturing	13	31
造纸及纸制品业	Papermaking and Paper Products	45	50
印刷和记录媒介复制业	Printing and Record Processing	64	104
文教、工美、体育和娱乐用品制造业	Stationery, Education, Art, Sport and Entertainment Products	65	72
石油加工、炼焦及核燃料加工业	Petroleum Processing, Coking Products and Nuclear Fuel Processing	13	12
化学原料及化学制品制造业	Raw Chemical Material and Chemical Products	351	411
医药制造业	Medical and pharmaceutical Products	202	252
化学纤维制造业	Chemical Fibers	8	9
橡胶和塑料制品业	Rubber Products and Plastic Products	113	175
非金属矿物制品业	Nonmetal Material Products	281	421
黑色金属冶炼及压延加工业	Smelting and Processing of ferrous Metals	30	30
有色金属冶炼及压延加工业	Smelting and Processing of Nonferrous Metals	44	68
金属制品业	Metal Products	198	255
通用设备械制造业	Ordinaryly Machinery Manufacturing	243	302
专用设备制造业	Special Purpose Equipment Manufacturing	261	316
汽车制造业	Automobile Manufacturing	480	561
铁路、船舶、航空航天和其他运输设备制造业	Realway, Ship, Aircraft and Other Transport Equipment Manufacturing	65	66
电气机械及器材制造业	Electric Machinery and Equipment	271	303
通信设备、计算机及其他电子设备制造业	Telecommunication Equipment, Computer and Other Electronic Equipment Manufacturing	199	244
仪器仪表制造业	Instruments, Meters Machinery	77	80
其他制造业	Other Manufacturing	19	21
废弃资源和废旧材料回收加工业	Waste Resources and Junk Material Recycled	21	23
金属制品、机械和设备修理业	Repairing of Metal and Mechanical Equipment	8	11
电力、热力的生产和供应业	Electric Power, Steam and Hot Water Production and Supply	18	33
煤气生产和供应业	Gas Production and Supply	1	5
水的生产和供应业	Tap Water Production and Supply	5	12

有研发机构的企业(个) Number of Enterprises with R & D Units (unit)		R&D人员合计(人) R & D Personels (person)		R&D经费支出(万元) Funding for R & D Expenditure (10 000 yuan)		新产品开发经费支出(万元) Funding for New Product Development Expenditures (10 000 yuan)		新产品销售收入(万元) Revenue of New Product Sales (10 000 yuan)	
2018	2019	2018	2019	2018	2019	2018	2019	2018	2019
33	54	2919	4078	84093	99318	107205	134988	1615248	1662571
46	72	2792	3174	94500	122231	119521	113177	1327423	1144732
2	4	703	438	19439	11975	23011	23271	495498	416215
56	85	6137	7764	86787	132130	113427	153856	3209930	3823652
12	15	1498	2069	19824	35565	34985	40674	682209	945645
2	7	940	869	16232	8234	18977	12073	615813	720177
18	25	1351	1424	31269	40280	29292	38687	670027	678039
4	13	358	648	6364	11262	18166	18160	270168	316586
10	15	1458	1810	45848	58718	39861	60835	791168	974580
13	30	1984	2954	39242	72560	52218	82301	644025	1109222
16	23	1309	2242	30708	40005	40245	52858	757971	959816
3	7	496	379	8568	52946	36259	52767	736359	968103
126	184	15729	16795	497029	531102	347504	403721	8266304	9343121
89	131	10609	9805	328242	253207	366892	316809	3328940	3860736
3	3	299	201	6930	4214	5628	6241	310725	284284
37	66	3072	4101	73097	111711	106047	138459	1862433	2002377
87	164	8145	9290	223087	286266	216035	327356	3778816	4493588
16	16	3781	3751	205207	315529	314152	448161	3609651	3601772
14	26	2404	2806	98078	78326	60642	63343	2941161	3365783
88	118	5863	6468	167974	166458	195183	228622	3231712	3378413
72	110	7060	8126	171125	207266	199210	250284	2679605	3322852
88	132	7667	8014	156161	187001	205439	269814	2768871	2679963
166	221	27391	25060	1012838	980309	1196371	1363408	17457803	17030434
23	24	8430	6572	201496	123418	209748	161801	1313464	1233829
85	126	11844	11122	387116	395216	466175	444802	7590112	7769724
70	103	19190	20001	870711	1068124	947351	1255882	9668669	11133241
16	28	2135	2083	48231	49814	57273	71914	566502	669676
7	5	604	985	16621	19750	25772	21297	227118	115514
7	15	648	886	26713	47024	48391	46146	1051612	1203445
2	4	393	756	11372	14322	8935	17120	149261	239061
4	13	1172	1748	28950	57725	23938	32665	120267	250695
	1	28	142	1813	3062	1969	3732	41060	48675
2	2	60	128	1103	2859	2346	1203	73504	84456

17-8 全省高新技术产业发展情况(2019)
Statistics on High and New Technology Industry Development of the Whole Province(2019)

单位:亿元 (100 million yuan)

项目	Item	全省 the Whole Province	增幅(%) Increase(%)
"四上"高新技术产业增加值	**Four Up Added Value of High-tech Industry**	**8817.43**	**11.3**
其中:高新制造业增加值	Added Value of High-tech Manufacturing	6379.07	9.2
高新建筑业增加值	Added Value of High-tech construction	917.88	14.6
高新服务业增加值	Added Value of High-tech Service	1520.48	18.3
高新制造业产值*	Output Value of High-tech Manufacturing	26249.35	7.7
高新制造业产品出口交货值*	Export Value of High-tech Manufacturing	1269.16	3.2
高新制造业产品销售收入*	Revenue of High-tech Manufacturing	26224.15	7.9
"四下"高新技术产业增加值	Four Up Added Value of High-tech Industry	105.40	11.3

17-9 市州高新技术产业发展情况(2019)

Statistics on Development of High and New Technology Industryof Cities and Prefectures(2019)

单位:亿元 (100 million yuan)

		增加值 Value Added	增加值* Value Added	增速* Increase(%)
全省合计	**Total of the Province**	**8922.86**	**8817.43**	**11.3**
武汉市	Wuhan	4224.71	4167.27	11.8
黄石市	Huangshi	388.43	386.59	12.6
十堰市	Shiyan	395.47	368.18	11.1
宜昌市	Yichang	644.65	639.63	12.1
襄阳市	Xiangyang	1022.22	1019.18	11.7
鄂州市	Ezhou	186.90	186.08	14.6
荆门市	Jingmen	344.93	343.45	10.7
孝感市	Xiaogan	320.94	318.40	9.7
荆州市	Jingzhou	373.34	372.91	16.7
黄冈市	Huanggang	209.27	208.04	2.8
咸宁市	Xianning	239.30	238.20	13.1
随州市	Suizhou	172.69	171.12	5.4
恩施州	Enshi	30.78	30.45	9.3
仙桃市	Xiantao	110.30	109.65	9.4
潜江市	Qianjiang	138.07	137.57	20.8
天门市	Tianmen	120.70	120.55	12.0
神农架林区	Shennongjia	0.16	0.16	4.3

注:带"*"号的指标口径为规模以上高新企业。

Note:Data with "*" cover above designated size(the same below).

17-10 申报登记省、部级以上成果分类及经济效益
Classification and Economic Benefits of Scientific Achievements Applied and Registered above Provincial and Ministry Level

单位:项 (unit)

项 目	Item	2000	2005	2010	2015	2016	2017	2018	2019
成果总类	**Total Calsses of Achievement**	**571**	**717**	**750**	**1933**	**2022**	**1600**	**1365**	**1580**
一、按成果水平分类	Grouped by Level								
国际首创/领先	International Innovation/ Leading	19	28	52	130	166	90	100	108
国际先进	Internationl Advanced Technology	97	172	195	373	324	203	204	199
国内首创/领先	Domestic Innovation/ Leading	276	394	362	743	685	465	291	380
国内先进	Domestic Advanced Technology	84	72	69	413	299	226	140	221
其它	Others	18	3	39	216	500	556	565	672
二、按成果类型分类	Grouped by Type								
基础理论研究	Basic Theory Research	37	15	15	16	17	20	40	60
应用开发研究	Applicable Development	494	669	717	1875	1974	1540	1300	1384
其它	Others	40	33	18	42	31	40	25	136
三、按成果产业属性分类	Grouped by Sector Property								
工业类成果	Industrial Achievements	145	225	226	693	579	643	374	517
农业类成果	Agricultural Achievements	79	129	124	320	334	218	176	210
医学类成果	Medical Achievements	199	291	231	394	467	144	209	342
其他类成果	Others	148	74	169	526	642	595	606	519
四、按成果完成单位分类	Grouped by Units								
高等院校完成	Institutions of Higher Education	149	169	137	198	283	308	453	491
研究单位完成	Scientific Research Institutions	92	92	64	99	122	86	100	120
厂矿企业完成	Industrial and Mineral Enterprises	137	176	303	1233	1206	1006	595	854
其他单位完成	Others	193	280	246	403	411	200	217	123
五、经济效益 (亿元)	Economic Benefits (100 million yuan)								
总收入	Total Income	78.33	199.5		379.48	492.26	457.23	257.7	
本年度节约资金	Capital Saved in This Year	6.33	28.28	36.85	23.19	77.647	135.95	11.42	

17-11 科学技术协会组织与活动
Organizations and Activities of Scientific and Technological Association

项　目		Item		2018	2019
一、机构与人员		**Organizations and Personels**			
1.省级学会	(个)	Provincal Institute	(unit)	146	152
会员	(人)	Members	(person)	166185	159216
高级(资深)会员	(人)	Senoir Members	(person)	22954	35647
外国会员	(人)	Foreign Members	(person)	16	38
2.市、州学会数	(个)	City and Prefecture Institute	(unit)	338	347
3.省级科协	(个)	Provincal Scientific Assosiations	(unit)	1	1
市、州科协	(个)	City and Prefecture Scientific Assosiations	(unit)	13	13
县(区)科协	(个)	County (District) Scientific Assosiations	(unit)	102	102
二、学术活动省级学会及县以上科协		**Academic Activities Provincial Institutes and Scientific Assosiations above County level**			
国内学术会议	(次)	Domestic Academic Conference	(time)	467	333
参加人数	(人次)	Number of Person Participated	(person-time)	92675	71829
论文数	(篇)	Number of Scholary Paper	(piece)	11073	6940
境内国际学术会议	(次)	Domestic International Academic Conference	(time)	33	34
参加人数	(人次)	Number of Person Participated	(person-time)	9857	12870
论文数	(篇)	Number of Scholary Paper	(piece)	2526	2507
三、科普活动省级学会及县以上科协		**Science and Technology Popularization Activities**			
举办科普宣讲活动	(次)	Events of Science Popularization Lectures	(time)	5055	4996
宣讲活动受众人数	(人次)	People Participated	(person-time)	3781496	3712863
举办实用技术培训	(次)	Technical Training	(time)	846	3864
实用技术培训人数	(人次)	People Participated	(person-time)	432599	350765
播放科技广播、影视节目	(分钟)	Scientific Radio and Video Programs	(mimute)	213748	64735
参加活动科技人员	(人次)	People Participated	(person-time)	62459	9582
四、青少年科技教育省级学会及县以上科协		**Education in Science and Technology for the Adolescents Provincial Institutes and Scientific Assosiations above County level**			
举办青少年科技竞赛	(项)	Adolescent Technology Competition	(unit)	118	148
参加人数	(人次)	Number of Person Participated	(person-time)	846542	749579
获奖人数	(人次)	Number of Person Rewarded	(person-time)	28050	27710
举办青少年科学营	(次)	Adolescent Technology Campus		37	42
参加人数	(人次)	Number of Person Participated	(person-time)	8595	7696
举办青少年科技教育培训	(次)	Adolescent Technology Education Training		382	769
培训人数	(人次)	Number of Person Participated	(person-time)	538404	438355
五、科普基础设施建设县以上科协		**Infrastructure Construction of Science Popularization Scientific Assosiations above County Level**			
科技场馆	(个)	Science and Technology Museum	(unit)	66	75
建筑面积	(平方米)	Construction Area	(square metre)	211614	220902
展厅面积	(平方米)	Exhibition Area	(square metre)	95397	109729
全年参观人数	(人次)	Year-round Visitor	(person-time)	3429435	3665951
科普活动站	(个)	Science Popularization Station	(unit)	2005	2421
科普画廊建筑面积	(平方米)	Science Popularization Gallery Construction Area	(square metre)	118565	87836
六、为科技工作者服务省级学会及县以上科协		**Serve for Scientists Provincial Institutes and Scientific Assosiations above County level**			
反映科技工作者建议	(条)	Reported Suggestions of Scientists		631	522
其中:获上级领导批示的建议	(条)	Answered by Leaders		128	6
答复人大政协代表(委员)提案	(件)	Replied Proposal of NPC and CPPCC Representatives(Committees)	(piece)	19	39
科学道德与学风建设宣讲活动	(场次)	Preach Ethics of Science		66	181
宣讲活动受众人数	(人次)	Number of Audience	(person-time)	24289	10785
技术创新方法培训班	(场次)	Technology Innovation Training Class		46	121
继续教育培训班	(场次)	Continuing Education Class		77	305
继续教育(培训)人次	(人次)	Number of People Completed Courses	(person-time)	19561	23268
通过媒体宣传科技工作者	(人)	Propagating Scientific and Technology Workers	(person)	2074	3255
表彰奖励科技工作者	(人次)	Rewarded Scientific and Technology Workers	(person-time)	1514	1012

17-12 专利受理量、批准量及分布状况

Number of Patent Applications Examination, Approval and Distribution

单位:项 (unit)

项目	Item	受理量 Number of Patent Applications Examined 2005	2010	2018	2019	批准量 Number of Patent Applications Approved 2005	2010	2018	2019
合计	**Total**	**11534**	**31311**	**129820**	**141411**	**3860**	**17362**	**64106**	**73940**
发明	Creations and Inventions	2038	7410	54918	47517	733	2025	11393	14178
实用新型	Utility Models	4835	12792	63780	81220	2238	10431	44350	50159
外观设计	Designs	4661	11109	11122	12674	889	4906	8363	9603
在合计中	**Of This Total**								
个人	Individual	7400	10844	25567	23183	2189	4990	10345	10698
大专院校	Universities and Colleges	1365	3265	21585	21253	574	1972	10304	11897
科研单位	Insitutions of Scientific Research	182	1112	3150	3090	101	532	1162	1681
工矿企业	Industrial and Mineral Enterprises	2305	15856	76678	89863	901	9744	41504	47884
机关团体	Government Agencies and Organizations	283	234	2840	4022	98	124	791	1780

17-13 按市州分三种专利申请与授权状况(2019)

Three Kinds of Patent Applications and Granted by Citiesand Prefectures(2019)

单位:项 (item)

市、州	Municipalities and Prefecture	申请 当年累计 Patent Application Total of year	发明 Invention	实用新型 New type of practicial Utility	外观设计 Design	授权 当年累计 Authorization Total of year	发明 Invention	实用新型 New type of practicial Utility	外观设计 Design
全省合计	**Total of the Province**	**141411**	**47517**	**81220**	**12674**	**73940**	**14178**	**50159**	**9603**
武汉市	Wuhan	76907	33201	38622	5084	39126	11745	23327	4054
黄石市	Huangshi	5029	1088	3607	334	2960	101	2588	271
十堰市	Shiyan	5085	1287	3398	400	2544	57	2177	310
宜昌市	Yichang	9864	2021	7423	420	7093	694	6049	350
襄阳市	Xiangyang	9201	2267	6173	761	4121	365	3219	537
鄂州市	Ezhou	2044	746	1134	164	744	70	518	156
荆门市	Jingmen	4457	1041	2888	528	2607	259	1949	399
孝感市	Xiaogan	5384	1339	3291	754	3077	320	2167	590
荆州市	Jingzhou	6202	1019	4008	1175	3674	207	2632	835
黄冈市	Huanggang	6275	1424	3779	1072	2603	120	1784	699
咸宁市	Xianning	4336	601	3134	601	2158	83	1589	486
随州市	Suizhou	1883	154	1271	458	993	34	672	287
恩施州	Enshi	1680	374	792	514	762	54	394	314
仙桃市	Xiantao	846	155	480	211	546	35	326	185
潜江市	Qianjiang	696	99	547	50	307	24	240	43
天门市	Tianmen	1489	684	662	143	577	6	495	76
神农架林区	Shennongjia	33	17	11	5	48	4	33	11

17-14 各类技术合同签定及执行情况
Signing and Implementation of Various Technical Contracts

项 目	Item	合同数(项) Number of Contracts (unit)	合同金额(万元) Value of Contracts (10 000 yuan)
2012	**2012**	**12908**	**2345655**
技术开发合同	Technology Development Contracts	7698	1000226
技术转让合同	Technology Transfer Contracts	447	482601
技术咨询合同	Technology Consultation Contracts	1391	87457
技术服务合同	Technology Service Contracts	3372	775371
2013	**2013**	**14909**	**4187410**
技术开发合同	Technology Development Contracts	9473	1614052
技术转让合同	Technology Transfer Contracts	574	342631
技术咨询合同	Technology Consultation Contracts	1082	238981
技术服务合同	Technology Service Contracts	3780	1991746
2014	**2014**	**21696**	**6017367**
技术开发合同	Technology Development Contracts	11695	1398146
技术转让合同	Technology Transfer Contracts	518	279765
技术咨询合同	Technology Consultation Contracts	1496	389802
技术服务合同	Technology Service Contracts	7987	3949654
2015	**2015**	**22787**	**8300672**
技术开发合同	Technology Development Contracts	11318	2155738
技术转让合同	Technology Transfer Contracts	547	390390
技术咨询合同	Technology Consultation Contracts	1408	316786
技术服务合同	Technology Service Contracts	9514	5437758
2016	**2016**	**24248**	**9277311**
技术开发合同	Technology Development Contracts	11637	2512842
技术转让合同	Technology Transfer Contracts	696	385274
技术咨询合同	Technology Consultation Contracts	1819	372867
技术服务合同	Technology Service Contracts	10096	6006327
2017	**2017**	**24742**	**10658791**
技术开发合同	Technology Development Contracts	10646	2040680
技术转让合同	Technology Transfer Contracts	871	486457
技术咨询合同	Technology Consultation Contracts	869	614678
技术服务合同	Technology Service Contracts	12356	7516976
2018	**2018**	**28835**	**12371856**
技术开发合同	Technology Development Contracts	10855	2226298
技术转让合同	Technology Transfer Contracts	874	375116
技术咨询合同	Technology Consultation Contracts	1649	1135005
技术服务合同	Technology Service Contracts	15457	8635437
2019	**2019**	**39511**	**14496286**
技术开发合同	Technology Development Contracts	14773	2772441
技术转让合同	Technology Transfer Contracts	1085	543611
技术咨询合同	Technology Consultation Contracts	2190	1278283
技术服务合同	Technology Service Contracts	21463	9901949

17-15 全省技术买卖情况(2019)
Purchase and Selling of Technology of the Whole Province (2019)

卖方类别 Type of the Seller 买方类别 Type of the Buyer	合计 Total		机关法人 Organ Corporations		事业法人 Institutions Corporations		社团法人 Associations Corporations	
	合同数(项) Number of Contracts	成交额(万元) Contracted Value (10 000 yuan)	合同数(项) Number of Contracts	成交额(万元) Contracted Value (10 000 yuan)	合同数(项) Number of Contracts	成交额(万元) Contracted Value (10 000 yuan)	合同数(项) Number of Contracts	成交额(万元) Contracted Value (10 000 yuan)
总计 Total	**39511**	**14496294**	**708**	**351686**	**14407**	**2017830**	**29**	**7078**
机关法人 Departments	8605	4122233	549	293845	3666	1140184	14	4170
事业法人 Institutions	5713	707031	1	230	4086	264187	4	746
社团法人 Social Groups	145	20418	54	16,643.92	70	1603		
企业法人 Corporations	24335	9212992	86	33768	6405	481296	5	142
自然人 Natural Person	185	61085			26	2736		
其他组织 Other Organizations	528	372534	18	7199	154	127824	6	2020

17-15 续表 continued

卖方类别 Type of the Seller 买方类别 Type of the Buyer	企业法人 Corporations		自然人 Natural Person		其他组织 Other Organizations	
	合同数(项) Number of Contracts	成交额(万元) Contracted Value (10 000 yuan)	合同数(项) Number of Contracts	成交额(万元) Contracted Value (10 000 yuan)	合同数(项) Number of Contracts	成交额(万元) Contracted Value (10 000 yuan)
总计 Total	**24123**	**11967314**	**45**	**11462**	**199**	**140924**
机关法人 Departments	4344	2662312	5	1856	27	19866
事业法人 Institutions	1619	441160	3	708		
社团法人 Social Groups	21	2172				
企业法人 Corporations	17675	8584820	18	2506	146	110460
自然人 Natural Person	154	56221	3	1183	2	945
其他组织 Other Organizations	310	220629	16	5209	24	9653

17-16 地震观测及地方地震工作情况

Statistics on Earthquake Observation and Local Efforts on Earthquake Works

项 目	Item	2017	2018	2019
职工总数 (人)	Total Number of Staff and Workers (person)	389	383	384
专业技术人员 (人)	Professtional Technical Personel (person)	298	294	299
高级技术人员 (人)	Senior Technical Personel (person)	86	98	101
市州级地震局 (个)	Number of Earthquake Agency (unit)	17	17	17
重点县地震办公室 (个)	Number of Earthquake Offices in Key Counties (unit)	32	32	32
地方地震工作人员 (人)	Local Seismologist (person)	736	778	611
地震观测台(网)人员 (人)	Number of Staff in Earthquake Observation Station (person)	60	60	58
#观测技术人员 (人)	#Technical Personel (person)	59	59	57
地震台站 (个)	Earthquake Observation Station (unit)	47	54	54
国家台	National Station	5	5	6
省级台	Provincial Station	42	49	48
GPS测量 (千米/点)	GPS Measurement (km/point)	125000/250	100000/200	60000/150
流动重力测量 (千米/点)	Flow Gravity Measurement (km/point)	130000/550	180000/840	80000/660

17-17 气象部门基本情况

Basic Conditions of Meteorological Department

项 目	Item	2000	2005	2010	2015	2017	2018	2019
一、气象观测人员总数 (人)	Total Number of Staff in Meteorological Depaartment (person)	333	375	378	446	384	382	376
地面观测	Groud Observation	285	320	330	376	315	313	315
高空观测	Upper Air Observation	24	18	18	34	28	30	25
雷达观测	Radar Observation	24	20	30	36	41	39	36
特种观测	Special Observation							
二、气象台站总数 (个)	Total Number of Meteorological Obervatory (unit)	85	87	87	89	89	89	89
气象台	Meteorological Obervatory	13	14	14	14	14	14	14
气象站	Weather Station	70	71	71	73	73	73	73
独立农试站	Independent Agricultural Station	2	2	2	2	2	2	2
三、卫星云图接收站点数 (个)	Number of Stations Receiving Satellite Image (unit)	11	25	15	17	18	18	18
极轨卫星	Polar Orbiting Meteorological Satellite	2	23	5	4	5	5	5
同步卫星	Geostationary Satellite	9	7	10	13	13	13	13
四、拥有雷达数 (部)	Number of Radar Owned (unit)	11	12	15	14	15	15	15
3厘米	3 cm	2	2	1	1	1	1	1
5厘米	5 cm	2	1	1				
10厘米	10 cm	3	5	10	10	11	11	11
1波段	1 Wave Band			3	3	3	3	3

17-18 质量技术监督检查情况
Statistics on Supervision and Examination of Quality Technology

年份 Year	机构(个) Institutions (unit)	职工人数(人) Number of Staff and Workers (person)	#专业技术人员 #Professional Technic Personel	经费收入(万元) Revenue (10 000 yuan)	经费支出(万元) Expenditures (10 000 yuan)	固定资产(万元) Fixed Assets (10 000 yuan)	#仪器设备 #Equipment and Devices	计量器具检定台(万套件) Number of Measuring Equipment Tested (10 000 units)	#衡具 #Measuring Instrument	#强制检定 #Compulsory Test
1980	88	1211	327	308	306	1667	512	60		
1985	107	1668	356	640	515	3234	1402	146	36	
1990	105	3299	1409	3063	2610	7994	3760	136	68	118
1995	167	6275	2121	10095	10374	21213	6327	150	64	140
1996	102	2265	1252	3237	3177	6985	3261	136	61	108
1997	101	2337	1337	3491	3418	6751	3680	150	62	110
1998	106	2479	1439	4 079	4034	6314	3810	126	50	100
1999	105	2531	1446	4 515	4532	6732	3713	120	43	103
2000	104	2790	1478	4 568	4853	8829	5286	150	43	105
2001	91	1632	911	3005	2899	6537	3881	132	33	65
2002	360	9583	4059	36371	34024	39461	9806	165	40	138
2003	403	9137	3960	44450	41317	47323	12114	154	45	118
2004	376	9034	4703	50520	48383	53579	14549	128	23	114
2005	398	9046	3953	59089	56152	62607	19986	120	22	98
2006	398	9050	4094	67864	64078	72440	23840	119	22	110
2007	393	9065	4072	79698	75988	81822	26984	119	19	102
2008	392	9055	3732	93140	89653	94547	27832	109	16	96
2009	395	9077	3718	111477	110965	111627	35047	128	18	107
2010	388	9133	3815	116319	109915	129113	38963	125	17	119
2011	387	8828	3693	134901	135563	150114	44143	142	15	135
2012	385	8997	3645	153332	146310	159772	45440	175	16	155
2013	383	8981	3655	197287	180390	183786	57740	199	15	188
2014	379	8420	3160	191091	177558	234080	64785	202	20	156
2015	409	8297	2996	206214	202262	248957	80114	261	20	232
2016	409	8452	2816	227598	225075	275586	83466	265	17	183
2017	360	7957	2543	266322	272889	392739	115357	323	15	268
2018	35	1829	1298	91850	91850	150937	34847	280	20	241
2019								221	13	180

注：因改革指标统计口径发生变化。

Note: Changes have taken place in the statistical scope of indicators as a result of the reform.

17-19 标准事业基本情况
Basic Statistics on Stand ard Enterprises

项　目		Item		2000	2005	2010	2015	2017	2018	2019
质量监督机构	(个)	Quality Supervision Institution	(unit)	86	99	99	99	99		
制定标准	(项)	Standard Established	(unit)	29	36	81	92	111	103	45
修定标准	(项)	Standard Revised	(unit)			4	11	8	7	1
废止标准	(项)	Standard Abolished	(unit)						196	
受检产品质量监督	(种)	Number of Products under Quality Supervision	(kind)	99			59	65	68	182
质量监督检测	(批次)	Quality Supervision Test	(batch)	20093	26548	40288	4797	4537	4720	9362
标准文件馆藏	(万件)	Standard Document Collection	(10 000 units)	25	22	30	140	136.94	146.63	150.86

17-20 档案事业基本情况
Basic Statistics on Archives

指 标		Item		2016	2017	2018	2019
各级各类档案馆数量	(个)	Number of Institutions	(unit)				
国家综合档案馆		National Comprehensive Archives		115	115	115	118
专门档案馆		National Special Archives		14	14	8	10
部门档案馆		Department Archives		4	4	6	7
各级各类档案馆馆藏		Number of Collections					
全宗	(个)	Fonds	(unit)	16033	16350	16070	16788
案卷	(万卷)	Archives	(10 000 volumes)	1748	1717	1639	1600
以件为保管单位档案	(万件)	Archives	(10 000 pieces)	972	970	1400	1416
照片	(万张)	Photos	(10 000 sheets)	140	152	125	128
馆藏资料	(万册)	Files	(10 000 volumes)	226.80	270	190	190
国家综合档案馆面积	(万平方米)	The Area of National Comprehensive Archives	(10 000 square meters)				
总建筑面积		Floor Space		25.3	30.0	36.5	43.7
库房面积		The Area of Storerooms		10.27	10.35	12.2	16
全省档案专业技术职称人员	(人)	Full-time Personnel	(person)				
研究馆员		Research Librarian		24	32	32	36
副研究馆员		Associate Research Librarian		161	178	205	252
馆员		Librarian		562	564	578	615
助理馆员		Associate Librarian		397	418	465	439
全省档案馆本年度利用档案		Utilized Archives					
利用档案人数	(万人次)	Use of Material	(10 000 person-times)	44.28	47.70	51.5	42
利用档案卷次	(万人次)	Number of Archives Used	(10 000 person-times)	99.42	101.50	108	119
举办展览	(个)	Display Organized	(unit)	564	311	347	154
接待参观	(万人次)	Visitors	(10 000 person-times)	60	43	21	74
全省本年编研档案资料		Materials Edited This Year					
公开出版种数	(种)	Number of Materials Open Published	(kind)	80	83	68	68
公开出版字数	(万字)	Number of Words Open Published	(10 000 words)	2838.80	2297.00	2065	2843
内部参考种数	(种)	Number of Materials for Inner Reference	(kind)	292	257	125	105
内部参考字数	(万字)	Number of Words for Inner reference	(10 000 words)	3120	4028	1831	2302

17-21 各级各类学校数
Number of Schools by Type and Level

单位:所 (unit)

学校分类	Type of Shool	2010	2012	2013	2014	2015	2016	2017	2018	2019
普通高等学校	Regular Institutions of Higher Education	120	122	123	123	126	129	128	128	128
#地方院校	#Local Schools	112	114	115	115	118	121	120	120	120
中等职业学校	Secondary Vocation Schools	413	332	310	301	289	289	289	270	272
普通中学	Regular Middle School	2787	2622	2576	2552	2545	2558	2573	2597	2612
#初中	#Junior High Schools	2184	2047	2013	2011	2013	2026	2041	2066	2080
城区	Urban	362	507	509	535	548	582	591	606	622
镇区	Township	671	953	945	955	968	967	978	987	986
乡村	Rural	1151	587	559	521	497	477	472	473	472
高中	Senior High School	603	575	563	541	532	532	532	531	532
城区	Urban	243	318	318	314	311	321	324	326	334
镇区	Township	278	220	212	201	193	188	187	186	180
乡村	Rural	82	37	33	26	28	23	21	19	18
小学	Primary School	7749	6614	5746	5513	5398	5383	5378	5396	5405
城区	Urban	685	1007	997	1061	1062	1124	1145	1168	1186
镇区	Township	937	1629	1536	1556	1543	1545	1558	1554	1543
乡村	Rural	6127	3978	3213	2896	2793	2714	2675	2674	2676
特殊教育学校	Special Education School	76	77	80	83	83	84	84	84	85
幼儿园	Kindergarten	4395	5321	6011	6491	6814	7500	7825	8273	8925
技工学校	School of Technology	206			131	132	124	146	106	102

17-22 各级各类学校在校学生数

Number of Enrolments of Formal Education by Type and Level

单位:人 (person)

学校分类	Type of Shool	2005	2010	2014	2015	2016	2017	2018	2019
普通高等学校	Regular Institutions of Higher Education	1012665	1296920	1419699	1408738	1399948	1398805	1435937	1498070
#地方院校	#Local Schools	824960	1098570	1216228	1207217	1200494	1201675	1239161	1300869
中等职业学校	Secondary Vocation Schools	606014	903834	372601	364893	375637	371206	369424	391910
普通中学	Regular Middle School	4466879	3418299	2294899	2241286	2259904	2306544	2411314	2505863
#初中	#Junior High Schools	3172392	2180937	1375940	1365319	1414864	1487131	1587795	1653660
城区	Urban	494739	413930	538778	547028	589002	617505	662668	699973
镇区	Township	750903	848967	627833	625858	646844	683979	728647	750020
乡村	Rural	1926750	918040	209329	192433	179018	185647	196480	203667
高中	Senior High School	1294487	1237362	918959	875967	845040	819413	823519	852203
城区	Urban	541404	427334	529827	512284	509424	498096	499625	522707
镇区	Township	553411	633319	357324	332446	311557	297857	300016	305926
乡村	Rural	199672	176709	31808	31237	24059	23460	23878	23570
小学	Primary School	4291881	3655512	3211598	3358095	3461337	3545680	3665794	3764794
城区	Urban	787812	713491	1120918	1202479	1307462	1387044	1485467	1590927
镇区	Township	593090	974019	1209864	1281967	1321295	1357390	1400250	1420425
乡村	Rural	2910979	1968002	880816	873649	832580	801246	780077	753442
特殊教育学校	Special Education School	9444	15349	11080	11057	11831	13953	16177	28774
幼儿园	Kindergarten	594481	1118360	1538200	1625793	1699519	1760387	1740534	1777926
技工学校	School of Technology	136000	229000	93400	89400	79156	77910	80570	83311

17-23　各级各类学校招生数
Number of Entrants of Formal Education by Type and Level

单位:人　　(person)

学校分类	Type of Shool	2005	2010	2014	2015	2016	2017	2018	2019
普通高等学校	Regular Institutions of Higher Education	315560	387612	400307	391157	397623	406668	426561	458777
#地方院校	#Local Schools	269042	337621	350391	342310	349234	358168	377924	409947
中等职业学校	Secondary Vocation Schools	273789	283610	126656	132594	132075	127224	127901	144955
普通中学	Regular Middle School	1469777	1053418	749560	740206	782004	797433	834520	866676
#初中	#Junior High Schools	1011186	657947	454284	461592	504948	526205	557084	565300
城区	Urban	162324	132571	178772	182684	209080	216945	231237	243404
镇区	Township	241579	251823	206959	213860	232105	242165	256601	253499
乡村	Rural	607283	273553	68553	65048	63763	67095	69246	68397
高中	Senior High School	458591	395471	295276	278614	277056	271228	277436	301376
城区	Urban	187976	138260	168688	161996	166665	165373	167496	184206
镇区	Township	197496	199177	116662	106275	102144	98286	101784	108398
乡村	Rural	73119	58034	9926	10343	8247	7569	8156	8772
小学	Primary School	567411	680166	597543	625609	623202	624961	672176	657842
城区	Urban	113284	126070	203429	217723	233312	247024	279771	291063
镇区	Township	81622	176073	217982	232628	231143	231915	248857	237942
乡村	Rural	372505	378023	176132	175258	158747	146022	143548	128837
特殊教育学校	Special Education School	1038	2047	2113	2047	2413	2294	2850	5549
幼儿园	Kindergarten	396082	761044	656652	613990	575076	594869	610815	568080
技工学校	School of Technology	73000	57000	38000	34700	34694	31620	32880	34316

17-24 各级各类学校毕业生数
Number of Graduates of Formal Education by Type and Level

单位:人 (person)

学校分类	Type of Shool	2005	2010	2014	2015	2016	2017	2018	2019
普通高等学校	Regular Institutions of Higher Education	51932	187920	331303	388621	393627	394423	374796	383037
#地方院校	#Local Schools	26461	144529	285599	339709	344834	345217	326982	336345
中等职业学校	Secondary Vocation Schools	125593	129436	335776	125735	111352	114889	116775	116755
普通中学	Regular Middle School	883828	1438503	1288944	778302	753920	733571	728464	773757
#初中	#Junior High Schools	718015	1055083	854395	461384	448251	444035	452823	499686
城区	Urban	198402	169257	149922	179771	186265	186696	188206	211418
镇区	Township	61909	239870	326945	213005	203963	201644	208107	227187
乡村	Rural	457704	645956	377528	68608	58023	55695	56510	61081
高中	Senior High School	165813	383420	434549	316918	305669	289536	275641	274071
城区	Urban	98353	161281	147307	183878	185881	175490	167712	168575
镇区	Township	41382	164517	228146	121045	111441	106219	100059	97217
乡村	Rural	26078	57622	59096	11995	8347	7827	7870	8279
小学	Primary School	1160203	1020710	611620	466221	499292	524455	552516	561501
城区	Urban	281706	149766	120208	170042	190560	200923	213495	225046
镇区	Township	84207	134340	160359	180809	194145	205853	217964	218168
乡村	Rural	794290	736604	331053	115370	114587	117679	121057	118287
特殊教育学校	Special Education School	1310	1498	2261	1112	1246	1278	1515	1724
幼儿园	Kindergarten				617733	640751	668141	698146	662895
技工学校	School of Technology	24848	45000		30000	27034	21944	21698	22878

17-25 各级各类学校教职工数
Number of Faculties at Schools by Type and Level

单位:人　　(person)

学校分类	Type of Shool	2000	2005	2010	2015	2016	2017	2018	2019
普通高等学校	Regular Institutions of Higher Education	72265	107459	123491	129118	131014	131395	129164	131228
#地方院校	#Local Schools	35120	73079	89205	96039	96571	96612	95510	96865
中等职业学校	Secondary Vocation Schools	28816	36658	40985	27532	27672	26595	25937	25951
普通中学	Regular Middle School	237500	273146	263055	246443	244193	244964	248406	256597
城区	Urban	97054	75581	68468	108438	113631	116058	120037	125912
镇区	Township	28889	78027	107371	106896	103052	102185	101651	103982
乡村	Rural	111557	119538	87216	31109	27510	26721	26718	26703
小学	Primary Schools	299994	232888	211247	197577	196452	196951	193885	197743
城区	Urban	84877	47727	42100	60500	64156	66552	67886	71861
镇区	Township	23515	33532	51059	71355	72377	72747	72017	72568
乡村	Rural	191602	151629	118088	65722	59919	57652	53982	53314
特殊教育学校	Special Education School	1676	1679	1744	1955	2028	2043	2099	2162
幼儿园	Kindergarten	40484	33094	66202	134279	152252	165810	179255	200730
技工学校	School of Technology	13070	9934		9383	8597	8122	8214	8517

17-26 各级各类学校专任教师数

Number of Full-time Teachers of Schools by Type and Level

单位:人 (person)

学校分类	Type of Shool	2000	2005	2010	2015	2016	2017	2018	2019
普通高等学校	Regular Institutions of Higher Education	30363	59009	74685	83444	83517	83507	83403	85276
#地方院校	#Local Schools	15995	43240	57264	65440	65068	64929	64535	66122
中等职业学校	Secondary Vocation Schools	15549	24036	28476	20550	20657	20211	19891	20452
普通中学	Regular Middle School	198486	233517	227962	198342	195685	194963	195766	200037
#初中	#Junior High Schools	154543	169084	156836	131325	129157	129034	129756	133135
城区	Urban	49752	31803	30409	46819	49710	49985	51413	54226
镇区	Township	13138	39851	59014	63263	61032	61150	60549	60927
乡村	Rural	91653	97430	67413	21243	18415	17899	17794	17982
高中	Senior High School	43943	64433	71126	67017	66528	65929	66010	66902
城区	Urban	27663	28330	26883	39755	40852	41106	41228	42279
镇区	Township	10336	27235	35091	24716	23609	22851	22829	22822
乡村	Rural	5944	8868	9152	2546	2067	1972	1953	1801
小学	Primary School	274979	215693	196078	200158	202014	203304	203576	208322
城区	Urban	75377	42127	37873	62736	67632	71194	74043	78800
镇区	Township	21459	30351	47480	72318	74021	74630	74912	76379
乡村	Rural	178143	143215	110725	65104	60361	57480	54621	53143
特殊教育学校	Special Education School	1231	1317	1477	1682	1741	1765	1799	1889
幼儿园	Kindergarten	29889	20018	38494	68761	78005	84613	89995	98612
技工学校	School of Technology	6182	7064		7794	7639	6456	6421	6753

17-27 各级各类学校专任教师学历分类

Statistics on Academic Degree of Full-Time Teachers at Schools by Type and Level

单位:人　　(person)

学历分类	Type of School	2015	2016	2017	2018	2019
一、中等职业学校	Secondary Vocational School	20550	20657	20211	19891	20452
高等学校本科毕业及以上	Graduated from Universities and Above	18105	18344	18343	18116	18639
高等学校专科毕业	Graduated from Colleges	2308	2145	1756	1687	1733
高中阶段及以下	Degree Below Senior High School	137	168	112	88	80
二、普通中学	Regular Secondary Schools	198342	195685	194963	195766	200037
高等学校本科毕业及以上	Graduated from Universities and Above	158861	159582	162148	165138	171439
高等学校专科毕业	Graduated from Colleges	38500	35415	32095	29972	28079
中专、高中毕业的	Graduated from Secondary and High Schools	981	688	720	656	519
三、小学	Primary School	200158	202014	203304	203576	208322
中师、高中毕业及以上的	Graduated from Teacher Schools and Degrees Above	199969	201896	203206	203417	208222
四、幼儿园(不包括园长)	Kindergarten (President is Excluded)	68761	78005	84613	89995	98612
中师、高中毕业及以上的	Graduate from Teacher Schools and Degrees Above	66395	75600	82408	87779	96279

17-28 高等学校分类别情况

单位:所、人

学校分类	Type of School	2000 学校数 Number of Colleges and Universities	2000 在校生数 Students Enrollment in Schools	2000 招生数 New Enroll-ment	2000 毕业生数 Graduates	2005 学校数 Number of Colleges and Universities	2005 在校生数 Students Enrollment in Schools	2005 招生数 New Enroll-ment	2005 毕业生数 Graduates
总计	**Total**	**54**	**346568**	**139666**	**51932**	**85**	**989754**	**306775**	**184706**
综合大学	Comprehensive Universities	6	79303	28489	13871	10	196454	48591	48617
理工院校	Colleges and Universities of Science	11	124501	47724	18603	49	545277	181361	92857
农业院校	Colleges and Universities of Agriculture	2	13111	4311	1775	1	15715	3999	2763
林业院校	Colleges and Universities of Forestry	4	10770	4095	1068	1	1678	1062	121
医药院校	Colleges and Universities of Medicine	7	39694	17186	5950	3	26534	7686	5238
师范院校	Colleges and Universities of Teacher-Training	4	26218	9923	4466	5	52581	15687	12960
语文院校									
财经院校	Colleges and Universities of Finance	1	2482	974	448	6	93524	30319	12771
政法院校	Colleges and Universities of Politics and Law	1	2787	915	515	3	12389	3416	2369
体育院校	Colleges and Universities of Physical Education	2	2255	749	318	1	8837	2735	1154
艺术院校	Colleges and Universities of Art	2	12719	4298	2584	4	8834	4378	814
民族院校	Colleges and Universities of Minority Groups	14	32728	21002	2334	2	27931	7539	5042

Classification of Higher Education Institutions

(unit, person)

2010				2018				2019			
学校数 Number of Colleges and Universities	在校生数 Students Enrollment in Schools	招生数 New Enroll-ment	毕业生数 Graduates	学校数 Number of Colleges and Universities	在校生数 Students Enrollment in Schools	招生数 New Enroll-ment	毕业生数 Graduates	学校数 Number of Colleges and Universities	在校生数 Students Enrollment in Schools	招生数 New Enroll-ment	毕业生数 Graduates
120	**1290243**	**386984**	**327208**	**128**	**1435937**	**426561**	**374796**	**128**	**1498070**	**458777**	**383037**
8	166008	44736	39434	8	168260	42747	41025	8	172050	44470	39521
74	773095	238873	202148	81	863162	267592	230748	81	909945	294817	239104
1	18239	4600	3892	1	18641	4642	4505	1	18721	4628	4406
1	5721	2051	1461	1	9025	3390	2935	1	10170	4015	2728
4	38173	10979	10031	4	39788	10183	10401	4	40394	10820	9989
7	78905	24018	18007	8	107250	32388	26982	8	108909	32827	30449
				1	10350	2849	1857	1	10750	2888	2271
12	123204	37315	30366	11	128466	37390	32700	11	133603	37819	31175
4	11698	2877	4157	4	13969	4798	4498	4	14750	4978	4121
2	14826	4298	2855	3	16884	4318	3844	3	17196	4530	4063
5	26179	8000	6898	4	20411	6427	5460	4	21881	7130	5433
2	34195	9237	7959	2	39731	9837	9841	2	39701	9855	9777

17-29 大学、中专专任教师职称情况

Statistics on Ranks and Titles of Full-Time Teachers at Schools of Various Levels

单位：人 (person)

职称	Ranks and Titles	2000	2005	2010	2014	2015	2016	2017	2018	2019
普通高等学校专任教师数	**Number of Full-Time Teachers of Regular Higher Education Institutions**	**30363**	**59009**	**74685**	**82821**	**83444**	**83517**	**83507**	**83403**	**85276**
正高级	Senoir	3253	6434	8674	10622	10901	10955	11237	11538	11847
副高级	Associate Senoir	9448	17843	22047	25927	26572	27072	27764	28150	28892
中级	Junior	9847	19169	26077	31273	30983	31186	31009	30650	30727
初级	Primary	5741	10311	13656	10544	9981	9379	8314	7961	7977
无职称	No Title	2074	5252	4231	4455	5007	4925	5183	5104	5833
中等职业学校专任教师数	**Number of Full-Time Teachers of Specialized Schools**	**15549**	**24036**	**28476**	**21905**	**20550**	**20657**	**20211**	**19891**	**20452**
正高级	Senoir					97	96	75	63	70
副高级	Associate Senoir	3523	5152	6441	5507	5262	5170	5109	4601	4691
中级	Junior	7229	11467	12935	10040	9258	9263	8889	9027	8996
初级	Primary	4399	5889	7229	5289	4961	4988	4724	4698	4705
无职称	No Title	398	1528	1871	1069	972	1140	1414	1502	1990

17-30 各级各类学校校舍建筑面积情况(2019)

Statistics on Floor Space of School Houses under Construction in Schools by Type and Level(2019)

单位：万平方米 (10 000 sq.m)

项目	Item	学校占地面积	校舍建筑面积	其中：教学及辅助用房
普通中学	Regular Middle School	10709.9	4672.5	1566.2
城区	Urban	4425.3	2126.0	794.7
镇区	Township	4882.2	2015.4	609.6
乡村	Rural	1402.4	531.1	161.9
其中：初中	#Junior High Schools	6737.8	2684.9	938.8
城区	Urban	1901.7	868.0	367.7
镇区	Township	3566.0	1355.3	426.5
乡村	Rural	1270.1	461.6	144.6
其中：高中	Senior High School	3972.1	1987.7	627.4
城区	Urban	2523.7	1258.1	426.9
镇区	Township	1316.2	660.1	183.2
乡村	Rural	132.3	69.5	17.3
小学	Primary School	9530.1	3112.4	1539.9
城区	Urban	1956.0	885.0	498.5
镇区	Township	3239.2	1113.9	546.1
乡村	Rural	4334.9	1113.5	495.3
特殊学校	Special Education School	74.0	36.6	16.6
城区	Urban	42.9	23.0	10.3
镇区	Township	25.8	11.7	5.4
乡村	Rural	5.3	1.9	0.9

17-31 初中毕业生升入高中和小学毕业生升入初中的升学率
Statistics on Proportion of Middle-School Students Entering High School and Proportion of Primary-School Students Entering Middle School

年份 Year	初中毕业生升入高中升学率 Proportion of Middle-School Students Entering High-School			小学毕业生升学率 Proportion of Primary-School Students Entering Middle-School		
	初中毕业生数(万人) Number of Middle-School Graduates (10 000 persons)	高中招生数(万人) Number of High-School Graduates (10 000 persons)	升学率(%) Proportion of Students Entering Schools of Higher Level(%)	小学毕业生数(万人) Number of Primary School Graduates (10 000 persons)	初中招生数(万人) Number of Middle-School Graduates (10 000 persons)	升学率(%) Proportion of Students Entering Schools of Higher Level(%)
1965	7.60	3.75	49.40	29.60	24.95	84.30
1975	49.25	31.26	63.50	116.05	110.11	94.90
1978	98.80	43.33	43.90	132.37	119.46	90.30
1980	52.23	25.04	47.70	107.64	88.93	82.60
1985	49.92	19.13	38.30	104.89	69.21	66.00
1990	51.71	16.78	32.50	89.96	66.63	74.10
1995	57.85	19.88	34.40	90.76	80.53	88.70
1996	59.33	19.86	33.50	90.19	83.59	92.70
1997	64.70	21.29	32.90	95.35	89.30	93.70
1998	69.23	24.53	35.40	103.75	96.10	92.60
1999	69.60	27.20	39.10	111.24	101.40	91.20
2000	71.80	31.43	43.80	116.02	109.06	94.00
2001	76.34	35.31	46.30	121.00	113.49	93.80
2002	82.93	42.45	51.20	122.17	120.07	98.30
2003	91.61	39.61	43.20	118.70	117.83	99.30
2004	99.32	42.97	43.30	109.93	109.69	99.80
2005	105.51	45.86	43.50	102.07	101.85	99.80
2006	106.18	45.55	42.90	94.66	97.07	102.60
2007	99.77	43.98	44.10	83.29	87.27	104.80
2008	96.10	43.91	45.70	71.51	77.75	108.70
2009	92.38	42.38	45.90	64.68	69.63	107.70
2010	85.44	39.55	46.30	61.16	65.79	107.60
2011	77.14	36.20	46.90	58.34	61.92	106.10
2012	57.58	32.75	56.90	51.38	51.09	99.40
2013	53.37	31.65	59.30	48.94	48.78	99.70
2014	47.71	29.53	61.90	45.19	45.43	100.50
2015	46.14	27.86	60.39	46.62	46.16	99.01
2016	44.83	27.71	61.81	49.93	50.49	101.13
2017	44.40	27.12	61.08	52.45	52.62	100.33
2018	45.28	27.74	61.27	55.25	55.71	100.83
2019	49.97	30.14	60.31	56.15	56.53	100.68

17-32 小学学龄儿童入学率
Statistics on Proportion of Children at Schooling Age Entering Primary Schools

年份 Year	学龄儿童数(万人) Number of Children at Schooling Age (10 000 person)	已入学学龄儿童数(万人) Number of Children Entering School (10 000 persons)	入学率(%) Proportion of Students Entering Schools of Higher Level (%)
1975	629.50	611.00	97.10
1978	616.86	597.73	96.90
1980	594.80	576.86	97.00
1985	496.69	489.38	98.50
1990	485.00	480.32	99.00
1991	556.39	549.35	98.70
1992	571.44	563.44	98.60
1993	574.54	566.84	98.70
1994	599.47	593.88	99.10
1995	637.12	632.34	99.20
1996	661.72	658.38	99.50
1997	681.52	678.95	99.60
1998	685.87	682.53	99.50
1999	669.16	665.88	99.50
2000	641.60	638.57	99.50
2001	585.99	583.29	99.50
2002	538.02	535.98	99.60
2003	490.29	488.68	99.70
2004	440.03	438.66	99.70
2005	397.52	396.11	99.70
2006	363.99	362.14	99.50
2007	345.49	344.77	99.80
2008	340.59	340.08	99.90
2009	343.63	342.74	99.70
2010	350.95	350.82	99.96
2011	362.77	362.74	99.96
2012	317.15	317.06	99.97
2013	320.48	320.41	99.98
2014	315.77	315.72	99.99
2015	330.72	330.69	99.99
2016	340.52	340.51	100.00
2017	349.22	349.22	100.00
2018	360.88	360.88	100.00
2019	370.30	370.30	100.00

17-33 各级各类学校服务的人口及每万人口中在校学生数
Statistics on Number of Population Served by Schools of Various Types and Levels and Number of Students at School per 10000 Persons

项 目	Item	2000	2005	2010	2014	2015	2016	2017	2018	2019
每一学校服务的人口数（万人）	**Number of Population Served by Each School (10 000 persons)**									
普通高等学校	Regular Institutions of Higher Education	111.63	70.95	47.70	47.28	46.44	45.62	46.11	46.23	46.30
成人高等学校	Adults Higher Education	188.37	354.76	408.86	415.43	417.96	420.36	421.57	422.64	423.36
普通中等专业学校	Specialized Secondary School	29.69	13.80	13.86	19.32	20.25	20.36	20.42	21.91	21.79
普通高中	RegualrHigh-School					11.00	11.06	11.09	11.14	11.14
普通初中	Regualr Middle-School					2.91	2.90	2.89	2.86	2.85
小学	Primary School	0.26	0.48	0.74	1.05	1.08	1.09	1.10	1.10	1.10
幼儿园	Kindergarten	1.61	2.58	1.30	0.90	0.86	0.78	0.75	0.72	0.66
每万人口中的学生数（人）	**Number of Students at School per 10 000 Persons (person)**									
普通高等学校	Regular Institutions of Higher Education	57.49	167.91	226.58	244.10	240.75	258.96	237.01	242.68	252.75
成人高等学校	Adults Higher Education	35.94	37.05	45.79	47.31	40.78	34.64	30.38	33.15	38.73
普通中等专业学校	Specialized Secondary School	46.22	100.48	157.90	64.06	62.36	63.83	62.89	62.43	66.12
普通高中	RegualrHigh-School					149.70	143.59	138.84	139.18	143.78
普通初中	Regualr Middle-School					233.33	240.42	251.97	268.34	279.00
小学	Primary School	1107.77	711.64	638.63	552.20	573.89	588.16	600.76	619.54	635.19
幼儿园	Kindergarten	120.56	98.57	195.38	264.48	277.84	288.79	298.27	294.16	299.97

17-34　各级各类学校每个专任教师负担的学生数
Statistics on Student-Teacher Ratio by Type and Level of School

单位:人　(person)

项　目	Item	2000	2005	2010	2012	2013	2014	2015	2016	2017	2018	2019
普通高等学校	Regular Institutions of Higher Education	11.41	15.86	17.37	17.18	17.35	17.14	15.73	15.63	17.52	18.31	18.49
中等职业学校	Secondary Vocation School	17.92	25.21	31.74	21.03	18.23	17.01	17.76	18.18	18.37	18.57	19.16
普通中学	Regular High School	17.68	19.13	15.00	12.49	12.04	11.37	11.30	11.55	11.83	12.32	12.53
#初中	#Junior Middle Schools	18.19	18.76	13.91	11.16	10.94	10.30	10.40	10.95	11.53	12.24	12.42
高中	Senior High School	15.89	20.09	17.40	15.16	14.17	13.49	13.07	12.70	12.43	12.48	12.74
小学	Primary School	24.28	19.90	18.64	17.04	16.7	16.12	16.78	17.13	17.44	18.01	18.07
幼儿园	Kindergarten	24.31	29.70	29.05	27.58	25.52	24.41	23.64	21.79	20.81	19.34	18.03

注:2018年起,教育监测指标口径发生变化。
Note: Since 2018, the scope of educational monitoring indicators has changed.

17-35 各级学校女学生和女教师数
Number of Female Students and Female Teachers at School of Various Types and Levels

单位:万人 (10 000 persons)

项　　目		Item	2000	2016	2018	2019
一、女学生数		Number of Female Students				
普通高等学校		Regular Institutions of Higher Education	11.93	68.15	70.81	73.76
中等专业学校		Specialized Secondary School	14.33	17.10	16.33	17.10
普通中学		Regualr High School	155.66	103.44	111.72	116.34
小学		Primary School	317.45	157.50	166.46	171.52
二、女学生占学生总数	%	Percentage of Female Students in School				
普通高等学校		Regular Institutions of Higher Education	34.4	48.6	49.2	49.1
中等专业学校		Specialized Secondary School	51.4	45.5	44.2	43.6
普通中学		Regualr High School	44.4	45.8	46.3	46.4
小学		Primary School	47.5	45.5	45.4	45.6
三、女教师数		Number of Female Teachers				
普通高等学校		Regular Institutions of Higher Education	1.02	3.77	3.87	4.00
中等专业学校		Specialized Secondary School	0.60	0.63	0.67	0.72
普通中学		Regualr High School	6.26	8.35	8.83	9.25
小学		Primary School	12.07	11.50	12.58	13.32
四、女教师占教师总数	%	Percentage of Female Teachers in School				
普通高等学校		Regular Institutions of Higher Education	33.60	45.10	46.4	47.0
中等专业学校		Specialized Secondary School	38.50	43.10	45.2	45.8
普通中学		Regualr High School	31.50	42.70	45.1	46.2
小学		Primary School	43.90	57.00	61.8	63.9

17-36 各级各类成人学校在校学生数

Number of Adult Students Enrolled at Schools by Type and Level

单位:万人 (10 000 persons)

各类学校	Item	2000	2005	2010	2014	2015	2016	2017	2018	2019
成人高等学校	Adult Higher Education	21.66	22.34	26.21	27.51	23.86	20.39	17.93	19.62	22.96
广播电视大学	Radio and TV Universities	2.78	2.52	0.54	0.33	0.35	0.20	0.13	0.11	0.09
职工大学	Schools of Higher Education for Staff	1.36	0.22	0.04						
管理干部学院	Colleges for Management and Caders	0.90	0.60	0.35	0.02	0.00	0.02	0.01	0.02	0.01
教育学院	Pedagogical College	0.94	0.89	0.37	0.23	0.18	0.17	0.17	0.24	0.29
普通高等学校办函授部、夜大学	Correspondence and Evening College Run by Regualr High Education	15.16	18.11	24.91	26.93	23.33	20.00	17.61	19.25	22.55
成人中等学校	Secondary Schools for Adults	139.75	35.90	81.77	39.46	28.16	34.71	27.41	20.65	20.06
中学	Middle School	0.61	2.42	3.69	3.67	3.36	3.37	3.36	3.16	3.16
技术培训学校	Technical Training Schools	131.86	33.48	78.08	35.79	24.80	31.35	24.04	17.5	16.91

注:成人高等学校学生数是本、专科学生数。
Note:The number of students in Adults Higher Education refers to the number of students in vocational schools.

17-37 研究生基本情况
Basic Conditions about Post-Graduates

单位:人 (person)

项目	Item	2014	2015	2016	2017	2018	2019
高等学校在校研究生数	Number of Post-graduates at School in Institutions of Higher Education	114260	117085	119676	133085	145060	157673
攻读博士学位研究生	Post-graduate Studying for Doctor's Degree	21509	22049	23088	24284	25213	27450
攻读硕士学位研究生	Post-graduate Studying for Master's Degree	92751	95036	96588	108801	119847	130223
招收研究生数	New Students Enrollment	38867	39785	40014	51011	51877	54139
攻读博士学位研究生	Post-graduate Studying for Doctor's Degree	4891	4940	5023	5366	5982	6473
攻读硕士学位研究生	Post-graduate Studying for Master's Degree	33976	34845	34991	45645	45895	47666
毕业研究生数	Number of Graduates	31992	34116	34838	34774	36595	38790
攻读博士学位研究生	Post-graduate Studying for Doctor's Degree	4038	3520	3669	3888	4294	3958
攻读硕士学位研究生	Post-graduate Studying for Master's Degree	27954	30596	31169	30886	32301	34832
科研单位在学研究生数	Number of Post-graduates Studying in Research Institutions	2399	2812	2443	2502	2640	2705
攻读博士学位研究生	Post-graduate Studying for Doctor's Degree	845	883	925	935	979	999
攻读硕士学位研究生	Post-graduate Studying for Master's Degree	1554	1929	1518	1567	1661	1706
招收研究生数	New Students Enrollment	790	778	791	821	871	871
攻读博士学位研究生	Post-graduate Studying for Doctor's Degree	246	237	251	243	250	248
攻读硕士学位研究生	Post-graduate Studying for Master's Degree	544	541	540	578	621	623
毕业研究生数	Number of Graduates	624	615	634	629	607	650
攻读博士学位研究生	Post-graduate Studying for Doctor's Degree	208	196	205	214	199	224
攻读硕士学位研究生	Post-graduate Studying for Master's Degree	416	419	429	415	408	426

主要统计指标解释

科技活动 指在自然科学、农业科学、医药科学、工程与技术科学、人文与社会科学领域(简称科学技术领域)中,与科技知识的产生、发展、传播和应用密切相关的有组织的活动。可分为研究与试验发展(R&D)、研究与试验发展成果应用及相关的科技服务三类活动。该定义是联合国教科文组织考虑成员国特别是发展中国家开展科技统计工作的需要,而对科技活动所作的统计界定。

科技活动人员 指直接从事科技活动、以及专门从事科技活动管理和为科技活动提供直接服务,累计的实际工作时间占全年制度工作时间10%及以上的人员。(1)直接从事科技活动的人员包括:在独立核算的科学研究与技术开发机构、高等学校、各类企业及其他事业单位内设的研究室、实验室、技术开发中心及中试车间(基地)等机构中从事科技活动的研究人员、工程技术人员、技术工人及其它人员;虽不在上述机构工作,但编入科技活动项目(课题)组的人员;科技信息与文献机构中的专业技术人员;从事论文设计的研究生等。(2)专门从事科技活动管理和为科技活动提供直接服务的人员,包括:独立核算的科学研究与技术开发机构、科技信息与文献机构、高等学校、各类企业及其他事业单位主管科技工作的负责人,专门从事科技活动的计划、行政、人事、财务、物资供应、设备维护、图书资料管理等工作的各类人员,但不包括保卫、医疗保健人员、司机、食堂人员、茶炉工、水暖工、清洁工等为科技活动提供间接服务的人员。该指标用来反映投入科技活动人力的规模。

科学家与工程师 指科技活动人员中具有高、中级技术职称(职务)的人员和不具有高、中级技术职称(职务)的大学本科及以上学历人员。该指标用来反映投入科技活动人力的素质。

研究与试验发展(R&D) 指在科学技术领域,为增加知识总量,以及运用这些知识去创造新的应用进行的系统的创造性的活动,包括基础研究、应用研究、试验发展三类活动。国际上通常采用R&D活动的规模和强度指标反映一国的科技实力和核心竞争力。

专业技术人员 指从事专业技术工作和专业技术管理工作的人员,即企事业单位中已经聘任专业技术职务从事专业技术工作和专业技术管理工作的人员,以及未聘任专业技术职务,现在专业技术岗位上工作的人员。包括工程技术人员,农业技术人员,科学研究人员,卫生技术人员,教学人员,经济人员,会计人员,统计人员,翻译人员,图书资料、档案、文博人员,新闻出版人员,律师、公证人员,广播电视播音人员,工艺美术人员,体育人员,艺术人员及企业政治思想工作人员,共十七个专业技术职务类别。用来反映科技人力资源情况。

科技活动经费筹集 指从各种渠道筹集到的计划用于科技活动的经费,包括政府资金、企业资金、事业单位资金、金融机构贷款、国外资金和其他资金等。反映各社会经济主体对促进科技进步所做的努力。

新产品 指采用新技术原理、新设计构思研制、生产的全新产品,或在结构、材质、工艺等某一方面比原有产品有明显改进,从而显著提高了产品性能或扩大了使用功能的产品。既包括政府有关部门认定并在有效期内的新产品,也包括企业自行研制开发,未经政府有关部门认定,从投产之日起一年之内的新产品。用来反映科技产出及对经济增长的直接贡献。

专利 是专利权的简称,是对发明人的发明创造经审查合格后,由专利局依据专利法授予发明人和设计人对该项发明创造享有的专有权。包括发明、实用新型和外观设计。反映拥有自主知识产权的科技和设计成果情况。

发明 指对产品、方法或者其改进所提出的新的技术方案。是国际通行的反映拥有自主知识产权技术的核心指标。

普通高等学校 指按照国家规定的设置标准和审批程序批准举办的,通过全国普通高等学校统一招生考试,招收高中毕业生为主要培养对象,实施高等教育的全日制大学、独立设置的学院和高等专科学校、高等职业学校和其他机构。

大学、独立设置的学院主要实施本科层次以上教育,高等专科学校、高等职业学校实施专科层次教育,其他机构是承担国家普通招生计划任务不计校数的机构。包括普通高等学校分校和批准筹建的普通高等学校等。

成人高等学校 指按照国家规定的设置标准和审批程序批准举办的,通过全国成人高等学校统一招生考试,招收具有高中毕业或同等学历的在职从业人员为主要培养对象，利用函授、业余、脱产等多种形式对其实施高等学历教育的学校。包括职工高等学校、农民高等学校、管理干部学院、教育学院、独立函授学院、广播电视大学、其他机构等。其他机构是承担国家成人招生计划任务不计校数的机构。

Explanatory Notes on Main Statistical Indicators

Scientific and Technological Activities (S&T Activities) refer to organized activities which are closely related with the creation, development, dissemination and application of the scientific and technical knowledge in the fields of natural sciences, agricultural science, medical science, engineering and technological science, humanities and social sciences (referred to as scientific and technological fields). S&T activities can be classified in to 3 categories: research and development (R&D) activities, application of R&D results, and related S&T services. This statistical definition is made by UNICHIEF for scientific and technological activities to meet the need of carrying out statistical work in this field for its member countries in particular those developing countries.

Personnel Engaged in S&T Activities refer to personnel directly engaged in S&T activities, in the management of S&T activities, and in providing direct service to S&T activities, who spend over 10% of the total working hours in a year in S&T activities. (1) Personnel directly engaged in S&T activities include researchers, engineers, technicians and other related personnel engaged in S&T activities in independent-accounting R&D institutions, institutions of higher learning, and in research institutes, laboratories, technology development centers and central experiment workshops under enterprises and institutions. Also included are people working in S&T research project teams, professional and technical personnel working in S&T information archiving institutes, and graduate students working on the design of their thesis. (2) Personnel engaged in the management of S&T activities and in providing direct service to S&T activities include senior management people responsible for S&T activities in independent-accounting R&D institutions, S&T information archiving institutes, institutions of higher learning, and in enterprises and institutions where S&T activities are undertaken. Also included are people responsible for the planning, administration, personnel management, financial management, logistics supply, equipment maintenance, information and library management that are related with S&T activities. People providing indirect services are excluded, such as security, medical service, drivers, plumbers, cleaners and those providing catering and related service. This indicator reflects the size of personnel engaged in S&T activities.

Scientists and Engineers refer to persons engaged in S&T activities who have obtained titles of senior and middle level professional positions, and those without such position but have completed university or higher education. This indicator reflects the quality of personnel engaged in S&T activities.

Research and Development (R&D) refers to systematic and creative activities in the field of science and technology aiming at increasing the knowledge and using the knowledge for new application. R&D includes 3 categories of activities: basic research, applied research and experiments and development. The scale and intensity of R&D are widely used internationally to reflect the strength of S&T and the core competitiveness of a country in the world.

Professional and Technical Personnel refer to persons engaged in professional and technical work or in the management of professional and technical activities, i.e., people with professional or technical positions who are engaged in professional and technical work or in the management of professional and technical activities, and people without professional or technical positions but are working on professional or technical posts. They include professionals and technicians working in 17 categories of technical occupations including engineering, agriculture, scientific researches, medical service, teaching, economic research and application, accounting, statistics, translation, libraries, archives, cultural and museum service, journalism and publication, lawyers, notarization service, radio and television broadcasting, handicraft and fine arts, sports, performing art, and political workers in enterprises. This indicator reflects the condition of human resources in S&T.

Funding for S&T Activities refers to funds obtained from various sources for S&T activities, including government funds, self–raised funds by enterprises, self–raised funds by institutions, loans from financial institutions, foreign funds and other funds. This indicator reflects the efforts made by various social economic entities in promoting the development of S&T.

New Products refer to new products produced with new technology and new design, or products that represent noticeable improvement in terms of structure, material, or production process so as to improve significantly the character or function of the older versions. They include new products certified by relevant government agencies within the period of certification, as well as new products designed and produced by enterprises within a year without certification by government agencies. This indictor reflects the direct contribution of S&T output to economic growth.

Patent is an abbreviation for the patent right and refers to the exclusive right of ownership by the inventors or designers for the creation or inventions, given from the patent offices after due process of assessment and approval in accordance with the Patent Law. Patents are granted for inventions, utility models and designs. This indicator reflects the achievements of S&T and design with independent intellectual property.

Inventions refer to the new technical proposals to the products or methods or their modifications. This is universal core indicator reflecting the technologies with independent intellectual property.

Regular Institutions of Higher Learning refer to educational establishments set up according to the government evaluation and approval procedures, enrolling graduates from senior secondary schools and providing higher education courses and training for senior professionals. They include full–time universities, colleges, high professional schools, high professional vocational schools and others.

Universities and colleges are mainly providing undergraduate courses; those high professional schools and high professional vocational schools are mainly providing professional trainings; and others refer to educational establishments, which are responsible for enrolling students but not covered in the total number of schools, including: branch schools of universities and colleges, and universities and colleges that have been proved and prepared to construct.

Institutions of Higher Learning for Adults refer to educational establishments, set up in line with relevant rules approved by the government, enrolling staff and workers with senior secondary school or equivalent education, and providing higher education courses in many forms of correspondence, spare time, or full time for adults. Professionals thus trained receive a qualification equivalent to graduates studying regular courses at regular universities, colleges and professional colleges. Institutions of higher learning for adults include schools of high education for staff and workers, schools of high education for peasants, colleges for management cadres, pedagogical colleges, independent correspondence colleges, Radio and TV universities and other educational establishments. Other educational establishments are responsible for enrolling adult students but not covered in the number of schools.

18 卫生和社会服务

Public Health and Social Services

资料整理人员：谢　涛

18-1 卫生机构数

Number of Health Care Institutions

单位：个 (unit)

年份 Year	总计 Total	医院 Hospitals	综合医院 General Hospitals	中医医院 Hosptials Specialized in Traditional Chinese Medicine	专科医院 Specialized Hosptials	基层医疗卫生机构 Basic Medical Institutions	社区卫生服务中心(站) Community Health Service Centers	街道卫生院 Urban Health Centers	乡镇卫生院 Township Health Centers
2006	10052	575	401	82	82		664	55	1140
2007	11093	580	393	83	93		1089	53	1160
2008	10305	593	389	86	106		1115	48	1155
2009	32790	614	409	86	105		1142	48	1134
2010	34269	602	394	87	107		1294	44	1149
2011	35625	608	393	91	111	34509	1278	34	1161
2012	35240	650	414	95	126	34063	1220	34	1165
2013	35631	711	444	98	153	34042	1231	36	1152
2014	36077	771	483	102	169	34503	1175	36	1150
2015	36173	869	532	109	208	34569	1189	29	1140
2016	36261	928	550	115	237	34706	1236	31	1136
2017	36323	976	567	117	261	34742	1173	25	1137
2018	36397	996	561	123	280	34821	1148	21	1139
2019	35479	1034	561	126	311	33893	1149	23	1129

注：卫生事业机构数从2009年起包含村卫生室数量。
Note: The statistics of health care units, hospital beds and health care professionals started to include the village clinics since 2009.

18-1 续表 continued

单位：个 (unit)

年 份 Year	总 计 Total						
			专业公共卫生机构				
	村卫生室 Village Clinices	门诊部(所) Outpatient Department	Specialized Public Health Institutions	疾病预防控制中心 Center for Disease Control and Prevention	专科疾病防治院(所/站) Specialized Disease Prevention & Treatment Institution	妇幼保健院(所/站) Women and Children Care Agencies	卫生监督所(中心) Health Inspection Institution(center)
2006		7116		114	116	95	72
2007		7677		113	118	100	83
2008		6871		110	109	99	93
2009	22405	6936		112	87	99	97
2010	24112	6729		115	84	100	98
2011	25204	6832	425	112	83	100	98
2012	24976	6668	438	111	83	100	109
2013	24941	6682	779	113	75	101	102
2014	24919	7223	696	112	76	100	103
2015	24796	7415	577	113	76	103	107
2016	24788	7515	559	115	74	104	109
2017	24633	7774	537	115	73	102	110
2018	24397	8116	504	115	74	103	107
2019	23230	8362	488	112	75	101	106

18-2 卫生机构人员数
Number of Persons Engaged in Health Care Institutions

单位：万人 (10 000 persom)

年 份 Year	总 计 Total	卫生技术人员 Medical Technical Personel	执业(助理)医师 Licensed (Assistant) Doctors	执业医师 Licensed Doctors	注册护士 Pegistertered Nurses	药师(士) Pharmacist	乡村医生和卫生员 Village Doctors and Assistants	每千人口医生数(人) Number of Doctors per 1000 Population (person)
1970	10.30	8.33	4.15		1.83			1.03
1975	15.05	11.85	4.91		2.05			1.11
1980	19.94	15.59	6.32		3.09			1.35
2006	26.53	21.80	9.01		7.06			1.49
2007	27.80	22.70	9.20	7.65	7.69			1.52
2008	28.48	23.38	9.20	7.7	8.06			1.51
2009	33.71	24.70	9.79	8.22	8.73		3.86	1.59
2010	34.95	25.58	9.95	8.37	9.38	1.77	4.15	1.62
2011	36.52	26.81	10.21	8.53	10.21	1.77	4.41	1.66
2012	38.64	28.87	10.91	9.01	11.57	1.74	4.30	1.89
2013	41.12	30.93	11.72	9.65	12.79	1.77	4.29	1.90
2014	43.82	33.55	12.61	10.39	14.40	1.78	4.22	2.17
2015	47.55	36.76	13.60	11.22	16.51	1.82	4.09	2.32
2016	49.54	38.54	14.24	11.74	17.52	1.85	4.04	2.42
2017	51.04	39.97	14.76	12.23	18.43	1.87	3.96	2.50
2018	52.18	41.08	15.19	12.66	19.08	1.87	3.74	2.57
2019	52.98	41.95	15.50	12.97	19.59	1.87	3.45	2.62

注：卫生人员数从2009年起包含村卫生室卫生人员数量。
Note:The statistics of health care units, hospital beds and health care professionals started to include the village clinics since 2009.

18-3 卫生机构床位数
Number of Beds in Health Care Institutions

单位:万张 (10 000 beds)

年份 Year	总计 Total	医院 Hospitals	基层医疗卫生机构 Basic Medical Institutions	乡镇卫生院 Township Health Centers	专业公共卫生机构 Specialized Public Health Institutions	每千人口卫生机构床位数(张) Beds of Medical InstitutionsPer 1000Population (bed)
1970	6.14	5.56				1.38
1975	9.90	9.02				2.05
1980	12.59	11.22				2.40
1985	14.70	11.52				2.34
1990	16.34	13.16				2.45
1991	16.52	13.43				2.47
1992	16.62	13.46				2.44
1993	16.30	13.48				2.41
1994	16.13	13.40				2.36
1995	15.78	13.08				2.29
1996	14.42	13.08				2.24
1997	15.30	13.08				2.24
1998	15.09	13.03				2.21
1999	14.90	12.91				2.07
2000	14.96	12.99				2.18
2001	14.62	12.91				2.18
2002	12.72	8.53				2.12
2003	13.59	9.39				2.26
2004	13.78	9.52				2.29
2005	13.96	9.67				2.31
2006	14.24	9.81				2.35
2007	15.06	10.36				2.48
2008	16.73	11.32				2.75
2009	18.72	12.66		4.33		2.82
2010	20.04	13.50		4.64		3.26
2011	22.40	15.20	6.23	5.05	0.96	3.63
2012	25.30	17.38	6.83	5.58	1.09	4.38
2013	28.82	20.05	7.47	6.18	1.32	4.97
2014	31.83	22.20	8.15	6.77	1.48	5.47
2015	34.38	24.66	8.39	6.90	1.57	5.87
2016	36.16	25.73	8.82	7.21	1.61	6.14
2017	37.53	26.95	8.93	7.27	1.65	6.36
2018	39.35	28.15	9.49	7.77	1.71	6.65
2019	40.65	29.12	9.81	8.06	1.71	6.86

18-4 分等级医疗卫生机构情况(2019)
Health Care Institutions by Level(2019)

单位:个 (Unit)

项目	Iem	合计 Total	三级 Thrid-level	二级 Second-level	一级 First-level	其他 Others
医院	Hospitals	1034	136	343	269	286
其中:综合医院	General Hospitals	561	70	161	175	155
中医医院	Hosptials Specialized in Traditional Chinese Medicine	126	21	65	23	17
中西医结合医院	Hospitals of Traditional Chinese Medicine and Western Medicine	23	4	5	9	5
民族医院	Minortiy Hospitals	2		2		
专科医院	Specialized Hosptials	311	41	110	60	100
妇幼保健院	Women and Children Care Agencies	96	12	82		2
专科疾病防治院	Specialized Prevention & Treatment Centers	13		2	3	8

18-5 医院业务工作开展情况
Basic Statistics on Hospital Business

项 目	Item	2000	2005	2010	2015	2018	2019
机构数 (个)	Number of Institutions (unit)	507	574	603	869	996	1034
诊疗总人次数 (万人次)	Number of Clients (10 000 person-times)	4616.20	5452.11	7710.20	12111.16	14171.37	15063.05
#门、急诊人次数 (万人次)	#Number of Outpacients and Emergency (10 000 person-times)	4396.10	5107.19	7533.44	11721.98	13834.99	14617.36
出院人数 (万人)	Number of discharged Patients (10 000 persons)	158.93	219.45	423.28	780.05	936.34	993.54
死亡 (万人)	Dead (10 000 persons)	1.59	2.28	3.13	3.81	4.59	4.67
病死率 (%)	Rate of Death from Illness (%)	1.08	1.04	0.74	0.49	0.49	0.47
病床平均周转次数 (次)	Average times of Beds Usage (time)	18.7	24.0	32.5	34.0	35.1	35.5
病床平均工作日 (日)	Average Day of Beds Usage (day)	218.8	268.2	350.4	337.4	338.2	336.1
病床使用率 (%)	Utilization Rate of Beds (%)	59.94	73.49	96.01	92.44	92.65	92.09
出院者平均住院日 (日)	Average Days for Hospitalization Discharged (day)	11.1	10.7	10.5	9.8	9.4	9.3

18-6 农村村级卫生组织情况
Statistics on Health Care Institutions at Village Level

项 目	Item	2000	2005	2010	2015	2018	2019
村设置的医疗点数 (个)	Medical care Station Set by Villages (unit)	26879	21136	24057	24795	24397	23230
#村或集体办	#Set by Villages or Collective Set	14666	11207	15395	15495	15268	14452
联合办	Set with Village Doctors	4640	3777	2815	2984	3090	2765
医院设点	Set by Hospital	2403	2410	3348	3559	3505	3410
私人办	Set by Individual	4344	2907	1833	1922	1587	1254
其他	Others	826	835	666	835	947	1349
乡村医生和卫生员人数 (人)	Number of Village Doctors and Medical Working Personel (person)	57511	34417	41473	40897	37358	34460
#乡村医生	#Village Doctors	44490	33375	40425	38970	35619	32780
卫生员	Medical Working Persone	1301	1042	1048	1927	1739	1680

主要统计指标解释

卫生机构 包括医疗机构、疾病预防控制中心(防疫站)、采供血机构、卫生监督及监测(检验)机构、医学科研和在职培训机构、健康教育所等。

医疗机构 包括医院、社区卫生服务中心(站)、疗养院、卫生院、门诊部、诊所(卫生所、医务室)、妇幼保健院(所、站)、专科疾病防治院(所、站)、急救中心(站)和临床检验中心。医疗机构分为非赢利性医疗机构和赢利性医疗机构。

医院 包括综合医院、中医医院、中西医结合医院、民族医院、各类专科医院和护理院。

卫生技术人员 指卫生机构中医生、护理人员 、药剂人员、检验人员等卫生技术人员。

医生 指在医疗、预防保健机构工作且取得《执业医师证书》的执业医师和执业助理医师。

Explanatory Notes on Main Statistical Indicators

Health Care Institutions include medical institutions, disease prevention and control centers (epidemic prevention stations), blood gathering and supplying institutions, health supervision and inspection (check up) institutions, medicinal scientific research and on–job training institutions, health education and so on.

Medical Organizations include hospitals, health service centers (stations) of communities, nursing homes, health centers, clinics, clinics (health stations and infirmaries), maternity and child care agencies (centers and stations), special disease prevention and curing agencies (centers and stations), first aid centers (stations) and clinical inspection centers. Medical organizations are grouped by two types: profit–making and non–profit–making medical organizations.

Hospitals include polyclinics, traditional Chinese medical hospitals, hospitals integrated with traditional Chinese therapeutics and western therapeutics, ethical hospitals, various specialties hospitals and nursing hospitals.

Medical Technical Personnel refers to doctors, assistant nurses, pharmacists, and laboratory technicians working in medical institutions.

Doctors refer to certified physicians and certified assistant physicians with certifications working in medical and health care and prevention agencies.

19 文化和体育

Culture and Sports

资料整理人员：谢　涛

19-1 文化事业机构、人员数
Number of Cultural Institutions and Personnel

单位:个、人 (unit, person)

项 目	Item	2013	2014	2015	2016	2017	2018	2019
艺术业机构	Art Performing Institution	363	328	340	366	538	550	456
#剧团	#Troupes	307	273	282	308	473	489	390
#剧场	#Theater	53	52	58	58	65	61	66
文物事业机构	Historical Relics Institutions	291	300	302	310	325	326	336
#博物馆	#Museums	170	174	175	183	199	200	213
图书馆事业机构	Library Institutions	112	112	112	112	116	115	116
群众文化事业机构	Public Culture Institutions	1382	1390	1399	1402	1406	1406	1405
文化馆	Cultural Centers	120	121	122	123	125	125	124
文化站	Art Center	1262	1269	1277	1279	1281	1281	1281
艺术业人员数	Number of People Engaged in Art Performing	10384	9774	10596	9969	12785	13200	11672
#剧团人员	#Staff in Troupes	9005	8520	8999	8699	11464	11853	10857
#剧场人员	#Staff in Theater	1367	1241	1597	1270	1321	1347	1085
文物事业人员数	Number of Historical Relics Staffs	4713	4928	5025	5162	5428	5557	5563
#博物馆人员	#Number of staff in Library	3360	3380	3449	3556	3956	4032	4218
图书馆事业人员数	Number of People Engaged in Library	2226	2231	2212	2198	2204	2128	2101
群众文化事业人员数	Number of People Engaged in Public Art	4912	5045	4869	4945	5037	5099	5162
文化馆人员	Number of People in Cultural Centers	2270	2294	2230	2220	2189	2158	2076
文化站人员	Number of People in Art Centers	2642	2751	2639	2725	2848	2941	3086
#乡镇文化站	#Township Cultural Stations	2046	2234	2109	2159	2258	2344	2460

19-2 公共图书馆发展情况
Development Statistics on Public Libraries

项 目	Item	2015	2016	2017	2018	2019
机构数 (个)	Number of Library (unit)	112	112	116	115	116
藏书数 (万册)	Total Collections (10 000 volumes)	3003	3318	3597	3910	4221
书架单层总长度 (万米)	Total Length of Bookshelves (10 000 m)	54	56	55	55	57
有效借书证数图书流通情况 (万个)	Valid Library card number (10 000 units)	144	167	187	212	220
公共图书馆流通人次 (万人次)	Number of Circulation The public library circulation (10 000 person-times)	1955	2082	2388	2577	2646
册次 (万册数)	Volume-time (10 000 volume-times)	1816	1882	2136	2210	2298
为读者服务举办各种活动次数 (次)	Service for Readers Times (time)	3615	4874	5236	4875	5508
参加人数 (万人次)	Number of Readers Involved (10 000 person-times)	163	233	231	278	290
当年新购图书 (万册)	New Books Purchaesd in 2017 (10 000 volume-times)	185	296	284	359	304
图书费 (万元)	Purchase Expenses (10 000 yuan)	7302	7948	8358	8244	8844

19-3 公共图书馆藏书及分类情况
Statistics on Books and classification in Public Libraries

单位:万册 (10 000 volumes)

年份 Year	合计 Total	#外 文 #Foreign	#古 籍 #Ancient	#图书 #New Books	其它藏量 Other Reserves
1996	1472	82	97		
1997	1533	81	97		
1998	1599	81	96		
1999	1643	81	96		
2000	1678	82	97		
2001	1709	83	98		
2002	1759	81	99		
2003	1819	83	98		
2004	1867		94		
2005	1923		97		
2006	1981		100		
2007	2037		96		
2008	2106		97		
2009	2181		96		
2010	2361		95		
2011	2410		98	1860	453
2012	2521		98	2008	415
2013	2648		99	2156	393
2014	2822		101	2295	426
2015	3003		101	2462	441
2016	3318		98	2752	468
2017	3597		98	2963	536
2018	3910		97	3259	554
2019	4221		97	3547	577

19-4 图书、报纸、期刊出版情况
Statistics on Publication of Books, Newspapers and Periodicals

项 目	Item	2000	2005	2010	2015	2016	2017	2018	2019
一、图书出版种数 (种)	**Category of Library Books Published (kind)**	**4529**	**6535**	**10464**	**15543**	**15105**	**13590**	**13419**	**13077**
新出版 (种)	New Publications (kind)	2443	3739	6328	8932	7911	7404	6852	5952
总印数 (千册)	Total Prints (1 000 volume)	288416	345510	275330	262997	270444	229726	268349	316620
总印张 (千印张)	Total Number of Paper Printed (1 000 pages)	1552128	2495183	1997639	2250020	2236382	1883288	2099493	2364196
二、杂志出版种数 (种)	**Category of Magazines Published (kind)**	**391**	**407**	**407**	**412**	**414**	**415**	**415**	**416**
总印数 (千册)	Total Prints (1000 volume)	220280	196800	300770	251249	185441	143353	118719	104927
总印张 (千印张)	Total Number of Paper Printed (1 000 pages)	746145	745526	1482345	1458924	1027425	757916	599399	517162
三、报刊出版种数 (种)	**Category of Newspapers and Periodicals Published (kind)**	**164**	**193**	**130**	**129**	**129**	**129**	**129**	**129**
总印数 (千份)	Total Prints (1 000 copies)	1342282	1956980	1816720	1539203	1226957	1064036	899099	736887
总印张 (万印张)	Total Number of Paper Printed (10 000 pages)	339434	520833	889514	538040	348483	297345	240632	209377

19-5 艺术活动、群众文化活动、图书馆及博物馆活动情况
Statistics on Art Activities, Public Culture Activities, Library and Museum

项 目	Item	2000	2005	2010	2015	2017	2018	2019
艺术表演团体	Art Performance Troupes							
演出场次 (万场次)	Number of Performances (10 000shows)				3.85	6.46	6.69	5.17
国内演出观众人数 (万人次)	Number of Domestic Audience (10 000 person-times)				2902	4151	4426	6119
艺术表演场馆	Art Performance Places							
演(映)出场次 (万场次)	Number of Performances (10 000shows)				3.49	5.35	6.74	5.20
观众人次 (万人次)	Number of Audience (10 000 person-times)				288	322	308.2	297.5
群众文化活动	Public Culture Activities							
举办展览个数 (个)	Number of Expo Displayed (unit)	2785	2653	4276	4399	5970	6309	6332
举办训练班结业人数 (万人次)	Number of Training Activities (10 000 person-times)	9.90	13.00	10.80	97.6	144.2	159.3	163.1
图书馆活动	Library Activities							
书刊文献外借人次 (千人次)	Number of Circulation (1000 person-times)				9918	11816	11429	12212
图书流通册次 (千册)	Number of Circulation (1000 volumes)	9485	9267	18462	18164	21363	22103	22976
博物馆活动	Museum Activities							
基本陈列展览 (个)	Displays Exhibition (unit) (unit)	210	218	686	964	1096	1003	1140
参观人数 (千人次)	Visitors (1000 persons) (time)	1819	2194	19212	26239	34709	39224.6	41099.7

19-6 文化、文物事业经费支出及基本建设情况
Basic Conditions about Expenditures and Constructionon Culture and Historical Relics

单位:万元 (10 000 yuan)

项　目	Item	2015	2016	2017	2018	2019
文化、文物事业经费支出总计	**Total Expenditures on Culture and Historical Relics**	**450545**	**571068**	**706865**	**847487**	**1391964**
文化事业	Culture	338057	416761	515684	663402.9	1221224
艺术表演团体	Art Performing Groups	63525	74001	93532	103203.2	112134.8
艺术表演场所	Art Performing Places	9784	10828	22924	26723.3	20671.5
图书馆	Library	50295	49833	58296	62460.6	62709.3
群众文化	Public Culture	51708	68180	81421	54823.2	49353.8
中等专业学校	Secondary Vocation School	12412	22985	21508		
干部训练	Cadre Taining					
其他文化事业	Others	150333	191165	27946	19070.2	19848.5
文物事业	Historical Relics	112488	154307	191181	184084.1	170740.5
博物馆	Museum	59126	101517	103765	113859.2	112266.1
文物事业机构	Institutions of Historical Relics	21621	24814	57771	43886	50445
其它文物事业	Others	31741	27976	29645	26338.9	8029.4
文化、文物基本建设	Investment in Culture & Historical	35872	45187	76822	30509.7	16576.4
完成投资	Relics Cause Construction					
文化事业	Culture Cause	17955	25945	40955	13205.5	2296.8
文物事业	Historical Relics Cause	17917	19242	35867	17304.2	14279.6

19-7 广播电视从业人员基本情况(2019)
Basic Statistics on Personnel Engaged in Broadcasting and Television(2019)

单位：人 (person)

项目	Item	全省合计 Total of the Province	省级 Provincial Level	市州级 Municiple and Prefecture Level	县级 County Level
从业人员	Personel	37165	23597	5496	8072
其中:长期职工	#Long-term Staff and Workers	36004	22750	5445	7809
按岗位分:	Classified by Job Division:				
管理人员	Management Personel	7021	3441	1280	2300
专业技术人员	Professional Technical Personel	5836	4152	755	929
编辑、记者	Editors and Reporters	6486	2198	1898	2390
播音员、主持人	Announcers and Hosts	1139	336	408	395
按学历分:	Classified by Academic Qualifications:				
研究生及以上	#Graduate and Above	1588	1176	282	130
本科及大专	Undergraduate and Post-secondary	27468	15943	4816	6709
高中及以下	High School and Below	8109	6478	398	1233
按职称分:	Classified According to Occupation:				
正高	Senior	299	237	60	2
副高	Vice-senior	1229	738	411	80
中级	Medium	6671	3150	1664	1857
初级及以下	Primary and Below	17931	12226	2414	3291
按年龄分:	Classified by Age:				
35岁以下	35 and Below	13076	9182	1707	2187
36岁至50岁	36-50	18430	11315	2794	4321
50岁以上	50 and Above	5659	3100	995	1564

19-8 广播电视传输覆盖情况
Statistics on Broadcasting and TV Coverage Rating

项 目	Item	2010	2015	2016	2017	2018	2019
广播综合人口覆盖率 (%)	Broadcasting Coverage Rate (%)	98.10	99.08	99.33	99.38	99.68	99.79
电视综合人口覆盖率 (%)	TV Coverage Rate (%)	98.11	98.98	99.15	99.32	99.58	99.7
有线电视实际用户数 (万户)	Cable Television Users (10 000 household)	894.07	1067.80	1060.80	1082.94	1082.77	1071.48
中短波发射台 (座)		26	28	28	28	28	26
中短波发射机 (部)		76	88	89	90	89	91
中短波发射机功率 (千瓦)		1256	1391	1401	1391	1376	1400
调频电视转播发射台 (座)	FM and Television Transmitting Stations (set)		481	478	201	181	404
调频发射机 (部)	FM Transmitters (set)	584	484	486	1214	438	372
调频发射机功率 (千瓦)	Power of FM Transmitters (kw)	520.31	623.69	633.97	749.86	727.65	728.96
电视发射机 (座)	Television Transmitting Station (set)			751	671	739	1397
电视发射机功率 (千瓦)	Power of Television Transmitters (kw)	592.22	598.69	590.21	566.05	585.12	727.23
微波线路站数/长度 (座/公里)	Length of Micro-Wave Route Per Station (set/km)	121/2961.05	126/2875.05	122/2829.05	99/3165.70	73/2158.6	63/2073.9

注:2017年起调频发射机台统计口径发生变化。
Note: Since 2017, the Statistical Caliber of FM transmitter has changed.

19-9 广播电视宣传、节目制作和电影活动
Radio and Television Promotion, Program Production and Film Activities

项　目	Item	2005	2010	2017	2018	2019
广播电台 (座)	Broadcasting Station (unit)	11	11	5	5	1
电视台 (座)	TV Station (unit)	12	12	5	5	1
广播电视台 (座)	Radiated TV Station (unit)	71	71	78	79	82
广播节目套数 (套)	Number of Radio Programs (unit)	81	85	90	94	96
广播平均日播音时间 (小时)	Average Broadcasting Hour per Week (h)	1040.40	1225.65	1367.14	1466	1443
广播节目年制作能力 (万小时)	Annual Capacity of Radio Program Production (10 000 h)	20.59	23.54	23.99	24.29	24.67
电视节目套数 (套)	Number of TV Programs (unit)	113	114	117	117	116
电视平均周播出时间 (万小时)	Average TV Hour per Week (10 000 h)	1.05	1.26	1.37	1.38	1.35
电视节目年制作能力 (万小时)	Annual Capacity of TV program Production (10 000 h)	7.93	9.48	10.00	10.37	8.8
电视剧制作 (部/集)	Production of TV Series (episode)	11/208	11/314	4/182	5/215	2/91
城市电影活动	Movie of city					
放映场次数 (万场)	Times Projected (10 000 times)			400.6	465.1	517.7
观众人数 (千人次)	Number of the audience (1000 person-times)			83127	84619.7	8190.4

19-10 分单位类型、分人员类型体育系统从业人员数(2019)

Number of Staff and Workers in Sports Commissions by Unit Type and Personnel Type(2019)

单位:人 (person)

项目	Item	合计 Total	公务员 Civilian	管理人员 Administrator	专业技术人员 小计 Subtotal	专业技术人员 其中:教练员 Coach	专业技术人员 其中:科研人员 Scientific research personnel	专业技术人员 其中:卫生技术人员 Health technical personnel	运动员 Athlete	工勤人员 Worker	其他 Others
合计	Total	6238	976	1270	929	845	60	24	1053	402	1608
体育行政机关	Sports Administrative Authority	1293	976	156	14	14				60	87
运动项目管理部门(优秀运动队)	Sports Management Department	1137		181	193	190		3	733	5	25
本科院校	Undergraduate School	1236		159	76	38	38		298	65	638
体育运动学校	Sports School for athelets	570		71	192	186	6		1	27	279
少年儿童体育学校	Sports School for Kids	553		103	283	282	1		18	26	123
体育中学	Middle School for Athelets	37		3	13	13				3	18
训练基地	Training Base	147		71	27	27			3	28	18
体育场馆	Stadium	675		287	87	86		1		162	139
体育科研机构	Sports Science Reaserch Institution	43		6	35		15	20			2
其他事业单位	Other Institution	533		221	9	9				24	279
其它	Others	14		12						2	

19-11 等级裁判员、运动员情况
Number of Athletes and Referees in Grades

单位:人 (person)

项 目	Item	2000	2005	2010	2013	2014	2015	2016	2017	2018	2019
等级裁判员合计	**Number of Referees in Grades**	**1195**	**787**	**1504**	**2335**	**1725**	**3021**	**1206**	**1910**	**1625**	**924**
国际裁判	International Referees								6	6	6
国家级裁判	National Referees	29	25	24	27		4	2	21	39	29
一级裁判	First Grade	143	115	352	377	394	317	176	416	471	288
二级裁判	Second Grade	1023	647	1128	1931	1331	2700	1028	1467	1109	601
等级运动员合计	**Number of Athletes in Grade**	**418**	**1149**	**1639**	**2109**	**2111**	**1556**	**2036**	**1987**	**1814**	**1692**
国际运动健将	International Master of Sports	6		1		4	4			23	9
运动健将	Master of Sports	36	36	21	61	41	68	5	5	50	111
一级运动员	First Grade	10	247	180	214	359	316	427	382	408	367
二级运动员	Second Grade	366	866	1437	1834	1707	1168	1604	1600	1333	1205

19-12 体育竞赛成果情况
Statistics on Achievement in Sports Competition

项目	Item	2000	2005	2010	2015	2016	2017	2018	2019
世界比赛获奖牌数（枚）	**Number of Medals Won in InternationalGames (unit)**	**13**	**5**	**12**	**66**	**107**	**116**	**113**	**169**
金牌	Gold Medal	4	3	2	29	50	48	60	73
银牌	Silver Medal	6	2	3	32	32	28	27	50
铜牌	Bronze Medal	3		7	5	25	40	26	46
亚洲比赛获奖牌数（枚）	**Number of Medals Won in Asia Games (unit)**	**5**	**7**	**13**	**35**	**44**	**34**	**51**	62
金牌	Gold Medal	4	5	8	17	23	18	17	**30**
银牌	Silver Medal		2	4	9	16	10	21	16
铜牌	Bronze Medal	1		1	9	5	6	13	16
全国比赛获前六名（人）	**Top Six Places in National Games (person)**		**155**	**134**	**502**	**655**	**651**	**855**	1266
第一名	First Place	35	24	21	75	116	107	172	**230**
第二名	Second Place	22	23	21	78	102	123	149	218
第三名	Third Place	21	27	17	85	131	124	167	275
第四名	Fourth Place	35	24	23	76	91	99	125	159
第五名	Fifth Place	29	31	30	109	126	135	153	238
第六名	Sixth Place	26	26	22	79	89	63	89	146

19-13 新建健身场地设施情况(2019)
Situation of New-Built Fitness Facilities(2019)

项目	Item	合计 Total	村级农民体育健身工程 Town-based Peasant Fitness Project	乡镇体育健身工程 County-based Fitness Project	全民健身路径工程 Citizen "Fitness Path" Project	全民健身活动中心 Citizen Fitness Center
数量 (个)	Number (unit)	769	200	100		25
器材件数 (件)	Number of Instrument (piece)					
场地面积 (平方米)	Area (sq. m)	1109396	106800	835960		68250
场地长度 (米)	Length (m)	1055482				
投资总额 (万元)	Total Investment (10 000 Yuan)	36513	4000	10000		8533

19-13 续表

项目	Item	户外健身场地设施 Outdoor Fitness Facilities					其他场地设施 Other Fitness Facilities
		体育公园 Fitness Park	全民健身广场 Citizen Fitness Square	户外体育营地 Outdoor Fitness Center	社区运动场地 Community-based Fitness Square	健身步道 Fitness Path	
数量 (个)	Number (unit)	7		21	78	338	
器材件数 (件)	Number of Instrument (piece)						
场地面积 (平方米)	Area (sq. m)	95800		2586			
场地长度 (米)	Length (m)					1055482	
投资总额 (万元)	Total Investment (10 000 Yuan)	7800		1550		4630	

19-14 分市州文化及相关产业"三上"法人单位数(2019)
Number of Corporate Units of Cultural and Related Industries above Designated Size by Cities and Prefectures(2019)

单位:个 (unit)

地 区	Region	"三上"法人单位数 Legal Persons	规上文化制造业 Cultual Manufacturing	限上文化批发和零售业 Wholesale and Rerail of Culture	规上文化服务业 Services of Culture
全 省	**Province**	**2845**	**848**	**580**	**1417**
武汉市	Wuhan	972	105	111	756
黄石市	Huangshi	85	25	25	35
十堰市	Shiyan	115	21	41	53
宜昌市	Yichang	411	128	71	212
襄阳市	Xiangyang	266	71	89	106
鄂州市	Ezhou	47	19	7	21
荆门市	Jingmen	127	54	37	36
孝感市	Xiaogan	160	108	31	21
荆州市	Jingzhou	113	36	45	32
黄冈市	Huanggang	205	127	37	41
咸宁市	Xianning	131	71	18	42
随州市	Suizhou	46	22	5	19
恩施州	Enshi	80	15	40	25
仙桃市	Xiantao	46	21	17	8
潜江市	Qianjiang	15	9	2	4
天门市	Tianmen	22	16	4	2
神农架	Shennongjia	4			4

19-15 分市州规模以上文化制造业企业基本情况(2019)

Statistics on Culture-Related Manufacturing Enterprises above Designated Size by Cities and Prefectures(2019)

单位:万元 (10 000 yuan)

地区	Region	企业单位数(个) Number of Enterprises(unit)	年末从业人员(人) Engaged Person at Year-end(person)	资产总计 Total Assets	营业收入 Business Revenue	税金及附加 Taxes and Extra Charges on Business	营业利润 Operating Profit	应交增值税 Value-added Tax Payable
全省	**Province**	**848**	**139395**	**12394985**	**17902282.5**	**159207.2**	**1016347.3**	**470384.5**
武汉市	Wuhan	105	16838	3283699.3	3020650.9	12203.1	164817.2	65951.2
黄石市	Huangshi	25	5080	254212.7	311241.7	2279.3	14907.6	3218.9
十堰市	Shiyan	21	1768	203786.4	196977.5	3761.7	21719.1	6589.1
宜昌市	Yichang	128	27535	2257585.0	2866479.0	18448.2	125975.2	75753.1
襄阳市	Xiangyang	71	12661	797545.4	2180617.2	10633.6	148316.0	51637.6
鄂州市	Ezhou	19	2354	262843.6	691939.1	4466.8	43081.2	18919.9
荆门市	Jingmen	54	7602	923702.5	1394354.7	18219.9	66117.5	31888.9
孝感市	Xiaogan	108	16915	1182218.7	2746686.7	50711	140605.6	91918.7
荆州市	Jingzhou	36	5187	435612.6	510363.4	6379.2	15414.8	10733.9
黄冈市	Huanggang	127	18383	1130713.5	1324798.2	8278.8	89686.2	28419.1
咸宁市	Xianning	71	7722	554279.4	987288.2	8574.1	67855.7	25526.6
随州市	Suizhou	22	4181	212175.2	448905.3	3224.8	37707.4	24326.1
恩施州	Enshi	15	1380	41268.5	72290.9	418.1	1171.4	1951.2
仙桃市	Xiantao	21	4364	411634.1	509260.8	4605.8	33977.0	16739.7
潜江市	Qianjiang	9	1606	210424.2	199276.8	5524.4	14536.9	8328.6
天门市	Tianmen	16	5819	233283.8	441152.1	1478.4	30458.5	8481.9
神农架	Shennongjia							

19-16 分市州限额以上文化批发和零售企业基本情况(2019)
Statistics on Culture-Related Wholesale and Retail Enterprises above Designated Size by Cities and Prefectures(2019)

单位:万元 (10 000 yuan)

地 区	Region	企业单位数(个) Number of Enterprises(unit)	年末从业人员(人) Engaged Person at Year-end(person)	资产总计 Total Assets	营业收入 Business Revenue	营业税金及附加 Taxes and Extra Charges on Business	营业利润 Operating Profit	应交增值税 Value-added Tax Payable
全 省	**Province**	**580**	**22607**	**3104866.6**	**4382658.4**	**53438.8**	**205239.7**	**63891.6**
武汉市	Wuhan	111	9342	1967588.3	2017486.4	7306.7	63404.0	14321.4
黄石市	Huangshi	25	501	33225.4	76960.9	245.2	3994.8	1527.6
十堰市	Shiyan	41	980	45738.9	106160.2	2485	6841.9	4265.4
宜昌市	Yichang	71	2140	190577.2	458295.8	3943.3	18651.3	7114.2
襄阳市	Xiangyang	89	1664	96596.9	360791.7	29558.9	34242.4	6532.9
鄂州市	Ezhou	7	146	5811.2	12645.8	51.0	33.7	890.1
荆门市	Jingmen	37	758	384701.1	546038.6	2259.2	43038.4	13644.3
孝感市	Xiaogan	31	2508	86796.7	223779.8	762.5	5679.0	4694.1
荆州市	Jingzhou	45	971	63490.2	176427.7	3653.4	3957.3	2654.6
黄冈市	Huanggang	37	1087	55811.9	123121.6	1120.5	4768.7	2656.3
咸宁市	Xianning	18	395	22157.4	95227.9	788.4	8088.4	2616.1
随州市	Suizhou	5	93	1605.9	6708.6	109.1	1478.2	303.9
恩施州	Enshi	40	1265	83536.2	90998.0	456.6	2948.2	1257.1
仙桃市	Xiantao	17	442	25689.0	39914.1	431.2	6452.2	838.2
潜江市	Qianjiang	2	139	20905.7	24654.9	147.3	232.5	173.8
天门市	Tianmen	4	176	20634.6	23446.4	120.5	1428.7	401.6
神农架	Shennongjia							

19-17 分市州规模以上文化服务业企业基本情况(2019)
Statistics on Culture-Related Service Enterprises above Designated Sizeby Cities and Prefectures(2019)

单位:万元 (10 000 yuan)

地 区	Region	企业单位数(个) Number of Enterprises(unit)	年末从业人员(人) Engaged Person at Year-end(person)	资产总计 Total Assets	营业收入 Business Revenue	营业税金及附加 Taxes and Extra Charges on Business	营业利润 Operating Profit	应交增值税 Value-added Tax Payable
全 省	**Province**	**1417**	**270674**	**42131676.5**	**17248348.9**	**247568.8**	**1495015.6**	**442943.9**
武汉市	Wuhan	756	227189	31852097.4	15592966.8	217354.3	1318314.6	392415.4
黄石市	Huangshi	35	2023	195275.2	64972.7	612.6	-4022.2	2031.4
十堰市	Shiyan	53	3052	334818.6	105477.1	1816.4	6529.8	4574.2
宜昌市	Yichang	212	14976	2867851.8	613291	7947.8	82858.9	19343.1
襄阳市	Xiangyang	106	5339	454949.4	261437.8	3990.5	12368.8	5138.5
鄂州市	Ezhou	21	916	184954.9	33429.5	528.4	-718.1	543.8
荆门市	Jingmen	36	2535	2349061.9	113795.9	10717.4	14467.8	2791.7
孝感市	Xiaogan	21	1253	111532.9	41683.2	677.4	1553.3	1743.2
荆州市	Jingzhou	32	3632	156312.9	117236.7	662.4	6307.0	3725.7
黄冈市	Huanggang	41	2433	1331215.4	82967.4	986.6	23300.3	1905.7
咸宁市	Xianning	42	2150	1138880.7	59369.9	923.5	6671.0	2048.6
随州市	Suizhou	19	1052	91749.8	31718.6	264.2	751.8	870.9
恩施州	Enshi	25	2042	835867.1	73455.6	676	15380.9	3475.1
仙桃市	Xiantao	8	1238	31059.7	24601.7	238.2	8347.8	1405.6
潜江市	Qianjiang	4	95	7967.5	4488.0	70.4	439.0	147.9
天门市	Tianmen	2	65	2586.8	3692.7	19.2	163.6	168.3
神农架	Shennongjia	4	684	185494.5	23764.3	83.5	2301.3	614.8

主要统计指标解释

文化事业机构 指从事专业文化工作和为专业文化工作服务的独立建制的单位。不包括这些单位另外举办独立核算的其他机构和各部门的业余文化组织。该指标主要反映文化事业机构发展规模水平。

艺术表演团体 指从事戏曲、音乐、舞蹈、杂技等专业艺术表演，有独立帐户的单位，不包括半工半艺、半农半艺和民间职业剧团。该指标主要反映全国专业艺术表演团体发展规模水平。

艺术表演观众人数(人次) 指售票、包场演出或民族地区免费演出的艺术表演观众人次数，不包括彩排审查和内部观摩演出的观看人次数。该指标主要反映全国观看专业艺术表演团体演出的效益规模。

等级运动员 是指经考核正式批准授予运动员称号的运动员，等级称号由高到低依次为国际级运动健将、运动健将、一级运动员、二级运动员、三级运动员。

广播节目综合人口覆盖率 指根据国家广电总局制定的《广播电视人口覆盖率统计技术标准和方法》进行统计调查的，在对象区能接收到由中央、省、地区或县通过无线、有线或卫星等技术方式传播的各级广播节目的人口数占全国总人口数的百分比。

电视节目综合人口覆盖率 指根据国家广电总局制定的《广播电视人口覆盖率统计技术标准和方法》进行统计调查的，在对象区能接收到由中央、省、地区或县通过无线、有线或卫星等技术方式传播的各级电视节目的人口数占全国总人口数的百分比。

Explanatory Notes on Main Statistical Indicators

Cultural Institutions refer to units, which have their own organizational system and independent accounting system and specialize in or serve cultural development. They exclude other establishments run by these cultural institutions and amateur cultural groups established by various departments. This indicator reflects the development of cultural units.

Art Troupe refers to the troupe which is engaged in drama, opera, music, dance, acrobatics or other art performance, opens independent accounts with banks and has self-supporting accounting system; excluding the troupes which are engaged partly in industrial or agricultural activities, partly in art performance and the professional troupes organized by the people. This indicator reflects the development of national professional art troupes.

Number of Audience at Art Performance refers to the number of attendants at commercial shows, completely booked shows or free shows given in minority national areas, and does not include the number of spectators at rehearsals for examination and internal shows for study.

Certified Grade Athletes refer to those who are awarded the title of athletes through assessment. The titles rank from high to low as: international level athletes, national level athletes, first grade athletes, second grade athletes and third grade athletes.

Radio Coverage of Population refers to the percentage of population, which can receive central, provincial, city, prefecture, and county radio programs relayed by wireless, cable, satellite and other technical means, in the surveying area, to national total population, according to Statistical Standard and Method on Television and Radio Coverage of Population established by the State Administration of Broadcasting, Film and Television.

Television Coverage of Population refers to the percentage of population, which can receive central, provincial, city, prefecture, and county television programs relayed by wireless, cable, satellite and other technical means, in the surveying area, to national total population, according to Statistical Standard and Method on Television and Radio Coverage of Population established by the State Administration of Broadcasting, Film and Television.

20 公共管理及其他

Public Management and Other

资料整理人员：谢　涛

20-1 工会组织情况
Basic Statistics on Labor Union

年 份 Year	工会基层组织数(个) Number of Grassroot Labor Union Organizations (unit)	全省已建工会的基层单位职工与会员人数(万人) Number of Grassroot Staff and Workers and Members of Established Labor Union in the Province(10 000 persons)				工会专职工作人员人数(万人) Number of Full-time Workers in Labor Union (10 000 persons)
		职工人数 Number of Staff and Workers	#女职工 #Women Workers	会员人数 Number of Members	#女会员 #Women Members	
1975	18872	280.22	83.18	174.72	56.24	0.87
1980	22802	387.95	139.20	299.41	94.91	1.04
1985	25286	484.68	192.32	404.58	156.62	2.76
1990	33990	559.00	227.00	498.00	198.00	3.40
1995	28461	564.34	230.90	511.11	207.49	1.81
1996	28459	584.30	238.16	527.09	213.08	2.88
1997	20151	472.60	192.65	419.72	168.89	2.68
1998	17488	445.80	183.90	400.90	163.90	2.30
1999	18976	442.97	178.21	396.90	155.03	3.18
2000	45251	532.31	197.81	475.57	176.87	2.45
2001	111309	728.94	218.68	660.82	198.25	2.45
2004	50391	755.90	276.69	721.46	262.74	2.95
2005	54893	856.07	298.78	771.95	279.94	3.09
2006	61627	904.15	314.67	856.95	296.39	3.76
2007	69886	1004.92	358.44	972.30	345.64	3.94
2008	79048	1099.78	382.72	1073.22	377.43	4.48
2009	83436	1160.45	418.82	1127.68	411.12	4.75
2010	88647	1220.52	437.50	1184.88	429.00	5.80
2011	107995	1319.08	462.18	1267.28	453.11	6.10
2012	120561	1336.09	491.49	1292.06	481.87	6.44
2013	130513	1348.45	494.94	1312.16	487.57	6.36
2014	130326	1325.35	495.91	1285.13	487.36	6.67
2015	130118	1355.78	505.27	1301.52	490.43	6.61
2016	131582	1385.96	515.29	1338.23	503.98	6.62
2017	132619	1395.86	516.85	1351.90	506.90	6.62
2018	133850	1384.92	517.48	1343.47	508.34	4.55
2019	131588	1394.14	521.80	1346.14	509.47	4.71

注：因文革期间工会统计中断，表中1975年数据根据年平均增长值推算。
Note:The data in 1975 were calculated by the average growth rate because Labor Union statistics had been suspended in the period of "The Great Cultural Revolution".

20-2 基层政权和村(居)委会情况

Basic Statistics on Grassroots Regime and Village Committees

单位:个 (unit)

年份 Year	镇 Township	乡 Villages	街道办事处 Regional Office	居委会个数 Number of Committees	村委会个数 Number of Village Committees
1986	859	3700	178	3257	32796
1987	836	1257	186	3394	32738
1988	828	1260	215	3483	32354
1989	840	1143	298	3545	32094
1990	849	1123	293	3573	32703
1991	849	1121	307	3709	32595
1992	852	1117	297	3830	32716
1993	857	1097	214	3921	32674
1994	864	1092	218	3998	32636
1995	865	1038	236	4110	32547
1996	823	567	252	4170	32486
1997	840	552	252	4287	32393
1998	847	543	253	4364	32293
1999	850	488	271	4425	32187
2000	860	466	283	3619	32001
2001	735	228	250	3468	31191
2002	738	224	272	3265	27667
2003	735	224	273	3351	27127
2004	738	224	274	3356	26470
2005	733	217	277	3465	29534
2006	737	210	277	3545	25828
2007	734	210	279	3653	25722
2008	735	207	285	3794	25551
2009	740	204	283	3882	25517
2010	741	199	290	3983	25763
2011	742	194	297	4051	25643
2012	746	188	298	4032	25575
2013	757	175	300	4208	25452
2014	761	170	302	4187	25448
2015	761	168	304	4294	25109
2016	759	168	307	4390	25064
2017	761	165	308	4401	24970
2018	762	163	310	4528	23392
2019	760	162	327	4631	22653

20-3　提供住宿的社会服务床位数

Beds of Social Welfare Institutions with Accommodations

单位:万张　　　　(10 000 beds)

年份 Year	床位数 Number of Beds	#养老 The Aged	#儿童 Child	#其他 Other
2012	25.4	23.7	0.7	0.6
2013	25.2	23.4	0.7	0.6
2014	27.7	23.3	0.8	0.7
2015	24.3	22.5	0.5	0.8
2016	25.7	23.9	0.5	0.8
2017	25.4	23.6	0.4	0.8
2018	23.6	22.4	0.4	0.6
2019	26.6	25.5	0.4	0.7

注:2018年社会服务床位数不含优抚(军休)床位数。
Note: The number of social service beds in 2018 does not include the number of special care (military rest) beds.

20-4　社会救助情况

Statistics on Social Assistance

单位:万人　　　　(10 000 persons)

年份 Year	城市居民最低生活保障人数 Number of Urban Residents Receiving Minimum Living Allowance	农村居民最低生活保障人数 Number of Rural Residents Receiving Minimum Living Allowance	城镇特困人员救助供养人数 Urban Households Livelihood Guaranteed in Five Aspects	农村特困人员救助供养人数 Rural Households Livelihood Guaranteed in Five Aspects
2012	129.5	230.7		
2013	125.9	235.7		
2014	107.1	221.6		
2015	84.6	159.5		
2016	55.3	138.2		
2017	45.9	137.9		
2018	37.8	133.8	0.8	24.8
2019	31.8	139.3	1.0	24.3

20-5 社会保险基本情况
Basic Conditions about Social Insurance

年 份	失业保险 Unemployment Insurance		城镇职工基本养老保险 Basic Endowment Insurance for Urban and Rural Employees		工伤保险年末参保人数	年末参加生育保险人数	基本医疗保险 Basic medical insurance	
year	年末参保人数(万人) Participants at Year-end (10 000 persons)	全年发放失业保险金(亿元) Unemployed Relief Released (100 million yuan)	年末参保职工人数(万人) Participants at Year-end (10 000 persons)	年末参保离退休人数(万人) Retirees (10 000 persons)	(万人) Participants at Year-end (10 000 persons)	(万人) Number of People Participated in Maternity Insurance at Year-end (10 000 persons)	年末职工参保人数(万人) Urban residents participanting in insurance at Year-end (10 000 persons)	年末城乡居民参保人数(万人) Rural residents participanting in insurance at Year-end (10 000 persons)
1996	392.9	0.4	353.2		177.6	137.8		
1997	381.2	0.5	355.8		188.5	165.5		
1998	378.2	0.5	413.1	107.4	190.0	168.8		
1999	517.6	0.6	455.3	122.4	183.8	189.0		
2000	459.6	1.6	465.6	130.4	185.0	191.3		
2001	420.8	3.2	474.4	136.6	182.3	182.1		
2002	416.1	5.4	532.7	154.5	183.2	182.7		
2003	390.1	5.6	554.5	167.5	189.2	182.1		
2004	391.3	4.0	586.1	194.7	187.2	179.9		
2005	391.5	4.0	597.6	206.4	230.3	175.9		
2006	395.5	3.7	630.2	220.5	275.5	194.5		
2007	405.4	3.8	651.4	235.3	328.0	225.0		
2008	422.6	3.6	671.7	252.4	350.7	315.4		
2009	437.0	3.6	701.9	273.7	396.5	350.6		
2010	464.5	3.9	749.1	301.3	444.5	388.7	847.8	
2011	496.0	3.7	766.0	341.4	467.3	412.9	902.8	
2012	501.4	3.8	801.4	367.3	505.8	444.7	921.2	
2013	511.9	4.2	822.0	396.0	541.0	457.9	922.8	
2014	520.9	5.1	847.0	419.3	576.7	480.6	933.3	
2015	531.2	5.8	874.9	440.6	640.1	500.2	949.4	
2016	542.5	7.7	897.1	457.9	651.1	511.9	960.99	
2017	565.4	7.6	1020.5	526.1	656.6	522.1	1018.89	4606.3
2018	590.3	10.1	1047.5	554.1	675.6	540.0	1053.95	4532.21
2019	618.2	8.8	1100.5	584.3	717.6	577.7	1093.17	4469.42

20-6 参加基本养老保险人数

Number of Persons Participated in Basic Endowment Insurance

单位:万人 (10 000 persons)

年份 Year	合计 Total	职工 Number of Employees	企业(含其他) Enterprises (including others)	离退休人员 Number of Retirees	企业(含其他) Enterprises (including others)	城乡居民基本养老保险
1996	353.2	353.2	353.2			
1997	355.8	355.8	355.8			
1998	520.5	413.1	413.1	107.4	107.4	
1999	577.7	455.3	455.3	122.4	122.4	
2000	596.0	465.6	465.6	130.4	130.4	
2001	611.0	474.4	474.4	136.6	136.6	
2002	687.2	532.7	481.5	154.5	147.2	
2003	722.0	554.5	501.1	167.5	158.6	
2004	780.8	586.1	530.6	194.7	184.5	
2005	804.0	597.6	539.8	206.4	195.1	
2006	850.7	630.2	570.0	220.5	207.5	
2007	886.7	651.4	602.6	235.3	223.0	
2008	924.1	671.7	628.7	252.4	238.7	
2009	975.6	701.9	660.5	273.7	259.2	
2010	1050.4	749.1	690.9	301.3	258.3	
2011	1107.4	766.0	725.5	341.4	325.6	
2012	1168.7	801.4	757.8	367.3	351.2	
2013	1217.9	822.0	779.1	396.0	379.7	
2014	1266.2	847.0	802.5	419.3	402.1	
2015	1315.5	874.9	830.7	440.6	422.9	
2016	1355.0	897.1	853.8	457.9	439.5	
2017	3806.7	1020.5	907.5	526.1	471.1	2260.1
2018	3884.2	1047.5	918.9	554.1	484.3	2282.5
2019	4029.7	1100.5	970.9	584.3	498.9	2344.9

注:2017年起,基本养老保险参保人数包括参加城乡居民基本养老保险人数。

Note: starting from 2017, the number of participants in basic old-age insurance shall include the number of urban and rural residents participating in Basic old-age insurance.

20-7 婚姻登记和离婚情况
Statistics on Marriage Registrationand Divorce

年份 Year	准予登记结婚(对) Marriage Registeration Granted (couple)	初婚(人) First Marriage (person)	再婚(人) Digamist(person)	离婚(对) Divorce (couple)	离婚率(‰) Rate of Divorce (‰)
1986	402315	785319	19311	6322	0.25
1987	417552	809808	25296	6660	0.26
1988	362654	698447	26861	7389	0.29
1989	413460	801171	25749	9203	0.35
1990	408688	790477	26899	9477	0.35
1991	424708	820092	29324	9584	0.35
1992	463279	897899	28659	10793	0.39
1993	425276	822044	28508	11937	0.43
1994	457324	884817	29831	12910	0.46
1995	482063	930832	33294	13340	0.46
1996	442532	851577	33487	14590	0.50
1997	426460	820615	32305	21260	0.72
1998	399900	763163	36637	24711	0.84
1999	376961	716175	37747	19519	0.66
2000	353781	673294	34268	21255	0.71
2001	335421	632188	38654	22077	0.74
2002	321517	605055	37979	24003	0.80
2003	329256	614244	44268	29375	0.98
2004	381472	710633	52311	46369	1.54
2005	394093	717495	70691	53394	1.77
2006	445672	822294	69050	57682	1.91
2007	485278	896768	73788	65876	2.17
2008	542251	1025496	59006	76003	2.49
2009	565400	1058851	71949	81133	2.84
2010	570810	1068715	72905	89549	3.11
2011	626912	1169771	84053	98874	3.18
2012	615861	1155365	76357	109862	3.81
2013	645767	1201344	90190	127604	4.40
2014	621946	1182271	61621	133723	4.60
2015	572954	1079852	66056	144684	4.90
2016	513823	971991	55655	160236	5.40
2017	472102	853124	91080	175815	5.96
2018	437777	749195	126359	177022	5.98
2019	389339	631495	147183	188388	6.36

20-8 残疾人基本情况
Basic Statistics on Disabled Persons

项目		Item		2018	2019
康复		Rehabilitation			
视力残疾康复服务人数	(人)	Rehabilitation of Persons with Visual Disability	(persons)	70593	55195
听力语言残疾康复服务人数	(人)	Rehabilitation of Persons with Hearing and Speech Disability	(persons)	35016	29729
肢体残疾康复服务人数	(人)	Rehabilitation of Persons with Physical Disability	(persons)	223370	200865
智力残疾康复服务人数	(人)	Rehabilitation of Persons with Intellectual Disability	(persons)	39700	35877
精神病防治康复服务人数	(人)	Rehabilitation institutions for the disabled	(unit)	90024	95743
残疾人康复机构	(个)	Assistive appliance service organization	(unit)	214	202
辅助器具服务机构	(个)			55	122
教育		Education			
特殊教育普通高中在校生	(人)	Students at Special Education Senior High Schools	(persons)	233	325
高等院校录取残疾考生	(人)	Disabled Students Admitted to Higher Education Institutions	(persons)	417	453
就业					
当年新增残疾人就业人数	(人)	Number of new invalids employed in the year	(persons)	17800	18197
社会保障		Social Security	(persons)		
残疾居民参加城乡社会养老保险	(人)	Disabled residents in Urban and Rural Social endowment Insurance		1551982	1319113
扶贫		Poverty Alleviation			
培训残疾人	(人)	Trained persons with disabilities	(persons)	22247	25422
维权		Rights Protection			
残疾人法律援助工作站	(个)	Legal aid workstation for persons with disabilities	(unit)	65	71
残疾人法律救助工作站办理的案件	(件)	Barrier Free Home Renovation for Poor PWDs	(households)	108	92
残疾人机动轮骑车燃油补贴	(人)	Fuel Subsidy for Motor Wheelchairs of PWDs	(persons)	34686	20713
组织建设		Organization Development			
残疾人专职委员	(人)	Full-time commissioner for Persons with Disabilities	(persons)	19184	18598
残疾人人口库持证残疾人	(万人)	PWDs with Disability Certificate in the PWD Database	(10 000 persons)	155.6	157.6

20-9 刑事案件发、破案情况
Statistics on Occurrenceand Clearing Up of Criminal Cases

指 标	Item	2000	2005	2010	2014	2015	2016	2017	2018	2019
刑事案件立案总数 (件)	Number of Criminal Cases Occurred (case)	114866	147004	221735	265260	299522	275707	233670	210296	198736
刑事案件破案总数 (件)	Number of Criminal Cases Cleared (case)	72796	71455	76401	90652	77355	69775	83723	65766	66026
刑事案件破案率 (%)	Rate of Criminal Cases Cleared (%)	63.4	48.6	34.5	34.2	25.8	25.3	35.8	31.3	33.2

20-10 交通事故与火灾情况
Basic Statistics on Traffic Accidents and Fire Accidents

指 标	Item	2000	2005	2010	2014	2015	2016	2017	2018	2019
交通事故处理发生件数 (起)	Number of Traffic Accidents (case)	20148	9585	6465	5268	4627	19269	16292	23540	27086
死亡人数 (人)	Deaths (person)	3792	2417	1967	1771	1694	6560	5976	5562	5157
受伤人数 (人)	Injuries (person)	16492	10555	7684	5468	4638	18111	15791	26300	30950
折合经济损失 (万元)	Losses Converted into Money (10 000 yuan)	7041	4958	3294	5071	5176	9801	10583	14542	15075
火灾发生数 (起)	Number of Fire Accsidents (case)	6780	9356	9333	2322	2121	1964	12460	13578	14528
死亡人数 (人)	Deaths (person)	54	56	17	2	3	4	16	23	19
受伤人数 (人)	Injuries (person)	106	47	7	10	3	12	19	7	4
折合经济损失 (万元)	Losses Converted into Money (10 000 yuan)	1754	1945	3565	5520	4142	4380	8400	6807	11221

注:2017年起,火灾情况统计口径发生变化。
Note: Since 2017, the statistics of fire situation has changed.

20-11 审查批捕、起诉情况

Statistics on Examination, Arrest and Prosecution

项 目	Item	2000	2005	2010	2014	2015	2016	2017	2018	2019
受理批捕件数 (件)	Number of Cases (case)	20378	19846	9120	28267	28860	28605	31560	33558	36821
受理批捕人数 (人)	Number of People Arrested (person)	31245	29427	13391	38379	38400	38587	42891	48246	53372
批准逮捕 (人)	Number of Arrests Granted (person)	25114	27063	12081	32398	32400	31332	34254	37966	43162
不批捕人数 (人)	Number of Non-Arrest (person)	4329	1522	1001	5305	5388	6588	7955	9445	9566
受理审查起诉件数 (件)	Number of Cases Received (case)	17660	21966	10028	39980	42337	43596	50365	50368	59672
受理审查起诉人数 (人)	Number of Prosecution Accepted (person)	25416	33410	15280	55410	57002	58036	67253	69446	83574
起诉人数 (人)	Prosecutor (person)	22396	26926	11600	45740	46609	48207	50726	53682	67456
不起诉人数 (人)	Non-prosecutor (person)	1019	982	329	2115	2235	2369	3082	3924	4715

20-12 律师、公证、调解工作基本情况
Basic Statistics on Lawyers, Notarization and Mediation

项 目	Item	2005	2010	2014	2015	2016	2017	2018	2019
一、律师工作	**Lawyers**								
律师事务所 (个)	Number of Lawyer Office (person)	387	466	595	665	717	806	852	901
专职律师	Number of Full-Time Lawyer	3722	5869	8502	9419	10314	11388	12258	13324
兼职律师	Number of Part-Time Lawyer	165	252	351	363	376	363	381	408
担任法律顾问 (家)	Number of Units with Legal Advisors (unit)	9565	12059	16973	34772	55269	24059	20850	27685
民事案件诉讼代理 (件)	Agent of Civil Cases (case)	27079	45403	64479	79913	81013	101474	107078	129117
刑事诉讼辩护及代理 (件)	Defender and Agent of Criminal Cases (case)	11341	17724	18155	19076	20457	16440	22934	37597
非诉讼法律事务 (件)	Agent of Non-Litigious Legal Affairs (case)	34674	37521	24928	26276	21731	20130	15144	24980
咨询和代书 (万人次)						16.4	12.6	6.8	7.1
二、公证工作	**Notarization**								
公证机构 (个)	Number of Notary Offices (unit)	118	116	117	117	117	112	108	109
#公证员	#Notaries	455	353	397	424	449	429	386	377
公证员助理	Assistant Notaries	62	167	236	254	256	239	299	329
办理公证文件 (万件)	Number of Domestic Notarized Document (10 000 cases)	31.04	32.65	35.84	42.04	47	48.2	38.3	38.1
#涉外公证 (件)	#Foreign Notarized Documents (case)	65498	79723	107445	113143	112384	106257	83172	94889
三、人民调解工作	**People's Mediation**								
人民调解委员会 (万个)	Number of People's Mediation Committees (10 000 units)	3.7	3.62	3.36	3.37	3.32	3.3	3.1	3.0
调解人员 (万人)	Number of Mediators (10 000 persons)	17.2	20.43	14.51	14.73	14.28	14.1	11.7	11.9
调解纠纷总数 (万件)	Number of Disputes Mediated (10 000 cases)	21.62	22.85	32.13	32.15	31.03	33.2	31.4	30.3
调解成功总数 (万件)	Number of Successful Mediation (10 000 cases)	21.13	22.14	31.5	31.44	30.46	32.6	30.9	29.7

20-13 公证文书分类情况
Related Notarial Documents by Type

单位：件 (case)

分类	Item	2018	2019
合计	**Total**	383385	381123
出生、生存、死亡	Births、Survival 、Death	11664	11939
学历、经历、职称、身份	Academic Degree、Personal Experience、Title、Identity	9499	9949
收养子女、亲属关系、婚姻状况	Children Adoption、Kinship、Marital Status	13892	17441
继承权	Rights of Inheritance	54783	63251
遗嘱	Testament	1672	2697
委托书	Trust Deed	92388	78358
公司章程	Chapter of Company	23	48
副本与原本相符	Confirmation of Copy and Photo-offset	77546	55333
	Copies to Originals		
证书(执照)	Operation Document	16595	20577
声明书	Declaration	16489	22229
合同(协议)	Contract(Agreement)	20934	21481
受、未受刑事处分	Criminal Record & Uncriminal Record	11124	12642
其他	Others	56776	65178

20-14 履行法律监督情况
Supervision on Law Enforcement

单位：人、件 (person, case)

项 目	Item	2000	2005	2010	2014	2015	2016	2017	2018	2019
监督公安机关立案件数	Number of Cases Registered by Public Security	247	554	1088	2429	1412	1107	2109	2909	1332
监督追捕人数	Number of Criminals Hunted under Supervision	300	204	903	2253	1985	1830	2572	3688	2405
监督追诉人数	Number of People Being Prosecuted	61	78	1130	2347	1484	1359	1927	2003	3699
刑事抗诉件数	Number of Cases Against Crimnal Prosecutions	192	123	119	470	433	467	505	501	307
监督刑罚执行纠错人次	Person-times of Error Correction of Execution of Punishment	3546	51	499	4362	3700	3440	1869	2385	2097
民事行政监督抗诉件数	Number of Counterappeal Civil Cases	894	514	432	218	155	114	94	80	78

20-15 调解民间纠纷分类
Civil Disputes Mediation by Type

项 目	Item	调解纠纷(件) Number of Disputes Mediated (case)				各种纠纷所占比重(%) Proportion (%)			
		2016	2017	2018	2019	2016	2017	2018	2019
合计	**Total**	**72599**	**84051**	**92094**	**109192**	**100**	**100**	**100**	**100**
婚姻	Marriage	18442	19924	20049	20119	25.4	23.7	21.77	18.43
继承	Rights of Inheritance	702	813	844	877	1	1	0.92	0.8
房地产开发	Real Estate Development	1061	15	51	15	1.5	0.02	0.06	0.01
运输合同	Transportation Contracts	315	385	296	614	0.4	0.5	0.32	0.56
买卖合同	Selling and Purchasing Contracts	6911	6096	6539	8798	9.5	7.3	7.1	8.06
借款合同	Loans Contracts	14862	18012	22359	27192	20.5	21.4	24.28	24.9
劳动争议	Labor Disputes	2956	3169	3523	4417	4.1	3.8	3.83	4.05
人格权	Personal Rights	14541	1112	1158	1247	20	1.3	1.26	1.14
所有权	Right of Ownership	1267	172	207	212	1.7	0.2	0.22	0.19
其他	Others	11542	34353	37068	45701	15.9	40.9	40.25	41.85

20-16 人民法院审理一审案件情况
Statistics on First Instance Cases in People's Court

单位：件 (case)

年份 Year	收案 Cases Received	刑事 Criminal Cases	民商事 Civil Cases	海事海商 Maritime	行政 Administration
1985	63079	12709	40660	26	
1990	227618	29086	166960		568
1995	257312	21391	174908	456	4359
1998	252403	17763	171025	606	6368
1999	238715	19598	151191	647	6247
2000	228804	19204	146838	618	6754
2001	251003	21741	222702	745	6560
2002	211464	19548	188163	525	3753
2003	193780	18943	171282	488	3555
2004	172889	18833	150682	592	3374
2005	155478	19672	132585	745	3221
2006	156885	19914	133584	606	3387
2007	161728	21719	137328	459	2681
2008	165099	22364	140072	746	2663
2009	173032	23481	147319	710	2232
2010	179631	22963	154299	781	2369
2011	280572	25074	249792	1458	5706
2012	395414	31489	354789	1501	9136
2013	422427	31621	387593	1914	3213
2014	344515	33931	306601	1951	3983
2015	316619	37034	272384	2022	7201
2016	326240	37309	281705	2212	7226
2017	375458	40309	327020	2245	8129
2018	431278	41332	380752	1813	9194
2019	484877	48702	426876	1608	9299

注：一审案件指人民法院按照诉讼级别管辖按第一审程序审理的案件。
Note: First instance cases refer to cases in the first instance process in People's Court.

20-17 人民法院刑事一审案件收结案情况

Statistics on End of First Instance Cases in People's Court of Criminal Lawsuits

单位：件 (case)

项 目	Item	收案 Cases Received				结案 Cases Closed			
		2016	2017	2018	2019	2016	2017	2018	2019
合 计	**Total**	37309	39641	41332	48702	38326	40309	41104	48233
危害公共安全罪	Crimes Harming Public Security	9633	10814	12349	16565	9760	10913	12369	16544
破坏社会主义市场经济秩序罪	Crimes Harming Socialism Market Economy Order	1449	1556	1683	1909	1438	1579	1668	1800
侵害公民人身权利民主权利罪	Offences Against Citizens' Personal and Democratic Rights	6429	6077	5889	5891	6600	6312	5862	5868
侵犯财产罪	Property Violation	9887	10624	9851	10329	10167	10773	9806	10225
妨害社会管理秩序罪	Crimes Harming Social Management Order	8528	9182	10452	13162	8658	9309	10214	12943
危害国防利益罪	Crimes Harimg National Defense Interests	13	12	12	27	14	12	13	26
贪污贿赂罪	Corruption and Bribe	1160	1164	931	679	1478	1218	951	691
渎职罪	Malversation	207	208	163	138	207	192	219	133
其他	Others	3	4	2	2	4	1	2	3
合计中含自诉案件	Self-Suing Cases	218	230	436	385	212		345	317

20-18 人民法院刑事案件中青少年犯罪情况
Statistics on Juvenile Delinquency in People's Court of Criminal Lawsuits

单位：人 (person)

年份 Year	刑事犯罪总数 Total Number of Criminal Cases	青少年犯罪（不满25周岁） Juvenile Delinquency (Under the age of 25)	不满18周岁 Juvenile Age under 18	已满18周岁不满25周岁 Age 18-25	青少年罪犯刑事罪犯率% Percentage of Juvenile Delinquency in Criminal Cases %
1999	20534	6836	1302	5534	33.3
2000	20076	5922	1279	4643	29.5
2001	22911	6597	1774	4823	28.8
2002	20868	5669	1901	3768	27.2
2003	20908	6207	2328	3879	29.7
2004	20429	5838	2633	3205	28.6
2005	21669	6283	2939	3344	29.0
2006	22876	6933	2945	3988	30.3
2007	17368	7459	3131	4328	43.0
2008	26682	6810	3030	3780	25.5
2009	28507	7700	2930	4770	27.0
2010	27928	7058	2287	4771	25.3
2011	29280	7263	2229	5034	24.8
2012	35419	7327	2050	5277	20.7
2013	33871	5398	1365	4033	15.9
2014	34599	4721	1170	3551	13.6
2015	43918	6011	1084	4927	13.7
2016	40797	4731	668	4063	11.6
2017	41654	5028	852	4176	12.1
2018	46356	6084	654	5430	13.1
2019	61572	7393	821	6572	12.0

20–19 人民法院民事一审案件收结案情况(2019)

Statistics on end of First Instance Cases in People's Court of Civil Lawsuits

单位：件 (case)

项 目	Item	收案 Cases Received	结案 Cases Ended	调解 Mediated	判决 Judgement	驳回 Cases Rejected	撤诉 Cases Withdraw	其他 Others
合 计	**Total**	**426876**	**428204**	**104349**	**202095**	**13965**	**101691**	**6104**
婚姻家庭	Marriage	60755	61215	19834	27458	658	12656	609
继承	Rights of Inheritance	1965	2048	849	786	37	353	23
知识产权	Intelligence Property Rights	18254	16892	544	5867	2871	7499	111
房地产开发	Real Estate Development	97	84	13	41	12	12	6
运输合同	Transportation Contracts	1572	1465	592	549	37	250	37
买卖合同	Selling and Purchasing Contracts	28626	28604	8479	11033	666	7627	799
借款合同	Loans Contracts	104085	105271	26633	54612	3403	19629	994
劳动争议	Labor Disputes	14724	14712	3750	7075	789	2446	652
海事海商	Martial Commerce	1608	1654	353	877	12	394	18
人格权	Personal Right	4624	4737	1101	2635	108	865	28
特别程序	Special Procedure	2007	1820	14	1348	111	323	24
破产	Bankruptcy	610	722	20	317	90	277	18
所有权及与其相关合同	Rights of Ownership and Relevant Contracts	1020	989	198	462	55	251	23
其他	Others	186929	187991	41969	89035	5116	49109	2762

注：结案中含上年旧存。
Note: The statistics of ended cases include statistics of last year.

20–20 人民法院行政一审案件收结案情况(2019)

Statistics on end of First Instance Cases in People's Court of Administration (2019)

单位：件 (case)

项 目	Item	收案 Cases Received	结案 Cases Ended	驳回起诉 Rejected	准予撤诉 Withdraw	其他 Others
合 计	**Total**	**9299**	**9673**	**2794**	**1932**	**4947**
土 地	Land	444	526	224	74	228
公 安	Public Security	508	478	106	133	239
城 建	City Construction	956	936	330	121	485
交通运输	Transportation	82	80	8	10	62
工 商	Industry and Commerce	175	182	51	55	76
环 保	Environment	55	49	2	19	28
林 业	Forestry	67	69	15	12	42
税 务	Taxes	18	21	3	9	9
卫 生	Sanitary and Hygiene	17	15	5	2	8
其 他	Others	6977	7317	2050	1497	3770

主要统计指标解释

基本养老保险

1.(参保)职工人数:指报告期末按照国家法律、法规和有关政策规定参加基本养老保险并在社保经办机构已建立缴费记录档案的职工人数,包括中断缴费但未终止养老保险关系的职工人数,不包括只登记未建立缴费记录档案的人数。

2.(参保)离退休人员人数:指报告期末参加基本养老保险的离休、退休和退职人员的人数。

3.基本养老保险基金收入:指根据国家有关规定,由纳入基本养老保险范围的缴费单位和个人按国家规定的缴费基数和缴费比例缴纳的养老保险基金,以及通过其他方式取得的形成基金来源的收入。包括单位和职工个人缴纳的基本养老保险费、基本养老保险基金利息收入、上级补助收入、下级上解收入、转移收入、财政补贴和其他收入。

4.基本养老保险基金支出:指按照国家政策规定的开支范围和开支标准从养老保险基金中支付给参加基本养老保险的离休、通休、退职人员个人的养老金、丧葬抚恤补助,以及由于保险关系转移、上下级之间调剂资金等原因而发生的支出。包括离休金、退休金、退职金、各种补贴、医疗费、死亡丧葬补助费、抚恤救济费、社会保险经办机构管理费、补助下级支出、上解上级支出、转移支出、其他支出等。

5.基本养老保险基金累计结余:指截止报告期末基本养老保险基金收支相抵后的累计余额。

离休、退休、退职人员　指正式办理了离休、退休、退职手续,并享受相应的离休、退休、退职待遇的人员。

基本医疗保险

1.参保人数:指报告期末按国家有关规定参加基本医疗保险的人数。包括参加保险的职工人数和退休人员人数。

2.基金收入:指根据国家有关规定,由纳入基本医疗保险范围的缴费单位和个人,按国家规定的缴费基数和缴费比例缴纳的基金,以及通过其他方式取得的形成基金来源的款项,包括:单位缴纳的社会统筹基金收入、个人缴纳的个人账户基金收入、财政补贴收入、利息收入、其他收入。

3.基金支出:指按照国家政策规定的开支范围和开支标准从社会统筹基金中支付给参加基本医疗保险的职工和退休人员的医疗保险待遇支出,和从个人帐户基金中支付给参加基本医疗保险的职工和退休人员的医疗费用支出,以及其他支出。包括:住院医疗费用支出、门急诊医疗费用支出、个人账户基金支出、其他支出。

4.基金累计结余:指截止报告期末基本医疗保险的社会统筹和个人帐户基金累计结余金额。包括银行存款、财政专户、债券投资和其他。

失业保险

1.参保人数:指报告期末按照国家法律、法规和有关政策规定参加了失业保险的城镇企业事业单位的职工及地方政府规定参加失业保险的其他人员的人数。

2.失业保险基金收入:指按照规定从企业、事业及其他单位筹集的失业保险费及其他并入失业保险基金收入的总额。包括单位和个人缴纳的失业保险费、失业保险基金利息收入、上级补助收入、下级上解收入、转移收入、财政补贴和其他收入。

3.失业保险基金支出:指报告期内为保障失业人员和下岗职工基本生活、促进其再就业等支出的基金总额。包括失业救济金、医疗费、死亡丧葬补助费、抚恤救济费、转业训练费支出、失业保险经办机构管理费、补助下级支出、上解上级支出、转移支出和其他支出。

4.基金累计结余:指截止报告期末失业保险基金收支相抵后的累计余额。

工伤保险

1.参加保险人数: 指报告期末依据国家有关规定参加工伤保险的职工人数。

2.享受保险待遇人数: 指劳动者因工负伤致残、死亡或因患职业病致残,根据有关规定享受工伤保险待遇职工或供养直系亲属人数。包括伤残人数、职业病人数、因工死亡人数、供养直系亲属人数。

3.基金收入: 指根据国家有关规定,由参加工伤保险的单位按国家规定的缴费基数和缴费比例缴纳的工伤保险基金,以及通过其他形式取得的形成基金来源的款项。包括:单位缴纳的社会统筹基金收入、财政补贴收入、利息收入、其他收入。

4.基金支出: 指按照国家政策规定的开支范围和开支标准从工伤保险基金中支付给参加工伤保险的人员及供养直系亲属工伤保险待遇支出及其他支出。包括工伤医疗费、伤残补助金、工亡补助金、护理费、丧葬补助费、工伤预防费用、职业康复费用和其他支出。

5.基金累计结余: 指截止报告期末工伤保险基金累计结余金额。包括银行存款、财政专户、债券投资和其他。

生育保险

1.参保人数: 指报告期末依据有关规定参加生育保险的职工人数。

2.基金收入: 指根据国家有关规定,由参加生育保险的单位按照国家规定的缴费基数和缴费比例缴纳的生育保险基金,以及通过其他方式取得的形成基金来源的款项,包括:单位缴纳的基金收入、利息收入和其他收入。

3.基金支出: 指按照国家政策规定的开支范围和开支标准,从生育保险基金中支付给参加生育保险的职工,因妊娠、分娩和计划生育手术而享受的待遇及其他支出。包括:生育津贴、医疗费用支出及其他支出。

4.基金累计结余: 指截止报告期末生育保险基金累计结余金额。包括银行存款、财政专户、债券投资和其他。

离休、退休、退职人员保险福利费用 指离休、退休、退职人员实际得到的生活费用总额,包括从社会保险经办机构和单位得到的费用。

1.离休金:指按规定支付给离休人员的生活费用。

2.退休金:指按规定支付给退休人员的生活费用。

3.退职生活费:指按规定支付给退职人员的生活费用。

4.医疗卫生费:指单位直接支付给离休、退休、退职人员的医疗费、住院费以及住院伙食补助等费用。

5.其他:指离休金、退休金、退职生活费和医疗卫生费以外的其他保险福利费用,如丧葬抚恤救济费、生活补贴、物价补贴、冬季取暖补贴等。

律师 指依法取得律师执业证书,担任法律顾问,民事(刑事、行政)案件代理人、刑事案件辩护人、办理非诉讼业务,解答法律询问,代写法律事务文书等,为社会提供法律服务的人员。

公证人员 指在公证处工作的人员总称,包括公证处主任、副主任、公证员、公证员助理(助理公证员)和其他从事辅助性工作的人员。

公证文书 指公证处根据当事人申请,依照事实和法律,按照法定程序制作的,具有法律效力的司法证明文书。根据公证书用途和使用地,公证书分为国内公证书、国内经济公证书、涉外民事公证书、涉外经济公证书四类。

调解员 指在人民调解委员会担负调解民间纠纷工作的人员,包括调解委员会的委员和调解小组的调解员。该指标主要反映从事人民调解工作的人员数量。

调解民间纠纷 指调解委员会按照法律规定,根据自愿原则,用说服教育的方法调解民间发生的有关民事权利和义务争执的件数,包括调解成功数和调解未成功数。该指标主要反映人民调解委员会的工作量。

立案 指人民检察院对受理的报案、控告、举报或自首及自行发现的犯罪线索、犯罪嫌疑人进行初步调查后,认为存在职务犯罪事实和应追究刑事责任,并决定作为刑事案件进行侦查的诉讼活动,是追究犯罪的开始。该指标主要反映人民检察院依法将职务犯罪线索作为刑事案件进行侦查的诉讼活动。

大案 指贪污、贿赂案数额在5万元以上,挪用公款案数额在10万元以上,集体私分、巨额财产来源不明、隐瞒境外存款案数额在50万元以上以及按照《人民检察院直接受理的渎职、侵权重、特大案件标准(试行)》认定的案件。该指标主要反映人民检察院立案查办的职务犯罪案件中经济损失大、社会危害严重的案件。

要案 指县、处级以上干部的犯罪案件。该指标主要反映国家工作人员中县、处级以上干部因职务犯罪被人民检察院依法立案侦查的情况。

决定逮捕 指人民检察院对直接受理、自行侦查的案件,认为需要逮捕犯罪嫌疑人时,依据法律做出的逮捕决定。该指标主要反映人民检察院对直接受理的案件行使决定逮捕权的情况。

批准逮捕 指人民检察院对公安机关、国家安全机关、监狱管理机关提出逮捕的犯罪嫌疑人进行审查，根据事实，依法做出逮捕决定。该指标主要反映人民检察院对提请逮捕机关提请逮捕犯罪嫌疑人进行审查后依法做出批准逮捕决定的情况。

决定起诉 指人民检察院对公安机关、国家安全机关、监狱管理机关和检察机关内设机构反贪污贿赂部门等移送起诉的案件进行审查，根据事实，做出提起公诉的案件。该指标主要反映人民检察院对各种刑事案件向人民法院提起公诉的情况。

申诉 指经检察机关信访部门审查处理后，移送到检察机关申诉部门的申诉案件，包括不服检察机关处理决定和不服法院刑事判决和裁定的申诉的案件。

受理劳动争议案件数 指劳动争议仲裁委员会根据国家有关规定，对劳动争议当事人的申请予以审查，符合受理条件而正式立案、准备处理的劳动争议案件数。

Explanatory Notes on Main Statistical Indicators

Basic Medical Care Insurance:

1. Number of people participating in the insurance programme refers to people participating in the basic medical care insurance programme according to related regulations by the end of reference period, including number of staff and workers and retirees participating in this insurance programme.

2. Revenue of insurance programme refer to payments made by employers and individuals participating in medical care insurance programs in accordance with the basis and proportion stipulated in state regulations, and income from other sources that become source of medical insurance fund, including income of social comprehensive funds paid by employers, income from individual accounts, government financial subsidies, interest income and other income.

3. Expenses of insurance programme refer to payment made from social comprehensive funds to those retired and resigned people covered in basic medical care insurance within the scope and standards of expenditure according to related national policies, and medical care payment made from individual accounts to staff and workers and retirees, and other expenses, including medical expenses of hospital inpatients, medical expenses for outpatients and emergency patients, payment from individual accounts and other expenditure.

4. Balance of basic medical care insurance refer to the balance of medical care insurance of social comprehensive funds and individual accounts at the end of the reference period, including bank savings, special fiscal accounts, investment in bonds and others.

Unemployment Insurance

1. Number of people covered refers to staff and workers in urban enterprises or institutions who have participated in unemployment insurance programme in line relevant policies and regulations, and other people who have participated according to local government regulations, by the end of reference period.

2. Revenue of unemployment insurance refer to payments made by employers and individuals participating in unemployment insurance programme in accordance with relevant regulations and other income contributed to this programme, including unemployment insurance premium made by employers and individuals, interest income, subsidies from higher level agencies, income as transfer from subordinate agencies, transferred income, government financial subsidies and other income.

3. Expenses of unemployment insurance refer to total expenses during the reference period to guarantee the basic livelihood of unemployed people and laid-off staff and workers and to encourage their re-employment. Included are unemployment relief, medical fees, funeral subsidies, compensation pension, training expenses, management fees for unemployment insurance agencies, subsidies to lower level agencies, expenses as transfer to higher level agencies, transferred expenditure and other expenditure.

4. Balance of unemployment insurance refer to the balance of unemployment revenue deducting unemployment expenses at the end of the reference period.

Work Injury Insurance

1. Number of people covered refers to staff and workers who have participated in work injury insurance programme in line with relevant national regulations.

2. Number of beneficiaries refers to staff and workers and their direct dependents who can, in line with relevant regulations, benefit from work injury insurance, as a result of work injury leading to disability or death of the staff/worker, or occupational disease leading to disability. Included in this category are number of injured and disabled people, number of people with occupational diseases, number of deaths at work places, and number of direct dependents.

3. Revenue of work injury insurance refer to payments made by employers participating in work injury insurance programs in accordance with the basis and proportion stipulated in state regulations, and income from other sources that become source of work injury insurance fund, including income of social comprehensive funds paid by employers, government financial subsidies, interest income and other income.

4. Expenses of work injury insurance refer to payments made from work injury insurance funds to those who participated in the work injury insurance programme and their direct dependents within the scope and standards of expenditure according to related national policies, and other expenditure, including medical fees for work injury, injury and disability subsidies, death subsidies, nursing fees, funeral subsidies, injury prevention fees, rehabilitation fees for occupational diseases and other expenditure.

5. Balance of work injury insurance refer to the balance of the work injury funds at the end of the reference period, including bank savings, special fiscal account, investment in bonds and others.

Maternity Insurance

1. Number of people covered refers to staff and workers who have participated in maternity insurance programme according to relevant regulation at the end of the reporting period.

2. Revenue of maternity insurance refers to payments made by employers participating in maternity insurance programs in accordance with the basis and proportion stipulated in state regulations, and income from other sources that become source of maternity insurance fund, including income of funds paid by employers, interest income and other income.

3. Expenses of maternity insurance refer to payments made from maternity insurance funds to staff and workers who participated in maternity insurance programme within the scope and standards of expenditure according to related national policies, expenses paid for pregnancy, child delivery or surgeries related to family planning, and other expenditure, including allowance for child bearing, medical fees and other expenditure.

4. Balance of the maternity insurance refers to the balance of the maternity insurance funds at the end of reference period, including bank savings, special fiscal account, investment in funds and others.

Insurance and Welfare Funds for Retirees refer to the total payment for living expenses actually received by retirees, including payment received from social insurance management agencies and units.

1. Pensions for retired veteran cadres refer to living expenses paid to retired veteran cadres according to related regulations.

2. Pensions for retirement refer to living expenses paid to retired staff and workers according to related regulations.

3. Living allowances for resigned staff and workers refer to living expenses paid to resigned staff and workers according to related regulation.

4. Medical care expenses refer to medical fees, hospitalization cost and per diem subsidies during hospitalizations paid by employers directly to retirees.

5. Others refer to insurance and welfare payments other than the above-mentioned payments, including funeral subsidies, living allowances, price subsidies and heating subsidies during winter.

Lawyers are certified legal workers according to law, and who are employed by legal counseling firms to act as legal advisers, agents in criminal or civil lawsuits, or defenders in criminal lawsuits, or to handle non–litigious legal affairs, to advise on matters of law or to write legal papers for others, and provide service to the public.

Notary Personnel refers to people working for notary offices including: directors, deputy director, notaries, assistant notaries, and other people providing assistance.

Notary Documents refer to the judicatory notary documents drawn up by the request of the party and are in accordance with facts and laws and following certain legal proceedings. According to usage and locality, the notary documents are divided into following 4 types: domestic notary documents, domestic economic notary documents, foreign–related civil notary documents and foreign–related economic notary documents.

Mediators refer to workers on peoples mediation committees responsible for mediating in civil disputes and cases of slight infraction of the law. They include members of the mediation committees and mediators of mediation groups. This indicator reflects the number of people engaged in meditation.

Mediation of Civil Disputes refers to number of cases made by mediation committees in mediating in civil disputes concerning civil rights and duties through persuasion and education in accordance with the provisions of law on a voluntary basis, so as to solve disputes by helping the parties involved come to an agreement and understanding, including those unsuccessful ones. This indicator reflects the workload of the mediation committees.

Acceptance of Case refers to the decision made by the people's procuratorate office on reported cases, prosecution, impeachment, surrender, self–found criminal clues or suspects after initial investigation to confirm the act of crime and to start legal proceedings of the case as criminal case.

Large Cases refer to cases involving a corruption or bribery of over 50,000 yuan, or a misappropriation of over 100,000 yuan. Cases of collectively illegal possession of public funds, unstated sources of large properties, or disguised overseas savings deposits involving 500,000 yuan, or a case that has been defined by the "Standard on Serious and Large Cases of Misconduct and Tortious that Directly Accepted by People's Procurators Office (trial)". This indicator mainly reflects number of accepted cases of job–related criminals that caused serious economic losses or extremely harmful to the society.

Key Cases refer to cases committed by government officials with a ranking of division director or county administrator. This indicator mainly reflects the recorded and spied on cases by the people's procurators offices toward government official with a ranking of division director or county administrator.

Decision on Arrest refers to decision made by people's procurators office, in accordance with laws, to arrest the suspect(s) in the cases that are accepted and to be investigated by procurators office. This indicator mainly reflects the implementation of the decision on arrest by people's procurators office.

Approval for Arrest refers to the decision made by people's procurators office, in accordance with laws and relevant facts, to approve the arrest of the suspect(s) that is proposed by the public security departments, state security departments or authority of prisons. This indicator reflects approved arrests made by people's procurators office that are proposed by related departments.

Decision on Prosecution refers to the decision made by people's procurators office, in accordance with laws and relevant facts, to institute proceedings to the people's court against the suspect(s) of criminal cases handed over by the public security departments, state security departments or authority of prisons, or by the anti–corruption departments within the procurators office. This indicator reflects the condition of the prosecutions made by people's procurators office toward the people's court.

Appeals refer to cases transferred to the appeal departments of procurator's offices after initial review by departments dealing with complaint letters and calls of the public. Included are appeals against decisions made by procurator's offices and appeals against court rules and verdicts.

Number of Labor Dispute Cases Accepted refers to the number of cases of labor dispute submitted that, after being reviewed by the labor dispute arbitration committees in line with the relevant national regulations, are accepted and registered for treatment.

Basic Pension Insurance

1.Number of staff and workers covered refer to staff and workers participating in basic pension insurance programme in line with national laws, regulations and related policies by the end of reference period, who have already had payment records in social security management agencies, including those who interrupt payment without terminating the insurance programme. Those who have registered in the programme with no payment records are not included.

2. Number of retirees participating in basic pension insurance programme refer to number of retirees participating in basic pension insurance programme by the end of reference period.

3. Revenue of basic pension insurance refer to payments made by employers and individuals participating in pension insurance programs in accordance with the basis and proportion stipulated in state regulations, and income from other sources that become source of pension insurance fund, including the premium paid by employers and staff and works, interest income, subsidies from higher level agencies, income as transfer from subordinate agencies, transferred income, government financial subsidies and other income.

4. Expenses of basic pension insurance refer to payment made to those retired and resigned people covered in pension insurance program in terms of pension or compensation within the scope and standards of expenditure according to related national policies, and expenditure occurred due to shift of the insurance relationship or adjustment of funds among agencies, including pension for resigned people, pension for retired people, pension for people quitting jobs, various subsidies, medical fees, funeral subsidies, compensation pension, management fees for social security agencies, expenses on subsidies to lower subordinates, expenses as transfer to agencies at higher level, transferred expenditure and other expenditure.

5. Balance of basic pension insurance refers to the balance of basic pension insurance at the end of the reference period after deducting expenses from revenue.

Retired or Resigned Personnel refers to people who have formally completed formalities for their retirement or quitting work and enjoy the corresponding retirement treatments.

21 "长江经济带"国民经济和社会发展主要指标

Main Indicators of National Economic and Social Development by Yangtze River Economic Zone

资料整理人员：文　静

21-1 长江经济带国民经济和社会发展主要指标(2017年)
Main Indicators of National Economic and Social Development by Yangtze River Economic Zone(2017)

指 标	Item	全国总计 National Total	长江经济带 Yangtze River Economic Zone	占全国比重(%) As Percentage of National Total
总人口(年末) (万人)	Population at Year-end (10 000 persons)	139008.0	59501.1	42.9
国内(地区)生产总值 (亿元)	Gross Domestic Product (100 million yuan)	827121.7	370998.5	43.8
第一产业	Primary Industry	65467.6	26943.8	43.4
第二产业	Secondary Industry	334622.6	156817.0	44.1
第三产业	Tertiary Industry	427031.5	187237.7	43.6
地方一般公共预算收入(亿元)	General Public Budget Revenue (100 million yuan)	91469.4	41014.2	44.8
地方一般公共预算支出(亿元)	General Public Budget Expenditure (100 million yuan)	173228.3	74041.4	42.7
社会消费品零售总额 (亿元)	Total Retail Sales of Consumer Goods (100 million yuan)	366261.6	154891.2	42.6
货物进出口总额 (亿元)	Total Value of Imports and Exports(RMB 100 million yuan)	278101.0	121330.6	43.6
出口	Exports	153311.2	71644.2	46.7
进口	Imports	124789.8	49686.5	39.8
主要农产品产量	Output of Major Farm Products			
谷物 (万吨)	Cereal (10 000 tons)	61520.5	21980.6	35.7
棉花 (万吨)	Cotton (10 000 tons)	565.3	52.2	9.2
油料 (万吨)	Oil-bearing Crops (10 000 tons)	3475.2	1514.1	43.6
主要工业产品产量	Output of Major Industrial Products			
原煤 (亿吨)	Coal (100 million tons)	35.2	4.3	12.3
天然气 (亿立方米)	Natural Gas (100 million cu.m)	1480.3	436.2	29.5
水泥 (万吨)	Cement (10 000 tons)	233084.1	117771.2	50.5
粗钢 (万吨)	Crude Steel (10 000 tons)	83138.1	27684.5	33.3
钢材 (万吨)	Rolled Steel (10 000 tons)	104642.1	34364.9	32.8
汽车 (万辆)	Motor Vehicles (10 000 sets)	2901.8	1325.4	45.7
发电量 (亿千瓦小时)	Electricity (100 million kwh)	64951.4	25784.2	39.7
铁路营业里程 (公里)	Length of Railways in Operation (km)	126969.9	37384.6	29.4
公路里程 (公里)	Length of Highways (km)	4773468.8	2081433.8	43.6
#高速公路	Expressway	136448.5	53631.2	39.3
客运量 (万人)	Passenger Traffic (10 000 persons)	1848620.1	902986.7	50.3
货运量 (万吨)	Freight Traffic (10 000 tons)	4804850.4	2045406.3	43.3
邮政业务总量 (亿元)	Business Volume of Postal Services (100 million yuan)	9763.7	4645.9	47.6
电信业务总量 (亿元)	Business Volume of Postal Services (100 million yuan)	27596.7	11671.6	42.5
普通高等学校数 (个)	Number of Regular Institutions of Higher Education(unit)	2631.0	1131.0	43.0
本专科在校学生数 (万人)	Graduates of Undergraduates and College Students (10 000 persons)	2753.6	1173.5	42.6
医院数 (个)	Number of Hospitals (unit)	31056.0	12840.0	41.3
执业(助理)医师 (万人)	Licensed (Assistant) Doctors (10 000 persons)	339.0	142.2	41.9
医院床位数 (万张)	Number of Beds of Medical Institutions (10 000 beds)	612.0	269.8	44.1

注：长江经济带：包括上海、江苏、浙江、安徽、江西、湖北、湖南、重庆、四川、贵州、云南。

Note: a) Yangtze River Economic Zone includes: Shanghai, Jiangsu, Zhejiang, Anhui, Jiangxi, Hubei, Hunan, Chongqing, Sichuan, Guizhou, Yunnan.

21-2 长江经济带国民经济和社会发展主要指标(2018年)
Main Indicators of National Economic and Social Development by Yangtze River Economic Zone (2018)

指 标	Item	全国总计 National Total	长江经济带 Yangtze River Economic Zone	占全国比重(%) As Percentage of National Total
总人口(年末) (万人)	Population at Year-end (10 000 persons)	139538.0	59873.0	42.9
国内(地区)生产总值 (亿元)	Gross Domestic Product (100 million yuan)	900309.5	402985.2	44.1
第一产业	Primary Industry	64734.0	27822.9	43.0
第二产业	Secondary Industry	366000.9	166486.2	44.2
第三产业	Tertiary Industry	469574.6	208676.1	44.1
地方一般公共预算收入(亿元)	General Public Budget Revenue (100 million yuan)	97903.4	43823.9	44.8
地方一般公共预算支出(亿元)	General Public Budget Expenditure (100 million yuan)	188196.3	80969.1	43.0
社会消费品零售总额 (亿元)	Total Retail Sales of Consumer Goods (100 million yuan)	380986.9	161574.1	42.9
货物进出口总额 (亿元)	Total Value of Imports and Exports(RMB 100 million yuan)	305008.1	133828.7	43.9
出口	Exports	164127.8	76017.0	46.3
进口	Imports	140880.3	57811.7	41.0
主要农产品产量	Output of Major Farm Products			
谷物 (万吨)	Cereal (10 000 tons)	61003.6	21714.0	35.6
棉花 (万吨)	Cotton (10 000 tons)	610.3	42.9	7.0
油料 (万吨)	Oil-bearing Crops (10 000 tons)	3433.4	1531.8	44.6
主要工业产品产量	Output of Major Industrial Products			
原煤 (亿吨)	Coal (100 million tons)	36.8	3.9	10.7
天然气 (亿立方米)	Natural Gas (100 million cu.m)	1602.7	466.1	29.1
水泥 (万吨)	Cement (10 000 tons)	220770.7	114858.4	52.0
粗钢 (万吨)	Crude Steel (10 000 tons)	92800.9	29683.5	32.0
钢材 (万吨)	Rolled Steel (10 000 tons)	110551.7	35549.0	32.2
汽车 (万辆)	Motor Vehicles (10 000 sets)	2781.9	1234.7	44.4
发电量 (亿千瓦小时)	Electricity (100 million kwh)	71117.7	27491.1	38.7
铁路营业里程 (公里)	Length of Railways in Operation (km)	131651.3	39043.9	29.7
公路里程 (公里)	Length of Highways (km)	4846531.7	2117275.0	43.7
#高速公路	Expressway	142593.2	55690.5	39.1
客运量 (万人)	Passenger Traffic (10 000 persons)	1732646.6	857563.9	49.5
货运量 (万吨)	Freight Traffic (10 000 tons)	5152731.6	2183615.2	43.1
邮政业务总量 (亿元)	Business Volume of Postal Services (100 million yuan)	12345.2	5920.7	48.0
电信业务总量 (亿元)	Business Volume of Postal Services (100 million yuan)	65633.9	28252.4	43.1
普通高等学校数 (个)	Number of Regular Institutions of Higher Education(unit)	2663.0	1147.0	43.1
本专科在校学生数 (万人)	Graduates of Undergraduates and College Students (10 000 persons)	2831.0	1208.2	42.7
医院数 (个)	Number of Hospitals (unit)	33009.0	13635.0	41.3
执业(助理)医师 (万人)	Licensed (Assistant) Doctors (10 000 persons)	360.7	150.5	41.7
医院床位数 (万张)	Number of Beds of Medical Institutions (10 000 beds)	652.0	287.4	44.1

注：长江经济带：包括上海、江苏、浙江、安徽、江西、湖北、湖南、重庆、四川、贵州、云南。

Note: a) Yangtze River Economic Zone includes: Shanghai, Jiangsu, Zhejiang, Anhui, Jiangxi, Hubei, Hunan, Chongqing, Sichuan, Guizhou, Yunnan.

21-3 长江经济带国民经济和社会发展主要指标(2019年)
Main Indicators of National Economic and Social Development by Yangtze River Economic Zone (2019)

指 标	Item	全国总计 National Total	长江经济带 Yangtze River Economic Zone	占全国比重(%) As Percentage of National Total
总人口(年末) (万人)	Population at Year-end (10 000 persons)	140005.0	60205.8	42.9
国内(地区)生产总值 (亿元)	Gross Domestic Product (100 million yuan)	990865.1	457805.2	46.5
第一产业	Primary Industry	70466.7	30603.7	43.4
第二产业	Secondary Industry	386165.3	182341.8	47.3
第三产业	Tertiary Industry	534233.1	244859.7	46.2
地方一般公共预算收入(亿元)	General Public Budget Revenue (100 million yuan)	101080.6	45128.6	44.6
地方一般公共预算支出(亿元)	General Public Budget Expenditure (100 million yuan)	203743.2	88504.2	43.4
社会消费品零售总额 (亿元)	Total Retail Sales of Consumer Goods (100 million yuan)	408017.2	198801.4	48.7
货物进出口总额 (亿元)	Total Value of Imports and Exports(RMB 100 million yuan)	315627.3	139828.7	44.3
出口	Exports	172373.6	80124.3	46.5
进口	Imports	143253.7	59704.4	41.7
主要农产品产量	Output of Major Farm Products			
谷物 (万吨)	Cereal (10 000 tons)	61369.7	21543.7	35.1
棉花 (万吨)	Cotton (10 000 tons)	588.9	37.4	6.3
油料 (万吨)	Oil-bearing Crops (10 000 tons)	3493.0	1560.4	44.7
主要工业产品产量	Output of Major Industrial Products			
原煤 (亿吨)	Coal (100 million tons)	38.5	3.7	9.7
天然气 (亿立方米)	Natural Gas (100 million cu.m)	1761.7	541.4	30.7
水泥 (万吨)	Cement (10 000 tons)	234430.6	120915.7	51.6
粗钢 (万吨)	Crude Steel (10 000 tons)	99541.9	32911.1	33.1
钢材 (万吨)	Rolled Steel (10 000 tons)	120456.9	39130.6	32.5
汽车 (万辆)	Motor Vehicles (10 000 sets)	2567.7	1089.7	42.4
发电量 (亿千瓦小时)	Electricity (100 million kwh)	75034.3	28713.3	38.3
铁路营业里程 (公里)	Length of Railways in Operation (km)	139926.4	42795.2	30.6
公路里程 (公里)	Length of Highways (km)	5012495.8	2230326.0	44.5
#高速公路	Expressway	149571.2	58801.3	39.3
客运量 (万人)	Passenger Traffic (10 000 persons)	1760435.7	828795.9	48.9
货运量 (万吨)	Freight Traffic (10 000 tons)	4713624.4	2066338.9	44.7
邮政业务总量 (亿元)	Business Volume of Postal Services (100 million yuan)	16229.6	7634.3	47.0
电信业务总量 (亿元)	Business Volume of Postal Services (100 million yuan)	106810.7	46795.6	43.9
普通高等学校数 (个)	Number of Regular Institutions of Higher Education(unit)	2688.0	1159.0	43.1
本专科在校学生数 (万人)	Graduates of Undergraduates and College Students (10 000 persons)	3031.5	1288.6	42.5
医院数 (个)	Number of Hospitals (unit)	34354.0	14365.0	41.8
执业(助理)医师 (万人)	Licensed (Assistant) Doctors (10 000 persons)	386.7	162.3	42.0
医院床位数 (万张)	Number of Beds of Medical Institutions (10 000 beds)	686.7	304.6	44.4

注：长江经济带：包括上海、江苏、浙江、安徽、江西、湖北、湖南、重庆、四川、贵州、云南。

Note: a) Yangtze River Economic Zone includes: Shanghai, Jiangsu, Zhejiang, Anhui, Jiangxi, Hubei, Hunan, Chongqing, Sichuan, Guizhou, Yunnan.

22 县域经济主要指标

Main Economic Indicators of Counties

资料整理人员：王静敏　周　真

22-1 县域经济主要指标(2019)

Main Economic Indicators of Counties (2019)

指标名称	Item	地区生产总值(亿元) Gross Regional Product(100 million yuan)
蔡甸区	Caidian District	400.53
江夏区	Jiangxia District	948.80
黄陂区	Huangpi District	1071.09
新洲区	Xinzhou District	951.61
阳新县	Yangxin County	290.43
大冶市	Daye City	680.69
郧阳区	Yun County	166.86
郧西县	Yunxi County	92.55
竹山县	Zhushan County	115.28
竹溪县	Zhuxi County	84.54
房县	Fang County	119.56
丹江口市	Danjiangkou City	290.61
夷陵区	Yiling District	541.67
远安县	Yuanan County	181.79
兴山县	Xingshan County	130.58
秭归县	Zigui County	164.49
长阳县	Changyang Tujia A.C.	159.38
五峰县	Wufeng Tujia A.C.	81.76
宜都市	Yidu City	679.24
当阳市	Dangyang City	509.19
枝江市	Zhijiang City	580.69
襄州区	Xiangzhou District	735.33
南漳县	Nanzhang County	296.39
谷城县	Gucheng County	408.43
保康县	Baokang County	137.01
老河口市	Laohekou City	388.66
枣阳市	Zaoyang City	674.91
宜城市	Yicheng City	367.73
梁子湖区	Liangzihu District	98.74
华容区	Huarong District	423.21
鄂城区	Echeng District	618.11
东宝区	Dongbao District	406.81
京山市	Jingshan City	430.10
沙洋县	Shayang County	335.85
钟祥市	Zhongxiang City	561.03
孝南区	Xiaonan District	429.59
孝昌县	Xiaochang County	139.06

22-1 续表1 continued

指标名称	Item	地区生产总值(亿元) Gross Regional Product(100 million yuan)
大悟县	Dawu County	182.76
云梦县	Yunmeng County	215.44
应城市	Yingcheng City	396.22
安陆市	Anlu City	260.70
汉川市	Hanchuan City	677.63
荆州区	Jingzhou District	350.05
江陵县	Jiangling County	115.90
公安县	Gongan County	332.35
监利县	Jianli County	310.04
石首市	Shishou City	223.49
洪湖市	Honghu City	306.15
松滋市	Songci City	343.78
黄州区	Huangzhou District	258.54
团风县	Tuanfeng County	122.25
红安县	Hongan County	199.11
罗田县	Luotian County	158.85
英山县	Yingshan County	121.62
浠水县	Xishui County	251.03
蕲春县	Qichun County	265.61
黄梅县	Huangmei County	247.12
麻城市	Macheng City	374.13
武穴市	Wuxue City	324.47
咸安区	Xian'an District	381.77
嘉鱼县	Jiayu County	288.96
通城县	Tongcheng County	166.06
崇阳县	Chongyang County	153.34
通山县	Tongshan County	137.99
赤壁市	Chibi City	466.85
曾都区	Zengdu District	535.54
随　县	Sui Country	270.12
广水市	Guangshui City	356.56
恩施市	Enshi City	379.52
利川市	Lichuan City	204.89
建始县	Jianshi County	120.48
巴东县	Badong County	127.46
宣恩县	Xuanen County	79.05
咸丰县	Xianfeng County	96.18
来凤县	Laifeng County	84.66
鹤峰县	Hefeng County	67.13
仙桃市	Xiantiao City	868.47
潜江市	Qianjiang City	812.63
天门市	Tianmen City	650.82

22-1　续表 2 continued

指标名称	Item	固定资产投资增速(%) Growth rate of fixed asset investment(%)	社会消费品零售总额(亿元) Total Retail Sales of Consumer Goods (100 million yuan)	地方一般公共预算收入(万元) General Public Budget Revenue of Local Governments (10 thousand yuan)
蔡甸区	Caidian District	21.8	144.54	400465
江夏区	Jiangxia District	12.0	301.98	918470
黄陂区	Huangpi District	22.5	331.78	685505
新洲区	Xinzhou District	17.6	444.97	482669
阳新县	Yangxin County	12.5	166.60	181616
大冶市	Daye City	12.7	353.59	504502
郧阳区	Yun County	13.5	100.29	103985
郧西县	Yunxi County	14.2	65.38	50890
竹山县	Zhushan County	13.1	69.76	65873
竹溪县	Zhuxi County	13.2	49.33	52641
房　县	Fang County	13.8	73.84	73989
丹江口市	Danjiangkou City	11.4	112.47	125039
夷陵区	Yiling District	13.3	170.59	241086
远安县	Yuanan County	9.4	62.07	98098
兴山县	Xingshan County	13.2	45.45	83218
秭归县	Zigui County	12.2	60.79	80003
长阳县	Changyang Tujia A.C.	12.3	66.14	76430
五峰县	Wufeng Tujia A.C.	5.9	29.33	33786
宜都市	Yidu City	12.7	148.05	235321
当阳市	Dangyang City	12.1	179.82	181096
枝江市	Zhijiang City	13.1	182.65	190118
襄州区	Xiangzhou District	12.2	259.88	351901
南漳县	Nanzhang County	12.0	145.62	114858
谷城县	Gucheng County	12.5	152.12	149366
保康县	Baokang County	11.9	67.97	96354
老河口市	Laohekou City	12.1	157.34	205180
枣阳市	Zaoyang City	11.2	272.61	270468
宜城市	Yicheng City	12.4	147.76	173019
梁子湖区	Liangzihu District	-6.4	28.74	45313
华容区	Huarong District	15.4	216.36	67245
鄂城区	Echeng District	12.8	176.77	132990
东宝区	Dongbao District	15.2	239.29	193700
京山市	Jingshan City	14.4	188.62	180074
沙洋县	Shayang County	7.2	116.85	100078
钟祥市	Zhongxiang City	7.6	233.69	206592
孝南区	Xiaonan District	12.4	226.02	194615
孝昌县	Xiaochang County	12.1	89.14	106656

22-1 续表3 continued

指标名称	Item	固定资产投资增速(%) Growth rate of fixed asset investment(%)	社会消费品零售总额(亿元) Total Retail Sales of Consumer Goods (100 million yuan)	地方一般公共预算收入(万元) General Public Budget Revenue of Local Governments (10 thousand yuan)
大悟县	Dawu County	11.8	116.60	112679
云梦县	Yunmeng County	12.0	154.90	141327
应城市	Yingcheng City	12.4	191.08	171717
安陆市	Anlu City	12.3	153.04	116006
汉川市	Hanchuan City	12.6	282.38	256332
荆州区	Jingzhou District	15.7	207.75	177189
江陵县	Jiangling County	15.9	58.48	51615
公安县	Gongan County	0.7	195.50	137749
监利县	Jianli County	15.2	199.35	95398
石首市	Shishou City	15.0	140.35	86435
洪湖市	Honghu City	16.4	166.10	105502
松滋市	Songci City	16.2	168.11	182100
黄州区	Huangzhou District	14.4	175.79	76128
团风县	Tuanfeng County	15.6	46.27	61241
红安县	Hongan County	11.1	94.00	166442
罗田县	Luotian County	7.9	90.62	80640
英山县	Yingshan County	9.2	48.74	54057
浠水县	Xishui County	10.0	178.46	102823
蕲春县	Qichun County	11.4	164.63	141343
黄梅县	Huangmei County	11.4	171.63	108227
麻城市	Macheng City	11.5	186.08	208382
武穴市	Wuxue City	10.9	176.56	203318
咸安区	Xian'an District	12.2	161.85	209193
嘉鱼县	Jiayu County	11.4	78.74	124684
通城县	Tongcheng County	12.3	81.19	82591
崇阳县	Chongyang County	11.3	77.67	83506
通山县	Tongshan County	11.8	73.27	66310
赤壁市	Chibi City	10.9	150.38	203582
曾都区	Zengdu District	11.4	283.30	175721
随　县	Sui Country	11.2	168.90	76030
广水市	Guangshui City	11.3	150.10	135557
恩施市	Enshi City	18.5	215.78	228585
利川市	Lichuan City	17.9	120.60	119476
建始县	Jianshi County	2.6	76.95	68751
巴东县	Badong County	17.3	77.63	67168
宣恩县	Xuanen County	2.4	51.60	39587
咸丰县	Xianfeng County	17.6	55.53	47295
来凤县	Laifeng County	17.8	48.69	42198
鹤峰县	Hefeng County	17.5	39.03	31268
仙桃市	Xiantiao City	11.4	418.27	346310
潜江市	Qianjiang City	12.4	291.98	275016
天门市	Tianmen City	4.3	403.52	213553

22-1 续表4 continued

指标名称	Item	外贸出口(亿元) Total Exports (100 million yuan)	城镇常住居民人均可支配收入(元) Per Capita Disposable Income of Urban Households (yuan)	农村常住居民人均可支配收入(元) Per Capita Disposable Income of Rural Households (yuan)
蔡甸区	Caidian District	35.30	38213	23035
江夏区	Jiangxia District	13.80	38265	23903
黄陂区	Huangpi District	170.14	38799	23195
新洲区	Xinzhou District	16.89	35432	22097
阳新县	Yangxin County	12.26	28576	13147
大冶市	Daye City	27.29	42814	21531
郧阳区	Yun County	7.06	30551	11365
郧西县	Yunxi County	4.79	29103	10961
竹山县	Zhushan County	5.34	28630	11147
竹溪县	Zhuxi County	1.73	28246	11044
房　县	Fang County	6.19	30260	11109
丹江口市	Danjiangkou City	3.71	32022	12575
夷陵区	Yiling District	9.81	40322	22149
远安县	Yuanan County	8.67	36630	20612
兴山县	Xingshan County	31.53	31611	13625
秭归县	Zigui County	8.26	30517	11596
长阳县	Changyang Tujia A.C.	6.17	31606	11671
五峰县	Wufeng Tujia A.C.	1.54	29285	11482
宜都市	Yidu City	26.10	40326	22753
当阳市	Dangyang City	2.62	38065	22746
枝江市	Zhijiang City	18.23	37065	23082
襄州区	Xiangzhou District	45.31	34773	20578
南漳县	Nanzhang County	23.08	34632	17430
谷城县	Gucheng County	16.05	35765	17904
保康县	Baokang County	9.13	31128	13132
老河口市	Laohekou City	21.88	37549	20468
枣阳市	Zaoyang City	12.10	38544	20005
宜城市	Yicheng City	20.37	34836	20154
梁子湖区	Liangzihu District	0.24	26374	14907
华容区	Huarong District	10.40	31019	20420
鄂城区	Echeng District	8.21	36174	20726
东宝区	Dongbao District	10.00	39486	20798
京山市	Jingshan City	9.20	35609	20570
沙洋县	Shayang County	7.00	35324	20224
钟祥市	Zhongxiang City	4.30	35625	21101
孝南区	Xiaonan District	7.48	38216	20167
孝昌县	Xiaochang County	4.17	31076	12131

22-1 续表5 continued

指标名称	Item	外贸出口(亿元) Total Exports (100 million yuan)	城镇常住居民人均可支配收入(元) Per Capita Disposable Income of Urban Households (yuan)	农村常住居民人均可支配收入(元) Per Capita Disposable Income of Rural Households (yuan)
大悟县	Dawu County	3.94	31391	12459
云梦县	Yunmeng County	22.61	36320	20643
应城市	Yingcheng City	5.15	36915	20918
安陆市	Anlu City	6.77	35202	17608
汉川市	Hanchuan City	28.04	36468	20302
荆州区	Jingzhou District	6.97	40050	21082
江陵县	Jiangling County	1.30	32148	17003
公安县	Gongan County	6.84	34348	19784
监利县	Jianli County	4.03	31993	18317
石首市	Shishou City	5.46	33635	18644
洪湖市	Honghu City	6.83	33454	18583
松滋市	Songci City	6.16	34367	19052
黄州区	Huangzhou District	7.24	36153	17554
团风县	Tuanfeng County	1.54	28925	13501
红安县	Hongan County	1.43	29433	12420
罗田县	Luotian County	4.12	29277	12036
英山县	Yingshan County	2.01	28285	12901
浠水县	Xishui County	4.58	31060	15183
蕲春县	Qichun County	10.25	30779	14967
黄梅县	Huangmei County	8.01	32197	16204
麻城市	Macheng City	3.93	32932	14011
武穴市	Wuxue City	21.74	34248	16848
咸安区	Xian'an District	7.95	36536	18247
嘉鱼县	Jiayu County	6.53	33334	18938
通城县	Tongcheng County	7.42	31570	16361
崇阳县	Chongyang County	4.62	29698	15892
通山县	Tongshan County	2.61	27654	12518
赤壁市	Chibi City	19.07	34420	18703
曾都区	Zengdu District	14.11	35010	19236
随　县	Sui Country	21.53	29142	18226
广水市	Guangshui City	4.88	31681	17928
恩施市	Enshi City	1.14	34300	12050
利川市	Lichuan City	1.16	31429	11533
建始县	Jianshi County	0.14	29680	11560
巴东县	Badong County	0.84	30183	11471
宣恩县	Xuanen County	0.78	29446	11396
咸丰县	Xianfeng County	0.91	29588	11476
来凤县	Laifeng County	0.45	30334	11342
鹤峰县	Hefeng County	0.75	29929	12153
仙桃市	Xiantiao City	54.54	34541	19891
潜江市	Qianjiang City	18.90	34627	19494
天门市	Tianmen City	10.74	31753	18138

22-1 续表6 continued

指标名称	Item	农业总产值(亿元) Total Value of Agricultural Output (100 million yuan)	粮食产量(万吨) Output of Grain (10 000 tons)	油料产量(万吨) Output of Oil-bearing Crops(10 000 tons)	猪肉产量(万吨) Pork of Meat (10 000 tons)
蔡甸区	Caidian District	77.02	11.68	0.94	1.01
江夏区	Jiangxia District	165.51	20.13	2.69	3.81
黄陂区	Huangpi District	202.36	30.06	5.33	4.54
新洲区	Xinzhou District	137.48	21.42	3.91	2.21
汉南区	Hannan District	25.00		0.06	0.99
阳新县	Yangxin County	91.63	29.34	5.55	3.09
大冶市	Daye City	80.23	24.04	5.35	2.48
郧阳区	Yun County	50.42	20.20	2.21	3.82
郧西县	Yunxi County	39.19	12.17	1.93	1.23
竹山县	Zhushan County	51.23	14.79	5.12	1.11
竹溪县	Zhuxi County	40.03	14.40	2.87	1.36
房县	Fang County	56.07	9.89	2.42	1.34
丹江口市	Danjiangkou City	54.55	9.45	1.32	1.26
夷陵区	Yiling District	113.85	20.25	2.76	5.01
远安县	Yuanan County	35.85	7.98	1.45	1.67
兴山县	Xingshan County	24.33	5.21	0.91	1.80
秭归县	Zigui County	49.04	8.32	1.74	3.62
长阳县	Changyang Tujia A.C.	70.38	10.81	1.48	3.98
五峰县	Wufeng Tujia A.C.	38.72	9.54	0.37	2.05
宜都市	Yidu City	84.64	9.80	2.18	3.91
当阳市	Dangyang City	142.77	46.03	5.68	4.73
枝江市	Zhijiang City	142.78	31.53	4.17	4.86
襄州区	Xiangzhou District	184.45	127.28	12.62	4.73
南漳县	Nanzhang County	84.16	43.26	1.60	5.15
谷城县	Gucheng County	68.19	26.42	1.96	3.52
保康县	Baokang County	37.66	13.18	1.66	1.95
老河口市	Laohekou City	83.40	34.34	2.09	4.39
枣阳市	Zaoyang City	177.60	124.18	6.50	5.07
宜城市	Yicheng City	96.83	64.94	6.84	3.73
梁子湖区	Liangzihu District	55.68		1.38	
华容区	Huarong District	48.68		1.54	
鄂城区	Echeng District	68.79		1.39	
东宝区	Dongbao District	38.95		2.36	
京山市	Jingshan County	110.95	70.34	4.95	4.70
沙洋县	Shayang County	122.05	88.84	11.17	4.09
钟祥市	Zhongxiang City	135.77	95.31	9.35	8.10
孝南区	Xiaonan District	63.29	23.53	3.38	1.45
孝昌县	Xiaochang County	63.53	25.46	3.75	2.25

22-1 续表7 continued

指标名称	Item	农业总产值 (亿元) Total Value of Agricultural Output (100 million yuan)	粮食产量 (万吨) Output of Grain (10 000 tons)	油料产量 (万吨) Output of Oil-bearing Crops(10 000 tons)	猪肉产量 (万吨) Pork of Meat (10 000 tons)
大悟县	Dawu County	68.20	28.29	6.00	1.99
云梦县	Yunmeng County	66.03	24.28	2.22	2.12
应城市	Yingcheng City	88.98	34.42	2.32	2.32
安陆市	Anlu City	67.61	43.42	1.98	3.58
汉川市	Hanchuan City	127.04	51.84	2.96	3.90
荆州区	Jingzhou District	76.86	40.62	2.07	2.19
江陵县	Jiangling County	47.57	50.42	4.33	1.77
公安县	Gongan County	122.45	87.47	9.62	3.35
监利县	Jianli County	185.24	127.12	12.38	3.66
石首市	Shishou City	74.09	29.73	3.63	3.34
洪湖市	Honghu City	149.85	65.29	7.94	2.42
松滋市	Songci City	77.59	50.52	2.71	5.95
黄州区	Huangzhou District	26.29	4.20	0.57	0.41
团风县	Tuanfeng County	28.72	11.04	1.39	0.47
红安县	Hongan County	43.03	17.23	8.18	2.85
罗田县	Luotian County	49.23	25.12	3.28	0.96
英山县	Yingshan County	57.62	10.59	1.42	0.94
浠水县	Xishui County	112.95	39.61	6.19	3.00
蕲春县	Qichun County	91.68	45.01	5.43	3.24
黄梅县	Huangmei County	88.58	46.99	6.41	3.12
麻城市	Macheng City	107.15	35.50	9.76	3.28
武穴市	Wuxue City	94.64	33.34	5.58	4.97
咸安区	Xian'an District	55.70	21.78	5.42	2.83
嘉鱼县	Jiayu County	82.82	17.13	1.44	0.77
通城县	Tongcheng County	45.85	17.01	1.61	3.27
崇阳县	Chongyang County	49.33	21.80	2.49	3.92
通山县	Tongshan County	34.56	11.20	1.17	2.38
赤壁市	Chibi City	84.47	27.53	4.60	1.13
曾都区	Zengdu District	57.85	25.11	1.38	3.90
随　县	Sui Country	122.34	78.11	3.14	3.62
广水市	Guangshui City	100.65	39.24	5.40	3.70
恩施市	Enshi City	55.97	20.91	2.02	4.67
利川市	Lichuan City	65.87	31.94	1.49	3.02
建始县	Jianshi County	42.00	20.64	1.83	3.49
巴东县	Badong County	41.65	20.23	2.64	3.50
宣恩县	Xuanen County	34.45	11.96	0.68	3.36
咸丰县	Xianfeng County	36.55	20.14	1.96	3.43
来凤县	Laifeng County	27.58	13.30	0.98	1.46
鹤峰县	Hefeng County	25.06	7.22	0.51	1.27
仙桃市	Xiantiao City	155.67	72.31	12.37	4.10
潜江市	Qianjiang City	141.73	59.57	4.11	4.27
天门市	Tianmen City	149.64	81.17	11.27	4.82

附录 全国分省主要指标

Major Indicators by Region

附录1-1　分地区行政区划
Divisions of Administrative Areas by Regions

单位:个　　　　(unit)

省级区划名称	provinces, Autonomous Regions and Municipalities	地级 Number of Regions at Prefecture Level	#地级市 Cities at Prefecture Level	县级 Number of Regions at County Level	#市辖区 Districts under the Jurisdiction of Cities	#县级市 Cities at County Level	#县 Counties	#自治县 Autponomous Counties
全 国	**National Total**	**333**	**293**	**2846**	**965**	**387**	**1323**	**117**
北 京	Beijing			16	16			
天 津	Tianjin			16	16			
河 北	Hebei	11	11	168	47	21	94	6
山 西	Shanxi	11	11	117	26	11	80	
内蒙古	Inner Mongolia	12	9	103	23	11	17	
辽 宁	Liaoning	14	14	100	59	16	17	8
吉 林	Jilin	9	8	60	21	20	16	3
黑龙江	Heilongjiang	13	12	121	54	21	45	1
上 海	Shanghai			16	16			
江 苏	Jiangsu	13	13	96	55	22	19	
浙 江	Zhejiang	11	11	90	37	20	32	1
安 徽	Anhui	16	16	105	44	9	52	
福 建	Fujian	9	9	85	29	12	44	
江 西	Jiangxi	11	11	100	27	11	62	
山 东	Shangdong	16	16	137	57	27	53	
河 南	Henan	17	17	158	53	22	83	
湖 北	**Hubei**	**13**	**12**	**103**	**39**	**25**	**36**	**2**
湖 南	Hunan	14	13	122	36	18	61	7
广 东	Guangdong	21	21	122	65	20	34	3
广 西	Guangxi	14	14	111	41	9	49	12
海 南	Hainan	4	4	23	8	5	4	6
重 庆	Chongqing			38	26		8	4
四 川	Sichuan	21	18	183	54	18	107	4
贵 州	Guizhou	9	6	88	15	9	52	11
云 南	Yunnan	16	8	129	17	17	66	29
西 藏	Tibet	7	6	74	8		66	
陕 西	Shaanxi	10	10	107	30	6	71	
甘 肃	Gansu	14	12	86	17	5	57	7
青 海	Qinghai	8	2	44	7	4	26	7
宁 夏	Ningxia	5	5	22	9	2	11	
新 疆	Xinjiang	14	4	106	13	26	61	6
香港特别行政区	Hong Kong Special Administrative Region							
澳门特别行政区	Macao Special Administrative Region							
台 湾 省	Taiwan							

续表 附录1-1 coutinued

单位:个 (unit)

省级区划名称	provinces,Autonomous Regions and Municipalities	乡镇级 Number of Regions at Townships Level	#镇数 towns	#乡数 Towns	#街道 Street Communities
全 国	**National Total**	**38727**	**20988**	**9222**	**8515**
北 京	Beijing	333	143	38	152
天 津	Tianjin	248	126	3	119
河 北	Hebei	2255	1156	790	308
山 西	Shanxi	1396	577	612	207
内蒙古	Inner Mongolia	1024	508	270	246
辽 宁	Liaoning	1355	640	201	514
吉 林	Jilin	937	426	182	329
黑龙江	Heilongjiang	1240	557	345	338
上 海	Shanghai	215	106	2	107
江 苏	Jiangsu	1261	718	40	503
浙 江	Zhejiang	1360	619	259	482
安 徽	Anhui	1498	968	271	259
福 建	Fujian	1107	653	270	184
江 西	Jiangxi	1563	828	570	165
山 东	Shangdong	1824	1087	68	669
河 南	Henan	2451	1173	618	660
湖 北	**Hubei**	**1249**	**760**	**162**	**327**
湖 南	Hunan	1937	1134	392	411
广 东	Guangdong	1606	1114	11	481
广 西	Guangxi	1250	806	312	132
海 南	Hainan	218	175	21	22
重 庆	Chongqing	1029	629	172	228
四 川	Sichuan	3440	1926	1065	449
贵 州	Guizhou	1440	837	315	288
云 南	Yunnan	1405	679	540	186
西 藏	Tibet	697	142	534	21
陕 西	Shaanxi	1312	975	21	316
甘 肃	Gansu	1357	892	337	128
青 海	Qinghai	403	144	222	37
宁 夏	Ningxia	240	103	90	47
新 疆	Xinjiang	1077	387	489	200
香港特别行政区	Hong Kong Special Administrative Region				
澳门特别行政区	Macao Special Administrative Region				
台湾省	Taiwan				

注:乡镇级总数包含河北省、新疆维吾尔族自治区的各一个区公所。

Note: The total number of township level including one district public of Hubei Province and Xinjiang Uygur Autonomous region respectively.

附录1-2 分地区按三次产业分法人单位数(2018)

Number of Legal Entities by Three Strata of Industry and Region(2018)

单位:个 (unit)

地区	Region	法人单位数 Corporate Units	第一产业 Primary Industry	第二产业 Secondary Industry	第三产业 Tertiary Industry
全 国	**National Total**	**21787273**	**1224**	**4626235**	**17159814**
北 京	Beijing	988483	43	60550	927890
天 津	Tianjin	291151	2	58229	232920
河 北	Hebei	1150955	55	315838	835062
山 西	Shanxi	462193	36	73378	388779
内蒙古	Inner Mongolia	297176	66	50137	246973
辽 宁	Liaoning	600313	29	130808	469476
吉 林	Jilin	187449	31	33009	154409
黑龙江	Heilongjiang	256191	150	43301	212740
上 海	Shanghai	440696	8	64674	376014
江 苏	Jiangsu	2053630	30	633703	1419897
浙 江	Zhejiang	1545153	110	480460	1064583
安 徽	Anhui	813279	64	180608	632607
福 建	Fujian	702826	19	155460	547347
江 西	Jiangxi	454387	24	100611	353752
山 东	Shangdong	1801301	17	439203	1362081
河 南	Henan	1279238	31	223621	1055586
湖 北	**Hubei**	**853168**	**13**	**156392**	**696763**
湖 南	Hunan	622764	12	103144	519608
广 东	Guangdong	3126550	54	696146	2430350
广 西	Guangxi	490277	75	66474	423728
海 南	Hainan	100096	12	13667	86417
重 庆	Chongqing	512470	127	77501	434842
四 川	Sichuan	761937	38	119589	642310
贵 州	Guizhou	348149	15	71833	276301
云 南	Yunnan	453286	63	70658	382565
西 藏	Tibet	47215		12191	35024
陕 西	Shaanxi	532220	20	103742	428458
甘 肃	Gansu	229632	10	31121	198501
青 海	Qinghai	72869	18	10840	62011
宁 夏	Ningxia	68817	15	11792	57010
新 疆	Xinjiang	243402	37	37555	205810

附录1-3 分地区按行业分法人单位数(2018)
Number of Legal Entities by Entities by Sector and Region(2018)

单位:个 (unit)

地区	Region	法人单位数 Corporate Units	#农、林、牧、渔业 Agriculture, Forestry, Animal husbandry, Fishery	#采矿业 Mining Industry	#制造业 Manufacturing	#电力、热力、燃气及水的生产和供应业 Electricity, Gas and Water Production and Supply	#建筑业 Construction	批发和零售业 Wholesale and Retail Trades
全国总计	**National Total**	**21787273**	**232818**	**70191**	**3269606**	**110714**	**1218463**	**6499161**
北京	Beijing	988483	456	78	25646	1193	35130	273387
天津	Tianjin	291151	449	72	39739	813	18846	79142
河北	Hebei	1150955	9885	4842	218111	5484	89523	358174
山西	Shanxi	462193	7053	5942	36079	4452	28707	141041
内蒙古	Inner Mongolia	297176	7267	3879	22169	2902	21994	85930
辽宁	Liaoning	600313	8449	3659	89332	3073	36767	178057
吉林	Jilin	187449	6364	989	20273	1590	10572	46950
黑龙江	Heilongjiang	256191	4758	1664	26101	2284	13859	69493
上海	Shanghai	440696	286	2	49395	193	16214	127314
江苏	Jiangsu	2053630	14591	370	513458	5033	119569	613999
浙江	Zhejiang	1545153	2794	841	424775	5240	51741	465896
安徽	Anhui	813279	16525	1237	112646	5608	62462	242064
福建	Fujian	702826	4332	1567	116023	6582	32300	236338
江西	Jiangxi	454387	6779	2998	63136	7566	27569	119751
山东	Shangdong	1801301	24243	2358	310428	6280	124512	598403
河南	Henan	1279238	35426	3588	138461	4971	78034	408979
湖北	**Hubei**	**853168**	**13944**	**2579**	**92277**	**5520**	**57256**	**257986**
湖南	Hunan	622764	20486	3779	62538	6800	30795	154878
广东	Guangdong	3126550	7173	2401	572121	9714	116949	966082
广西	Guangxi	490277	6683	2672	37551	3290	23669	142714
海南	Hainan	100096	885	172	3719	418	9553	22146
重庆	Chongqing	512470	3590	1428	55196	2291	19330	176115
四川	Sichuan	761937	6090	3411	65249	5982	46075	187084
贵州	Guizhou	348149	1503	4326	46302	2089	19521	91682
云南	Yunnan	453286	5227	5434	34606	2975	28058	141696
西藏	Tibet	47215	319	314	3758	261	7938	7292
陕西	Shaanxi	532220	6065	4418	41926	3229	57251	147183
甘肃	Gansu	229632	4238	1227	15209	1628	13473	58213
青海	Qinghai	72869	512	493	4727	684	5035	17087
宁夏	Ningxia	68817	862	496	6678	473	4349	18271
新疆	Xinjiang	243402	5584	2955	21977	2096	11412	65814

附录1-3 续表1 continued

单位:个 (unit)

地区	Region	*交通运输、仓储和邮政业 Traffic, Transport, Storage and Postal Industry	*住宿和餐饮业 Accommodation and Catering Services	*信息传输、软件和信息技术服务业 Information Transmission, Software and Computer Services	金融业 Financial Intermediation	*房地产业 Real Estate	*租赁和商务服务业 Leasing and Business Services
		法人单位数 Corporate Units					
全国总计	**National Total**	**577233**	**431323**	**919879**	**137934**	**744924**	**2551306**
北京	Beijing	19175	34458	77133	12796	26884	184751
天津	Tianjin	13792	4935	17802	4988	10832	39513
河北	Hebei	31074	15538	39141	3681	45063	99299
山西	Shanxi	14626	8427	17399	2401	16757	45373
内蒙古	Inner Mongolia	11040	4358	8256	1721	11617	32688
辽宁	Liaoning	21938	8862	28833	3673	22196	64493
吉林	Jilin	5824	2625	6495	1312	7454	16861
黑龙江	Heilongjiang	9398	2706	10182	1487	9574	24764
上海	Shanghai	16002	20445	23484	9539	21457	69898
江苏	Jiangsu	59043	25927	72799	6925	59246	188239
浙江	Zhejiang	32133	24951	55067	16965	46052	157725
安徽	Anhui	24424	16738	30440	3270	26697	90577
福建	Fujian	16714	12861	32791	3347	18144	69411
江西	Jiangxi	17144	6697	15310	1649	13547	48714
山东	Shangdong	52848	28234	58722	5783	51380	171491
河南	Henan	26433	21284	56112	3001	46303	126282
湖北	**Hubei**	**22591**	**17622**	**39431**	**2875**	**31427**	**93706**
湖南	Hunan	13686	11646	24880	2011	20714	65296
广东	Guangdong	72787	52913	165633	30364	117254	514187
广西	Guangxi	13253	8451	18658	2387	21498	68961
海南	Hainan	2254	2691	5804	588	10393	14719
重庆	Chongqing	11711	26373	22734	1818	16578	64049
四川	Sichuan	18551	16832	31631	3394	25144	92162
贵州	Guizhou	7709	17053	8179	1509	11596	35243
云南	Yunnan	10675	14348	15285	2948	14998	48736
西藏	Tibet	684	1139	1097	336	627	5692
陕西	Shaanxi	13403	11321	20798	2399	19993	57625
甘肃	Gansu	5000	5899	4146	1550	7331	19942
青海	Qinghai	1588	2095	1785	354	2545	9806
宁夏	Ningxia	2575	1201	1462	576	2119	6878
新疆	Xinjiang	9158	2693	8390	2287	9504	24225

附录1-3　续表2 continued

单位:个 (unit)

地 区	Region	法人单位数 Corporate Units *科学研究和技术服务 Research and Technical Service	*水利、环境和公共设施管理业 Water, Environment and Public Facilities Management	*居民服务、修理和其他服务业 Resident Services、Repair and Other Services	*教 育 Education	*卫生和社会工作 Health and Social Work	*文化、体育和娱乐业 Culture, Sports and Entertainment	*公共管理、社会保障和社会组织 Public Management、Social Security and Social Organization
全国总计	**National Total**	**1275579**	**148860**	**497292**	**665883**	**272504**	**566593**	**1597010**
北 京	Beijing	154092	7346	36756	21236	6607	53882	17477
天 津	Tianjin	25989	1732	7237	5749	2262	7395	9864
河 北	Hebei	51677	7420	22280	28623	10764	23852	86524
山 西	Shanxi	21099	5510	11377	15682	6896	13635	59737
内蒙古	Inner Mongolia	13102	3785	6932	10805	4926	7343	36462
辽 宁	Liaoning	30154	3710	12599	19103	11409	12712	41294
吉 林	Jilin	9485	1519	4078	8344	4405	4205	28104
黑龙江	Heilongjiang	15612	2346	4816	11671	6162	6496	32818
上 海	Shanghai	26067	2228	17678	9227	4933	12599	13735
江 苏	Jiangsu	129379	10920	41016	36601	30041	44141	82333
浙 江	Zhejiang	61583	8556	26474	37929	12391	36470	77570
安 徽	Anhui	41985	6426	21003	25508	11564	21353	52752
福 建	Fujian	27310	4849	15468	20876	6262	19022	58629
江 西	Jiangxi	16779	3033	7990	19188	8524	10752	57261
山 东	Shangdong	93529	10758	33873	43057	18784	37583	129035
河 南	Henan	75709	9631	25048	60451	20369	34229	104927
湖 北	**Hubei**	**56306**	**8162**	**20009**	**25978**	**12539**	**23539**	**69421**
湖 南	Hunan	45379	6462	13286	31778	11858	24155	72337
广 东	Guangdong	194574	11067	62395	71352	17810	61695	80079
广 西	Guangxi	28686	4524	11192	26800	5822	11599	51867
海 南	Hainan	5537	876	3084	5239	1298	3140	7580
重 庆	Chongqing	21164	3162	17501	16561	6476	16975	29418
四 川	Sichuan	42513	6044	19026	34127	16751	26469	115402
贵 州	Guizhou	11100	3373	13950	15828	5569	9258	42359
云 南	Yunnan	21870	4061	13888	15492	5887	14315	52787
西 藏	Tibet	1461	205	673	1038	575	1013	12793
陕 西	Shaanxi	28134	5486	13423	20247	11463	13799	54057
甘 肃	Gansu	7564	1895	5882	12540	3992	5870	54033
青 海	Qinghai	3370	970	1778	2358	1462	1766	14454
宁 夏	Ningxia	2235	527	1741	3049	869	1647	12809
新 疆	Xinjiang	12135	2277	4839	9446	3834	5684	39092

附录1-4　分地区年末常住人口
Population at Year-end by Regions

单位：万人　　　　(10 000 persons)

地区	Region	2012	2013	2014	2015	2016	2017	2018	2019
全　国	**National Total**	**135404**	**136072**	**136782**	**137462**	**138271**	**139008**	**139538**	**140005**
北　京	Beijing	2069	2115	2152	2171	2173	2171	2154	2154
天　津	Tianjin	1413	1472	1517	1547	1562	1557	1560	1562
河　北	Hebei	7288	7333	7384	7425	7470	7520	7556	7592
山　西	Shanxi	3611	3630	3648	3664	3682	3702	3718	3729
内蒙古	Inner Mongolia	2490	2498	2505	2511	2520	2529	2534	2540
辽　宁	Liaoning	4389	4390	4391	4382	4378	4369	4359	4352
吉　林	Jilin	2750	2751	2752	2753	2733	2717	2704	2691
黑龙江	Heilongjiang	3834	3835	3833	3812	3799	3789	3773	3751
上　海	Shanghai	2380	2415	2426	2415	2420	2418	2424	2428
江　苏	Jiangsu	7920	7939	7960	7976	7999	8029	8051	8070
浙　江	Zhejiang	5477	5498	5508	5539	5590	5657	5737	5850
安　徽	Anhui	5988	6030	6083	6144	6196	6255	6324	6366
福　建	Fujian	3748	3774	3806	3839	3874	3911	3941	3973
江　西	Jiangxi	4504	4522	4542	4566	4592	4622	4648	4666
山　东	Shangdong	9685	9733	9789	9847	9947	10006	10047	10070
河　南	Henan	9406	9413	9436	9480	9532	9559	9605	9640
湖　北	**Hubei**	**5779**	**5799**	**5816**	**5852**	**5885**	**5902**	**5917**	**5927**
湖　南	Hunan	6639	6691	6737	6783	6822	6860	6899	6918
广　东	Guangdong	10594	10644	10724	10849	10999	11169	11346	11521
广　西	Guangxi	4682	4719	4754	4796	4838	4885	4926	4960
海　南	Hainan	887	895	903	911	917	926	934	945
重　庆	Chongqing	2945	2970	2991	3017	3048	3075	3102	3124
四　川	Sichuan	8076	8107	8140	8204	8262	8302	8341	8375
贵　州	Guizhou	3484	3502	3508	3530	3555	3580	3600	3623
云　南	Yunnan	4659	4687	4714	4742	4771	4801	4830	4858
西　藏	Tibet	308	312	318	324	331	337	344	351
陕　西	Shaanxi	3753	3764	3775	3793	3813	3835	3864	3876
甘　肃	Gansu	2578	2582	2591	2600	2610	2626	2637	2674
青　海	Qinghai	573	578	583	588	593	598	603	608
宁　夏	Ningxia	647	654	662	668	675	682	688	695
新　疆	Xinjiang	2233	2264	2298	2360	2398	2445	2487	2523

注：以上数据为年度人口抽样调查推算数据。
Note:Above data are the estimates from the annual national sample survey of population.

附录1-5 分地区年末城镇人口比重
Proportion of Urban Populations at Year-end by Region

单位:% (%)

地区	Region	2010	2011	2012	2013	2014	2015	2016	2017	2018	2019
全 国	**National Total**	**49.95**	**51.27**	**52.57**	**53.73**	**54.77**	**56.10**	**57.35**	**58.52**	**59.58**	**60.60**
北 京	Beijing	85.96	86.20	86.20	86.30	86.35	86.50	86.50	86.50	86.50	86.60
天 津	Tianjin	79.55	80.50	81.55	82.01	82.27	82.64	82.93	82.93	83.15	83.48
河 北	Hebei	44.50	45.60	46.80	48.12	49.33	51.33	53.32	55.01	56.43	57.62
山 西	Shanxi	48.05	49.68	51.26	52.56	53.79	55.03	56.21	57.34	58.41	59.55
内蒙古	Inner Mongolia	55.50	56.62	57.74	58.71	59.51	60.30	61.19	62.02	62.71	63.37
辽 宁	Liaoning	62.10	64.05	65.65	66.45	67.05	67.35	67.37	67.49	68.10	68.11
吉 林	Jilin	53.35	53.40	53.70	54.20	54.81	55.31	55.97	56.65	57.53	58.27
黑龙江	Heilongjiang	55.66	56.50	56.90	57.40	58.01	58.80	59.20	59.40	60.10	60.90
上 海	Shanghai	89.30	89.30	89.30	89.60	89.60	87.60	87.90	87.70	88.10	88.30
江 苏	Jiangsu	60.58	61.90	63.00	64.11	65.21	66.52	67.72	68.76	69.61	70.61
浙 江	Zhejiang	61.62	62.30	63.20	64.00	64.87	65.80	67.00	68.00	68.90	70.00
安 徽	Anhui	43.01	44.80	46.50	47.86	49.15	50.50	51.99	53.49	54.69	55.81
福 建	Fujian	57.10	58.10	59.60	60.77	61.80	62.60	63.60	64.80	65.82	66.50
江 西	Jiangxi	44.06	45.70	47.51	48.87	50.22	51.62	53.10	54.60	56.02	57.42
山 东	Shangdong	49.70	50.95	52.43	53.75	55.01	57.01	59.02	60.58	61.18	61.51
河 南	Henan	38.50	40.57	42.43	43.80	45.20	46.85	48.50	50.16	51.71	53.21
湖 北	**Hubei**	**49.70**	**51.83**	**53.50**	**54.51**	**55.67**	**56.85**	**58.10**	**59.30**	**60.30**	**61.00**
湖 南	Hunan	43.30	45.10	46.65	47.96	49.28	50.89	52.75	54.62	56.02	57.22
广 东	Guangdong	66.18	66.50	67.40	67.76	68.00	68.71	69.20	69.85	70.70	71.40
广 西	Guangxi	40.00	41.80	43.53	44.81	46.01	47.06	48.08	49.21	50.22	51.09
海 南	Hainan	49.80	50.50	51.60	52.74	53.76	55.12	56.78	58.04	59.06	59.23
重 庆	Chongqing	53.02	55.02	56.98	58.34	59.60	60.94	62.60	64.08	65.50	66.80
四 川	Sichuan	40.18	41.83	43.53	44.90	46.30	47.69	49.21	50.79	52.29	53.79
贵 州	Guizhou	33.81	34.96	36.41	37.83	40.01	42.01	44.15	46.02	47.52	49.02
云 南	Yunnan	34.70	36.80	39.31	40.48	41.73	43.33	45.03	46.69	47.81	48.91
西 藏	Tibet	22.67	22.71	22.75	23.71	25.75	27.74	29.56	30.89	31.14	31.54
陕 西	Shaanxi	45.76	47.30	50.02	51.31	52.57	53.92	55.34	56.79	58.13	59.43
甘 肃	Gansu	36.12	37.15	38.75	40.13	41.68	43.19	44.69	46.39	47.69	48.49
青 海	Qinghai	44.72	46.22	47.44	48.51	49.78	50.30	51.63	53.07	54.47	55.52
宁 夏	Ningxia	47.90	49.82	50.67	52.01	53.61	55.23	56.29	57.98	58.88	59.86
新 疆	Xinjiang	43.01	43.54	43.98	44.47	46.07	47.23	48.35	49.38	50.91	51.87

注:2010年数据为根据当年人口普查数据推算的数据;其余年份数据根据年度人口抽样调查推算。
Note:Data of 2010 is based on the current census data extrapolated; While the rest are based on the annual sanple survey of population .

附录1-6 地区生产总值(2019年)
Gross Regional Product (2019)

单位:亿元 (100 million yuan)

地区	Region	地区生产总值 Gross Regional Product	三次产业增加值 Value-Added by Three Strata of Industry			分行业增加值 Value-Added by Sector		
			第一产业 Primary Industry	第二产业 Secondary Industry	第三产业 Tertiary Industry	农林牧渔业 Agriculture, Forestry, Animal Husbandry and Fishery	工业 Industry	建筑业 Construction
北京	Beijing	35371.28	113.69	5715.06	29542.53	116.20	4241.10	1513.67
天津	Tianjin	14104.28	185.23	4969.18	8949.87	191.61	4394.27	693.76
河北	Hebei	35104.52	3518.44	13597.26	17988.82	3727.50	11503.03	2129.89
山西	Shanxi	17026.68	824.72	7453.09	8748.87	874.87	6569.51	894.76
内蒙古	Inner Mongolia	17212.53	1863.19	6818.88	8530.46	1893.38	5514.34	1304.54
辽宁	Liaoning	24909.45	2177.77	9531.24	13200.44	2266.70	8164.55	1482.05
吉林	Jilin	11726.82	1287.32	4134.82	6304.68	1333.42	3347.82	808.63
黑龙江	Heilongjiang	13612.68	3182.45	3615.21	6815.03	3267.44	3291.05	419.16
上海	Shanghai	38155.32	103.88	10299.16	27752.28	110.10	9670.68	716.16
江苏	Jiangsu	99631.52	4296.28	44270.51	51064.73	4610.84	37825.32	6493.54
浙江	Zhejiang	62351.74	2097.38	26566.60	33687.76	2146.23	22840.53	3779.55
安徽	Anhui	37113.98	2915.70	15337.90	18860.38	3068.93	11454.85	3905.71
福建	Fujian	42395.00	2596.23	20581.74	19217.03	2690.85	16170.45	4482.03
江西	Jiangxi	24757.50	2057.56	10939.83	11760.11	2135.69	8965.81	1980.99
山东	Shandong	71067.53	5116.44	28310.92	37640.17	5476.47	22985.13	5441.91
河南	Henan	54259.20	4635.40	23605.79	26018.01	4860.38	18413.21	5272.97
湖北	**Hubei**	**45828.31**	**3809.09**	**19098.62**	**22920.60**	**4014.00**	**16087.33**	**3073.13**
湖南	Hunan	39752.12	3646.95	14946.98	21158.19	3850.19	11630.55	3327.00
广东	Guangdong	107671.07	4351.26	43546.43	59773.38	4478.51	39398.46	4255.07
广西	Guangxi	21237.14	3387.74	7077.43	10771.97	3492.03	5277.57	1816.05
海南	Hainan	5308.93	1080.36	1099.03	3129.54	1119.07	588.71	514.47
重庆	Chongqing	23605.77	1551.42	9496.84	12557.51	1581.15	6656.72	2840.12
四川	Sichuan	46615.82	4807.24	17365.33	24443.25	4937.70	13365.66	4123.48
贵州	Guizhou	16769.34	2280.56	6058.45	8430.33	2408.03	4545.97	1517.06
云南	Yunnan	23223.75	3037.62	7961.58	12224.55	3096.08	5301.51	2664.64
西藏	Tibet	1697.82	138.19	635.62	924.01	142.07	131.72	503.90
陕西	Shaanxi	25793.17	1990.93	11980.75	11821.49	2098.01	9609.70	2482.96
甘肃	Gansu	8718.30	1050.48	2862.42	4805.40	1087.61	2319.75	552.99
青海	Qinghai	2965.95	301.90	1159.75	1504.30	306.03	817.49	342.26
宁夏	Ningxia	3748.48	279.93	1584.72	1883.83	297.66	1270.02	316.17
新疆	Xinjiang	13597.11	1781.75	4795.50	7019.86	1888.39	3861.66	1037.29

注:1.表中数据为初步核算数。
2.本表绝对数按当年价格计算,指数按不变价格计算。
1.Data in this table are preliminary data.
2.Level data in this table are calculated at current prices while indices at constant prices.

1-6 续表 1 continued

单位:亿元 (100 million yuan)

地区	Region	批发和零售业 Wholesale and Retail Trades	交通运输、仓储和邮政业 Transport, Storage and Post	住宿和餐饮业 Hotels and Catering Services	金融业 Financial Intermediation	房地产业 Real Estate	其他 Others	人均地区生产总值(元) Per Capita Gross Regional Product (yuan)
北京	Beijing	2856.89	1025.33	540.36	6544.77	2620.79	15912.17	164220
天津	Tianjin	1372.27	787.73	169.14	1907.86	1238.45	3349.19	90371
河北	Hebei	2947.53	2916.01	389.04	2416.13	2310.00	6765.39	46348
山西	Shanxi	1361.61	1006.82	207.05	1174.01	1081.74	3856.31	45724
内蒙古	Inner Mongolia	1448.34	1202.71	361.54	874.88	892.20	3720.60	67852
辽宁	Liaoning	2164.38	1313.36	317.61	1985.18	1471.41	5744.21	57191
吉林	Jilin	759.11	574.40	192.61	837.89	778.83	3094.12	43475
黑龙江	Heilongjiang	1005.33	533.00	237.06	995.36	671.93	3192.35	36183
上海	Shanghai	5023.23	1650.44	458.86	6600.60	3300.72	10624.53	157279
江苏	Jiangsu	10901.27	3157.21	1540.21	7529.61	8057.76	19515.76	123607
浙江	Zhejiang	7470.08	1962.13	1092.28	5004.37	4356.87	13699.69	107624
安徽	Anhui	3429.23	1973.87	759.36	2345.64	2870.49	7305.90	58496
福建	Fujian	4242.89	1484.58	656.65	2875.35	2689.62	7102.58	107139
江西	Jiangxi	2103.31	1083.72	447.40	1557.50	1895.01	4588.06	53164
山东	Shandong	9744.83	3636.06	1173.68	4177.35	4348.67	14083.43	70653
河南	Henan	4010.80	2970.41	1150.16	2793.94	3419.58	11367.75	56388
湖北	**Hubei**	**3347.05**	**2233.45**	**1248.46**	**2783.57**	**3680.34**	**9360.98**	**77387**
湖南	Hunan	4022.92	1556.52	922.40	1960.07	2777.26	9705.21	57540
广东	Guangdong	11153.04	3466.42	1878.20	8881.41	9223.62	24936.34	94172
广西	Guangxi	1758.95	902.04	376.87	1469.45	1798.82	4345.36	42964
海南	Hainan	533.03	246.93	269.18	392.23	497.86	1147.45	56507
重庆	Chongqing	2192.06	977.14	501.98	2087.95	1473.04	5295.61	75828
四川	Sichuan	4194.68	1468.52	1149.18	3121.87	3399.12	10855.61	55774
贵州	Guizhou	1269.90	709.88	417.18	1060.02	632.24	4209.06	46433
云南	Yunnan	2389.22	1113.14	599.45	1406.08	1410.42	5243.21	47944
西藏	Tibet	104.51	47.76	41.90	121.89	54.50	549.56	48902
陕西	Shaanxi	1880.44	1059.86	428.31	1708.33	1305.59	5219.97	66649
甘肃	Gansu	646.28	438.39	158.27	862.33	470.49	2182.20	32995
青海	Qinghai	160.83	123.18	50.75	262.96	127.49	774.96	48981
宁夏	Ningxia	200.85	178.21	53.72	302.01	148.09	981.75	54217
新疆	Xinjiang	766.09	953.72	181.89	1015.31	509.95	3382.81	54280

1-6 续表 2 continued

地区	Region	构成(地区生产总值=100) Composition (GRP=100)			指数(上年=100) Indices (preceding year=100)				
		第一产业 Primary Industry	第二产业 Secondary Industry	第三产业 Tertiary Industry	地区生产总值 Gross Regional Product	第一产业 Primary Industry	第二产业 Secondary Industry	第三产业 Tertiary Industry	人均地区生产总值 Per Capita Gross Regional Product
北京	Beijing	0.3	16.2	83.5	106.1	97.5	104.5	106.4	106.5
天津	Tianjin	1.3	35.2	63.5	104.8	100.2	103.2	105.9	104.6
河北	Hebei	10.0	38.7	51.3	106.8	101.6	104.9	109.4	106.2
山西	Shanxi	4.8	43.8	51.4	106.2	102.1	105.7	107.0	105.8
内蒙古	Inner Mongolia	10.8	39.6	49.6	105.2	102.4	105.7	105.4	105.0
辽宁	Liaoning	8.7	38.3	53.0	105.5	103.5	105.7	105.6	105.7
吉林	Jilin	11.0	35.2	53.8	103.0	102.5	102.6	103.3	103.5
黑龙江	Heilongjiang	23.4	26.6	50.1	104.2	102.4	102.7	105.9	104.7
上海	Shanghai	0.3	27.0	72.7	106.0	95.0	100.5	108.2	105.7
江苏	Jiangsu	4.3	44.4	51.3	106.1	101.3	105.9	106.6	105.8
浙江	Zhejiang	3.4	42.6	54.0	106.8	102.0	105.9	107.8	105.0
安徽	Anhui	7.9	41.3	50.8	107.5	103.2	108.0	107.7	106.5
福建	Fujian	6.1	48.5	45.3	107.6	103.5	108.3	107.3	106.7
江西	Jiangxi	8.3	44.2	47.5	108.0	103.0	108.0	109.0	107.4
山东	Shandong	7.2	39.8	53.0	105.5	101.1	102.6	108.7	105.2
河南	Henan	8.5	43.5	48.0	107.0	102.3	107.5	107.4	106.5
湖北	**Hubei**	**8.3**	**41.7**	**50.0**	**107.5**	**103.2**	**108.0**	**107.8**	**107.2**
湖南	Hunan	9.2	37.6	53.2	107.6	103.2	107.8	108.1	107.1
广东	Guangdong	4.0	40.4	55.5	106.2	104.1	104.7	107.5	104.5
广西	Guangxi	16.0	33.3	50.7	106.0	105.6	105.7	106.2	105.1
海南	Hainan	20.3	20.7	59.0	105.8	102.5	104.1	107.5	104.7
重庆	Chongqing	6.6	40.2	53.2	106.3	103.6	106.4	106.4	105.4
四川	Sichuan	10.3	37.3	52.4	107.5	102.8	107.5	108.5	107.0
贵州	Guizhou	13.6	36.1	50.3	108.3	105.7	109.8	107.8	107.6
云南	Yunnan	13.1	34.3	52.6	108.1	105.5	108.6	108.3	107.4
西藏	Tibet	8.2	37.4	54.4	108.1	104.6	107.0	109.2	106.0
陕西	Shaanxi	7.7	46.4	45.8	106.0	104.0	105.5	106.8	105.4
甘肃	Gansu	12.0	32.8	55.1	106.2	105.8	104.7	107.2	105.7
青海	Qinghai	10.2	39.1	50.7	106.3	104.6	106.3	106.5	105.4
宁夏	Ningxia	7.5	42.3	50.3	106.5	103.2	106.7	106.8	105.5
新疆	Xinjiang	13.1	35.3	51.6	106.2	105.3	103.7	108.1	104.5

附录1-7　分地区居民消费价格指数
Consumer Price Index by Region

(上年=100)　(Previous Year = 100)

地 区	Region	2012	2013	2014	2015	2016	2017	2018	2019
全 国	**National Total**	**102.6**	**102.6**	**102.0**	**101.4**	**102.0**	**101.6**	**102.1**	**102.9**
北 京	Beijing	103.3	103.3	101.6	101.8	101.4	101.9	102.5	102.3
天 津	Tianjin	102.7	103.1	101.9	101.7	102.1	102.1	102.0	102.7
河 北	Hebei	102.6	103.0	101.7	100.9	101.5	101.7	102.4	103.0
山 西	Shanxi	102.5	103.1	101.7	100.6	101.1	101.1	101.8	102.7
内蒙古	Inner Mongolia	103.1	103.2	101.6	101.1	101.2	101.7	101.8	102.4
辽 宁	Liaoning	102.8	102.4	101.7	101.4	101.6	101.4	102.5	102.4
吉 林	Jilin	102.5	102.9	102.0	101.7	101.6	101.6	102.1	103.0
黑龙江	Heilongjiang	103.2	102.2	101.5	101.1	101.5	101.3	102.0	102.8
上 海	Shanghai	102.8	102.3	102.7	102.4	103.2	101.7	101.6	102.5
江 苏	Jiangsu	102.6	102.3	102.2	101.7	102.3	101.7	102.3	103.1
浙 江	Zhejiang	102.2	102.3	102.1	101.4	101.9	102.1	102.3	102.9
安 徽	Anhui	102.3	102.4	101.6	101.3	101.8	101.2	102.0	102.7
福 建	Fujian	102.4	102.5	102.0	101.7	101.7	101.2	101.5	102.6
江 西	Jiangxi	102.7	102.5	102.3	101.5	102.0	102.0	102.1	102.9
山 东	Shangdong	102.1	102.2	101.9	101.2	102.1	101.5	102.5	103.2
河 南	Henan	102.5	102.9	101.9	101.3	101.9	101.4	102.3	103.0
湖 北	**Hubei**	**102.9**	**102.8**	**102.0**	**101.5**	**102.2**	**101.5**	**101.9**	**103.1**
湖 南	Hunan	102.0	102.5	101.9	101.4	101.9	101.4	102.0	102.9
广 东	Guangdong	102.8	102.5	102.3	101.5	102.3	101.5	102.2	103.4
广 西	Guangxi	103.2	102.2	102.1	101.5	101.6	101.6	102.3	103.7
海 南	Hainan	103.2	102.8	102.4	101.0	102.8	102.8	102.5	103.4
重 庆	Chongqing	102.6	102.7	101.8	101.3	101.8	101.0	102.0	102.7
四 川	Sichuan	102.5	102.8	101.6	101.5	101.9	101.4	101.7	103.2
贵 州	Guizhou	102.7	102.5	102.4	101.8	101.4	100.9	101.8	102.4
云 南	Yunnan	102.7	103.1	102.4	101.9	101.5	100.9	101.6	102.5
西 藏	Tibet	103.5	103.6	102.9	102.0	102.5	101.6	101.7	102.3
陕 西	Shaanxi	102.8	103.0	101.6	101.0	101.3	101.6	102.1	102.9
甘 肃	Gansu	102.7	103.2	102.1	101.6	101.3	101.4	102.0	102.3
青 海	Qinghai	103.1	103.9	102.8	102.6	101.8	101.5	102.5	102.5
宁 夏	Ningxia	102.0	103.4	101.9	101.1	101.5	101.6	102.3	102.1
新 疆	Xinjiang	103.8	103.9	102.1	100.6	101.4	102.2	102.0	101.9

附录1-8 分地区全体居民人均可支配收入与消费支出
Per Capita Disposable Income and Consumption Expenditure of Urban and Rural Households by Region

单位:元 (yuan)

地区	Region	可支配收入 Disposable Income		消费支出 Expenses on Consumption	
		2018	2019	2018	2019
全国总计	**National Total**	**28228**	**30733**	**19853**	**21559**
北 京	Beijing	62361	67756	39843	43038
天 津	Tianjin	39506	42404	29903	31854
河 北	Hebei	23446	25665	16722	17987
山 西	Shanxi	21990	23828	14810	15863
内蒙古	Inner Mongolia	28376	30555	19665	20743
辽 宁	Liaoning	29701	31820	21398	22203
吉 林	Jilin	22798	24563	17200	18075
黑龙江	Heilongjiang	22726	24254	16994	18111
上 海	Shanghai	64183	69442	43351	45605
江 苏	Jiangsu	38096	41400	25007	26697
浙 江	Zhejiang	45840	49899	29471	32026
安 徽	Anhui	23984	26415	17045	19137
福 建	Fujian	32644	35616	22996	25314
江 西	Jiangxi	24080	26262	15792	17650
山 东	Shangdong	29205	31597	18780	20427
河 南	Henan	21964	23903	15169	16332
湖 北	**Hubei**	**25815**	**28319**	**19538**	**21567**
湖 南	Hunan	25241	27680	18808	20479
广 东	Guangdong	35810	39014	26054	28995
广 西	Guangxi	21485	23328	14935	16418
海 南	Hainan	24579	26679	17528	19555
重 庆	Chongqing	26386	28920	19248	20774
四 川	Sichuan	22461	24703	17664	19338
贵 州	Guizhou	18430	20397	13798	14780
云 南	Yunnan	20084	22082	14250	15780
西 藏	Tibet	17286	19501	11520	13029
陕 西	Shaanxi	22528	24666	16160	17465
甘 肃	Gansu	17488	19139	14624	15879
青 海	Qinghai	20757	22618	16557	17545
宁 夏	Ningxia	22400	24412	16715	18297
新 疆	Xinjiang	21500	23103	16189	17397

注:本表按当年价格计算。
Note:The table is calculated at current prices.

附录1-9 分地区城镇居民人均可支配收入与消费支出

Per Capita Disposable Income and Consumption Expenditure of Urban Households by Region

单位:元 (yuan)

地区	Region	可支配收入 Disposable Income		消费支出 Expenses on Consumption	
		2018	2019	2018	2019
全国总计	**National Total**	**39251**	**42359**	**26112**	**28063**
北京	Beijing	67990	73849	42926	46358
天津	Tianjin	42976	46119	32655	34811
河北	Hebei	32977	35738	22127	23483
山西	Shanxi	31035	33262	19790	21159
内蒙古	Inner Mongolia	38305	40782	24437	25383
辽宁	Liaoning	37342	39777	26448	27355
吉林	Jilin	30172	32299	22394	23394
黑龙江	Heilongjiang	29191	30945	21035	22165
上海	Shanghai	68034	73615	46015	48272
江苏	Jiangsu	47200	51056	29462	31329
浙江	Zhejiang	55574	60182	34598	37508
安徽	Anhui	34393	37540	21523	23782
福建	Fujian	42121	45620	28145	30946
江西	Jiangxi	33819	36546	20760	22714
山东	Shangdong	39549	42329	24798	26731
河南	Henan	31874	34201	20989	21972
湖北	**Hubei**	**34455**	**37601**	**23996**	**26422**
湖南	Hunan	36698	39842	25064	26924
广东	Guangdong	44341	48118	30924	34424
广西	Guangxi	32436	34745	20159	21591
海南	Hainan	33349	36017	22971	25317
重庆	Chongqing	34889	37939	24154	25785
四川	Sichuan	33216	36154	23484	25367
贵州	Guizhou	31592	34404	20788	21402
云南	Yunnan	33488	36238	21626	23455
西藏	Tibet	33797	37410	23029	25637
陕西	Shaanxi	33319	36098	21966	23514
甘肃	Gansu	29957	32323	22606	24454
青海	Qinghai	31515	33830	22998	23799
宁夏	Ningxia	31895	34328	21977	24161
新疆	Xinjiang	32764	34664	24191	25594

注:本表按当年价格计算。

Note:The table is calculated at current prices.

附录1-10 分地区农村居民人均可支配收入与消费支出
Per Capita Disposable Income and Consumption Expenditure of Rural Households by Region

单位:元 (yuan)

地区	Region	可支配收入 Disposable Income		消费支出 Expenses on Consumption	
		2018	2019	2018	2019
全国总计	**National Total**	**14617**	**16021**	**12124**	**13328**
北京	Beijing	26490	28928	20195	21881
天津	Tianjin	23065	24804	16863	17843
河北	Hebei	14031	15373	11383	12372
山西	Shanxi	11750	12902	9172	9728
内蒙古	Inner Mongolia	13803	15283	12661	13816
辽宁	Liaoning	14656	16108	11455	12030
吉林	Jilin	13748	14936	10826	11457
黑龙江	Heilongjiang	13804	14982	11417	12495
上海	Shanghai	30375	33195	19965	22449
江苏	Jiangsu	20845	22675	16567	17716
浙江	Zhejiang	27302	29876	19707	21352
安徽	Anhui	13996	15416	12748	14546
福建	Fujian	17821	19568	14943	16281
江西	Jiangxi	14460	15796	10885	12497
山东	Shangdong	16297	17775	11270	12309
河南	Henan	13831	15164	10392	11546
湖北	**Hubei**	**14978**	**16391**	**13946**	**15328**
湖南	Hunan	14093	15395	12721	13969
广东	Guangdong	17168	18818	15411	16949
广西	Guangxi	12435	13676	10617	12045
海南	Hainan	13989	15113	10956	12418
重庆	Chongqing	13781	15133	11977	13112
四川	Sichuan	13331	14670	12723	14056
贵州	Guizhou	9716	10756	9170	10222
云南	Yunnan	10768	11902	9123	10260
西藏	Tibet	11450	12951	7452	8418
陕西	Shaanxi	11213	12326	10071	10935
甘肃	Gansu	8804	9629	9065	9694
青海	Qinghai	10393	11499	10352	11343
宁夏	Ningxia	11708	12858	10790	11465
新疆	Xinjiang	11975	13122	9421	10318

注:本表按当年价格计算。
Note:The table is calculated at current prices.

附录1-11 分地区一般公共预算收入
General Public Budget Revenue by Region

单位:亿元 (100 million yuan)

地 区	Region	2014	2015	2016	2017	2018	2019
地方总计	**Region Total**	**75876.6**	**83002.0**	**87239.4**	**91469.4**	**97903.4**	**101076.8**
北 京	Beijing	4027.2	4723.9	5081.3	5430.8	5785.9	5817.1
天 津	Tianjin	2390.4	2667.1	2723.5	2310.4	2106.2	2410.3
河 北	Hebei	2446.6	2649.2	2849.9	3233.8	3513.9	3742.7
山 西	Shanxi	1820.6	1642.4	1557.0	1867.0	2292.7	2347.6
内蒙古	Inner Mongolia	1843.7	1964.5	2016.4	1703.2	1857.6	2059.7
辽 宁	Liaoning	3192.8	2127.4	2200.5	2392.8	2616.1	2652.0
吉 林	Jilin	1203.4	1229.4	1263.8	1210.9	1240.9	1116.9
黑龙江	Heilongjiang	1301.3	1165.9	1148.4	1243.3	1282.6	1262.6
上 海	Shanghai	4585.6	5519.5	6406.1	6642.3	7108.1	7165.1
江 苏	Jiangsu	7233.1	8028.6	8121.2	8171.5	8630.2	8802.4
浙 江	Zhejiang	4122.0	4809.9	5302.0	5804.4	6598.2	7048.0
安 徽	Anhui	2218.4	2454.3	2672.8	2812.4	3048.7	3182.5
福 建	Fujian	2362.2	2544.2	2654.8	2809.0	3007.4	3052.7
江 西	Jiangxi	1881.8	2165.7	2151.5	2247.1	2373.0	2486.5
山 东	Shangdong	5026.8	5529.3	5860.2	6098.6	6485.4	6526.6
河 南	Henan	2739.3	3016.1	3153.5	3407.2	3766.0	4041.6
湖 北	**Hubei**	**2566.9**	**3005.5**	**3102.1**	**3248.3**	**3307.1**	**3388.4**
湖 南	Hunan	2262.8	2515.4	2697.9	2757.8	2860.8	3007.0
广 东	Guangdong	8065.1	9366.8	10390.4	11320.3	12105.3	12651.5
广 西	Guangxi	1422.3	1515.2	1556.3	1615.1	1681.4	1811.9
海 南	Hainan	555.3	627.7	637.5	674.1	752.7	814.1
重 庆	Chongqing	1922.0	2154.8	2227.9	2252.4	2265.5	2134.9
四 川	Sichuan	3061.1	3355.4	3388.9	3578.0	3911.0	4070.7
贵 州	Guizhou	1366.7	1503.4	1561.3	1613.8	1726.9	1767.4
云 南	Yunnan	1698.1	1808.1	1812.3	1886.2	1994.3	2073.5
西 藏	Tibet	124.3	137.1	156.0	185.8	230.4	222.0
陕 西	Shaanxi	1890.4	2060.0	1834.0	2006.7	2243.1	2287.7
甘 肃	Gansu	672.7	743.9	787.0	815.7	871.1	850.2
青 海	Qinghai	251.7	267.1	238.5	246.2	272.9	282.1
宁 夏	Ningxia	339.9	373.4	387.7	417.6	436.5	423.6
新 疆	Xinjiang	1282.3	1330.9	1299.0	1466.5	1531.4	1577.6

附录1-12 分地区一般公共预算支出
General Public Expenditure by Region

单位:亿元 (100 million yuan)

地 区	Region	2014	2015	2016	2017	2018	2019
地方总计	**Region Total**	**129215.5**	**150335.6**	**160351.4**	**173228.3**	**188196.3**	**203758.9**
北 京	Beijing	4524.7	5737.7	6406.8	6824.5	7471.4	7408.3
天 津	Tianjin	2884.7	3232.4	3699.4	3282.5	3103.2	3508.7
河 北	Hebei	4677.3	5632.2	6049.5	6639.2	7726.2	8313.7
山 西	Shanxi	3085.3	3423.0	3428.9	3756.4	4283.9	4713.1
内蒙古	Inner Mongolia	3880.0	4253.0	4512.7	4529.9	4831.5	5097.9
辽 宁	Liaoning	5080.5	4481.6	4577.5	4879.4	5337.7	5761.4
吉 林	Jilin	2913.2	3217.1	3586.1	3725.7	3789.6	3933.4
黑龙江	Heilongjiang	3434.2	4020.7	4227.3	4641.1	4676.8	5011.6
上 海	Shanghai	4923.4	6191.6	6918.9	7547.6	8351.5	8179.3
江 苏	Jiangsu	8472.4	9687.6	9982.0	10621.0	11657.4	12573.6
浙 江	Zhejiang	5159.6	6646.0	6974.3	7530.3	8629.5	10053.0
安 徽	Anhui	4664.1	5239.0	5523.0	6203.8	6572.2	7391.0
福 建	Fujian	3306.7	4001.6	4275.4	4684.2	4832.7	5097.3
江 西	Jiangxi	3882.7	4412.5	4617.4	5111.5	5667.5	6402.6
山 东	Shangdong	7177.3	8250.0	8755.2	9258.4	10101.0	10736.8
河 南	Henan	6028.7	6799.4	7453.7	8215.5	9217.7	10176.3
湖 北	**Hubei**	**4934.1**	**6132.8**	**6423.0**	**6801.3**	**7258.3**	**7967.7**
湖 南	Hunan	5017.4	5728.7	6339.2	6869.4	7479.6	8091.8
广 东	Guangdong	9152.6	12827.8	13446.1	15037.5	15729.3	17314.1
广 西	Guangxi	3479.8	4065.5	4441.7	4908.6	5310.7	5849.0
海 南	Hainan	1099.7	1239.4	1376.5	1444.0	1691.3	1859.1
重 庆	Chongqing	3304.4	3792.0	4001.8	4336.3	4540.9	4847.8
四 川	Sichuan	6796.6	7497.5	8008.9	8694.8	9707.5	10349.6
贵 州	Guizhou	3542.8	3939.5	4262.4	4612.5	5029.7	5921.4
云 南	Yunnan	4438.0	4712.8	5018.9	5713.0	6075.0	6770.1
西 藏	Tibet	1185.5	1381.5	1588.0	1681.9	1970.7	2180.9
陕 西	Shaanxi	3962.5	4376.1	4389.4	4833.2	5302.4	5721.6
甘 肃	Gansu	2541.5	2958.3	3150.0	3304.4	3772.2	3956.7
青 海	Qinghai	1347.4	1515.2	1524.8	1530.4	1647.4	1863.7
宁 夏	Ningxia	1000.5	1138.5	1254.5	1372.8	1419.1	1438.4
新 疆	Xinjiang	3317.8	3804.9	4138.3	4637.2	5012.5	5269.1

附录1-13 分地区电力消费量
Electricity Consumption by Region

单位:亿千瓦时 (10 000 KW/h)

地区	Region	2012	2013	2014	2015	2016	2017	2018	2019
北京	Beijing	874.3	913.1	937.1	952.7	1020.3	1066.9	1142.4	1166.4
天津	Tianjin	722.5	774.5	794.4	800.6	807.9	805.6	861.4	878.4
河北	Hebei	3077.7	3251.2	3314.1	3175.7	3264.5	3441.7	3665.7	3856.1
山西	Shanxi	1765.8	1832.3	1822.6	1737.2	1797.2	1990.6	2160.5	2261.9
内蒙古	Inner Mongolia	2016.8	2181.9	2416.7	2542.9	2605.0	2891.9	3353.4	3653.0
辽宁	Liaoning	1899.9	2008.5	2038.7	1984.9	2037.4	2135.5	2302.4	2401.5
吉林	Jilin	637.0	653.8	667.8	652.0	667.6	703.0	750.6	780.4
黑龙江	Heilongjiang	827.9	845.2	859.4	869.0	896.6	928.6	973.9	995.6
上海	Shanghai	1353.4	1410.6	1369.0	1405.5	1486.0	1526.8	1566.7	1568.6
江苏	Jiangsu	4580.9	4956.6	5012.5	5114.7	5458.9	5807.9	6128.3	6264.4
浙江	Zhejiang	3210.6	3453.1	3506.4	3553.9	3873.2	4192.6	4532.8	4706.2
安徽	Anhui	1361.1	1528.1	1585.2	1639.8	1795.0	1921.5	2135.1	2300.7
福建	Fujian	1579.5	1700.7	1855.8	1851.9	1968.6	2112.7	2313.8	2402.3
江西	Jiangxi	867.7	947.1	1018.5	1087.3	1182.5	1294.0	1428.8	1535.7
山东	Shangdong	3794.6	4083.1	4223.5	5117.0	5390.7	5430.2	5916.8	6218.7
河南	Henan	2747.7	2899.2	2919.6	2879.6	2989.2	3166.2	3417.7	3364.2
湖北	**Hubei**	**1507.9**	**1629.8**	**1656.5**	**1665.2**	**1763.1**	**1869.0**	**2071.4**	**2214.3**
湖南	Hunan	1346.5	1423.1	1430.9	1447.6	1495.7	1581.5	1745.2	1864.3
广东	Guangdong	4619.4	4830.1	5235.2	5310.7	5610.1	5959.0	6323.4	6695.9
广西	Guangxi	1153.9	1237.7	1308.0	1334.3	1359.6	1444.9	1702.7	1907.2
海南	Hainan	210.3	232.0	251.9	272.4	287.3	305.0	326.8	354.6
重庆	Chongqing	723.5	813.3	867.2	875.4	924.9	996.5	1114.5	1160.2
四川	Sichuan	1830.7	1949.0	2014.8	1992.4	2101.0	2205.2	2459.5	2635.8
贵州	Guizhou	1046.7	1126.3	1173.7	1174.2	1241.8	1384.9	1482.1	1540.7
云南	Yunnan	1315.9	1459.8	1529.4	1438.6	1410.5	1538.1	1679.1	1812.0
西藏	Tibet	27.8	30.7	34.0	40.5	49.2	58.2	69.0	77.6
陕西	Shaanxi	1066.7	1152.2	1226.0	1221.7	1357.1	1494.7	1594.2	1682.8
甘肃	Gansu	994.6	1073.2	1095.5	1098.7	1065.2	1164.4	1289.5	1288.0
青海	Qinghai	602.2	676.3	723.2	658.0	637.5	687.0	738.3	716.5
宁夏	Ningxia	741.8	811.2	848.8	878.3	886.9	978.3	1064.8	1083.9
新疆	Xinjiang	1151.5	1539.8	1900.2	2160.3	2316.5	2542.8	2138.3	2867.6

注:数据来源于中国电力企业联合会,2019年为快报数。

Note: Data are from China Electricity Council, the data of 2019are preliminary statistics.

附录1-14 分地区按领域分固定资产投资(不含农户)比上年增长情况(2019)

Growth Rate of Total Investment (Excluding Rural Households) over Preceding Year by Region and Field (2019)

单位:% (%)

地 区	Region	2016	2017	2018	2019
全国总计	**National Total**	**8.1**	**7.2**	**5.9**	**5.4**
北 京	Beijing	5.9	5.3	-5.5	-2.4
天 津	Tianjin	8.0	0.5	-5.6	13.9
河 北	Hebei	8.4	5.3	6.0	6.1
山 西	Shanxi	0.8	6.3	5.7	9.3
内蒙古	Inner Mongolia	10.1	-7.2	-28.3	6.8
辽 宁	Liaoning	-63.5	0.1	3.7	0.5
吉 林	Jilin	10.1	1.4	1.6	-16.3
黑龙江	Heilongjiang	5.5	6.2	-4.7	6.3
上 海	Shanghai	6.3	7.2	5.2	5.1
江 苏	Jiangsu	7.5	7.5	5.5	5.1
浙 江	Zhejiang	10.9	8.6	7.1	10.1
安 徽	Anhui	11.7	11.0	11.8	9.2
福 建	Fujian	9.3	13.9	11.5	5.9
江 西	Jiangxi	14.0	12.3	11.1	9.2
山 东	Shandong	10.5	7.3	4.1	-8.4
河 南	Henan	13.7	10.4	8.1	8.0
湖 北	**Hubei**	**13.1**	**11.0**	**11.0**	**10.6**
湖 南	Hunan	13.8	13.1	10.0	10.1
广 东	Guangdong	10.0	13.5	10.7	11.1
广 西	Guangxi	12.8	12.8	10.8	9.5
海 南	Hainan	11.7	10.1	-12.5	-9.2
重 庆	Chongqing	12.1	9.5	7.0	5.7
四 川	Sichuan	13.1	10.6	10.2	8.6
贵 州	Guizhou	21.1	20.1	15.8	1.0
云 南	Yunnan	19.8	18.0	11.6	8.5
西 藏	Tibet	23.2	23.8	9.8	-2.1
陕 西	Shaanxi	12.3	14.6	10.4	2.5
甘 肃	Gansu	10.5	-40.3	-3.9	6.6
青 海	Qinghai	9.9	10.5	7.3	5.0
宁 夏	Ningxia	8.2	3.0	-18.2	-10.3
新 疆	Xinjiang	-5.1	20.0	-25.2	2.5

附录1-15 分地区房地产开发企业(单位)房屋施工、竣工面积和商品房销售面积

Real Estate Development Enterprises (Units)' Region Housing Construction, Completion and Sales of Commercial Space Area by Region

单位:万平方米 (10 000 sqm)

地 区	Region	房屋施工面积 Housing Construction Area		房屋竣工面积 Housing Completed Area		商品房销售面积 Sales of Commercial Area	
		2018	2019	2018	2019	2018	2019
全国总计	**National Total**	**822300**	**893821**	**93550**	**95942**	**171654**	**171558**
北 京	Beijing	12963	12515	1558	1343	696	939
天 津	Tianjin	10324	11453	2092	1656	1250	1479
河 北	Hebei	28172	29853	2390	2680	5252	5283
山 西	Shanxi	16950	19549	1408	2739	2361	2366
内蒙古	Inner Mongolia	15054	15889	1416	951	2008	2008
辽 宁	Liaoning	24217	23787	2274	1818	3935	3696
吉 林	Jilin	12080	12404	1520	1222	2074	2122
黑龙江	Heilongjiang	10588	11441	1203	1204	1913	1684
上 海	Shanghai	14672	14803	3116	2670	1767	1696
江 苏	Jiangsu	62673	65687	8536	9369	13484	13973
浙 江	Zhejiang	44537	49605	5190	5739	9755	9378
安 徽	Anhui	41128	43591	4488	5674	10038	9229
福 建	Fujian	32826	34140	3739	2882	6213	6456
江 西	Jiangxi	20739	23557	2032	2231	6201	6459
山 东	Shangdong	69063	75767	10513	10179	13455	12727
河 南	Henan	54686	57567	6655	6571	13990	14278
湖 北	**Hubei**	**31316**	**33825**	**2774**	**2559**	**8865**	**8602**
湖 南	Hunan	35782	40045	4161	3975	9239	9104
广 东	Guangdong	79935	86825	7615	9956	14336	13847
广 西	Guangxi	25399	29807	2193	2038	6213	6712
海 南	Hainan	9575	9222	1187	1302	1432	829
重 庆	Chongqing	27227	27987	4083	5069	6536	6105
四 川	Sichuan	44066	49114	5635	4580	12211	12979
贵 州	Guizhou	21953	27775	1280	955	5182	5323
云 南	Yunnan	21800	26314	1447	1844	4532	4835
西 藏	Tibet	359	764	50	19	73	128
陕 西	Shaanxi	24618	27728	1525	1782	4119	4401
甘 肃	Gansu	9429	10977	752	674	1596	1705
青 海	Qinghai	2549	2922	320	133	448	481
宁 夏	Ningxia	6048	5937	1214	1011	1026	1010
新 疆	Xinjiang	11575	12970	1183	1117	1452	1724

注:商品房销售面积包括期房面积和现房面积。

Note: Commercial housing sales area include the area of completed and future houses sold.

附录1-16 分地区房地产开发企业(单位)投资和商品房销售额

Investment and Commercial Housing Sales of Real Estate Development Company (Units)

单位:亿元 (100 million yuan)

地区	Region	房地产开发投资额 Real Estate Development Investment		商品房销售额 Commercial Housing Sales		#住宅 #Residential	
		2018	2019	2018	2019	2018	2019
全国总计	**National Total**	**120263.5**	**132194.3**	**149972.7**	**159725.1**	**126392.6**	**139440.0**
北京	Beijing	3873.4	3838.4	2377.0	3371.0	1971.1	3032.4
天津	Tianjin	2424.5	2727.8	2006.6	2294.1	1816.5	2132.5
河北	Hebei	4476.4	4347.1	4035.0	4138.6	3567.3	3714.6
山西	Shanxi	1376.6	1656.5	1610.6	1631.8	1473.2	1425.4
内蒙古	Inner Mongolia	882.8	1041.9	1113.9	1243.9	909.0	1104.1
辽宁	Liaoning	2599.3	2834.0	2967.3	3049.1	2615.8	2814.9
吉林	Jilin	1175.9	1315.5	1452.4	1581.5	1233.5	1373.5
黑龙江	Heilongjiang	944.4	958.0	1320.3	1268.2	1112.3	1070.0
上海	Shanghai	4033.2	4231.4	4751.5	5203.8	3864.0	4457.2
江苏	Jiangsu	10982.3	12009.3	14527.3	16259.6	12693.9	14894.8
浙江	Zhejiang	9944.9	10683.0	14089.8	14352.1	12096.3	12723.1
安徽	Anhui	5974.1	6670	7077.0	6823.5	6174.8	6126.7
福建	Fujian	4940.3	5673.1	6579.5	6938.8	5074.5	5685.3
江西	Jiangxi	2174.9	2239.1	4219.9	4710.4	3524.3	4038.0
山东	Shangdong	7553.0	8614.9	10065.7	10271.2	8682.8	9287.1
河南	Henan	7015.5	7464.6	8055.3	9010.0	6903.8	8016.9
湖北	**Hubei**	**4693.1**	**5111.7**	**7531.4**	**7751.8**	**6591.4**	**6903.7**
湖南	Hunan	3945.9	4445.5	5354.0	5578.0	4377.4	4721.4
广东	Guangdong	14412.2	15852.2	18742.1	19748.2	15595.3	16758.0
广西	Guangxi	3004.1	3814.4	3826.5	4366.2	3330.7	3913.4
海南	Hainan	1715.0	1336.2	2083.3	1275.8	1832.0	1090.6
重庆	Chongqing	4248.8	4439.3	5272.7	5129.4	4442.9	4457.8
四川	Sichuan	5697.9	6573.2	8532.3	9666.7	6621.2	7869.0
贵州	Guizhou	2349.2	2990.8	2921.0	3183.6	2278.1	2527.4
云南	Yunnan	3247.2	4151.4	3406.8	3846.2	2690.8	3255.8
西藏	Tibet	92.6	129.6	52.8	96.8	42.9	81.2
陕西	Shaanxi	3534.7	3903.6	3407.4	3960.2	2808.8	3359.2
甘肃	Gansu	1116.4	1257.8	922.3	1019.3	774.6	907.1
青海	Qinghai	351.8	406.3	289.9	367.3	224.1	295.6
宁夏	Ningxia	449.6	403.1	517.7	573.9	420.6	498.5
新疆	Xinjiang	1033.4	1074.0	863.3	1034.3	648.6	877.9

附录1-17 按收发货人所在地分分地区货物进出口总额(2019)
Total Value of Imports and Exports of Goods by Region and Location of Importers/Exporters (2019)

(按收发货人所在地分)

(Location of Importers/Exporters)

单位:亿美元 (100 million US dollors)

地 区	Region	进出口 Total	出 口 Exports	进 口 Imports
全 国	**National Total**	**45761.3**	**24990.3**	**20771.0**
北 京	Beijing	4161.6	750.0	3411.6
天 津	Tianjin	1066.5	437.9	628.5
河 北	Hebei	580.4	343.8	236.6
山 西	Shanxi	209.7	116.9	92.8
内蒙古	Inner Mongolia	159.1	54.7	104.5
辽 宁	Liaoning	1052.8	454.5	598.3
吉 林	Jilin	189.0	47.0	142.0
黑龙江	Heilongjiang	271.0	50.7	220.3
上 海	Shanghai	4938.9	1990.0	2948.9
江 苏	Jiangsu	6295.3	3948.3	2347.0
浙 江	Zhejiang	4472.3	3345.9	1126.4
安 徽	Anhui	687.5	404.1	283.3
福 建	Fujian	1931.2	1201.7	729.5
江 西	Jiangxi	509.3	362.1	147.2
山 东	Shandong	2963.0	1614.5	1348.5
河 南	Henan	824.7	542.2	282.5
湖 北	**Hubei**	**571.5**	**360.0**	**211.5**
湖 南	Hunan	628.9	445.5	183.5
广 东	Guangdong	10361.8	6291.8	4070.0
广 西	Guangxi	682.1	377.5	304.6
海 南	Hainan	131.5	49.9	81.7
重 庆	Chongqing	839.7	538.0	301.7
四 川	Sichuan	980.6	563.9	416.7
贵 州	Guizhou	65.7	47.4	18.3
云 南	Yunnan	337.0	150.2	186.7
西 藏	Tibet	7.0	5.4	1.6
陕 西	Shaanxi	510.5	272.2	238.3
甘 肃	Gansu	55.1	19.1	36.1
青 海	Qinghai	5.4	2.9	2.5
宁 夏	Ningxia	34.9	21.6	13.3
新 疆	Xinjiang	237.1	180.4	56.7

附录1-18 按境内目的地和货源地分分地区货物进出口总额(2019)

Total Value of Imports and Exports of Goods by Region and Location of Place of Destination or Origin in China (2019)

(按境内目的地和货源地分)

(Location of Place of Destination or Origin in China)

单位:亿美元 (100 million US dollors)

地区	Region	进出口 Total	出口 Exports	进口 Imports
全国	**National Total**	**45761.3**	**24990.3**	**20771.0**
北京	Beijing	1122.3	265.1	857.2
天津	Tianjin	1363.7	412.5	951.1
河北	Hebei	946.5	480.6	466.0
山西	Shanxi	228.5	147.3	81.2
内蒙古	Inner Mongolia	201.1	73.8	127.4
辽宁	Liaoning	1337.2	558.0	779.2
吉林	Jilin	192.4	52.8	139.6
黑龙江	Heilongjiang	248.8	56.3	192.5
上海	Shanghai	4733.6	1698.5	3035.1
江苏	Jiangsu	6785.1	4029.8	2755.3
浙江	Zhejiang	4517.2	3395.8	1121.4
安徽	Anhui	637.9	398.6	239.4
福建	Fujian	1747.6	1087.8	659.7
江西	Jiangxi	443.9	291.9	152.0
山东	Shandong	3580.3	1710.6	1869.7
河南	Henan	879.8	593.0	286.8
湖北	**Hubei**	**537.5**	**318.7**	**218.8**
湖南	Hunan	421.3	263.3	158.0
广东	Guangdong	11837.0	7196.1	4641.0
广西	Guangxi	653.4	193.3	460.1
海南	Hainan	171.7	48.5	123.3
重庆	Chongqing	755.8	497.2	258.6
四川	Sichuan	1040.6	526.2	514.4
贵州	Guizhou	69.4	52.1	17.3
云南	Yunnan	334.5	144.8	189.7
西藏	Tibet	6.2	5.6	0.6
陕西	Shaanxi	490.9	265.8	225.1
甘肃	Gansu	53.7	22.1	31.6
青海	Qinghai	4.8	2.3	2.5
宁夏	Ningxia	41.9	27.8	14.1
新疆	Xinjiang	372.8	171.7	201.1

附录1-19 分地区农林牧渔业总产值及增长速度(2019)

Gross Output Value and Growth Rate of Farming, Forestry, Animal Husbandry and Fisheryby Region(2019)

地区	Region	农林牧渔业总产值(亿元) Forestry, Animal Husbandry Fishery (100 million yuan)	#农业 #Agriculture	#林业 #Forestry	#牧业 #Livestock	#渔业 #Fishing	农林牧渔业总产值比上年增长(%) Previous Year (%)
全国总计	**National Total**	**123967.9**	**66066.5**	**5775.7**	**33064.3**	**12572.4**	**2.8**
北 京	Beijing	281.7	102.3	115.6	49.3	5.3	-6.3
天 津	Tianjin	414.4	202.9	24.9	100.4	71.4	0.6
河 北	Hebei	6061.5	3114.9	231.4	2035.4	212.5	1.9
山 西	Shanxi	1626.5	936.8	101.3	478.6	6.9	2.0
内蒙古	Inner Mongolia	3176.3	1606.3	100.9	1390.5	27.8	2.1
辽 宁	Liaoning	4368.2	1912.0	117.4	1479.5	669.6	3.0
吉 林	Jilin	2442.7	1014.1	68.1	1239.6	40.1	2.3
黑龙江	Heilongjiang	5930.0	3774.5	193.9	1671.8	123.1	2.5
上 海	Shanghai	284.8	145.8	18.3	48.2	55.0	-7.3
江 苏	Jiangsu	7503.2	3828.6	162.0	1213.0	1741.0	0.7
浙 江	Zhejiang	3355.2	1595.0	185.5	395.2	1080.9	1.8
安 徽	Anhui	5162.1	2365.4	351.3	1628.9	521.3	2.3
福 建	Fujian	4636.6	1774.8	417.3	914.4	1361.7	3.6
江 西	Jiangxi	3481.3	1624.3	342.8	888.9	476.5	3.0
山 东	Shangdong	9671.7	4914.4	197.7	2412.1	1397.4	0.8
河 南	Henan	8541.8	5408.6	140.8	2316.5	118.2	3.0
湖 北	**Hubei**	**6681.9**	**3257.9**	**258.5**	**1521.5**	**1152.7**	**3.5**
湖 南	Hunan	6405.1	3052.1	430.7	2003.1	441.8	3.2
广 东	Guangdong	7175.9	3530.2	408.5	1404.1	1524.8	3.5
广 西	Guangxi	5498.8	3102.3	410.5	1189.7	538.9	4.8
海 南	Hainan	1689.4	819.6	106.4	300.8	390.9	2.6
重 庆	Chongqing	2337.8	1397.5	113.1	679.5	105.3	2.8
四 川	Sichuan	7889.3	4395.0	372.2	2647.9	263.5	2.6
贵 州	Guizhou	3889.0	2535.7	275.4	829.6	57.7	5.9
云 南	Yunnan	4935.7	2680.2	395.5	1600.7	105.4	5.6
西 藏	Tibet	212.8	94.9	3.5	108.4	0.1	7.7
陕 西	Shaanxi	3536.8	2445.8	106.1	757.2	31.4	4.3
甘 肃	Gansu	1887.6	1306.4	38.1	395.6	2.0	5.8
青 海	Qinghai	454.4	181.3	11.3	250.8	3.9	4.6
宁 夏	Ningxia	584.8	330.8	11.2	197.8	17.4	3.1
新 疆	Xinjiang	3850.6	2616.3	62.6	915.3	27.5	3.5

注:本表绝对数按当年价格计算,指数按可比价格计算。总产值包括农林牧渔专业及辅助性活动产值。

Note: Data in value terms in this table are calculated at current prices, while the indices are calculated at constant prices.Gross output value includes professional and support services for agriculture, forestry, animal husbandry and fishery.

附录1-20 分地区主要农产品产量(2019)
Output of Major Farm Products by Region(2019)

单位:万吨 (10 000 tons)

地区	Region	粮食 Food	油料 Oil feed	棉花 Cotton	糖料 sugar	蔬菜 Vegetables	水果 Fruit
全国总计	**National Total**	**66384.3**	**3493.0**	**588.9**	**12169.1**	**72102.6**	**27400.8**
北 京	Beijing	28.8	0.3	0.0		111.5	59.9
天 津	Tianjin	223.3	0.4	1.8		242.8	57.4
河 北	Hebei	3739.2	119.5	22.7	64.3	5093.1	1391.5
山 西	Shanxi	1361.8	13.7	0.3	0.1	827.8	862.7
内蒙古	Inner Mongolia	3652.5	228.7	0.0	629.6	1090.8	280.4
辽 宁	Liaoning	2430.0	97.7	0.0	14.6	1885.4	820.7
吉 林	Jilin	3877.9	81.8		2.9	445.4	153.9
黑龙江	Heilongjiang	7503.0	11.5		41.6	655.4	165.0
上 海	Shanghai	95.9	0.8	0.0	0.4	268.1	48.1
江 苏	Jiangsu	3706.2	94.3	1.6	7.4	5643.7	983.6
浙 江	Zhejiang	592.1	31.9	0.8	44.7	1903.1	744.1
安 徽	Anhui	4054.0	161.4	5.6	10.9	2213.6	706.3
福 建	Fujian	493.9	22.0	0.0	26.3	1570.7	727.2
江 西	Jiangxi	2157.5	120.8	6.6	62.4	1581.8	693.3
山 东	Shangdong	5357.0	289.0	19.6		8181.1	2840.2
河 南	Henan	6695.4	645.5	2.7	11.9	7368.7	2589.7
湖 北	**Hubei**	**2725.0**	**313.9**	**14.4**	**27.9**	**4086.7**	**1010.2**
湖 南	Hunan	2974.8	239.2	8.2	34.2	3969.4	1062.0
广 东	Guangdong	1240.8	110.2		1434.6	3528.0	1768.6
广 西	Guangxi	1332.0	71.6	0.1	7490.7	3636.4	2472.1
海 南	Hainan	145.0	8.7		114.5	572.0	456.1
重 庆	Chongqing	1075.2	65.2		8.1	2008.8	476.4
四 川	Sichuan	3498.5	367.4	0.3	37.2	4639.1	1136.7
贵 州	Guizhou	1051.2	103.0	0.0	62.8	2734.8	442.0
云 南	Yunnan	1870.0	62.5	0.0	1569.7	2304.1	860.3
西 藏	Tibet	103.9	5.7			77.5	2.4
陕 西	Shaanxi	1231.1	60.1	0.8	0.1	1897.4	2012.8
甘 肃	Gansu	1162.6	63.2	3.3	26.5	1388.8	710.1
青 海	Qinghai	105.5	28.9		0.0	151.9	3.7
宁 夏	Ningxia	373.2	7.7		0.1	565.9	258.6
新 疆	Xinjiang	1527.1	66.4	500.2	445.3	1458.8	1604.8

注:水果产量含果用瓜产量。

Note:Fruit production contain fruit with a melon production.

附录1-20　续表 continued

单位:万吨　　(10 000 tons)

地区	Region	肉类 Meat	#猪肉 #Pork	#牛肉 #Beef	#羊肉 #Sheep Meat	奶类 Dairy
全国总计	**National Total**	**7758.8**	**4255.3**	**667.3**	**487.5**	**3297.6**
北京	Beijing	5.1	2.3	0.7	0.4	26.4
天津	Tianjin	30.4	15.6	2.5	0.8	47.4
河北	Hebei	433.4	241.9	57.2	31.0	433.8
山西	Shanxi	91.0	56.8	6.6	8.0	92.3
内蒙古	Inner Mongolia	264.6	62.6	63.8	109.8	582.9
辽宁	Liaoning	367.9	189.4	29.6	6.8	134.7
吉林	Jilin	243.2	108.3	41.9	4.7	40.0
黑龙江	Heilongjiang	237.1	135.2	45.5	12.7	467.0
上海	Shanghai	10.8	8.9	0.0	0.2	29.7
江苏	Jiangsu	274.5	146.2	2.9	6.5	62.4
浙江	Zhejiang	94.3	60.2	1.3	2.3	15.5
安徽	Anhui	402.8	197.8	9.5	18.8	33.8
福建	Fujian	255.2	103.0	2.1	2.2	15.0
江西	Jiangxi	299.8	206.8	13.1	2.3	7.3
山东	Shangdong	704.0	254.7	73.3	36.9	234.5
河南	Henan	560.4	344.4	36.2	28.1	208.5
湖北	**Hubei**	**349.2**	**243.0**	**16.0**	**9.9**	**13.4**
湖南	Hunan	459.4	348.5	19.0	15.9	6.3
广东	Guangdong	412.1	221.9	4.1	2.0	13.9
广西	Guangxi	380.0	192.1	12.4	3.5	8.7
海南	Hainan	67.1	29.5	2.2	1.2	0.2
重庆	Chongqing	163.8	112.1	7.3	6.8	4.2
四川	Sichuan	559.5	353.4	36.4	27.1	66.8
贵州	Guizhou	205.9	150.3	21.5	5.0	5.3
云南	Yunnan	405.9	287.5	39.0	20.0	66.7
西藏	Tibet	28.4	0.8	21.2	5.8	48.2
陕西	Shaanxi	109.5	80.9	8.5	9.3	159.7
甘肃	Gansu	101.7	48.0	22.7	25.0	44.7
青海	Qinghai	37.4	7.7	14.6	13.9	35.5
宁夏	Ningxia	33.5	7.8	11.5	10.4	183.4
新疆	Xinjiang	170.7	37.6	44.5	60.3	209.4

附录1-21　分地区规模以上工业企业主要经济指标（2019）

Main Indicators of Industrial Enterprises above Designated Size by Region（2019）

单位：亿元　　(100 million yuan)

地 区	Region	营业收入 Business Revenue	营业成本 Business Cost	销售费用 Selling expenses	管理费用 Administrative Expenses	财务费用 Finance Expenses	利润总额 Total Profit
全国总计	**National Total**	**1057824.9**	**889442.1**	**31177.6**	**52275.2**	**11443.1**	**61995.5**
北 京	Beijing	22856.4	18874.8	1235.0	1241.9	237.2	1683.5
天 津	Tianjin	18717.6	15884.5	427.7	852.0	134.5	1212.0
河 北	Hebei	40416.9	35203.5	902.4	1456.7	543.5	2013.1
山 西	Shanxi	21123.5	17142.5	662.9	1140.8	710.5	1184.0
内蒙古	Inner Mongolia	16233.1	13001.6	431.2	620.1	430.5	1431.7
辽 宁	Liaoning	30365.5	25783.3	817.1	1296.6	428.7	1332.0
吉 林	Jilin	14024.4	11538.0	587.0	749.9	126.2	740.5
黑龙江	Heilongjiang	9916.6	8150.6	318.7	540.1	139.5	389.1
上 海	Shanghai	38841.0	31312.3	1489.8	2722.9	77.3	2874.5
江 苏	Jiangsu	118768.3	100600.0	3638.4	6346.7	922.8	6733.8
浙 江	Zhejiang	74962.5	62649.5	2312.8	4508.9	753.7	4759.5
安 徽	Anhui	37042.2	31600.0	972.1	1689.6	381.2	2159.6
福 建	Fujian	56921.8	49145.3	1300.1	2071.6	379.2	3815.1
江 西	Jiangxi	34851.5	30156.0	709.8	1350.6	235.3	2158.8
山 东	Shangdong	84541.9	73322.6	2177.6	3439.2	1154.1	3669.4
河 南	Henan	48544.5	41987.7	1007.4	1665.2	673.0	2762.4
湖 北	**Hubei**	**45212.9**	**37950.4**	**1394.5**	**2072.7**	**411.5**	**2867.8**
湖 南	Hunan	37310.8	30558.3	1192.2	2407.7	352.5	1870.8
广 东	Guangdong	146517.7	122278.5	5076.4	9385.1	725.9	8915.3
广 西	Guangxi	17433.4	15134.7	388.4	607.8	188.5	777.7
海 南	Hainan	2280.7	1769.0	132.0	89.6	38.0	171.6
重 庆	Chongqing	20793.9	17729.1	616.5	993.7	178.7	1102.8
四 川	Sichuan	43811.1	36334.4	1481.7	1880.3	533.7	2900.0
贵 州	Guizhou	9292.1	6982.0	324.7	433.3	207.3	867.2
云 南	Yunnan	14612.6	11428.7	395.1	556.5	318.7	879.9
西 藏	Tibet	288.3	233.5	9.5	28.9	9.4	5.2
陕 西	Shaanxi	24526.8	19642.8	619.1	1036.4	361.2	2167.0
甘 肃	Gansu	9151.8	7953.7	146.0	275.9	199.4	251.8
青 海	Qinghai	2339.3	1914.7	55.9	113.4	117.4	-541.9
宁 夏	Ningxia	4824.9	4027.7	85.4	205.4	166.8	218.1
新 疆	Xinjiang	11301.0	9152.3	270.1	495.9	306.7	623.4

附录1-21　续表 continued

单位:亿元　(100 million yuan)

地区	Region	亏损企业亏损总额 Total Loss of Loss-making Enterprise	流动资产合计 Total Current Assets	应收票据及应收账数 Bill and Accounts Received	存货 Inventory	产成品 Finished Products	资产总计 Total Assets	负债合计 Total Liability
全国总计	**National Total**	**9414.6**	**587317.3**	**174019.8**	**117780.2**	**43283.8**	**1191375.3**	**673949.8**
北　京	Beijing	328.3	19049.6	5154.2	2727.2	995.9	52444.2	22273.5
天　津	Tianjin	234.7	10565.5	3091.8	2137.8	718.2	21563.0	12596.9
河　北	Hebei	264.9	21645.5	5895.5	4375.6	1545.1	46788.1	28114.0
山　西	Shanxi	345.2	17015.9	3513.9	2184.8	821.5	41434.5	29550.5
内蒙古	Inner Mongolia	279.1	10850.6	2499.2	1625.7	583.3	31314.0	19093.3
辽　宁	Liaoning	425.9	19380.6	5257.1	4410.4	1381.2	38850.8	24563.6
吉　林	Jilin	275.1	8040.3	2048.4	1756.4	775.8	16710.4	9926.3
黑龙江	Heilongjiang	188.3	7170.6	1611.6	1402.4	426.4	16396.8	9610.8
上　海	Shanghai	263.9	25415.0	8638.9	4965.9	1603.7	44031.5	20770.7
江　苏	Jiangsu	998.2	69481.8	25504.0	14359.8	5559.4	120515.1	63786.6
浙　江	Zhejiang	479.5	46665.5	16196.2	9504.7	3863.4	84743.5	46706.6
安　徽	Anhui	236.2	19246.2	6827.7	3720.1	1469.4	38104.2	21536.5
福　建	Fujian	206.9	19803.8	5439.1	4477.4	1771.0	38755.6	19705.4
江　西	Jiangxi	106.2	13028.9	3493.0	2843.3	1061.0	26200.8	13771.9
山　东	Shangdong	618.7	53271.9	12873.0	11022.4	4287.5	99292.1	63392.9
河　南	Henan	380.7	23625.4	6183.8	4417.7	1486.1	50712.0	28864.1
湖　北	**Hubei**	**255.8**	**19703.2**	**6018.6**	**4126.9**	**1599.9**	**42224.4**	**21810.0**
湖　南	Hunan	197.9	13147.2	4267.9	2994.3	1055.8	28705.2	14569.7
广　东	Guangdong	940.5	83743.5	26927.6	17051.1	6352.2	137930.4	77910.9
广　西	Guangxi	155.9	9189.8	2388.1	2008.0	756.4	18371.6	11704.5
海　南	Hainan	21.0	1439.9	328.4	233.9	71.5	3285.1	1722.4
重　庆	Chongqing	239.9	9749.2	3512.6	1761.9	697.0	20188.0	11461.1
四　川	Sichuan	244.0	20251.0	5970.4	4015.3	1466.7	47022.1	26220.0
贵　州	Guizhou	181.0	6896.6	1319.7	1375.8	304.2	15521.8	9515.9
云　南	Yunnan	174.4	7946.9	1610.6	2331.0	571.1	21063.0	12147.2
西　藏	Tibet	32.0	444.8	57.8	35.3	9.7	1692.6	888.7
陕　西	Shaanxi	168.3	13231.4	3249.5	2342.0	950.5	35183.3	18937.5
甘　肃	Gansu	131.4	4316.8	1048.8	1150.9	363.8	12153.0	7622.8
青　海	Qinghai	692.5	2097.4	599.2	335.7	112.4	6671.5	4857.3
宁　夏	Ningxia	78.9	3665.7	838.9	761.8	193.0	10682.7	6518.8
新　疆	Xinjiang	269.3	7236.8	1654.4	1324.6	430.7	22824.1	13799.1

附录1-22　分地区主要工业产品产量(2019)
Output of Major Industrial Products by Region(2019)

地区	Region	原煤(万吨) Raw Coal (10 000 tons)	原油(万吨) Crude Oil (10 000 tons)	天然气(亿立方米) Natural gas (100 million cu.m)	布(亿米) Cloth (100 million meters)	农用氮、磷、钾化肥(万吨) Chemical Fertilizers (10 000 Tons)	水泥(万吨) Cement (10 000 tons)	生铁(万吨) Pig Iron (10 000 tons)	粗钢(万吨) Crude steel (10 000 tons)
全国总计	**National Total**	**384633.2**	**19101.4**	**1761.7**	**575.6**	**5731.2**	**235012.1**	**80936.5**	**99634.2**
北　京	Beijing	36.1		29.7			318.8		
天　津	Tianjin		3111.9	34.9	3.7	16.4	687.7	2073.1	2194.8
河　北	Hebei	5075.2	550.0	5.8	15.8	186.7	10523.8	21774.4	24157.7
山　西	Shanxi	98795.4		64.6	0.2	400.6	5257.5	5557.1	6039.1
内蒙古	Inner Mongolia	109068.1	11.8	22.1		515.4	3377.7	2303.1	2653.7
辽　宁	Liaoning	3292.0	1053.3	6.2	0.9	38.1	4677.4	6855.6	7361.9
吉　林	Jilin	1255.6	385.7	10.3	0.3	29.0	1815.0	1257.1	1356.6
黑龙江	Heilongjiang	5390.9	3110.0	45.7	0.1	46.6	1989.6	800.7	896.1
上　海	Shanghai		39.1	12.5	1.2	1.0	441.5	1490.1	1640.3
江　苏	Jiangsu	1102.7	151.4	12.2	114.9	200.6	16072.3	7347.6	12017.1
浙　江	Zhejiang			0.0	126.0	50.4	13441.0	835.5	1350.7
安　徽	Anhui	10989.5		2.1	10.7	271.3	14018.8	2530.0	3222.5
福　建	Fujian	845.7			106.2	90.3	9475.0	1038.1	2390.3
江　西	Jiangxi	503.6		0.0	10.4	29.8	9691.3	2218.0	2524.5
山　东	Shangdong	11918.1	2237.8	5.1	53.6	425.5	14643.0	5770.1	6357.0
河　南	Henan	10937.8	251.1	3.0	15.2	416.5	10496.6	2573.8	3299.1
湖　北	**Hubei**	**40.8**	**53.6**	**4.9**	**57.6**	**569.6**	**11626.0**	**2765.2**	**3611.5**
湖　南	Hunan	1473.5			2.1	59.5	11251.2	1973.9	2385.7
广　东	Guangdong		1475.1	112.1	22.9	15.8	16895.5	2086.1	3229.1
广　西	Guangxi	406.2	50.3	0.2	0.2	34.8	12093.0	1466.1	2662.7
海　南	Hainan		30.5	1.0		65.6	2019.0		
重　庆	Chongqing	1171.4		65.1	2.0	83.6	6757.7	611.0	920.9
四　川	Sichuan	3396.6	8.4	441.4	17.6	451.9	14184.6	2131.3	2733.3
贵　州	Guizhou	13167.9		3.2	0.3	372.4	11061.1	351.2	442.3
云　南	Yunnan	5522.9				296.9	12907.4	1788.0	2154.7
西　藏	Tibet						1080.9		
陕　西	Shaanxi	63630.0	3543.2	473.4	9.0	127.6	6642.7	1237.1	1430.7
甘　肃	Gansu	3684.6	58.1	0.1		22.6	4450.1	659.1	877.8
青　海	Qinghai	1286.5	228.0	64.0		560.7	1348.8	151.9	178.8
宁　夏	Ningxia	7476.9			0.6	45.4	1889.7	120.8	308.6
新　疆	Xinjiang	24165.3	2752.1	342.0	4.0	306.5	3877.1	1170.6	1236.9

附录1-22 续表 continued

地区	Region	钢材(万吨) Rolled Steel (10 000 tons)	汽车(万辆) Car (10 000 units)	家用电冰箱(万台) Household Refrigerators (10 000 units)	房间空气调节器(万台) Air Conditioners (10 000 units)	移动通信手持机(万台) Mobile Handset (10 000 units)	微型计算机设备(万台) Micro-computer Equipment (10 000 units)	发电量(亿千瓦小时) Power generation (Billion kilowatt hours)
全国总计	**National Total**	**120477.4**	**2552.8**	**7904.3**	**790.5**	**170100.6**	**34163.2**	**75034.3**
北京	Beijing	170.7	164.0			8373.3	513.2	464.1
天津	Tianjin	5455.0	104.1	44.6		11.5		733.0
河北	Hebei	28409.6	105.0		38.4			3297.7
山西	Shanxi	5594.2	6.5			1862.2		3361.7
内蒙古	Inner Mongolia	2563.8						5495.1
辽宁	Liaoning	7254.4	79.2	178.2	3.5	46.1	3.0	2072.9
吉林	Jilin	1544.2	288.9					946.4
黑龙江	Heilongjiang	782.0	18.9			259.5		1111.9
上海	Shanghai	1819.7	274.9	33.8	4.2	4173.2	1121.7	822.1
江苏	Jiangsu	14211.4	82.8	1068.1		5003.8	6032.3	5166.4
浙江	Zhejiang	3468.2	99.1	567.9	104.6	4652.6	277.7	3537.6
安徽	Anhui	3158.4	77.6	2505.9		81.7	2253.8	2886.7
福建	Fujian	3737.7	16.9			1802.9	2192.4	2578.0
江西	Jiangxi	2795.7	49.1	93.3		4897.6		1375.9
山东	Shangdong	9289.4	77.7	732.5		1177.2	0.9	5897.2
河南	Henan	3838.0	60.9	251.6		21744.1		2888.3
湖北	**Hubei**	**3771.6**	**224.0**	**539.9**		**3920.0**	**1270.2**	**2957.5**
湖南	Hunan	2451.6	56.1			1262.9	128.8	1559.4
广东	Guangdong	4510.5	311.7	1631.4	638.4	70502.8	5784.7	5051.0
广西	Guangxi	3346.7	183.0			594.7	245.1	1846.3
海南	Hainan							345.7
重庆	Chongqing	1136.4	138.3			17431.9	7614.3	811.6
四川	Sichuan	3308.2	61.9	99.5	1.4	14811.4	6584.2	3923.9
贵州	Guizhou	707.7	4.6	157.6		3289.1	0.1	2206.5
云南	Yunnan	2323.3	10.0			2792.2	140.6	3465.6
西藏	Tibet							85.5
陕西	Shaanxi	2037.5	54.7			1409.9		2193.2
甘肃	Gansu	936.7	0.1					1630.5
青海	Qinghai	180.6						886.1
宁夏	Ningxia	306.2						1766.0
新疆	Xinjiang	1367.9	2.5					3670.5

附录1-23 分地区建筑业总产值和房屋面积(2019)

Total Output Value of Construction and Building Area by Region (2019)

单位:亿元、万平方米　　(100 million yuan、10000sq.m)

地区	Region	总产值 Total Output	房屋施工面积 Floor Space under Construction	房屋竣工面积 Floor Space Completed
全国总计	**National Total**	**248445.8**	**1441644.8**	**402410.9**
北　京	Beijing	11999.4	80556.8	10932.1
天　津	Tianjin	4096.5	15616.9	2371.7
河　北	Hebei	5848.0	34994.7	8939.3
山　西	Shanxi	4653.3	16990.3	3836.4
内蒙古	Inner Mongolia	1086.1	5785.4	1459.9
辽　宁	Liaoning	3554.6	15312.8	4335.0
吉　林	Jilin	1863.1	7987.5	2935.2
黑龙江	Heilongjiang	1181.4	3430.2	1301.4
上　海	Shanghai	7812.7	50918.9	9232.0
江　苏	Jiangsu	33103.6	255297.7	77899.5
浙　江	Zhejiang	20390.2	182718.5	43545.6
安　徽	Anhui	8503.3	48611.4	15706.7
福　建	Fujian	13164.4	76606.3	17810.5
江　西	Jiangxi	7944.8	33897.5	14869.3
山　东	Shangdong	14269.3	83686.1	21925.7
河　南	Henan	12701.0	64256.1	20736.2
湖　北	**Hubei**	**16979.6**	**92042.2**	**33907.9**
湖　南	Hunan	10800.6	65247.3	21041.9
广　东	Guangdong	16633.4	84392.3	22174.0
广　西	Guangxi	5407.3	29487.8	8685.7
海　南	Hainan	366.0	2309.5	485.0
重　庆	Chongqing	8223.0	36557.8	13618.3
四　川	Sichuan	14668.2	61743.0	20341.0
贵　州	Guizhou	3714.9	15929.5	4131.0
云　南	Yunnan	6122.1	19766.7	6805.4
西　藏	Tibet	220.3	348.2	242.7
陕　西	Shaanxi	7883.9	35276.5	6769.8
甘　肃	Gansu	1916.4	10689.9	2686.7
青　海	Qinghai	460.7	904.6	396.3
宁　夏	Ningxia	601.4	2251.2	679.1
新　疆	Xinjiang	2276.7	8031.4	2609.7

附录1-24 分地区建筑业劳动生产率(2019年)
Labor Productivity of Construction by Region (2019)

单位:元/人 (yuan/person)

地 区	Region	企业个数(个) Number of Enterprises(unit)	从事建筑业活动的从业人员平均人数(万人) Average number of Employed Persons(ten thousand people)	按建筑业总产值计算的劳动生产率(元/人) Productivity of Labour (Yuan / person)	人均竣工产值(元/人)Per capita Output Value(Yuan / person)	人均施工面积(平方米/人)Per capita Construction Area (M2/person)
全国总计	**National Total**	**103814**	**6216.5**	**399656**	**199203**	**231.9**
北 京	Beijing	2694	208.3	576000	250568	386.7
天 津	Tianjin	1799	97.1	421878	191494	160.8
河 北	Hebei	2502	97.0	602872	257564	360.8
山 西	Shanxi	2999	113.1	411623	148197	150.3
内蒙古	Inner Mongolia	1026	26.7	406307	158268	216.4
辽 宁	Liaoning	5323	87.8	404956	180153	174.5
吉 林	Jilin	2388	42.3	440074	261263	188.7
黑龙江	Heilongjiang	1850	38.9	303720	170198	88.2
上 海	Shanghai	2438	126.3	618646	328319	403.2
江 苏	Jiangsu	9356	912.1	362924	268154	279.9
浙 江	Zhejiang	7256	620.2	328747	180822	294.6
安 徽	Anhui	4446	198.7	428005	180054	244.7
福 建	Fujian	5830	488.7	269391	121830	156.8
江 西	Jiangxi	3094	203.2	390924	212401	166.8
山 东	Shangdong	7299	345.1	413499	181833	242.5
河 南	Henan	6739	314.2	404291	235673	204.5
湖 北	Hubei	4565	251.3	675817	320724	366.3
湖 南	Hunan	2986	294.6	366599	187401	221.5
广 东	Guangdong	6643	349.4	476056	185652	241.5
广 西	Guangxi	1630	142.8	378628	186424	206.5
海 南	Hainan	213	8.3	441509	209607	278.6
重 庆	Chongqing	2939	236.1	348288	159255	154.8
四 川	Sichuan	5826	416.7	352004	147564	148.2
贵 州	Guizhou	1449	90.9	408857	151270	175.3
云 南	Yunnan	3156	181.4	337460	127260	109.0
西 藏	Tibet	278	6.7	328179	146023	51.9
陕 西	Shaanxi	3066	171.1	460863	146115	206.2
甘 肃	Gansu	1654	54.2	353876	143305	197.4
青 海	Qinghai	389	10.5	439073	228643	86.2
宁 夏	Ningxia	662	20.5	293969	146576	110.0
新 疆	Xinjiang	1319	62.5	364412	168768	128.6

附录1-25　分地区社会消费品零售总额
Total Retail Sales of Consumer Goods by Region

单位:亿元　　(100 million yuan)

地　区	Region	2012	2013	2014	2015	2016	2017	2018	2019
全国总计	**National Total**	**214432.7**	**242842.8**	**271896.1**	**300930.8**	**332316.3**	**366261.6**	**380986.9**	**411649.0**
北　京	Beijing	8123.5	8872.1	9638.0	10338.0	11005.1	11575.4	11747.7	12270.1
天　津	Tianjin	3921.4	4470.4	4738.7	5257.3	5635.8	5729.7	5533.0	5516.1
河　北	Hebei	9254.0	10516.7	11820.5	12990.7	14364.7	15907.6	16537.1	17934.2
山　西	Shanxi	4506.8	5139.3	5717.9	6033.7	6480.5	6918.1	7338.5	7909.2
内蒙古	Inner Mongolia	4572.5	5114.2	5657.6	6107.7	6700.8	7160.2	7311.1	7610.6
辽　宁	Liaoning	9304.2	10581.4	11857.0	12787.2	13414.1	13807.2	14142.8	15008.6
吉　林	Jilin	4772.9	5426.4	6080.9	6651.9	7310.4	7855.8	7520.4	7777.2
黑龙江	Heilongjiang	5491.0	6251.2	7015.3	7640.2	8402.5	9099.2	9317.4	9898.4
上　海	Shanghai	7840.4	8557.0	9303.5	10131.5	10946.6	11830.3	12668.7	13497.2
江　苏	Jiangsu	18411.1	20878.2	23458.1	25876.8	28707.1	31737.4	33230.4	35291.2
浙　江	Zhejiang	14199.6	15970.8	17835.3	19784.7	21970.8	24308.5	25007.9	27176.4
安　徽	Anhui	6142.8	7044.7	7957.0	8908.0	10000.2	11192.6	12100.1	13377.7
福　建	Fujian	7256.5	8275.3	9346.7	10505.9	11674.5	13013.0	14317.4	15749.7
江　西	Jiangxi	4123.3	4696.1	5292.6	5925.5	6634.6	7448.1	7566.4	8421.6
山　东	Shangdong	19651.9	22294.8	25111.5	27761.4	30645.8	33649.0	33605.0	35770.6
河　南	Henan	10915.6	12426.6	14005.0	15740.4	17618.4	19666.8	20594.7	22733.0
湖　北	**Hubei**	**9682.4**	**11035.9**	**12449.3**	**14003.2**	**15649.2**	**17394.1**	**18333.6**	**20224.2**
湖　南	Hunan	8318.7	9509.5	10723.5	12024.0	13436.5	14854.9	15638.3	17239.5
广　东	Guangdong	22677.1	25453.9	28471.1	31517.6	34739.1	38200.1	39501.1	42664.5
广　西	Guangxi	4516.6	5133.1	5772.8	6348.1	7027.3	7813.0	8291.6	8873.0
海　南	Hainan	950.2	1090.9	1224.5	1325.1	1453.7	1618.8	1717.1	1808.3
重　庆	Chongqing	4403.0	5055.8	5710.7	6424.0	7271.4	8067.7	7977.0	8667.3
四　川	Sichuan	9622.0	11001.0	12393.0	13877.7	15601.9	17480.5	18254.5	20144.3
贵　州	Guizhou	2266.3	2601.2	2936.9	3283.0	3709.0	4154.0	3971.2	4174.2
云　南	Yunnan	3597.9	4112.6	4632.9	5103.2	5722.9	6423.1	6826.0	7539.2
西　藏	Tibet	277.9	322.2	364.5	408.5	459.4	523.3	597.6	649.3
陕　西	Shaanxi	4571.6	5245.0	5918.7	6578.1	7367.6	8236.4	8938.3	9598.7
甘　肃	Gansu	2064.4	2368.8	2668.3	2907.2	3184.4	3426.6	3428.3	3692.4
青　海	Qinghai	480.3	549.6	620.8	691.0	767.3	839.0	835.6	880.8
宁　夏	Ningxia	590.5	668.5	737.2	789.6	850.1	930.4	935.8	984.5
新　疆	Xinjiang	1916.1	2179.5	2436.5	2606.0	2825.9	3044.6	3187.0	3361.6

附录1-26 分地区网上零售额(2019)
Online Retail Sale by Region(2019)

地区	Region	网上零售额(亿元) Online Retail Sales (100 million yuan)	比上年增长(%) Growth Rata(%)	其中:实物商品网上零售额(亿元) Online Retail Sales in Goods (100 million yuan)	比上年增长(%) Growth Rata(%)
全国总计	**National Total**	**106324.2**	**16.5**	**85239.5**	**19.5**
北京	Beijing	8675.7	18.6	6503.8	24.5
天津	Tianjin	2239.4	72.2	1931.5	95.8
河北	Hebei	2403.5	19.4	2108.4	25.5
山西	Shanxi	563.6	6.5	304.0	20.1
内蒙古	Inner Mongolia	440.5	19.0	196.1	29.2
辽宁	Liaoning	1426.4	22.2	1094.4	24.7
吉林	Jilin	524.9	15.0	286.7	31.6
黑龙江	Heilongjiang	669.0	19.5	370.1	31.8
上海	Shanghai	10418.5	16.8	8424.5	16.4
江苏	Jiangsu	9896.1	6.9	8361.4	8.7
浙江	Zhejiang	16315.7	12.4	12815.5	14.8
安徽	Anhui	2400.7	18.4	1973.1	20.7
福建	Fujian	4894.5	19.1	4298.4	22.7
江西	Jiangxi	1588.2	29.5	1374.1	38.6
山东	Shangdong	4109.0	15.8	3445.0	19.6
河南	Henan	2255.8	19.4	1750.0	27.6
湖北	**Hubei**	**2860.0**	**10.1**	**2384.4**	**17.7**
湖南	Hunan	1840.5	10.8	1351.8	26.8
广东	Guangdong	22828.2	19.1	19819.1	19.3
广西	Guangxi	820.0	10.4	444.3	16.9
海南	Hainan	373.2	0.6	99.2	-14.0
重庆	Chongqing	1082.1	5.0	683.0	22.1
四川	Sichuan	3318.1	22.5	2557.5	25.2
贵州	Guizhou	477.6	5.2	245.2	6.6
云南	Yunnan	821.8	30.5	442.0	30.4
西藏	Tibet	52.5	26.6	26.3	45.1
陕西	Shaanxi	1043.5	3.9	722.9	3.6
甘肃	Gansu	330.6	14.3	114.0	32.3
青海	Qinghai	67.2	27.6	28.8	43.5
宁夏	Ningxia	105.2	22.5	43.0	11.5
新疆	Xinjiang	202.0	26.5	157.7	33.4

附录1-27 分地区客运量和旅客周转量(2019)

Passenger Traffic and Turnover Volume of Passenger Traffic by Region(2019)

地 区	Region	客运量 (万人) Passenger Traffic (10 000 Persons)	#铁路 Railway	#公路 Highway	#水运 Waterway	旅客周转量 (亿人公里) Turnover Volume of Passenger Traffic (100 million person-kms)	#铁路 Railway	#公路 Highway	#水运 Waterway
全国总计	**National Total**	**1760436**	**366002**	**1301173**	**27267**	**35349**	**14706.6**	**8857.1**	**80.2**
北 京	Beijing	62977	14825	48151		264	158.9	104.8	
天 津	Tianjin	17679	5332	12206	141	287	208.5	78.7	0.2
河 北	Hebei	44733	13013	31719	1	1311	1089.5	221.5	0.1
山 西	Shanxi	22305	8153	14010	142	396	236.7	158.8	0.1
内蒙古	Inner Mongolia	12158	5640	6518		313	211.6	101.6	
辽 宁	Liaoning	70266	15137	54599	530	945	656.9	282.4	6.0
吉 林	Jilin	31599	8623	22881	94	425	276.2	148.6	0.1
黑龙江	Heilongjiang	29751	11223	18212	317	429	289.4	139.3	0.4
上 海	Shanghai	16442	12834	3168	441	227	117.7	108.5	0.8
江 苏	Jiangsu	120298	23739	94475	2084	1566	863.9	698.2	3.7
浙 江	Zhejiang	101893	24309	72799	4785	1129	743.3	378.4	6.9
安 徽	Anhui	59275	13410	45643	222	1165	824.3	340.2	0.3
福 建	Fujian	45761	12741	31199	1821	589	396.2	190.0	2.7
江 西	Jiangxi	58069	11938	45933	198	984	739.7	244.2	0.3
山 东	Shangdong	68920	17325	49581	2014	1338	831.0	492.6	14.4
河 南	Henan	109297	17709	91281	307	1799	1099.0	699.0	0.7
湖 北	**Hubei**	**87432**	**17216**	**69584**	**632**	**1200**	**803.5**	**392.1**	**4.8**
湖 南	Hunan	101428	15626	84162	1641	1443	1006.0	433.5	3.5
广 东	Guangdong	142326	38699	101012	2614	2126	1023.0	1093.0	9.7
广 西	Guangxi	47085	11777	34539	770	817	481.3	332.7	3.5
海 南	Hainan	14187	3085	9366	1736	130	52.6	73.7	4.1
重 庆	Chongqing	60153	8407	50990	756	488	239.2	243.0	5.7
四 川	Sichuan	91668	17352	72387	1930	873	433.2	437.7	1.8
贵 州	Guizhou	93756	7196	84255	2305	833	354.0	471.5	7.5
云 南	Yunnan	38381	6553	30681	1147	441	187.9	251.3	2.3
西 藏	Tibet	1365	345	1020		45	18.1	27.2	
陕 西	Shaanxi	70761	11461	59015	285	804	523.6	279.7	0.5
甘 肃	Gansu	42133	5969	36085	80	647	419.1	227.8	0.1
青 海	Qinghai	6313	1148	5071	94	128	78.1	50.0	0.1
宁 夏	Ningxia	5754	666	4905	183	87	40.9	46.0	0.1
新 疆	Xinjiang	20276	4550	15726		415	303.1	111.4	
不分地区	Not Classified by Region	65993				11705			

注:不分地区合计为民航完成数。
Note: The total passenger traffic not classified by region is civil aviation completion.

附录1-28 分地区货运量和货物周转量(2019)
Freight Traffic and Turnover Volume of Freight Traffic by Region(2019)

地区	Region	货运量(万吨) Freight Traffic (10 000 tons)	#铁路 Railway	#公路 Highway	#水运 Waterway	货物周转量(亿吨公里) Turnover Volume of Freight Traffic (100 million ton-km)	#铁路 Railway	#公路 Highway	#水运 Waterway
全国总计	**National Total**	**4706493**	**431773**	**3435480**	**747225**	**199287**	**30074.7**	**59636.4**	**103963.0**
北京	Beijing	22808	484	22325		1089	813.7	275.7	
天津	Tianjin	50093	9888	31250	8955	2662	517.1	599.4	1546.0
河北	Hebei	242445	26823	211461	4160	13563	4937.2	8027.2	599.0
山西	Shanxi	192192	91321	100847	24	5466	2774.7	2691.6	0.1
内蒙古	Inner Mongolia	182702	71828	110874		4587	2632.3	1954.5	
辽宁	Liaoning	178253	21199	144556	12498	8921	1231.6	2662.5	5027.3
吉林	Jilin	43193	5962	37217	14	1803	539.9	1262.8	0.1
黑龙江	Heilongjiang	50475	12073	37623	780	1615	814.4	795.1	5.6
上海	Shanghai	121124	487	50656	69981	30325	14.6	839.2	29471.1
江苏	Jiangsu	261711	6463	164578	90670	9944	329.7	3234.8	6379.5
浙江	Zhejiang	289011	4450	177683	106878	12392	236.1	2082.1	10073.7
安徽	Anhui	368248	7997	235269	124982	10246	753.5	3267.6	6224.7
福建	Fujian	134419	4840	87317	42263	8292	194.1	962.5	7135.6
江西	Jiangxi	150950	5065	135554	10331	3860	564.6	3040.3	255.4
山东	Shangdong	309410	25527	266124	17758	10166	1524.5	6746.2	1895.5
河南	Henan	219024	10905	190883	17235	8659	2146.4	5299.8	1212.3
湖北	**Hubei**	**188133**	**5480**	**143549**	**39105**	**6132**	**938.7**	**2268.1**	**2925.6**
湖南	Hunan	189740	4554	165096	20090	2594	855.4	1316.7	421.5
广东	Guangdong	358288	10172	239744	108371	27373	301.2	2564.0	24508.3
广西	Guangxi	183036	8405	142751	31881	3989	752.8	1470.9	1765.5
海南	Hainan	18456	1133	6770	10552	1648	16.8	40.8	1590.5
重庆	Chongqing	112970	1911	89965	21094	3614	208.2	952.6	2453.4
四川	Sichuan	177283	7718	162668	6896	2711	877.7	1527.5	305.6
贵州	Guizhou	83402	5523	76205	1674	1235	641.6	548.5	45.2
云南	Yunnan	122727	4886	117145	696	1552	519.4	1015.2	17.4
西藏	Tibet	4025	55	3969		154	39.9	114.5	
陕西	Shaanxi	154749	44751	109801	197	3482	1750.1	1731.4	0.6
甘肃	Gansu	63610	5366	58228	16	2496	1516.7	979.6	
青海	Qinghai	14945	3223	11722		398	271.6	126.3	
宁夏	Ningxia	42511	8151	34360		651	213.6	437.4	
新疆	Xinjiang	84423	15133	69290		1948	1146.4	801.8	
不分地区	Not Classified by Region	92139			124	5717			103.7

注:不分地区合计中包括管道运输企业、民航运输企业、中国远洋海运集团有限公司下属海外公司及中海集团香港有限公司完成量。货运量和货物周转量的全国总计等于分省数与不分地区数据之和。

Note:The total amount of not classified by region includes pipeline transportation enterprises, civil aviation transportation enterprises, overseas ompanies affiliated to COSCO and COSCO Hong Kong Limited. The national total of freight volume and freight turnover volume is equal to the sum of provincial and regional data.

中国统计出版社最新图书简目

(仅供参考,以实际出版为准)

统计资料

中国统计年鉴 中国统计摘要 中国第三产业统计年鉴
中国第三次全国农业普查综合资料 国际统计年鉴 金砖国家联合统计手册
中国-东盟国家统计手册 中国农村统计年鉴 中国县域统计年鉴
中国农产品价格调查年鉴 中国城市统计年鉴 中国价格统计年鉴
中国贸易外经统计年鉴 中国零售和餐饮连锁企业统计年鉴 中国商品交易市场统计年鉴
大中型批发零售和住宿餐饮企业统计年鉴 中国住户调查年鉴 中国工业统计年鉴
中国环境统计年鉴 中国能源统计年鉴 中国建筑业统计年鉴
中国房地产统计年鉴 中国固定资产投资统计年鉴 中国对外直接投资统计公报
中国人口和就业统计年鉴 中国劳动统计年鉴 中国社会统计年鉴
中国科技统计年鉴 中国高技术产业统计年鉴 全国企业创新调查年鉴
中国文化及相关产业统计年鉴 2018年时间利用调查资料 中国妇女儿童状况统计资料
中国基本单位统计年鉴 中国教育统计年鉴 中国教育经费统计年鉴
中国民族统计年鉴 中国残疾人事业统计年鉴

省级综合统计年鉴系列

北京 天津 河北 山西 内蒙古 辽宁 吉林 黑龙江 上海 江苏 浙江 安徽 福建 江西 山东 河南 湖北 湖南 广东 广西 海南 重庆 四川 贵州 云南 西藏 陕西 甘肃 青海 宁夏 新疆 新疆生产建设兵团

市(县)级综合统计年鉴系列

滨海新区 石家庄 唐山 邯郸 保定 沧州 邢台 廊坊 承德 衡水 秦皇岛 张家口 太原 大同 阳泉 长治 晋城 朔州 晋中 运城 忻州 临汾 吕梁 呼和浩特 呼和浩特新城区 鄂尔多斯 包头 沈阳 大连 长春 吉林 延吉 四平 通化 松原 哈尔滨 齐齐哈尔 黑龙江垦区 上海浦东新区 南京 无锡 徐州 常州 苏州 南通 连云港 淮安 盐城 扬州 镇江 泰州 宿迁 江阴 丹阳 海门 杭州 宁波 温州 嘉兴 湖州 绍兴 金华 衢州 舟山 台州 丽水 合肥 安庆 马鞍山 福州 厦门 宁德 漳州 龙岩 南昌 九江 上饶 新余 抚州 萍乡 赣州 吉安 景德镇 济南 青岛 潍坊 枣庄 日照 滕州 郑州 洛阳 平顶山 三门峡 商丘 信阳 济源 汝州 武汉 十堰 荆州 宜昌 荆门 咸宁 长沙 广州 深圳 惠州 东莞 汕尾 南宁 柳州 桂林 梧州 来宾 河池 防城港 海口 三亚 成都 贵阳 黔南 毕节 昆明 西安 咸阳 延安 宝鸡 安康 铜川 汉中 榆林 兰州 庆阳 银川 乌鲁木齐 兵团一师 兵团十师

调查年鉴系列

天津 内蒙古 上海 浙江 福建 河南 湖北 湖南 广东 广西 重庆 四川 云南 甘肃 宁夏

统计方法应用/实用手册

实用SAS统计分析教程 Python数据分析基础 统计公文知识问答 领导干部统计知识问答
乡镇统计人员岗位知识培训系列教材: 辅助调查员岗位基础知识 乡镇统计人员岗位基础知识
县级统计人员岗位知识培训系列教材: Excel在统计工作中的应用 简明统计分析
地市级统计人员岗位知识培训系列教材: 统计报告与演示 中国国民经济核算体系(2016)基础知识
全国统计专业技术资格考试系列考试用书: 统计业务知识(第四版) 统计业务知识学习指导与习题
全国统计专业技术资格考试系列考试用书: 统计相关知识(第四版) 统计相关知识学习指导与习题

统计通俗读物/统计科普图书

我国20个统计指标的历史变迁 联合国工业发展组织: 2016年工业发展报告
中国古代统计发展史 理解国民账户

重点图书

波澜壮阔四十年 砥砺奋进铸就辉煌——改革开放40年与时俱进的中国统计
新编英汉汉英统计大词典 中国国民经济核算体系2016 国民经济行业分类注释
挑大学选专业2019—考研择校指南 挑大学选专业2019—高考志愿填报指南 中华医学统计百科全书

中国统计出版社发行部电话: (010) 63376907 63376908 同棋行书店电话: 68783171 68783172
地址: 北京市丰台区西三环南路甲6号 邮政编码: 100073 网址: http://www.zgtjcbs.com